THE AMERICAN CINEMA

DIRECTORS
AND
DIRECTIONS
1929–1968

by Andrew Sarris

DA CAPO PRESS
NEW YORK

Library of Congress Cataloging in Publication Data

Sarris, Andrew.
  The American cinema: directors and directions, 1929–1968 / by
Andrew Sarris; with new afterword by the author.—1st Da Capo Press
ed.
      p.   cm.
  Originally published: 1st ed. New York: Dutton, 1968.
  Includes index.
  ISBN 0-306-80728-9 (alk. paper)
  1. Motion picture producers and directors—United States—Biogra-
phy—Dictionaries. I. Title.
PN1998.2.S266   1996
791.43′0233′0922—dc20
[B]   96-19944
                                                                      CIP

First Da Capo Press edition 1996

This Da Capo Press paperback edition of *The American Cinema*
is an unabridged republication of the edition published in
Chicago in 1985, with birth and death dates emended.
It is reprinted by arrangement with Dutton Signet,
a division of Penguin Books USA, Inc.

Published by Da Capo Press, Inc.
A Subsidiary of Plenum Publishing Corporation
233 Spring Street, New York, N.Y. 10013

Manufactured in the United States of America

To Molly

ACKNOWLEDGMENTS I am deeply indebted to Stephen Gottlieb, Michael McKegney, Eugene Archer, and Patrick Bauchau for their stimulating comments on the manuscript. I am grateful also to Jonas Mekas for his kindness in providing a haven for my critical opinions in the pages of *Film Culture* and *The Village Voice*.

CONTENTS

PREFACE   15

INTRODUCTION   19

I. PANTHEON DIRECTORS   39

CHARLES CHAPLIN   40

ROBERT FLAHERTY   42

JOHN FORD   43

D. W. GRIFFITH   49

HOWARD HAWKS   52

ALFRED HITCHCOCK   56

BUSTER KEATON   61

FRITZ LANG   63

ERNST LUBITSCH   65

F. W. MURNAU   68

MAX OPHULS   69

JEAN RENOIR   73

JOSEF VON STERNBERG   74

ORSON WELLES   77

II. THE FAR SIDE OF PARADISE   83

ROBERT ALDRICH   84

FRANK BORZAGE   85

FRANK CAPRA   87

GEORGE CUKOR   88

CECIL B. DE MILLE   90

BLAKE EDWARDS   91

SAMUEL FULLER   93

GREGORY LA CAVA   94

JOSEPH LOSEY   95

ANTHONY MANN   98

LEO MCCAREY   99

VINCENTE MINNELLI   100

OTTO PREMINGER   102

NICHOLAS RAY   107

DOUGLAS SIRK   109
GEORGE STEVENS   110
ERICH VON STROHEIM   111
PRESTON STURGES   112
KING VIDOR   117
RAOUL WALSH   119

III. **EXPRESSIVE ESOTERICA**   **123**
BUDD BOETTICHER   124
ANDRE DE TOTH   125
STANLEY DONEN   126
CLIVE DONNER   127
ALLAN DWAN   128
TAY GARNETT   129
SETH HOLT   130
PHIL KARLSON   131
JOSEPH H. LEWIS   132
ALEXANDER MACKENDRICK   133
ROBERT MULLIGAN   134
GERD OSWALD   135
ARTHUR PENN   135
LOWELL SHERMAN   136
DONALD SIEGEL   137
ROBERT SIODMAK   138
JOHN M. STAHL   139
FRANK TASHLIN   140
JACQUES TOURNEUR   141
EDGAR G. ULMER   142
ROLAND WEST   143

IV. **FRINGE BENEFITS**   **145**
MICHELANGELO ANTONIONI   146
LUIS BUÑUEL   146
CLAUDE CHABROL   147
RENÉ CLAIR   148
RENÉ CLÉMENT   149
SERGEI EISENSTEIN   149
G. W. PABST   150
ROMAN POLANSKI   151
ROBERTO ROSSELLINI   152

FRANÇOIS TRUFFAUT 152
LUCHINO VISCONTI 153

V. **LESS THAN MEETS THE EYE** 155
JOHN HUSTON 156
ELIA KAZAN 158
DAVID LEAN 159
ROUBEN MAMOULIAN 160
JOSEPH L. MANKIEWICZ 161
LEWIS MILESTONE 162
CAROL REED 163
WILLIAM WELLMAN 164
BILLY WILDER 165
WILLIAM WYLER 167
FRED ZINNEMANN 168

VI. **LIGHTLY LIKABLE** 171
BUSBY BERKELEY 172
HENRY CORNELIUS 173
JOHN CROMWELL 173
MICHAEL CURTIZ 174
HARRY D'ARRAST 176
DELMER DAVES 176
EDMUND GOULDING 177
BYRON HASKIN 178
HENRY HATHAWAY 178
GARSON KANIN 180
BURT KENNEDY 180
ALEXANDER KORDA 181
ZOLTAN KORDA 182
MITCHELL LEISEN 182
MERVYN LE ROY 183
FRANKLIN SCHAFFNER 184
GEORGE SIDNEY 185
ANDREW L. STONE 186
CHARLES WALTERS 186
JAMES WHALE 187

VII. **STRAINED SERIOUSNESS** 189
RICHARD BROOKS 190

JACK CLAYTON 190

JULES DASSIN 191

RICHARD FLEISCHER 191

BRYAN FORBES 192

JOHN FRANKENHEIMER 193

SIDNEY J. FURIE 194

NORMAN JEWISON 194

STANLEY KUBRICK 195

RICHARD LESTER 196

ALBERT LEWIN 197

SIDNEY LUMET 197

KAREL REISZ 198

TONY RICHARDSON 199

ROBERT ROSSEN 199

JOHN SCHLESINGER 201

JOHN STURGES 201

ROBERT WISE 202

VIII. ODDITIES, ONE-SHOTS, AND NEWCOMERS 205

LINDSAY ANDERSON 206

GEORGE AXELROD 206

JOHN BOORMAN 207

MARLON BRANDO 207

PETER BROOK 208

JOHN CASSAVETES 209

JAMES CLAVELL 209

HAROLD CLURMAN 209

FRANCIS FORD COPPOLA 210

ROGER CORMAN 210

DESMOND DAVIS 211

THEODORE J. FLICKER 211

BERNARD GIRARD 211

ROBERT GIST 212

CURTIS HARRINGTON 212

HARVEY HART 213

BEN HECHT AND CHARLES MACARTHUR 213

HOWARD HUGHES 213

GENE KELLY 214

BUZZ KULIK 214

CHARLES LAUGHTON   215
IRVING LERNER   215
IDA LUPINO   216
ROBERT MONTGOMERY   216
MIKE NICHOLS   217
CHRISTIAN NYBY   218
ROBERT PARRISH   218
SAM PECKINPAH   219
FRANK PERRY   219
ABE POLONSKY   220
STUART ROSENBERG   220
ELLIOT SILVERSTEIN   221
ALEXANDER SINGER   221
JACK SMIGHT   222
PETER TEWKSBURY   222
PETER WATKINS   223
JOHN WAYNE   223
JACK WEBB   224
PAUL WENDKOS   224
CORNELL WILDE   225
MICHAEL WINNER   225
BUD YORKIN   226

IX. SUBJECTS FOR FURTHER RESEARCH   227
CLARENCE BROWN   228
TOD BROWNING   228
JAMES CRUZE   229
PAUL FEJOS   230
SIDNEY FRANKLIN   231
WILLIAM K. HOWARD   231
REX INGRAM   232
HENRY KING   233
MALCOLM ST. CLAIR   234
VICTOR SEASTROM   235
MAURICE TOURNEUR   236

X. MAKE WAY FOR THE CLOWNS!   237
W. C. FIELDS   238
JERRY LEWIS   239

HAROLD LLOYD   **245**

THE MARX BROTHERS   **246**

MAE WEST   **248**

XI. **MISCELLANY**   **251**

MICHAEL ANDERSON   **252**

LASLO BENEDEK   **252**

JOHN BRAHM   **253**

JACK CONWAY   **253**

HUBERT CORNFIELD   **254**

WILLIAM DIETERLE   **255**

ROY DEL RUTH   **255**

GORDON DOUGLAS   **256**

PHILIP DUNNE   **257**

VICTOR FLEMING   **258**

JACK GARFEIN   **259**

STUART HEISLER   **259**

STANLEY KRAMER   **260**

JOSHUA LOGAN   **260**

DAVID MILLER   **261**

JEAN NEGULESCO   **262**

JOSEPH M. NEWMAN   **262**

ELLIOTT NUGENT   **263**

ARCH OBOLER   **264**

RICHARD QUINE   **264**

LESLIE STEVENS   **265**

EDWARD SUTHERLAND   **265**

BURT TOPPER   **266**

W. S. VAN DYKE   **266**

DON WEIS   **267**

TERENCE YOUNG   **268**

AFTERWORD: THE AUTEUR THEORY REVISITED   **269**

DIRECTORIAL CHRONOLOGY 1915–1967   **279**

DIRECTORIAL INDEX   **311**

PREFACE

The need for an updated film history is self-evident. Time keeps marching on, with new movies arriving and old movies acquiring new perspectives. Lewis Jacobs's *The Rise of the American Film* stopped at 1939. The forties, the fifties, the sixties have had to shift for themselves, a few thousand features a decade spreading memories and associations so widely, indiscriminately, and unpredictably that no conceivable chronicle could ever serve as a final judgment on the subject. Far from rendering final judgments, this book is intended to reappraise the American sound film from the transitory vantage point of 1968. The sociologically oriented film historians — Jacobs, Grierson, Kracauer, Rotha, Griffith, Leyda, Sadoul, *et al.*—looked on the Hollywood canvas less as an art form than as a mass medium. Hollywood directors were regarded as artisans rather than as artists, and individual movies were less often aesthetically evaluated than topically synopsized. Inevitably, something was left out, and that something is the very personal art of the talkies, an art that has flourished through nearly forty years of obtrusive obscurity. The evidence was on the screen all the time, but no one bothered to look very hard.

Still, if my distinguished predecessors tended to focus on the forest at the expense of the trees, they did endow film scholarship with a commendable seriousness of purpose. A serious approach to old movies is particularly indispensable at a time when the very existence of old movies is jeopardized by the shocking negligence of the so-called film industry, and at a time also when the appreciation of old movies is hindered by the pernicious frivolities of pop, camp, and trivia. The enemies of cinema have found their new battle cry in the condescending cackle one hears in so-called art houses. This book is intended for those perennial cinephiles, the solitary moviegoers.

For practical purposes, the term "American" should be

more precisely defined. Since the criteria of selection for this historical survey are aesthetic rather than social or industrial, "American" will embrace many undubbed English-language films produced abroad. As much as this encroachment on British and international cinema may smack of imperialistic presumption, the doctrine of directorial continuity within the cultural marketplace of the English language takes precedence here over ethnographic considerations. This point of view is perhaps more representative of New York, a distribution center, than of Hollywood, a production center. The distinction is not worth an extended debate, but it might be noted that we do not intend to overemphasize "Americana" in American films. It is this exaggerated concern with what is "distinctively" American that has led to the unfortunate denigration of Ophuls, Sternberg, and Lubitsch for their alleged exoticism. *That* is carrying social consciousness too far.

As for what constitutes a movie by our temporary definition, the necessary evil of specialization must be invoked. Quite simply, a movie is a movie is a movie. It is what most people are thinking of when they propose "going to the movies." It is generally encumbered by a plot, actors who portray characters, and a running time of one hour or more. This hardly represents the totality of cinema, especially in these feverish times. The vast realms of documentary, animated and experimental film-making are pointedly excluded. Flaherty is mentioned arbitrarily for the sake of an aesthetic principle; otherwise, the survey is limited to what has been variously described as the narrative, fictional, theatrical, commercial, conventional, hybrid, and impure motion picture. Even such popular fare as comedy two-reelers, serials and television films are ignored here because of the problems of historical classification. The feature film that emerged full-grown from the head of Cinema's Zeus, D. W. Griffith, happens to be the subject under scrutiny. Let us say for the moment that this is just one kind of cinema, but the one that most people would identify, rightly or wrongly, as *the* Cinema.

The framework of this book appeared originally in the Spring 1963 *Film Culture* (No. 28), and aroused considerable controversy. Many critics objected to my placing directors in categories, particularly categories with whimsical titles. After some thought, I have decided to retain the categories and even expand them. There is no such thing as an objective film history. Each historian weights his presentation by the arrangement of chapters, the length of paragraphs, the tone of sentences, the choice of words. The historian's categories are usually implicit in his text, but he usually strives to preserve the spurious façade of "objectivity" by not seeming to have strong opinions. I choose to make my categories explicit for the convenience of my readers. Also, I feel that marginal distinctions are the most important distinctions a critic can make. They indicate a critical sensibility at work over the entire expanse of the cinema, not just in the currently fashionable sectors. To put it bluntly, many alleged authorities on film disguise their ignorance of the American cinema as a form of intellectual superiority. I have no quarrel with such snobbery, but there is no point in compromising with it. There are now enough dedicated moviegoers in the reading public to make the most adventurous speculations seem more reasonable than they did in 1963.

The film titles that are in italics in the individual filmographies represent the highlights of a director's career. The implied valuation is relative in that the worst film of a great director may be more interesting though less successful than the best film of a fair to middling director. Hence, by arranging the directors in categories we maintain some perspective on careers as coherent identities whereas the italics make the distinction between those movies that made it and those that did not. All in all, the italics both in the filmographies and in the directorial chronology from 1915 to 1967 near the end of the book are intended as guides for the film enthusiast who lacks the lifetime in the darkness to check out every possibility of personal expression in the cinema.

TOWARD A THEORY OF FILM HISTORY

I. The Forest and the Trees

The cinema by any definition is still very young, but it is already old enough to claim not only its own history but its own archaeology as well. The earliest artifacts have been traced back to the 1880's and 1890's in the United States, France, or England, depending on the nationality of the archaeologist. Conflicting proofs and patents of invention have been submitted for Thomas A. Edison, William Kennedy Laurie Dickson, William Friese-Greene, Louis Aimé Augustin Le Prince, Louis and Auguste Lumière, and many other shadowy figures out of the nineteenth-century camera obscura of art, science, and capitalism.

To the extent that the cinema is a creature of the scientific spirit, it has inherited expectations of infinite development and improvement. It is as if this machine art were designed to transcend the vagaries of human inspiration. A Shakespeare may appear once in a millennium, but the express train of twentieth-century history cannot wait a century or even a decade for the world to be remade from the moonbeams of a movie projector. Too much was expected of the medium, and too little was demanded of its scholars. The extravagant rhetoric of disillusionment obscured the incredibly perfunctory attention given to thousands upon thousands of movies. Therefore the first task of a theory of film history is to establish the existence of these thousands of movies as a meaningful condition of the medium.

Even though most movies are only marginally concerned with the art of the cinema, the notion of quality is difficult to grasp apart from the context of quantity. Comprehension becomes a function of comprehensiveness. As more movies are seen, more cross-references are assembled. Fractional responsibilities are more precisely defined; personal signatures are more clearly discerned.

It follows that comprehensive film scholarship from primary sources depends for its motivation upon a pleasurable response to the very act of moviegoing. Conversely, the compleat film historian must be recruited from the ranks of the authentic moviegoers rather than the slummers from the other arts. Not that an uncritical enthusiasm for movies is desirable in our chronicler. Film history devoid of value judgments would degenerate into a hobby like bridge or stamp collecting, respectable in its esoteric way, but not too revelatory. Or, as has been more the fashion, the collectivity of movies could be clustered around an idea, usually a sociological idea befitting the mindlessness of a mass medium.

The trouble up to now has been not seeing the trees for the forest. But why should anyone look at thousands of trees if the forest itself be deemed aesthetically objectionable? Of course, the forest to which I refer is called Hollywood, a pejorative catchword for vulgar illusionism. Hollywood is a foresty word rather than a treesy word. It connotes conformity rather than diversity, repetition rather than variation. The condescending forest critic confirms his preconceptions by identifying those elements that Hollywood movies have in common. Thus he also justifies his random sampling of Hollywood's output. If you've seen one, you've seen 'em all. And if you've seen a few, you certainly don't need to see them all. Hence the incessant carping on Hollywood "clichés:" Boy Meets Girl. The Happy Ending. The Noble Sacrifice. The Sanctity of Marriage. The Gangster Gets His Just Deserts. The Cowboy Outdraws the Villain. Girl and Boy Feel a Song Coming On. Presumably if you've laughed at one such convention, you've laughed at them all.

There is no denying that Hollywood movies emerge through a maze of conventions. Pressures from the studio, the censor, and the public have left their mark on film history. There is no artistic justification for the handcuffing of Burgess Meredith's George after he has mercifully shot the Lennie of Lon Chaney, Jr., in *Of Mice and Men*. Nor for the arrest of Gale Sondergaard at the end of *The Letter*. Nor for the mysterious going-away tears shed by Carole Lombard's Amy in *They Knew What They Wanted*. The citations of censor-dictated punishments of crime and sin could take up volumes and volumes. Hollywood movies have been hobbled also by front-office interference and a Scribean script policy that decreed the simplest, singlest, and most vulgar motivations for characters.

But the forest critic is not concerned with particulars. It is the system that he despises. It is the system that he blames for betraying the cinema. This curious feeling of betrayal dominates most forest histories to the point of paranoia. Somewhere on the western shores of the United States, a group of men have gathered to rob the cinema of its birthright. If the forest critic be politically oriented, he will describe these coastal conspirators as capitalists. If aesthetically oriented, he will describe them as philistines. Either way, an entity called the cinema has been betrayed by another entity called Hollywood. It is hard to find a parallel to this stern attitude in any of the other arts. A bad novel is not reviewed as if the author and publisher had betrayed literature. A bad painting is not castigated for disgracing the medium that produced Poussin and Delacroix. Perhaps the closest parallel can be found in certain critical attitudes toward the type of play performed on Broadway, London's West End, and the Parisian boulevards. The factor shared by theatre and cinema in this regard is the possession of buildings in which the public gathers to watch plays or films as the particular edifice complex dictates. The forest critic cannot help wondering what would happen if these buildings were consecrated to what he considers to be genuine art. What he seeks is the union of crowd spectacle with coterie taste. His generally liberal leanings convince him that the masses can indeed be saved from their own vulgarities.

The forest critic is not entirely lacking in historical proofs of betrayal. An unimpeachable witness such as George Stevens has testified: "When the movie industry was young, the film-maker was its core and the man who handled the business details his partner. . . . When he finally looked around, he found his partner's name on the door. Thus the film-maker became the employee, and the man who had the time to attend to the business details became the head of the studio." The so-called system can be blamed for the blighted careers of D. W. Griffith, Josef von Sternberg, Orson Welles, Erich von Stroheim, and Buster Keaton, and for the creative frustrations of innumerable other directors. The problem with these examples is that in most instances the forest critics repudiated the afflicted directors long before the industry curtailed their careers. Forest critics have never championed individuality for its own sake. A Griffith has been denounced for not keeping up with the times. A Sternberg has been condemned for his preoccupation with eroticism. A Welles has been flayed for his flamboyant egotism. The principle of the forest has been upheld at the expense of tne topmost trees, and this is indeed the supreme irony of forest criticism. Far from welcoming diversity, the forest critic seeks a new uniformity. He would have Hollywood march off en masse like Birnam Wood to whatever Dunsinane the forest critic desires. Instead of one version of *The Grapes of Wrath,* there would be three hundred. Instead of one biography of Émile Zola, there would be a thousand critiques of anti-Semitism throughout the ages. Every movie would deal Realistically with a Problem in Adult Terms, or employ the Materials of the Medium in a Creative Manner. Thus the goals of forest criticism are ultimately impersonal. If John Ford decides to make a thirties adventure movie like *Seven Women* in the sixties, he is hopelessly out of step with cinemah. Similarly Charles Chaplin's *Countess from Hong Kong,* Orson Welles's *Falstaff,* and Howard Hawks's *El Dorado* are not synchronized with the express train of history. The medium marches on at its own pace. It is impervious to the melancholy twilight periods of its greatest artists.

The forest critic has had recourse to other snobberies over the years, and brief rebuttals to the battle cries of foreign "art" films, documentary, and the avant-garde might be in order at this point. In fact, the same careless arguments are heard today. The same rebuttals obviously apply.

THE FOREIGN FILM IS BETTER: The first serious cults of the foreign film sprang up in the twenties around the German and Russian cinemas, notable respectively for expressive camera mobility and revolutionary theories of montage. The giants of this era were Murnau, Lang, and Pabst in Germany, and Eisenstein, Pudovkin, and Dovjenko in Russia. The French cinema of Renoir, Vigo, Becker, Cocteau, Pagnol, Duvivier, Carné, Feyder, and Autant-Lara attracted some cultists in the thirties and early forties. The Italian neorealism of Rossellini, Visconti, and De Sica dominated the late forties and early fifties. The current line of the xenophiles among American critics is less localized. Hollywood's alleged betters may be found in Sweden (Ingmar Bergman), Denmark (Carl Dreyer), Japan (Mizoguchi,

Kurosawa, Ozu), India (Satyajit Ray), Poland (Has, Polanski, Skolimowski, Wajda), not to mention the familiar hunting grounds of France, Italy, and England. Film for film, Hollywood can hold its own with the rest of the world. If there have been more individualized works from abroad, there have also been fewer competent ones. If Hollywood yields a bit at the very summit, it completely dominates the middle ranges, particularly in the realm of "good-bad" movies and genres. Invidious comparisons are inevitable to some extent because of the arithmetic of distribution. Since a lower percentage of foreign films are available in America, indiscriminate viewing of Hollywood movies leads to an unscientific sampling of merit. Language barriers and the sheer exoticism of the unknown contribute to critical distortions. By the same token, American movies are often overrated abroad.

DOCUMENTARY FILMS ARE MORE REALISTIC THAN FICTIONAL MOVIES, HENCE MORALLY AND AESTHETICALLY SUPERIOR: One might just as well say that books of nonfiction are more truthful than novels. A great deal of semantic confusion is caused here by the duality of the cinema as a recording medium like the printing press, phonography, radio, lithography, and television, and as an art form.

AVANT-GARDE FILMS POINT THE WAY FOR COMMERCIAL MOVIES: It is difficult to think of any technical or stylistic innovations contributed by the avant-garde. Avant-garde critics and film-makers have had to be dragged screaming into the eras of sound, color, and wide-screen. Avant-garde impulses seem to be channeled toward the shattering of content taboos, political, religious, and sexual. Luis Buñuel and René Clair have come out of the avant-garde, and some think that Cocteau never left it, but few avant-garde mannerisms stand for long the withering gaze of the camera.

Though the forest critic may still point to foreign "art" films, the documentary, and the avant-garde, he knows full well that the masses he wants to save are enthralled more by ordinary movies than by lofty cinema. He himself is fascinated by the vulgar spectacles he deplores in his scholarly treatises, and in his fascination is the secret of his yearning. If the stupidities on the screen can stir even his own refined sensibilities, what ecstasies would he not experience if the dream mechanism were controlled by tastes comparable to his own? Greta Garbo edited by the *Partisan Review,* and all that. The forest critic cannot admit even to himself that he is beguiled by the same vulgarity his mother enjoys in the Bronx. He conceals his shame with such cultural defense mechanisms as pop, camp, and trivia, but he continues to sneak into movie houses like a man of substance visiting a painted woman. If he understood all the consequences involved, he would not want movies liberated from their vulgar mission. He appreciates the fact that always and everywhere there were temples of temptation dedicated to the kind of furtive pleasure that was mercifully free from the stink of culture. Nonetheless his intellectual guilt compels him to deny serious purpose and individual artistry to the mass spectacles he has been educated to despise.

The forest critic makes the mistake of crediting the power of the medium for making a "bad" movie seem entertaining. He overlooks the collectivity of creation in which "good" and "bad" can co-exist. Greta Garbo is genuinely "good" in *Camille* and Robert Taylor is genuinely "bad." George Cukor's direction of Garbo is extraordinary, but his direction of Laura Hope Crews is much too broad. In that same year (1937) Ernst Lubitsch obtained a restrained performance from Miss Crews in *Angel.* Thus our notions of "good" and "bad" are cast adrift in a sea of relativity. The collectivity that makes the cinema the least personal of all the arts also redeems most movies from complete worthlessness. But collectivity is not necessarily impersonality. Collectivity may just as easily be a collection of distinctive individualities. Ideally the strongest personality should be the director, and it is when the director dominates the film that the cinema comes closest to reflecting the personality of a single artist. A film history could reasonably limit itself to a history of film directors. It would certainly be a good start toward a comprehensive film history, but it would hardly explain everything to be found in thousands of movies. Nor is there any theory that would explain everything for all time. The performances of Humphrey Bogart, for example, seem more meaningful today than they did in their own time. By contrast, the image of Greer Garson has faded badly.

Film history is both films *in* history and the history of films.

The forest critic tends to emphasize the first approach at the expense of the second. He treats the movies of the thirties as responses to the Great Depression. By this criterion, few movies met their responsibilities to the oppressed and the underprivileged. For every *I Was a Fugitive from a Chain Gang* and *Our Daily Bread,* there were a score of "Thou Swell" romances in which money was no object. Yet the escapism of the thirties was as much a reflection of the Great Depression as any topical film on unemployment. The most interesting films of the forties were completely unrelated to the War and the Peace that followed. Throughout the sound era, the forest critic has been singling out the timely films and letting the timeless ones fall by the wayside. Unfortunately, nothing dates faster than timeliness. Hence the need for perpetual revaluation.

The theory of film history toward which this book is directed aims at nothing more than taking the moviegoer out of the forest and into the trees. The thousands of sound films in the English language exist for their own sake and under their own conditions. They constitute their own history, be it sublime or ridiculous or, as is more likely, a mixture of both. This particular study will start at the top with the bundles of movies credited to the most important directors, and work downward, director by director, movie by movie, year by year, toward a survey of what was best in American sound movies between 1929 and 1966. This survey is obviously a labor of love beyond the boundaries of art. The movies have been their own justification. Piece by piece, scene by scene, moment by moment, they have paralleled my own life. I was born in the midst of the convulsions over sound. I grew up with the talkies. Film history constitutes a very significant portion of my emotional autobiography. Fortunately, the resources of archives, television, museums, and revival houses make it possible to reappraise nostalgic memories in the clear, cold light of retrospection. Old movies come out of their historical contexts, but they must be judged ultimately in the realm of now.

II. The Auteur Theory

I first employed the term "auteur theory" in an article entitled "Notes on the Auteur Theory in 1962" (*Film . Culture* No. 27, Winter 1962–63). The article was written in what I thought was a modest, tentative, experimental manner. It was certainly not intended as the last word on the subject. Indeed, it invited debate in a dialectical spirit of pooled scholarship, though without much hope of attracting attention in a publication with a readership of less than ten thousand. I had been writing articles in *Film Culture* for seven years without fueling any fires of controversy, but on this occasion a spark was ignited in far-off San Francisco by a lady critic with a lively sense of outrage. As often happens, the attack on the theory received more publicity than the theory itself. Unfortunately, the American attacks on the auteur theory only confirmed the backward provincialism of American film criticism. Not that the auteur theory is beyond criticism. Far from it. What is beyond criticism is the historical curiosity required to discuss any critical theory on film. A character in Bernardo Bertolucci's *Before the Revolution* observes that you can argue only with those with whom you are in fundamental agreement. "Let us polemicize," a Polish critic once wrote me. The affectionate aggressiveness of this attitude demands a modicum of mutual respect and a tradition of scholarly community sadly lacking in American film criticism.

First of all, the auteur theory, at least as I understand it and now intend to reaffirm it, claims neither the gift of prophecy nor the option of extracinematic perception. Directors, writers, actors (even critics) do not always run true to form, and the critic can never assume that a bad director will always make a bad film. No, not always, but almost always, and that is the point. What is a bad director but a director who has made many bad films? Hence, the auteur theory is a theory of film history rather than film prophecy. Of the directors listed in this book's Pantheon, Flaherty, Griffith, Keaton, Lubitsch, Murnau, and Ophuls are dead. Lang, Renoir, and Sternberg are involuntarily inactive, Chaplin, Ford, and Welles involuntarily intermittent. Only Hawks and Hitchcock of this group still enjoy reasonable commercial viability as they pass into their seventies, but it is difficult to imagine that their ultimate critical standing will be at stake in the next few seasons. Auteur criticism has been accused of sentimentality toward old directors. In Hollywood, particularly, you're only as good as your last picture, and no one in that power-oriented micropolis wants to waste time on has-beens. Since auteur criticism is based on an awareness of the past, it finds the work of old directors rich in associations. Not the work of all old directors, however. William Wellman, Henry King, and Frank Lloyd are not without their defenders, but the sum totals of their careers reveal more debits than credits. The ranking of directors is based on total rather than occasional achievement.

But why rank directors at all? Why all the categories and lists and assorted drudgeries? One reason is to establish a system of priorities for the film student. Another is the absence of the most elementary academic tradition in cinema. The drudgeries in the other, older, arts are performed by professional drudges. Film scholarship remains largely an amateur undertaking. In America especially, a film historian must double as a drudge. The rankings, categories, and lists establish first of all the existence of my subject and then my attitude toward it. "Taste," Paul Valéry remarked, "is made of a thousand distastes." François Truffaut's *Politique des auteurs,* first promulgated in the *Cahiers du Cinému* No. 31 of January 1954, can be credited (or blamed) for the polemical stance of the term "auteur."

Politique des auteurs referred originally to the policy at *Cahiers* to be for some directors and against others. For Truffaut, the best film of Delannoy was less interesting than the worst film of Renoir. This was an extreme example of the *politique* in action. It served as a shock statement for the criticism of cruelty. The term "auteur" is more perplexing, as I should be the first to recognize after all the controversies the term has caused me. Strictly speaking, "auteur" means "author," and should be so translated when the reference is to literary personalities. When Truffaut writes of Gide or Giraudoux, and refers to them incidentally as "auteurs," there is no special point being made, and "author" is both an adequate and accurate translation. It is another matter entirely when Truffaut describes Hitchcock and Hawks as "auteurs." "Author" is neither adequate nor accurate as a translation into English mainly because of the inherent literary bias of the Anglo-American cultural Establishment. In terms of this bias, Ingmar Bergman did not become an author until his screenplays were published in cold print. The notion that a non-literary director can be the author of his films is difficult to grasp in America. Since most American film critics are either literary or journalistic types with no aspirations or even fantasies of becoming film directors, the so-called auteur theory has had rough sledding indeed. Truffaut's greatest heresy, however, was not in his ennobling direction as a form of creation, but in his ascribing authorship to Hollywood directors hitherto tagged with the deadly epithets of commercialism. This was Truffaut's major contribution to the anti-Establishment ferment in England and America.

However, Truffaut cannot be considered a systematic historian of the American cinema. Nor a comrade in arms for Anglo-American auteurists and New Critics. Truffaut, Godard, Chabrol, Rohmer, Rivette, and other *Cahiers* critics may have stimulated the Anglo-American New Criticism into being, but they did not long sustain its heresies. Of course, even *Cahiers* criticism was never so monolithic as its more vulgar American antagonists supposed. Nor were (or are) all French critics and periodicals camped under the *Cahiers* standard. Nor does the *nouvelle vague* constitute a continuing advertisement for auteur criticism. The critics of each country must fight their own battles within their own cultures, and no self-respecting American film historian should ever accept Paris as the final authority on the American cinema.

If Truffaut's "Politique des auteurs" signaled a break with anything, it was with a certain segment of the French cinema that was dominated (in Truffaut's view) by a handful of scriptwriters. The target was the well-upholstered, well-acted, carefully motivated "Tradition of Quality" represented by Claude Autant-Lara, Marcel Carné, René Clair, René Clément, Henri Clouzot, André Cayatte, Jean Delannoy, Marcel Pagliero, and a host of even lesser figures. This "Old Guard" was responsible for films like *Devil in the Flesh, The Red and the Black, Forbidden Games, Gervaise, Wages of Fear, Diabolique, Justice Is Done,* and *Symphonie Pastorale,* in short, what American reviewers considered the class of French film-making into the late fifties. Against these alleged creatures of fashion, Truffaut counterposed Jean Renoir, Max Ophuls, Robert Bresson, Jacques Becker, Jean Cocteau, and Jacques Tati as authentic auteurs.

Truffaut was involved in nothing less than changing the course of the French cinema. His bitterest quarrels were with film-makers, whereas the bitterest quarrels of the New Critics in England and America were with other critics. Truffaut's critical antagonists in Paris were generally not guilty of condescending to the American cinema. The editors of *Positif* may have preferred Huston to Hitchcock, and the MacMahonists may have preferred Losey to Hawks, but no faction had to apologize for its serious analyses of American movies. Even the French Marxists denounced the more capitalistic output from Hollywood in intellectually respectful terms. Long before the giddy rationalizations of pop, camp, and trivia, French critics were capable of discussing such lowbrow genres as Westerns and *policiers* with a straight face. The fact that many French critics had small English and less American actually aided them in discerning the visual components of a director's style.

Nevertheless a certain perversity in Truffaut's position still haunts the auteur theory and the New Criticism. Truffaut used American movies as a club against certain snobbish tendencies in the French cinema. This suggests the classic highbrow gambit of elevating lowbrow art at the expense of middle-brow art. Auteur critics are particularly vulnerable to the charge of preferring trash to art because they seek out movies in the limbo of cultural disrepute. An anti-auteur critic can score points simply by citing the titles of alleged auteur masterpieces. Without having seen the films, is anyone likely to believe that *Kiss Me Deadly* is more profound than *Marty,* that *Seven Men from Now* is more artistically expressive than *Moby Dick,* that *Baby Face Nelson* is more emotionally effective than *The Bridge on the River Kwai,* that *Bitter Victory* is more psychologically incisive than *The Defiant Ones,* that *Rio Bravo* is more morally committed than *The Nun's Story,* that *Gun Crazy* will outlive *The Heiress* or that *Psycho* will be admired long after *A Man for All Seasons* has been forgotten? Again, these propositions cannot be seriously debated. One kind of critic refuses to cope with a world in which a movie called *Baby Face Nelson* could possibly be superior to *The Bridge on the River Kwai.* The other kind of critic refuses to believe that a movie called *Baby Face Nelson* could possibly be less interesting than *The Bridge on the River Kwai.* One of the fundamental correlations in auteur criticism is that between neglected directors and neglected genres. To resurrect Ford and Hawks, it is necessary also to resurrect the Western. To take Minnelli seriously, it is necessary to take musicals seriously. However, auteur criticism is quite distinct from genre criticism. Genre criticism of the Western, for example, presupposes an ideal form for the genre. Directors may deviate from this form, but only at their own peril. The late Robert Warshow's celebrated essay on the Western described how a variety of directors failed to achieve Warshow's idealized archetype of the genre. By contrast, auteur criticism of the Western treats the genre as one more condition of creation.

Ultimately, the auteur theory is not so much a theory as an attitude, a table of values that converts film history into directorial autobiography. The auteur critic is obsessed with the wholeness of art and the artist. He looks at a film as a whole, a director as a whole. The parts, however entertaining individually, must cohere meaningfully. This meaningful coherence is more likely when the director dominates the proceedings with skill and purpose. How often has this directorial domination been permitted in Hollywood? By the most exalted European standards, not nearly enough. Studio domination in the thirties and forties was the rule rather than the exception, and few directors had the right of final cut. Educated Americans were brought up on the jaundiced Hollywood chronicles of F. Scott Fitzgerald, Nathanael West, John Dos Passos, Ring Lardner, and John O'Hara. The vulgar but vital producer-entrepreneur was the sun king in these sagas, and sensitive literary types were left out in the shade. In retrospect, however, the studio system victimized the screenwriter more than the director. It was not merely a question of too many scribes spoiling the script, although most studios deliberately assigned more than one writer to a film to eliminate personal idiosyncrasies, whereas the director almost invariably received sole credit for direction regardless of the studio influences behind the scenes. This symbol of authority was not entirely lacking in substance even in Hollywood, or perhaps especially in Hollywood where the intangibles of prestige loom large. There were (and are) weak and strong directors as there were weak and strong kings, but film history, like royal history, concerns those who merely reign as well as those who actually rule. Indeed, the strength of a John Ford is a function of the weakness of a Robert Z. Leonard just as the strength of a Louis XIV is a function of the weakness of a Louis XVI. The strong director imposes his own personality on a film; the weak director allows the personalities of others to run rampant. But a movie is a movie, and if by chance Robert Z. Leonard should reign over a respectable production like *Pride and Prejudice,* its merits are found elsewhere than in the director's personality, let us say in Jane Austen, Aldous Huxley, Laurence Olivier, Greer Garson, and a certain tradition of gentility at Metro-Goldwyn-Mayer. Obviously, the auteur theory cannot possibly cover every vagrant charm of the cinema. Nonetheless, the listing of films by directors remains the most reliable index of quality available to us short of the microscopic evaluation of every film ever made.

Even the vaunted vulgarity of the movie moguls worked in favor of the director at the expense of the writer. A producer was more likely to tamper with a story line than with a visual style. Producers, like most people, understood plots in literary rather than cinematic terms. The so-called "big" pictures were particularly vulnerable to front-office interference, and that is why the relatively conventional genres offer such a high percentage of sleepers. The culturally ambitious producer usually disdained genre films, and the fancy dude writers from the East were seldom wasted on such enterprises. The auteur theory values the personality of a director precisely because of the barriers to its expression. It is as if a few brave spirits had managed to overcome the gravitational pull of the mass of movies. The fascination of Hollywood movies lies in their performance under pressure. Actually, no artist is ever completely free, and art does not necessarily thrive as it becomes less constrained. Freedom is desirable for its own sake, but it is hardly an aesthetic prescription.

However, the auteur critic does not look to the cinema for completely original artistic experiences. The cinema is both a window and a mirror. The window looks out on the real world both directly (documentation) and vicariously (adaptation). The mirror reflects what the director (or other dominant artist) feels about the spectacle. Modern cinema tends to fog up the window in order to brighten the reflection. It would seem that a theory that honored the personality of a director would endorse a cinema in which a director's personality was unquestionably supreme. Paradoxically, however, the personalities of modern directors are often more obscure than those of classical directors who were encumbered with all sorts of narrative and dramatic machinery. The classical cinema was more functional than the modern cinema. It knew its audience and their expectations, but it often provided something extra. This something extra is the concern of the auteur theory.

The auteur theory derives its rationale from the fact that the cinema could not be a completely personal art under even the best of conditions. The purity of personal expression is a myth of the textbooks. The camera is so efficient a manufacturer of "poetic" images that even a well-trained chimpanzee can pass as a "film poet." For all its viciousness and vulgarity, the Hollywood system imposed a useful discipline on its directors. The limited talents of a Gregory La Cava could be focused on an exquisite department-store-window whimsy involving Claudette Colbert and a family of mannequins. The genre expectations of *She Married Her Boss* took care of the rest of the movie, but in those few moments in the department-store window, the La Cava touch was immortalized as a figure of style.

Nonetheless the auteur theory should not be defended too strenuously in terms of the predilections of this or that auteur critic. Unfortunately, some critics have embraced the auteur theory as a shortcut to film scholarship. With a "you-see-it-or-you-don't" attitude toward the reader, the particularly lazy auteur critic can save himself the drudgery of communication and explanation. Indeed, at their worst, auteur critiques are less meaningful than the straightforward plot reviews that pass for criticism in America. Without the necessary research and analysis, the auteur theory can degenerate into the kind of snobbish racket that is associated with the merchandizing of paintings. The burden of proof remains with the critic, auteur-oriented or otherwise, and no instant recipes of aesthetic wisdom will suffice. Welles is not superior to Zinnemann "of course," but only after an intensive analysis of all their respective films. Where the auteur critic parts company with the anti-auteur critic is in treating every Welles film as well as every Zinnemann film as part of a career whole. The auteur critic thus risks the resentment of the reader by constantly judging the present in terms of the past. The auteur critic must overcome this resentment by relating the past to the present in the most meaningful way possible. Fortunately, readers are becoming more rather than less knowledgeable about the past with each passing year.

Ian Cameron's article "Films, Directors and Critics" in *Movie* of September 1962 raises an interesting objection to the auteur theory: "The assumption which underlies all the writing in *Movie* is that the director is the author of a film, the person who gives it any distinctive quality. There are quite large exceptions, with which I shall deal later. On the whole we accept the cinema of directors, although without going to the farthest-out extremes of the *la politique des auteurs* which makes it difficult to think of a bad director making a good film and almost impossible to think of a good director making a bad one."

Cameron was writing particularly of the policy at *Cahiers du Cinéma* in which the films of favored directors were invariably assigned to the specialists in those directors. The result was that no favored director was ever panned. Ironically, Cameron and his colleagues found themselves in the same bind in *Movie* when David Lean's *Lawrence of Arabia* came up for consideration. Since none of the *Movie* critics liked Lean or the film enough to search for meanings in the mise-en-scène, *Lawrence* was left in the lurch without any review at all. Cameron defended the exclusion on the grounds that the best review of any film will be written by the critic who best understands the film, usually because he is the most sympathetic to it. Cameron, like the editors of *Cahiers,* thus upheld the criticism of enthusiasm as a criterion for his publication. Why does this sound so heretical in the United States? Simply because most movie reviewers fancy themselves as magistrates of merit and paid taste consultants for the public. The "best" movie reviewer is the "toughest" movie reviewer, and a reputation is made and measured by the percentage of movies the reviewer pans. The more movies panned, the more honest the reviewer. Everyone knows how assiduously the movie companies seek to corrupt the press. Hence, what better proof of critical integrity than a bad notice? Besides, the journalistic beat of the movie reviewer takes in all movies, not just the ones he likes. The highbrow critic can pick and choose; the lowbrow reviewer must sit and suffer. Walter Kerr has defined the difference between reviewing and criticism as the difference between assuming that your reader has not seen the work in question and assuming that he has. Reviewing is thus a consumer report for the uninitiated; criticism a conversation with one's equals. It is the economic structure of the cinema that gives the reviewer more power than the critic, but whereas in the other arts the critic makes up in academic prestige what he lacks in the market power of the reviewer, the film scholar has until very recently lacked both power and prestige. That is why film scholars can be slandered as "cultists" by philistinish movie reviewers.

However, the more fastidious film publications neglect their obligations to the medium by restricting their critiques to the films and directors they like. The film scholar should see as much as possible and write about as much as possible. To avoid passing judgment on a film because of lack of sympathy is an act of intellectual arrogance. Nothing should be beneath criticism or contempt. I take a transcendental view of the role of a critic. He must aspire to totality even though he knows that he will never attain it. This transcendental view disposes of the either/or tone of many opponents of the auteur theory. This tone suggests that the critic must make an irrevocable choice between a cinema of directors and a cinema of actors, or between a cinema of directors and a cinema of genres, or between a cinema of directors and a cinema of social themes, and so on. The transcendental view of the auteur theory considers itself the first step rather than the last stop in a total history of the cinema. Eventually we must talk of everything if there is enough time and space and printer's ink. The auteur theory is merely a system of tentative priorities, a pattern theory in constant flux. The auteur critic must take the long view of cinema as if every film would survive in some vault forever. Auteur criticism implies a faith in film history as a continuing cultural activity. The last thing an auteur critic desires is to keep a reader from seeing a movie. Debate is encouraged, but the auteur critic is committed to the aesthetic values he has derived from the artists who have inspired him. The auteur critic seeks to communicate the excitement he has felt to his readers, but he does not substitute his own sensibility for that of the artist under analysis. The ideal auteur critic should sacrifice his own personality to some extent for the sake of illuminating the personality of the director. In practice, however, no critic can entirely escape the responsibility of his own values. Elucidation must yield at some point to evaluation. All that is meaningful is not necessarily successful. John Ford's sentimentality in *The Informer* is consistent with the personality he expresses throughout his career, but the film suffers from the sentimentality just the same. Alfred Hitchcock's *Marnie* makes a meaningful statement about sexual relationships, but the script and acting leave much to be desired. *Red Line—7000* is no less personal a project for Howard Hawks than *El Dorado,* but there is all the difference in the world between the self-parody of *Red Line* and the self-expression of *El Dorado.* Orson Welles manifests his vision of the world with more lucidity and grace in *The Magnificent Ambersons* than in *Macbeth,* and Sternberg is more poetic, if less personal, in *Morocco* than in *Anatahan.* Even the greatest directors have their ups and downs. No one has ever suggested the contrary. At a certain level of achievement, however, even the failures of a director can be fascinating. Actually, a careful analysis of a director's career often turns up neglected masterpieces that replace the "official" masterpieces. Ford, for example, is seldom cited for *Steamboat 'Round the Bend* and *The Searchers,* but these films look more interesting today than *The Informer* and *The Grapes of Wrath.*

The best directors generally make the best films, but the directors must be discovered through their films. "That was a good movie," the critic observes. "Who directed it?" When the same answer is given over and over again, a pattern of performance emerges. The critic can talk about meaning and style in the work of a director. But how does a critic determine whether a movie is good or bad? This is a more difficult question. At first, there was only the vaguest idea of what a movie should be like to qualify as a work of art. Then as more and more movies were made, it was possible to impose relative standards. D. W. Griffith was the first great film-maker simply because his films were so much more accomplished than anyone else's.

After Griffith, film criticism became richer in associations. If Aristotle had been alive to write a *Poetics* on film, he would have

begun with D. W. Griffith's *Birth of a Nation* as the first definition of a feature film as a work of bits and pieces unified by a
central idea. Griffith is thus one of the definitions of cinema.
Subsequent definitions include Murnau, Lang, Lubitsch, Flaherty, Eisenstein, Dreyer, Hitchcock, Renoir, Ford, *et al.* In
every instance, the film preceded the film-maker in the critic's
consciousness. The films have continued to accumulate more
than fifty years after *Birth of a Nation*. The bits and pieces have
multiplied beyond measure. The auteur theory is one of several
methods employed to unify these bits and pieces into central
ideas.

To look at a film as the expression of a director's vision is not
to credit the director with total creativity. All directors, and not
just in Hollywood, are imprisoned by the conditions of their craft
and their culture. The reason foreign directors are almost invariably given more credit for creativity is that the local critic is
never aware of all the influences operating in a foreign environment. The late Robert Warshow treated Carl Dreyer as a solitary
artist and Leo McCarey as a social agent, but we know now that
there were cultural influences in Denmark operating on Dreyer.
Day of Wrath is superior by any standard to *My Son John,* but
Dreyer is not that much freer an artist than McCarey. Dreyer's
chains are merely less visible from our vantage point across the
Atlantic.

The art of the cinema is the art of an attitude, the style of a
gesture. It is not so much *what* as *how*. The *what* is some aspect
of reality rendered mechanically by the camera. The *how* is what
the French critics designate somewhat mystically as mise-en-
scène. Auteur criticism is a reaction against sociological criticism that enthroned the *what* against the *how*. However, it would
be equally fallacious to enthrone the *how* against the *what*. The
whole point of a meaningful style is that it unifies the *what* and
the *how* into a personal statement. Even the pacing of a movie
can be emotionally expressive when it is understood as a figure of
style. Of course, the best directors are usually fortunate enough
to exercise control over their films so that there need be no glar-
ing disparity between *what* and *how*. It is only on the intermediate and lower levels of film-making that we find talent wasted
on inappropriate projects.

Not all directors are auteurs. Indeed, most directors are virtually anonymous. Nor are all auteurs necessarily directors. There is much more of Paddy Chayefsky than of Arthur Hiller in *The Americanization of Emily,* which is another way of saying that *Emily* is written but not really directed. Players, particularly comic players, are their own auteurs to varying degrees. It can be argued that Leo McCarey directed the funniest picture of the Marx Brothers in *Duck Soup,* but he can hardly be credited with molding their anarchic personalities. The trouble with the Marx Brothers, in comparison with Chaplin, Keaton, and Lloyd in the silent era, was that they never controlled their own films either as directors or producers. W. C. Fields did his most memorable turns as unrelated bits of vaudeville in the muck of third-rate scenarios. We remember fragments more than we remember films. Even Garbo was of only fragmentary interest in Robert Z. Leonard's *Susan Lennox — Her Fall and Rise.* Would Garbo's image be as lustrous today without her performances in *Camille* (George Cukor), *Ninotchka* (Ernst Lubitsch), and *Queen Christina* (Rouben Mamoulian)? Good sequences in bad movies can be cited *ad infinitum, ad gloriam.* How about good performances by bad actors? Or good novels by bad novelists? Good and bad seem to become less frivolous matters with acting and writing than with direction. Most cultivated people know what they like and what is art in acting and writing, but direction is a relatively mysterious, not to say mystical, concept of creation. Indeed, it is not creation at all, but rather a very strenuous form of contemplation. The director is both the least necessary and most important component of film-making. He is the most modern and most decadent of all artists in his relative passivity toward everything that passes before him. He would not be worth bothering with if he were not capable now and then of a sublimity of expression almost miraculously extracted from his money-oriented environment.

I.
PANTHEON
DIRECTORS

These are the directors who have transcended their technical problems with a personal vision of the world. To speak any of their names is to evoke a self-contained world with its own laws and landscapes. They were also fortunate enough to find the proper conditions and collaborators for the full expression of their talent. Works of special interest in each director's filmography are indicated by italics.

CHARLES CHAPLIN (1889–1977)

FILMS: 1914—Making a Living, Kid Auto Races at Venice, Mabel's Strange Predicament, Between Showers, A Film Johnnie, Tango Tangles, His Favorite Pastime; Cruel, Cruel Love; The Star Boarder, Mabel at the Wheel, Twenty Minutes of Love; Caught in a Cabaret, Caught in the Rain, A Busy Day, The Fatal Mallet, Her Friend the Bandit, The Knockout, Mabel's Busy Day, Mabel's Married Life, Laughing Gas, The Property Man, The Face on the Barroom Floor, Recreation, The Masquerader, His New Profession, The Rounders, The New Janitors, Those Love Pangs, Dough and Dynamite, Gentlemen of Nerve, His Musical Career, His Trysting Place, Tillie's Punctured Romance, Getting Acquainted, His Prehistoric Past. 1915—His New Job, A Night Out, The Champion, In the Park, The Jitney Elopement, The Tramp, By the Sea, Work, A Woman, The Bank, Shanghaied, A Night in the Show. 1916—Carmen, Police, The Floorwalker, The Fireman, The Vagabond, *One* A.M., The Count, *The Pawnshop,* Behind the Screen, *The Rink.* 1917 —*Easy Street, The Cure, The Immigrant, The Adventurer.* 1918— Triple Trouble, *A Dog's Life,* The Bond, *Shoulder Arms.* 1919— *Sunnyside,* A Day's Pleasure. 1920—*The Kid.* 1921—The Idle Class. 1922—Pay Day. 1923—*The Pilgrim, A Woman of Paris.* 1925—*The Gold Rush.* 1928—*The Circus.* 1931—*City Lights.* 1936—*Modern Times.* 1940—*The Great Dictator.* 1947—*Monsieur Verdoux.* 1952—*Limelight.* 1957—A King in New York (unreleased in New York). 1967—The Countess from Hong Kong.

Chaplin's "primitive" Sennett films are listed above because the evolution of the actor preceded the evolution of the director. The apparent simplicity of Chaplin's art should never be confused with lack of technique. For Chaplin, his other self on the screen has always been the supreme object of contemplation, and the style that logically followed from this assumption represents the antithesis to Eisenstein's early formulations on montage. The late André Bazin brilliantly analyzed this fundamental opposition between montage and the one-scene sequence thus: "If burlesque triumphed before Griffith and montage, it is because most of the gags came out of a comedy of space, of the relation of man to objects and to the exterior world. Chaplin, in *The Circus,* is actually in the lion's cage and both are enclosed in a single frame on the screen." However, Chaplin, unlike Keaton, eventually subordinated his physical ties to the exterior world to the interior, almost schizophrenic relationship between director and actor. The physical objects that remained mechanical props in Keaton's cinema became universal symbols in Chaplin's. The breathtaking ballet with a global balloon in *The Great Dictator* derives its effect, not from the physical properties of balloons, but from a symbolic extension of megalomania. The circle Chaplin traces on the ground in *The Circus* is less an image in space than an image of time and life. The loss of plasticity and specificity in Chaplin's films coincided with a loss of humor and a gain of meaning. Ultimately Chaplin lost most of his audience, and in *Limelight* he celebrated the occasion by imagining his own death, a conception of sublime egoism unparalleled in the world cinema. To imagine one's own death, one must imagine the death of the world, that world which has always dangled so helplessly from the tips of Chaplin's eloquent fingertips.

Chaplin dabbled in Marxian (*Modern Times*) and Brechtian (*Monsieur Verdoux*) analysis, but the solipsism of his conceptions negated the social implications of his ideas. The idea of the actor has always contradicted the idea of the masses, just as the close-up has always distorted the long view of history. Chaplin's sensitivity to the eternal perverseness of woman further clouded his vision of the world. What, after all, is the final close-up of *City Lights* but the definitive image of a man who feels tragically unworthy of his beloved?

Chaplin has been criticized for abandoning the Tramp, a creature who had engulfed his creator in the public's mind. Chaplin might be criticized with equal justice for having grown old and reflective. The bitter melancholy of *Limelight* carries over into *A King in New York,* a film widely misunderstood as an anti-American tract. For Chaplin, however, America is like Dawn Addams, a fantasy and a delusion, a marvelous world that he may yet revisit but that he will never reconquer. Viewed as a whole, Chaplin's career is a cinematic biography on the highest level of artistic expression.

Chaplin the director was denied Chaplin the actor on only two occasions: *A Woman of Paris* (1923) and *The Countess from Hong Kong* (1967). Even in these two relatively objective enterprises, Chaplin makes cameo appearances. Curiously, *A Woman of Paris* was considered ahead of its time, and *The Countess from Hong Kong* behind its time, but both movies reveal Chaplin's roots in the theatre. Without Chaplin's physical grace at the center of the action, all the stage machinery becomes more visible. Yet Chaplin communicates his own personality to such disparate players as Adolphe Menjou, Edna Purviance, Marlon Brando, and Sophia Loren. The continuity of his career is maintained even in the absence of his acting persona, which proves that in the cinema feelings are expressed *through* actors, not *by* actors.

ROBERT FLAHERTY (1884–1951)

FILMS: 1922—*Nanook of the North*. 1926—Moana. 1927—White Shadows of the South Seas (with W. S. Van Dyke). 1931—*Tabu* (with F. W. Murnau). 1934—*Man of Aran*. 1937—Elephant Boy (with Zoltan Korda). 1948—*Louisiana Story*. Shorts: 1925—The Pottery Maker. 1927—The Twenty-Four Island. 1931—Industrial Britain. 1942—The Land.

Robert Flaherty was not merely the "father" of the documentary but also one of its few justifications. Actually, his films slip so easily into the stream of fictional cinema that they hardly seem like documentaries at all. From the beginning, Flaherty intuitively sensed the limitations of the impersonal camera and the restrictions of the formal frame. By involving himself in his material, he established a cinematic principle that parallels Werner Heisenberg's Uncertainty Principle in physics, namely, that the mere observation of nuclear (and cinematic) particles alters the properties of these particles. One of the most beautiful moments in the history of the cinema was recorded when Nanook smilingly acknowledged the presence of Flaherty's camera in his igloo. The director was not spying on Nanook or attempting to capture Nanook's life in the raw. He was collaborating with Nanook on a representation rather than a simulation of existence. What Flaherty understood so well was the potential degeneration of the documentary into voyeurism when the images of the camera were not reprocessed in the mind of the artist.

Tabu remains an interesting footnote to Flaherty's career, and his clash with Murnau acquires a fateful inevitability in retrospect. Where Flaherty expressed man's adaptability to nature, Murnau pondered on man's place in the universe. Where Flaherty was concerned with the rhythm of living, Murnau was obsessed with the meaning of life.

Flaherty was written off by some schools of documentary in the thirties for his presumed exoticism. The charge made more sense in the days when people believed that documentaries could reform the world. Today Flaherty seems touchingly romantic in his desire to find people who have escaped the corruption of civilization. Flaherty's cinema is one of the last testaments of the "cult of nature," and, as such, is infinitely precious.

JOHN FORD (1895–1973)

FILMS: 1917—The Tornado, The Trail of Hate, The Scrapper, The Soul Herder, Cheyenne's Pal, Straight Shooting, The Secret Man, A Marked Man, Bucking Broadway. 1918—Phantom Riders, Wild Women, Thieves' Gold, The Scarlet Drop, Hell Bent, Delirium, A Woman's Fool, Three Mounted Men. 1919—Roped, A Fight for Love, The Fighting Brothers, Bare Fists, The Gun Packers, Riders of Vengeance, The Last Outlaw, The Outcasts of Poker Flat, Ace of the Saddle, Rider of the Law, A Gun Fightin' Gentleman, Marked Men. 1920—The Prince of Avenue A, The Girl in Number 29, Hitchin' Posts, Just Pals. 1921—The Big Punch, The Freeze-Out, The Wallop, Desperate Trails, Action, Sure Fire, Jackie. 1922—Little Miss Smiles, Silver Wings, The Village Blacksmith. 1923—The Face on the Bar-Room Floor, Three Jumps Ahead, Cameo Kirby. 1924—Hoodman Blind, North of Hudson Bay, The Iron Horse, Hearts of Oak. 1925—Lightnin', Kentucky Pride, The Fighting Heart, Thank You. 1926—The Blue Eagle, The Shamrock Handicap, Three Bad Men. 1927—Upstream. 1928—Four Sons, Mother Machree, Napoleon's Barber, Riley the Cop. 1929—Strong Boy, Black Watch, Salute. 1930—*Men Without Women,* Born Reckless, *Up the*

River, The Seas Beneath. 1931—The Brat, *Arrowsmith.* 1932—
Air Mail, Flesh. 1933—Pilgrimage, *Doctor Bull.* 1934—*The Lost
Patrol,* The World Moves On, *Judge Priest.* 1935—*The Whole
Town's Talking, The Informer, Steamboat 'Round the Bend.* 1936—
The Prisoner of Shark Island, Mary of Scotland, The Plough and the
Stars. 1937—Wee Willie Winkie, *The Hurricane.* 1938—Four
Men and a Prayer, Submarine Patrol. 1939—*Stagecoach, Young
Mr. Lincoln,* Drums Along the Mohawk. 1940—*The Grapes of
Wrath, The Long Voyage Home.* 1941—*Tobacco Road,* Sex Hy-
giene (Army documentary), *How Green Was My Valley.* 1942—
The Battle of Midway (Navy documentary). 1943—December 7th,
We Sail at Midnight (Navy documentaries). 1945—*They Were Ex-
pendable.* 1946—*My Darling Clementine.* 1947—The Fugitive.
1948—*Fort Apache,* Three Godfathers. 1949—*She Wore a Yel-
low Ribbon.* 1950—When Willie Comes Marching Home, *Wagon-
master, Rio Grande.* 1951—This Is Korea (Navy documentary).
1952—What Price Glory, *The Quiet Man.* 1953—*Mogambo.*
1954—*The Sun Shines Bright.* 1955—*The Long Gray Line,*
Mister Roberts. 1956—*The Searchers.* 1957—*The Wings of
Eagles, The Rising of the Moon.* 1958—The Last Hurrah. 1959—
Gideon of Scotland Yard, Korea (documentary), *The Horse Soldiers.*
1960—Sergeant Rutledge. 1961—*Two Rode Together.* 1962—
The Man Who Shot Liberty Valance. 1963—How the West Was
Won (with Henry Hathaway and George Marshall), *Donovan's Reef.*
1964—Cheyenne Autumn. 1965—Young Cassidy (finished and
signed by Jack Cardiff), 1966—*Seven Women.*

If John Ford had died or retired at the end of 1929, he would
have deserved at most a footnote in film history. *The Iron Horse*
and *Four Sons* attracted some attention in their time, and seem to
be the only Ford silents in the American museum repertory. *The
Iron Horse* is clearly influenced by Griffith, and *Four Sons* by
Murnau. Neither work is a revelation in itself, though there are
privileged moments in these films that belong to Ford alone.
Above all, there is a nostalgia for lost innocence on the family
level of history. Ford's technical competence has been established even at this early stage in his career, but up to 1929 he
cannot be considered one of the major artists of the medium. His
personal vision has not been developed to the level of a Lubitsch
or a Lang at this stage of film history.

If Ford had died or retired at the end of 1939, he would have deserved at least a paragraph for *The Informer* and *Stagecoach,* the former allegedly the first creative American sound film, and the latter representing the renaissance of the Western. He would now be a faded, dated establishment figure like Marcel Carné, a vulnerable target for all the New Critics after Bazin. Dated also would be the calculated expressionism and maudlin sentimentality of *The Informer.* Ford's style still lingered in the shadow of Murnau's in 1935, but no one had seemed to notice *Steamboat 'Round the Bend* and *The Whole Town's Talking* that same year. Ford has never been sufficiently appreciated for the verve and snap of his visual storytelling. Critics of the thirties always joked about the fact that the Hollywood system compelled Ford to make three *Wee Willie Winkie*s for every *Informer.* The joke, then as now, was on the critics. Despite the monstrous mythology of Shirley Temple, *Wee Willie Winkie* contains extraordinary camera prose passages from the wide-eyed point of view of a child. What the critical establishment of the thirties admired in Ford was his ability to avoid so-called woman's pictures despite studio pressures. Nor was Ford too much interested in the fancier forms of sexual intrigue. Being Irish and Catholic and action-oriented to boot, he tended to gravitate to public places where men spoke their minds openly. The Left has always been puritanical, but never more so than in the thirties when Hollywood's boy-girl theology threatened to paralyze the class struggle. In such an epoch, even an Irish-Catholic conservative like Ford could be mistaken for a progressive force.

Ford's critical reputation reached its peak and then began its decline during the forties. *The Grapes of Wrath, The Long Voyage Home* and *How Green Was My Valley* firmly established Ford as *the* Hollywood director despite the extraordinary challenges of Orson Welles and Preston Sturges. The New Dealish propaganda of *The Grapes of Wrath* has dated badly, as has John Steinbeck's literary reputation. Ford's personal style was particularly inimical to Steinbeck's biological conception of his characters. Where Steinbeck depicted oppression by dehumanizing his characters into creatures of abject necessity, Ford evoked nostalgia by humanizing Steinbeck's economic insects into heroic champions of an agrarian order of family and community. By the time of *How Green Was My Valley,* Ford had mastered his narrative style to the point that he could embroider it with those pauses and contemplations that expressed his feelings. Even in *Tobacco Road,* Charlie Grapewin's Jeeter Lester was transformed from a greedy barnyard animal to a seedy but serious mainstay of tradition. Ford had more in common with Welles than anyone realized at the time. Ford was forty-six when he made *How Green Was My Valley,* and Welles was only twenty-five when he made *Citizen Kane,* but both films are the works of old men, the beginnings of a cinema of memory.

Ford's *The Battle of Midway* is ostensibly a documentary, but it is as personal a statement as any of his fiction films. He focuses here on the ordinary scale by which the most gallant heroes are measured. It is not the battle itself that intrigues Ford, but the weary faces of rescued fliers plucked out of the Pacific after days of privation. World War II was the last war to be endorsed by the intellectual establishment as a valid artistic subject. Ford proceeded into the fifties to photograph the Korean war, an act symptomatic of his downfall with the taste-makers.

Only the Lindsay Anderson–Gavin Lambert generation of *Sequence* and *Sight and Sound* kept Ford's reputation alive in the period beginning with *They Were Expendable* in 1945 and ending with *The Sun Shines Bright* in 1954. The British critics could appreciate Ford for the flowering of his personal style at a time when the rest of the world (this critic included) were overrating Carol Reed and David Lean for the efficient, impersonal technicians that they were. Finally, the New Critics in London and Paris rediscovered Ford after he had been abandoned even by the *Sequence–Sight and Sound* generation. The last champions of John Ford have now gathered around *Seven Women* as a beacon of personal cinema.

The late André Bazin damaged Ford's reputation with New Critics by describing Ford's technique as a hangover from the scenario-dominated thirties. Bazin overrated the use of deep-focus in *The Little Foxes* as the antithesis to Ford's "invisible editing" in *Stagecoach.* What Ford had been evolving all through his career was a style flexible enough to establish priorities of expression. He could dispose of a plot quickly and efficiently when he had to, but he could always spare a shot or two for a mood that belonged to him and not to the plot. A Ford film, particularly a late Ford film, is more than its story and characterizations; it is also the director's attitude toward his milieu and its codes of conduct. There is a fantastic sequence in *The Searchers* involving a brash frontier character played by Ward Bond. Bond is drinking some coffee in a standing-up position before going out to hunt some Comanches. He glances toward one of the bedrooms, and notices the woman of the house tenderly caressing the Army uniform of her husband's brother. Ford cuts back to a full-faced shot of Bond drinking his coffee, his eyes tactfully averted from the intimate scene he has witnessed. Nothing on earth would ever force this man to reveal what he had seen. There is a deep, subtle chivalry at work here, and in most of Ford's films, but it is never obtrusive enough to interfere with the flow of the narrative. The delicacy of emotion expressed here in three quick shots, perfectly cut, framed, and distanced, would completely escape the dulled perception of our more literary-minded film critics even if they deigned to consider a despised genre like the Western. The economy of expression that Ford has achieved in fifty years of film-making constitutes the beauty of his style. If it had taken him any longer than three shots and a few seconds to establish this insight into the Bond character, the point would not be worth making. Ford would be false to the manners of a time and a place bounded by the rigorous necessity of survival.

Ford's major works can be traced in a rising parabola from *Steamboat 'Round the Bend* to *Seven Women,* but even when Ford is in less than top form there are marginal compensations. His sentimentality extends to his casting not only of leads but also of the most minute bit roles. As Jean Mitry once observed, there is a John Ford world with a distinctive look to it. *How Green Was My Valley* established Maureen O'Hara as the definitive Ford heroine just as *Stagecoach* established John Wayne as the definitive John Ford hero. The extraordinary rapport of the Wayne-O'Hara team through *Rio Grande, The Quiet Man,* and *Wings of Eagles* adds a sexual dimension to Ford's invocation of tradition in human experience. *How Green Was My Valley* is also notable for introducing Ford's visual treatment of the past as a luminous memory more real than the present, and presumably more than the heroic future. Ford and Hawks, the directors closest to the Griffith tradition, project different aspects of Griffith's personality: Ford the historical perspective and unified vision of the world, and Hawks the psychological complexity and innate nobility of characterization.

Ford can never become fashionable again for the rigidly ideological critics of the Left. Too many of his characters wear uniforms without any tortuous reasoning why. Even the originally pacifistic *What Price Glory* is transformed by Ford into a nostalgic celebration of military camaraderie with the once-raucous Charmaine emerging from the dim shadows as an idealization of the Chivalric Code. As a director, Ford developed his craft in the twenties, achieved dramatic force in the thirties, epic sweep in the forties, and symbolic evocation in the fifties. His style has evolved almost miraculously into a double vision of an event in all its vital immediacy and yet also in its ultimate memory image on the horizon of history.

Ford's failures tend to be objective rather than subjective in that he tends to be faithful to his own feelings at the expense of his material. *Mary of Scotland* is patently biased in favor of Mary against Elizabeth even in Maxwell Anderson's blank-minded verse version. Ford completes the travesty of historical objectivity by treating Katharine Hepburn's Mary as a soft-focused, unfairly slandered Madonna of the Scottish moors. (Curiously, it is not until *Seven Women* that Ford can bear to look at women with a degree of sexual ambiguity.) *When Willie Comes Marching Home* seemed to be a Preston Sturges project that Ford directed with undue seriousness, and *The Last Hurrah* lost much of its satiric sparkle in the transition from novel into film. *The Fugitive,* like *The Informer,* runs counter to Ford's sense of order. Graham Greene's renegade priest and Liam O'Flaherty's renegade informer are clearly beyond Ford's comprehension, and in both instances Ford's casual Catholicism cannot grapple with the causal Catholicism in the two novels. Nor with the Left-wing politics of the two novelists. *Cheyenne Autumn* is a failure simply because Ford cannot get inside the Indians he is trying to ennoble.

Ultimately, Ford's cinema must be considered a continent full of mountain peaks and desert valleys. *The Horse Soldiers* is weakest when the characters are talking abstractly about war, but the march of the little boy soldiers lingers in the mind long after all the dialogues have been forgotten. Tyrone Power may have played very broadly in *The Long Gray Line,* but who can forget the first materialization of his family at the kitchen table or Maureen O'Hara's standing in the doorway and watching a son-substitute go off to war. Ford is more than the sum of his great moments, however. A storyteller and poet of images, he made his movies both move and be moving.

D. W. GRIFFITH (1875–1948)

FILMS (partial list 1908–1914): 1908—The Adventures of Dollie, For the Love of Gold, After Many Years, The Taming of the Shrew, The Song of the Shirt. 1909—Edgar Allan Poe, The Curtain Pole, The Politician's Love Story, The Voice of the Violin, The Medicine Bottle, The Drunkard's Reformation, The Suicide Club, Resurrection, The Cricket on the Hearth, What Drink Did, The Violin Maker of Cremona, The Lonely Villa, Her First Biscuits, A Convict's Sacrifice, The Mended Lute, The Sealed Room; 1776: or, The Hessian Renegades; In Old Kentucky, Leather Stockings, Pippa Passes, A Change of Heart, In the Watches of the Night, Through the Breakers, Lines of White on a Sullen Sea, Nursing a Viper, The Restoration, The Light That Came, The Red Man's View, A Corner in Wheat. 1910—In Old California, As It Is in Life, The Unchanging Sea, Ramona, In the Season of Buds, A Child of the Ghetto, The Face at the Window, Muggsy's First Sweetheart, The House with Closed Shutters, The Usurer, Rose o' Salem Town, The Iconoclast, That Chink at Golden Gulch, The Message of the Violin, Waiter No. 5, The Lesson. 1911—The Two Paths, The Italian Barber, His Trust, His Trust Fulfilled, The Manicure Lady, What Shall We Do with Our Old, Fisher Folk, The Lily of the Tenements, The Heart of a Savage, A Decree of Destiny, The Lonedale Operator, The Spanish Gypsy, Paradise Lost, How She Triumphed, Enoch Arden, The Primal Call, Fighting Blood, The Last Drop of Water, The Squaw's Love, The Revenue Man and the Girl, Her Awakening, The Battle, Through Darkened Vales, The Miser's Heart, The Failure, A Terrible Discovery. 1912—For His Son, A Mender of Nets, The Goddess of Sagebrush Gulch, A Girl and Her Trust, The Female of the Species, The Lesser Evil, The Old Actor, A Temporary Truce, Lena and the Geese, Man's Lust for Gold, Man's Genesis, The Sands of Dee, A

Change of Spirit, A Pueblo Legend, An Unseen Enemy, A Feud in the Kentucky Hills, The Musketeers of Pig Alley, My Baby, Friends, The Massacre, The New York Hat, The God Within, Greed, The One She Loved. 1913—Broken Ways, The Sheriff's Baby, The Mothering Heart, The Battle at Elderbush Gulch, Judith of Bethulia, The Battle of the Sexes. 1914—The Escape, Home Sweet Home, The Avenging Conscience, The Mother and the Law. 1915—*The Birth of a Nation.* 1916—*Intolerance.* 1918—*Hearts of the World,* The Great Love, The Greatest Thing in Life. 1919—A Romance of Happy Valley, The Girl Who Stayed at Home, *Broken Blossoms, True Heart Susie,* The Fall of Babylon, The Mother and the Law, Scarlet Days, The Greatest Question. 1920—The Idol Dancer, The Love Flower, *Way Down East.* 1921—*Dream Street.* 1922— *Orphans of the Storm,* One Exciting Night. 1923—*The White Rose.* 1924—America, *Isn't Life Wonderful?* 1925—Sally of the Sawdust, That Royle Girl. 1926—Sorrows of Satan. 1928—Drums of Love, The Battle of the Sexes. 1929—Lady of the Pavements. 1930 —*Abraham Lincoln.* 1931—*The Struggle.* 1940—One Million, B.C. (signed by Hal Roach, but reputedly directed by Griffith).

It is about time that D. W. Griffith was rescued from the false pedestal of an outmoded pioneer. The cinema of Griffith is no more outmoded, after all, than the drama of Aeschylus. When one observes in the bird-in-a-cage telephone-booth image in Hitchcock's *The Birds* a derivation of a similarly objective viewpoint in Griffith's *Broken Blossoms,* the alleged antiquity of Griffith becomes more dubious than ever. Only in film history is half a century treated as a millennium. This is particularly true of the liberal, technological, or Marxist historians who have embraced a theory of Progress in contradistinction to all other arts. By their standards, the cinema does not rise or fall, as do all other arts, in relation to the artists involved. Instead, the cinema is subject to a certain mystical process of evolution by which Griffith's Babylonian crane shots are on the bottom rung of a ladder that mounts to Eisenstein's Odessa Steps. Conversely, the fallacious assumption that the cinema rose progressively from Griffith to Murnau to Eisenstein in the period from 1915 through 1928 implies that the cinema was betrayed from 1929 onward. The fact remains that Griffith, Murnau, and Eisenstein had differing visions of the world, and their technical "contributions" can never be divorced from their personalities. The recent rediscovery of Griffith in New York and Paris centered not on the relatively familiar landmarks, *The Birth of a Nation* and *Intolerance,* but on such underrated masterpieces as *Broken Blossoms, True Heart Susie, Way Down East, Dream Street,* and *Orphans of the Storm.*

We might observe that Griffith's silent films, like Sternberg's and Stroheim's, are often carelessly evaluated in terms of their absurd titles. When Griffith is mistakenly called naïve, the titles of his films are usually responsible even when the images belie them. However, in recent years, both Jean Renoir and Josef von Sternberg have explicitly repudiated the titles connecting their films. Griffith was certainly not a writer in any serious literary sense, but a film-maker of extraordinary complexity and depth. When Richard Barthelmess first confronts Lillian Gish in *Broken Blossoms,* the subtle exchange of emotions between the two players would defy the art of the greatest novelist, but the scene is almost invariably measured by the dime-magazine title that "explains" it. The same critics and historians who denounced the intrusion of dialogue into the silent film were guilty of reducing the glorious images of the silent cinema to the feeble conventions of the explanatory title. Very early in his career, Griffith mastered most of the technical vocabulary of the cinema, and then proceeded to simplify his vocabulary for the sake of greater psychological penetration of the dramatic issues that concerned him. Like all great artists, his art had become so deceptively simple by the time of *Abraham Lincoln* that most critics assumed that he was in decline. Yet today the stark simplicity of *Lincoln* looks infinitely greater than the once-fashionable razzle-dazzle of Mamoulian's *Applause.*

The debt that all film-makers owe to D. W. Griffith defies calculation. Even before *The Birth of a Nation,* he had managed to synthesize the dramatic and documentary elements of the modern feature film. He traced the paths of his players across natural landscapes without the slightest trace of incongruity. Indeed, the rural countryside of *True Heart Susie* and *The White Rose* is in complete harmony with the careless rapture of Lillian Gish and Mae Marsh. For Griffith, a tree was more than a tree. Its strength and vulnerability expressed metaphorically the emotional life of his heroines. Modern audiences have lost this sense of psychological harmony with nature to the extent that the trees in, say, Antonioni's compositions serve as metaphors of cosmic indifference. The harmonies of Griffith have become the dissonances of Antonioni. The moral order to which Griffith's scenarios refer no longer exists. What remains to delight the modern connoisseur are torrents and torrents of classical acting, forceful, direct and full-bodied, cleanly and inventively directed with full psychological accountability. Literary pundits may see great profundities in Monica Vitti's inscrutable smile, but it is much harder for an actress to express feelings like joy and fear than to let her director express them for her with literary metaphors of vision. Lillian Gish is an infinitely greater actress than Monica Vitti because Griffith's cinema demands a rediscovery of behavioral reality, whereas Antonioni's divests characters of their personalities for the sake of a literary statement on alienation and boredom.

Griffith devised a grammar of emotions through his expressive editing. The focal length of his lens became a function of feeling. Close-ups not only intensified an emotion; they shifted characters from the republic of prose to the kingdom of poetry. Griffith's privileged moments are still among the most beautiful in all cinema. They belong to him alone, since they are beyond mere technique. Griffith invented this "mere" technique, but he also transcended it.

HOWARD HAWKS (1896–1977)

FILMS: 1926—The Road to Glory, Fig Leaves. 1927—The Cradle Snatchers, Paid to Love. 1928—*A Girl in Every Port,* Fazil, The Air Circus. 1929—Trent's Last Case. 1930—*The Dawn Patrol.* 1931—The Criminal Code. 1932—The Crowd Roars, *Scarface,* Tiger Shark. 1933—Today We Live. 1934—*Twentieth Century,* Viva Villa! (completed and signed by Jack Conway). 1935—Barbary Coast. 1936—*Ceiling Zero, The Road to Glory,* Come and Get It (with William Wyler). 1938—*Bringing Up Baby.* 1939—*Only Angels Have Wings.* 1940—*His Girl Friday.* 1941—Sergeant York, Ball of Fire. 1943—*Air Force.* 1944—*To Have and Have Not.* 1946—*The Big Sleep.* 1948—*Red River,* A Song Is Born.

1949—*I Was a Male War Bride.* 1952—*The Big Sky, Monkey Business,* O'Henry's Full House (The Ransom of Red Chief episode). 1953—*Gentlemen Prefer Blondes.* 1955—The Land of the Pharaohs. 1959—*Rio Bravo.* 1962—*Hatari!* 1964—*Man's Favorite Sport.* 1965—Red Line—7000. 1967—*El Dorado.*

Howard Hawks was until recently the least known and least appreciated Hollywood director of any stature. His name is not mentioned in the indices of Kracauer's *Theory of Film, Grierson on Documentary* (which discusses many Hollywood directors), Lewis Jacobs's *The Rise of the American Film,* and Roger Manvell's *Penguin Film* series. Paul Rotha's *The Film Till Now* makes one brief reference to Hawks: "A very good all-rounder" [who] "stays in the mind with *The Crowd Roars, Scarface, Ball of Fire,* and *The Big Sleep."* By contrast, Hawks had been greatly admired in France since *Scarface* in 1932. But then it was easier to see *Scarface* in Paris than in New York through the thirties and forties. Many revival houses featured a double bill of *The Public Enemy* and *Little Caesar,* but *Scarface* was always withheld from circulation by the Howard Hughes interests. (It would be interesting to know where and when the late Robert Warshow saw *Scarface,* to which he refers briefly in his famous essay on *The Gangster as Tragic Hero.*) Once Hawks was discovered, however, he revealed a consistent personal style and view of the world. If anything, *Man's Favorite Sport, Red Line —7000,* and *El Dorado* are quintessentially and self-consciously Hawksian. The same lines and basic situations pop up in film after film with surprisingly little variation. Call it classicism or cliché, the fact remains that for a director whose credentials are so obscure to English-speaking critics, Hawks has retained a surprising degree of control over his assignments, choosing the ones he wanted to do, and working on the scripts of all his films. The Hawksian hero acts with remarkable consistency in a predominantly male universe.

If Ford's heroes are sustained by tradition, the Hawksian hero is upheld by an instinctive professionalism. Even during the Depression, Hawksian characters were always gainfully employed. The idea that a man is measured by his work rather than by his ability to communicate with women is the key to Hawksian masculinity, as the converse is the key to Antonioni's femininity. Whereas Ford's attitude to his women can be defined in terms of chivalry, the Hawksian woman is a manifestation of the director's gallantry.

Like his heroes, Howard Hawks has lived a tightrope existence, keeping his footing in a treacherous industry for more than forty years without surrendering his personal identity. It is impossible to single out any one of his films as a definitive summation of his career, and it is unlikely that he will ever discard the mask of the commercial film-maker, although he comes very close in *El Dorado* when one of his characters recites Poe's "Eldorado" almost as a tribute to perceptive French criticism of both Poe and Hawks.

Throughout his career Hawks has adjusted to technological changes without blazing a trail for others to follow. He came late to the talking film after Vidor, Lubitsch, von Sternberg, and Mamoulian had explored its potentialities, extremely late to the color film, and, despite an honorable effort in *Land of the Pharaohs,* he does not seem to have been enchanted by the world of the wide screen. His technique is a function of his personality and the material with which he has chosen to work. His scenarios, which invariably emphasize action within a short time span, do not lend themselves to decorative mannerisms. When he has been confronted with epic subjects in *Red River* and *Land of the Pharaohs,* he has split his story into two short segments of time a decade or so apart. He has never used a flashback, and even in the thirties he seldom resorted to the degenerative montage of time lapses. His tracking, cutting, and framing have never attracted much attention in themselves, and this is not so much a virtue as it may seem. Critics who argue that technique should not call attention to itself are usually critics who do not wish to call attention to technique. If Hawks does not choose to use technique as reflective commentary on action, it is because his personality expresses a pragmatic intelligence rather than a philosophical wisdom.

Hawks has an uncanny technical flair for establishing the mood of the film at the outset and sustaining this mood to the end. The atmosphere established in the opening fog-enshrouded shots of *Barbary Coast, Road to Glory* and *Only Angels Have*

Wings casts a spell that is uniquely Hawksian. The opening, wordless sequences in *Rio Bravo* present all the moral issues of the film. The low-angle shot of Wayne looking down at Martin with sorrowful disdain tells the audience all it has to know about the two men, and Hawks even tilts his camera to isolate the relationship from its background and to intensify the reciprocal feelings of shame and disappointment. However, Hawks never tilts his camera again in the film, and the intensity of the opening tapers off into comic understatement. This is typical of the director's tendency to veer away from dramatization and verbalization of feelings that are implicit in the action.

Hawks consciously shoots most of his scenes at the eye level of a standing onlooker. Consequently, even his spectacles are endowed with a human intimacy which the director will not disturb with pretentious crane shots. Hawks will work within a frame as much as possible, cutting only when a long take or an elaborate track might distract his audience from the issues in the foreground of the action. This is good, clean, direct, functional cinema, perhaps the most distinctively American cinema of all. It is certainly not the last word on the art of film-making, but its qualities are more unusual than most critics have imagined. However, even at the time of their release, the Hawks films were generally liked for their solid professionalism. The director has worked with the most distinguished cameramen in Hollywood: Gregg Toland, Lee Garmes, James Wong Howe, Tony Gaudio, Ernest Haller, Russell Harlan, and Sid Hickox. Hawks himself has never been less than a professional, but he has been more as well. His technique has served ultimately to express his personal credo that man is the measurer of all things.

Aside from a few gibes at red-baiting in *His Girl Friday,* Hawks has never indicated any specific political orientation. The religious lunatic in *Twentieth Century,* the revivalism in *Sergeant York,* and the mordant piety after the brutal fact in *Red River* constitute what little there is of religion in the world of Howard Hawks. Except for *Sergeant York,* Hawks has never dealt with the very poor as a class, and except for *Bringing Up Baby,* he has never dealt with the very rich as a class. To the best of my memory there has never been a divorce or a gratuitous suicide in any of the director's films. Hawks rejected *Fourteen*

Hours as a directorial assignment because he explicitly disapproved of the theme of suicide as a form of neurotic escape. (Henry Hathaway later accepted this assignment.) Curiously, however, *Dawn Patrol, Today We Live, Ceiling Zero,* and *Road to Glory* have quasi-suicidal climaxes in which characters accept fatal missions, but the moral arithmetic balances out because in each instance the martyr is a replacement in an obligatory situation. However, it may be significant that all these sacrificial episodes occurred in films of the thirties, an era in which the Hawksian virtues were most appropriate. A director of parts as well as a unified whole, Hawks has stamped his distinctively bitter view of life on adventure, gangster and private-eye melodramas, Westerns, musicals, and screwball comedies, the kind of thing Americans do best and appreciate least. Now that his work has been thoroughly revived and revaluated throughout the English-speaking world, there is little point in belaboring the point for the few remaining stragglers who maintain that his art is not really Art with a serving of espresso in the lobby. That one can discern the same directorial signature over a wide variety of genres is proof of artistry. That one can still enjoy the genres for their own sake is proof of the artist's professional urge to entertain.

ALFRED HITCHCOCK (1899–1980)

FILMS: 1925—The Pleasure Garden. 1926—The Mountain Eagle, The Lodger. 1927—Downhill, Easy Virtue, The Ring. 1928 —*The Farmer's Wife,* Champagne, The Manxman. 1929—*Blackmail.* 1930—Juno and the Paycock, *Murder.* 1931—The Skin Game. 1932—East of Shanghai, Number Seventeen. 1935—*The Man Who Knew Too Much, The 39 Steps,* Strauss' Great Waltz. 1936—*Secret Agent.* 1937—*Sabotage.* 1938—*The Lady Vanishes, A Girl Was Young.* 1939—Jamaica Inn. 1940—*Rebecca, Foreign Correspondent.* 1941—Mr. and Mrs. Smith, *Suspicion.* 1942—*Saboteur.* 1943—*Shadow of a Doubt.* 1944—Lifeboat. 1945—Spellbound. 1946—*Notorious.* 1947—The Paradine Case. 1948—Rope. 1949—*Under Capricorn.* 1950—*Stage Fright.* 1951—*Strangers on a Train.* 1953—*I Confess.* 1954— *Dial M for Murder, Rear Window.* 1955—*To Catch a Thief, The*

Trouble with Harry. 1956—*The Man Who Knew Too Much, The Wrong Man.* 1958—*Vertigo.* 1959—*North by Northwest.* 1960 —*Psycho.* 1963—*The Birds.* 1964—Marnie. 1966—*Torn Curtain.* 1969—Topaz, Frenzy.

Alfred Hitchcock is the supreme technician of the American cinema. Even his many enemies cannot begrudge him that distinction. Like Ford, Hitchcock cuts in his mind, and not in the cutting room with five different setups for every scene. His is the only contemporary style that unites the divergent classical traditions of Murnau (camera movement) and Eisenstein (montage). (Welles, for example, owes more to Murnau, whereas Resnais is closer to Eisenstein.) Unfortunately, Hitchcock seldom receives the visual analysis he deserves in the learned Anglo-American periodicals devoted ostensibly to the art of the cinema. Pages and pages will be expended on Resnais's synchronized tracks in *Last Year at Marienbad,* but the subtler diminuendo of Hitchcock's cross-tracking in the American remake of *The Man Who Knew Too Much* will pass by unnoticed. Truffaut, Chabrol, and Resnais can pay homage to Hitchcock, but the Anglo-American admirers of Truffaut, Chabrol, and Resnais will continue to pass off Hitchcock as a Continental aberration. "The Master of Suspense" is thus virtually without honor in his own countries.

Hitchcock's art is full of paradoxes. *The Birds,* for example, reveals a rigorous morality coupled with a dark humor, but the theme of complacency that runs through all his work is now so explicit that it is generally misunderstood. Hitchcock requires a situation of normality, however dull it may seem on the surface, to emphasize the evil abnormality that lurks beneath the surface. Hitchcock understands, as his detractors do not, the crucial function of counterpoint in the cinema. You cannot commit a murder in a haunted house or dark alley, and make a meaningful statement to the audience. The spectators simply withdraw from these bizarre settings, and let the décor dictate the action. It is not Us up there on the screen, but some play actors trying to be sinister. However, when murder is committed in a gleamingly sanitary motel bathroom during a cleansing shower, the incursion of evil into our well-laundered existence becomes intolerable. We may laugh nervously or snort disgustedly, but we shall never be quite so complacent again. Hitchcock's repeated invasions of everyday life with the most outrageous melodramatic devices have shaken the foundations of the facile humanism that insists that people are good, and only systems evil, as if the systems themselves were not functions of human experience. Much of the sick, perverse, antihumanistic humor sweeping through America today is an inevitable reaction to the sickening sentimentality of totalitarianism masquerading as all-encompassing humanism. Hitchcock has never been accepted as part of this fashionable sickness, and his unfashionableness is all to his credit. He insists, almost intolerantly, upon a moral reckoning for his characters and for his audience. We can violate the Commandments at our own psychic peril, but we must pay the price in guilt at the end. Hitchcock can be devious, but he is never dishonest.

Hitchcock's reputation has suffered from the fact that he has given audiences more pleasure than is permissible for serious cinema. No one who is so entertaining could possibly seem profound to the intellectual puritans. Furthermore, did not Santayana once observe that complete understanding extinguishes pleasure? No matter. Hitchcock's art will always delight the specialist because so much of it is rendered with an air of casualness. The iron is encased in velvet, the irony in simplicity—simplicity, however, on so many levels that the total effect is vertiginously complex. Beneath the surface melodrama of every Hitchcock film is a lively comedy of manners. In this regard, *The Farmer's Wife* of 1928 displays Hitchcock's flair for satiric pantomime much as Dreyer's *Master of the House* reveals the Great Dane apart from the shadow of eternity. Hitchcock's style is alive to the expressive potentialities of the slightest encounter. His cutting is the means by which he contradicts what people say by what they do. In the beginning of his career, he was attracted to montage as a mental language. In *Murder* (1930) a sleuth-type character thinks of the hot meal he is missing at home in order to stay at a dingy hotel, and Hitchcock cuts to a spatially abstract shot of roast duckling purely as a mental expression of a gourmet's grief. Hitchcock quickly abandoned this experiment in favor of the intricate editing of objects and glances within a scene. His films abound with objects as visual correlatives—the missing finger in *The 39 Steps*, the crashing cymbals (not symbols) in both versions (1935 and 1956) of *The Man Who Knew Too Much*, the milk chocolates on the assembly line in *Secret Agent*, the knife and time bomb in *Sabotage*, the doctored drink in *The Lady Vanishes*, the twitching eye in *A Girl Was Young*, the monogrammed pillowcase in *Rebecca*, the reverse-sailing windmills in *Foreign Correspondent*, the conjugally crossed skis in *Mr. and Mrs. Smith*, the sinister glasses of milk in *Suspicion* and *Spellbound*, the magisterial Statue of Liberty in *Saboteur*, the incriminating ring in *Shadow of a Doubt*, the concealed compass in *Lifeboat*, the key to the winecellar in *Notorious*, the hypnotic portrait in *The Paradine Case*, the omnipresent trunk in *Rope*, the shrunken head in *Under Capricorn*, the bloodstained doll in *Stage Fright*, the incriminating cigarette lighter in *Strangers on a Train*, the falling bicycle in *I Confess*, the latchkeys in *Dial M for Murder*, the wedding ring in *Rear Window*, the cat in *To Catch a Thief*, the bothersome corpse in *The Trouble with Harry*, the hallucinatory coiffure in *Vertigo*, the crop duster in *North by Northwest*, the motel shower in *Psycho*, the besieged telephone booth in *The Birds*, the papier-mâché flames in *Torn Curtain*. Hitchcock's objects are never mere props of a basically theatrical mise-en-scène, but rather the very substance of his cinema. These objects embody the feelings and fears of characters as object and character interact with each other in dramas within dramas.

The late James Agee perceived the novelistic nuances of Hitchcock's visual storytelling in *Notorious*, but most American reviewers have failed to appreciate the Hitchcockian virtues of vividness and speed as artistic merits. Hitchcock's economy of expression can be compared favorably to that of any of his colleagues or imitators. There is, for example, a Hitchcockian touch in John Huston's direction of *Reflections in a Golden Eye*. Marlon Brando's Captain Penderton is following a private with whom he is obsessed. There is a sound of a car crash behind Brando. The private and his buddies all turn to look at the crash. Brando keeps staring at the private. The Hitchcockian equivalent of this sequence occurs in *Strangers on a Train* at a tennis match involving a troubled participant played by Farley Granger. The visual coup of the sequence is the familiar joke of spectators at a tennis match swiveling their heads back and forth to follow the action. All heads swivel but one—that of a psychopathic murderer played by Robert Walker. The difference of camera placement and editing between the Hitchcock sequence and the Huston sequence is the difference between visual directness and visual obliqueness. Hitchcock gives the audience the point immediately with a device designed for maximum vividness. Huston's effect is slower in making its point. Paradoxically, however, Hitchcock is more oblique psychologically than Huston. Hitchcock's characters are ostensibly obsessed by the issues of a contrived melodrama. The Walker character has proposed to the Granger character an exchange of murders so that the police would be left without a plausible motive for either murder. The Granger character has never taken the proposition seriously enough to reject it flatly, and he is horrified to discover that he is an accomplice to one murder and expected to keep his end of the bargain by committing another. Walker stalks Granger everywhere, most memorably at the tennis match. It is only under the surface of the melodrama that the darker humor of homosexual obsessiveness comes into play as an added layer of meaning. Huston's treatment of homosexuality is much closer to the surface. Indeed, the Brando characterization of Captain Penderton is less subtle and repressed than the Carson McCullers original out of her Gothic novel. Hitchcock is ultimately more cinematic; Huston more literary. Hitchcock operates on many levels, Huston only on one. The beauty of Hitchcock's style is a function of its speed and efficiency in operating a time mechanism. Huston's personality is not expressed so much through the medium itself as in a sour reaction to its emotional facility.

Hitchcock has worked with big stars from Nita Naldi to Julie Andrews and from Ivor Novello to Paul Newman, but he has generally managed to impart Hitchcockian humor to the most distinctive personalities. The ultra-Hitchcockian performances are those of James Stewart in *Rope, Rear Window, The Man Who Knew Too Much,* and *Vertigo* and Cary Grant in *Suspicion, Notorious, To Catch a Thief,* and *North by Northwest.* Stewart and Grant gave Hitchcock the means he could not have got from any other actors. In return, Hitchcock gave Stewart and Grant meanings they could not have got from any other director. Nonetheless Hitchcock has seldom been the favorite director of his players. Thespians traditionally prefer weaker wills and more adaptable visions of life.

BUSTER KEATON (1895–1966)

FILMS: Roscoe ("Fatty") Arbuckle two-reelers, directed by and starring Arbuckle: 1917—The Butcher Boy, Rough House, His Wedding Night, Fatty at Coney Island, Oh, Doctor!; Out West. 1918 —The Bell Boy, Goodnight Nurse, Moonshine, The Cook. 1919— A Desert Hero, Backstage, A Country Hero, The Garage. 1920— The Saphead (feature film directed by Winchell Smith and starring Keaton). Two- and three-reelers produced by and starring Keaton: 1920—The High Sign (written and directed by Keaton and Eddie Cline), One Week, Convict 13, The Scarecrow, Neighbors. 1921— The Haunted House, Hard Luck, The Goat (written and directed by Keaton and Malcolm St. Clair), The Playhouse (directed by Keaton and Cline), *The Boat,* The Paleface. 1922—*Cops,* My Wife's Relations, The Blacksmith, *The Frozen North, The Electric House, Daydreams.* 1923—*Balloonatics,* The Love Nest (directed by Keaton). Features produced by and starring Keaton: 1923—The Three Ages (directed by Keaton and Cline), *Our Hospitality* (directed by Keaton and Jack Blystone). 1924—*Sherlock Jr.* (directed by Keaton), *The Navigator* (directed by Keaton and Donald Crisp). 1925—Seven Chances (directed by Keaton), Go West (directed by Keaton). 1926 —*Battling Butler* (directed by Keaton), *The General* (directed by Keaton and Clyde Bruckman). 1927—*College* (directed by James Horne), *Steamboat Bill Jr.* (directed by Charles "Chuck" Reisner). 1928—The Cameraman (directed by Edward Sedgwick, Jr.). 1929 —Spite Marriage (directed by Sedgwick). 1930—Free and Easy (directed by Sedgwick). Doughboys (directed by Sedgwick). 1931— Speak Easily (directed by Sedgwick). 1932—Parlor, Bedroom and Bath (directed by Sedgwick), The Passionate Plumber (directed by Sedgwick). 1933—Sidewalks of New York (directed by Jules White and Zion Myers), What, No Beer? (directed by Sedgwick).

Keaton appeared in close to sixty films after 1933, most memorably in *San Diego I Love You, Sunset Boulevard, Limelight,* and

A Funny Thing Happened on the Way to the Forum, but only in *Limelight* with Chaplin was there a spark of the creative fire behind the deadpan mask. Even Samuel Beckett contributed to the desecration of the Keaton mask by involving the actor of absurdity before its time in a dreary exercise called *Film,* the most pretentious title in all cinema.

That Buster Keaton had regained a certain critical eminence before his death is due largely to the tireless efforts of the film cultists in the little magazines. What the late James Agee described as the "Golden Age of Comedy" (and Silence) has been distilled into the precious essence of Chaplin and Keaton or Keaton and Chaplin. (By contrast, the intermittent inspiration of Lloyd, Langdon, Arbuckle, Sennett, Laurel and Hardy, et al., seems relatively one-dimensional.) The difference between Keaton and Chaplin is the difference between poise and poetry, between the aristocrat and the tramp, between adaptability and dislocation, between the function of things and the meaning of things, between eccentricity and mysticism, between man as machine and man as angel, between the girl as a convention and the girl as an ideal, between the centripetal and the centrifugal tendencies of slapstick. Keaton is now generally acknowledged as the superior director and inventor of visual forms. There are those who would go further and claim Keaton as pure cinema as opposed to Chaplin's essentially theatrical cinema. Keaton's cerebral tradition of comedy was continued by Clair and Tati, but Keaton the actor, like Chaplin the actor, has proved to be inimitable. Ultimately, Keaton and Chaplin complement each other all the way down the line to that memorably ghostly moment in *Limelight* when they share the same tawdry dressing room as they prepare to face their lost audience.

Keaton's most striking visual coups involve the collision between an irresistible farce and an immovable persona. Immovable and imperturbable. At least on the surface. Time has transformed the surface calm of Keaton's countenance into a subtle beauty. There is a moment in *The General* when Keaton, exasperated by the stupidity of his Southern Belle sweetheart, makes a mock gesture to choke her, but then kisses her instead. This kiss constitutes one of the most glorious celebrations of heterosexual love in the history of the cinema. Unlike Chaplin, Keaton does not idealize women as projections of his own romantic fantasies. Keaton is more like Chabrol in *Les Bonnes Femmes* in perceiving the beauty of women through all their idiocies and irritations. Their beauty and their indispensability. Keaton accepts woman as his equal with clear-eyed candor, whereas Chaplin's misty-eyed mysticism is the façade of a misogynist.

A complete revival of Keaton's career is promised for 1968. Until that fateful moment of reappraisal, the evidence of *Cops, Sherlock Jr., The Navigator,* and *The General* is sufficient to stamp Keaton as the most enduringly modern of classical directors. A stylistic footnote is in order here. When Jean-Luc Godard frames Jean-Paul Belmondo in an iris improvised out of Jean Seberg's rolled-up magazine spyglass, the knowledgeable film aesthete identifies this mannerism in *Breathless* as a tribute to Samuel Fuller's iris frame in *Forty Guns.* Fuller's viewpoint represented that of a real spyglass. *Breathless* was released in Paris in 1960 and in New York in 1961. *Forty Guns* came out in New York in 1957. Back in 1926, Keaton devised the same iris frame (in *The General*) out of a tablecloth burned through by a careless cigar. Keaton's Confederate fugitive, hiding under a Union table, sees his sweetheart through the hole in the tablecloth as in a locket tintype. It is a measure of Keaton's classicism that he conceals this poetic effect within a contrived plot. By contrast, Fuller and Godard flaunt the effect in a manner that can be described as self-consciously decadent.

FRITZ LANG (1890–1976)

FILMS: 1919—Halb-Blut, Der Herr der Liebe, Die Spinnen (Part One): Der Goldene See, Hara Kiri, Die Spinnen (Part Two): Das Brillanten Schiff. 1920—Das Wandernde Bild. 1921—Vier um die Frau, Der Müde Tod. 1922—*Dr. Mabuse, Der Spieler.* 1924 —*Die Niebelungen.* 1926—*Metropolis.* 1928—*Spione,* Frau im Mond. 1932—*M;* Das Testament von Dr. Mabuse. 1933—Liliom. American period: 1936—*Fury.* 1937—*You Only Live Once.* 1938 —You and Me. 1940—The Return of Frank James. 1941— Western Union, *Manhunt.* 1943—*Hangmen Also Die.* 1945— *Ministry of Fear, The Woman in the Window, Scarlet Street.* 1946—

Cloak and Dagger. 1948—Secret Beyond the Door. 1950—House by the River, American Guerilla in the Philippines. 1952—*Rancho Notorious,* Clash by Night. 1953—The Blue Gardenia, *The Big Heat.* 1954—Human Desire. 1955—*Moonfleet.* 1956—While the City Sleeps, Beyond a Reasonable Doubt. 1960—Journey to the Lost City (English-German languages). 1961—*The Thousand Eyes of Dr. Mabuse.*

Fritz Lang's cinema is the cinema of the nightmare, the fable, and the philosophical dissertation. Lang's apparent weaknesses are the consequences of his virtues. He has always lacked the arid sophistication lesser directors display to such advantage. Lang's plots generally go inexplicably sour or sentimental at the very end. His characters never develop with any psychological precision, and his world lacks the details of verisimilitude that are so important to realistic critics. However, Lang's vision of the world is profoundly expressed by his visual forms. Where Renoir's *The Human Beast* is the tragedy of a doomed man caught up in the flow of life, Lang's remake, *Human Desire,* is the nightmare of an innocent man enmeshed in the tangled strands of fate. What we remember in Renoir are the faces of Gabin, Simon, and Ledoux. What we remember in Lang are the geometrical patterns of trains, tracks, and fateful camera angles. If Renoir is humanism, Lang is determinism. If Renoir is concerned with the plight of his characters, Lang is obsessed with the structure of the trap. It must be stressed that Lang's cinema has not declined over the years. The same objections can be directed at both *Metropolis* and *Moonfleet,* and yet both films share the same bleak view of the universe where man grapples with his personal destiny, and inevitably loses. The last sea image of *Moonfleet* is Lang's chilling reconstruction of the legend of the Flying Dutchman. There is something of the voyeur in Lang; vide the flashlight sequence in *Metropolis* and the false mirror in the last *Mabuse.* His films take place in a closed world, but their formal brilliance and intellectual conceptions are incontestable. Lang is the cerebral tragedian of the cinema, and his lapses into absurdity are the evidence of a remote sagacity, an intellect that transforms images into ideas.

A curious pattern of paranoia runs through Lang's films from the first *Mabuse* in 1922 to the last in 1961. The pattern persists in his best Hollywood films—*Fury, You Only Live Once, Manhunt, Hangmen Also Die, Ministry of Fear, The Woman in the Window, Scarlet Street, Rancho Notorious,* and *The Big Heat.* As the servant of an allegedly optimistic film industry, Lang is singularly successful in undercutting audience expectations of a moral balance regained. Lang's prevailing image is that of a world ravaged and in flames. The hero is nearly burned to death in *Fury* and actually shot to death with his wife in *You Only Live Once.* The hero's wife is raped and murdered in *Rancho Notorious,* as is her child in a direct evocation of the bouncing-ball murder of the innocents in Lang's *M.* The hero's wife in *The Big Heat* is blown up when she presses the starter of the car, and her husband must then not only revenge her death but also assuage his guilt at being the intended victim of the bomb-planter. The most memorable violence in *The Big Heat* involves, not explosives, however, but scaldingly hot coffee flung in Gloria Grahame's face by Lee Marvin, and later, in a revenge worthy of Kriemhild, in Marvin's face by Grahame. In view of these outrages, Lang's violent mise-en-scène implies, the world must be destroyed before it can be purified.

Nonetheless Lang makes sentimental exceptions to this paranoia in the pure, trustworthy love of beautiful girls, a love capable of destroying the most intricately insidious conspiracies ever devised by evil minds. Romantic love with its intimations of Christian self-sacrifice flows through both the German and American periods of Lang's career, as strongly in *Spione* as in *The Ministry of Fear.* Sentimental exceptions aside, Lang might argue that in a century that has spawned Hitler and Hiroshima, no artist can be called paranoiac; he *is* being persecuted.

ERNST LUBITSCH (1892–1947)

FILMS: 1915–1918—twelve comedy shorts. 1918—Die Augen der Mumie Ma (The Eyes of the Mummy), The Ballet Girl, Carmen. 1919—Meyer from Berlin; My Wife, the Movie Star; The Schwab Maiden, The Oyster Princess, Rausch (Intoxication), *Mad-*

ame Dubarry (Passion), *Die Puppe* (The Doll). 1920—Kohlhiesel's Daughters, Romeo and Juliet in the Snow, Sumurun (One Arabian Night), Anne Boleyn (Deception). 1921—The Wildcat. 1922— The Loves of Pharaoh. 1923—Die Flamme (Montmartre). American period: 1923—Rosita. 1924—*The Marriage Circle,* Three Women, Forbidden Paradise. 1925—Kiss Me Again, *Lady Windermere's Fan.* 1926—*So This Is Paris.* 1927—The Student Prince. 1928—The Patriot, Eternal Love. 1929—*The Love Parade.* 1930 —Paramount on Parade (with Edmund Goulding, Victor Schertzinger, Rowland V. Lee, Edward Sutherland, Lother Mendes, Frank Tuttle, Dorothy Arzner, Edwin H. Knopf, Victor Heerman, Otto Brower), *Monte Carlo.* 1931—*The Smiling Lieutenant.* 1932— The Man I Killed, *One Hour With You* (Cukor directed from Lubitsch plan, signed by Lubitsch), *Trouble in Paradise,* If I Had a Million (with King Vidor, James Cruze, Norman Z. McLeod, Stephen S. Roberts, William A. Seiter, Norman Taurog, Bruce Humberstone). 1933—*Design for Living.* 1934—*The Merry Widow.* 1937— *Angel.* 1938—Bluebeard's Eighth Wife. 1939—*Ninotchka.* 1940 —*The Shop Around the Corner.* 1941—That Uncertain Feeling. 1942—*To Be or Not to Be.* 1943—*Heaven Can Wait.* 1946— *Cluny Brown.* 1948—That Lady in Ermine (completed by Otto Preminger after Lubitsch's death, signed by Lubitsch).

In the well-mannered, good-natured world of Ernst Lubitsch, grace transcends purpose. *To Be or Not to Be,* widely criticized as an inappropriately farcical treatment of Nazi terror, bridges the abyss between laughter and horror. For Lubitsch, it was sufficient to say that Hitler had bad manners, and no evil was then inconceivable. What are manners, after all, but the limits to man's presumption, a recognition that we all eventually lose the game of life but that we should still play the game according to the rules. A poignant sadness infiltrates the director's gayest moments, and it is this counterpoint between sadness and gaiety that represents the Lubitsch touch, and not the leering humor of closed doors. Describing Lubitsch as the continental sophisticate is as inadequate as describing Hitchcock as the master of suspense. Garbo's pixilated speech in *Ninotchka* is pitched delicately between the comic and the cosmic, and in one breathtaking moment, Garbo and Lubitsch sway on the tightrope between grace and purpose.

Lubitsch was always the least Germanic of German directors, as Lang was the most Germanic. The critics were always so obsessed with what Lubitsch naughtily left off the screen that they never fully evaluated what was left on. It seems incredible that Lubitsch's silent *Lady Windermere's Fan* was an improvement on Wilde's original. Everyone remembers Wilde's epigrams, which were largely irrelevant to the plot, but Lubitsch redeemed Wilde's silly melodramatics through the sardonic wit of his images and players. There were many Lubitsch imitators in the thirties, but none could penetrate beyond the master's most superficial mannerisms.

Lubitsch's German period ran between 1915 and 1923, the American period from 1923 to the director's death in 1947, or three times as long. Consequently, Lubitsch, unlike Lang and Murnau, is more an American director than a German director, and must be evaluated accordingly, particularly after 1933 for such neglected masterpieces as *Design for Living, The Merry Widow, Angel, The Shop Around the Corner, To Be or Not to Be, Heaven Can Wait,* and *Cluny Brown,* all in all, a dazzling display of stylistic unity transcending varied source materials. The conventional critics of the time decided that Gary Cooper and Fredric March were miscast for *Design for Living,* Chevalier was too old for *The Merry Widow,* Marlene Dietrich too stiff for *Angel,* James Stewart and Margaret Sullavan too cute for *The Shop Around the Corner,* Carole Lombard and Jack Benny too disparate for *To Be or Not to Be,* Gene Tierney and Don Ameche too guileless for *Heaven Can Wait,* and Jennifer Jones and Charles Boyer too strained for *Cluny Brown.* And that was that. However, Lubitsch has had the last laugh in that the magical qualities of his films have survived the topical distractions of his detractors. If *Angel* evokes Pirandello as *The Shop Around the Corner* evokes Molnar, it is because Lubitsch taught the American cinema the importance of appearances for appearance's sake (Pirandello) and the indispensability of good manners (Molnar). Lubitsch was the last of the genuine continentals let loose on the American continent, and we shall never see his like again because the world he celebrated had died—even before he did—everywhere except in his own memory.

F. W. MURNAU (1889–1931)

FILMS: 1919—Der Knabe in Blau. 1920—Satanas, Sehn-sucht, Der Buckelige und die Tänzerin, Der Januskopf, Abend . . . Nacht . . . Morgen, Der Gang in die Nacht. 1921—Marizza, Gennant die Schmugglermadonna; Schloss Vogeloed. 1922—*Nosferatu*, Der Brennende Acker, Phantom. 1923—Die Austreibung. 1924—Die Finanzen des Grossherzogs, *The Last Laugh*. 1926—Tartuffe, *Faust*. 1927—*Sunrise*. 1928—Four Devils. 1930—Our Daily Bread (City Girl). 1931—*Tabu* (with Robert Flaherty).

The tradition Murnau represents is that of the director who decides how much of the world will be revealed to his audience. The aesthetic of camera movement over montage implies the continuousness of a visual field outside the frame of a film. What we see on the screen is what the director has chosen to show us. He could have shown us more or less or something else, but he chose to show us what he has shown us for a specific purpose. In *Faust,* the screen is momentarily dark. Suddenly it is illuminated by a candle, and we see a man carrying the candle down some stairs. The man, the candle, the stairs have materialized out of the darkness. The world has been manifested by the director. Spottiswoode or Arnheim would demystify this luminous moment by explaining the technical processes involved, but they could never fully express the magical effect of these processes upon an audience. This is the difference between viewing the cinema as the sum of its machinery and regarding it as the creation of its artists. Any director can track if he has the facilities at his disposal. Any director can illuminate a dark screen. But only Murnau could have given the meanings and moods to tracking and lighting that he did.

The limiting factor in Murnau's cinema is his conception of characters in terms of universals. His Everyman in *Faust, The Last Laugh, Sunrise,* and *Tabu* is no man in particular, and paradoxically, no man in general. Murnau's characters, like Lang's, are creatures of their private destinies. The director's fateful camera angles, again like Lang's, constitute the signature of a modern tragedian. Murnau's enclosed cosmos even in *Tabu* is the logical consequence of studio cinema, and the ultimate presumption of his mise-en-scène. It might be supposed that after the extraordinary artistry of *Sunrise* and *Tabu,* Murnau's future in the American cinema seemed limitless. His tragic death in a car accident shortly after he had signed a Paramount contract removed for all time the staggering possibilities of a Murnau-Sternberg-Lubitsch triumvirate at one studio. On the other hand, the acute pessimism of *Tabu* seems today a fitting testament for a suicidally inclined artist.

Murnau's influence on the cinema has proved to be more lasting than Eisenstein's. Murnau's moving camera seems a more suitable style for exploring the world than does Eisenstein's dialectical montage, and the trend in modern movies has been toward escaping studio sets so as to discover the real world. Also, the modern cinema tends to be less manipulative and more expressionistic, less concerned with how the audience feels than with how the artist feels. The trolley ride from the country to the city in *Sunrise* is one of the most lyrical passages in the world cinema. It is also a prophetic passage in that it heralds the cinema of the future as the art of the traveler. Back in the silent era Murnau saw cinema as an international language to the extent of printing signs in Esperanto in *The Last Laugh.* Murnau never really made the transition to the sound film, but it is difficult to see how his style could have been adversely affected by the elimination of titles as breaks in the continuousness of his visual field. Indeed, there is a sequence in *Sunrise* in which music and pantomime are directly substituted for speech, as if the cinema were not silent at all, but merely straining to be heard through a technological barrier.

MAX OPHULS (1902–1957)

FILMS: 1930—Dann Schon Lieber Lebertran. 1931—Die Lachende Erben, Die Verliebte Firma. 1932—*Die Verkaufte Braut, Liebelei.* 1933—Une Histoire d'Amour, On a Vole un Homme. 1934—*La Signora di Tutti.* 1935—*Divine.* 1936—Komödie um

Geld, Ave Maria of Schubert (short), La Valse Brilliante (short) *La Tendre Ennemie.* 1937—Yoshiwara. 1938—Werther. 1939—Sans Lendemain. 1940—De Mayerling à Sarajevo. 1947—*The Exile.* 1948—*Letter from an Unknown Woman.* 1949—*Caught, The Reckless Moment.* 1950—*La Ronde.* 1951—*Le Plaisir.* 1953 —*Madame de . . .* 1955—*Lola Montès* (released in mutilated English-language version, Sins of Lola Montes, in New York, 1959).

The cinema of Max Ophuls translates tracking into walking. His fluid camera follows his characters without controlling them, and it is this stylistic expression of free will that finally sets Ophuls apart from Murnau and Hitchcock. However, the track is such a conspicuous element of film technique that Ophuls has never been sufficiently appreciated for his other merits. Even when he is most bitter, he never descends to caricature. His humor is never malicious, his irony never destructive. Like Renoir, he was one of the first genuinely international directors, the kind of artist who did not slur over national differences in the name of a spurious universality, but who defined national differences as functions of a larger unity. Consequently, Ophuls's American films, particularly *Caught* and *The Reckless Moment,* express a perceptive vision of America's glamorous fantasies (*Caught*) and the obsessive absorption with family at the expense of society (*The Reckless Moment*). Conversely, his treatment of European subjects in *The Exile* and *Letter from an Unknown Woman* lent grace and sensibility to the American cinema at a time when it was reeling from its false realism.

We claim Max as our own only to the extent that he happened to pass in our midst during his long voyage to sublimity. His influence was not so decisive as Murnau's or so pervasive as Renoir's. In the final analysis, Ophuls is, like all great directors, inimitable, and if all the dollies and cranes in the world snap to attention when his name is mentioned, it is because he gave camera movement its finest hours in the history of the cinema. When Joan Fontaine mounts the staircase to her lover's apartment for the last time, Ophuls's camera slowly turns from its vantage point on a higher landing to record the definitive memory-image of love. For a moment we enter the privileged sanctuary of remembrance, and *Letter from an Unknown*

Woman reverberates forever after with this intimation of mortality. Love, the memory of love, the mortality of love comprise the Ophulsian heritage. If Ophuls seemed inordinately devoted to baroque opulence, his devotion was nevertheless strong-minded enough to contemplate an underlying human vanity tinged with sadness at its impending doom. The sensuous fabrics and surfaces of the Ophulsian world never completely obscure the grinning skeletons in the closets, and luxury never muffles tragedy.

The main point is that Ophuls is much more than the sum of all his camera movements. What elementary aestheticians overlook in Ophuls is the preciseness of his sensibility. His women may dominate subjectively, but his men are never degraded objectively. James Mason in *Caught* does not know what Barbara Bel Geddes is feeling when he proposes to her, but Ophuls conveys through the acting sensibility of Mason that a man need not understand what a woman feels to be capable of providing love. The Bergman-Antonioni problem of communication between the sexes does not arise in Ophuls simply because the director recognizes the two separate spheres of men and women. The Ophulsian view is never feminist, like Mizoguchi's, or feminine like Bergman's and Antonioni's. No Ophulsian male, for example, is ever caught with his pants down like Gunnar Bjornstrand in *Smiles of a Summer Night* or Gabriele Ferzetti in *L'Avventura,* and no Ophulsian female ever displays the smug complacency toward her own moral superiority evidenced in the superior expressions of Eva Dahlbeck and Monica Vitti. We have instead the desperate effort of Wolfgang Liebeneiner in *Liebelei* to recapture his lost innocence with Magda Schneider on a sleigh ride that is mystically reprised by the camera after they both have died. It is not merely the moving camera that expresses the tragedy of lost illusions, but the preciseness of the playing. There is a direct link between Liebeneiner and Gérard Philipe's jaded count in *La Ronde* looking deep into Simone Signoret's eyes to find something he has forgotten forever. There is the same delicacy of regret nearly twenty years apart.

Some critics, particularly in England, have objected to the softening of Schnitzler's cynicism in the Ophuls versions of *Liebelei* and *La Ronde,* not to mention the Ophulsian rendering of De Maupassant in *Le Plaisir.* Ophuls himself once observed that

Schnitzler wrote *Liebelei* after *Reigen,* and not before. The implication is clear. It is cynicism, and not idealism, that is generally the mark of youthful immaturity, or rather it is the cynic who is generally the most foolish romantic. A cynic delights in the trivial deceptions lovers practice on each other, and his attitude is particularly fashionable in a culture dedicated to the happy ending. There is a time in every film critic's life when he thinks that Billy Wilder is more profound than John Ford, and that nastiness is more profound than nobility. However, the acquiring of moral wisdom comes with mortal awareness, and vice begins paying back all its youthful debts to virtue. At such a moment, Ophuls becomes more profound than Schnitzler and De Maupassant, and *Madame de* becomes infinitely more tragic than *The Bicycle Thief.* By showing man in his direst material straits, De Sica and Zavattini imply a solution to his problems. Ophuls offers no such comforting consolation. His elegant characters lack nothing and lose everything. There is no escape from the trap of time. Not even the deepest and sincerest love can deter the now from its rendezvous with the then, and no amount of self-sacrifice can prevent desire from becoming embalmed in memory. *"Quelle heure est-il?"* ask the characters in *La Ronde,* but it is always too late, and the moment has always passed.

This is the ultimate meaning of Ophulsian camera movement: time has no stop. Montage tends to suspend time in the limbo of abstract images, but the moving camera records inexorably the passage of time, moment by moment. As we follow the Ophulsian characters, step by step, up and down stairs, up and down streets, and round and round the ballroom, we realize their imprisonment in time. We know that they can never escape, but we know also that they will never lose their poise and grace for the sake of futile desperation. They will dance beautifully, they will walk purposively, they will love deeply, and they will die gallantly, and they will never whine or whimper or even discard their vanity. It will all end in a circus with Lola Montès selling her presence to the multitudes, redeeming all men both as a woman and as an artistic creation, expressing in one long receding shot, the cumulative explosion of the romantic ego for the past two centuries.

JEAN RENOIR (1894–1979)

FILMS: 1924—La Fille de l'Eau. 1926—*Nana.* 1927—Charleston, Marquitta. 1928—La Petite Marchande d'Allumettes. 1929—*Tire au Flanc,* Le Tournoi, Le Petit Chaperon Rouge, La P'tite Lili, Le Bled. 1931—On Purge Bébé, *La Chienne.* 1932—La Nuit du Carrefour, *Boudu Sauve des Eaux.* 1933—Chotard et Compagnie. 1934—*Toni, Madame Bovary.* 1935—*Le Crime de Monsieur Lange.* 1936—La Vie Est à Nous, *Une Partie de Campagne,* Les Bas Fonds. 1937—*La Bête Humaine.* 1939—*La Regle du Jeu.* 1940—La Tosca (with C. Koch and Luchino Visconti). 1941—*Swamp Water.* 1943—This Land Is Mine. 1944—Salute to France (allegorical documentary). 1945—*The Southerner.* 1946 —*Diary of a Chambermaid.* 1947—*The Woman on the Beach.* 1951—*The River.* 1954—*The Golden Coach.* 1956—*French Can Can.* 1957—*Paris Does Strange Things.* 1960—*Le Dejeuner sur l'Herbe.* 1961—Dr. Cordelier. 1963—*The Elusive Corporal* (Renoir wrote and produced Une Vie sans Joie in 1924, and Albert Dieudonne directed.)

Renoir's career is a river of personal expression. The waters may vary here and there in turbulence and depth, but the flow of personality is consistently directed to its final outlet in the sea of life. If the much-abused term "humanism," could be applied to Renoir's art and to no one else's, it might still provide an accurate definition for his work as a whole. In Renoir's films, man's natural surroundings are almost always prominently featured, and it is this emphasis on man in his environment photographed by an unblinking camera that is the true precursor of neorealism. As Murnau represents the formal antithesis to Eisenstein's montage principles, Renoir represents the thematic alternative to Eisenstein's dialectic. However, the fact that Renoir is a warm director and Eisenstein a cold one cannot be explained entirely through forms and themes. Directorial personality is, as always, the crucial determinant of a film's temperature. Murnau, after all, is cold, and Ophuls is warm, and both move their cameras. Chaplin is warm, and Keaton is cold, and both have evolved from the Sennett tradition. Lubitsch is warm, and Preminger is cold, and both are descended from the Viennese school. However, Renoir's preoccupation with his actors implies a concern with the unifying principles of humanity. *The Diary of a Chambermaid* is Renoir's definitive Resistance film. Never before had his characterizations been so Manichean. On one side were the fascists, the reactionaries, and the opportunists, and on the other, the enlightened aristocrats and the people, and the issue between the two groups could be resolved only by violence. Yet, before and after his committed periods, whether Marxist or patriotic, Renoir developed the themes of brotherly accommodation. Consequently, Renoir's career is not merely biography but also history. He has never looked back to an imaginary Golden Age, and he has never exploited past successes. The easy paths of cynicism and sentimentality have never appealed to him, and his unyielding sincerity is one of the glories of the cinema. If Renoir had not come to America in 1940, his work might have developed into an elaboration of the class structure as seen from the multiple viewpoint of *The Rules of the Game*. Renoir's American experience undoubtedly contributed to his transition from objectivity to subjectivity. In the American cinema, one must ultimately root for one side or another. The exceptions to this rule, most notably Hitchcock and Preminger, only confirm the rule. However, Renoir's conversion was only surface deep, and the multiple viewpoint was never really abandoned even in *The Diary of a Chambermaid*. The problem with most conventional critiques of Renoir's films is that humanism is invariably associated with crudity of expression, but there is nothing crude about Renoir's technique once its purposes have been fully understood. Only when style is confused with meaningless flourishes does Renoir's economy of expression seem inadequate for textbook critics.

JOSEF VON STERNBERG (1894–1969)

FILMS: 1925—*The Salvation Hunters*. 1926—The Sea Gull, The Exquisite Sinner. 1927—*Underworld*. 1928—*Last Command*, The Dragnet, *Docks of New York*. 1929—The Case of Lena Smith,

Thunderbolt. 1930—*The Blue Angel, Morocco.* 1931—*Dishonored, An American Tragedy.* 1932—*Shanghai Express,* Blonde Venus. 1934—*The Scarlet Empress.* 1935—*The Devil is a Woman,* Crime and Punishment. 1936—The King Steps Out. 1937 —*Claudius* (unfinished). 1939—Sergeant Madden. 1941—*The Shanghai Gesture.* 1944—The Town. 1952—Macao. 1954— *Anatahan.* 1957—Jet Pilot.

Although Josef von Sternberg's directorial career spans almost thirty years, he was a meaningful force in the cinema primarily between 1927 and 1935, an interval we might ironically designate as his Paramount Period. Until very recently, even his work of this period had not been seriously evaluated since the midthirties, when movies were supposed to crackle crisply to the proletarian point. Sternberg was then considered slow, decadent, and self-indulgent, while gloriously ambiguous Marlene Dietrich was judged too rich for the people's blood—it was a time for bread, not cake. Paradoxically, Sternberg and Dietrich look deeper and more dazzling than ever, while most of the cinema of the bread lines looks excessively mannered.

Even today, however, the art of Josef von Sternberg is too often subordinated to the mystique of Marlene Dietrich, with whom the director was associated in seven of his more familiar movies. Unfortunately, the Svengali-Trilby publicity that enshrouded *The Blue Angel, Morocco, Dishonored, Shanghai Express, Blonde Venus, The Scarlet Empress,* and *The Devil Is a Woman* obscured the more meaningful merits not only of these particular works but of Sternberg's career as a whole. In fact, the director's filtered feminine mystique neither originated nor disappeared with Marlene Dietrich, but ecstatically embraced such other photogenic features as those of Georgia Hale, Evelyn Brent, Betty Compson, Olga Baclanova, Esther Ralston, Fay Wray, Sylvia Sidney, Frances Dee, Laraine Day, Gene Tierney, and Janet Leigh. It is also part of the record that he made films before *The Blue Angel* and after *The Devil Is a Woman.* At all times, Sternberg's cinema of illusion and delusion has transcended the personality of even his most glittering star the better to reflect his own vision.

In a sense, Sternberg entered the cinema through the camera rather than the cutting room, and thus became a lyricist of light and shadow rather than a master of montage. The control he achieved over his studio surroundings encouraged him to concentrate on the spatial integrity of his images rather than on their metaphorical juxtaposition. Sternberg's cinema, for better or worse, represents a distinctively Germanic camera movement— from Murnau and Lang—in contrast to Eisenstein's fashionably Marxist montage.

Even today, however, critics and audiences may be reluctant to endorse Sternberg's story sense. Apart from "classical" assignments like *An American Tragedy* and *Crime and Punishment,* his plots seem farfetched, his backgrounds bizarre, and his character motivations obscure, at least by conventional standards of storytelling. As in a dream, he has wandered through studio sets representing Imperial Russia (*The Last Command, The Scarlet Empress*), China (*Shanghai Express, The Shanghai Gesture*), North Africa (*Morocco*), Spain (*The Devil Is a Woman*), Austria (*The Case of Lena Smith, Dishonored*), France (*The Exquisite Sinner*), and Germany (*The Blue Angel*). Even his American locales focus primarily on the dregs or fringes of society from the festive criminality of *Underworld, The Dragnet* and *Thunderbolt* to the bawdy, brawling backwaters and back streets of *The Salvation Hunters, Docks of New York,* and *Blonde Venus.* Everyday life, as such, seldom appears in Sternberg's cinema. His characters generally make their entrance at a moment in their lives when there is no tomorrow. Knowingly or unknowingly, they have reached the end or the bottom, but they will struggle a short time longer, about ninety minutes of screen time, to discover the truth about themselves and those they love. Although there is much violence and death in Sternberg's world, there is relatively little action. The various murders, duels, executions, suicides, and assaults serve merely as poetic punctuation for lives drifting to their destination in reflective repose. Death in this context is less a conclusion than a termination. The paradox of violence without action is supplemented by the paradox of virtue without morality. There are no codes or systems in these dream worlds; the characters retain their civilized graces despite the most desperate struggles for psychic survival, and it is their poise under pressure, their style under stress, that grants them a measure of heroic stature and stoic calm.

Sternberg's films are poetic without being symbolic. We need not search for slumbering allegories of Man and God and Life, but rather for a continuous stream of emotional autobiography. Sternberg's exoticism is, then, less a pretense than a pretext for objectifying personal fantasies. His equivalent literary genre is not the novel or the short story or the theatrical spectacle, but the closet drama unplayable but for the meaningful grace of gesture and movement. There persists an erroneous impression that the art of a *Morocco* or a *Shanghai Express* consists of the magnifying of trivialities. Yet there is nothing trivial about the size of Sternberg's emotions, and nothing disproportionate in the means employed to express them, critics from John Grierson to Susan Sontag notwithstanding. Also there is conscious humor in the director's awareness of his own absurdity, though some spectators still imagine they are laughing *at* Sternberg when they are merely laughing *with* him. The colorful costumes, the dazzling décors, the marble-pillared palaces merely underscore by ironic contrast the painfully acquired wisdom of the all too human prisoners of grandiose illusions. The limitations of this aesthetic are self-evident. An insufficient grasp of one's time and place is hardly a positive virtue even for the most lyrical poet. It is only when we look around at the allegedly significant cinema of Sternberg's contemporaries that we recognize the relative stature of a director who chose to write with a camera in the first person long before Alexandre Astruc's *caméra-stylo* made such impious subjectivity fashionable and such personal poetry comprehensible.

ORSON WELLES (1915–1985)

FILMS: 1941—*Citizen Kane.* 1942—*The Magnificent Ambersons,* Journey into Fear (signed by Norman Foster). 1946—The Stranger. 1948—*Lady from Shanghai.* 1950—Macbeth. 1955—*Othello.* 1958—*Touch of Evil.* 1962—*Mr. Arkadin.* 1963—The Trial. 1967—*Falstaff.* 1968—*The Immortal Story.*

That Welles, the aging *enfant terrible* of the American Cinema, is still the youngest indisputably great American director is an ominous symptom of decadence in the industry as a whole. It can even be argued that Welles's films are now less American than European in outlook and that in ten years or less there may be no American cinema of great artistic significance. It is more likely, however, that we are too dazzled by the phantasms of the sixties to perceive their ultimate aesthetic contours.

With *Mr. Arkadin* and *The Trial,* Welles's career took a curious turn. This Man from Mars who projected radio dynamics to that RKO-Radio classic *Citizen Kane* went surprisingly sour on the sound track. The ear of the expatriate had lost contact with the nuances of American speech. It may be no accident that Welles has gradually turned away from the psychological density of the fictionalized biography (*Citizen Kane*) and the filmed novel (*The Magnificent Ambersons*) to the psychological abstractions of fantasy (*Lady from Shanghai*), allegory (*Touch of Evil*), fable (*Mr. Arkadin*), hallucination (*The Trial*), and reverie (*Falstaff*).

Welles seemed to have been rehearsing all his life for *Falstaff,* and it is not surprising that he should be carted away in a coffin like one of Murnau's vampires in *Nosferatu.* Indeed, Welles has been the foremost German expressionist in the Anglo-Saxon world ever since *Citizen Kane* infected the American cinema with the virus of artistic ambition. The conventional American diagnosis of his career is decline, pure and simple, but decline is never pure and never simple. Welles began his career on such a high plateau that the most precipitous decline would not affect his place in the Pantheon. *Citizen Kane* is still the work that influenced the cinema more profoundly than any American film since *Birth of a Nation.* If the thirties belong to Lubitsch's subtle grace and unobtrusive cutting, the forties belong to the Wellesian resurrection of Murnau's portentous camera angles. The decade of plots gave way to a decade of themes, and the American cinema had lost its innocence and charm forever. From the beginning, Welles imposed a European temperament on the American cinema. Even today, Arthur Penn acknowledges the influence of Welles. Certainly the cinema is no poorer for having inspired a young man from Wisconsin to act out his Faustian fantasies on the screen until they consumed him.

The Wellesian persona looms large in Wellesian cinema.

Apart from *The Magnificent Ambersons,* in which his presence was exclusively vocal narration, every Welles film is designed around the massive presence of the artist as autobiographer. Call him Hearst or Falstaff, Macbeth or Othello, Quinlan or Arkadin, he is always at least partly himself, ironic, bombastic, pathetic, and, above all, presumptuous. The Wellesian cinema is the cinema of magic and marvels, and everything, and especially its prime protagonist, is larger than life. The dramatic conflict in a Welles film often arises from the dialectical collision between morality and megalomania, and Welles more often than not plays the megalomaniacal villain without stilling the calls of conscience. Curiously, Welles is far from being his own best actor. Actually, no actor-director in history has been as generous to his colleagues. Through less than a dozen films the roll call of distinguished performances is long indeed: Joseph Cotten, Dorothy Comingore, Ray Collins, Everett Sloane, George Colouris, Agnes Moorehead, Dolores Costello, Anne Baxter, Richard Bennett, Edward G. Robinson, Glenn Anders, Suzanne Cloutier, Charlton Heston, Janet Leigh, Joseph Calleia, Akim Tamiroff, Peter Van Eyck, Michael Redgrave, Suzanne Flon, Katina Paxinou, Romy Schneider, John Gielgud, Keith Baxter, with extraordinarily honorable mention to such limited performers as Tim Holt (as the last of the Ambersons) and Rita Hayworth (as the spectacularly mythic Lady from Shanghai shattered irrevocably in a hall of mirrors, a superb metaphor for the movie career of Orson Welles).

French critics, most notably André Bazin, hailed *Citizen Kane* after the war for its single-take, deep-focus scenes as improvements upon the traditional Hollywood crosscutting (or *champ-contre-champ*) inside a master scene. However, most moviegoers tend to identify Welles stylistically more for his eccentric camera angles and swooping camera movements than for the relative stability of his staging. The world of Orson Welles is the world of the runaway artist who pauses every so often to muse over what he has lost or left behind. Quiet and frenzy alternate in this world, as do nostalgia and adventure. There is stylistic alternation as well between dynamic progressions through the plot and décor and very formal compositions of the characters. Mark Shivas has established a Welles-Hitchcock contrast both thematically and technically with the observation that Welles is concerned with the ordinary feelings of extraordinary people and Hitchcock with the extraordinary feelings of ordinary people. Whereas Welles flourishes in baroque settings, Hitchcock functions in commonplace settings. To a limited extent, at least, Wellesian cinema is as much the cinema of the exhibitionist as Hitchcockian cinema is the cinema of the voyeur.

The Trial deserves a derisory footnote all its own, but with reservations. Since everything Welles had done since *Citizen Kane* and *The Magnificent Ambersons* had been denounced as a betrayal of his talent, it is possible to sympathize with his decision to hurl Kafka at the culture-mongers. The final irony of this absurd situation is that *The Trial* is the most hateful, the most repellent, and the most perverted film Welles ever made. What seemed even to his steadfast admirers a glorious opportunity has dissolved into a fatal temptation. Welles asserts in the prologue that his story has the logic of a dream, but Welles on Kafka, like Mondrian's white on white, is less logical than superfluous, less a dream of something than a dream of a dream of something. Indeed, *The Trial* is in its brilliantly accomplished way as much of a dead end as Minnelli's *Ziegfeld Follies,* which demonstrated that the most hackneyed backstage plot was preferable to no plot at all, and as Resnais's *Last Year at Marienbad,* which demonstrated that ambiguity was less appealing as a subject than as an attitude. Paradoxically, what have always seemed the least meaningful elements of a movie—the surface plot, the apparent subject, the objective background—are also the most necessary. Once a director soars off into time and space without a calendar and an atlas, he loses that force of gravity without which a movie cannot address itself to an audience. By this standard and many others, *Touch of Evil* and *The Lady from Shanghai* are superior to *The Trial*.

The key to the director (as well as *Mr. Arkadin*) is revealed when Orson Welles (alias Gregory Arkadin) tells the story of a frog and a scorpion meeting by a river. When the scorpion asks to ride across the river on the frog's back, the frog demurs: "If I take you on my back, you will sting me, and your sting is fatal." The scorpion responds with a plausible argument: "Where is the logic in that? If I sting you, we both will drown." The frog, a logical creature, then agrees to transport the scorpion, but he no sooner reaches the middle of the river than he feels a deadly sting in his back. "Where is the logic in this?" croaks the dying frog as he begins to sink below the surface. "This is my character," replies the doomed scorpion, "and there is no logic in character."

II.
THE
FAR
SIDE
OF
PARADISE

These are the directors who fall short of the Pantheon either because of a fragmentation of their personal vision or because of disruptive career problems.

ROBERT ALDRICH (1918–1983)

FILMS: 1953—The Big Leaguer. 1954—World for Ransom, *Apache, Vera Cruz.* 1955—*Kiss Me Deadly, The Big Knife.* 1956 —Autumn Leaves, *Attack!* 1959—The Angry Hills, Ten Seconds to Hell. 1961—The Last Sunset. 1962—*What Ever Happened to Baby Jane?* 1963—Sodom and Gomorrah. 1964—Four for Texas. 1965—*Hush, Hush . . . Sweet Charlotte.* 1966— *Flight of the Phoenix.* 1967—*The Dirty Dozen.* 1968—The Legend of Lylah Claire. 1969—The Killing of Sister George.

Robert Aldrich has emerged as one of the most strikingly personal directors of the past two decades. His style is notable for its violence even in genres that subsist on violence. His projects have ranged from the elegant escapism of *Vera Cruz* and *Autumn Leaves* to the explicit social protest of *Apache, Attack!,* and *The Big Knife* to the garish gargoyle-watching of *What Ever Happened to Baby Jane?* and *Hush, Hush . . . Sweet Charlotte* to the genuinely democratic treatment of dropouts in *Flight of the Phoenix* and *The Dirty Dozen,* the latter film so commercially successful that it enabled Aldrich to purchase his own movie studio. *Kiss Me Deadly* is perhaps his most perplexing and revealing work, poised as it is on the controversial boundary line between an unfashionable genre and a transcendent attitude toward the genre's moral implications. *Kiss Me Deadly* is not only the best Mickey Spillane screen adaptation; it is also a testament to Aldrich's anarchic spirit.

Except for his baroque sessions with Bette Davis and Joan Crawford, Aldrich can be classified as a moralist in a man's world. His films have a distinctively personal signature, largely through a handful of character players who follow him from film to film. Along with such other underrated genre stylists as Nicholas Ray, Joseph Losey, and Anthony Mann, Aldrich was discovered by European critics long before American reviewers deigned to acknowledge his existence. In recent years his reputation has fluctuated from film to film, but he has achieved a degree of freedom as a producer-director largely on a lucky gamble involving the chemical combustibility of Bette Davis and Joan Crawford in *What Ever Happened to Baby Jane?* Aldrich's direction of his players generally creates a subtle frenzy on the screen, and his visual style suggests an unstable world full of awkward angles and harsh transitions. His films are invariably troubled by intimations of decadence and disorder. The titles of even his lesser films — *World for Ransom, Autumn Leaves, Ten Seconds to Hell, The Last Sunset, Sodom and Gomorrah* — suggest a mood befitting the Decline of the West.

FRANK BORZAGE (1893–1961)

FILMS: 1918—Flying Colors, Until They Get Me, The Gun Woman, Shoes That Danced, Innocents' Progress, Society for Sale, An Honest Man, Who Is to Blame?, The Ghost Flower, The Curse of Iku. 1919—Toton, Prudence of Broadway, Whom the Gods Destroy. 1920—*Humoresque.* 1921—The Duke of Chimney Butte. 1922—Get Rich Quick Wallingford, Bank Day, Silent Shelby, Billy Jim, The Good Provider, Valley of Silent Men, The Pride of Palomar. 1923—Children of Dust, Nth Commandment, Song of Love. 1924—The Age of Desire, Secrets. 1925—The Lady, Daddy's Gone a' Huntin', Wages for Wives, The Circle, Lazybones. 1926—Marriage License, The First Year, The Dixie Merchant, Early to Wed. 1927—*Seventh Heaven.* 1928—*Street Angel.* 1929—*The River, Lucky Star, They Had to See Paris.* 1930—Song o' My Heart, Liliom. 1931—*Bad Girl,* Doctor's Wives, As Young as You Feel. 1932—*A Farewell to Arms,* After Tomorrow, Young America. 1933—*A Man's Castle,* Secrets. 1934—*No Greater Glory, Little Man What Now,* Flirtation Walk. 1935—*Living on Velvet,* Stranded, Shipmates Forever. 1936—*Desire,* Hearts Divided. 1937 —*History Is Made at Night, Green Light,* The Big City, Mannequin. 1938—*Three Comrades,* The Shining Hour. 1939—Disputed Passage. 1940—*The Mortal Storm,* Strange Cargo, Flight Command. 1941—Smilin' Through, The Vanishing Virginian. 1942—Seven Sweethearts. 1943—Stage-door Canteen, His Butler's Sister. 1944—Till We Meet Again. 1945—The Spanish Main. 1946—I've Always Loved You, The Magnificent Doll. 1947— That's My Man. 1948—*Moonrise.* 1958—China Doll. 1959— The Big Fisherman.

Frank Borzage was that rarity of rarities, an uncompromising romanticist. Anglo-Saxon film historians have generally underrated Borzage on the assumption that the director's romanticism was a commercially motivated betrayal of realism. Yet, the way of the romanticist is usually much harder than that of the realist. Audiences generally prefer realism, at least on the surface; and intimate love stories have always been box-office poison. On the rare occasions when romanticism seems to be popular, it is usually the false romanticism of Hathaway's *Peter Ibbetson* or Wyler's *Wuthering Heights,* romantic subjects directed coldly by unromantic directors, the coldness disguised in the former instance by the photography of Lee Garmes, and in the latter by the music of Alfred Newman. Borzage never needed dream worlds for his suspensions of disbelief. He plunged into the real world of poverty and oppression, the world of Roosevelt and Hitler, the New Deal and the New Order, to impart an aura to his characters, not merely through soft focus and a fluid camera, but through a genuine concern with the wondrous inner life of lovers in the midst of adversity. His anti-Nazi films—*Little Man, What Now* and *Three Comrades*—were far ahead of their time, emotionally if not politically. Borzage's objection to Hitler was a curious one. What Hitler and all tyrants represented most reprehensibly was an invasion of the emotional privacy of individuals, particularly lovers, those blessed creatures gifted with luminous rapport. *History Is Made at Night* is not only the most romantic title in the history of the cinema but also a profound expression of Borzage's commitment to love over probability. Borzage's cinema is typified by his extraordinary treatment of Janet Gaynor and Margaret Sullavan, actresses with screen personalities molded by Borzage. Jean Arthur and Gail Russell fitted into the Borzage tradition on their first and only tries, and Borzage's actors, notably Spencer Tracy, Charles Boyer, and James Stewart, were made to discard Hollywood's traditionally cynical attitudes toward love. Many of Borzage's projects, particularly toward the end of his career, were indisputably trivial in conception, but the director's personality never faltered, and when the glorious opportunity of *Moonrise* presented itself, Borzage was not stale or jaded. This, if anything, is the moral of the *auteur* theory.

FRANK CAPRA (1897–1991)

FILMS: 1926—*The Strong Man.* 1927—*Long Pants,* For the Love of Mike. 1928—That Certain Feeling, So This Is Love, The Matinee Idol, The Way of the Strong, Say It with Sables, Submarine, Power of the Press. 1929—Younger Generation, Donovan Affair, Flight. 1930—Ladies of Leisure, Rain or Shine. 1931—Dirigible, Miracle Woman, *Platinum Blonde.* 1932—Forbidden, *American Madness.* 1933—*Bitter Tea of General Yen, Lady for a Day.* 1934 —*It Happened One Night,* Broadway Bill. 1936—*Mr. Deeds Goes to Town.* 1937—*Lost Horizon.* 1938—*You Can't Take It with You.* 1939—*Mr. Smith Goes to Washington.* 1941—*Meet John Doe.* 1944—Arsenic and Old Lace. 1942–1945—Co-directed seven war documentaries. 1946—*It's a Wonderful Life.* 1948— *State of the Union.* 1950—Riding High. 1951—Here Comes the Groom. 1959—A Hole in the Head. 1961—*Pocketful of Miracles.*

With *Meet John Doe,* Frank Capra crossed the thin line between populist sentimentality and populist demogoguery. Capra's political films—*Meet John Doe, You Can't Take It With You, Mr. Smith Goes to Washington*—had always implied a belief in the tyranny of the majority, but John Doe embodied in Gary Cooper a barefoot fascist, suspicious of all ideas and all doctrines, but believing in the innate conformism of the common man. Capra's Shangri-la Hilton in *Lost Horizon* was an anti-intellectual paradise, a rest home for the troubled mind, with even the eternal problems of aging and dying miraculously banished from consideration. At that point, Capra stopped the world and got off. After years of relative inactivity, Capra returned almost triumphantly with the new look in conformity, Frank Sinatra, and a more nervous brand of sentimentality labeled: *Hole in the Head.* In *Pocketful of Miracles,* Capra quoted Pascal to the effect that the heart has its own reasons. Capra's remake of his own *Lady for a Day* was disastrously but touchingly dated.

Capra is a genuine auteur, and there is no mistaking his point of view. The Kaufman and Hart *You Can't Take It with You* on Broadway related the story of an eccentric family that chose to live on the basis of its unconventional impulses. The Capra-Riskin version transformed the eccentric family into a spokesman for all the little people in the world, and perverted the play's stuffy businessman into a bloated shark of Wall Street (a thirties specialty of Edward Arnold) beyond even Eisenstein's power of caricature.

Capra's flair for improvisation was evident throughout his career. This flair made his fortune in *It Happened One Night,* the sleeper of its year and the death knell of the more deliberately expressionistic experiments of Sternberg (*The Scarlet Empress*), Lubitsch (*The Merry Widow*), and Milestone (*Hallelujah, I'm a Bum*). Capra's boisterous humor seemed in tune with the mood of Depression audiences, but there runs through most of his films a somber Christian parable of idealism betrayed and innocence humiliated. The obligatory scene in most Capra films is the confession of folly in the most public manner possible. Indeed, Spencer Tracy's hapless presidential Candidate in *State of the Union* (1948) seems to anticipate George Romney by two decades.

GEORGE CUKOR (1899–1983)

FILMS: 1930—*The Royal Family of Broadway* (with Cyril Gardner), Grumpy (with Cyril Gardner), Virtuous Sin (with Louis Gasnier). 1931—*Tarnished Lady,* Girls About Town. 1932—*One Hour with You* (directed by Cukor from Lubitsch plan, signed by Lubitsch), *A Bill of Divorcement, What Price Hollywood,* Rockabye. 1933—*Dinner at Eight, Little Women,* Our Betters. 1935—*David Copperfield, Sylvia Scarlett.* 1936—Romeo and Juliet. 1937—*Camille.* 1938—*Holiday,* Zaza. 1939—*The Women.* 1940—*The Philadelphia Story,* Susan and God. 1941—A Woman's Face, Two-Faced Woman. 1942—Her Cardboard Lover. 1943—Keeper of the Flame. 1944—*Gaslight,* Winged Victory. 1948—*A Double Life.* 1949—*Adam's Rib; Edward, My Son.* 1950—A Life of Her Own, Born Yesterday. 1952—The Model and the Marriage Broker, *The Marrying Kind, Pat and Mike.* 1953—*The Actress.* 1954—*A Star Is Born, It Should Happen to You.* 1956—*Bhowani Junction.* 1957—Les Girls, Wild Is the Wind. 1960—*Heller in Pink Tights,*

Let's Make Love, Song Without End (begun and signed by Charles Vidor). 1962—The Chapman Report. 1964—My Fair Lady.

George Cukor's filmography is his most eloquent defense. When a director has provided tasteful entertainments of a high order consistently over a period of more than thirty years, it is clear that said director is much more than a mere entertainer. Mere entertainers seldom entertain for more than five years, and then only intermittently. Even Cukor's enemies concede his taste and style, but it has become fashionable to dismiss him as a woman's director because of his skill in directing actresses, a skill he shares with Griffith, Chaplin, Renoir, Ophuls, Sternberg, Welles, Dreyer, Bergman, Rossellini, Mizoguchi, *ad infinitum, ad gloriam.* Another argument against Cukor is that he relies heavily on adaptations from the stage and that his cinema consequently lacks the purity of the Odessa Steps. This argument was refuted in principle by the late André Bazin. There is an honorable place in the cinema for both adaptations and the non-writer director; and Cukor, like Lubitsch, is one of the best examples of the non-writer auteur, a creature literary film critics seem unable to comprehend. The thematic consistency of Cukor's career has been achieved through a judicious mixture of selection and emphasis. The director's theme is imagination, with the focus on the imaginer rather than on the thing imagined. Cukor's cinema is a subjective cinema without an objective correlative. The husbands never appear in *The Women,* and Edward never appears in *Edward, My Son.* Most critics would argue that this merely proves Cukor's slavish fidelity to his playwrights, but the fact remains that most directors attempt to make plays more "cinematic" by moving outdoors and adding characters and extras. Not Cukor. *Bhowani Junction* and *Heller in Pink Tights* demonstrate that Cukor is fully capable of exploiting exteriors when they serve his purposes. The opening Central Park sequence in *The Marrying Kind* is one of the most graceful exercises in open-air film-making in the history of the cinema, and the corresponding sequence in *It Should Happen to You* is not far behind. Yet, when characters have to thrash out their illusions and problems across the kitchen table, Cukor glides through his interiors without self-conscious reservations about what is "cinematic" and what is not. It is no accident that many of Cukor's characters are thespians of one form or another. John Barrymore and Marie Dressler in *Dinner at Eight,* Ina Claire in *Royal Family of Broadway,* Katharine Hepburn and Cary Grant in *Sylvia Scarlett,* Judy Garland and James Mason in *A Star Is Born,* Jean Simmons in *The Actress,* Marilyn Monroe in *Let's Make Love,* and even Sophia Loren, De Sica's alleged earth mother, in *Heller in Pink Tights.* Even when Cukor's characters do not appear formally behind the footlights, they project an imaginative existence. W. C. Fields is pure ham in *David Copperfield,* and Katharine Hepburn is pure ego in *The Philadelphia Story,* and Cukor is equally sympathetic to the absurdities of both. *Les Girls* is Cukor's *Rashomon,* but where Kurosawa argues that all people are liars, Cukor suggests that all people tell the truth in their fashion. Even when imagination extends to transvestism in *Adam's Rib* and *Sylvia Scarlett,* Cukor retains an indulgent affection for the misguided brashness of Katharine Hepburn. The theme is consistent; the pattern is established. Cukor is committed to the dreamer, if not to the content of the dream. He is a genuine artist.

CECIL B. DE MILLE (1881–1959)

FILMS: 1913—*The Squaw Man.* 1914—The Virginian, The Call of the North, What's His Name, The Man from Home, Rose of the Rancho. 1915—The Girl of the Golden West, The Warrens of Virginia, The Unafraid, The Captive, Wild Goose Chase, The Arab, Chimmie Fadden, Kindling, Maria Rosa, Carmen, Temptation, Chimmie Fadden Out West, *The Cheat.* 1916—The Golden Chance, The Trail of the Lonesome Pine, The Heart of Nora Flynn, The Dream Girl. 1917—Joan the Woman, A Romance of the Redwoods, The Little American, The Woman God Forgot, The Devil Stone. 1918—The Whispering Chorus, Old Wives for New, We Can't Have Everything, Till I Come Back to You, The Squaw Man. 1919—*Don't Change Your Husband,* For Better, for Worse, *Male and Female.* 1920—Why Change Your Wife, Something to Think About. 1921—Forbidden Fruit, The Affairs of Anatol. 1922—Fool's Paradise, Saturday Night, Manslaughter. 1923—Adam's Rib, The Ten Commandments. 1924—Triumph, Feet of Clay. 1925—The Golden Bed, The Road to Yesterday. 1926—The Volga

Boatman. 1927—*The King of Kings.* 1928—The Godless Girl. 1929—Dynamite. 1930—Madame Satan. 1931—The Squaw Man. 1932—*The Sign of the Cross.* 1933—This Day and Age. 1934—Four Frightened People, *Cleopatra.* 1935—*The Crusades.* 1936—*The Plainsman.* 1938—*The Buccaneer.* 1939—*Union Pacific.* 1940—*North West Mounted Police.* 1942—*Reap the Wild Wind.* 1944—The Story of Dr. Wassell. 1947—*Unconquered.* 1949—Samson and Delilah. 1952—*The Greatest Show on Earth.* 1956—The Ten Commandments.

It is inevitable that the mere mention of Cecil B. de Mille will evoke complacent laughter in some quarters, and bristling patriotic speeches in others. If De Mille had the right enemies, he also had the wrong friends. De Mille was neither a primitive like Fuller nor a populist like Capra. Although he appealed to audiences, he never manipulated them. He remained faithful to the literary tradition of Cooper's Leatherstocking Tales and to the dramatic conventions of David Belasco. Griffith, Chaplin, Lubitsch, Murnau, Eisenstein, Ford, Hawks, Capra, Welles, Renoir, Ophuls, and all the others came and went without influencing his style in the slightest. Ironically, his films look much better today than their reputations would indicate. De Mille's cross-reference is Frank Lloyd, and interested or rather disinterested critics might profitably compare De Mille's *Union Pacific* with Lloyd's *Wells Fargo,* or De Mille's *Reap the Wild Wind* with Lloyd's *Rulers of the Sea,* or De Mille's *The Crusades* with Lloyd's *If I Were King.* The comparison in each instance is almost fantastically favorable to De Mille. Where Lloyd's spectacles are dull, heavy, and monotonous; De Mille's are well paced and logically constructed. De Mille relished complications in his narratives, and he may have been the last American director who enjoyed telling a story for its own sake. He may also have been the last Victorian, although the Late George Orwell would probably have held out for Salvador Dali.

BLAKE EDWARDS (1922–   )

FILMS: 1955—Bring Your Smile Along. 1956—He Laughed Last. 1957—*Mr. Cory.* 1958—This Happy Feeling, The Perfect Furlough. 1959—*Operation Petticoat.* 1960—High Time. 1961

—*Breakfast at Tiffany's*. 1962—Experiment in Terror. 1963—
Days of Wine and Roses. 1964—*The Pink Panther, Shot in the
Dark*. 1965—*The Great Race*. 1966—*What Did You Do in the
War, Daddy?* 1967—*Gunn*. 1968—The Party. 1969—Darling
Lili.

Edwards seemed until 1963 to merit only cult recognition. I
wrote at that time: "As Blake Edwards's stock has risen, Richard
Quine's has fallen. Where Edwards has a decisive edge is in the
conviction he applies to a bright, if artificial style. Despite occasional lapses in taste and increasingly frequent bursts of visual
flamboyance, Edwards confirms on a minor scale what Lubitsch
established on a major scale, and that is the correlation of buoy-
ancy with conviction. It follows that Edwards operates most
effectively with the thinly lacquered dramas of *Mr. Cory* and
Breakfast at Tiffany's and the transparently farcical water colors
of *This Happy Feeling, The Perfect Furlough, Operation Petticoat* and *High Time*. In the more realistic black-and-white
worlds of *Experiment in Terror* and *Days of Wine and Roses*, the
removal of the director's rose-colored glasses reveals an unpleasant vision of the plastic forms of urban life."

Since 1963, Edwards has emerged from the ranks of commissioned directors with such personal works as *The Pink Panther,
Shot in the Dark, The Great Race, What Did You Do in the War,
Daddy?* and *Gunn*. His films manage to be funny in spite of repeated violations of the axioms of classical slapstick. (Was it
Proust who said that we say "in spite of" when we mean "because
of"?) One axiom insists that audiences will laugh at a man slip-
ping on a banana peel only if nothing is seriously hurt except his
dignity but that if he fractures his leg the audience will not see
the humor of the situation. Unfortunately for the axiom, Blake
Edwards is one writer-director who has got some of his biggest
laughs out of jokes that are too gruesome for most horror films.

Another axiom is that any farcical pratfall must be constructed from a probable premise. Yet *A Shot in the Dark*
lurches from improbability to improbability without losing its
comic balance. For example, when Peter Sellers inserts a still-
ignited cigarette lighter inside his raincoat, the ensuing slapstick
with smoke and flame is unsatisfactory. Part of the élan of using a

cigarette lighter derives from the courtly symbolism of controlled virility involved in the extinction of the flame of sex. No matter. Edwards leapfrogs over the lighter gag by opening a door in someone's face and sending him out the window, and only the most captious critic has a chance to raise the question of logic. By the same token, the custard-pie sequence in *The Great Race* transcends the psychology of slapstick to qualify as the last spasm of action painting in the Western world.

For a time Edwards seemed to be following in the footsteps of Billy Wilder, with somewhat more visual style and somewhat less verbal crackle. But their paths have diverged. Wilder is a curdled Lubitsch, romanticism gone sour, 78 rpm played at 45, an old wordling from Vienna perpetually sneering at Hollywood as it engulfs him. Edwards is more a new breed, post-Hitler, post-Freud, post-sick-joke, with all the sticky sentimentality of electronic music. The world he celebrates is cold, heartless, and inhuman, but the people in it manage to preserve a marginal integrity and individuality. Edwards has become a stylistic influence in the cinema, and his personality and script dominate Ralph Nelson's *Soldier in the Rain* the way Lubitsch's personality once dominated Cukor's *One Hour with You*.

SAMUEL FULLER (1911–   )

FILMS: 1949—*I Shot Jesse James*. 1950—The Baron of Arizona, *The Steel Helmet*. 1951—*Fixed Bayonets*. 1952—*Park Row*. 1953—*Pickup on South Street*. 1954—Hell and High Water. 1955—*House of Bamboo*. 1957—*China Gate, Run of the Arrow, Forty Guns*. 1959—The Crimson Kimono. 1960—Verboten! 1961—*Underworld U.S.A.* 1962—*Merrill's Marauders*. 1963—*Shock Corridor*. 1965—The Naked Kiss. 1968—Caine.

Fuller is an authentic American primitive whose works have to be seen to be understood. Seen, not heard or synopsized. His first film, *I Shot Jesse James,* was constructed almost entirely in close-ups of an oppressive intensity the cinema had not experienced since Dreyer's *The Passion of Joan of Arc*. Fuller's script was so compressed that there was no room for even one establishing atmosphere shot or one dramatically irrelevant scene in which characters could suggest an everyday existence. The excitement Fuller arouses in critics sensitive to visual forms is equaled by the horror he arouses in critics of the Left for the lack of social perspective in his films. The cinematic opposition between Right and Left is exemplified in the different approaches of Fuller's *China Gate* and Mankiewicz's *The Quiet American*. Where Fuller thrusts all his political ideas forward with his few characters carrying all the ideological burdens of the Cold War and American-Asian relations, Mankiewicz is always receding from his characters to allow the larger spectacle of the Indo-Chinese masses to serve as a political context. Mankiewicz's adaptation of Greene's personal plot is anecdotal, microcosmic, symbolic. With Fuller, the distinction between the personal plot and its political context evaporates with the first leggy sprawl of Angie Dickinson. Fuller's ideas are undoubtedly too broad and oversimplified for any serious analysis, but it is the artistic force with which his ideas are expressed that makes his career so fascinating to critics who can rise above their political prejudices. Admittedly, it is absurd to attribute the depradations of Indians (*Run of the Arrow*) and neo-Nazis (*Verboten!*) to some universal juvenile delinquency, but Fuller's perversity and peculiarly Old Testament view of retribution carries the day in both instances. It is time the cinema followed the other arts in honoring its primitives. Fuller belongs to the cinema, and not to literature and sociology.

GREGORY LA CAVA (1892–1949)

FILMS: 1924—The New School Teacher, Restless Wives. 1925—Womanhandled. 1926—Let's Get Married, So's Your Old Man, Say It Again. 1927—Paradise for Two, *Running Wild*, Tell It to Sweeney. 1928—The Gay Defender, Feel My Pulse, Half a Bride. 1929—Saturday's Children, Big News. 1930—His First Command. 1931—Laugh and Get Rich, Smart Woman. 1932—Symphony of Six Million, Age of Consent, *The Half-Naked Truth*. 1934 —Affairs of Cellini, What Every Woman Knows. 1935—Private Worlds, *She Married Her Boss*. 1936—*My Man Godfrey*. 1937—

Stage Door. 1939—Fifth Avenue Girl. 1940—Primrose Path. 1941—*Unfinished Business.* 1942—Lady in a Jam. 1947—Living in a Big Way.

Gregory La Cava's best films—*She Married Her Boss, My Man Godfrey, Stage Door,* and *Unfinished Business*—reveal a flair for improvisation and a delicate touch with such expert comediennes as Claudette Colbert, Carole Lombard, Katharine Hepburn, Ginger Rogers, and Irene Dunne. The seduction scene of Irene Dunne and Preston Foster in *Unfinished Business,* like that of Jean Arthur and Joel McCrea in Stevens's *The More the Merrier,* demonstrates the conflict between Hollywood's erotic images and its laundered scripts. Significantly, La Cava was most effective when he could work between the lines of his scenarios and against the conventions of his plots. W. C. Fields credited La Cava with the best comedy mind in Hollywood next to Fields's own, and *Life* magazine once reproduced La Cava's on-the-set sketches for the Billy Rose takeoff in *Unfinished Business.* Of such trifles was the legend of La Cava fashioned. However, the La Cava touch never became as famous as the Lubitsch touch even after the New York Film Critics Circle singled out La Cava's direction of *Stage Door* for an award in 1937. The La Cava touch was mainly touches, whereas the Lubitsch touch expressed a distinctive vision of the world. La Cava's more solemn projects—*What Every Woman Knows, The Affairs of Cellini, Private Worlds,* and *Primrose Path*—suffer from structural deficiencies. He is remembered now for a few interludes of antic desperation in the midst of the Depression.

JOSEPH LOSEY (1909–1984)

FILMS: 1948—The Boy with Green Hair. 1950—*The Lawless.* 1951—*The Prowler;* M; *The Big Night.* 1953—Stranger on the Prowl. 1954—The Sleeping Tiger. 1956—Finger of Guilt. 1957—*Time Without Pity.* 1958—The Gypsy and the Gentleman. 1960—*Chance Meeting.* 1962—*The Concrete Jungle.* 1964—*The Servant.* 1965—*These Are the Damned,* Eva. 1966—*King* *and Country, Modesty Blaise.* 1967—*Accident.* 1968—Boom!, Secret Ceremony.

Joseph Losey may not actually thrive on controversy, but he seems to arouse it on every level, from the most vulgar to the most esoteric. Originally an exile from the Hollywood blacklist, he seemed by all indications to belong to the committed Left. In quick succession, he was embraced by a rightist faction in *Cahiers du Cinéma,* enthroned by *Movie,* and repudiated by *Sight and Sound.* Realist critics have always resisted the intensity and sweep of his style, the steady hysteria of his actors, the violence of his plots. By any standards, Losey's is a technique that calls attention to itself or, more properly, to the personal feelings of Joseph Losey.

Losey has spent most of his career on commissioned projects that mixed melodrama with social significance. The movies of his Hollywood period—*The Boy with Green Hair, The Lawless, The Prowler, M,* and *The Big Night*—have gained in interest over the years as the exaggerations of a style have become more expressive of an era. The stage director of Charles Laughton in Bertolt Brecht's *Galileo* and the screen director of Harold Pinter's scripts for *The Servant* and *Accident,* Losey seems always to have aspired beyond the presumed limitations of genre movies. The High Art Game is an understandable temptation to the movie director, particularly in the culturally beleaguered Anglo-American cinema. Indeed, *The Servant* and *Accident* have done more for Losey's general reputation than all his other pictures put together.

Ironically, Losey's personality comes through more clearly and forcefully in such relatively neglected works as *Time Without Pity, Chance Meeting, The Concrete Jungle, King and Country,* and *Modesty Blaise.* Like many directors, Losey seems more effective when he transcends conventions than when he avoids them altogether. Genre movies give him the distancing he needs to writhe expressively on the screen. By contrast, movies about Life and Time and The World seem to make him relatively subdued, functional, and impersonal. Losey's dilemma is not unique. With *Accident,* Losey has escaped the clutches of the cultists to fall into the hands of the snobs. Certainly, nothing could be more fashionable than serving as the house director of the Burtons after Mike Nichols and Franco Zeffirelli. Only time will tell if such fashion will be fatal to Losey's artistic personality.

Losey's best performers are almost invariably male—Van Heflin in *The Prowler,* Dirk Bogarde in *The Sleeping Tiger, The Servant, King and Country, Modesty Blaise,* and *Accident,* Stanley Baker in *Chance Meeting, The Concrete Jungle, Eva,* and *Accident,* Michael Redgrave and Leo McKern in *Time Without Pity,* Patrick McGee in *The Concrete Jungle,* Oskar Werner in *Chance Meeting,* James Fox in *The Servant,* Tom Courtenay in *King and Country,* Terence Stamp in *Modesty Blaise.* There are pleasant enough feminine portrayals in Losey's *œuvre;* Gail Russell in *The Lawless,* Evelyn Keyes in *The Prowler,* Sarah Miles and Wendy Craig in *The Servant,* Viveca Lindfors in *These Are the Damned,* and Vivian Merchant in *Accident* come immediately to mind. But the feminine role in Losey's world is strictly subordinate because of the histrionic hysteria of his actors. Men simply cannot cope with their lives and social institutions, and they crack up with very lyrical results. Meanwhile the women stand by to pick up the pieces. They cope because of their ability to compromise with reality, an ability Losey frankly admires. Unfortunately, the best roles are the least stable. Hence, Losey's actresses are usually denied the great scene-stealing moments of psychic dissolution.

Losey has been criticized for the precision and fluidity of his camera style, but it is through his excesses that he most successfully projects a redeeming sense of humor. When Stanley Baker is jilted at the door by Jeanne Moreau in *Eva,* Losey's steep overhead camera angle makes the humiliation deliciously funny in a nonsadistic way. Losey is playing a joke on his own portentousness. Conversely, *Modesty Blaise* is a more serious enterprise than it seems precisely because of the strenuousness of its levity. Losey is joking about matters concerning the relations of men and women, relations that affect him deeply. There is also in Losey's films time and again that psychic spasm, that futile gesture a character makes to register a personal protest against cosmic injustice. In Losey's world, both sex and politics are out of joint, and if Losey's style is baroque or expressionistic, it is a very nervous baroque or expressionistic. With the disintegration of the male, Yeats's center cannot hold, and anarchy is loosed upon the world.

ANTHONY MANN (1906–1967)

FILMS: 1942—Dr. Broadway, Moonlight in Havana. 1943—Nobody's Darling. 1944—My Best Gal, Strangers in the Night. 1945—The Great Flamarion, Two o'Clock Courage, Sing Your Way Home. 1946—Strange Impersonation, The Bamboo Blonde. 1947—Desperate, Railroaded, *T-Men.* 1948—Raw Deal. 1949—*Reign of Terror, Border Incident, Side Street.* 1950—*Devil's Doorway,* The Furies, *Winchester 73.* 1951—*The Tall Target.* 1952 —*Bend of the River.* 1953—*The Naked Spur,* Thunder Bay. 1954 —*The Glenn Miller Story.* 1955—*The Far Country, Strategic Air Command, The Man from Laramie.* 1956—*The Last Frontier,* Serenade. 1957—*Men in War,* The Tin Star. 1958—*God's Little Acre, Man of the West.* 1960—Cimarron. 1961—El Cid. 1964—The Fall of the Roman Empire. 1965—The Heroes of Telemark. 1968—A Dandy in Aspic.

Anthony Mann (not to be confused with dreary Daniel and Delbert) directed action movies with a kind of tough-guy authority that never found favor among the more cultivated critics of the medium. His Westerns stand out today as geological excavations of a neglected genre. Writer Philip Yordan once remarked that the ideal film-maker would combine Anthony Mann's exteriors with Nicholas Ray's interiors, the implication being that both Mann and Ray were artistically incomplete.

Back in 1963, I was impressed more with Mann's manner than with his meaning: "Anthony Mann is a style without a theme. His Westerns are distinguished by some of the most brilliant photography of exteriors in the history of the American cinema, and yet it is impossible to detect a consistent thematic pattern in his work. His best films—*Man of the West, The Last Frontier, Men in War, The Naked Spur, Bend of the River*—are directed with psychological intensity and an undercurrent of didacticism. His most didactic film, *Tin Star,* is also one of his weakest. Curiously, Mann's visual style is the American style which most closely resembles that of Antonioni in the literal progression through landscapes from the vegetable to the mineral world as in *Man of the West* and *Il Grido* down to the ultimate decadence of *El Cid* and *L'Eclisse*."

The eight films Mann made with James Stewart are especially interesting today for their insights into the uneasy relationships between men and women in a world of violence and action. Stewart, the most complete actor-personality in the American cinema, is particularly gifted in expressing the emotional ambivalence of the action hero. Mann and Stewart between them suggest that there is more than meets the eye in such reputed potboilers as *Winchester 73, Bend of the River, The Naked Spur, Thunder Bay, The Glenn Miller Story, The Far Country, Strategic Air Command,* and *The Man from Laramie.* Mann's best period lasted little more than a decade between *T-Men* in 1947 and a spread in *Life* magazine for this sleeper and *Man of the West* (in 1958), notable to the general public mainly for Julie London's epochal striptease in a Western. Unfortunately, Universal pictures were seldom taken seriously during this period by anyone except Manny Farber and the French critics, and Mann, like Sirk, was overlooked by the American critical establishment until it was too late for his career to find a firmer footing than obscure cult interest.

LEO MC CAREY (1898–1969)

FILMS: 1929—The Sophomore, Red Hot Rhythm. 1930—Let's Go Native, Wild Company, Part Time Wife. 1931—Indiscreet. 1932—The Kid from Spain. 1933—*Duck Soup.* 1934 —Six of a Kind, Belle of the Nineties. 1935—*Ruggles of Red Gap.* 1936—The Milky Way. 1937—*The Awful Truth, Make Way for Tomorrow.* 1939—*Love Affair.* 1942—Once Upon a Honeymoon. 1944—*Going My Way.* 1945—*The Bells of St. Mary's.* 1948—Good Sam. 1952—*My Son John.* 1957—*An Affair to Remember.* 1958—Rally Round the Flag, Boys. 1962—Satan Never Sleeps.

Leo McCarey represents a principle of improvisation in the history of the American film. Noted less for his rigorous direction than for his relaxed digressions, McCarey has distilled a unique blend of farce and sentimentality in his best efforts. He has worked with some of the most notable eccentric stars in Hollywood—Laurel and Hardy, the Marx Brothers, Harold Lloyd, Eddie Cantor, Mae West, Victor Moore, and later, and more normally, Cary Grant, Irene Dunne, Charles Boyer, Ingrid Bergman, and Bing Crosby. Jean Renoir once remarked that Leo McCarey understood people better than any other Hollywood director. McCarey's moments may outlive his movies, be it Charles Laughton reciting the Gettysburg Address in *Ruggles of Red Gap* or, even more memorably from that same film, Binnie Barnes teaching Roland Young to play the drums; or Victor Moore saying goodbye to Beulah Bondi in *Make Way for Tomorrow* or Irene Dunne speaking to Maria Ouspenskaya in *Love Affair* or Barry Fitzgerald embracing his mother in *Going My Way* or Cary Grant and Irene Dunne reminiscing about their lost marriage in *The Awful Truth*. After enough great moments are assembled, however, a personal style must be assumed even though it is difficult to describe.

McCarey and Capra seem to go together like ham and eggs. They both started at about the same time in the twenties with the same kind of gag training. They both slipped unobtrusively into the sound era, and didn't hit their stride until the mid-thirties. Both declined in the late forties, virtually faded away in the early fifties, and returned in the late fifties. Both won two Oscars for direction, Capra for *Mr. Deeds Goes to Town* in 1936 and *You Can't Take It with You* in 1938, McCarey for *The Awful Truth* in 1937 and *Going My Way* in 1944. There is on film a record of a thirties Oscar ceremony during which Capra and McCarey playfully wrestled on stage for a golden statuette they both coveted. It is perhaps at that very golden moment that their joint preeminence was officially recognized, a very brief moment before the surge of John Ford and Orson Welles.

VINCENTE MINNELLI (1903–1986)

FILMS: 1943—*Cabin in the Sky*, I Dood It. 1944—*Meet Me in St. Louis*. 1945—*The Clock, Yolanda and the Thief*. 1946—

Ziegfeld Follies, Undercurrent. 1948—*The Pirate.* 1949—*Madame Bovary.* 1950—Father of the Bride. 1951—*An American in Paris,* Father's Little Dividend. 1953—*The Bad and the Beautiful,* The Story of Three Loves (Minnelli did Mademoiselle episode with Leslie Caron, Farley Granger, Ethel Barrymore, and Gottfried Reinhardt; the first episode with James Mason and Moira Shearer and the third with Kirk Douglas and Pier Angeli), *The Band Wagon.* 1954 —The Long, Long Trailer; Brigadoon. 1955—*Cobweb,* Kismet. 1956—Lust for Life, Tea and Sympathy. 1957—Designing Woman. 1958—Gigi, *The Reluctant Debutante.* 1959—*Some Came Running.* 1960—Bells Are Ringing, *Home from the Hill.* 1962—*Four Horsemen of the Apocalypse, Two Weeks in Another Town.* 1963—The Courtship of Eddie's Father. 1964—Goodbye Charlie. 1965—The Sand Piper.

Minnelli's reputation has undergone several metamorphoses in a quarter of a century. His Garland-Kelly-Astaire-Charisse-Caron musicals deserve a chapter of their own in any ultimate history of the medium. Minnelli's stylistic flourishes awed even the late James Agee back in the forties, and Stephen Longstreet of the Screenwriters' Guild once attacked the director for distracting audiences from dialogue with fancy camera angles in the 1945 Judy Garland–Robert Walker romance, *The Clock.* Needless to say, no screenwriter today would dare make a comparable objection. *Cabin in the Sky, Meet Me in St. Louis, Yolanda and the Thief,* and *The Pirate* made him the darling of the *Sequence* and *Sight and Sound* generation sparked by Lindsay Anderson, Karel Reisz, Gavin Lambert, and Tony Richardson. This was the period in which his art was more visual than personal, more decorative than meaningful. His Hollywood reputation reached its crest with two curiously depressing musicals, *An American in Paris* and *Gigi.* It suddenly became apparent that Minnelli had an unusual, somber outlook for musical comedy. *The Band Wagon,* his best musical, fitted in with his tendency toward negative thinking as Fred Astaire sang "I Want to Be by Myself " as an unheeding world passed him by and a sympathetic mise-en-scène lyricized loneliness.

A new generation of cinéastes adopted Minnelli for his garish fifties and sixties dramas, most notably *The Bad and the Beautiful, Cobweb, Somé Came Running, Home From the Hill, Four*

Horsemen of the Apocalypse, and *Two Weeks in Another Town.* Mark Shivas, Ian Cameron, and V. F. Perkins of *Movie* were particularly perceptive in analyzing Minnelli's dreamlike style with subjects of substance. Unfortunately, the new Minnelli became anathema to most of the Anglo-American critical Establishment, and in 1968 he finds himself exiled back on the musical beat with an intransigent Barbra Streisand.

Nonetheless, the Pirandellian pyrotechnics of *Two Weeks in Another Town,* a self-conscious sequel to his masterpiece on moviemaking, *The Bad and the Beautiful,* summed up his career and the American cinema as a whole with what amounted to Hollywood's final blast at Cinecitta. As a side dividend, *Last Year at Marienbad* and *La Dolce Vita* will never look the same again. Jean-Luc Godard provided a footnote to Minnelli's career by having his protagonist in *Contempt* wear his hat in the bathtub in *un hommage* to Dean Martin from *Some Came Running.* By contrast, François Truffaut exiled Minnelli from the "Politique des Auteurs" by describing him as *"un ésclave."* Truffaut's intolerance toward Hollywood directors has increased markedly since he became their rival instead of their *raisonneur,* but he is especially unfair to a director who has always regarded himself as more of a stylist than an auteur. Furthermore, Minnelli has always required relatively luxurious projects upon which to lavish his taste. If he has a fatal flaw as an artist, it is his naïve belief that style can invariably transcend substance and that our way of looking at the world is more important than the world itself. Critic-film-makers like Godard and Truffaut pay lip service to these doctrines, but they don't really believe them. Only Minnelli believes implicitly in the power of his camera to transform trash into art, and corn into caviar. Minnelli believes more in beauty than in art.

OTTO PREMINGER (1905–1986)

FILMS: 1936—Under Your Spell. 1937—Danger—Love at Work. 1943—Margin for Error. 1944—In the Meantime, Darling; *Laura.* 1945—A Royal Scandal, *Fallen Angel.* 1946—Centennial

Summer. 1947—Forever Amber, *Daisy Kenyon.* 1948—That Lady in Ermine (begun and signed by Ernst Lubitsch). 1949—The Fan, *Whirlpool.* 1950—*Where the Sidewalk Ends,* The Thirteenth Letter. 1953—*Angel Face,* The Moon is Blue. 1954—*River of No Return,* Carmen Jones. 1955—The Court-Martial of Billy Mitchell, *The Man with the Golden Arm.* 1957—*Saint Joan.* 1958—*Bonjour Tristesse.* 1959—Porgy and Bess, *Anatomy of a Murder.* 1960 —Exodus. 1962—*Advise and Consent.* 1963—The Cardinal. 1965—*In Harm's Way, Bunny Lake Is Missing.* 1966—Hurry Sundown. 1968—Skidoo!

Laura is Preminger's *Citizen Kane,* at least in the sense that Otto's detractors, like Orson's, have never permitted him to live it down. For his part, Preminger refuses to accept any responsibility whatsoever for the films he directed before *Laura* in 1944. There is admittedly a streak of Foxphorescent giddiness running through the frames of *Under Your Spell* (1936), *Danger—Love at Work* (1937), *Margin for Error* (1943), and *In the Meantime, Darling* (1944). However, Preminger is hardly unique in his disdain for the fruits of his early experience. Fred Zinnemann has never been eager to reminisce about *Kid Glove Killer, Eyes in the Night, Little Mr. Jim,* and *My Brother Talks to Horses.* George Stevens undoubtedly prefers to jump straight to *Alice Adams* without pausing for *Cohens and Kellys in Trouble, Bachelor Bait,* and *Kentucky Kernels.* Vincente Minnelli's mystique does not encompass *I Dood It* any more than Robert Aldrich boasts of *The Big Leaguer,* and Josef von Sternberg would probably prefer to forget his close-up of Grace Moore's tonsils in *The King Steps Out.*

There is no easy moral to draw from the evolution of Preminger's style since he left Fox in the early fifties to become his own producer. Ironically, it was only when Preminger began blowing his own horn from *The Moon Is Blue* onward that his earliest films came into focus. His enemies have never forgiven him for being a director with the personality of a producer. Perhaps they subconsciously resent him for not ruining himself with the excesses of a creative folly. Culture heroes like Sternberg and Stroheim and Ophuls and Welles have acquired, rightly or wrongly, a legendary reputation for profligacy. Preminger's legend is that of the cosmic cost accountant, a ruthless creature who will mangle the muse for the sake of a shooting schedule.

The story is told in the trade of the day Preminger shot the Saint-Newman hilltop scene in *Exodus*. During the last take, the shadow of the boom fell across the couple. It was too late for a retake because the sun had gone. Preminger decided to let the shadow stand rather than return to the location the next day for a retake that would disrupt his shooting schedule. Some finicky aesthetes might write this decision off as sloppy craftsmanship, but for Preminger it is a question of survival. The fact is that he has not enjoyed a major critical and commercial success since *Anatomy of a Murder* in 1959. His frugality, and his frugality alone, has kept him from drowning in a sea of red ink. Almost alone of the new tribe of producer-directors, Preminger has accepted the responsibility of freedom, as well as the lesson of a shrinking market.

But what is the artistic point of all these crass production stories? Or as Dwight Macdonald might put it, what's art to Preminger or Preminger to art? Indeed, serious film criticism of Hollywood movies is always impaled upon the point that Hollywood directors are not profoundly articulate about their alleged art. In this respect, Preminger is not a "good" interview. He will freely concede that more is read into his films by some critics than he consciously put there. He neither abuses his detractors nor embraces his defenders. He seems to enjoy the effect he creates with his outrageous personality, a personality that serves also as a mask. To read all sorts of poignant profundities in Preminger's inscrutable urbanity would seem to be the last word in idiocy, and yet there are moments in his films when the evidence on the screen is inconsistent with one's deepest instincts about the director as a man. It is at these moments that the serenity of his style seems to transcend the limitations of his sensibility.

It is ultimately Preminger's manner, rather than his matter, that should concern us most deeply. Otherwise, his extraordinary eclecticism in subject matter would make him a poor choice indeed for a career analysis. What is one to say of a taste in scripts oscillating between Oscar Wilde and Kathleen Winsor, Bernard Shaw and F. Hugh Herbert, Nelson Algren and Allen Drury, Françoise Sagan and Leon Uris? Thematic consistency is hardly Preminger's hobgoblin. The secret of his style is else-where. One critic has called it fairness, another the ambiguity of objectivity. Its technical correlative is the perversely objective camera viewpoint that keeps his characters in the same frame. Why does Preminger present his spectacle in this way? As he himself explains, he came from the theatre where he was accus-tomed to looking at drama as a spatial whole. Consequently, his deepest instincts are always opposed to montage. Without an in-bred instinct for cutting, he is not able to execute the movie gags for which Hollywood has developed an original cinematographic language. It follows almost logically that Preminger's projects, more often than not, have a solemn, somber quality. His melo-dramas at Fox, particularly *Laura, Fallen Angel, Whirlpool, Where the Sidewalk Ends,* and his RKO loan-out, *Angel Face,* are all moodily fluid studies in perverse psychology rather than crackling suspense movies. The characters click even as the ac-tion falters. The reviewer in search of crackling melodrama would mark Preminger down as a failure in most of these films, possibly all except *Laura.* Even his comedies are too fluid to en-compass the obligatory reaction shots. *The Moon is Blue* comes out being a little sad, and *Bonjour Tristesse,* far from being a merry Gallic romp, is transformed by Preminger's color/black-and-white duality into a tragedy of time and illusion.

Where Richard Brooks displays a tendency to transform art into trash, Preminger displays a tendency to transform trash into art. His most recent plots have been big, violent, and vulgar. *Exodus, Advise and Consent, The Cardinal, In Harm's Way,* and *Hurry Sundown* are all derived from bloated novels on big sub-jects. Unfortunately, Preminger does not entirely transcend his material on any occasion. Nor does he reshape it sufficiently to his own taste. He is similarly passive with his players. John Wayne and Patricia Neal are as admirable in *In Harm's Way* as Paula Prentiss, Tom Tryon, and Patrick Neal are deplorable. For every John Huston in *The Cardinal* there is unfortunately a Lee J. Cobb in *Exodus.* Where Michael Caine and Jane Fonda are original creations in *Hurry Sundown,* Robert Hooks and Diahann Carroll degenerate into dull stereotypes. Individual scenes can be magnificent—the prison raid in *Exodus,* the shipboard sequences with the President in *Advise and Consent,* the Viennese ballroom scene in *The Cardinal,* and the opening dance scene in *In Harm's Way* invoking in one slowly moving shot the entire Glenn Millerish *Zeitgeist* of the forties. Too often, however, Preminger seems to destroy what he so lovingly creates. This is part of his ambiguity as an artist, a key perhaps to a cynicism far deeper and infinitely more destructive than Billy Wilder's.

Still, every Preminger film, even his most ill-fated, bears the signs of an overall conception and the stigmata of a personal attitude. If a *Centennial Summer* or a *Porgy and Bess* fails of execution, it is not because Preminger lacked a discernible approach toward these musicals, but rather because the various elements in the genre failed to coalesce in terms of the director's conception. By contrast, *Carmen Jones* succeeds on its own questionable terms as the Preminger musical par excellence—drab, austere, and completely depoeticized.

During his career Preminger has moved into direct competition or comparison with other directors. *A Royal Scandal* and *The Fan* pointed up Preminger's relationship to Lubitsch, as did obviously *That Lady in Ermine,* which Preminger finished after Lubitsch's death. Lubitsch is generally given the edge in these sectors and for good reasons. However, it is not entirely fair to Preminger to place him out of his time. As Lubitsch was the unobtrusive cutting of the twenties and thirties, Preminger is the camera movement and long takes of the fifties and sixties. If Lubitsch summed up his time, Preminger was ahead of it in his Fox period. The Lubitsch virtues have disappeared from the cinema, and we are the poorer for it, but Preminger anticipated the conditions that would cause their disappearance. The grace and precision of Lubitsch's sensibility seem out of place in a world consecrated to the most grotesque explosions of the ego. Preminger's impassive gaze—accepting the good with the bad, the beautiful with the ugly, the sublime with the mediocre—is both more appropriate and more merciful.

We are left with a director who has made at least four masterpieces of ambiguity and objectivity—*Laura, Bonjour Tristesse, Advise and Consent,* and *Bunny Lake Is Missing,* a director who sees all problems and issues as a single-take two-shot, the stylistic expression of the eternal conflict, not between right and wrong, but between the right-wrong on one side and the right-wrong on the other, a representation of the right-wrong in all of us as our share of the human condition. In the middle of the conflict stands Otto Preminger, right-wrong, good-bad, and probably sincere-cynical.

NICHOLAS RAY (1911–1979)

FILMS: 1949—*They Live by Night,* Knock on Any Door, A Woman's Secret. 1950—*In a Lonely Place,* Born to Be Bad. 1951—Flying Leathernecks, *On Dangerous Ground.* 1952—*The Lusty Men.* 1954—*Johnny Guitar.* 1955—*Run for Cover, Rebel Without a Cause.* 1956—Hot Blood, *Bigger Than Life.* 1957—The True Story of Jesse James. 1958—*Bitter Victory, Wind Across the Everglades,* Party Girl. 1961—*The Savage Innocents,* King of Kings. 1963—55 Days at Peking.

Nicholas Ray has been the cause célèbre of the auteur theory for such a long time that his critics, pro and con, have lost all sense of proportion about his career. Nicholas Ray is not the greatest director who ever lived; nor is he a Hollywood hack. The Truth lies somewhere in between. It must be remembered that *They Live by Night, The Lusty Men, Rebel Without a Cause,* and *Bigger Than Life* are socially conscious films by any standards, and that *Knock on Any Door* is particularly bad social consciousness on the Kramer-Cayatte level. His form is not that impeccable, and his content has generally involved considerable social issues. Ray has always displayed an exciting visual style. For example, if one compares *They Live by Night* with Huston's *The Asphalt Jungle*—and these two films are strikingly similar in mood, theme, and plot—one will notice that where Ray tends to cut between physical movements, Huston tends to cut between static compositions. Ray's style tends to be more kinetic, Huston's more plastic, the difference between dance and sculpture. If Ray's nervous direction has no thematic meaning, he would be a minor director indeed. Fortunately, Ray does have a theme, and a very important one; namely, that every relationship establishes its own moral code and that there is no such thing as abstract morality. This much was made clear in *Rebel Without a Cause* when James Dean and his fellow adolescents leaned back in their seats at the planetarium and passively accepted the proposition that the universe itself was drifting without any frame of reference. Even though Ray's career has been plagued by many frustrations, none of his films lacks some burst of inspiration. *Johnny Guitar* is his most bizarre film, and probably his most personal. Certainly, we can sympathize with Everson and Fenin trying to relate this "Western" to the William S. Hart tradition, and finding Ray lacking; but this is the fallacy of writing about genres. *Johnny Guitar* has invented its own genre. Philip Yordan set out to attack McCarthyism, but Ray was too delirious to pay any heed as Freudian feminism prevailed over Marxist masochism, and Pirandello transcended polemics.

Henri Agel, the French film historian, has linked the romanticism of Nicholas Ray to that of Frank Borzage, and the link is not inapt. The agonizingly adolescent intensity of the lovers in *They Live by Night* (Farley Granger and Cathy O'Donnell) and *Rebel Without a Cause* (James Dean and Natalie Wood) invests the lovers with a privileged aura reminiscent of such Borzage classics as *Seventh Heaven, The River, A Man's Castle, History Is Made at Night,* and *Moonrise.* However, Ray's world is more clouded with moral ambiguity than Borzage's. Ray's characters are inflicted with all the psychic ills of the fifties. Paranoia is provided by Humphrey Bogart at the emotional expense of Gloria Grahame in *In a Lonely Place.* Arthur Kennedy's ingratitude in *The Lusty Men* costs Robert Mitchum his life. Jealousy of Joan Crawford is the murderous motivation of Mercedes McCambridge in *Johnny Guitar;* jealousy and envy of Richard Burton is the murderous motivation of Curt Jurgens in *Bitter Victory.* James Mason suffers from delusions of grandeur in *Bigger than Life,* and Robert Ryan from disillusion with mankind in *On Dangerous Ground.* By contrast, a savage instinct for honor saves two civilized figures of the law (Christopher Plummer and Peter O'Toole) from two of nature's outlaws (Burl Ives and Anthony Quinn) in *Wind Across the Everglades* and *The Savage Innocents* respectively, and—despite the reviewers of the time —impressively. Nicholas Ray's reputation does not depend upon undue rationalization. His films are the indisputable records of a very personal anguish that found artistic expression for little more than a decade.

DOUGLAS SIRK (1900–1987)

FILMS: German career (as Detlef Sierk): 1935—April, April; Das Mädchen vom Moorhof, Stutzen der Gesellschaft. 1936—Das Hofkonzert, La Chanson du Souvenir, Schlussakkord. 1937—La Habanera, Zu Neuen Ufern. American career (as Douglas Sirk): 1943—Hitler's Madman. 1944—*Summer Storm.* 1946—*A Scandal in Paris.* 1947—Lured. 1948—Sleep My Love. 1949—Shockproof, Slightly French. 1950—Mystery Submarine. 1951—The First Legion, Thunder on the Hill, The Lady Pays Off, Weekend with Father. 1952—No Room for the Groom, *Has Anybody Seen My Gal?*, Meet Me at the Fair. 1953—*Take Me to Town, All I Desire.* 1954—Taza, Son of Cochise; *Magnificent Obsession,* Sign of the Pagan. 1955—*Captain Lightfoot.* 1956—*All That Heaven Allows,* There's Always Tomorrow, *Battle Hymn.* 1957—*Written on the Wind,* Interlude. 1958—*The Tarnished Angels, A Time to Love and a Time to Die.* 1959—*Imitation of Life.*

Time, if nothing else, will vindicate Douglas Sirk as it has already vindicated Josef von Sternberg. Formal excellence and visual wit are seldom as appreciated at first glance as are the topical sensations of the hour. Yet, *The Defiant Ones* and *On the Beach* are already dead, whereas *Written on the Wind* and *Tarnished Angels* become more impressive with each passing year. Sirk requires no extreme rationalization, and his films require no elaborate defense. The evidence of his style is visible on the screen. It is a personal style, distinct from the impressive technological apparatus of the Universal-MCA-Decca complex. David Miller's *Back Street* and Norman Jewison's *Forty Pounds of Trouble* can serve as decisive cross-references against the theoreticians of studios as auteurs. Even before Sirk came to Universal, he displayed his audacious talent in films like *Summer Storm, A Scandal in Paris,* and *Lured.* The essence of Sirkian cinema is the direct confrontation of all material, however fanciful and improbable. Even in his most dubious projects, Sirk never shrinks away from the ridiculous, but by a full-bodied formal development, his art transcends the ridiculous, as form comments on content. Whereas John Stahl transcended the lachrymose dramas of *Imitation of Life* and *Magnificent Obsession* through the incisiveness of his dark humor. If it be true, as veteran Polish director Aleksander Ford once observed, that the cinema of tomorrow is the cinema of wide screen and color, then Sirk's formal achievements will have helped lead the way into a more sensuous future. Visual style is never an end in itself, and it cannot be ultimately defended except as it relates to a director's taste and sensibility. Any visual style can be mechanically reproduced, but without the linkage to a directorial personality, the effect is indeed mechanical. Sirk's taste is exquisite, and hence, inimitable. One big obstacle to an appreciation of his *œuvre* is an inbred prejudice to what Raymond Durgnat has called the genre of the female weepies as opposed to the male weepies, particularly the kind from Italy that are hailed as "humanist."

GEORGE STEVENS (1904–1979)

FILMS: 1933—Cohens and Kellys in Trouble. 1934—Bachelor Bait, Kentucky Kernels. 1935—*Alice Adams,* Laddie, Nitwits, Annie Oakley. 1936—*Swing Time.* 1937—Quality Street, A Damsel in Distress. 1938—Vivacious Lady. 1939—*Gunga Din.* 1940—Vigil in the Night. 1941—*Penny Serenade.* 1942—*Woman of the Year, The Talk of the Town.* 1943—*The More the Merrier.* 1948—*I Remember Mama.* 1951—*A Place in the Sun.* 1953—*Shane.* 1956—*Giant.* 1959—The Diary of Anne Frank. 1965—The Greatest Story Ever Told.

George Stevens was a minor director with major virtues before *A Place in the Sun,* and a major director with minor virtues after. His instinctive sentimentality has always been intelligently restrained and carefully graded. He served his apprenticeship with Laurel and Hardy two-reelers, and thus learned all the techniques of the slow buildup. Indeed, his dawdling direction of comedy is the slowest in the business. The farcical dénouements of *Vivacious Lady, Woman of the Year, The Talk of the Town,* and *The More the Merrier* now seem interminable despite the behavioral charm of the performers. By contrast, Katharine

Hepburn's incandescent performance in *Alice Adams* remains a tribute to the slow fire of Stevens's direction. Also, *Swing Time* is the best of the Astaire-Rogers musicals, *Gunga Din* the most entertaining of the juvenile Kipling movies, *Penny Serenade* the most honorable of the child-adoption tearjerkers, and *I Remember Mama* the most restrained of the immigrant-family sagas.

All in all, his little movies have outlasted his big ones. The technique of Stevens's American Dream *Sun-Shane-Giant* trilogy that once seemed accomplished now seems labored. *Shane,* particularly, now looks overelaborated in terms of its genre and material, particularly in comparison with the greater spontaneity of Ford and Hawks. Stevens has gained more emotional mileage out of massive slow dissolves than has any other American director, but the emotional linkage of slow dissolves is an effect we now associate more with the thirties than with the fifties. The concentric classicism of the Stevens frame, shot after shot, once looked almost like an official style for national epics. Unfortunately, Stevens ended up looking ponderously old-fashioned in *The Diary of Anne Frank* and *The Greatest Story Ever Told.* What happened to Stevens is that his talent, like that of many of his colleagues, was strained to the breaking point by the massive projects of the fifties. His best days were in the thirties and forties when a movie was just a movie and when any extra care in the direction was conspicuously personal.

ERICH VON STROHEIM (1885–1957)

FILMS: 1918—Blind Husbands. 1919—The Devil's Passkey. 1922—*Foolish Wives,* Merry-Go-Round. 1925—*Greed, The Merry Widow.* 1928—*The Wedding March,* Queen Kelly. 1932—̂ Walking Down Broadway.

Stroheim, like Welles, was often suspected of yielding to the temptation of martyrdom. Film-making, like life, is full of compromises and accommodations, but Stroheim seemed as intransigent on trivial issues as on major ones. What difference did it make, after all, if his royal troops wore the right underwear under their uniforms. Was not this realism carried to idiocy? One might similarly reproach Abel Gance for applying a hundred superimpositions when the audience was aware of only four or five, or Eisenstein for criticizing Korda for not varying the tonality of *Rembrandt* to express the chromatic evolution of the painter as if more than twenty people in the world would get the point. The mark of genius is an obsession with irrelevant detail. Stroheim knew as well as anyone that the commercial exhibition of movies precluded a realistic style that simply accumulated details until the audience was crushed by the sheer weight of the details, but he also understood that realism could not be faked by suggestion or elided by conceptual montage. His films establish a distinction between things as essences and things as appearances.

Stroheim's art is made even more complex by the flamboyant perversity of his personality. A false opposition has been established between Stroheim and Griffith on the grounds of sophistication of film content, but in some ways Stroheim was more Victorian than Griffith, just as cynicism is often more naïve than passion. Perhaps the most remarkable aspect of Stroheim's style is its technical chastity. *The Wedding March,* made in 1928 when Murnau was at the peak of his influence, does not contain a single camera movement. Ultimately, Stroheim's obsessive realism, even in the most romantic settings, anchored his camera to his compositions. Lacking his distinctive personality, his films would have been unbearably literal, and the limitations of his realism would have been more apparent.

However, Stroheim's realism anticipated the sound era in that he established a sense of milieu more through composition than through montage, and also in that he created characterizations less through pantomime than through contextual detail. (His own performances were models of stiff-necked imperturbability, but colorful withal.) Ironically, Stroheim, like Murnau, was to be denied genuine opportunities with the sound film his silent films had heralded.

PRESTON STURGES (1898–1959)

FILMS: 1940—*The Great McGinty, Christmas in July.* 1941 —*The Lady Eve.* 1942—*Sullivan's Travels, The Palm Beach*

Story. 1944—*The Miracle at Morgan's Creek, Hail the Conquering Hero, The Great Moment.* 1947—*Mad Wednesday.* 1948—Unfaithfully Yours. 1949—The Beautiful Blonde from Bashful Bend. 1957—The French They Are a Funny Race.

Acknowledged as the foremost satirist of his time, Preston Sturges enjoyed his greatest vogue between 1940 and 1944, when his pungent wit and frenetic slapstick exploded on such targets as Tammany Hall politics, advertising, American fertility rites, hero and mother worship. Within the context of a Sturges film, a gangster could declare with ringing, heavily accented conviction: "America is a land of great opportunity." An underpaid clerk could rise to fame and fortune by coining the slogan "If you can't sleep, it isn't the coffee. It's the bunk." A sign in a flophouse could remind its denizens: "Have you written to Mother?" Sturges repeatedly suggested that the lowliest boob could rise to the top with the right degree of luck, bluff, and fraud. The absurdity of the American success story was matched by the ferocity of the battle of the sexes. In *The Lady Eve,* when Henry Fonda plaintively confesses, "Snakes are my life," Barbara Stanwyck snaps back, "What a life!" The climax of *Palm Beach Story* finds Rudy Vallee serenading Claudette Colbert's upstairs window while the object of his affections is being seduced by the subject of hers, Joel McCrea.

What distinguishes Sturges from his contemporaries is the frantic congestion of his comedies. The Breughel of American comedy directors, Sturges created a world of peripheral professionals—politicians, gangsters, executives, bartenders, cabdrivers, secretaries, bookies, card sharps, movie producers, doctors, dentists, bodyguards, butlers, inventors, millionaires, and derelicts. These were not the usual flotsam and jetsam of Hollywood cinema, but self-expressive cameos of aggressive individualism. With the determinism of the Sturges plots, these infinitely detailed miniatures served as contingent elements, and it is these elements, and the single-take, multiple viewpoint sequences formally demanded by these elements, that establish the comedies of Preston Sturges as comedy/not tragedy rather than merely comedy/ha ha.

Sturgean comedy was influenced both by the silent antics of Charles Chaplin, Buster Keaton, and Harold Lloyd in the twenties, and by the crackling verbal rhythms of Howard Hawks, Frank Capra, Leo McCarey and Gregory La Cava in the thirties. Sturges contributed to this distinguished tradition mainly through the unusual density of his scripts. His films were noted for the hilarious side effects of character and bit actors. It was not unusual for a gravel-voiced bus driver to use the word "paraphrase" or for a hoodlum to invoke the ruinous symmetry of "Samson and Delilah, Sodom and Gomorrah." A stereotyped performer like Eric Blore was virtually rediscovered savoring the line: "I positively swill in his ale." Similarly, Edgar Kennedy was resurrected from two-reelers to play an inspired bartender reacting to a customer asking for his first drink ever: "Sir, you rouse the artist in me." The Sturges stock company was particularly noted for the contrasting personalities of William Demarest, the eternal roughneck, and Franklin Pangborn, the prissy prune.

Sturges was criticized at his peak by James Agee and Manny Farber for an ambivalence in his work derived from a childhood conflict between a culturally demanding mother and an admired businessman foster father. This unusually Freudian analysis of the director's work, unusual, that is, for its time, sought to explain the incongruity of continental sophistication being challenged by American pragmatism. Sturges himself was seen as an uneasy mixture of savant and wise guy. On the one hand, his extreme literacy, rare among Hollywood screenwriters, enabled him to drop words like "ribaldry" and "vestal" into their proper contexts without a pretentious thud. On the other, he seemed unwilling to develop the implications of his serious ideas. His flair for props and gadgets suited the popularly recalled image of the young inventor of kissproof lipstick.

His reputation today is based mainly on the eight films he directed for Paramount. *The Great McGinty,* a vigorous satire of big-city politics marked by lusty performances from Akim Tamiroff as the Boss and Brian Donlevy as the hobo elevated to governor, was the pilot film of the writer-director movement in Hollywood. Most directors had previously risen from the ranks of studio technicians and stage directors. After Sturges led the way, John Huston, Billy Wilder, Dudley Nichols, Clifford Odets, Nunnally Johnson, Robert Rossen, Samuel Fuller, Frank Tashlin, and Blake Edwards followed from the writer's cubicle to the director's chair. *Christmas in July* lingered over a Depression mood as Dick Powell and Ellen Drew played an engaged couple trying to make ends meet on a combined salary of forty dollars a week. The vagaries of luck and the cruelties of practical jokes developed the plot in a disturbing manner that was later to be recognized as the director's trademark.

The Lady Eve, a sophisticated comedy with Henry Fonda and Barbara Stanwyck, was hailed by *The New York Times* as the best film of 1941. Sturges circumvented the censors with a rowdy blackout technique that began where the more discreet "Lubitsch touch" had left off. (The difference between the Lubitsch smile and the Sturges guffaw is the difference between winking at what is happening behind closed doors and laughing at what happens when the doors are flung open. Lubitsch treated sex as the dessert of a civilized meal of manners; Sturges, more in the American style, served sex with all the courses. Despite its ribaldry and gusto, the Sturges manner was never coarse and tasteless.) An adroit manipulation of mistaken identity aided Sturges in preserving the technical morality of the marriage contract for the oppressive censors of his time. The duet in *The Lady Eve* was later enlarged into the quartet of *Palm Beach Story* in which Joel McCrea, Claudette Colbert, Mary Astor, and Rudy Vallee were perpetually confused and obsessed by the permutations of what Sturges leeringly defined as "Subject A."

Sullivan's Travels, a Swiftian glimpse of Hollywood and its occasional flirtations with social consciousness, is generally considered the most profound expression of the director's personality. Dedicating the film to the world's clowns and mountebanks, Sturges forthrightly defended the muse of comedy against the presumably more serious demands of society. Like Shakespeare's *A Winter's Tale,* the film pivots in one poetic pirouette from the sunny to the somber when an old derelict is trapped in a metal jungle of switch rails, and is unable to avoid an oncoming train.

The Miracle of Morgan's Creek and *Hail the Conquering Hero* represented the director's original vision of small-town America from which Eddie Bracken emerged as a Sturges folk hero. In *Miracle,* Bracken has "greatness thrust upon him" when his frolicsome V-girl sweetheart, Betty Hutton, is thoughtful enough to transcend her disgrace with sextuplets. In *Hero,* Bracken survives the ordeal of a 4-F self-exposed as a false war hero, and again he is redeemed by the generous emotions of his girl friend, Ella Raines. Especially and disturbingly timely was the intense performance of ex-prizefighter Freddie Steele, in the film an orphanage-bred marine hero with a severe mother complex.

After 1944, when he left Paramount to form a short-lived partnership with Howard Hughes, Sturges's career suffered a precipitous decline. His three subsequent Hollywood films were remote from the tastes of their time, and during his long exile in the fifties, his one realized European project, the bilingual *Les Carnets de Major Thompson* (*The French They Are a Funny Race*) was unsuccessful. His present reputation is that of a period director who ultimately lost contact with his audience. Even at the time of his greatest success, he was overshadowed by the emotions aroused by the war and the stylistic revolution introduced with *Citizen Kane.* He received an Academy Award for the script of *The Great McGinty* in 1940, and was nominated twice in 1944 for *The Miracle of Morgan's Creek* and *Hail the Conquering Hero,* though again as a writer rather than as a director.

His directorial style depended more on the pacing of action and dialogue than on visual texture and composition. His canvas was flat, his sense of space shallow. Sturges employed long, uncut, "single-take" scenes to establish the premises of his elaborate scripts, but when he shifted to slapstick, he often cut to reactions before the action had been terminated. His instinct for timing comedy montage made his films the funniest of their era in terms of audience laughter. He was capable of cinematic license with a talking horse or a portrait that changed expressions. When he wanted to speed up the plot, he dispensed with dialogue and let the crisp movement and montage of silent farce fill the screen with hurtling bodies. In *Mad Wednesday,* he went so far as to begin with the last reel of Harold Lloyd's 1925 classic, *The Freshman,* after which he attempted to re-create Lloyd's vertiginous comedy effects with even wilder Sturges variations. As a screenwriter, he had pioneered in the development of the intricate flashback with *The Power and the Glory* in 1933, and his directed scenarios remain models of structural complexity.

KING VIDOR (1894–1982)

FILMS: 1913–1918—Short Subjects. 1918—The Turn in the Road. 1919—Better Times, The Other Half, Poor Relations, *The Jack-Knife Man.* 1920—The Family Honor. 1921—The Sky Pilot, Love Never Dies, Conquering the Women; Woman, Wake up. 1922—The Real Adventure, Dusk to Dawn, Alice Adams, Peg o' My Heart. 1923—The Woman of Bronze, Three Wise Fools, Wild Oranges, Happiness. 1924—Wine of Youth, His Hour, Wife of the Centaur. 1925—Proud Flesh, *The Big Parade,* La Bohème. 1926— Bardelys the Magnificent. 1928—*The Crowd, Show People.* 1929 —*Hallelujah!* 1930—Not So Dumb, Billy the Kid. 1931—*Street Scene, The Champ.* 1932—Bird of Paradise, Cynara. 1933—The Stranger's Return. 1934—*Our Daily Bread,* The Wedding Night. 1935—*So Red the Rose.* 1936—The Texas Rangers. 1937— *Stella Dallas.* 1938—*The Citadel.* 1939—*Northwest Passage.* 1940 —Comrade X. 1941—H. M. Pulham, Esq. 1944—An American Romance. 1947—*Duel in the Sun,* On Our Merry Way. 1949— *The Fountainhead.* Beyond the Forest. 1951—Lightning Strikes Twice. 1952—Japanese War Bride, *Ruby Gentry.* 1955—*Man Without a Star.* 1956—*War and Peace.* 1959—Solomon and Sheba.

King Vidor is a director for anthologies. He has created more great moments and fewer great films than any director of his rank. Vidor's is an unusually intuitive talent, less grounded than most in theory. The classics of his humanistic museum period— *The Big Parade, The Crowd, Hallelujah*—are no less uneven or more impressive than the classics of his delirious modern pe- riod—*Duel in the Sun, The Fountainhead, Ruby Gentry.*

Vidor's vitality seems ageless, and his plastic force is espe- cially appropriate for partings and reunions, and the visual op- position of individuals to masses, both social and physical. Vidor's is an architectural cinema with none of Lang's deter- minism or Antonioni's decadence. There are occasions in the cinema when two directors confront the same visual problem and thus provide a convenient cross-reference. Such a cross-reference occurs in Siegel's *Hell Is for Heroes* and Sanders's *War Hunt* when a wounded soldier dies in the midst of his screams as he is being carried to a medic. On a purely technical level, Siegel's treatment is decisively superior in the judicious use of a traveling overhead shot. Similarly, Vidor and Milestone cross each other's path in *The Big Parade* and *All Quiet on the Western Front*. In the Vidor, an enraged American soldier pursues a German into a shell hole. When the American sees that the German is wounded, he is unable to finish the job, but gives his enemy a cigarette instead. In the Milestone, a German soldier bayonets a Frenchman, and then asks his victim's forgiveness. Both scenes are contrived to express human brotherhood, and thereby attack the idea of War. Both scenes involve two figures in a depressed and isolated enclosure. The two-shot is almost mandatory here for both directors because cross-cutting would destroy the meaning of the scene. If two figures are shown in the same frame, a bond is established between them. Cross-cutting would establish separateness and opposition as the point of view changed back and forth. Both Vidor and Milestone understood this much, and thus the issue of montage never arises. Yet, though these scenes are identical in meaning and broadly equivalent in technical execution, the Vidor is both more moving and aesthetically superior to the Milestone. Why? Well, not because the Vidor came first. Most film critics under fifty probably saw the Milestone before they saw the Vidor. Not because Vidor has been arbitrarily designated as a better director than Milestone. One superficial advantage the Vidor possesses is that it is a silent sequence in a silent film, while the Milestone is handicapped by an inexperienced Lew Ayres reciting excessively literary dialogue. The scene in both cases involves soldiers who speak different languages, and so the Milestone imposes a suspension of disbelief unnecessary in the Vidor. The Vidor does not even have to break the continuity of the visual field with titles, and so one of the great advantages of the talkies—their visual continuum—does not help Milestone in this instance.

The personalities of the actors must also be considered somewhat, and in this instance, the advantage is with Vidor. John Gilbert and his German comrade are closer together in age than are

Lew Ayres and a middle-aged Raymond Griffith. The Vidor pair convey more strongly the idea of vital youth wasted in war, while the Milestone pair suggest abstractions of humanity rather than individuals. Ultimately, however, the issue between the two scenes is resolved by the oldest criterion of the cinema, good old camera placement, an aesthetic factor that was as decisive in 1895 as it is today. Vidor moves much closer to his characters, and thus achieves greater dramatic intensity. By staying farther back, Milestone emphasizes the pictorialism of the scene, the frame in which the spectacle unfolds rather than the spectacle itself. Vidor's treatment is more forceful than Milestone's, and hence more emotionally satisfying. We remember the faces of the two protagonists, and not the spectacle as a whole. Thus, in this one sequence, two careers fall into place. Vidor's plasticity versus Milestone's pictorialism. Engagement versus disengagement. An auteur versus a technician. The auteur theory can only record the evidence on the screen. It can never prejudge it. Vidor is superior to Milestone.

RAOUL WALSH (1887–1980)

FILMS: 1912—Life of Villa. 1915—The Regeneration, Carmen. 1916—Honor System, Blue Blood and Red, The Serpent. 1917 —Betrayed, The Conqueror, The Pride of New York, The Innocent Sinner, Silent Lie. 1918—Woman and the Law, This Is the Life, The Prussian Cur, On the Jump, Every Mother's Son, I'll Say So. 1919— Evangeline, Should a Husband Forgive? 1920—From Now On, The Deep Purple, The Strongest. 1921—The Oath, Serenade. 1922 —Kindred of the Dust. 1923—Lost and Found. 1924—The Thief of Bagdad. 1925—East of Suez, The Spaniard. 1926—The Wanderer, The Lucky Lady, The Lady of the Harem, *What Price Glory?* 1927—The Monkey Talks, The Loves of Carmen. 1928— *Sadie Thompson*, The Red Dance, Me Gangster. 1929—Hot for Paris, *In Old Arizona* (with Irving Cummings), *The Cock-Eyed World*. 1930—The Big Trail. 1931—The Man Who Came Back, Women of All Nations, Yellow Ticket. 1932—Wild Girl, Me and My Gal. 1933—Sailor's Luck, The Bowery, Going Hollywood. 1935—Under Pressure, Baby Face Harrington, Every Night at Eight. 1936—Klondike Annie, Big Brown Eyes, Spendthrift. 1937

—You're in the Army Now, When Thief Meets Thief, Artists and Models, Hitting a New High. 1938—College Swing. 1939—St. Louis Blues, *The Roaring Twenties.* 1940—Dark Command, *They Drive by Night.* 1941—*High Sierra, The Strawberry Blonde,* Manpower, *They Died with Their Boots On.* 1942—*Desperate Journey, Gentleman Jim.* 1943—Background to Danger, *Northern Pursuit.* 1944—Uncertain Glory. 1945—*Objective Burma, Salty O'Rourke,* The Horn Blows at Midnight. 1946—*The Man I Love.* 1947—*Pursued, Cheyenne.* 1948—Silver River, *One Sunday Afternoon,* Fighter Squadron. 1949—*Colorado Territory, White Heat.* 1951—Along the Great Divide, *Captain Horatio Hornblower, Distant Drums.* 1952—*Glory Alley, The World in His Arms,* Blackbeard the Pirate. 1953—Sea Devils, *A Lion Is in the Streets, Gun Fury.* 1954—Saskatchewan. 1955—*Battle Cry, The Tall Men.* 1956—The Revolt of Mamie Stover, The King and Four Queens. 1957—*Band of Angels.* 1958—The Naked and the Dead, The Sheriff of Fractured Jaw. 1959—A Private's Affair. 1960—Esther and the King. 1961—Marines, Let's Go.

If the heroes of Ford are sustained by tradition, and the heroes of Hawks by professionalism, the heroes of Walsh are sustained by nothing more than a feeling for adventure. The Fordian hero knows why he is doing something even if he doesn't know how. The Hawksian hero knows how to do what he is doing even if he doesn't know why. The Walshian hero is less interested in the why or the how than in the what. He is always plunging into the unknown, and he is never too sure what he will find there. There is a pathos and vulnerability in Walsh's characters lacking in the more self-contained Ford and Hawks counterparts. Where Ford shifts from the immediacy of the slightly depressed heroic angle to the horizon line of history, and Hawks remains at eye level, Walsh often moves to the slightly elevated angle of the lost child in the big world. One of the most stunning shots of this nature occurs in *Captain Horatio Hornblower* when Walsh's camera recedes and rises slowly to present the lonely image of Gregory Peck, ridiculously gallant in his period costume and yet foreshortened into the lost son of his mother. The *Time* reviewer of *White Heat* has perceptively observed that Raoul Walsh was the only Hollywood director who could have got away with a shot of James Cagney sitting on his mother's lap. The principle of counterpoint operates here. Only the most virile director can effectively project a feminine vulnerability in his characters. Only an actor like Bogart could effectively hold Ava Gardner's dead body in his arms, and wonder aloud why he could never remember the Spanish word for Cinderella. Only a tough actor like Garfield could cry over the death of a friend in *The Breaking Point*. A sensitive actor like Brando was also perceptive enough to hold back his tears at Red Buttons's death in *Sayonara*. The other point that can be made about Walsh is that he has always possessed the necessary technical skills and artistic instincts to bring off the most ambitious physical spectacles. His best films are genuinely exciting, though neither profound nor pretentious. If there is no place in the cinema for the virtues and limitations of Raoul Walsh, there is even less place for an honestly pluralistic criticism.

III.
EXPRESSIVE
ESOTERICA

These are the unsung directors with difficult styles or unfashionable genres or both. Their deeper virtues are often obscured by irritating idiosyncrasies on the surface, but they are generally redeemed by their seriousness and grace.

BUDD BOETTICHER (1916–)

FILMS: 1944—One Mysterious Night. 1945—The Missing Juror; A Guy, A Gal and a Pal; Escape in the Fog, Youth on Trial. 1948—Assigned to Danger, Behind Locked Doors. 1949—Black Midnight. 1950—Killer Shark, The Wolf Hunters. 1951—*The Bullfighter and the Lady*, The Cimarron Kid. 1952—Red Ball Express, Bronco Buster, Horizons West. 1953—City Beneath the Sea, Seminole, The Man from the Alamo, Wings of the Hawk, East of Sumatra. 1955—*The Magnificent Matador*. 1956—*The Killer Is Loose, Seven Men from Now*. 1957—*Decision at Sundown, The Tall T*. 1958—*Buchanan Rides Alone*. 1959—*Ride Lonesome, Westbound*. 1960—*The Rise and Fall of Legs Diamond, Comanche Station*. 1968—The Carlos Arruza Story.

Does anyone know where Budd Boetticher is? The last we heard, our gifted friend was on his way to Mexico to make a movie on bullfighting, his third. Be that what it may, Boetticher is one of the most fascinating unrecognized talents in the American cinema. How many admirers of Peckinpah's *Ride the High Country* recognize this film as an attempted summation of the incredibly consistent Boetticher–Randolph Scott–Harry Joe Brown series of Westerns, which from 1956 on, established a new style in the genre? Constructed partly as allegorical Odysseys and partly as floating poker games where every character took turns at bluffing about his hand until the final showdown, Boetticher's Westerns expressed a weary serenity and moral certitude that was contrary to the more neurotic approaches of other directors on this neglected level of the cinema. Similarly, *The Rise and Fall of Legs Diamond* is a minor classic in the perverse *Scarface* tradition. One wonders where directors like Boetticher find the energy and the inspiration to do such fine work, when native critics are so fantastically indifferent that they probably couldn't tell a Boetticher film apart from a Selander or worse. This unyielding taste and dedication is what makes the American cinema so exciting and, at times, so miraculous.

Whatever his action setting, be it the corrida, the covered wagon, or the urban underworld, Boetticher is no stranger to the nuances of *machismo,* that overweening masculine pride that provides both a style and a fatal flaw to his gun-wielding or cape-flourishing characters. Boetticher's films strip away the outside world to concentrate on the deadly confrontations of male antagonists. No audience is required for the final showdown. It is man to man in an empty arena on a wide screen before a very quiet, elemental camera. Elemental but not elementary. Boetticher's timing of action is impeccable. He is not a writer-director like Burt Kennedy or Sam Peckinpah, but he is a much better storyteller.

ANDRE DE TOTH (1900–   )

FILMS: 1944—None Shall Escape, *Dark Waters.* 1947— *Ramrod,* The Other Love. 1948—*Pitfall.* 1949—Slattery's Hurricane. 1951—Man in the Saddle. 1952—Carson City, *Springfield Rifle,* Last of the Comanches. 1953—House of Wax, The Stranger Wore a Gun, Thunder Over the Plains. 1954—Riding Shotgun, Crime-Wave, The Bounty Hunters, Tanganyika. 1955—*The Indian Fighter.* 1957—Monkey on My Back, Hidden Fear. 1959—The Two-Headed Spy, *Day of the Outlaw.* 1960—Man on a String. 1961 —Morgan the Pirate, The Mongols. 1964—Gold for the Caesars. 1968—Play Dirty.

André de Toth's most interesting films reveal an understanding of the instability and outright treachery of human relationships. *Ramrod, Pitfall, Springfield Rifle, The Indian Fighter,* and *Day of the Outlaw* are unusually unpleasant explorations of failed love and trust. The assorted villainies seem more like the natural order of things than like mere contrivances of melodrama. Raymond Burr's soft-spoken Machiavellian schemer in *Pitfall* and Paul Kelly's quietly desperate traitor in *Springfield Rifle* are memorably de Tothian in their adaptability to a world of conflicting interests.

STANLEY DONEN (1924–   )

FILMS: 1949—*On the Town* (with Gene Kelly). 1951—Royal Wedding. 1952—*Singin' in the Rain* (with Gene Kelly), Love Is Better than Ever, Fearless Fagan. 1953—*Give a Girl a Break.* 1954—*Seven Brides for Seven Brothers,* Deep in My Heart. 1955—*It's Always Fair Weather* (with Gene Kelly). 1957—*Funny Face, The Pajama Game* (with George Abbott), Kiss Them for Me. 1958—*Indiscreet, Damn Yankees.* 1960—Once More with Feeling, Surprise Package, The Grass is Greener. 1963—*Charade.* 1966 —Arabesque. 1968—*Two for the Road,* Bedazzled.

Stanley Donen has always seemed to function best as a hyphenated director. He was dismissed for a time as Gene Kelly's invisible partner on such Golden-Age Metro musicals as *On the Town, Singin' in the Rain,* and *It's Always Fair Weather.* When the Metro bubble burst, Donen moved to Warners with *The Pajama Game* and *Damn Yankees,* two transposed Broadway musicals seemingly dominated by George Abbott's vigorously theatrical pacing. Even when Donen received sole directorial credit, his more notable efforts seemed only marginally personal. *Seven Brides for Seven Brothers,* for example, is stamped (and stomped) with Michael Kidd's muscular choreography; *Funny Face* is graced with Richard Avedon's witty fashion photography. In all these tandem operations, Donen clearly lacks the stylistic presence of a Vincente Minnelli. As for Donen's relatively personal musicals, *Royal Wedding* and *Give a Girl a Break* are peculiarly somber affairs with only intermittent flashes of inspiration, while *Deep in My Heart* is virtually a complete disaster. His nonmusical comedies have been either relentlessly trivial (*Love Is Better than Ever, Fearless Fagan*) or nervously ververbalized (*Kiss Them for Me, Once More with Feeling, Surprise Package, The Grass Is Greener*).

Where Donen has come closest to projecting a personal style is in *Indiscreet,* a comedy that eventually collapses under the weight of Norman Krasna's plot indiscretions, but not before Donen reveals the serious temperament necessary for high comedy. His timing is sharp, and he seems at home with an elegant cast; in this instance the height of elegance represented by Cary Grant and Ingrid Bergman. After flirtations with black comedy, op art, and half-baked Hitchcock imitations in *Charade* and *Arabesque,* Donen has found his own road back with *Two for the Road.* The director's serious temperament is well suited to the offbeat casting of Audrey Hepburn with Albert Finney, the stylishly brittle script of Frederic Raphael (*Nothing but the Best, Darling*), and the tinkly romantic score of Henry Mancini. It would seem that if Donen is to be involved in good movies in the future, it will be more as a genial catalyst than as a creative force. Donen seems too much the congenital team player ever to display a marked individuality, and the Donen "touch" remains as elusive as ever. Certainly, *Bedazzled* owes infinitely more of its personal style to Dudley Moore and Peter Cook than to Stanley Donen, whereas a relative newcomer like Joseph McGrath seems already to have stolen Donen's thunder with the psychedelic portions of *Casino Royale* and the more dazzling than *Bedazzled* Dudley Moore capers in *30 Is a Dangerous Age, Cynthia!* Still, if a director acts as a pleasant enough catalyst long enough, he may come to be accepted as a creator if only in the most passive form permitted the claim of creation.

CLIVE DONNER (1926–   )

FILMS: 1956—The Secret Place. 1958—Heart of a Child. 1959—Marriage of Convenience. 1960—The Sinister Man. 1962 —*Some People.* 1964—*The Guest (The Caretaker)*, *Nothing but the Best.* 1965—*What's New Pussycat?* 1967—Luv. 1968—Here We Go Round the Mulberry Bush. 1969—Alfred the Great.

Clive Donner has emerged in recent years as a gifted stylist with an eye for contemporaneous detail. He has been particularly fortunate in his writers, notably Frederic Raphael (*Nothing but the Best*), Harold Pinter (*The Caretaker*), Woody Allen (*What's New Pussycat?*), and Murray Schisgal (*Luv*). Donner's scenarists aside, he seems to be emerging as Britain's answer to Vincente

Minnelli. Donner, like Lester, seems to have anticipated the transformation of England from mum to mod. It remains to be seen if the prophet can avoid being swallowed up by his own revolution. With Donner it is not so much a question of aesthetics versus ethics as of decorative complicity versus dramatic conflict. In this sense, the mod mushiness of *Here We Go Round the Mulberry Bush* marks an ominous turn in Donner's career.

ALLAN DWAN (1885–1981)

FILMS (partial list 1911–1917): 1914—Wildflower, The Straight Road. 1915—A Girl of Yesterday, Jordan Is a Hard Road, The Pretty Sister of Jose, The Dancing Girl, David Harum. 1916—Betty of Greystone, The Habit of Happiness, The Half-Breed, The Good Bad Man, Manhattan Madness, An Innocent Magdalene. 1917—Panthea, The Fighting Odds. 1918—A Modern Musketeer, Mr. Fix-It, Bound in Morocco, He Comes Up Smiling. 1919—Cheating Cheaters, Soldiers of Fortune, The Dark Star, Getting Mary Married. 1920—Luck of the Irish, A Splendid Hazard, The Forbidden Thing. 1921—The Perfect Crime, A Broken Doll, In the Heart of a Fool, The Scoffer. 1922—The Sin of Martha Queed, Superstition, *Robin Hood.* 1923—Zaza, Glimpses of the Moon, Lawful Larceny, Big Brother. 1924—Her Love Story, Manhandled, A Society Scandal, The Wages of Virtue, Argentine Love. 1925—Night Life in New York, Stage Struck, Coast of Folly. 1926—Sea Horses, Padlocked, Tin Gods, Summer Bachelors. 1927—The Music Master, The Joy Girl; East Side, West Side. 1928—French Dressing, Big Noise. 1929—*The Iron Mask,* Tide of Empire, Frozen Justice, The Far Call, South Sea Rose. 1930—What a Widow! 1931—Man to Man, Chances, Wicked. 1932—While Paris Sleeps. 1934—The Morning After. 1935—Black Sheep, Beauty's Daughter. 1936—The Song and Dance Man, Human Cargo, High Tension, Fifteen Maiden Lane. 1937—Woman Wise, That I May Live, One Mile from Heaven, Heidi. 1938—Rebecca of Sunnybrook Farm, Josette, *Suez.* 1939—The Three Musketeers, The Gorilla, *Frontier Marshall.* 1940—Sailor's Lady, Young People, Trail of the Vigilantes. 1941—Look Who's Laughing, Rise and Shine. 1942—Friendly Enemies, Here We Go Again. 1943—Around the World. 1944—Abroad with Two Yanks, *Up in Mabel's Room.* 1945—*Brewster's Millions, Getting Gertie's Garter.* 1946—*Rendezvous with Annie.* 1947—Calendar Girl, Northwest Outpost. 1948—The Inside Story, Angel in Exile. 1949—*Sands of Iwo Jima*. 1950—Surrender. 1951—Belle Le Grande, The Wild Blue Yonder. 1952—I Dream of Jeannie, Montana Belle. 1953—Woman They Almost Lynched, Sweethearts on Parade, Flight Nurse. 1954—*Silver Lode*, Cattle Queen of Montana, Passion. 1955—Escape to Burma, Pearl of the South Pacific, *Tennessee's Partner*. 1956—Slightly Scarlet, *Hold Back the Night*. 1957—*The River's Edge, The Restless Breed*. 1958—Enchanted Island. 1961—Most Dangerous Man Alive.

Dwan's career is still being mined for a possibly higher assay of gold to dross. Recent findings—*Silver Lode, The Restless Breed, The River's Edge*—represent a virtual bonanza of hitherto unexplored classics. It is too early to establish any coherent pattern to Dwan's career as a whole, but it may very well be that Dwan will turn out to be the last of the old masters. *Silver Lode* displays a classic circularity of remembered technique, unifying the varied themes of the film by repeating the same images in different contexts. From the Fairbanks period in the silents, to unassuming comedies in the thirties and forties, and to Westerns in the fifties, Dwan has been as active as he has been obscure. Yet, one can recall *Brewster's Millions* and *Rendezvous with Annie* with fond pleasure unprompted by the alleged mystiques of the *auteur* theory. Consequently, there may be much more to be said about Dwan.

TAY GARNETT (1894–1977)

FILMS: 1928—Celebrity, *The Spieler*. 1929—Flying Fools, Oh Yeah! 1930—Officer O'Brien, *Her Man*. 1931—Bad Company. 1932—*One Way Passage*, Prestige, Okay America. 1933—Destination Unknown, SOS Iceberg. 1935—China Seas, She Couldn't Take It, Professional Soldier. 1937—Love Is News, *Slave Ship, Stand-In*. 1938—Joy of Living, Trade Winds. 1939—*Eternally Yours*. 1940—Slightly Honorable, *Seven Sinners*. 1941—Cheers for Miss Bishop. 1942—My Favorite Spy. 1943—Bataan, The Cross of Lorraine. 1944—Mrs. Parkington. 1945—*The Valley of Decision*. 1946—*The Postman Always Rings Twice*. 1947—Wild Harvest. 1949—A Connecticut Yankee in King Arthur's

Court. 1950—The Fireball. 1951—Soldiers Three, *Cause for Alarm*. 1952—One Minute to Zero. 1953—Main Street to Broadway. 1954—The Black Knight. 1956—Seven Wonders of the World. 1960—*The Night Fighter.*

Inconsistency is the hobgoblin of Tay Garnett's career, and inconsistency can never be defined satisfactorily. The director of *Her Man, One-Way Passage, The Postman Always Rings Twice,* and *The Night Fighter* stays in the mind despite the lack of an overall pattern in his work. Curiously, the director's fondness for *China Seas* and *The Cross of Lorraine* is as inexplicable as the underground reputations of *Stand-In* and *Cause for Alarm,* but critical values are always topsy-turvy at this level of filmmaking. For the moment, Garnett's ultimate reputation is still unusually elusive. Even as a footnote to Marlene Dietrich's career, the rowdy humor of *Seven Sinners* could tip the scales in the director's favor. The recent loans from the Cinémathèque française of such early Garnetts as *The Spieler* and *Her Man* suggest that Garnett's personality is that of a rowdy vaudevillian, an artist with the kind of rough edges that cause the overcivilized French sensibility to swoon in sheer physical frustration. One of Garnett's most distinguished defenders is the British critic Raymond Durgnat. *Her Man,* according to Durgnat, is superior to Hawks's chilling *A Girl in Every Port* because of, rather than in spite of, Garnett's period sentimentality. What lingers in the mind is James Gleason's knowing comedy relief from the travails of Helen Twelvetrees, the Frankie no less of the Frankie and Johnnie ballad, particularly the wickedly sophisticated bigotry implicit in the muttered exclamation, "There's an octoroon in the kindling." Memorable also in the 1930 *Her Man* are the extraordinarily fluid camera movements that dispel the myth of static talkies, a myth treated as gospel in the official film histories of the period.

SETH HOLT

FILMS: 1959—Nowhere to Go. 1962—*Taste of Fear.* 1964 —*Station Six—Sahara.* 1965—*The Nanny.* 1968—Danger Route.

Seth Holt seemed more promising when he was less accomplished. *The Nanny* fell somewhere between *What Ever Happened to Baby Jane?* and *Die, Die, My Darling* in the gallery of gargoyles. Though Holt is more polished than Aldrich and infinitely more talented than Narizzano, his virtues are things of bits and pieces. Still, there are moments in *Taste of Fear* and *Station Six—Sahara* when it seems that Holt has at least one great picture in him, but where is it and what would it be about?

PHIL KARLSON (1908–1985)

FILMS: 1944—A Wave, a WAC and a Marine. 1945—There Goes Kelly, G.I. Honeymoon, The Shanghai Cobra. 1946—Live Wires, Swing Parade of 1946, Dark Alibi, Behind the Mask, Bowery Bombshell, Wife Wanted. 1947—Black Gold, Louisiana. 1948—Adventures in Silverado, Rocky, Thunderhoof, Ladies of the Chorus. 1949—The Big Cat. 1950—The Iroquois Trail. 1951—Lorna Doone, Texas Rangers, Mask of the Avenger. 1952—Scandal Sheet, The Brigand. 1953—*99 River Street.* 1954—They Rode West. 1955—*Hell's Island, Tight Spot, Five Against the House, The Phenix City Story.* 1957—*The Brothers Rico.* 1958—*Gunman's Walk.* 1960—*Hell to Eternity*, Key Witness. 1961—The Secret Ways, The Young Doctors. 1962—*Kid Galahad.* 1963—Rampage. 1966—*The Silencers.* 1969—The Wrecking Crew.

Phil Karlson's career has had a peculiar rhythm all its own. He started slowly, and from 1944 through 1952, did little to attract attention. *Ladies of the Chorus* has acquired a retroactive cult composed of some of the admirers of the late Marilyn Monroe in her pristine state, but otherwise nothing much happens until *99 River Street.* Then, in 1955, a Karlson style emerges decisively in *Hell's Island, Tight Spot, Five Against the House,* and *The Phenix City Story,* pictures with more quality than prestige, interestingly ambiguous action heroes ranging from late John Payne to early Brian Keith. *The Brothers Rico* in 1957 is still Karlson's best film; and then a tapering off—*Gunman's Walk, Hell to Eternity, Key Witness, The Young Doctors, Rampage,* and *The Silencers,* the latter the best of the Dean Martin—Matt

Helm takeoffs on the Bond craze, but a deplorable genre all the same, despite Martin's charm and the goofy voluptuousness of Stella Stevens. *Kid Galahad,* Presley's best film since *Flaming Star,* and equally unsuccessful at the box office, represents another oasis in a desert of decline. Karlson may have had bad luck with projects, but the evidence of recession before full recognition is too strong to be denied. Karlson was most personal and most efficient when he dealt with the phenomenon of violence in a world controlled by organized evil. His special brand of lynch hysteria establishes such an outrageous moral imbalance that the most unthinkable violence releases the audience from its helpless passivity. Unfortunately, an American director gets nowhere making films like *The Brothers Rico.* The cosmopolitan genre prejudices are too strong.

JOSEPH H. LEWIS (1900–   )

FILMS: 1937—Courage of the West, Singing Outlaw, International Spy. 1938—The Spy Ring, Border Wolves, The Last Stand. 1940—Two-Fisted Rangers, Blazing Six-Shooters, Texas Stagecoach, The Man from Tumbleweeds, Boys of the City, The Return of Wild Bill, That Gang of Mine. 1941—The Invisible Ghost, Pride of the Bowery. 1942—Arizona Cyclone, Bombs Over Burma, The Silver Bullet, Secrets of a Co-ed, The Boss of Hangtown Mesa, The Mad Doctor of Market Street. 1944—Minstrel Man. 1945—*My Name Is Julia Ross.* 1946—So Dark the Night. 1947—The Swordsman. 1948—The Return of October. 1949—*The Undercover Man, Deadly Is the Female* (or *Gun Crazy*). 1950—Lady Without a Passport. 1952—Retreat, Hell! Desperate Search. 1953—Cry of the Hunted. 1955—*The Big Combo,* A Lawless Street. 1956—The Seventh Cavalry. 1957—*The Halliday Brand.* 1958—Terror in a Texas Town.

Back in the Spring 1962 issue of *Film Culture,* a critic, writing on "The High Forties Revisited," remarked: "If some bright new critic should awaken the world to the merits of Joseph Lewis in the near future, we will have to scramble back to his 1940 record: *Two-Fisted Rangers, Blazing Six-Shooters, Texas Stage-*

coach, The Man from Tumbleweeds, Boys of the City, Return of Wild Bill, and *That Gang of Mine.* Admittedly, in this direction lies madness." Well, madness is always preferable to smugness, and scramble we must because Lewis has been discovered. After several years of Poverty Row, he made *The Minstrel Man,* with Edgar G. Ulmer, no less, as his set designer. Then, in 1945, *My Name Is Julia Ross* became the sleeper of the year. From that point on, the director's somber personality has been revealed consistently through a complex visual style. It would seem that his career warrants further investigation. The director's one enduring masterpiece is *Gun Crazy,* a subtler and more moving evocation of American gun cult than the somewhat overrated *Bonnie and Clyde.* The performances of John Dall and Peggy Cummins in *Gun Crazy* suggest the vitality of the American action movie despite its relative obscurity.

ALEXANDER MACKENDRICK (1912–1993)

FILMS: 1950—*Tight Little Island.* 1952—*The Man in the White Suit.* 1953—*The Story of Mandy.* 1954—High and Dry. 1957—*Sweet Smell of Success.* 1965—*A Boy Ten Feet Tall,* A High Wind in Jamaica. 1967—Don't Make Waves. 1969—Mary, Queen of Scots.

Back in 1963, I asked, more rhetorically than realistically: "How much of *Sweet Smell of Success* is attributable to Mackendrick, and how much to Clifford Odets and James Wong Howe? What has happened to Mackendrick's career, and why? We miss Mackendrick without knowing exactly what we are missing."

Mackendrick returned to our attention in 1965, and his career has since followed the curious pattern of sexual sophistication and child-cult cultivation, but it is good to have him back. *A Boy Ten Feet Tall* and *A High Wind in Jamaica* revel in the emotional gusto of tall stories, while *Don't Make Waves* slashes the ethos of the California coast almost as savagely as *Sweet Smell of Success* did for New York. In both instances, the hustle projected by Tony Curtis found its ideal directorial correlative.

ROBERT MULLIGAN (1930–   )

FILMS: 1957—*Fear Strikes Out.* 1960—*The Rat Race,* The Great Impostor. 1961—Come September. 1962—Spiral Road. 1963—To Kill a Mockingbird, Love with the Proper Stranger. 1964 —*Baby, the Rain Must Fall.* 1965—*Inside Daisy Clover.* 1967— *Up the Down Staircase.* 1968—The Stalking Moon. 1969—The Piano Sport. 1970—Good Times, Bad Times.

Back in 1963, I confidently consigned Robert Mulligan to the ranks of the minor disappointments: "François Truffaut to the contrary notwithstanding, Robert Mulligan has struck out on six pitches. To recapitulate, two of the pitches were screwballs (*Fear Strikes Out* and *The Great Impostor*) which broke over the heart of the plate like miniatures of *Citizen Kane.* Two wild blooper pitches (*Come September* and *The Spiral Road*) should never have been swung at in the first place. *To Kill a Mockingbird* was the kind of sweeping literary curve which drives hitters (and directors) back to the minors for more seasoning. *The Rat Race* broke stupidly because that old spitball pitcher Garson Kanin was out there on the mound. Whatever the extenuating circumstances, Mulligan missed every pitch, good and bad. He has yet to make a satisfactory film despite at least two good opportunities. What Mulligan lacks is not technique, but the rudimentary artistic discernment to separate the wheat from the chaff in his material. His direction is unstressed, impersonal, and uncommitted. He never gives his more promising projects the necessary point of view, and he never salvages the impossible projects with the saving grace of humor. Mulligan's direction on every occasion is ultimately too frivolous to justify serious expectations that this competent technician will ever be anything more."

Five years later Mulligan has still not made an entirely satisfactory film, but an accumulation of bits and pieces of lyricism constitutes a vindication of sorts for the director. If Mulligan's movies still suffer from a lack of coherence, they manage nonetheless to establish behavioral beauties. Particularly memorable are the performances of Steve McQueen in *Baby, the Rain Must Fall* and Ellen O'Mara in *Up the Down Staircase*.

GERD OSWALD (1916–1989)

FILMS: 1956—*A Kiss Before Dying, The Brass Legend.* 1957 —*Crime of Passion, Fury at Showdown, Valerie.* 1958—Paris Holiday, *Screaming Mimi.* 1961—*Brainwashed.* 1966—Agent for H.A.R.M.

Except for such predoomed projects as *Paris Holiday* (with Bob Hope and Fernandel no less) and *Agent for H.A.R.M.,* Gerd Oswald has shown an admirable consistency, both stylistically and thematically, for a director in his obscure position. A fluency of camera movement is controlled by sliding turns and harsh stops befitting a cinema of bitter ambiguity. Oswald's success in imposing a personal style on such otherwise routine Westerns as *The Brass Legend* and *Fury at Showdown* on shooting schedules ranging from five to seven days should serve as an object lesson to young directors who complain that they lack the time to get their films just right. There are paranoiac overtones in all his films, and the anti-Nazi symbolism is never too hard to detect, even in a frontier *Rashomon* like *Valerie*. What is important is that Gerd Oswald has been making distinguished American films that are never reviewed in the fashionable weeklies and monthlies that feed off the fashionable and well-publicized projection-room circuit. Such indifference may be the epitaph for the inspired "sleeper."

ARTHUR PENN (1922–   )

FILMS: 1958—*The Lefthanded Gun.* 1962—*The Miracle Worker.* 1965—Mickey One. 1966—The Chase. 1967—*Bonnie and Clyde.*

Bonnie and Clyde has confirmed Penn's position as the American Truffaut, and what I have written in the past about Truffaut applies in some measure to Penn as well: "As an artist, Truffaut is torn between a love for his audience and a fear of emotional facility. As the best-liked director of the *nouvelle vague,* Truffaut is always tempted to be touching. His emotional commitment to and deep involvement with his players and characters generate emotional power with an occasional loss of intellectual perspective." Benton and Newman reportedly offered their script for *Bonnie and Clyde* to Truffaut and Godard, but luckily they obtained Penn instead. However, the tensions between the script and the direction were never fully resolved, and *Bonnie and Clyde* still seems excessively Europeanized for what it is supposed to be.

Nevertheless, for a stage director whose work suffers from an oppressive literalness of effect, Penn has revealed a distinctive flair for the cinema. The intense physicality of the performances in his films serves to counterbalance a strained reading of lines. A director of force rather than grace, Penn may yet reassert the plastic role of the actor in the scheme of things. Be that as it may, *The Lefthanded Gun* remains a tribute to the director's gifts of improvisation.

LOWELL SHERMAN (1885–1934)

FILMS: 1930—Lawful Larceny, The Pay Off. 1931—Bachelor Apartment, Royal Bed, High Stakes. 1932—*The Greeks Had a Word for Them,* Ladies of the Jury, False Faces. 1933—*She Done Him Wrong, Morning Glory,* Broadway Thru a Keyhole. 1934— Born to Be Bad. 1935—Night Life of the Gods.

Lowell Sherman deserves an esoteric niche all his own for the behavioral glories of Katharine Hepburn in *Morning Glory* and Mae West in *She Done Him Wrong.* Both as an actor and as a director, Sherman was gifted with the ability to express the poignancy of male lechery when confronted with female longing. His civilized sensibility was ahead of its time, and the sophistication of his sexual humor singularly lacking in malice.

DONALD SIEGEL (1912-1991)

FILMS: 1946—*The Verdict*. 1949—The Big Steal, Night unto Night. 1952—The Duel at Silver Creek, No Time for Flowers. 1953—Count the Hours, China Venture. 1954—*Riot in Cell Block 11, Private Hell 36*. 1955—An Annapolis Story. 1956—*Invasion of the Body Snatchers*, Crime in the Streets. 1957—*Baby Face Nelson*. 1958—Spanish Affair, *The Line-Up*, The Gun Runners. 1959—Hound Dog Man. 1960—Edge of Eternity, Flaming Star. 1962—*Hell Is for Heroes*. 1964—*The Killers*. 1967—Stranger on the Run. 1968—*Madigan*, Coogan's Bluff. 1969—Two Mules for Sister Sara.

Siegel's most successful films express the doomed peculiarity of the antisocial outcast. The director's gallery of loners assimilates an otherwise anomalous group of actors—Neville Brand (*Riot in Cell Block 11*), Steve Cochran (*Private Hell 36*), Mickey Rooney (*Baby Face Nelson*), Eli Wallach (*The Line-Up*), Elvis Presley (*Flaming Star*), Steve McQueen (*Hell Is for Heroes*), Lee Marvin (*The Killers*), Henry Fonda (*Stranger on the Run*), and Richard Widmark (*Madigan*). *Invasion of the Body Snatchers*, one of the few authentic science fiction classics, derives its horror from the systematic destruction of individual feeling by unearthly forces. On another level, *Invasion of the Body Snatchers* evokes wild humor through Siegel's matter-of-fact view of paranoia. Siegel's style does not encompass the demonic distortions of Fuller's, Aldrich's, Losey's, and, to a lesser extent, Karlson's. Siegel declines to implicate the world at large in the anarchic causes of his heroes. Nor does he adjust his compositions to their psychological quirks. The moral architecture of his universe is never undermined by the editing, however frenzied. Nevertheless, the final car chase in *The Line-Up* and the final shoot-up in *Madigan* are among the most stunning displays of action montage in the history of the American cinema. On the negative side, *No Time for Flowers* clearly fails to meet the awesome challenge of Lubitsch's *Ninotchka,* and Audie Murphy's stone-faced virtuousness in *The Gun Runners* seems beyond any director's control. For the present, Siegel seems most assured with the middle-budget action film, and it is to be hoped that he does not become a casualty of Hollywood's excluded middle.

ROBERT SIODMAK (1900–1973)

FILMS: 1927—*Menschen am Sonntag.* 1932—Stürme der Leidenschaft. 1933—Le Sexe Faible. 1937—Mister Flow. 1938 —Mollenard. 1939—Pièges. 1941—West Point Widow. 1942 —Fly by Night, My Heart Belongs to Daddy, The Night Before the Divorce. 1943—Someone to Remember, Son of Dracula. 1944—*Phantom Lady,* Cobra Woman, *Christmas Holiday.* 1945— *The Suspect, Uncle Harry.* 1946—*The Spiral Staircase, The Killers, The Dark Mirror.* 1947—Time Out of Mind. 1948—*Cry of the City.* 1949—*Criss Cross,* The Great Sinner, Thelma Jordan. 1950—Deported. 1951—The Whistle at Eaton Falls. 1952—*The Crimson Pirate.* 1954—Le Grand Jeu. 1955—Die Ratten. 1959— L'Affaire Nina B. 1962—Escape from East Berlin. 1963—Magnificent Sinner. 1968—Custer of the West.

Robert Siodmak's Hollywood films were more Germanic than his German ones, and that is as it should be. Why should Germans want to look at Germanic films? Only Americans are suitably impressed by this apparent triumph of form over content. Nevertheless, Siodmak's most successful projects—*Phantom Lady, Christmas Holiday, The Suspect, Uncle Harry, The Spiral Staircase, The Killers*—represent a fortuitous conjunction of such attractive actresses as Ella Raines, Dorothy McGuire, Ava Gardner, and even an absurdly lurid Deanna Durbin, with perverse subjects and expert technicians all whipped together with a heavy Teutonic sauce and served to the customers as offbeat art. After this period, Siodmak's personality, such as it is, becomes less distinctive, and the casual observer might mistake Siodmak's *Cry of the City* as a Dassin, and Dassin's *Brute Force* as a Siodmak. Now, virtually in retrospect, Siodmak evokes the garish Universal lighting of the forties, the music of Miklos Rozsa, Burt Lancaster in his falsely promising debut in *The Killers,* and

Maria Montez at her most deliriously defective in a dual role for *Cobra Woman*. And without Maria Montez we might have been spared Jack Smith's *Flaming Creatures*. However, Siodmak is not to blame for spawning those mutants of the medium, the moviepoids. He merely manipulated Hollywood's fantasy apparatus with taste and intelligence for a studio that has always been more devious than most.

JOHN M. STAHL (1886–1950)

FILMS: 1914–1917: No reliable index. 1918—Wives of Men. 1919—Her Code of Honor, Suspicion, A Woman Under Oath. 1920 —Women Men Forget, Woman in His House. 1921—The Child Thou Gavest Me, Sowing the Wind. 1922—The Song of Life, One Clear Call, Suspicious Wives. 1923—The Wanters, The Dangerous Age. 1924—Husbands and Lovers, Why Men Leave Home. 1925— Fine Clothes. 1926—Memory Lane, The Gay Deceiver. 1927— Lovers, In Old Kentucky. 1931—Seed, *Strictly Dishonorable*. 1932 —*Back Street*. 1933—*Only Yesterday*. 1934—*Imitation of Life*. 1935—*Magnificent Obsession*. 1937—Parnell. 1938—*Letter of Introduction*. 1939—*When Tomorrow Comes*. 1943—*Holy Matrimony, Immortal Sergeant*. 1944—*The Eve of St. Mark, The Keys of the Kingdom*. 1945—*Leave Her to Heaven*. 1947—The Foxes of Harrow, The Walls of Jericho.

John M. Stahl was a neglected pre-Sirkian figure whose career suddenly became illuminated after his death through an accident in film scholarship. A French film historian classified Stahl as a director with only one masterpiece, *Back Street* (1932). A quick recheck of Stahl's career for possible auteur analysis revealed a startling quality of consistency from 1932 on. For the most part, Stahl, like Sternberg and Sirk, was involved with outrageously improbable material. Hence, the disapprobation of the plot-obsessed American critics. *Holy Matrimony*, however, was a success by any standards. *Parnell* was actually one of the more creditable films of Clark Gable, and not the hopeless disaster its reputation would indicate. Stahl's strong point was sincerity and a vivid visual style. Who can forget Gene Tierney on horseback

spreading her father's ashes in *Leave Her to Heaven* or Margaret
Sullavan having one last tryst with her forgetful lover on the
second level of a duplex or Irene Dunne having a somber farewell dinner with hopelessly married Charles Boyer or Andrea
Leeds and her *Letter of Introduction* to Adolphe Menjou? Stahl
possessed the audacity of Sirk, but not the dark humor. Where
Stahl was capable of a straight, reverent treatment of *The Keys
of the Kingdom,* Sirk transformed *The First Legion* into a devas-
tating parody of the Jesuits. In *The Eve of St. Mark,* Stahl revealed a profound comprehension of the emotional implications
of two-shots as opposed to cross-cutting. At times, Stahl's conception of contrasts was as forceful as Sirk's. In *The Immortal
Sergeant,* for example, Henry Fonda is in the desert with a mental image of Maureen O'Hara emerging dripping wet from a
swimming pool. This is the cinema of audacity to the point of
madness, and yet always preferable to the relative sanity of dis-
cretion.

FRANK TASHLIN (1913–1972)

FILMS: 1952—The First Time, Son of Paleface. 1953—
Marry Me Again. 1955—*Artists and Models.* 1956—The Lieu-
tenant Wore Skirts, *Hollywood or Bust, The Girl Can't Help It.* 1957
—*Will Success Spoil Rock Hunter.* 1958—Rock-a-bye Baby,
Geisha Boy. 1959—Say One for Me. 1960—Cinderfella. 1962—
Bachelor Flat, It's Only Money. 1963—The Man from the Diners'
Club, *Who's Minding the Store?* 1964—*The Disorderly Orderly.*
1966—The Glass Bottom Boat, The Alphabet Murders. 1967—
Caprice. 1968—The Private Navy of Sgt. O'Farrell.

Back in 1963, I wrote on Tashlin thus: "Peter Bogdanovich and
Ian Cameron have analyzed Tashlin's career with great accuracy
and perception, and Jean-Luc Godard had already hailed Tashlin as the vanguard of a genuinely modern comedy style in the
cinema. What then is the problem with Tashlin? Simply that
there is a distinction between what is analyzed and what is directly experienced. In short, Tashlin sounds better than he plays.
One can approve vulgarity in theory as a comment on vulgarity,

but in practice all vulgarity is inseparable. Tashlin can still be given considerable leeway. An unrecognized comedy director in Hollywood at the present time can hardly write his own ticket, and studio interference is particularly damaging to farce conceptions. Casts are a special problem, also, but the suspicion persists that if Tashlin had not had Jerry Lewis and Jayne Mansfield, he would have invented their equivalents. To ridicule Jayne Mansfield's enormous bust in *Will Success Spoil Rock Hunter* may be construed as satire, indulgent or otherwise, but to ridicule Betsy Drake's small bust in the same film is simply unabashed vulgarity. Although Tashlin is impressively inventive, particularly with gadgets and animals, he has never been sympathetic enough to any of his characters to forego a laugh at their expense. The one possible exception is the sweet, anonymous British girl in *Bachelor Flat,* Tashlin's best film. Ultimately, frenetic farce, however inventive, is self-defeating without a theory of character. Up to now, Tashlin has dealt almost exclusively with caricatures instead of characters, and so unless we are entering an age of robot comedy, the problem of Tashlin will remain a problem of taste."

In five years, Tashlin has become sympathetically obsolete without ever becoming fashionable. What little Tashlin cult interest there was has now shifted almost entirely to Jerry Lewis, actor-director extraordinary. Tashlin himself has been reduced to relatively commissioned projects, and has proved himself time and again stylistically superior to material so odious as to seem an affront to Doris Day in her last filtered days on the screen. Tashlin's little victories, however reassuring to the *Politique,* are ultimately Pyrrhic.

JACQUES TOURNEUR (1904–1977)

FILMS: 1931—Tout Ça Ne Vaut Pas L'Amour. 1933—Toto, Pour Etre Aimé. 1934—Les Filles de la Concierge. 1939—They All Come Out, Nick Carter—Master Detective. 1940—Phantom Riders. 1941—Doctors Don't Tell. 1942—*Cat People.* 1943—*I Walked with a Zombie,* The Leopard Man. 1944—Days of Glory,

Experiment Perilous. 1946—*Canyon Passage.* 1947—Out of the Past. 1948—Berlin Express. 1949—Easy Living. 1950—Stars in My Crown, The Flame and the Arrow. 1951—Circle of Danger, Anne of the Indies. 1952—Way of a Gaucho. 1953—Appointment in Honduras. 1955—Stranger on Horseback, *Wichita.* 1956— *Great Day in the Morning,* Nightfall. 1958—*Curse of the Demon,* The Fearmakers. 1959—Timbuktu. 1960—The Giant of Marathon. 1963—The Comedy of Terrors. 1965—War Gods of the Deep.

Jacques Tourneur, son of the late Maurice Tourneur, brings a certain French gentility to the American cinema. At its best, this gentility lifts a Western like *Great Day in the Morning* to a new, unaccustomed level of subdued, pastel-colored sensibility. At its worst, this same gentility drains all the vitality out of a trivial, medieval exercise like *The Flame and the Arrow.* Tourneur's first films for Val Lewton—*The Cat People* and *I Walked with a Zombie*—possessed a subtler dramatic force than those of Wise and Robson. *Out of the Past* is still Tourneur's masterpiece, a civilized treatment of an annihilating melodrama. *Anne of the Indies* and *Way of a Gaucho,* two misguided Fox projects conceived in the last hectic days before Cinemascope, come off much better than anyone had any right to expect despite their intransigent exoticism. *Stranger on Horseback* and *Wichita* lack both excitement and the compensating sensibility of *Great Day in the Morning.* On the commercial downgrade, *Curse of the Demon, The Fearmakers, Timbuktu,* and *The Giant of Marathon* attest to Tourneur's unyielding pictorialism if little else. All in all, Tourneur's career represents a triumph of taste over force.

EDGAR G. ULMER (1904–1972)

FILMS: 1929—*Menschen am Sonntag* (with Robert Siodmak). 1933—Damaged Lives. 1934—*The Black Cat.* 1937—Green Fields (with Jacob Ben-Ami). 1938—The Singing Blacksmith. 1939 —Moon over Harlem. 1942—Tomorrow We Live. 1943—My Son, the Hero; Girls in Chains, Isle of Forgotten Sins, Jive Junction. 1944—*Bluebeard.* 1945—Strange Illusion, The Strange Woman. 1946—*Detour,* Club Havana, The Wife of Monte Cristo, Her Sister's Secret. 1947—Carnegie Hall. 1948—*Ruthless.* 1949—The Pirates of Capri. 1951—The Man From Planet X, St. Benny the Dip. 1952—Babes in Bagdad. 1955—*Murder Is My Beat, The Naked Dawn.* 1957—Daughter of Dr. Jekyll. 1960—Hannibal, The Amazing Transparent Man, Beyond the Time Barrier. 1961—*L'Atlantide.* 1965—The Cavern.

The French call him *un cinéaste maudit,* and directors certainly don't come any more *maudit.* But yes, Virginia, there is an Edgar G. Ulmer, and he is no longer one of the private jokes shared by auteur critics, but one of the minor glories of the cinema. Here is a career, more subterranean than most, which be signature of a genuine artist. Strictly speaking, most of Ulmer's films are of interest only to unthinking audiences or specialists in mise-en-scène. Yet, anyone who loves the cinema must be moved by *Daughter of Dr. Jekyll,* a film with a scenario so atrocious that it takes forty minutes to establish that the daugher of Dr. Jekyll is indeed the daughter of Dr. Jekyll. Ulmer's camera never falters even when his characters disintegrate. As the executor of the Murnau estate, he is faithful to his trust, and when his material is less impossible, his reflexes are still sharp for the meaningful challenges of *The Black Cat, Bluebeard, Ruthless, Murder Is My Beat, Detour,* and *The Naked Dawn.* That a personal style could emerge from the lowest depths of Poverty Row is a tribute to a director without alibis.

ROLAND WEST (1887–1952)

FILMS: 1918—De Luxe Annie. 1921—The Silver Lining, Nobody. 1923—The Unknown Purple. 1925—The Monster. 1926—*The Bat.* 1927—The Dove. 1929—*Alibi.* 1931—Bat Whispers, *Corsair.*

Roland West is one of the forgotten figures of the early thirties. The misty expressionism and delicate feelings of *Corsair* entitle this director to a place in film history. The cigar-chomping stoicism of Ned Sparks reflects West's sensitivity to the softer side of the cynical bootlegging genre. *Alibi* remains to be seen and saved from the limbo of legend.

IV.
FRINGE
BENEFITS

The following directors occupied such a marginal role in the American cinema that it would be unfair to their overall reputations to analyze them in this limited context in any detail, but a few comments may be in order.

MICHELANGELO ANTONIONI (1912–   )

FILMS: Documentaries: 1943–1947—Gente del Po. 1948—
N.U. 1948–1949—L'Amorosa Menzogna, Superstizione. 1949—
Sette Canne un Vestito. 1950—La Funivia del Faloria, La Villa dei
Mostri. 1955—Uomini in Più. Features: 1950—*Cronaca di un
Amore*. 1952—I Vinti. 1952–1953—La Signora Senza Camelie.
1953—Tentato Suicidio (episode in Love in the City). 1955—*Le
Amiche*. 1957—*Il Grido*. 1959–1960—*L'Avventura*. 1960—*La
Notte*. 1961—*L'Eclisse*. 1964—*The Red Desert*. 1966—*Blow-
Up*. 1969—Zabriskie Point.

Antonioni came, saw, and conquered the English-language
market on his very first try. When *Blow-Up* was screened in
Hollywood, the natives chortled with derision. Who was this
Mike Antonioni who thought he could walk in without a shred of
scripting and take over the cultural scene? What the Hollywood
factory workers failed to perceive was the underlying literary
framework of Antonioni's visual doodling. Antonioni had
become adept at exploiting the sentimental pessimism and sen-
sual prying of his age, and the American market was ripe for his
brilliant coup. Ripe to the tune of eight million dollars. In some
ways, Antonioni was more honest in *Blow-Up* than in *La Notte,
Eclipse,* and *The Red Desert,* films in which he sought to graft
Antoniennui onto the world at large. In *Blow-Up,* Antonioni
acknowledged for the first time his own divided sensibility, half
mod and half Marxist. Unlike Fellini, however, Antonioni converted his confession into a genuine movie that objectifies his ob-
sessions without whining or self-pity. As befits the classical tradition of movie-making, *Blow-Up* can be enjoyed by moviegoers
who never heard of Antonioni.

LUIS BUÑUEL (1900–1983)

FILMS: 1928—The Fall of the House of Usher, *Un Chien
Andalou*. 1930—*L'Age d'Or*. 1932—*Land Without Bread*. 1947

—Gran Casino. 1949—El Gran Calavera. 1950—*Los Olivados* (The Young and the Damned), Susana. 1951—Daughter of Deceit, A Woman Without Love, Ascent to Heaven. 1952—El Bruto, El Robinson Crusoe. 1953—Wuthering Heights, *Illusion Travels by Streetcar*. 1954—The River and Death. 1955—*The Criminal Life of Archibaldo Cruz*. 1956—La Mort en Ce Jardin. 1958—*Nazarin*. 1959—La fievre monte a El Pao. 1960—The Young One. 1961—*Viridiana*. 1962—*The Exterminating Angel*. 1965—Diary of a Chambermaid, *Simon of the Desert*. 1967—*Belle de Jour*. 1969—La Voie Lactée.

His English-language films—*Robinson Crusoe* and *The Young One*—indicate that he could have been one of Us if he had not hated everything Hollywood stands for. Buñuel had the talent to justify his anger and integrity, but too many people with only anger and integrity think that a brave anti-Hollywood posture will compensate for a lack of talent. It won't. Still, there may come a day when censorship gives up the ghost forever, and Hollywood is thrown to the few audacious spirits in the world, and Buñuel should head the list. Even in 1967, Buñuel's greatest and most beautiful film, the purest expression of surrealism in the history of the cinema, *Belle de Jour*, would probably face less censorship in America than in France.

CLAUDE CHABROL (1930–   )

FILMS: 1958—*Le Beau Serge, Les Cousins*. 1959—*Leda*. 1960—*Les Bonnes Femmes, Les Godelureaux*. 1961—*The Third Lover*, Seven Capital Sins (L'Avarice). 1962—*Ophelia, Landru*. 1964—Le Tigre Aime la Chair Fraiche. 1965—Marie-Chantal Contre le Docteur Kah, Le Tigre Se Parfume à la Dynamite, *Paris vu par . . . Chabrol*. 1966—La Ligne de Demarcation. 1968—The Champagne Murders, The Route to Corinth, *Les Biches*. 1969—La Femme Infidèle.

Claude Chabrol failed to find universality in Universal's *The Champagne Murders*, an exercise in international casting and bilingual shooting. Chabrol belongs in the French cinema as its foremost Hitchcockian, but with a decided Gallic accent.

Chabrol, more than Truffaut and Godard, has followed the Hollywood credo of keeping your hand in even when your heart isn't in it, thus perfecting your craft until the opportunity arrives for practicing your art once more. Ironically, Chabrol had become one of the forgotten figures of the *nouvelle vague* even though he turned out eight very personal and professional feature films while most of his colleagues were still floundering with fragments of films. Films is perhaps less the operative word for Chabrol than movies. Only time will tell if Chabrol's movies will outlive Godard's anticinema.

RENÉ CLAIR (1898–1981)

FILMS: 1923—Paris Qui Dort. 1924—*Entr'Acte.* La Fantôme du Moulin Rouge. 1925—Le Voyage Imaginaire. 1926 —La Proie du Vent. 1927—*The Italian Straw Hat.* 1928—Les Deux Timides, La Tour (Documentary). 1930—*Sous les Toits de Paris* (Under the Roofs of Paris). 1931—*Le Million.* 1932—*À Nous la Liberté.* 1933—Quatorze Juillet. 1935—Le Dernier Milliardaire. 1936—*The Ghost Goes West.* 1938—Break the News. 1939—Air Pur (incomplete). 1941—The Flame of New Orleans. 1942—I Married a Witch, Forever and a Day (one episode, replacing Alfred Hitchcock). 1944—It Happened Tomorrow. 1945— *And Then There Were None.* 1947—*Le Silence Est d'Or.* 1950— La Beauté du Diable (Beauty and the Devil). 1952—Les Belles de Nuit (Beauties of the Night). 1956—*Les Grandes Manoeuvres.* 1957—Porte de Lilas (Gates of Paris). 1960—La Française et l'Amour (Love and the Frenchwoman), episode "Le Mariage." 1961 —Tout l'Or du Monde. 1962—Les Quatre Vérité, episode, "Les Deux Pigeons." 1965—Les Fêtes Galantes.

Although Clair made several English-language and Hollywood films, his American period is generally blamed for his decline. The trouble with Clair's American career is that he was typed for fantasy and other fluff, and could never escape his niche. His most successful American film—*And Then There Were None* —confirmed that Clair needed a little realistic vinegar in his material in order to function. Even Agatha Christie's formula murders were preferable to the processions of ghosts and futurities in *I Married a Witch, The Ghost Goes West, It Happened Tomorrow*. Only Dietrich's intransigent corporeality redeemed *The Flame of New Orleans* from the spooky fate of Clair's other films. However, it must be reported honestly that Clair's decline began before he left France for Hollywood's lucre and that Clair never regained his footing back in Paris. *À Nous la Liberté, Le Million, Sous les Toits de Paris, The Italian Straw Hat* retain a certain classic value, but Clair, once too good to be called even the French Lubitsch, now seems more like the French Mamoulian.

RENÉ CLÉMENT (1913–   )

FILMS: 1946—*Le Bataille du Rail,* Le Pére Tranquille. 1947 —*Les Maudits (The Damned).* 1949—*The Walls of Malapaga.* 1950—Le Château de Verre. 1952—*Forbidden Games.* 1954— *Monsieur Ripois (Lovers, Happy Lovers).* 1956—*Gervaise.* 1958 —*This Angry Age.* 1959—*Purple Noon.* 1961—*Quelle Joie de Vivre.* 1963—The Day and the Hour. 1964—*Joy House.* 1966— Is Paris Burning?

The irony of René Clément was that his two best films— *Lovers, Happy Lovers* and *This Angry Age*—were both English-language productions and that Clément, more than such Americanophiles as Melville and Sautet, seemed to possess the necessary pragmatic temperament to become an American director. Unfortunately, since Clément took the plunge, his career has done likewise. The intermittent charm of a *Joy House* cannot compensate for the disastrous dullness of an *Is Paris Burning?*

SERGEI EISENSTEIN (1898–1948)

FILMS: 1924—Strike. 1925—Potemkin. 1927—October (Ten Days That Shook the World). 1929—The General Line. 1931— Que viva Mexico (not completed). 1938—Alexander Nevsky. 1941–1946—Ivan the Terrible, Parts I and II.

The time has come to stop blaming Eisenstein for every excess or inadequacy of montage. As it is, Eisenstein's *Film Form* and *Film Sense* have been almost as misunderstood as Stanislavsky's *An Actor Prepares,* with its legacy of mumbling mummers out of The Method. Furthermore, Eisenstein's montage classics have probably done more harm to American film criticism and film history than any other factor. The totalitarians of the Left embraced Eisenstein and montage as the first step toward brainwashing humanity, but the cinema quickly lent its manipulative social powers to Television. The cinema returned to formal excellence, abandoning the salvation of mankind as a criterion of criticism. Now there is a tendency to dismiss Eisenstein as irrelevant to modern aesthetics, and nothing could be further from the truth.

G. W. PABST (1885–1967)

FILMS: 1923—Der Schatz (The Treasure). 1924—Gräfin Donelli (Countess Donelli). 1925—*Die Freudlose Gasse (The Joyless Street).* 1926—*Geheimnisse Einer Seele (Secrets of a Soul),* Man Spielt Nicht mit der Liebe (Never Play Around with Love). 1927—*Die Liebe der Jeanne Ney (The Love of Jeanne Ney).* 1928 —Begierde (Desire). 1929—*Die Büchse der Pandora (Pandora's Box), Das Tagebuch Einer Verloren (The Diary of a Lost Girl),* Die Weisse Hölle vom Pitz Palu (The White Hell of Pitz Palu) (with Dr. Arnold Fanck). 1930—*Westfront 1918,* Skandal um Eva (Scandal About Eva). 1931—*Die Dreigroschenoper (The Three Penny Opera),* L'Opéra a Quat' Sous (French version of Die Dreigroschenoper), *Kamaradschaft.* 1932—La Tragédie de la Mine (French version of Kamaradschaft), L'Atlantide. 1933—Don Quichotte, Don Quixote (English version), De Haut en Bas, La Nuit. 1934—A Modern Hero. 1936—Mademoiselle Docteur. 1938—Le Drame de Shanghai, L'Esclave Blanche. 1939—Jeunes Filles en Détresse. 1940—Feuertaufe (Baptism of Fire). 1941—Komödianten. 1943 —Paracelsus. 1945—Der Fall Molander (The Molander Affair). 1948—*Der Prozess (The Trial).* 1949—Gehemnisvolle Tiefe. 1952—La Voce del Silenzio. 1953—Cose da Pazzi. 1954—Das

Bekenntnis der Ina Kahr (The Confession of Ina Kahr). 1955—*Der Letzte Akt* (*The Last Ten Days*), Es Geschah am 20. Juli '55 (It Happened on the 20th of July). 1956—Rosen Für Bettina; Durch die Wälder, Durch die Auen.

Pabst is cited here not for his American film *A Modern Hero,* but rather for the retroactive glory of Louise Brooks in *Diary of a Lost Girl* and *Lulu.* The preeminence of Miss Brooks as the beauty of the twenties indicates the classic nature of the cinema, and its built-in machinery for an appeal to the verdict of history.

ROMAN POLANSKI (1933–   )

FILMS: Shorts: 1957–1962—Two Men and a Wardrobe, When Angels Fall, The Fat and the Lean, Mammals. 1963—*Knife in the Water.* 1964—Les Plus Belles Escroqueries (Episode in Sketch Film). 1965—*Repulsion.* 1966—Cul-de-Sac. 1967—*The Fearless Vampire Killers.* 1968—*Rosemary's Baby.*

Roman Polanski has introduced a peculiarly European sensibility to the English-language cinema. His early short films were strongly influenced by the empty-world aesthetics of Beckett, Ionesco, and Pinter mixed with Polish cynicism, black humor, and Gothic horror. At his best, Polanski is genuinely unpredictable; at his worst, grievously pretentious. *Repulsion* contains too much undigested clinical material for comfort, but Polanski's handling of Catherine Deneuve anticipates in its perceptiveness Buñuel's definitive diagnosis of the devilish angel in *Belle de Jour. Cul-de-Sac* ultimately chokes on its incongruities as a kind of *Waiting for Godot* stranded in a Sir Walter Scott landscape. *The Fearless Vampire Killers* fails as a loving parody of a genre, but not before it has scored its well-calculated coups with a Jewish vampire unintimidated by the traditional malediction of the Cross, and a homosexual vampire rendering into reality one of the most frighteningly hilarious implications of the genre. Polanski's talent is as undeniable as his intentions are dubious.

ROBERTO ROSSELLINI (1906–1977)

FILMS: 1936—Dafné (short subject). 1937–1938—Prélude à l'Après-midi d'un Faune (short subject). 1939—Fantasia Sottomarina, Il Tacchino Prepotente, La Vispa Teresa (short subjects). 1940–1941—Il Ruscello Blanca (short subject). 1941—La Nave Bianca. 1942—Un Pilota Ritorna. 1943—Desiderio. 1944–1945 —*Open City*. 1946—*Paisan*. 1947–1948—*L'Amore*. 1948— La Macchina Ammazzacattivi. 1949—*The Flowers of St. Francis*. 1949–1950—Stromboli. 1951–1952—Envy (fifth sketch in The Seven Deadly Sins). 1952—*Europa 51* (The Greatest Love—released in America in 1954), Dov'e la Libertà. 1953—Ingrid Bergman sketch in We Are the Women, *Viaggio in Italia* (Strangers—released in America in 1955). 1954—Joan at the Stake, Fear. 1957— *India*. 1959—*General Della Rovere*. 1960—Era Notte a Roma, *Viva Italia!* 1961—*Vanina Vanini*. 1962—Anima Nera. 1963— First episode in RoGoPaG. 1965—Age of Iron (TV documentary). 1966—*La Prise de Pouvoir par Louis XIV* (TV film released in theatres abroad).

Rossellini's sublime films with Ingrid Bergman were years ahead of their time, and are not fully appreciated even today in America. For the record, *Stromboli, The Greatest Love, Strangers, Fear,* and *Joan at the Stake* constitute one of the most impressively biographical bodies of work in the history of the cinema. It might be noted also that Rossellennui preceded Antoniennui by several years.

FRANÇOIS TRUFFAUT (1932–1984)

FILMS: Short Subjects: 1954—Une Visite (16 mm.). 1957— Les Mistons. 1958—Une Histoire d'Eau (with Jean-Luc Godard). 1962—Antoine et Colette (Love at Twenty). Feature Films: 1959— *The Four Hundred Blows*. 1960—*Shoot the Piano Player*. 1961—

Jules and Jim. 1964—The Soft Skin. 1966—*Fahrenheit 451.* 1968 —The Bride Wore Black, Stolen Kisses, The Siren of Mississippi.

Truffaut made the jump into the English-language cinema despite his lacking command of the English language. *Fahrenheit 451* is consequently as verbally clumsy as it is visually graceful and emotionally expressive. Truffaut ran for cover back to the womb of the French language, but not before he had demonstrated that there was something irreducibly universal in the cinema of Babel. Truffaut's sympathetically perceptive book on Hitchcock was further proof of this universality up to a point beyond which lurked the misunderstandings of translation and the lost nuances within a culture.

LUCHINO VISCONTI (1906–1976)

FILMS: 1942—*Ossessione.* 1948—*La Terra Trema.* 1951— *Bellissima.* 1953—We Are the Women (Anna Magnani episode). 1954—*Senso.* 1957—*White Nights.* 1960—*Rocco and His Brothers.* 1962—*Boccaccio 70* (Romy Schneider episode). 1963—The Leopard. 1965—*Sandra.* 1967—The Stranger.

Luchino Visconti tried to break into the English-language market behind the blocking of Burt Lancaster, he of the broad shoulders and sullen expression. Lampedusa's *The Leopard* deserved much better than Lancaster, but the casting was typical of Visconti's bad luck in these matters. Back in the mid-fifties, Visconti had persuaded Ingrid Bergman and Marlon Brando to appear together in *Senso.* Visconti's casting coup of the decade was blithely vetoed by an Italian producer who preferred and substituted Alida Valli and Farley Granger! Valli was extraordinarily effective and Granger surprisingly so, but the emotional electricity was never turned on. Visconti has never received his due in America largely because his films were always ridiculously delayed in transit. American audiences have never seen *Ossessione* because of difficulties with the James M. Cain estate over the rights to *The Postman Always Rings Twice*. How differently would American highbrows have reacted to neorealism if its first example had been the sexual melodrama of *Ossessione* rather than the dramatic newsreel of Rossellini's *Open City*, and how much jittery photography would we have been spared from naïve Hollywood imitators of Rossellini's wobbly tripod? No one will ever know.

V.
LESS
THAN
MEETS
THE
EYE

These are the directors with reputations in excess of inspirations. In retrospect, it always seems that the personal signatures to their films were written with invisible ink.

JOHN HUSTON (1906–1987)

FILMS: 1941—*The Maltese Falcon.* 1942—In This Our Life, *Across the Pacific,* Report from the Aleutians (documentary). 1944 —*The Battle of San Pietro* (documentary). 1945—Let There Be Light (documentary). 1948—*The Treasure of the Sierra Madre, Key Largo.* 1949—*We Were Strangers.* 1950—*The Asphalt Jungle.* 1951—*The Red Badge of Courage.* 1952—*The African Queen.* 1953—Moulin Rouge. 1954—*Beat the Devil.* 1956—Moby Dick. 1957—Heaven Knows, Mr. Allison. 1958—The Barbarian and the Geisha, The Roots of Heaven. 1960—The Unforgiven. 1961—The Misfits. 1962—Freud. 1963—The List of Adrian Messenger. 1964—The Night of the Iguana. 1966—The Bible. 1967—Casino Royale, *Reflections in a Golden Eye.* 1969—Sinful Davey, A Walk with Love and Death.

The late James Agee canonized Huston prematurely in a *Life*-magazine auteur piece circa *Treasure of the Sierra Madre.* Agee was as wrong about Huston as Bazin was about Wyler, but Huston is still coasting on his reputation as a wronged individualist with an alibi for every bad movie. If it isn't Jack Warner, it's L. B. Mayer, and if it isn't L. B. Mayer, it's David O. Selznick, and if it isn't David O. Selznick, and if it isn't any of these, it's the whole rotten system of making movies. But who except Huston himself is to blame for the middle-brow banality of *Freud,* a personal project with built-in compromises for the "mass" audience. Huston has confused indifference with integrity for such a long time that he is no longer even the competent craftsman of *The Asphalt Jungle, The Maltese Falcon,* and *The African Queen,* films that owe more to casting coups than to directorial acumen. *Falcon,* particularly, is an uncanny match-up of Dashiell Hammett's literary characters with their visual doubles: Mary Astor, Humphrey Bogart, Sidney Greenstreet, Peter Lorre, and Elisha Cooke, Jr. Only Stendahl's Julien Sorel in search of Gérard Philipe can match *Falcon's* Pirandellian equation. Even in his palmier days, Huston displayed his material without projecting his personality. His technique has always been evasive, his camera often pitched at a standoffish angle away from the heart of the action. *Treasure of the Sierra Madre* and *Beat the Devil,* his two most overrated films, end with howling laughter on the sound track, an echo perhaps of the director laughing at his own feeble jokes.

Huston's dismaying decline notwithstanding, his theme has been remarkably consistent from *The Maltese Falcon* to *Reflections in a Golden Eye.* His protagonists almost invariably fail at what they set out to do, generally through no fault or flaw of their own. Unfortunately, Huston is less a pessimist than a defeatist, and his characters manage to be unlucky without the world being particularly out of joint. Huston's best film, *The Asphalt Jungle,* deals fittingly enough with collective defeat, and even his cast represents an interesting gallery of talented players who did not reach the heights they deserved: Sterling Hayden, the sensitive giant who never made the Wayne-Mitchum-Heston bracket; James Whitmore, who never became the second Spencer Tracy; Jean Hagen, who never obtained the dramatic-pathetic roles her talents demanded; Sam Jaffe, who never won an Oscar; Louis Calhern, who never mounted an adequate Lear although he was tall enough for tragedy; and Marc Lawrence, who never found his niche as the all-purpose villain. Only Marilyn Monroe was sprinkled with stardust after *Asphalt,* and Huston nearly finished her with the casual cruelty of *The Misfits.* The turning point in Huston's career was probably *Moby Dick.* In retrospect, he should have acted Ahab himself and let Orson Welles direct. This was his one gamble with greatness, and he lost, and like the cagey poker player he is, he has been playing it cool and corrupt ever since. *The List of Adrian Messenger,* a case in point, is so corrupt that even a fox hunt is in drag, not to mention *Beat the Devil,* which was consciously (and Capotishly) campy long before camp was even a gleam in Susan Sontag's eye.

As a stylist, Huston has always overloaded the physical with the moral. He never cared for that sissy stuff in drawing rooms where people try to communicate with each other through dialogue. Indeed, Huston's intimate scenes are often staged as if he were playing croquet with a sledgehammer. His antics with the two ridiculously graceful beach boys in *Night of the Iguana* are as false as the breast-thrusting jitterbug routine of the teenager in *The Asphalt Jungle* and all the nonsense with the wild horses in *The Misfits*. Movies are still primarily a dramatic medium, and if you can't establish characters indoors, you're not going to illuminate them with any clarity outdoors. Unfortunately, Huston, unlike Hawks, does not believe sufficiently in the action ethos to enjoy action for its own sake. A director like Cukor may choose to make himself comfortable inside, a director like Hawks outside, a director like Huston nowhere. Ultimately, Huston mistrusts his own dramatic material to the point that he makes excessively meaningful flourishes with the smokily suffused color in *Moulin Rouge* and the severely subdued color in *Reflections in a Golden Eye*. It must have looked good on the drawing board with *Moulin Rouge* color equaling artistic expression and *Reflections in a Golden Eye* colorlessness equaling sexual repression. Very little of the intended effect came through on the screen. Mere technique can never transcend conviction.

ELIA KAZAN (1909–   )

FILMS: 1945—*A Tree Grows in Brooklyn*. 1947—*Boomerang*, The Sea of Grass, Gentleman's Agreement. 1949—*Pinky*. 1950 —*Panic in the Streets*. 1951—*A Streetcar Named Desire*. 1952— *Viva Zapata!* 1953—Man on a Tightrope. 1954—*On the Waterfront*. 1955—*East of Eden*. 1956—Baby Doll. 1957—*A Face in the Crowd*. 1960—*Wild River*. 1961—*Splendor in the Grass*. 1963 —*America America*. 1969—The Arrangement.

Elia Kazan's position seemed dubious in 1963 when I wrote: "The Method of *A Streetcar Named Desire* has finally degenerated into the madness of *Splendor in the Grass*. Kazan's violence has always been more excessive than expressive, more mannered than meaningful. There is an edge of hysteria even to his pauses and silences, and the thin line between passion and neurosis has been crossed time and again. Yet, his brilliance with actors is incontestable. The revolutionary performances of Marlon Brando and the late James Dean are irrevocable, and *East of Eden,* though technically dated, is still a creditable achievement. Kazan's conscious efforts to adjust his personality to the classical forms of Ford (*Pinky, Wild River*) and Eisenstein (*Viva Zapata!*) were commendable if not entirely successful. Unfortunately, his career as a whole reflects an unending struggle between a stable camera and a jittery one. Significantly, his most nervous films—*Man on a Tightrope, Baby Doll,* and *Splendor in the Grass*—are ultimately his weakest. Kazan's gifts can never be written off entirely, but the evidence of decline is overwhelming."

Since 1963, Kazan has made one autobiographical film (*America America*) and written an autobiographical best-selling novel (*The Arrangement*) which he intends to film with Brando in the leading role. With an instinct more dramatic than epic, Kazan is nonetheless drifting into the realm of the epic. His art is more anguished and personal than ever before, less successful but more sympathetic. For the most part, however, it seems that Kazan intends to ignore his limitations rather than transcend them.

DAVID LEAN (1908–1991)

FILMS: 1942—*In Which We Serve* (with Noël Coward). 1945 —*Blithe Spirit.* 1946—*Brief Encounter.* 1947—*This Happy Breed, Great Expectations.* 1949—*One Woman's Story.* 1950— Madeleine. 1951—*Oliver Twist.* 1952—*Breaking Through the Sound Barrier.* 1954—*Hobson's Choice.* 1955—*Summertime.* 1957—Bridge on the River Kwai. 1962—Lawrence of Arabia. 1965—Dr. Zhivago.

David Lean was thanking the Motion Picture Academy for his second Oscar back in 1963 while I was writing: "Lean's career has reached the point where the modest virtues of *Brief Encounter* and *Great Expectations* have been inflated with the hot air of *Lawrence of Arabia* and *The Bridge on the River Kwai,* films as pointlessly obscure in their way as that most muddled of all murder mysteries, *Madeleine.* By the time Lean gets around to propounding a question, no one really cares about the answer. The sheer logistics of *Lawrence* and *Kwai* cannot support the luxury of a directorial point of view. Lean is even more of an enigma than Lawrence, but the cinema as an expressive art form is not receptive to enigmas. Now that Lean has been enshrined in the various Academies, whatever artistic sensibility he once possessed is safely embalmed in the tomb of the impersonal cinema. Looking back past the shifting sands of *Lawrence* and the tangled underbrush of *Kwai,* one can fondly remember the tasteful performances of Celia Johnson and Trevor Howard (*Brief Encounter*), Ralph Richardson and Nigel Patrick (*Breaking the Sound Barrier*), John Mills and Brenda de Banzie (*Hobson's Choice*), and Katharine Hepburn (*Summertime*), but these deviations from obfuscation are no longer the measure of a director whose next logical project is a spectacle on the riddle of the Sphinx."

Since 1963, David Lean has labored on but one additional superproduction, *Dr. Zhivago,* a work with more commercial than critical success, a work also of the most impeccable impersonality, and not even an Oscar to show for such self-abnegation. Not that Lean is particularly faithful to Pasternak's extravagant emotions. Lean and his scenarist Robert Bolt are too coldly British for rousing Russian rhetoric. Ultimately, Dr. Zhivago suffers most from too little literary fat and too much visual Lean.

ROUBEN MAMOULIAN (1898–1987)

FILMS: 1929—*Applause.* 1931—*City Streets.* 1932—*Dr. Jekyll and Mr. Hyde, Love Me Tonight.* 1933—*Queen Christina,* Song of Songs. 1934—We Live Again. 1935—Becky Sharp. 1936 —*The Gay Desperado.* 1937—High, Wide and Handsome. 1939 —Golden Boy. 1940—The Mark of Zorro. 1941—Blood and Sand. 1942—Rings on Her Fingers. 1948—Summer Holiday. 1957—Silk Stockings.

Mamoulian's tragedy is that of the innovator who runs out of innovations. *Applause* and *City Streets* have been amply honored in the textbooks for helping to break the sound barrier, and *Becky Sharp* is usually cited in any tract on the color film. The obviousness of Mamoulian's technique, like King's in *Tol'able David,* is ideal for anthologies. Unfortunately, while Mamoulian was performing his technical acrobatics, Lubitsch, Vidor, Sternberg, Hawks, and Ford swept into the sound era without breaking their stride. Except for *Applause,* Mamoulian's films date badly. *Love Me Tonight* is imitation Lubitsch with too many camera angles. *High, Wide and Handsome* misapplies Busby Berkeley's crane choreography to the great outdoors, and *The Gay Desperado,* not without its charms, resembles an impersonal operetta. The innovator has become an imitator, and the rest is mediocrity.

JOSEPH L. MANKIEWICZ (1909–1993)

FILMS: 1946—Dragonwyck, Somewhere in the Night. 1947 —The Late George Apley, *The Ghost and Mrs. Muir.* 1948— Escape. 1949—*Letter to Three Wives, House of Strangers.* 1950— *No Way Out, All About Eve.* 1951—*People Will Talk.* 1952— *Five Fingers.* 1953—*Julius Caesar.* 1954—*Barefoot Contessa.* 1955—*Guys and Dolls.* 1958—*The Quiet American.* 1959— *Suddenly Last Summer.* 1963—Cleopatra. 1967—The Honey Pot. 1969—Couples, The Bawdy Bard.

The cinema of Joseph L. Mankiewicz is a cinema of intelligence without inspiration. His best films—*All About Eve* and *The Barefoot Contessa*—bear the signature of a genuine auteur. Turn off the sound track, and *The Barefoot Contessa* is closer to Lewin's *Pandora and the Flying Dutchman* than to Ophuls' *Lola Montès.* Mankiewicz' sensibility is decidedly more refined than Lewin's, but his technique is almost as pedestrian. With *Five Fingers,* Mankiewicz set out to prove that he could execute a technical exercise as well as anyone, and he failed honorably. *Cleopatra* and *The Honey Pot* should not be considered the last word on this intelligent American cinéaste because once his limitations are conceded, there is nothing wrong in enjoying his gibes at the Philistines. Mankiewicz' cranky liberalism sometimes gets the better of him, particularly when he wrenches scenes out of their context to inveigh against the evils of farm subsidies (*People Will Talk*) and oil-depletion allowances (*The Barefoot Contessa*). He despises the lechery of fat, greasy plutocrats, the disloyalty of opportunists, and the hypocrisy of moralists, but these commendable attitudes reflect a naïve morality unable to cope with the political hallucinations of Graham Greene (*The Quiet American*) and the sexual traumas of Tennessee Williams (*Suddenly Last Summer*). Although his wit scratches more than it bites, it is undeniable enough to place his area of greatest aptitude somewhere between the brittle worlds imitative of Oscar Wilde (*All About Eve*) and F. Scott Fitzgerald (*The Barefoot Contessa*). His vibrant women —Susan Hayward (*House of Strangers*), Bette Davis, and Anne Baxter (*Eve*), Danielle Darrieux (*Five Fingers*) and Ava Gardner (*Contessa*) —shine with special brilliance from midnight to the three o'clock in the morning of the soul.

LEWIS MILESTONE   (1895–1980)

FILMS: 1925—Seven Sinners. 1926—The Caveman, The New Klondike. 1927—*Two Arabian Knights*. 1928—The Garden of Eden, *The Racket*. 1929—The Betrayal, New York Nights. 1930 —*All Quiet on the Western Front*. 1931—*The Front Page*. 1932 —*Rain*. 1933—*Hallelujah, I'm a Bum*. 1934—The Captain Hates the Sea. 1935—Paris in Spring. 1936—Anything Goes. *The General Died at Dawn*. 1940—The Night of Nights, *Of Mice and Men*, Lucky Partners. 1941—My Life with Caroline. 1943—Edge of Darkness, The North Star. 1944—The Purple Heart. 1946—*A Walk in the Sun, The Strange Love of Martha Ivers*. 1948—*Arch of Triumph*, No Minor Vices. 1949—The Red Pony. 1950—Halls of Montezuma. 1952—Kangaroo, Les Miserables. 1953—Melba. 1955—They Who Dare. 1959—Pork Chop Hill. 1960—Ocean's Eleven. 1962—Mutiny on the Bounty.

A formalist of the Left, Milestone was hailed as the American Eisenstein after *All Quiet on the Western Front* and *The Front Page*. It is of course possible, though not highly probable, that Eisenstein himself might have ended up directing the Clan in *Ocean's Eleven* if he had remained in Hollywood. Just think of all the opportunities for dialectical montage in Las Vegas! Where else is the naked structure of capitalism so garishly visual? Unfortunately, Milestone's fluid camera style has always been dissociated from any personal viewpoint. The director's cynical detachment is more appropriate to the stylized surfaces of *The General Died at Dawn* and *The Night of Nights* than to the realistic depths of *All Quiet* and *Of Mice and Men*. A propagandist in press releases only, Milestone is almost the classic example of the uncommitted director. From the beginning, his editing was mechanical rather than analytical, and his tracking synthetic rather than expressive. Socially conscious film historians were therefore needlessly agitated by the miscellaneousness of his projects. *Anything Goes* or *The North Star:* What difference does it make? It might be said in Milestone's defense that he has never discriminated against doomed projects like *Rain* and *The Arch of Triumph*. His professionalism is as unyielding as it is meaningless, and not even the seismic eruptions of *Mutiny on the Bounty* can faze him.

CAROL REED (1906–1976)

FILMS: 1936—Midshipman Easy, Laburnum Grove. 1937—Talk of the Devil, Bank Holiday. 1938—No Parking, Climbing High, A Girl Must Live, Penny Paradise. 1939—*The Stars Look Down* (1941 in New York), *Night Train* (1940 in New York). 1940—The Girl in the News, *Kipps*, The Young Mr. Pitt. 1942–1945—Documentaries: The New Lot, The Way Ahead, The True Glory (with Garson Kanin). 1947—*Odd Man Out.* 1949—*Fallen Idol.* 1950—*The Third Man.* 1952—*The Outcast of the Islands.* 1953—*The Man Between.* 1956—A Kid for Two Farthings, Trapeze. 1958—The Key. 1960—Our Man in Havana. 1963—The Running Man. 1965—The Agony and the Ecstasy. 1968—Oliver!

The decline of Carol Reed since *Outcast of the Islands* is too obvious to be belabored. The director of *Odd Man Out, The Fallen Idol,* and *The Third Man* displayed undeniable talent and feeling at one time, particularly with ensemble acting. His modulated sound tracks seemed impressive in an era when understatement was generally overrated. Similarly, his editing of off-angle compositions produced a misleading impression of visual complexity. Today the technique of even his "golden" period looks too turgid (*Odd Man Out*), too fastidious (*The Fallen Idol*), and too elaborate (*The Third Man*). Nowhere does the director's personality grip the literary themes of F. L. Green, Graham Greene, and Joseph Conrad. From *The Man Between* to that man on the ceiling—*Michelangelo*—Reed steadily lost control of his medium as his feigned objectivity disintegrated into imperviousness. Reed's career demonstrates that a director who limits himself to solving technical problems quickly lapses into the decadence of the inappropriate effect. For example, Reed's fateful camera angles in *The Key* only emphasize the dishonesty of Carl Foreman's script.

Still, Reed's best films seem to have survived their director, particularly in the felicitous charm of Michael Redgrave's *Kipps,* Rex Harrison's agent in *Night Train,* and Emlyn Williams's rogue in the otherwise overrated *The Stars Look Down.* F. J. McCormick in *Odd Man Out* lingers in the mind, as do James Mason and Claire Bloom in *The Man Between,* Ralph Richardson in *Fallen Idol,* and Celia Johnson in *A Kid for Two Farthings.* Perhaps most memorable of all Reed readings is that of Conrad's heroic rhetoric in *Outcast of the Islands* by Trevor Howard and Ralph Richardson. If François Truffaut had understood and appreciated the English language, he would not have been in such a strategic position to write off Carol Reed, as it turned out, prematurely.

WILLIAM WELLMAN (1896–1975)

FILMS: 1923—The Man Who Won, Second Hand Love, Big Dan. 1924—The Vagabond Trail, Cupid's Fireman, Not a Drum Was Heard, The Circus Cowboy. 1926—When Husbands Flirt, The Boob, The Cat's Pajamas, You Never Know Women. 1927—*Wings.* 1928—Legion of Condemned, Ladies of the Mob, *Beggars of Life.* 1929—Chinatown Nights, The Man I Love, Woman Trap. 1930—Dangerous Paradise, Young Eagles, Maybe It's Love, Steel Highway. 1931—*The Public Enemy,* Other Men's Women, Star Witness, Night Nurse, Safe in Hell. 1932—Love is a Racket, *Hatchet Man,* So Big, Purchase Price, The Conquerors. 1933—Frisco Jenny, Central Airport, Lady of the Night, Lilly Turner, College Coach, *Heroes for Sale,* Midnight Mary, *Wild Boys of the Road.* 1934—

Looking for Trouble, Stingaree, *The President Vanishes*. 1935—The Call of the Wild, Robin Hood of El Dorado. 1936—Small Town Girl. 1937—*A Star Is Born, Nothing Sacred*. 1938—Men with Wings. 1939—*Beau Geste, The Light That Failed*. 1940—Reaching for the Sun. 1942—*Roxie Hart*, The Great Man's Lady, Thunder Birds. 1943—*Ox-Bow Incident*, Lady of Burlesque. 1944—Buffalo Bill. 1945—This Man's Navy, *Story of G.I. Joe*. 1946—Gallant Journey. 1947—Magic Town. 1948—The Iron Curtain, Happy Years, The Next Voice You Hear. 1949—*Battleground*. 1950—Across the Wide Missouri, Westward the Women. 1951—*Yellow Sky*. 1952—My Man and I. 1953—Island in the Sky. 1954—*High and the Mighty*, Track of the Cat. 1955—Blood Alley. 1956—*Goodbye, My Lady*. 1958—Darby's Rangers, Lafayette Escadrille.

With Wellman, crudity is too often mistaken for sincerity. What is at issue here is not the large number of bad films he has made, but a fundamental deficiency in his direction of good projects. On parallel subjects, he runs a poorer second to good directors than he should. *The Public Enemy* with Cagney should not be all that inferior to Hawks's *Scarface,* or *Nothing Sacred* with Lombard and Hecht to McCarey's *The Awful Truth,* or *Story of G.I. Joe* with Mitchum and Steele to Ford's *They Were Expendable.* Wellman, like Wyler, Huston, and Zinnemann, is a recessive director, one whose images tend to recede from the foreground to the background in the absence of a strong point of view. *Roxie Hart* is framed like a Sennett primitive without the Sennett pacing. *The Light That Failed* keeps floating back in its frame like a Sunday painting. *The Ox-Bow Incident* looks grotesque today with its painted backdrops treated like the natural vistas in a Ford Western. Again, a Hollywood director cannot be criticized for working with fake sets, but his technique can be called into question if it emphasizes the fakery. With Wellman, as with so many other directors, objectivity is the last refuge of mediocrity.

BILLY WILDER (1906–   )

FILMS: 1942—*The Major and the Minor*. 1943—*Five Graves to Cairo*. 1944—*Double Indemnity*. 1945—*The Lost Weekend*. 1948—The Emperor Waltz, *A Foreign Affair*. 1950—*Sun-*

set Boulevard. 1951—*Ace in the Hole.* 1953—*Stalag 17.* 1954—
Sabrina. 1955—The Seven Year Itch. 1957—Spirit of St. Louis,
Love in the Afternoon. 1958—*Witness for the Prosecution.* 1959—
Some Like It Hot. 1960—*The Apartment.* 1961—One, Two,
Three. 1963—Irma La Douce. 1964—*Kiss Me Stupid.* 1966—
The Fortune Cookie. 1969—Sherlock Holmes.

Billy Wilder is too cynical to believe even his own cynicism. Toward the end of *Stalag 17,* William Holden bids a properly cynical adieu to his prison-camp buddies. He ducks into the escape
tunnel for a second, then quickly pops up, out of character, with
a boyish smile and a friendly wave, and then ducks down for
good. Holden's sentimental waste motion in a tensely timed
melodrama demonstrates the cancellation principle in Wilder's
cinema. For example, the director's irresponsible Berlin films—
A Foreign Affair and *One, Two, Three*—have been wrongly
criticized for social irresponsibility. This is too serious a charge
to level at a series of tasteless gags, half anti-Left and half anti-
Right, adding up to Wilder's conception of political sophistication. Even his best films—*The Major and the Minor, Sunset
Boulevard, Stalag 17,* and *Some Like It Hot*—are marred by
the director's penchant for gross caricature, especially with peripheral characters. All of Wilder's films decline in retrospect because of visual and structural deficiencies. Only Laughton's
owlish performance makes *Witness for the Prosecution* look like
the tour de force it was intended to be, and only Jack Lemmon
keeps *The Apartment* from collapsing into the cellar of morbid
psychology. Wilder deserves full credit for these performances,
and for many of the other felicities that redeem his films from the
superficial nastiness of his personality. He has failed only to the
extent that he has been proved inadequate for the more serious
demands of middle-class tragedy (*Double Indemnity*) and social
allegory (*Ace in the Hole*). A director who can crack jokes about
suicide attempts (*Sabrina* and *The Apartment*) and thoughtlessly
brutalize charming actresses like Jean Arthur (*Foreign Affair*)
and Audrey Hepburn (*Sabrina*) is hardly likely to make a coherent film on the human condition.

If Billy Wilder's stock has risen slightly in recent years with
the escalation of satiric savagery in *Kiss Me Stupid* and *The For-*

tune Cookie, it is not so much because of the films themselves, but rather because Wilder has chosen to remain himself while almost everyone else has been straining to go mod. Curiously, Wilder seems to have completely abandoned the Lubitsch tradition he upheld ever so briefly with *Love in the Afternoon,* an Audrey Hepburn vehicle not without its cruelties toward agingly jaded Gary Cooper, but not without its beauties as well.

WILLIAM WYLER (1902–1981)

FILMS: 1926—Lazy Lightning, Stolen Ranch. 1927—Blazing Days, Hard Fists, Straight Shootin', The Border Cavalier, Desert Dust. 1928—Thunder Riders, Anybody Here Seen Kelly? 1929—The Shakedown, Love Trap. 1930—*Hell's Heroes,* The Storm. 1932—*A House Divided,* Tom Brown of Culver. 1933—Her First Mate, *Counsellor at Law.* 1935—The Good Fairy, *The Gay Deception.* 1936—Come and Get It (with Howard Hawks), *Dodsworth,* These Three. 1937—*Dead End.* 1938—*Jezebel.* 1939—*Wuthering Heights.* 1940—*The Letter,* The Westerner. 1941—*The Little Foxes.* 1942—Mrs. Miniver. 1943–1945—The Memphis Belle, The Fighting Lady (documentaries). 1946—*The Best Years of Our Lives.* 1949—The Heiress. 1951—*Detective Story.* 1952—Carrie. 1953—*Roman Holiday.* 1955—The Desperate Hours. 1956—*Friendly Persuasion.* 1958—The Big Country. 1959—Ben Hur. 1962—The Children's Hour. 1965—*The Collector.* 1966—How to Steal a Million. 1968—Funny Girl.

Back in 1963, I denounced a career that was inflating without expanding: "There is something poetically just in the announcement that William Wyler will direct *Sound of Music,* the *Ben Hur* of Broadway musicals, for Darryl F. Zanuck. If ever there were a prescription for elephantiasis, this is it. A French hack director once expressed his admiration for Wyler as 'the style without a style.' Precisely. *The Little Foxes* owes more to Toland's camera than to Wyler's direction, and *The Letter* still reverberates somewhat with the repressed passion of Bette Davis and James Stephenson. Otherwise, Wyler's career is a cipher as far as personal direction is concerned. What has become increasingly apparent in retrospect is a misanthropic tendency in Wyler's technique, particularly with romantic material like *Wuthering Heights* and *Roman Holiday*. It would seem that Wyler's admirers have long mistaken a lack of feeling for emotional restraint."

As it turned out, Robert Wise, and not William Wyler, directed *Sound of Music* with such straight-faced sobriety that this oversized marshmallow broke all box-office records. For his part, Wyler redeemed his reputation somewhat with *The Collector*, a project for which his meticulous craftsmanship was ideally suited. Welles has called Wyler not inaptly the great producer among directors. No matter. Wyler is back beating on the door of the bonanza musical with Barbra Streisand, no less, in *Funny Girl*. It is as if *The Collector* were an unforeseen interlude in the director's inevitably dismal destiny.

FRED ZINNEMANN (1907–)

FILMS: Short Subjects: 1938—A Friend Indeed, The Story of Dr. Carver, That Mothers Might Live, Tracking the Sleeping Death, They Live Again. 1939—Weather Wizards, While America Sleeps, Help Wanted!, One Against the World, The Ash Can Fleet, Forgotten Victory. 1940—The Old South, The Way in the Wilderness, The Great Meddler. 1941—Forbidden Passage, Your Last Act. 1942—The Lady or the Tiger? Features: 1935—Waves. 1942—Kid Glove Killer, Eyes in the Night. 1944—The Seventh Cross. 1946—Little Mr. Jim. 1947—My Brother Talks to Horses. 1948—*The Search.* 1949—*Act of Violence.* 1950—*The Men.* 1951—*Teresa.* 1952—*High Noon,* The Member of the Wedding. 1953—*From Here to Eternity.* 1955—Oklahoma! 1957—*A Hatful of Rain.* 1959—*The Nun's Story.* 1960—The Sundowners. 1963—Behold a Pale Horse. 1966—*A Man for All Seasons.*

Fred Zinnemann's career reflects the rise and fall of the realist aesthetic in Hollywood. He directed the first screen performances of Montgomery Clift (*The Search*) and Marlon Brando (*The Men*). His looseness and gentleness with actors contributed to the nice-guy image one does not usually associate with realists in Hollywood. Zinnemann is hardly a Stroheim. Indeed, his neatness and decorum constitute his gravest artistic defects. *The Search, Act of Violence, The Men,* and *Teresa* represented a period of promise. These films were not entirely devoid of modest virtues even though they were ultimately compromised by sentimental formulas. It is the payoff films—*High Noon, From Here to Eternity, The Nun's Story,* and *A Man for All Seasons* —that most vividly reveal the superficiality of Zinnemann's personal commitment. At its best, his direction is inoffensive; at its worst, it is downright dull. Zinnemann has finally settled down to being a semirealist, stepping gingerly around such subgenres as the moralistic melodrama (*Act of Violence*), the antipopulist anti-Western (*High Noon*), the empty sidewalk stage adaptation (*Member of the Wedding, A Hatful of Rain*), the pigpen musical (*Oklahoma!*), and the painless political allegory (*Behold a Pale Horse*). By draining every subject and every situation of any possible emotional excitement, Fred Zinnemann is now widely considered in academic circles as the screen's most honest director. Besides, he has two Oscars and four scrolls from the New York Film Critics Circle. His inclusion in any objective history of the American cinema is mandatory, but his true vocation remains the making of antimovies for antimoviegoers. Even the realism that once served as his rationale seems to have been displaced in fashionable circles by newfangled notions of stylization and distancing. No matter. Fred Zinnemann will plod on with all the solid virtues of the vestryman and the modest countenance of the truth-seeker. Perhaps there is not in Zinnemann enough of the redeeming outrageousness of the compulsive entertainer. In cinema, as in all art, only those who risk the ridiculous have a real shot at the sublime.

VI.
LIGHTLY
LIKABLE

These are talented but uneven directors with the saving grace of unpretentiousness.

BUSBY BERKELEY (1895–1976)

FILMS: 1935—*Gold Diggers of 1935*, Bright Lights, I Live for Love. 1936—Stagestruck. 1937—The Go-Getter, Hollywood Hotel. 1938—Men Are Such Fools, Garden of the Moon, Comet over Broadway. 1939—They Made Me a Criminal, *Babes in Arms,* Fast and Furious. 1940—Strike Up the Band, Forty Little Mothers. 1941 —Babes on Broadway, Blonde Inspiration. 1942—*For Me and My Gal.* 1943—The Gang's All Here. 1948—Cinderella Jones. 1949—*Take Me Out to the Ball Game.*

Busby Berkeley is a name that conjures up a certain form of spectacle in Hollywood musicals of the thirties. Although Berkeley's choreographic and directorial contributions span a period of over thirty years, his maximum influence was exerted mainly through the series of *Gold Digger* movies. It is customary for film historians to assume that Busby Berkeley's style of mass choreography and aerial cinematography were completely eclipsed by the relative grace and simplicity of the Fred Astaire-Ginger Rogers musicals. Actually, Berkeley and Astaire both overlapped and coexisted as stylistic alternatives for the Hollywood musical to follow. At his best, Berkeley's spectacle effects possessed a giddy, vertiginous, disorienting charm. If his musical numbers were larger than life, it was because he found Hollywood sound stages less constricting than the Broadway boards. Berkeley's vitality and ingenuity transcended the limitations of his sensibility, and he bequeathed to posterity an entertaining record of the audacity of an escapist era.

As a choreographer from the crane, Berkeley scrawled a kind of skywriting signature clearly visible from the sound stages of *42nd Street* (1933) to the circus grounds of *Jumbo* (1962). As a moderately entertaining director, he held the fort for the musical between the end of the Astaire-Rogers cycle and the beginning of the Minnelli-Donen-Kelly period. He can claim some of the credit for the spectacular evolution of Judy Garland and Gene Kelly into the titans of the Metro musical. If some of his socialized floral patterns do indeed look a bit naïve and prematurely anti-Astairish today, they did have their time and place in the depths of the Depression when the difference between quality and quantity did not seem too important. Taken as a whole, Berkeley's contributions deserve better than being consigned to the sniggerings of Camp followers. Busby Berkeley deserves enduring respect as the Méliès of the Musical.

My most poignant recollection of Berkeleyana is the "Lullaby of Broadway" number from *The Gold Diggers of 1935*. For years and years I retained the image of a playgirl plunging to her death from a skyscraper ballroom, and then the lingering contemplation of an empty apartment with a hungry kitten waiting to be fed and outside somewhere a chorus singing "Good night, baby" as if perchance to die was but to dream of a lullaby as a requiem mass. *The Gold Diggers of 1935* revisited turned out to be a long prologue, by turns cynical and fatuous, to a very short production number as a show within a show. I had almost begun to doubt my moviegoing memory when suddenly the playgirl plunged to her death and the traveling camera lingered over an empty apartment, and the lullaby engulfed the screen once more as it had once long ago in the darkest days of the Depression. The magic of Busby Berkeley had been miraculously reconfirmed.

HENRY CORNELIUS (1913–1958)

FILMS: 1949—*Passport to Pimlico.* 1951—The Galloping Major. 1954—*Genevieve.* 1955—I Am a Camera. 1960—Next to No Time.

He will be best remembered for *Genevieve,* a luminous comedy of the outdoors, a film glowing with a Defoe-like sense of property. Cornelius was a comic potentiality cut short by death; and, like many of the more colorful contributors to the British cinema, he was not British himself.

JOHN CROMWELL (1888–1979)

FILMS: 1929—*Close Harmony, Dance of Life.* 1930—*Street of Chance,* The Texan, For the Defense, Tom Sawyer. 1931—Scandal Sheet, Unfaithful, Vice Squad, Rich Man's Folly. 1932—World and the Flesh. 1933—Sweepings, Silver Cord, Double Harness, Ann Vickers. 1934—This Man Is Mine, Spitfire, *Of Human Bondage,* The Fountain. 1935—Village Tale, Jalna, I Dream Too Much. 1936 —Little Lord Fauntleroy, To Mary with Love, Banjo on My Knee. 1937—*The Prisoner of Zenda.* 1938—Algiers. 1939—*Made for Each Other,* In Name Only, Abe Lincoln in Illinois. 1940—Victory. 1941—*So Ends Our Night.* 1942—*Son of Fury.* 1944—*Since You Went Away.* 1945—*The Enchanted Cottage.* 1946—*Anna and the King of Siam.* 1947—Dead Reckoning, Night Song. 1950 —*Caged,* The Company She Keeps. 1951—The Racket. 1958— *The Goddess.* 1961—A Matter of Morals. 1963—*The Scavengers.*

From Nancy Carroll (*Close Harmony*) to Kim Stanley (*The Goddess*), the motto of Cromwell's cinema has been *cherchez la femme.* Whether by luck or design, his eclectic career has been redeemed by the iconographical contributions of Irene Dunne, Katharine Hepburn, Bette Davis, Madeleine Carroll, Mary Astor, Carole Lombard, Betty Field, Margaret Sullavan, Gene Tierney, Jennifer Jones, and Dorothy McGuire. Fortunately, Cromwell's formal deficiencies seldom obscure the beautiful drivers of his vehicles. Cromwell may be remembered ultimately as the perfect director for David O. Selznick, himself a noted connoisseur of feminine beauty. If Cromwell's career be but a footnote to film history, a footnote should be appended to that footnote for the curious sado-masochistic relationship between Hope Emerson and Eleanor Parker in *Caged,* that minor classic of repression.

MICHAEL CURTIZ (1888–1962)

FILMS: 1927—Moon of Israel, The Third Degree, A Million Bid, The Desired Woman, Good Time Charlie. 1928—Tenderloin. 1929—Noah's Ark, Glad Rag Doll, Madonna of Avenue A, Hearts in Exile. 1930—Mammy, Under a Texas Moon, The Matrimonial Bed. 1931—River's End, Bright Lights, God's Gift to Women, Soldier's Plaything. 1932—Woman from Monte Carlo, Strange Love of Molly Louvain, Doctor X, *Cabin in the Cotton.* 1933—*20,000 Years in Sing Sing,* History of the Wax Museum, The Keyhole, Private Detective 62, Goodbye Again, Kennel Murder Case, Female. 1934—Mandalay; Jimmy, the Gent; The Key, Brutal Agent. 1935 —Case of the Curious Bride, *Black Fury*, Front Page Woman, Little Big Shot, *Captain Blood*. 1936—The Walking Dead, Stolen Holiday, *Charge of the Light Brigade*. 1937—*Kid Galahad*, Mountain Justice, The Perfect Specimen. 1938—Gold Is Where You Find It, *The Adventures of Robin Hood* (with William Keighley), *Four Daughters*, Four's a Crowd, *Angels with Dirty Faces*. 1939— *Dodge City, Daughters Courageous, The Private Lives of Elizabeth and Essex, Four Wives*. 1940—Virginia City, *The Sea Hawk, Santa Fe Trail*. 1941—*The Sea Wolf*, Dive Bomber. 1942—*Casablanca, Yankee Doodle Dandy*, Captains of the Clouds. 1943—Mission to Moscow, This Is the Army. 1944—Passage to Marseilles, Janie. 1945—Roughly Speaking, *Mildred Pierce*. 1946—Night and Day. 1947—Life with Father, The Unsuspected. 1948—Romance on the High Seas. 1949—*Flamingo Road*, My Dream Is Yours, The Lady Takes a Sailor. 1950—*The Breaking Point*, Bright Leaf. 1951—Jim Thorpe—All-American, *Force of Arms*, I'll See You in My Dreams. 1952—The Will Rogers Story, The Jazz Singer. 1954 —The Boy from Oklahoma, The Egyptian, White Christmas. 1955 —We're No Angels. 1956—The Scarlet Hour, The Vagabond King, The Best Things in Life Are Free. 1957—The Helen Morgan Story. 1958—The Proud Rebel, King Creole. 1959—The Hangman, The Man in the Net. 1960—The Adventures of Huckleberry Finn, A Breath of Scandal. 1961—Francis of Assisi, The Comancheros.

Perhaps more than any other director, Curtiz reflected the strengths and weaknesses of the studio system in Hollywood. This most amiable of Warners' technicians faithfully served the studio's contract players from Dolores Costello to Doris Day. When one speaks of a typical Warners' film in the thirties and forties, one is generally speaking of a typical Curtiz film of those periods. He directed many of Bette Davis's lesser bread-and-butter vehicles, and shared the Errol Flynn cycle with Raoul Walsh. He guided James Cagney (*Yankee Doodle Dandy*) and Joan Crawford (*Mildred Pierce*) to Oscars, and saw the Lane sisters through the Depression. He helped project the memorably anarchic personalities of Cagney, Bogart, Garfield, and Muni in between other less memorable projects. After *Force of Arms,* his career went to the dogs. If many of the early Curtiz films are hardly worth remembering, none of the later ones are even worth seeing. What the collapse of studio discipline meant to Curtiz and to Hollywood was the bottom dropping out of routine film-making. The director's one enduring masterpiece is, of course, *Casablanca,* the happiest of happy accidents, and the most decisive exception to the auteur theory.

HARRY D'ARRAST (1897–1968)

FILMS: 1927—Service for Ladies, *A Gentleman of Paris,* Serenade. 1928—Magnificent Flirt, *Dry Martini.* 1930—*Raffles, Laughter.* 1933—*Topaze.* 1935—The Three Cornered Hat.

His wit was said to be as dry as his own *Dry Martini.* One of the more colorful directors of the late twenties and early thirties, Harry D'Arrast expressed some of the elegance of his time with grace and charm. *Laughter* and *Topaze,* seen today, seem fragile and vulnerable exceptions to the boisterousness of mass taste.

DELMER DAVES (1904–1977)

FILMS: 1943—Destination Tokyo. 1944—The Very Thought of You, Hollywood Canteen. 1945—Pride of the Marines. 1947 —*The Red House, Dark Passage.* 1948—To the Victor. 1949— A Kiss in the Dark, Task Force. 1950—*Broken Arrow.* 1951— Bird of Paradise. 1952—Return of the Texan. 1953—Treasure of the Golden Condor, Never Let Me Go. 1954—Demetrius and the Gladiators, Drum Beat. 1956—Jubal, *The Last Wagon.* 1957— *3:10 to Yuma.* 1958—*Cowboy,* Kings Go Forth, The Badlanders. 1959—The Hanging Tree, *A Summer Place.* 1961—Parrish, Susan Slade. 1963—Spencer's Mountain. 1964—*Youngblood Hawke.* 1965—The Battle of the Villa Fiorita.

If you have no kind thoughts for the authoritative absurdities of *Dark Passage, The Red House, A Summer Place, Rome Adventure* and *Youngblood Hawke,* read no further. Delmer Daves is the property of those who can enjoy stylistic conviction in an intellectual vacuum. The movies of Delmer Daves are fun of a very special kind. Call it Camp or call it Corn. The director does not so much transcend his material as mingle with it.

EDMUND GOULDING (1891–1959)

FILMS: 1925—Sun-Up; Sally, Irene and Mary. 1926—Paris. 1927—Women Love Diamonds. 1928—Love, The Trespasser, Paramount on Parade, Devil's Holiday. 1931—Reaching for the Moon, Night Angel. 1932—*Grand Hotel*, Blondie of the Follies. 1934—Riptide. 1935—The Flame Within. 1937—That Certain Woman. 1938—*White Banners, The Dawn Patrol.* 1939—*Dark Victory, We Are Not Alone, The Old Maid.* 1940—Till We Meet Again. 1941—*The Great Lie.* 1943—*The Constant Nymph, Claudia.* 1946—Of Human Bondage, *The Razor's Edge.* 1947—*Nightmare Alley.* 1949—Everybody Does It. 1950—*Mr. 880.* 1952—We're Not Married. 1953—Down Among the Sheltering Palms. 1956—*Teen Age Rebel.* 1958—Mardi Gras.

Goulding's career, like his talent, was discreet and tasteful. A vehicle director with something extra, he lent his most threadbare projects a feeling of concern. His best films—*Grand Hotel, The Constant Nymph, Claudia, The Razor's Edge,* and *Nightmare Alley*—are seldom attributed to him. *Grand Hotel* won an Academy Award in a year when he was not even nominated for direction. His remakes—*The Dawn Patrol* and *Till We Meet Again*—were markedly but not disgracefully inferior to the originals of Hawks and Garnett (*One-Way Passage*). Even when he remade his Gloria Swanson vehicle (*The Trespasser*) into a Bette Davis vehicle (*That Certain Woman*), he did not gain or lose much in the process. Plus and minus all the way down the line. *Dark Victory, The Old Maid,* and *The Great Lie* are afflicted by George Brent and excessive melodrama, but they are still much closer to Wyler's Davis counterparts, *Jezebel, The Letter,* and *The Little Foxes,* than anyone would have suspected at the time. Goulding not only enhanced his actresses—Greta Garbo, Bette Davis, Dorothy McGuire, Joan Fontaine, Gene Tierney—but also his supporting actresses—Geraldine Fitzgerald, Jane Bryan, Mary Astor, Anne Baxter, the latter two winning Oscars, and who can forget Marilyn Monroe in a bathing suit in *We're Not Married*?

BYRON HASKIN (1899–1984)

FILMS: 1927—Matinee Ladies, Irish Hearts, Ginsberg the Great. 1928—The Siren. 1947—*I Walk Alone*. 1948—Man-Eater of Kumaon. 1949—*Too Late for Tears*. 1950—Treasure Island. 1951—Tarzan's Peril, Warpath, Silver City. 1952—The Denver and the Rio Grande. 1953—The War of the Worlds, His Majesty O'Keefe. 1954—*The Naked Jungle*. 1955—Long John Silver, Conquest of Space. 1956—The First Texan, The Boss. 1958 —From the Earth to the Moon. 1959—Little Savage. 1960—September Storm. 1961—*Armored Command*. 1963—Captain Sinbad. 1964—Robinson Crusoe on Mars.

Byron Haskin's directorial career has seemed so incidental to the processes of personal expression in an impersonal industry that he must be praised indeed for as many as four achievements that linger in the memory, namely, *I Walk Alone, Too Late for Tears, The Naked Jungle,* and *Armored Command,* genre films all with unexpected deposits of feeling and comedy.

HENRY HATHAWAY (1898–1985)

FILMS: 1933—Wild Horse Mesa, Heritage of the Desert, Under the Tonto Rim, Sunset Pass, Man of the Forest, To the Last Man. 1934—*Come on Marines,* Last Round-Up, Thundering Herd, *The Witching Hour,* Now and Forever. 1935—*Lives of a Bengal Lancer, Peter Ibbetson*. 1936—*Trail of the Lonesome Pine;* Go West, Young Man. 1937—*Souls at Sea*. 1938—*Spawn of the North*. 1939—The Real Glory. 1940—Johnny Apollo, Brigham Young. 1941—*The Shepherd of the Hills, Sundown*. 1942—Ten Gentlemen from West Point, *China Girl*. 1944—*Home in Indiana, Wing and a Prayer*. 1945—Nob Hill, *The House on 92nd Street*.

1946—*The Dark Corner, 13 Rue Madeleine.* 1947—*Kiss of Death.* 1948—*Call Northside 777.* 1949—Down to the Sea in Ships. 1950—The Black Rose. 1951—*You're in the Navy Now, Rawhide, 14 Hours, The Desert Fox.* 1952—*Diplomatic Courier.* 1953—*Niagara,* White Witch Doctor. 1954—Prince Valiant, Garden of Evil. 1955—The Racers. 1956—The Bottom of the Bottle, 23 Paces to Baker Street. 1957—Legend of the Lost. 1958— *From Hell to Texas.* 1959—Woman Obsessed. 1960—*Seven Thieves, North to Alaska.* 1963—How the West Was Won (with John Ford and George Marshall). 1964—Circus World. 1965— *The Sons of Katie Elder.* 1966—*Nevada Smith.* 1968—5 Card Stud. 1969—True Grit.

Henry Hathaway is a director without complexes or neuroses even when his material is saturated with these modern accouterments. The lunacies of *14 Hours* and *Niagara* are treated with the grotesque straightforwardness of the action genre. The conventional distinctions between realism and romanticism are irrelevant to Hathaway's career. The legendary romanticism of *Peter Ibbetson* can now be clearly traced to Lee Garmes's camera, and the semidocumentary surfaces of *The House on 92nd Street, 13 Rue Madeleine,* and *Call Northside 777* can be dismissed as a passing fancy of the American cinema. Hathaway's charm consists chiefly of minor virtues, particularly a sense of humor, uncorrupted by major pretensions, but this charm is also a limiting factor. The professional detractors of Ford and Hawks almost invariably attempt to palm off Hathaway as a reasonable facsimile, but such a comparison is patently absurd. Hathaway has directed many likable films—*The Witching Hour, The Lives of a Bengal Lancer, Spawn of the North, Shepherd of the Hills, China Girl, From Hell to Texas,* and *North to Alaska.* Even *The Dark Corner,* a poor man's *Laura,* and *The Kiss of Death,* a conformist gangster film, have their merits. Unfortunately, Hathaway has directed, however amiably, too many clinkers. On balance, Hathaway has had a creditable career on Hollywood's roulette wheel, but nothing approaching the high plateau of Ford and Hawks. He is probably closer to Wellman, though Hathaway is neater and less pretentious.

GARSON KANIN (1912–   )

FILMS: 1938—*A Man to Remember,* Next Time I Marry. 1939—*The Great Man Votes, Bachelor Mother.* 1940—*My Favorite Wife,* They Knew What They Wanted. 1941—*Tom, Dick and Harry.* 1945—The True Glory (with Carol Reed). 1969—Where It's At.

As a playwright, Kanin tended to imitate George S. Kaufman. His direction of film comedies derived from Capra and McCarey to such an extent that *Cahiers du Cinéma* once erroneously listed Kanin's *My Favorite Wife* as a McCarey film. Even so, his work is not without charm and talent. However, his major contribution to the American cinema consists of the inventive scripts he provided George Cukor for the glorious Judy Holliday cycle of psychological comedies.

BURT KENNEDY (1923–   )

FILMS: 1961—The Canadians. 1964—*Mail Order Bride.* 1965—*The Rounders.* 1966—*The Money Trap,* The Return of the Seven. 1967—*Welcome to Hard Times,* The War Wagon. 1968—The Good Guys and the Bad Guys. 1969—Young Billie Young.

Burt Kennedy wrote the scripts for some of Budd Boetticher's best Westerns, but Kennedy's directorial style seems more discursive and less dramatic than Boetticher's. There is also more realistic and psychological clutter in Kennedy's mise-en-scène than in Boetticher's. Kennedy's directorial career has suffered from one false start (*The Canadians*) and six rides in almost as many directions. *Mail Order Bride* and *The Rounders* were low-key folksy exercises on the sexual mores of the New West. *The Money Trap* was unexpectedly poetic in its evocation of forties fakery and urban melodrama. *Welcome to Hard Times* rattled in its hard formal frame as a perverse statement of violence and sexuality in the allegorical West. The least personal of Kennedy's films were *The War Wagon*, a frolicsome vehicle for John Wayne and Kirk Douglas, and *The Return of the Seven*, a dried-up reprise of *The Magnificent Seven* of John Sturges. Kennedy's best films have been aided in no small measure by the weather-beaten talent and iconography of Glenn Ford, Henry Fonda, Rita Hayworth, Ricardo Montalban and Aldo Ray. An interestingly talented writer-director, Kennedy seems to direct his ideas somewhat too tightly and schematically at the expense of the natural flow of his narrative. Even at its best, Kennedy's direction seems too strained for his scenario.

ALEXANDER KORDA (1893–1956)

FILMS: HUNGARIAN PERIOD: 1916—Egy tiszti Kardbojt, Feher éjszakak, Vergödö szivek, Nagymama, Mesek az Ivógepröl, Egymillio fontos bankó. 1917—Magnas Miska, A Kétszivü férfi, Szent Pter Esernyöje, A Gölyakalifa, Magia, Faun, Harrison and Harrison, A Kétlelku Asszony. 1918—Az Aranyembrr, Mary Ann, Se Ki se be. 1919—Ave Caesar, Feher Rosza, A 111-es, Yamata. AUSTRIAN AND GERMAN PERIOD: 1920—Seine Majestät das Bettlekind. 1922—Herren der Meere, Eine Versunkene Welt, Samson und Dalila. 1923—Der Unbekannte Morgen. 1924—Jedermanns Frau, Tragödie in Hause Habsbourg. 1925—Der Tänzer meiner Frau. 1926—Madame wünscht keine Kinder. AMERICAN PERIOD: 1926—The Stolen Bride. 1927—*The Private Life of Helen of Troy*, Night Watch. 1928—The Yellow Lily. 1929—Love and the Devil, The Squall, Her Private Life. 1930—Women Everywhere, The Princess and the Plumber. FRENCH PERIOD: 1931—Rive Gauche, *Marius*. BRITISH PERIOD: 1931—Service for Ladies. 1932—Wedding Rehearsal. 1933—The Girl from Maxim's, *The Private Life of Henry VIII*. 1934—The Private Life of Don Juan. 1936—*Rembrandt*. 1940—Conquest of the Air. 1941—*Lady Hamilton*. 1945—*Vacation From Marriage*. 1947—An Ideal Husband.

Alexander Korda represented and indeed virtually created the Tradition of Quality in the British Cinema. He was generally underrated by the Marxist film historians because his unyielding gentility seemed an affront to the documentary movement. The fact remains that under his direction, Raimu and Pierre Fresnay in *Marius* and Charles Laughton in *The Private Life of Henry VIII* and *Rembrandt* provided some of the greatest and lustiest acting in the history of the cinema. When Korda is accused of excessive gentility, it might be well to remember that Bertolt Brecht himself derived the idea of his *Galileo* from the spectacle of Charles Laughton's tossing away his chewed-out chicken bones in *Henry VIII*.

ZOLTAN KORDA (1895–1961)

FILMS: 1935—Sanders of the River, Forget Me Not. 1937— *Elephant Boy,* Revolt in the Desert. 1938—Drums. 1939—*Four Feathers.* 1942—Jungle Book. 1943—*Sahara.* 1945—Counter-Attack. 1947—*The Macomber Affair,* A Woman's Vengeance. 1952—*African Fury* (Cry the Beloved Country). 1956—Storm Over the Nile.

He directed Paul Robeson and Canada Lee in Africa, and Sabu somewhere in Sabuland. He manned the most far-flung outposts of the British Empire. *Sahara* was the first film to popularize the spirit of the United Nations; and who can forget Ralph Richardson, C. Aubrey Smith, June Duprez, and the Fuzzy-Wuzzies in *Four Feathers*? He also directed the best stretch of Hemingway ever put on the screen (*The Macomber Affair*) and some of the most literate dialogue of Aldous Huxley (*A Woman's Vengeance*). Still, his career is longer on quality than personality, and it remains difficult to define him.

MITCHELL LEISEN (1898–1972)

FILMS: 1933—Cradle Song. 1934—Death Takes a Holiday, Murder at the Vanities. 1935—Behold My Wife, Four Hours to Kill, *Hands Across the Table.* 1936—Thirteen Hours by Air, Big Broadcast of 1937. 1937—*Swing High, Swing Low; Easy Living.* 1938—Big Broadcast of 1938, Artists and Models Abroad. 1939— *Midnight.* 1940—*Remember the Night,* Arise My Love. 1941—I

Wanted Wings, *Hold Back the Dawn*. 1942—The Lady Is Willing; Take a Letter, Darling. 1943—No Time for Love. 1944—*Lady in the Dark*, Frenchman's Creek, Practically Yours. 1945—Masquerade in Mexico. 1946—*Kitty, To Each His Own*, Suddenly It's Spring. 1947—*Golden Earrings*, Dream Girl. 1949—Bride of Vengeance, Song of Surrender. 1950—No Man of her Own, Captain Carey, U.S.A. 1951—*The Mating Season;* Darling, How Could You? 1952—Young Man with Ideas. 1953—Tonight We Sing. 1955—Bedeviled. 1957—The Girl Most Likely. 1967—Spree!

When Mitchell Leisen began at Paramount, the art was supplied by Lubitsch and Sternberg, and the junk by almost everyone else. Leisen occupied a middle position in the late thirties and early forties with such stylish productions as *Easy Living, Midnight, Remember the Night, Hold Back the Dawn,* and *Lady in the Dark*. The promotion of Preston Sturges and Billy Wilder from writers' cubicles to directors' chairs in the forties probably contributed to Leisen's decline. He soon found himself in the unenviable position of an expert diamond cutter working with lumpy coal. Yet, even the trivialities of *Kitty, Golden Earrings* and *The Mating Season* are not entirely devoid of directorial niceties.

MERVYN LE ROY (1900–1987)

FILMS: 1927—No Place to Go. 1928—Flying Romeos, Harold Teen. 1929—Naughty Baby, Hot Stuff, Broadway Daddy. 1930—Little Johnny Jones, Playing Around, Show Girl in Hollywood, Numbered Men, Broken Dishes, Top Speed, *Little Caesar*. 1931—Broad Minded, Too Young to Marry, *Five Star Final,* Local Boy Makes Good, Tonight or Never. 1932—*I Am a Fugitive from a Chain Gang,* High Pressure, Heart of New York, *Two Seconds*, Big City Blues, Three on a Match. 1933—*Hard to Handle*, Tugboat Annie, Elmer the Great, *Gold Diggers of 1933*, The World Changes. 1934—Heat Lightning, *Hi Nellie*, Happiness Ahead, *Sweet Adeline*. 1935—Oil for the Lamps of China, Page Miss Glory, I Found Stella Parish. 1936—Anthony Adverse, Three Men on a Horse. 1937—The King and the Chorus Girl, *They Won't Forget*. 1938—Fools for Scandal. 1940—*Waterloo Bridge, Escape*. 1941—*Blossoms in the Dust*, Unholy Partners. 1942—*Random Harvest, Johnny Eager*.

1943—Madame Curie. 1946—Without Reservations. 1948—Homecoming. 1949—In the Good Old Summertime, Any Number Can Play; East Side, West Side. 1951—Quo Vadis. 1952—Lovely to Look At, Million Dollar Mermaid. 1953—Latin Lovers. 1954—Rosemarie. 1955—Strange Lady in Town, *Mr. Roberts* (with John Ford). 1956—*The Bad Seed*, Toward the Unknown. 1958—No Time for Sergeants, Home Before Dark. 1959—The FBI Story. 1960—Wake Me When It's Over. 1961—The Devil at 4 o'Clock, A Majority of One. 1962—*Gypsy*. 1963—Mary, Mary. 1966—Moment to Moment. 1969—Downstairs at Ramsey's. 1970—The Thirteen Clocks.

From *Little Caesar* to *Gypsy*, Le Roy has converted his innate vulgarity into a personal style. As long as he is not mistaken for a serious artist, Le Roy can be delightfully entertaining. Divested of a spurious social consciousness, *I Am a Fugitive from a Chain Gang* and *They Won't Forget* are as much fun as *Waterloo Bridge* and *Random Harvest*. For all the jokes made about *Quo Vadis*, Le Roy's feeling for spectacle is clearly superior to Wyler's in the unendurable *Ben Hur*. His *Little Caesar* is feeble next to Hawks's *Scarface*, and his *Little Women* are far littler than Cukor's, but you can't have everything. His direction of Conrad Veidt and Norma Shearer in *Escape* and the haunting presence of Irene Dunne in *Sweet Adeline* make up for any numbers of clinkers.

FRANKLIN SCHAFFNER (1920–1989)

FILMS: 1963—The Stripper. 1964—*The Best Man*. 1965—*The War Lord*. 1968—Planet of the Apes. 1968—The Double Man.

The great commercial irony of Franklin Schaffner's career is that his silliest project—*Planet of the Apes*—will make more money than all his three other more serious projects put together. However, even the financially fruitful monkeyshines of *Planet of the Apes* are not too high a price to pay for maintaining Schaffner's place in a film industry that has not given his talents the opportunities they deserve. An alumnus of the Philco-Westinghouse "Golden Age" of television drama, Schaffner was particularly successful with the histrionic demands of *The Best Man,* and particularly sympathetic for his unrewarded ambitiousness with *The War Lord,* a film that dared to treat romantic heterosexual love as a sacred subject worthy of epic consideration.

GEORGE SIDNEY (1916–   )

FILMS: 1941—Free and Easy. 1942—Pacific Rendezvous. 1943—Pilot No. 5 . . . , Thousands Cheer. 1944—Bathing Beauty. 1945—*Anchors Aweigh.* 1946—The Harvey Girls, Holiday in Mexico. 1947—Cass Timberlane. 1948—*The Three Musketeers.* 1949—The Red Danube. 1950—*Annie Get Your Gun,* Key to the City. 1951—*Show Boat.* 1952—*Scaramouche.* 1953—*Kiss Me Kate.* 1955—Jupiter's Darling. 1956—*The Eddie Duchin Story.* 1957—*Jeanne Eagels,* Pal Joey. 1960—*Who Was That Lady?,* Pepe. 1963—*Bye Bye Birdie.* 1966—*The Swinger.* 1968—Half a Six-pence.

Alongside Sidney, Le Roy looks like a Bressonian director. It can be argued that Sidney has ruined more good musicals with more gusto than any director in history, but who else has directed Esther Williams and Kim Novak in their opulent periods with such a straight face? There is a point at which brassiness, vulgarity, and downright badness become virtues, and Sidney approached that point in *Scaramouche* and *Jeanne Eagels,* and was not too far behind with *The Three Musketeers* and *The Eddie Duchin Story.* Of course, *Kiss Me Kate* was regrettable, and *Pal Joey* was unforgivable, but Sidney has kept his hand in even when it seemed time and again that the musical gravy train had reached the last stop. Sidney's ability to shift gears after such disasters as *Holiday in Mexico, Jupiter's Darling,* and *Pepe* is a tribute to his tenacity. After all, every aesthete in New York, London, and Paris wants to make a musical, but Sidney just keeps making them by default. Ultimately, Sidney may deserve a footnote in film history as the only director to appreciate Ann-

Margret in such culturally disreputable frolics as *Bye Bye Birdie* and *The Swinger.*

ANDREW L. STONE (1902–)

FILMS: 1928—Two o'Clock in the Morning, Liebenstraum. 1930—Sombras de Gloria. 1932—Hell's Headquarters. 1938—Stolen Heaven, Say It in French. 1939—The Great Victor Herbert. 1941—The Hard-Boiled Canary. 1943—Stormy Weather, Hi Diddle Diddle. 1944—Sensations of 1945. 1950—Highway 301. 1952—Confidence Girl, *The Steel Trap.* 1955—*The Night Holds Terror.* 1956—*Julie.* 1958—*Cry Terror,* The Decks Ran Red. 1960—*The Last Voyage.* 1962—*The Password Is Courage.* 1964 —Never Put It in Writing. 1965—The Secret of My Success.

Since *The Steel Trap,* Andrew Stone and his fantastically helpful wife-editor have evolved a materialism without a dialectic, a form of film-making for those who brood over movie "boners." A tree is a tree to the Stones, but they don't shoot it in Griffith Park. If they want to blow up a train, they blow up a real train. If they want to sink an ocean liner, they sink a real ocean liner. This literal approach to catastrophes is pleasantly naïve in this neurotic age when everyone is afraid of his shadow and when what is truly frightening about things is not their essence but their appearance. One sobering deduction: If the Stones had made *On the Beach,* none of us would be around now to review it.

CHARLES WALTERS (1911–1982)

FILMS: 1947—*Good News.* 1948—*Easter Parade.* 1949— *The Barkleys of Broadway.* 1950—*Summer Stock.* 1951—Three Guys Named Mike, Texas Carnival. 1952—The Belle of New York. 1953—*Lilli, Torch Song.* 1955—The Glass Slipper, *The Tender Trap.* 1956—High Society. 1957—Don't Go Near the Water. 1959—*Ask Any Girl.* 1960—*Please Don't Eat the Daisies.* 1961 —Two Loves. 1962—*Jumbo.* 1964—The Unsinkable Molly Brown. 1966—Walk, Don't Run.

The late H. L. Mencken used to boast that he had never seen a movie, but toward the end of his life, this irascible cynic was induced to see *Lilli,* and he loved it! Charles Walters produces this effect almost inexplicably with the most dubious material. His sensibility is pitched at a certain level of fakery and remains there consistently. If the adjective "nice" could be defined with any precision, it would apply to most of his films. At the very least, his films almost invariably turn out being more entertaining than their subject and title would indicate. Walters is often too arch and affected for comfort, but his direction of players is never lacking in knowledgeable subtlety.

JAMES WHALE (1896–1957)

FILMS: 1930—*Journey's End.* 1931—*Waterloo Bridge, Frankenstein.* 1932—Impatient Maiden, *The Old Dark House.* 1933—The Kiss Before the Mirror, *The Invisible Man,* By Candlelight. 1934—*One More River.* 1935—*The Bride of Frankenstein,* Remember Last Night? 1936—*Show Boat.* 1937—The Road Back, The Great Garrick. 1938—*Sinners in Paradise,* Wives Under Suspicion, Port of Seven Seas. 1939—*The Man in the Iron Mask.* 1940—Green Hell. 1941—They Dare Not Love. 1949—Hello Out There (never released).

James Whale's career has been somewhat submerged by the Karloff cult. John Grierson managed to talk about *Frankenstein* without even mentioning Whale, but connoisseurs of horror films know that the real gem of the series was *The Bride of Frankenstein* with Whale's bizarre camera angles battling Ernest Thesiger's fruity performance for attention. Whale's overall career reflects the stylistic ambitions and dramatic disappointments of an expressionist in the studio-controlled Hollywood of the thirties.

VII.
STRAINED
SERIOUSNESS

These are talented but uneven directors with the mortal sin of pretentiousness. Their ambitious projects tend to inflate rather than expand.

RICHARD BROOKS (1912–1992)

FILMS: 1950—Crisis. 1951—The Light Touch. 1952—*Deadline U.S.A.* 1953—Battle Circus, Take the High Ground. 1954—*The Last Time I Saw Paris.* 1955—*Blackboard Jungle.* 1956—*The Last Hunt,* The Catered Affair. 1957—Something of Value. 1958—The Brothers Karamazov, *Cat on a Hot Tin Roof.* 1960—*Elmer Gantry.* 1962—*Sweet Bird of Youth.* 1964—Lord Jim. 1966—*The Professionals.* 1967—*In Cold Blood.*

Richard Brooks is attracted to violent subjects, but his direction lacks the force to express them. His punches are seen but not felt, and his films consequently lack any lasting impact. The director's superficiality is applied impartially to Dostoyevsky and Chayefsky, Tennessee Williams and Robert Ruark, Sinclair Lewis and Evan Hunter. Brooks's sub-Proustian visualization in *Sweet Bird of Youth* and his facile Freudianizing for *In Cold Blood* are particularly damning proofs of an imagination more shallow than fallow. There has to be something wrong with an artist who searches for the kind of material he knows he will shamefully compromise. Although most of his films display something of value on first viewing, none can take the high ground in retrospect. However, there are moments in *The Last Hunt* and *The Professionals* when Brooks seems to be projecting a prophetic disillusion with individualism and liberalism in America. The conception is provocative, but the execution is excessively rhetorical. As one of the breed of writer-directors, Brooks has a bad habit of saying what he means without showing what he feels.

JACK CLAYTON (1921–   )

FILMS: 1959—*Room at the Top.* 1961—*The Innocents.* 1964—The Pumpkin Eater. 1967—Our Mother's House.

Jack Clayton represents the last word in academic direction. Every project must find its appropriate style. *Room at the Top* was nervously angry-young-mannish, *The Innocents* fluidly Jamesian, *The Pumpkin Eater* palpitatingly Pinteresque, and *Our Mother's House* Gothically Dickensian. The only Clayton constant is impersonality, but such studied impersonality seems out of date.

JULES DASSIN (1911–   )

FILMS: 1942—Nazi Agent, The Affairs of Martha, Reunion in France. 1943—Young Ideas. 1945—A Letter for Evie. 1946—Two Smart People. 1947—*Brute Force.* 1948—*The Naked City.* 1949—*Thieves' Highway.* 1950—*Night and the City.* 1956—*Rififi.* 1958—He Who Must Die. 1960—*Never on Sunday.* 1962—Phaedra. 1964—*Topkapi.* 1966—10:30 P.M. Summer. 1968—Survival! 1969—Up Tight!

Confronting a career that verges on the grotesque, one might say that it is easier to drive a director out of Hollywood than to drive Hollywood out of a director. Dassin's softheaded social consciousness has never obscured his minor talents. After the lumpy proletarianism of *He Who Must Die,* the ludicrous escapades of *Never on Sunday* and *Phaedra* seem more appropriate to the delirious director of *Brute Force* and *Night and the City.* If the works of Dassin's Mercourial period are not particularly mercurial, neither is much of the other transatlantic cinema that presumes to graft European intellectualism to American intelligence. Dassin remains a lively director in a minor key, and it is difficult to understand today why anything more was ever expected of him. For the record, Dassin's most famous films, *The Naked City* and *Rififi,* are among his lesser works.

RICHARD FLEISCHER (1916–   )

FILMS: 1946—Child of Divorce. 1947—Banjo. 1948—*So This Is New York.* 1949—Make Mine Laughs, The Clay Pigeon,

Follow Me Quietly, Trapped. 1950—Armored Car Robbery. 1952
—*The Narrow Margin,* The Happy Time. 1953—Arena. 1954—
20,000 Leagues Under the Sea. 1955—*Violent Saturday, The Girl
on the Red Velvet Swing.* 1956—*Bandido,* Between Heaven and
Hell. 1958—*The Vikings.* 1959—*These Thousand Hills, Compul-
sion.* 1960—Crack in the Mirror. 1961—The Big Gamble. 1962—
Barabbas. 1966—Fantastic Voyage. 1967—Dr. Dolittle. 1968—
The Boston Strangler.

Responsible critics have advanced Fleischer as a candidate for
Walsh's laurels in the adventure category. Since *The Narrow
Margin,* Fleischer's career has sputtered, alas, at less than 50
percent efficiency. That is, even if the director be given the bene-
fit of the doubt for *Violent Saturday, The Girl on the Red Velvet
Swing, Bandido, The Vikings,* and *These Thousand Hills.* On the
theory that a director must be judged by all his films rather than
by his more bearable ones, the burden of proof falls on Fleischer's champions. *Crack in the Mirror* alone would be sufficient to disqualify most directors from serious consideration. As
for *Compulsion,* the subject is still in search of an abler director.
More damning to Fleischer's reputation is the striking vapidity
of *The Happy Time,* the Dunne-like turgidity of *Between
Heaven and Hell,* the elaborate pointlessness of *The Big Gamble,* and the muddled mindlessness of the *Fantastic Voyage.*
Fleischer does get some points for his strenuous efforts in the
physical cinema, an addiction perhaps inherited from his cartoonist father, Max Fleischer, whose *Gulliver's Travels* failed to
dent the Disney monopoly back in 1939.

BRYAN FORBES (1926–   )

FILMS: 1962—Whistle Down the Wind. 1963—The L-
Shaped Room. 1964—*Seance on a Wet Afternoon.* 1965—*King
Rat.* 1966—*The Wrong Box.* 1967—The Whisperers. 1968—
Deadfall. 1969—The Madwoman of Chaillot.

The Whisperers is an apt title for a Bryan Forbes project. Indeed, the world of Bryan Forbes is one of wisps and whispers.
Whistle Down the Wind was muted allegory, *The L-Shaped*

Room muted soap opera, *Seance on a Wet Afternoon* muted melodrama, *King Rat* muted adventure, and *The Wrong Box* muted slapstick. Always nibbling at nuances, always straining for subtlety, never quite breaking an egg to make an omelet, never quite exploding a theme into dramatic excitement, Forbes perpetually pursues the anticliché only to arrive at anticlimax.

JOHN FRANKENHEIMER (1930–   )

FILMS: 1957—*The Young Stranger.* 1961—*The Young Savages.* 1962—*All Fall Down,* Birdman of Alcatraz, *The Manchurian Candidate.* 1964—Seven Days in May. 1965—The Train. 1966—Seconds, *Grand Prix.* 1968—The Fixer. 1969—The Gypsy Moths.

A director of parts at the expense of the whole, Frankenheimer betrays his television origins by pumping synthetic technique into penultimate scenes as if he had to grab the audience before the commercial break. The selective eclecticism of his first film, influenced as it was by Stevens and Reed, has degenerated into an all-embracing academicism, a veritable glossary of film techniques. A director capable of alternating shock cuts and slow dissolves is obviously sweating over his technique. Instead of building sequences, Frankenheimer explodes them prematurely, preventing his films from coming together coherently. Until *The Manchurian Candidate,* it was difficult to differentiate between the contradictions in the director's style and the confusion inherent in his material. The vaguely environmental focus on delinquency, criminality, libertinism, and hypocrisy in *The Young Stranger, The Young Savages, All Fall Down,* and *Birdman of Alcatraz* suggested a modern form of social consciousness in search of more sophisticated means of expression. But with George Axelrod's efficient blueprint for a modern thriller, Frankenheimer simply bungled the assignment by dawdling over the motivations of intermediate sequences. When a director flunks the kind of technical exercise a Gerd Oswald or a Blake Edwards would have passed with honors, it becomes difficult to honor his more serious aspirations. Ironically, Frankenheimer's stylistic eclecticism was ideally suited to the monstrous challenge of *Grand Prix,* a multimedia movie to make the most captious critic speed-struck and carsick.

SIDNEY J. FURIE (1933 —   )

FILMS: 1961—The Snake Woman, Doctor Blood's Coffin, During One Night, Three on a Spree. 1962—The Young Ones. 1963 —The Boys, The Leather Boys. 1964—Wonderful Life. 1965— The Ipcress File. 1966—The Appaloosa. 1967—The Naked Runner. 1969—The Lawyer.

Sidney J. Furie may be the most obsessively clinical of modern directors. *The Ipcress File* is rather antiseptic in its anti-Bond mannerisms, but its father-fixation ending with its psychically battered hero in the position of choosing which pater to perforate adds a new dimension to the sick cinema. From the black leather jackets of *The Leather Boys* to Marlon Brando's Indian blanket in *The Appaloosa,* Furie seems to elevate fabric fetishism into a personal style. Furie's films are more interesting visually than dramatically, but if *The Naked Runner* be any indication of development, his work is becoming less affecting and more affected.

NORMAN JEWISON

FILMS: 1962—40 Pounds of Trouble. 1963—The Thrill of It All. 1964—Send Me No Flowers. 1965—The Art of Love, *The Cincinnati Kid*. 1966—The Russians Are Coming. 1967—*In The Heat of the Night*. 1968—The Thomas Crown Affair. 1969—Gaily, Gaily. 1971—Fiddler on the Roof.

Norman Jewison has been guided from the very beginning of his career by a commendable desire to escape from the confines of a studio set to the great outdoors of reality. After all, cinema should move, and preferably outdoors. As a director of actors,

Jewison is reasonably good with good people—Steve Mc-Queen, Tuesday Weld, and Edward G. Robinson in *The Cincinnati Kid,* Alan Arkin in *The Russians Are Coming,* Sidney Poitier and Rod Steiger for *In the Heat of the Night.* Unfortunately, Jewison's films suffer from the director's compulsion to be strenuously cinematic. Jewison does not so much direct as overdirect and too often to diminishing returns. The historical timing of such projects as *The Russians Are Coming* and *In the Heat of the Night* has been so fortuitous that Jewison has found himself somewhat undeservedly at the top of the heap.

STANLEY KUBRICK (1928–   )

FILMS: 1953—Fear and Desire. 1955—Killer's Kiss. 1956 —*The Killing.* 1957—*Paths of Glory.* 1960—Spartacus. 1962— *Lolita.* 1964—*Dr. Strangelove* 1968—2001: A Space Odyssey. 1971 —Napoleon.

Back in 1963, I wrote off Kubrick thus: "His métier is projects rather than films, publicité rather than cinéma. He may wind up as the director of the best coming attractions in the industry, but time is running out on his projected evolution into a major artist. His unfortunate tendency to misapply Ophulsian camera movements to trivial diversions, and his increasing reluctance to express an apparently perverse personality, suggest that his career is at a standstill of his own devising. *Lolita* is his most irritating failure to date. With such splendid material, he emphasized the problem without the passion, the badness without the beauty, the agony without the ecstasy. What doth it avail a director if a project be presold to the whole world and he loseth his soul?"

In the five years since 1963, Kubrick has made two films— *Dr. Strangelove* and *2001: A Space Odyssey.* All in all, he has directed six films in a dozen years. (*Fear and Desire* and *Killer's Kiss* can be written off as strained experiments.) The very fact that he makes few films seems to confirm his stature among his champions. There is supposedly too much care and integrity in Kubrick to make him work more often. *Dr. Strangelove* clicked with most sophisticates largely because its irreverence seemed modish at the time and also because some of Terry Southern's lines punctuated the proceedings with the kind of belly laughs Vladimir Nabokov's lines lacked in *Lolita*. Still, the failure of *Lolita* seems more interesting and more personal in retrospect than the success of *Dr. Strangelove*. After the satiric alienation of *Dr. Strangelove*, Kubrick spent five years and ten million dollars on a science-fiction project so devoid of life and feeling as to render a computer called Hal the most sympathetic character in a jumbled scenario. *2001: A Space Odyssey* also confirms Kubrick's inability to tell a story on the screen with coherence and a consistent point of view. Kubrick's tragedy may have been that he was hailed as a great artist before he had become a competent craftsman. However, it is more likely that he has chosen to exploit the giddiness of middle-brow audiences on the satiric level of *Mad* magazine. Ultimately, Stanley Kubrick shares with Claude Lelouch a naïve faith in the power of images to transcend fuzzy feelings and vague ideas. The ending of *2001* qualifies in its oblique obscurity as Instant Ingmar.

RICHARD LESTER (1932–   )

FILMS: 1962—Ring-A-Ding Rhythm. 1964—*A Hard Day's Night*. 1965—The Knack . . . and How to Get It, *Help!* 1966—A Funny Thing Happened on the Way to the Forum. 1967—How I Won the War. 1968—Petulia. 1969—From the Hip, The Bed Sitting Room.

Richard Lester is the most fragmented director this side of Jean-Luc Godard, and his fragmentation is becoming increasingly irritating. He was mistaken at first for the long-awaited satirist of television commercials, but he has degenerated into the servant of the form, though not of course the content, of these same commercials. From the highwater mark of *A Hard Day's Night*, he has fallen to the piecemeal polemics of *How I Won the War*. It is now clear that one Beatle close-up is worth a thousand Lester cutups.

ALBERT LEWIN (1894–1968)

FILMS: 1942—*The Moon and Sixpence.* 1945—*The Picture of Dorian Gray.* 1947—The Private Affairs of Bel Ami. 1951—*Pandora and the Flying Dutchman.* 1954—Saadia. 1957—The Living Idol.

Jean Renoir said it all when he observed that Albert Lewin was too much of a theoretician. There is an ironic moment in *Pandora and the Flying Dutchman,* Lewin's most memorable film, when Ava Gardner has just defaced James Mason's painting of her, and the doomed painter declares that the desecration introduces the element of accident to his art. Would that there were more room for accident in Lewin's clogged literary narrations and his naïve conception of refinement in the cinema, a refinement that presumes to vulgarize Wilde, De Maupassant, and even Somerset Maugham for the sake of bringing kulchur to the masses. Still, Lewin's cultural evangelism is less offensive than most, and there are even moments of cinematic lucidity in the midst of all his literary elucidation. George Sanders was the Lewin actor par excellence, bored, cynical, decadent, and a bit threadbare. The most memorable face in the Lewin gallery is Hurd Hatfield's as Dorian Gray, a casting coup that Oscar Wilde would have applauded. It is in the surface snobbery of Hatfield's face that Lewin's sensibility can best be measured.

SIDNEY LUMET (1924–   )

FILMS: 1957—*Twelve Angry Men.* 1958—Stage Struck. 1959—*That Kind of Woman,* The Fugitive Kind. 1962—*View from the Bridge, Long Day's Journey into Night.* 1964—Fail Safe. 1965—*The Pawnbroker, The Hill.* 1966—*The Group.* 1968—*Bye Bye Braverman,* The Appointment. 1969—The Sea Gull.

At its best, Lumet's direction is efficiently vehicular but pleasantly impersonal. Sophia Loren and Tab Hunter come off much better in *That Kind of Woman* than do the stronger-willed Anna Magnani and Marlon Brando in *The Fugitive Kind*. The moral is clear. Those who would be led, Lumet will guide. Those who would lead, Lumet will follow. He lacks the necessary temperament of a tyrant on the set, but insists on remaining a constitutional monarch. When his subjects are responsible, as in *Long Day's Journey into Night,* his services are valuable. In most other instances, only his innate good taste saves him from utter mediocrity.

Lumet has tended to be a more venturesome producer-director in the past five years, and though his films are invariably flawed, the very variety of the challenges constitutes a kind of entertainment. *Fail Safe* is funnier unintentionally than *Dr. Strangelove* is intentionally, but there is something manically impressive about Lumet's direction of Walter Matthau and Fritz Weaver. *The Pawnbroker* might have been subtitled *Harlem Mon Amour* if Lumet were capable of regarding the pretentiousness of the project with any humor, but the masochism of *The Pawnbroker,* like the sadism of *The Hill,* depends for its execution upon a humorless temperament. *The Deadly Affair* is a dismal exercise except for the bright cameos of Harry Andrews and Lynn Redgrave; *The Group* is at best well-modulated mediocrity, and *Bye Bye Braverman* as courageous in its conception as it is vulgar in its execution, but here too Joseph Wiseman and Sorrell Brooke are marvelous, and George Segal ultimately affecting. Unfortunately, Lumet shows no sign of ever rising above the middle-brow aspirations of his projects to become the master rather than the mimic of the current trend away from Hollywood.

KAREL REISZ (1926–   )

FILMS: 1961—*Saturday Night and Sunday Morning.* 1964—Night Must Fall. 1966—*Morgan!* 1968—Isadora.

Karel Reisz has moved from the kitchen-sink mannerisms of *Saturday Night and Sunday Morning* to the mod mannerisms of

Morgan! without missing a beat. *Night Must Fall* is a disaster that can be charitably forgotten, *Isadora* a future prospect that can be eagerly anticipated. Reisz may be remembered ultimately as the screen Pygmalion to Vanessa Redgrave's Galatea, a Galatea moreover who is as effectively mannered for Reisz as she is as excruciatingly mannered for everyone else.

TONY RICHARDSON (1928–1991)

FILMS: 1959—Look Back in Anger. 1960—The Entertainer. 1961—Sanctuary. 1962—*A Taste of Honey, The Loneliness of the Long Distance Runner.* 1963—*Tom Jones.* 1965—The Loved One. 1966—Mademoiselle. 1967—The Sailor from Gibraltar. 1968—The Charge of the Light Brigade. 1969—Laughter in the Dark.

Tony Richardson has become the most prolific and the most prosperous of the *Sight and Sound* crop of directors, and ultimately the least respected. His authors have included Osborne, Faulkner, Delaney, Sillitoe, Duras, Fielding, and Waugh, his players Burton, Bloom, Olivier, Da Banzie, Plowright, Evans, Finney, Bates, Tushingham, Melvin, Courtenay, Redgrave (Michael), Redmond, Fox, York, Cilento, Steiger, Morse, Moreau, Bannen, and many others of exceptional talent. Curiously, Richardson is as effective a stage director as he is ineffective a screen director. With all the talent at his disposal, it is not surprising that most of his films have a few stirring moments. By any standard, his career has gone downhill since *Tom Jones,* but even in such highly regarded clusters of bits and pieces as *A Taste of Honey* and *The Loneliness of the Long Distance Runner,* Richardson's direction lacks any genuinely unifying force or conviction.

ROBERT ROSSEN (1908–1966)

FILMS: 1947—*Johnny O'Clock, Body and Soul.* 1949—*All the King's Men.* 1951—The Brave Bulls. 1955—Mambo. 1956—

Alexander the Great. 1957—Island in the Sun. 1959—They Came to Cordura. 1961—*The Hustler*. 1964—*Lilith*.

Back in 1963, I wrote of Rossen: "For all their seriousness of purpose, Rossen's films prove only that aspiration is no substitute for inspiration. A moralizer rather than a moralist, the director is always trying to say more than his technique can express. His characters consequently have a tendency to run down after talking themselves out. In all fairness to the director, it must be recorded that Rossen lost four years at a time when his work still seemed promising. (*Mambo* can be charged off to McCarthy.) In retrospect, however, the dreariness of Rossen's direction is remarkably consistent. *All the King's Men* is more pretentious than Walsh's *A Lion Is in the Streets,* but less forceful and less coherent. Similarly, *The Brave Bulls* is more grandiloquent than Boetticher's *The Bullfighter and the Lady,* but less personal and less moving. The point is that Rossen had stronger literary material to begin with, but then dissipated his advantage over Walsh and Boetticher in the transition from script to screen. To compensate for the lack of a visual style, Rossen picks at his characters in the name of psychological realism. Huey Long, Alexander the Great, and the Hustler meet on the same ignoble plane to engage in bizarre intrigues. The low point of psychological (and physiological) realism in the American cinema was probably reached in *They Came to Cordura* when contrite Rita Hayworth sacrificed herself to villainous Van Heflin so that Gary Cooper could get a safe night's sleep. The scabrousness of this intrigue only enhances the power and glory of a similar gambit in Hawks' *Red River*."

Robert Rossen made only one additional film—*Lilith*—before his death, and it was a failure according to the critical consensus, but it somehow upgraded Rossen's reputation as an artist with more feeling than facility. Rossen was never a natural, but *Lilith* was his noblest and most lyrical failure. *Lilith* is closer to the ridiculous at its worst than to the sublime at its best, but Rossen did take the risk of being ridiculed for the sake of Jean Seberg's ambiguous beauty. If Rossen had never been overrated, he would now be due for cultish rediscovery for *Body and Soul, All the King's Men, Johnny O'Clock, The Hustler,* and, above all, *Lilith*.

JOHN SCHLESINGER (1926–   )

FILMS: 1962—A Kind of Loving. 1963—*Billy Liar.* 1965—*Darling.* 1967—Far from the Madding Crowd. 1969—Midnight Cowboy.

John Schlesinger has not yet fully arrived in his permanent position in film history; but, come what may, he will deserve at the very least a footnote as the discoverer of Julie Christie. Originally one of the wave of working-class subject directors, Schlesinger came into his own with *Darling,* Britain's answer to *La Dolce Vita,* and one of the key works in the evolution of the swinging cinema. Schlesinger represents a new blend of pragmatism and experimentation in film making. He is particularly skilled in the direction of dialogue. Dirk Bogarde and Lawrence Harvey in *Darling,* Tom Courtenay in *Billy Liar,* Alan Bates in *A Kind of Loving* and *Far from the Madding Crowd,* Peter Finch and Terence Stamp in *Crowd* constitute a gallery of inspired performances and an index of the enormous supply of gifted British actors available to the English-speaking cinema. Unfortunately, Schlesinger lacks the directorial coherence to tie together his intermittent inspirations.

JOHN STURGES (1911–1992)

FILMS: 1946—The Man Who Dared, Shadowed. 1947—Alias Mr. Twilight, For the Love of Rusty, Keeper of the Bees. 1948—Best Man Wins, Sign of the Ram. 1949—*The Walking Hills.* 1950—*Mystery Street,* The Capture, The Magnificent Yankee, Right Cross. 1951—*Kind Lady, The People Against O'Hara,* It's a Big Country. 1952—The Girl in White. 1953—Jeopardy, Fast Company, *Escape from Fort Bravo.* 1955—*Bad Day at Black Rock,* Underwater, The Scarlet Coat. 1956—*Backlash.* 1957—Gunfight at the O.K. Corral. 1958—The Old Man and the Sea, The Law and Jake Wade. 1959—*Last Train from Gun Hill,* Never So Few. 1960—*The Magnificent Seven.* 1961—By Love Possessed. 1962—

Sergeants Three. 1963—*The Great Escape,* A Girl Named Tamiko. 1965—The Satan Bug, The Hallelujah Trail. 1967—*The Hour of the Gun.* 1969—Marooned.

Long before *The Magnificent Seven,* John Sturges seemed to be striving, albeit unconsciously, to become the American Kurosawa, tortured, humorless, and self-consciously social. Come to think of it, is there much difference between Spencer Tracy's karate crusade in *Bad Day at Black Rock* and Toshiro Mifune's samurai swordplay in *Yojimbo?* If Kurosawa has an advantage here, it is because his personality is more attuned to violence and misanthropy. Unfortunately, it is hard to remember why Sturges's career was ever considered meaningful. How naïve it was, for example, to deduce that Sturges had solved the problems of Cinemascope by his allegorical groupings in the aforementioned *Bad Day at Black Rock.* Even in the era of *Mystery Street, The People Against O'Hara,* and *Escape From Fort Bravo,* the director's easily acquired reputation as an expert technician was incomprehensible. Where Daves attracts attention with his debasing crane, Kubrick with his meaningless tracks, and Wise with the IBM perforations of his montage, Sturges's stock-in-trade for superficial visual analysis is the wasteful pan. The fact that *The Great Escape* is as successful as *The Hallelujah Trail* is unsuccessful indicates not only that Steve McQueen is a more persuasive personality than Burt Lancaster but also that Sturges should work exclusively in the serious if not solemn action genre.

ROBERT WISE (1914—   )

FILMS: 1944—*Curse of the Cat People,* Mlle. Fifi. 1945—*The Body Snatcher,* A Game of Death. 1946—Criminal Court. 1947—Born to Kill. 1948—Mystery in Mexico, Blood on the Moon. 1949—*The Set-Up.* 1950—Two Flags West, Three Secrets. 1951—The House on Telegraph Hill, *The Day the Earth Stood Still.* 1952—The Captive City, Something for the Birds. 1953—Destination Gobi, The Desert Rats, So Big. 1954—*Executive Suite.* 1955—Helen of Troy. 1956—Tribute to a Bad Man, *Somebody Up There Likes Me.* 1957—This Could Be the Night, Until They Sail.

1958—Run Silent, Run Deep; *I Want to Live*. 1959—*Odds Against Tomorrow*. 1961—*West Side Story* (with Jerome Robbins). 1962—Two for the Seesaw. 1963—The Haunting. 1965—*The Sound of Music*. 1966—The Sand Pebbles. 1968—Star!

Robert Wise was marked as a director to watch very early in his career. Among Val Lewton alumni, he occupies a middle position between Jacques Tourneur at the top and Mark Robson at the bottom. His temperament is vaguely liberal, his style vaguely realistic; but after *The Sound of Music* and *The Sand Pebbles*, the stylistic signature of Robert Wise is indistinct to the point of invisibility. Even the unity-of-time experiment of *The Set-Up* and the click-clack cutting of *Executive Suite* seem to belong in another era entirely. Although montage is not out, as Bazin had once proclaimed, academic montage can no longer function as an adequate means of expression even for the cutter of *Citizen Kane* and *The Magnificent Ambersons*. What has happened to Wise in the fifties and sixties has happened to most technicians without a strong personality. The strained techniques of *Odds Against Tomorrow, Two for the Seesaw,* and *The Haunting* are more elaborate than expressive. For example, the split-screen conception borrowed from the stage version of *Two for the Seesaw* actually defeats the mood of the story. When two people are shown in the same frame, their loneliness is not being expressed visually. Still, Wise's conscientious craftsmanship is something of a virtue in these days of giddy chaos. The commercial success of *The Sound of Music* is a tribute to Wise's ability to treat the most sentimental material with a straight face.

VIII.
ODDITIES, ONE-SHOTS, AND NEWCOMERS

These are the eccentrics, the exceptions and the expectants, the fallen stars and the shooting stars. They defy more precise classification by their very nature.

LINDSAY ANDERSON (1923–1994)

FILMS: 1963—*The Sporting Life*. 1966—The White Bus. Short Subjects: Thursday's Children, O Dreamland. 1968—If.

Lindsay Anderson came to the cinema with a reputation as a controversial critic scornful of both Philistinism and dandyism. He has been associated with such oversimplified catchwords as "commitment" and "Free Cinema," but he has striven in *This Sporting Life* and *The White Bus* to express a subtle, supple, and highly individualized sensibility. Nonetheless there has been a tendency to lump Lindsay Anderson together with Karel Reisz, Tony Richardson, John Schlesinger, Jack Clayton, and Desmond Davis in the school of so-called British realism. Anderson, like his French counterparts swept ashore on the "New Wave," disdains such facile categories as mere journalistic conveniences. Both as critic and film-maker, he has remained skeptical of the alleged glories of improvisation. He believes firmly in the value of preparation both with scripts and performers, and he is not ashamed of adapting a novel to the screen. When he was the leading luminary of the *Sequence-Sight-and-Sound* generation of the late forties and early fifties, he revealed a taste capable of embracing simultaneously the works of John Ford, Jean Cocteau, and Vincente Minnelli. He has directed many plays, and has otherwise remained in the forefront of the New Look in British culture. It may be that Anderson is more a critical influence than a creative force. In this, Lindsay Anderson resembles such French critic-creators as Eric Rohmer and Jacques Rivette.

GEORGE AXELROD (1922—)

FILMS: 1966—*Lord Love a Duck*. 1968—The Secret Life of an American Wife.

George Axelrod had been involved as a controversial middleman between Max Shulman and Leo McCarey on *Rally Round the*

Flag, Boys! and between Truman Capote and Blake Edwards on *Breakfast at Tiffany's.* Axelrod, like Paddy Chayefsky, found the role of writer-producer peculiarly frustrating in an industry oriented more and more toward the director. *Lord Love a Duck* was Axelrod's opportunity to fall flat on his face, but he proved to be surprisingly adept at rendering his own very personal comic vision. Tuesday Weld under Axelrod's direction captured all the sweetness of Nabokov's *Lolita* so lacking in Kubrick's sour direction of Sue Lyon. In addition, Axelrod's zany direction of Roddy Macdowall, Martin West, Lola Albright, and Ruth Gordon revealed a variety of tone and mood hitherto unexpressed in his writing for Broadway and Hollywood.

JOHN BOORMAN (1933–   )

FILMS: 1965—Having a Wild Weekend. 1967—*Point Blank.* 1968—Hell in the Pacific. 1969—Rosencrantz and Guildenstern Are Dead.

John Boorman's sense of architecture in *Point Blank* is stunning, and the curiously bleak rather than cool intermingling of morality, sexuality, and violence makes *Point Blank* more edifying than either *Bonnie and Clyde* or *The Graduate.* There is a bit too much jazzy crosscutting à la Resnais, and Boorman often wallows in an effect, but his direction of Lee Marvin and Angie Dickinson make him a director to watch. Even if *Point Blank* should turn out to be a one-shot for its director, it would deserve lasting admiration for treading over the slick surfaces of evil with the squeaky shoes of morality.

MARLON BRANDO (1924–   )

FILM: 1961—One-Eyed Jacks.

For all his decadent narcissism and self-indulgence, Brando remains one of the most fascinating actors in the cinema. If he has reached the point where he is unable to or unwilling to take strong direction, self-direction would seem a wiser course than weak direction. *One-Eyed Jacks* is quite charming in a disorganized sort of way, with Brando's Western hero closer to Heathcliff than to Hopalong Cassidy, but *The Ugly American,* under Ken Englund's subservient direction, is completely worthless.

PETER BROOK (1925–   )

FILMS: 1953—The Beggar's Opera. 1960—Moderato Cantabile. 1962—*Lord of the Flies.* 1967—*Marat / Sade.* 1968—Tell Me Lies.

Peter Brook is interesting mainly as an emissary traveling freely and frequently between the modern theatre and the modern cinema. His films serve as extensions of his ideas about the ultimate direction and destination the cinema must follow. *Moderato Cantabile* is an exercise in languorous introspection of the Resnais–*Hiroshima Mon Amour* school. *The Lord of the Flies* is an expedition in search of inspired improvisation. Brook himself remains a stimulating and articulate spokesman for the growing interdependence of the theatre and the motion picture.

Marat / Sade and *Tell Me Lies* represent Brook's unsuccessful attempts to transpose the theatre of cruelty to the screen without any appreciable formal or intellectual erosion. Unfortunately, Brook has always been more intellectually provocative than artistically successful. *The Beggar's Opera, Moderato Cantabile, Lord of the Flies,* and *Marat / Sade* all looked better on the drawing board than on the screen despite impressive castings and performances of such as Olivier, Belmondo, Moreau, McGee, (Ian) Richardson, and the little boy who played Piggy. Brook seems to have used up all his artistic options from the extreme determinism of *Moderato Cantabile* to the extreme improvisation of *Lord of the Flies,* but *Tell Me Lies* provides an entirely new set of cinematic conceptions that miscarry in the messiest ways imaginable.

JOHN CASSAVETES (1929–1989)

FILMS: 1961—Shadows. 1962—Too Late Blues, A Child Is Waiting. 1968—Faces. 1969—Husbands.

John Cassavetes remains an unresolved talent, not entirely happy with the Establishment or against it. His direction, like his acting, hovers between offbeat improvisation and blatant contrivance. Somehow his timing always seems to be off a beat or two even when he understands what he is doing. Too much of the time he is groping when he should be gripping. At his best, however, he makes emotional contact with his material, and transforms his humblest players into breathing, feeling beings.

JAMES CLAVELL (1925–   )

FILMS: 1959—Five Gates to Hell. 1960—Walk Like a Dragon. 1967—To Sir, With Love. 1968—Where's Jack?

James Clavell teeters on the thin line between ideas and gimmicks as a writer and/or director of unusual subjects. He seems particularly attracted to interracial problem parables (*Walk Like a Dragon; To Sir, With Love*) and military adventure allegories (*Five Gates to Hell, The Great Escape, King Rat*). The latter two films are among the most effective entertainments dispensed respectively by directors John Sturges and Bryan Forbes. Clavell's own direction ranges from sub-Fuller (*Hell, Dragon*) to super-Kramer (*To Sir*).

HAROLD CLURMAN (1901–   )

FILM: 1946—Deadline at Dawn.

Back when the Group Theatre was camped in Hollywood, Clurman came up with a film that today resembles nothing so much as
a parody of poetic social consciousness. Yet there, in the middle
of all the fakery, was Susan Hayward, pure Brooklyn and pure
Hollywood, and infinitely more real and lasting than the WPA.

FRANCIS FORD COPPOLA (1939–   )

FILMS: 1962—Dementia. 1967—*You're A Big Boy Now*.
1968—Finian's Rainbow. 1969—The Rain People.

Francis Ford Coppola is probably the first reasonably talented
and sensibly adaptable directorial talent to emerge from a university curriculum in film-making. *You're A Big Boy Now*
seemed remarkably eclectic even under the circumstances. If the
direction of Nichols on *The Graduate* has an edge on Coppola's
for *Big Boy,* it is that Nichols borrows only from good movies
whereas Coppola occasionally borrows from bad ones. Curiously, Coppola seems infinitely more merciful to his grotesques
than does anything-for-an-effect Nichols. Coppola may be heard
from more decisively in the future.

ROGER CORMAN (1926–   )

FILMS: 1955—Apache Woman, The Intruder, Five Guns
West. 1957—Not of This Earth, Attack of the Crab Monsters,
Teenage Doll, Sorority Girl. 1958—War of the Satellites, I, Mob-
ster. 1959—A Bucket of Blood. 1960—The House of Usher. 1961
—The Pit and the Pendulum. 1962—Premature Burial, I Hate
Your Guts, Poe's Tales of Terror, Tower of London. 1963—*The
Raven*, The Young Racers, The Haunted Palace, *"X" The Man with
the X-Ray Eyes*. 1964—*The Masque of the Red Death*, The Secret
Invasion. 1966—*The Wild Angels*. 1967—*The St. Valentine's Day
Massacre*, The Trip.

Roger Corman's outstanding achievement to date is *The Masque
of the Red Death*, but on the whole he seems much stronger
visually than dramatically. His acting is usually atrocious, and

his feeling for dialogue uncertain. It is quite possible that he is miscast, like Mankiewicz, Wyler, and Wise, as a director, when he would be much more effective as a producer.

DESMOND DAVIS (1928–)

FILMS: 1964—*Girl With Green Eyes.* 1966—The Uncle, Time Lost and Time Remembered (I Was Happy Here). 1967—Smashing Time. 1969—A Nice Girl Like Me.

Desmond Davis has been sliding downhill since *Girl With Green Eyes,* itself a curious blend of folk caricature and *nouvelle vague* artiness. There is a distinctive sensibility at work in his films, but his means of expression are too muddled and pretentious. The idea of pairing Rita Tushingham and Lynn Redgrave in *Smashing Time* should have been resisted at all costs, and it is a measure of the director's excess that he should flaunt the frightening antisexual implications of this oddest of odd couples.

THEODORE J. FLICKER

FILMS: 1964—The Troublemaker. 1967—The President's Analyst.

Theodore J. Flicker is one of the few exemplars of the New Yorkish cabaret sensibility at large in Hollywood. Flicker seems aware of the pitfalls of excessively satiric conceptions, perhaps too aware. He seems overly conscious of the risks of audacity and insufficiently receptive to the opportunities. His gibes at J. Edgar Hoover and the CIA in *The President's Analyst* were welcome, but he seems too much of the time to be working the high trapeze of irreverence with the net of conformist calculation.

BERNARD GIRARD (1930–)

FILM: 1966—*Dead Heat on a Merry-Go-Round.* 1969—The Mad Room.

Bernard Girard has made an interesting debut as writer-director of *Dead Heat on a Merry-Go-Round,* but it is difficult to imagine where he can go from here. *Dead Heat* seems complete and definitive as the expression of a chilling sophistication in the treatment of the big caper genre. There is something so inhuman in the directorial attitude revealed that *Dead Heat* seems like a dead end.

ROBERT GIST

FILM: 1966—An American Dream.

An American Dream can be described with some affection as the worst picture of its year because of the hilarious misalliance of Mailer and Hollywood. Robert Gist's direction lingers in the mind in spite of, or perhaps because of, this very misalliance. His stylistic conviction deserves another chance with less intransigent material.

CURTIS HARRINGTON (1928–   )

FILMS: 1942–1955—Fall of the House of Usher, Crescendo, Renascence, Fragment of Seeking, Picnic, On the Edge, Dangerous Houses, The Assignation, The Wormwood Star (Experimental Shorts). 1961—Night Tide. 1966—Queen of Blood. 1967—Games.

Curtis Harrington is the most consciously Sternbergian of the cinéastes of the sixties, and his films reflect the triumph of décor over drama. *Games* comes closest to bridging the gap between the hopelessly self-indulgent symbolism of *Night Tide* and the very conventional attitude Harrington brings to the working out of his plots. Harrington probably needs most a producer like the late Val Lewton. Up to now, however, his films have lacked the finer instincts of Sternberg's. Harrington's glossy surfaces have the feel of Sternberg, but not the feelings.

HARVEY HART (1928–1989)

FILMS: 1965—*Bus Riley's Back in Town,* Dark Intruder. 1968 —The Sweet Ride.

Harvey Hart and his Canadian colleagues—Jewison, Furie, Narizzano, Hiller, et al.—seem stronger on technique than personality. Nonetheless Hart's direction of *Bus Riley's Back in Town* almost transcended the egregiousness of William Inge's maudlin memories of the Middle West.

BEN HECHT (1893–1964) &
CHARLES MACARTHUR (1895–1956)

FILMS: 1934—*Crime Without Passion.* 1935—Once in a Blue Moon, *The Scoundrel.* 1936—Soak the Rich. Hecht is credited with direction of three other films without MacArthur: 1940— *Angels Over Broadway* (with Lee Garmes). 1946—Specter of the Rose. 1952—Actors and Sin.

Ben Hecht and Charles MacArthur decided to beat Hollywood at its own game with their own special brand of Broadway sophistication. Together with Noel Coward, they fashioned in *The Scoundrel* the most entertaining exposure of Broadway's notion of sophistication ever filmed. Hecht and MacArthur were a great deal of fun, but they seem even more frivolous today than many of the Hollywood characters they ridiculed.

HOWARD HUGHES (1905–1976)

FILMS: 1930—Hell's Angels. 1943—The Outlaw.

Hughes has been caricatured and vilified from *The Barefoot Contessa* to *The Carpetbaggers.* He has been accused of destroying the American career of Jean Simmons, and of rejecting Bette Davis as an actress because she lacked sex appeal. The fact remains that his record as a director and a producer is far more interesting than his lurid reputation would indicate. Anyone who has produced *Scarface, Jet Pilot, Mad Wednesday, Angel Face,* and *Two Arabian Knights* cannot be all bad. To his credit, Hughes has never been as sanctimonious about his "art" as have those revered oracles of mediocrity, Samuel Goldwyn and Dore Schary. At the very least, Hughes is entitled to a sociological footnote for sponsoring the bosom craze that swept the world through Jane Russell's sullen bustiness in *The Outlaw*. (Two good reasons why every red-blooded American boy should see this movie are self-evident; the third exploded over Hiroshima in 1945.)

GENE KELLY (1912–1996)

FILMS: With Stanley Donen: 1949—*On the Town.* 1952— *Singin' in the Rain.* 1955—*It's Always Fair Weather.* Solo: 1956— Invitation to the Dance. 1957—The Happy Road. 1958—Tunnel of Love. 1962—Gigot. 1967—Guide for the Married Man. 1969 —Hello, Dolly.

The charm and brilliance of Gene Kelly's dancing has not carried over to his direction since the dissolution of his partnership with Donen. If Donen has since diminished, Kelly has completely disintegrated. Kelly's potentialities as a straight actor were never fully developed, and the Metro musical died before his musical ideas had been fully expressed. *Invitation to the Dance* was an uneasy mixture of Hollywood formulas and European pretensions, and *Gigot* was pure slop out of the gutters of an expatriate's Paris. Yet, *Singin' in the Rain* can never be tarnished by the subsequent derelictions of its participants.

BUZZ KULIK (1923–   )

FILMS: 1961—The Explosive Generation. 1963—*The Yellow Canary.* 1964—Ready for the People. 1967—*Warning Shot.* 1968—Sergeant Ryker, Villa Rides!, The Riot.

Buzz Kulik reveals an interesting glimmer of intelligence in *The Yellow Canary* and *Warning Shot*. He is from television, perhaps too much so. *Sergeant Ryker* has created considerable ill will by charging first-run movie prices for an attraction so obviously designed for television that the audience can almost see the test patterns.

CHARLES LAUGHTON (1899–1962)

FILM: 1955—*The Night of the Hunter.*

Rumor has it that the final shooting script of *The Night of the Hunter* was one-third Laughton, one-third James Agee, and one-third Davis Grubb. Be that what it may, *The Night of the Hunter* displays a striking visual style, almost semi-Germanic Griffith, which is completely lacking in the Huston-Agee-Forester *The African Queen* and the Windust-Agee-Crane *The Bride Came to Yellow Sky*. Moral: Directors, not writers, are the ultimate auteurs of the cinema, at least of cinema that has any visual meaning and merit.

IRVING LERNER (1909–   )

FILMS: 1954—Man Crazy. 1958—Edge of Fury, *Murder by Contract*. 1959—City of Fear. 1960—Studs Lonigan. 1963—Cry of Battle.

Murder by Contract is a minor classic of murderous understatement, and is all that need be said about Irving Lerner's career. Perhaps it is a mistake to treat films like *Murder by Contract* as means to an end or as overtures to grand operas. A director, like any artist, may have but one good work in his system. Often the promising work turns out to be the ultimate work, and *Murder by Contract* seems to fall into that category.

IDA LUPINO (1918–1995)

FILMS: 1949—Not Wanted. 1950—Outrage, Never Fear. 1951—Hard, Fast and Beautiful. 1953—The Bigamist, The Hitch-Hiker. 1965—The Trouble with Angels. Note: *Not Wanted* was actually directed by Elmer Clifton, but Ida Lupino produced and wrote the screenplay and presumably served her technical apprenticeship with the silent-movie veteran.

Ida Lupino's directed films express much of the feeling if little of the skill which she has projected so admirably as an actress. But while we are on the subject: Lillian Gish, that actress of actresses, once directed a film (*Remodeling Her Husband*—1921), and declared afterward that directing was no job for a lady. Simone de Beauvoir would undoubtedly argue the contrary, but relatively few women have put the matter to the test. Dorothy Arzner, Jacqueline Audrey, Mrs. Sidney Drew, Lilian Ducey, Julia Crawford Ivers, Frances Marion, Vera McCord, Frances Nordstrom, Mrs. Wallace Reid, Lois Weber, and Margery Wilson come to mind as little more than a ladies' auxiliary. (The unwary historian might also include such certified males as Monta Bell and Marion Gering). A special footnote must be devoted to the widow of Alexander Dovjenko, particularly for such séance productions as *Poem from the Sea* and *Years of Fire*. A longer and considerably more controversial footnote would be devoted to Leni Riefenstahl, more for the relative objectivity of her *Olympiad* than for the blatant contrivance of *Triumph of the Will*. The jury is still out on Vera Chytilova, Shirley Clarke, Juleen Compton, Joan Littlewood, Nadine Trintingnant, Agnes Varda, and Mai Zetterling.

ROBERT MONTGOMERY (1904–1981)

FILMS: 1946—Lady in the Lake. 1947—*Ride the Pink Horse*. 1949—*Once More, My Darling*. 1950—Eye Witness. 1960—Gallant Hours.

Robert Montgomery always admired James Cagney's acting, and Cagney always admired Montgomery's, but neither actor received the direction he deserved, except on the rarest occasions, Montgomery with Hitchcock (*Mr. and Mrs. Smith*) and Ford (*They Were Expendable*), Cagney with Walsh (*White Heat*) and Ray (*Run for Cover*). Montgomery directed Cagney in *Gallant Hours* period. Otherwise, Montgomery achieved some notoriety with his subjective camera in *Lady in the Lake,* coaxed a memorable performance out of Wanda Hendrix in *Ride the Pink Horse,* executed a charming *champ-contre-champ* joke in *Once More, My Darling;* and went to Britain to make *Eye Witness,* a film not entirely devoid of merit.

MIKE NICHOLS (1931–   )

FILMS: 1967—Who's Afraid of Virginia Woolf? 1968—*The Graduate.* 1969—Catch-22.

Everything Mike Nichols has touched on stage and screen has turned to gold if not glory. Why then do there remain little pockets of cultural resistance to his magical manipulation? He was criticized, perhaps unjustly, for taking *Virginia Woolf* out of doors into shivering cinematic reality. Richard Burton gave a good performance; Elizabeth Taylor was monotonously shrill; Sandy Dennis was excruciatingly mannered; George Segal was excessively bland. The film seemed to preen itself on its honesty. But why were the settings so expressively sloppy? Was this an example of the subtlety that Nichols was bringing to Hollywood? Many critics thought so. The public thought so. Mike Nichols stood up to receive the directorial award from the Directors Guild of America, but the calling of his name turned out to be a mistake. Fred Zinnemann, a director infinitely duller and more "honest" than Nichols, was tapped for the dry-as-dust academics of *A Man for All Seasons.*

Whereas Nichols merely transferred *Virginia Woolf,* he transcended *The Graduate.* Nichols was not cashing in on the Burtons and Edward Albee with *The Graduate.* Anne Bancroft,

Dustin Hoffman, and Katherine Ross had little marquee value of their own, and Charles Webb's novel little presold potency. Nichols had turned the trick with a neatly eclectic style borrowed from directors as disparate as Federico Fellini and George Stevens, Ingmar Bergman and Richard Lester, Michelangelo Antonioni and Orson Welles. His supporting actors were dreadfully caricatured. The suspicion persisted in shamefully skeptical circles that Nichols was more a tactician than a strategist and that he won every battle and lost every war because he was incapable of the divine folly of a personal statement. No American director since Orson Welles had started off with such a bang, but Welles had followed his own road, and that made all the difference. Nichols seems too shrewd ever to get off the main highway. His is the cinema and theatre of complicity. And the customer is always right except in the long view of eternity.

CHRISTIAN NYBY (1913–)

FILMS: 1951—*The Thing*. 1965—Operation C.I.A. 1967—First to Fight.

The Thing, with its understandable traces of Producer Howard Hawks and its unearthly traces of uncredited Orson Welles, remains an inexplicable incident in Nyby's otherwise negligible career.

ROBERT PARRISH (1916–)

FILMS: 1951—The Mob, *Cry Danger*. 1952—Assignment Paris, My Pal Gus. 1953—Shoot First. 1955—*The Purple Plain*, Lucy Gallant. 1957—*Fire Down Below*. 1958—Saddle the Wind. 1959—*The Wonderful Country*. 1963—In the French Style. 1965—Up from the Beach. 1967—The Bobo. 1968—Duffy. 1969—Doppelganger.

The Purple Plain stands out in the above list like a pearl among swine. What burst of Buddhist contemplation was responsible for such a haunting exception to such an exceptionable career? Apart from *The Purple Plain,* the films of Robert Parrish belong to a director who craves anonymity.

SAM PECKINPAH (1925–1984)

FILMS: 1962—The Deadly Companions, *Ride the High Country.* 1965—*Major Dundee.* 1968—The Wild Bunch.

Ride the High Country was considered the sleeper of its year, but was it? At first glance, the film represented a fusion of the Boetticher-Scott and Tourneur-McCrea traditions, but then it turned out that its director grudgingly accepted Randolph Scott and Joel McCrea and the myths they incarnated simply for the sake of daubs of atmospheric realism from Peckinpah's palette. *Ride the High Country* is thus in retrospect something new in anti-Westerns. The trials and tribulations of *Major Dundee* confirmed the pattern of Peckinpah's ambitions. Since Peckinpah considers himself too intellectual to tell a story, it remains to be seen whether he will be forceful enough to develop a theme.

FRANK PERRY (1930–   )

FILMS: 1962—*David and Lisa.* 1963—Ladybug, Ladybug. 1968—*The Swimmer,* Trilogy. 1969—Last Summer.

David and Lisa brought fame and fortune to Frank and Eleanor Perry, and everyone said it was a case of a good script awkwardly directed because Frank Perry had never directed a movie before, and it is generally assumed that direction is more a craft than an art as writing is more an art than a craft. Actually, *David and Lisa* is rather awkwardly written and rather interestingly directed. Despite the disaster of *Ladybug, Ladybug,* it would seem that more may be heard from the Perrys before *David and Lisa* is written off once and for all as a one-shot. At the very least, Perry deserves attention for the disciplined performances of Keir Dullea and Janet Margolin.

ABE POLONSKY (1910–   )

FILMS: 1948—*Force of Evil.* 1968—Willie Boy.

William Pechter's astute analysis of Polonsky's career in the Spring 1962 issue of *Film Quarterly* confirms that Polonsky's influence was decisive over Rossen's in Garfield's companion vehicle, *Body and Soul.* Polonsky, along with Chaplin and Losey, remains one of the great casualties of the anti-Communist hysteria of the fifties. *Force of Evil* stands up under repeated viewings as one of the great films of the modern American cinema, and Garfield's taxicab scene with Beatrice Pearson takes away some of the luster from Kazan's Brando-Steiger tour de force in *On the Waterfront.*

STUART ROSENBERG (1927–   )

FILMS: 1960—*Murder Inc.* (with Burt Balaban). 1961— Question 7. 1967—*Cool Hand Luke.* 1968—The April Fools. 1969 —The Lenny Bruce Story.

Stuart Rosenberg has had an intermittent movie career in between piling up prestigious credits in television. *Cool Hand Luke* is his most striking achievement to date and one of many recent manifestations of a tendency in the American cinema to use visual virtuosity as an end in itself. *Point Blank, Bonnie and Clyde,* and *In the Heat of the Night* are other examples of films that undercut the conventions of their genres by escaping the controlled studio environments in which the conventions were carefully contrived in terms of light and shadow. Rosenberg, like Boorman (*Point Blank*), Penn (*Bonnie and Clyde*), and Jewison (*In the Heat of the Night*) tends to a certain stylistic eclecticism in rendering scripts that strive very consciously for a Europeanized ambiguity. For all its effectiveness as entertainment, *Cool Hand Luke* seems too histrionic and exhibitionistic for comfort. What is wrong with *Cool Hand Luke* seems less a matter of compromise than miscalculation. Even in the midst of monumental mistakes, Rosenberg's direction is capable of tasteful touches. Nothing, particularly the villainy, ever gets completely out of hand.

ELLIOT SILVERSTEIN

FILMS: 1962—Belle Sommers. 1965—*Cat Ballou.* 1967— *The Happening.* 1969—A Man Called Horse.

Elliot Silverstein's directorial career virtually came out of nowhere with *Cat Ballou.* (*Belle Sommers* was not exactly nowhere, at least not in terms of quality, but Silverstein himself has preferred to begin his official career with *Cat Ballou* much as Preminger begins with *Laura,* Stevens with *Alice Adams* and Zinnemann with *The Search.*) *Cat Ballou* won an Oscar for Lee Marvin and the ire of serious admirers of the Western, a genre that traditionally defies parody and satire. Silverstein then stubbed his toe on *The Happening,* a generation-gap kidnaping comedy-melodrama that was as underrated by the reviewers as *Cat Ballou* was overrated. What is most distinctive about Silverstein's directorial personality is not so much a smart-alecky attitude toward his material as a penchant for Jewish humor in the unlikeliest situations.

ALEXANDER SINGER (1932–)

FILMS: 1961—*Cold Wind in August.* 1964—Psyche 59. 1965—Love Has Many Faces.

Alexander Singer's screen subjects have become increasingly sordid, and his career increasingly dubious. *Cold Wind in August* still sparkles with Lola Albright's distinctively hip brand of sensuality. Singer was almost as adept with Patricia Neal and Samantha Eggar in *Psyche 59,* but the fading stars and starlets of *Love Has Many Faces*—Lana Turner, Ruth Roman, and Virginia Grey—take the director into the dreaded country of camp. The suspicion persists that Singer is better than his material, but that there is something in the very worst material that attracts his attention. Curiously, Lana Turner, Ruth Roman, and Virginia Grey, and their assorted gigolos are more affecting than they have any right to be. Perhaps Singer has become the poet of the rejected woman while commercially exploiting the subject of the fallen woman.

JACK SMIGHT (1926–   )

FILMS: 1964—I'd Rather Be Rich. 1965—The Third Day. 1966—Harper, *Kaleidoscope.* 1968—The Secret War of Harry Frigg, *No Way to Treat a Lady,* The Illustrated Man. 1969—Rabbit, Run.

Jack Smight's directorial career has been settling into an interesting pattern. *Harper, Kaleidoscope,* and *No Way to Treat a Lady* are very weakly directed on the action and suspense levels. *Lady* is particularly unbelievable whenever New York City is integrated into the action as an exterior set. The same police car hurtles down the same academically neonized corridor of Forty-second Street three times in succession like a recurring refrain in a visual verse by Cocteau. Where Smight excels is in the tensions and humors of offbeat relationships enacted by Paul Newman and Arthur Hill in *Harper,* Susanna York, Clyde Revill, and Murray Melvin in *Kaleidoscope,* and George Segal and Lee Remick in *No Way to Treat a Lady.*

PETER TEWKSBURY (1924–   )

FILMS: 1964—*Sunday in New York,* Emil and the Detectives. 1967—Doctor, You've Got to Be Kidding. 1968—Stay Away, Joe.

Peter Tewksbury's direction is invariably more graceful than his material deserves. *Sunday in New York* was cursed with Norman Krasna's nasty plot contrivances despite the pleasant casting of Jane Fonda, Cliff Robertson, and Rod Taylor, not to mention the moderately miraculous metamorphosis of Jo Morrow from plump ingenue to sleek siren. *Emil and the Detectives* may have been handicapped somewhat by the demands of the Disney Organization, and *Doctor, You've Got to be Kidding* by one's preconceptions about Sandra Dee. Still, Tewskbury has persevered with his pleasantness, and such perseverance should be both recorded and rewarded.

PETER WATKINS (1935–   )

FILMS: 1967—The War Game, Privilege.

Peter Watkins would become the Cromwell of film directors if he were given half a chance, and he has been given at least one and a half chances. *The War Game* represents for some the triumph of content over form, for others the triumph of paranoia over perception. *Privilege* manages to be more hysterical than *The War Game* with less provocation. Watkins seems to feel strongly and deeply about the state of the world, but he is so lacking in humor and balance and distance that he would probably wail and whine in Paradise itself. Significantly fallacious is his insistence that Paul Jones's natural charm as a singer and performer be suppressed for the sake of the theme.

JOHN WAYNE (1907–1979)

FILMS: 1960—The Alamo. 1968—The Green Berets.

Rumor has it that the old master himself, John Ford, directed some of *The Alamo*. Nevertheless, Wayne's epic style reveals enough individual visual beauties amid the oratorical bombast to encourage another try on a less pretentious scale. Unfortunately, *The Green Berets* seems like another trap.

JACK WEBB (1920–1982)

FILMS: 1954—Dragnet. 1955—*Pete Kelley's Blues.* 1957—The D.I. 1959— –30–. 1961—The Last Time I Saw Archie.

Jack Webb's directed movies are rather peculiar manifestations of the techniques of his television series—*Dragnet.* Enormous close-ups of faces with clipped, understated dialogue, visual shouting combined with verbal whispering. The movies never clicked with the critics or the public, possibly because Webb's style was too controlled for the little he had to say.

PAUL WENDKOS (1922–   )

FILMS: 1957—*The Burglar.* 1958—*The Case Against Brooklyn,* Tarawa Beachhead. 1959—Gidget, *Face of a Fugitive,* Battle of the Coral Sea. 1960—Because They're Young. 1961—*Angel Baby,* Gidget Goes Hawaiian. 1963—Gidget Goes to Rome. 1966—Johnny Tiger. 1968—Guns of the Magnificent Seven, Attack on the Iron Coast. 1969—Hellboats.

Paul Wendkos is teetering somewhere between Arthur Penn and John Frankenheimer, with frequent detours to the *Gidget* genre. His ideas about the relationship between form and content are still scrambled, and his career thus far is consistent only in its inconsistency. Perhaps Welles is a dangerous influence on any young director. Welles can get away with a lot more than can his most devout disciples because the power of Welles's personality holds the most varied forms in some meaningful context. However, it would be a mistake to strike too Faustian a tone with Wendkos. The *Gidget* movies are not all that bad, and *The Burglar* and *Angel Baby* are not all that good.

CORNELL WILDE (1915–1989)

FILMS: 1956—*Storm Fear.* 1957—The Devil's Hairpin. 1958 —Maracaibo. 1963—Sword of Lancelot. 1966—*The Naked Prey.* 1967—*Beach Red.* 1969—The Raging Sea.

Cornell Wilde's first film, *Storm Fear,* was notable for its half-baked intensity and the actor-director's bizarre imitation of Marlon Brando after years of having other directors exploit Wilde's expressionless good looks. Wilde's turnabout was comparable to Dick Powell's at that moment when the sappiest tenor of the thirties became one of the toughest private eyes of the forties. Wilde's most recent efforts—*The Naked Prey* and *Beach Red* —are nothing if not ambitious. Wilde is still too bland as both actor and director to be given major consideration, but he does reveal a modestly likable personality in over its head with themes oversized for the talent and skill available.

MICHAEL WINNER (1935–   )

FILMS: 1966—You Must Be Joking!, The Girl Getters. 1967 —The Jokers. 1968—I'll Never Forget What's 'Is Name.

Michael Winner gives conformity a mod look in *The Girl Getters, The Jokers,* and *I'll Never Forget What's 'Is Name.* Winner's films condemn and ridicule the very youthful spirit they exploit. *The Girl Getters* is condescending to young people, *The Jokers* malicious, and *I'll Never Forget What's 'Is Name* destructively cynical. Winner's films manage to be slick and messy at the same time. There are intimations in *What's 'Is Name* of Ingmar Bergman's *Wild Strawberries,* but with Winner there are only sour raspberries.

BUD YORKIN (1926–   )

FILMS: 1963—Come Blow Your Horn. 1965—Never Too Late. 1967—*Divorce American Style*. 1968—Inspector Clouseau. 1969—Two Times Two.

Bud Yorkin served his apprenticeship with two Broadway comedies that gave tastelessness and vulgarity new dimensions. After *Come Blow Your Horn* and *Never Too Late,* the only possible direction was up, but *Divorce American Style* turned out to be surprisingly effective entertainment on its own terms, and Yorkin displayed a commendable sense of timing in his set comedy scenes.

IX.
SUBJECTS
FOR
FURTHER
RESEARCH

These are the directors whose work must be more fully evaluated before any final determination of the American cinema is possible. There may be other unknown quantities as well, but this list will serve for the moment as a reminder of the gaps.

CLARENCE BROWN (1890–1987)

FILMS: 1920—The Great Redeemer. 1922—The Light in the Dark. 1923—Don't Marry for Money, The Acquittal. 1924—The Signal Tower, Butterfly. 1925—Smouldering Fires, The Eagle, *The Goose Woman.* 1926—Kiki, *Flesh and the Devil.* 1928—Trail of '98. 1929—Woman of Affairs, Wonder of Women, Navy Blues. 1930—*Anna Christie, Romance.* 1931—Inspiration, A Free Soul, Possessed. 1932—*Emma,* Letty Lynton: The Son-Daughter. 1933 —Looking Forward, Night Flight. 1934—Sadie McKee, Chained. 1935—Anna Karenina, *Ah Wilderness!* 1936—Wife Versus Secretary, The Gorgeous Hussy. 1937—Conquest. 1938—Of Human Hearts. 1939—Idiot's Delight, The Rains Came. 1940—Edison, the Man. 1941—Come Live with Me, They Met in Bombay. 1943 —The Human Comedy. 1944—The White Cliffs of Dover. 1945 —*National Velvet.* 1946—*The Yearling.* 1947—Song of Love. 1949—*Intruder in the Dust.* 1950—To Please a Lady. 1951— Angels in the Outfield, When in Rome. 1952—Plymouth Adventure.

Clarence Brown's career is not without a certain amiability in its evolution from German Expressionism (*Flesh and the Devil*) to American Gothic (*Intruder in the Dust*). His best films are usually his most modest—*Anna Christie, Ah Wilderness!, National Velvet,* and *Emma.* His main claim to fame is that he was Garbo's favorite and most frequent director, but none of his efforts attained the peaks of *Ninotchka* (Ernst Lubitsch), *Camille* (George Cukor), and *Queen Christina* (Rouben Mamoulian).

TOD BROWNING (1882–1962)

FILMS: 1918—Which Woman, The Deciding Kiss, The Eyes of Mystery, Revenge, The Legion of Death. 1919—Unpainted Woman, Wicked Darling, Exquisite Thief, Set Free, Brazen Beauty, Petal on the Current. 1920—The Virgin of Stamboul, Bonnie, Bonnie Lassie. 1921—Outside the Law, No Woman Knows. 1922—

The Wise Kid, Man Under Cover, Under Two Flags. 1923—Drifting, White Tiger, The Day of Faith. 1924—The Dangerous Flirt. 1925—*The Unholy Three,* The Mystic, Dollar Down, Silk Stocking Sal. 1926—The Road to Mandalay, The Black Bird. 1927—The Show, The Unknown, London After Midnight. 1928—Big City. 1929—East Is East, Thirteenth Chair. 1930—Paid. 1931—*Dracula,* Iron Man. 1932—*Freaks.* 1933—Fast Workers. 1935—Mark of the Vampire. 1936—*The Devil-Doll.* 1939—Miracles for Sale.

The morbid cinema of Tod Browning seems to have been ahead of its time on some levels and out of its time on others. *Freaks* is memorable chiefly because of its impassive confrontation of the most monstrous deformities. By contrast, *Dracula* seems dully static in its elaborate expressionism. On a purely technical level, Browning seems less talented than Whale, not to mention Murnau (*Nosferatu*) and Dreyer (*Vampyr*) on the sublime level of obsessional horror. However, Browning's career is more meaningful than Whale's in terms of a personal obsession. Also, *Freaks* may be one of the most compassionate movies ever made.

JAMES CRUZE (1884–1942)

FILMS: 1919—Roaring Road, The Dub, Alias Mike Moran, Too Many Millions, You're Fired, Love Burglar. 1920—Hawthorne of the U.S.A., The Lottery Man, Mrs. Temple's Telegram, An Adventure in Hearts, Terror Island, What Happened to Jones. 1921—The Dollar a Year Man, Food for Scandal, Always Audacious, Charm School. A Full House, Crazy to Marry. 1922—One Glorious Day, Is Matrimony a Failure, The Dictator, The Old Homestead, Thirty Days. 1923—*The Covered Wagon, Hollywood, Ruggles of Red Gap,* To the Ladies. 1924—The Garden of Weeds, The Fighting Coward, The City that Never Sleeps, The Enemy Sex, *Merton of the Movies.* 1925—The Goose Hangs High, *Beggar on Horseback,* Welcome Home, Marry Me, The Pony Express. 1926—Mannequin, The Waiter from the Ritz, Old Ironsides. 1927—We're All Gamblers, On to Reno, The City, Gone Wild. 1928—Red Mark, Excess Baggage, Mating Call. 1929—Man's Man. 1930—Once a Gentleman, Great Gabbo, She Got What She Wanted. 1931—Salvation Nell. 1932—*Washington Merry-Go-Round*, If I Had a Million. 1933—Sailor Be Good, Racetrack, *I Cover the Waterfront*, Mr. Skitch. 1934—*David Harum*, Their Big Moment. 1935—Helldorado, Two Fisted. 1936—*Sutter's Gold*. 1937—The Wrong Road. 1938—Prison Nurse, Gangs of New York, Come On Leathernecks.

James Cruze has been saddled with the epic reputation of *The Covered Wagon*, one of the most disappointing of all "great classics." The evidence in *The Covered Wagon* and elsewhere suggests a rather lively if somewhat coarse sense of humor hindered to some degree by a very crude visual style. Cruze looked very old-fashioned throughout the thirties, but today such interesting museum pieces as *I Cover the Waterfront, David Harum*, and even the catastrophic *Sutter's Gold* seem endearingly dated.

PAUL FEJOS (1897–1963)

FILMS: HUNGARIAN PERIOD: 1920—The Black Captain, Pan, Hallucination. 1921—Le Revenant. 1923—The Rose of Eggert. HOLLYWOOD PERIOD: 1928—Last Moment, Lonesome. 1929—Broadway, The Last Performance. EUROPEAN PERIOD: 1932—Fantomas, Marie, The Condemned Balaton. 1933—Sonnenstrahl, Les Millions en Fuite. 1935—Prisoners, Le Hors la Loi, The Golden Smile. 1938—A Handful of Rice (Ceylonese documentary).

Fejos is a mysterious figure in the American cinema. He is regarded much more highly in France, both for *Lonesome* and for the European version of George Hill's *The Big House*. He left Hollywood at about the time of the sound changeover, and later found his way back to his native Hungary. *Lonesome* is a rather curious relic of Hollywood's changeover from eloquently expressive silence to coarse and clumsy sound. Many film historians were traumatized by the heartbreaking superiority of the last silents to the first talkies, and we are conditioned to invidious comparisons between the unpopular virtuosity of, say, *Docks of New York* as opposed to the popular vulgarity of, say, *The Singing Fool*. *Lonesome*, however, carried the contrast to the point of schizophrenia. A tender love story in its silent passages, *Lonesome* becomes crude, clumsy, and tediously tongue-tied in its "talkie" passages added to the finished film to make it that hybrid monstrosity of the period, a part-talkie. We know now that sound was as desirable as it was inevitable, but after seeing and hearing *Lonesome,* it is possible to appreciate the depth of an aesthete's despair at a time when the medium seemed a mess.

SIDNEY FRANKLIN (1893–1972)

FILMS: 1918—The Safety Curtain, Her Only Way, The Babes in the Woods, Treasure Island, Aladdin and the Wonderful Lamp, Jack and the Beanstalk, Six Shooter Andy, The Bride of Fear, Confession. 1919—Fan Fan, Probation Wife, Heart of Wetona, Forbidden City, Ali Baba and the Forty Thieves. 1920—The Heart of the Hills, The Hoodlum, Two Weeks. 1921—Not Guilty, Courage, Unseen Forces. 1922—The Primitive Lover, Smilin' Through, The Beautiful and the Damned, East Is West. 1923—Dulcy, Brass, Tiger Rose. 1924—Her Night of Romance. 1925—Learning to Love, Her Sister from Paris. 1926—Beverly of Graustark, The Duchess of Buffalo. 1928—The Actress. 1929—Wild Orchids, Last of Mrs. Cheney, Devil May Care. 1930—Lady of Scandal, A Lady's Morals, Soul Kiss. 1931—*The Guardsman, Private Lives.* 1933—Reunion in Vienna. 1934—Barretts of Wimpole Street. 1935—*The Dark Angel.* 1937—*The Good Earth.* 1957—The Barretts of Wimpole Street.

Sidney Franklin was a director dear to the heart of the legendary Irving J. Thalberg. Franklin was slow, deliberate, conscientious, and dull as were most of the Thalberg-Franklin productions. Perhaps the peak year was 1931 with Lunt and Fontanne transcribing Molnar's *The Guardsman* and Montgomery and Shearer doing the same for Coward's *Private Lives.* This was the era of Hollywood's most Anglicized gentility. We shall never see its equal again.

WILLIAM K. HOWARD (1899–   )

FILMS: 1921—What Love Will Do. 1922—Extra, Extra, Deserted at the Altar, Danger Ahead. 1923—Lucky Dan, The Fourth

Musketeer, Captain-Fly-By-Night, Let's Go. 1924—The Border Legion, East of Broadway, The Torrent. 1925—Code of the West, The Light of Western Stars, The Thundering Herd. 1926—Volcano, Red Dice, Bachelor Brides, Gigolo. 1927—*White Gold,* The Main Event. 1928—Ship Comes In, River Pirate. 1929—Christina, *The Valiant,* Love, Live and Laugh. 1930—Good Intentions, Scotland Yard. 1931—Don't Bet on Women, *Transatlantic,* Surrender. 1932 —Trial of Vivienne Ware, First Year, Sherlock Holmes. 1933— *Power and the Glory.* 1934—Cat and the Fiddle, This Side of Heaven, Evelyn Prentice. 1935—*Vanessa—Her Love Story,* Rendezvous, *Mary Burns—Fugitive.* 1936—*The Princess Comes Across.* 1937—*Fire Over England,* Murder on Diamond Row. 1939 —*Back Door to Heaven.* 1940—Money and the Woman. 1941— Bullets for O'Hara. 1942—Klondike Fury. 1943—Johnny Come Lately. 1944—When the Lights Go On Again. 1946—A Guy Could Change.

William K. Howard has a deserved reputation for individualistic intransigence. *White Gold, The Valiant, Power and the Glory, Mary Burns—Fugitive,* and *Back Door to Heaven* show the signs of a very personal touch. Unfortunately, Howard's films do not display the degree of talent necessary to overcome the problems of a difficult temperament. Film historians talk about the studio system and its effect on the greatest talents, but it is the intermediate talent that suffered the most, specifically the directors, like Howard, who were good, but not quite good enough.

REX INGRAM (1892–1950)

FILMS: 1918—His Robe of Honor, Humdrum Brown. 1920 —Shore Acres, Under Crimson Skies, The Day She Paid. 1921— *The Four Horsemen of the Apocalypse,* Hearts are Trumps, The Conquering Power. 1922—Turn to the Right, *Prisoner of Zenda,* Trifling Women. 1923—Where the Pavement Ends, *Scaramouche.* 1924—The Arab. 1926—Mare Nostrum, The Magician. 1927— A Garden of Allah. 1929—Three Passions. 1932—Baroud.

Rex Ingram is one of the forgotten directors of the film societies. His reputation, like Sternberg's, suffers from the charge of excessive pictorialism. Only a resurrection of his work can confirm the validity of the judgment. *The Four Horsemen of the Apocalypse* alone justifies a revaluation.

HENRY KING (1888–1982)

FILMS: 1912–1917—Short features for Lubin, Pathé, General Film Company, and Mutual. 1919—23½ Hours Leave, A Fugitive from Matrimony, Haunting Shadows. 1920—The White Dove, Uncharted Channels, One Hour Before Dawn, Help Wanted —Male, Dice of Destiny. 1921—When We Were 21, Mistress of Shenstone, Salvage, The Sting of the Lash, *Tol'able David*. 1922— The Seventh Day, Sonny, The Bond Boy, Fury. 1923—*The White Sister*. 1924—*Romola*. 1925—Sackcloth and Scarlet, Any Woman, *Stella Dallas*. 1926—Partners, *The Winning of Barbara Worth*. 1927—The Magic Flame. 1928—The Woman Disputed (Codirected with Sam Taylor). 1929—She Goes to War. 1930— Hell Harbor, Eyes of the World, *Lightnin'*. 1931—Merely Mary Ann, *Over the Hill*. 1932—The Woman in Room 13. 1933—*State Fair*, I Loved You Wednesday. 1934—Carolina, Marie Galante. 1935—*One More Spring, Way Down East*. 1936—The Country Doctor, Ramona. 1937—*Lloyd's of London*, Seventh Heaven. 1938 —*In Old Chicago, Alexander's Ragtime Band*. 1939—*Jesse James*, Stanley and Livingstone. 1940—Little Old New York, Maryland, Chad Hanna. 1941—A Yank in the RAF, Remember the Day. 1942 —The Black Swan. 1944—*The Song of Bernadette*, Wilson. 1945 —A Bell for Adano. 1946—*Margie*. 1947—The Captain from Castile. 1948—Deep Waters. 1949—The Prince of Foxes. 1950 —*Twelve o'Clock High, The Gunfighter*. 1951—I'd Climb the Highest Mountain. 1952—David and Bathsheba, *Wait Till the Sun Shines Nellie*, The Gift of the Magi episode in O. Henry's Full House, The Snows of Kilimanjaro. 1954—King of the Khyber Rifles. 1955 —Untamed, *Love Is a Many Splendored Thing*. 1956—Carousel. 1957—The Sun Also Rises. 1958—The Bravados. 1959—This Earth Is Mine. 1962—Tender Is the Night.

Would film history have been radically altered if Henry King had directed *The Grapes of Wrath* and John Ford *Jesse James,* instead of vice versa? Not likely. Ford lifted a Western like *Stagecoach* above its customary level of significance, whereas King muffed such fashionably liberal opportunities as *Wilson* and *A Bell for Adano*. The careers of Ford and King run a somewhat parallel course at Fox. Both directed Will Rogers; both did versions of *Lightnin'*, Ford in 1925, King in 1930; both dealt sincerely with rustic themes until that fateful day in 1935 when *Variety* headlined: STICKS NIX HICKS PIX. Henry King's place in the history books is attributable almost entirely to the happy accident of Pudovkin's admiration of *Tol'able David* with its broad strokes of expressive villainy. *Stella Dallas, The Winning of Barbara Worth, State Fair, In Old Chicago, The Song of Bernadette, Margie, Twelve o'Clock High,* and even *Love Is a Many Splendored Thing* and *The Bravados* are likable enough in their plodding intensity, but not quite forceful enough to compensate for the endless footage of studio-commissioned slop which King could never convert into anything personal or even entertaining. The one film for which he will probably be remembered longest is *The Gunfighter,* the most charming of the handle-bar-mustache anti-Westerns. But even at his best, King tended to be turgid and rhetorical in his storytelling style.

MALCOLM ST. CLAIR (1897–1952)

FILMS: 1925—On Thin Ice, Are Parents People, The Trouble with Wives, After Business Hours. 1926—*The Grand Duchess and the Waiter,* Good and Naughty, *A Woman of the World, A Social Celebrity, The Show-Off,* The Popular Sin. 1927—Knockout Reilly, Breakfast at Sunrise. 1928—Gentlemen Prefer Blondes, Sporting Goods, Beau Broadway, Fleet's In. 1929—Canary Murder Case, Side Street, Night Parade. 1930—Montana Moon, Dangerous Nan [sic] McGrew, Remote Control, Boudoir Diplomat. 1933—Goldie Gets Along. 1934—Olsen's Big Moment. 1936—Crack-Up. 1937—Time Out for Romance, Born Reckless, She Had to Eat, Dangerously Yours. 1938—A Trip to Paris, Safety in Numbers. 1939—Down on the Farm, Quick Millions. 1940—Young As You Feel, Meet the Missus. 1942—The Bashful Bachelor, The Man in the Trunk, Over My Dead Body. 1943—Two Weeks to Live, Jitterbugs, The Dancing Masters. 1944—The Big Noise. 1945—The Bull Fighters. 1948—Arthur Takes Over, Fighting Back.

St. Clair's silent films, particularly *The Grand Duchess and The Waiter* and *A Social Celebrity*, fizzed, and his sound films fizzled. It was as simple and as tragic as that.

VICTOR SEASTROM (VICTOR SJÖSTRÖM) (1879–1960)

FILMS: 1912—Trädgårdsmästaren (False Alarm), Ett Hemligt Giftermäl (A Secret Marriage), En Sommarsaga (A Tale of Summer), Lady Marions Sommarflirt (Lady Marion's Summer Romance), Det Var I Maj (It Was in May), Aktenskapsbyrän (The Marriage Bureau), Löjen Och Tärar (Laughter and Tears). 1913—Blodets Röst (The Voice of Blood), Ingebord Holm, Livets Konflikter (Life's Conflicts), Prästen (The Pastor), Kärlek Starkare Än Hat (Love Is Stronger Than Hate), Halvblod (Mixed Blood), Miraklet (The Miracle), Strejken (The Strike). 1914—Dömen Icke (Judge Not), Bra Flicka Reder Sig Själv (A Brave Girl Should Solve Her Problems by Herself), Sonad Skuld (Payment for Error), Högfjällets Dotter (Girl of the Snow), Hjärtan Som Mötas (Hearts According to Fashion), Gatans Barn (Children of the Street). 1915—Ev av de Mänga (One Among Many), Landshövdingens Dottrar (The Governor's Daughters), Skomakare Bliv Vid Din Läst (To Each His Calling), Judaspengar (The Wages of Judas), Skepp Som Mötas (The Meeting of Ships), I Prövningens Stund (The Hour of Trial), Havsgamar (The Scavengers of the Sea), Hon Segrade (She Triumphs). 1916—Therese, Dödskyssen (The Strange Adventure of the Engineer Lebell), Terje Vigen. 1917—*Berg-Ejvind Och Hans Hustru (The Outlaw's Wife)*, Tosen Frän Stormyrtorpe. 1918—*Ingmarssonerna* (I) (The Voice of the Ancestors), *Ingmarssonerna* (II) (The Voice of the Ancestors). 1919—Klostret I Sendomir (The Monastery of Sendomir), *Karin Ingsmarsdotter*, Hans Näds Testamente. 1920—*Körkarlen (The Phantom Carriage)*, Mästerman (Master Samuel). 1921—Vem Dömer? (Trial by Fire). 1922—Omringade Huset. 1923—Eld Omborg. 1924—Name the Man, *He Who Gets Slapped*. 1925—Confessions of a Queen, *The Tower of Lies*. 1926—*The Scarlet Letter*. 1928—*The Divine Woman, The Wind*, Masks of the Devil. 1930—A Lady to Love, Markurells I Wadköping, Väter und Söhne (German Version of Markurells I Wadköping). 1937—Under the Red Robe.

It is possible that Victor Seastrom was the world's first great director, even before Chaplin and Griffith. Seastrom and Stiller stand at that odd confluence of Scandinavian air and sky later to give artistic life to Dreyer and Bergman. Seastrom's American career is peculiarly uneven, *The Wind* standing up much better today than *The Scarlet Letter*. It is as if when Seastrom left Sweden, his artistic soul couldn't breathe. There was not enough air on the Hollywood sound stages.

MAURICE TOURNEUR (1876–1961)

FILMS: 1914—Mother, The Man of the Hour, The Wishing Ring, The Pit. 1915—Alias Jimmy Valentine, The Cub, Trilby, The Ivory Snuff Box, A Butterfly on the Wheel. 1916—The Pawn of Fate, The Hand of Peril, The Closed Road, The Rail Rider, The Velvet Paw. 1917—A Girl's Folly, The Whip, *The Pride of the Clan,* The Poor Little Rich Girl, The Undying Flame, The Law of the Land, Exile, Barbary Sheep, The Rise of Jennie Cushing. 1918— Rose of the World, A Doll's House, The Blue Bird, Prunella, Sporting Life, Woman. 1919—The White Heather, The Broken Butterfly, The Life Line. 1920—My Lady's Garter, Treasure Island, The Great Redeemer, The White Circle, Deep Waters, *The Last of the Mohicans.* 1921—The Bait, *The Foolish Matrons.* 1922—Lorna Doone. 1923—While Paris Sleeps, The Christian, The Isle of Lost Ships, The Brass Bottle, Jealous Husbands. 1924—Torment, The White Moth. 1925—Never the Twain Shall Meet, Sporting Life, Clothes Make the Pirate. 1926—Aloma of the South Seas, Old Loves and New, The Mysterious Island. EUROPEAN PERIOD: 1927— L'Équipage. 1929—Das Schiff der Verloren. 1930—Accusée Levez-Vous. 1931—Maison de Danses, Partir! 1932—Au Nom de la Loi, Les Gaîtés de l'Escalron. 1933—Les Deux Orphelines, Obsession. 1934—Le Voleur. 1935—Justin de Marseille, Königsmark. 1936—Samson, Avec le Sourire. 1938—Le Patriote, Katia. 1940—Volpone. 1941—Péchés de Jeunesse, Mam'zelle Bonaparte. 1942—La Main du Diable. 1943—La Val d'Enfer, Cécile Est Morte. 1947—Apres d'Amour. 1948—L'Impasse des Deux Anges.

Maurice Tourneur's early American films still remain to be explored in depth. Off the startling evidence of *The Last of the Mohicans* and Barbara Bedford's expressively perverse performance therein, it would seem that Tourneur is one of the leading stylists of the period, if not actually in a class by himself.

X.
MAKE
WAY
FOR
THE
CLOWNS!

These are the most conspicuous of the nondirectorial auteurs, and, as such, they cannot be subsumed under any directorial style. They are ultimately the funniest footnotes to the auteur theory.

W. C. FIELDS (1879–1946)

FILMS: 1915—Pool Sharks. 1925—Janice Meredith, *Sally of the Sawdust* (directed by D. W. Griffith). 1926—It's the Old Army Game (A. Edward Sutherland), That Royle Girl (D. W. Griffith), So's Your Old Man (Gregory La Cava). 1927—*Running Wild* (Gregory La Cava), Two Flaming Youths (John Waters), The Potters (Fred Newmeyer). 1928—Tillie's Punctured Romance (A. Edward Sutherland), Fools for Luck (Charles F. Reisner). 1930—*The Golf Specialist* (Monte Brice), Her Majesty Love (William Dieterle). 1932—*The Dentist* (Leslie Pierce), If I Had a Million (Eddie Cline), *Million Dollar Legs* (Eddie Cline), International House. 1933—*The Barber Shop* (Arthur Ripley), *The Fatal Glass of Beer* (Arthur Ripley), The Pharmacist (Arthur Ripley), Alice in Wonderland (Norman McLeod), Tillie and Gus (Francis Martin). 1934—*Six of a Kind* (Leo McCarey), You're Telling Me (Erle Kenton), Mrs. Wiggs of the Cabbage Patch (Norman Taurog), It's a Gift (Norman Taurog), The Old-Fashioned Way (William Beaudine), Mississippi (A. Edward Sutherland), *The Man on the Flying Trapeze* (Clyde Bruckman), *David Copperfield* (George Cukor). 1936—Poppy (A. Edward Sutherland). 1938—The Big Broadcast of 1938 (Mitchell Leisen). 1939—You Can't Cheat an Honest Man (George Marshall), 1940—*The Bank Dick* (Eddie Cline), My Little Chickadee (Eddie Cline). 1941—Never Give a Sucker an Even Break (Eddie Cline). 1942—Tales of Manhattan (Julien Duvivier). 1944—Follow the Boys (A. Edward Sutherland), Song of the Open Road (S. Sylvan Simon). 1945—Sensations of 1945 (Andrew Stone).

The vogue for W. C. Fields is concerned more with the comedian's astringent personality than with any particular form of cinema. W. C. Fields is enjoyed as a critical reaction against the prevailing saccharinity of the American cinema, or at least that part of the American cinema that is sufficiently inane to justify the wildest Fieldsian frenzies against Man and Woman. A combined misanthrope and misogynist, Fields virtually demolished the mythology of the American family in the opening reels of his most successful screen incarnation, *The Bank Dick*. Fields was especially appealing when he was bullying little children who had it all too much their own way on the screen in the thirties and forties. Less successful was Fields' one appearance with Mae West in *My Little Chickadee*. West brought out all the wizened, infantile sexlessness of Fields, and the pairing was more funny/ peculiar than funny/ha ha.

The Fields enthusiasts have amassed a considerable literature on their unheroic hero. The standard line about Fields was that he had the grace of a juggler, but few of his sight gags bear comparison with the more distinctively Fieldsian throwaway delivery of comic lines. With a talent more verbal than visual, it is difficult to appreciate the success of W. C. Fields in the silent cinema, but the fact remains that he functioned with comic effectiveness for silent directors as disparate as D. W. Griffith (*Sally of the Sawdust*) and Gregory La Cava (*Running Wild*). Some of his best comedy shorts were directed by Arthur Ripley. My favorite Fields line occurs on a golf course where, after he expresses the wish that his caddy lose a toenail, Fields hastily assures his female companion: "I was only fooling and pretending." The double disclaimer issues from Fields' lips with all the comic irony of Shakespeare's "Honest, honest Iago" from Othello's. All in all, Fields was a monstrous outgrowth of American Puritanism, and not even Dickens could have imagined such deviously and intransigently petty malice in any human being.

JERRY LEWIS (1928–   )

FILMS: DEAN MARTIN PERIOD: 1949—My Friend Irma (George Marshall). 1950—My Friend Irma Goes West (Hal Walker). 1951 —At War with the Army (Hal Walker), That's My Boy (Hal Walker). 1952—Sailor Beware (Hal Walker), Jumping Jacks (Norman Taurog). 1953—*The Stooge* (Norman Taurog), Scared Stiff (George Marshall), The Caddy (Norman Taurog). 1954—Money from Home (George Marshall), Living It Up (Norman Taurog), Three-Ring Circus (Joseph Pevney). 1955—You're Never Too Young (Norman Taurog), *Artists and Models* (Frank Tashlin). 1956 —Pardners (Norman Taurog), *Hollywood or Bust* (Frank Tashlin). SOLO PERIOD: 1957—The Delicate Delinquent (Don McGuire), The Sad Sack (George Marshall). 1958—Rock-a-Bye Baby (Frank Tashlin), The Geisha Boy (Frank Tashlin). 1959—Don't Give Up the Ship (Norman Taurog). 1960—Visit to a Small Planet (Norman Taurog), *The Bellboy* (Jerry Lewis), Cinderfella (Frank Tashlin). 1961—The Ladies' Man (Jerry Lewis), *The Errand Boy* (Jerry Lewis). 1962—*It's Only Money* (Frank Tashlin). 1963—*The Nutty Professor* (Jerry Lewis), Who's Minding the Store (Frank Tashlin). 1964—*The Patsy* (Jerry Lewis), The Disorderly Orderly (Frank Tashlin). 1965—The Family Jewels (Jerry Lewis), Boeing Boeing (John Rich). 1966—*Three On a Couch* (Jerry Lewis), Way . . . Way Out (Gordon Douglas). 1967—The Big Mouth (Jerry Lewis). 1968—Don't Raise the Bridge, Lower the River (Jerry Pasis).

If in this period of film history and polemics, I choose to take a stand *against* Jerry Lewis, I do so with certain preliminary qualifications. First, unlike some of my American colleagues, I think Jerry Lewis is worth discussing seriously as a bone of contention between American and French criticism. The principle involved in this instance is one of total cinema. What I always hoped the auteur theory would contribute to the American film scene was an expanding vision of the cinema as far as the eye of the beholder could see.

Second, Jerry Lewis cannot be considered an exclusively Cahierist cult figure. Lewis seems to be generally popular in France, and his strongest champions are to be found on the staff of *Positif,* a publication perpetually at war with *Cahiers.* (We will not speak here of a *Positif* critic who so resembles Jerry Lewis that hero-worship verges on narcissism.) Therefore, there are many arguments cited for Jerry Lewis undreamed of in the *Cahiers* aesthetic. The fact remains that Lewis has been blessed with French paradoxes and rationalizations denied to merely mortal *metteurs en scène* like Blake Edwards and Clive Donner. Serge Daney's elaborate analysis of the Edwardian cartoon fallacy in *The Great Race* would seem to pertain more appropriately to Jerry Lewis and his mentor, Frank Tashlin. It was Tashlin, after all, who started out as a cartoonist, not Edwards, and if anything distinguishes the Edwardian style, it is a cool, TV deadpan, verbal wit. I can think of a dozen Tashlin-Lewis gags that consist of contorting the human body into positions of linear distortion beyond muscular reality. The basic Edwards gag on the contrary denies its heroes the ability to transcend their physical limitations. Even when the Edwards characters wear animal masks, they retain their poise and sangfroid. Recall the climax of *The Pink Panther,* and compare it with the much admired (by the French) sequence in *The Patsy* where Hans Conried's hammy music teacher demolishes a room and inverts Jerry Lewis's Valentino eyebrows through the seismic acoustics of singing scales. Which of these two sequences owes more to the cartoon? The disinterested observer can make his own choice. Lest this point be misconstrued as unmotivated rationalization, let me add that I think *The Pink Panther, A Shot in the Dark,* and *What Did You Do in the War, Daddy?* are funnier than all the Lewis-Tashlin movies put together, but such a judgment leads to more complex considerations.

I have the impression that French critics see more in Lewis than mere comedy/ha-ha and that therefore the complaint that Lewis does not get all that many laughs is somewhat beside the point. The French critics often use Lewis as a club against American critics. In addition to the traditional argument about Americans being obtuse when it comes to analyzing their own art, there is the more cogent ploy about comedians and clowns being culturally underrated in their own time and place. Look at Chaplin, Keaton, Laurel and Hardy, and so on, the argument goes. How valid is this argument? Somewhat. Yet look at Wheeler and Woolsey and the Ritz Brothers. They look even worse in retrospect than they did at the time. However, until movies came along, clowns and comedians lacked any medium which could preserve their performances. There were legends and traditions, but no objective way of checking up on them, and there is consequently no verifiable classical criticism on performers. Who knows for sure how good David Garrick was or how adept Shakespeare's clowns? We of the cinema have to make up our own criteria as we go along, and our task is not made easier by the proliferation of categories. Jerry Lewis, for example, is not judged merely as a comic performer but as a comic creator. Cocteau has already been mentioned, and Molière cannot be far behind. Some skeptical observations on Lewis as an artist are therefore in order.

1. Jerry Lewis has become conscious, even self-conscious, about his own art. The Pirandellian ending of *The Patsy* is proof

enough of expanding ambitiousness. That the ending doesn't come off indicates that Lewis's aspiration now exceeds his ability.

2. There is a chasm between Lewis's verbal sophistication in nightclubs and sometimes on television and his simpering simplemindedness on the screen. The problem of Lewis is thus similar to the problem of Danny Kaye in developing a screen character consistent with the character of a manic entertainer, a Golem, no less, of grotesque comic energy. It follows that Americans would be more conscious of this split in Lewis than the French would be. Similarly, the people in the front row of the Paramount knew the moment that Danny Kaye was permanently corrupted by Royalty in the Palladium. It was that moment when Kaye reverently displayed Harry Lauder's walking stick. The wild boy from Brooklyn had gone posh, and that was the end of his frenzy and his timing. The Queen Mother had turned him into a national shrine.

3. The fact that Lewis lacks verbal wit on the screen doesn't particularly bother the French, who then patiently explain to us what we are missing in Sacha Guitry, which, in turn, is what they are missing in Preston Sturges, particularly in his Paramount Period.

4. It would be presumptuous of Americans to tell the French that Maurice Chevalier represents their national soul. Similarly, it is presumptuous to claim that Lewis's screen experiences represent something profound about America. If Lewis cannot make American audiences respond to his films, he is living on borrowed time appealing to the intellectual authority of the French.

5. Lewis appeals to unsophisticated audiences in the sticks and to ungenteel audiences in the urban slums; he is bigger on Forty-second Street, for example, than anyplace else in the city. Most urban reviewers limit even his most ambitious efforts to the most routine reviews, and the weekly and monthly reviewers barely acknowledge his existence. Little distinction is made between the films he or Tashlin directs and the potboilers turned out by Douglas and Taurog and Rich, and so on. This is one argument for the completeness of French criticism.

6. Throughout his screen career Lewis has played the innocent with themes of effeminacy and transvestism. During his

partnership with Dean Martin, Lewis played the old Ginger Rogers role in a remake of *The Major and the Minor,* the old Carole Lombard role in a remake of *Nothing Sacred* and the old Betty Hutton role in a remake of *The Miracle of Morgan's Creek.* Only recently Lewis himself parodied one of the songs from *West Side Story* by beginning the first bars thus: "Maria, I know a guy named Maria." This kind of borscht-circuit hipsterism puts a different construction on the screen simpleton on whom Lewis lavishes so much sentimentality with so much apparent affection. If he is not playing down to his audience, he is playing down to himself, and all for the dubious dividends of "universality."

7. Martin and Lewis were something unique in comedy teams. Most comedy teams—the Marx Brothers, Laurel and Hardy, Abbott and Costello, even the Beatles—have a certain internal cohesion that unites them against the world outside. That is to say that members of a comedy team have more in common with each other than with anyone else. Martin and Lewis, at their best—and that means not in any of their movies—had a marvelous tension between them. The great thing about them was their incomparable incompatibility, the persistent sexual hostility, the professional knowingness they shared about the cutthroat world they were in the process of conquering. I think of them as they were the night they chased Bob Hope and Bing Crosby off the stage. The atmosphere reeked with the odor of rotting royalty being overthrown by the new Zanies, or the night they pretended to be thrown off the stage by Tony Martin and Joe Louis, and they were on top of the world. If *The Nutty Professor* is Jerry Lewis's best picture, it is largely because of the recreation of Dean Martin in the Hyde-like Buddy Love, and the subsequent rebirth of the Martin-Lewis tension. (*The Nutty Professor* was not handicapped by Victor Young's lovely melody for *The Uninvited* ["Stella by Starlight"] nor by the starlit Stella Stevens the song seemed to caress.)

8. The argument about laughs is irrelevant because laughter is less decisive in this instance than love. The French critics love Jerry Lewis. Many Americans do not.

9. Lewis can be criticized for the weakness of his narrative

bridges between his big comedy sequences. *The Family Jewels* is badly acted throughout, but particularly in the setting-up scenes. Never trust an art or an artist lacking in a passion for detail.

10. This brings up the question of the feature-length film as the proper vehicle for farce with continuous belly laughs. The late James Agee commemorated the Chaplin one- and two-reelers in his classic essay on comedy. Rudi Blesch prefers the shorter Keaton features to the longer ones in his excellent biography of Buster. Laurel and Hardy were better in short features than long ones, and so the argument goes. Perhaps belly laughs are not enough to sustain a feature-length film. Screen farce, like screen pornography, may involve culturally embarrassing examinations of audience metabolism and endurance, examinations which may explain why modern audiences are seldom moved as emotionally as they think guiltily they ought to be by the five-act tragedies of Shakespeare. For Lewis, this may mean a renewed attention to plots, dialogue, and, above all, grading.

11. When Lewis decides he has something to say, it comes out conformist, sentimental and banal. He was quite funny laughing at Hedda Hopper's hat in *The Patsy,* but then he has to go spoil it all by letting dear Hedda make a speech about the importance of being sincere in Hollywood. The clown's speech in *The Family Jewels* might have been conceived in the mind of any smug superpatriot as a sermon on what showbiz folk owe dear old Uncle Sam. The point here is not Lewis's politics, but rather his sanctimoniousness. A John Ford can celebrate the bitter glories of established orders, but the man and the message are one, and the style expresses the essential unity of what Ford is and what he says. Lewis's sentimentality is not only embarrassingly tinny in this admittedly sublime context. It is self-righteous as well.

12. Still, it is unfair to say that Jerry Lewis takes himself too seriously to pretend otherwise. Nor can the French be blamed for ruining him as a comedian. He had nowhere to go but up, and his post-highbrow ones are clearly superior to his pre-highbrow ones. The trouble is that he has never put one brilliant comedy together from fade-in to fade-out. We can only wait and hope, but the suspicion persists that the French are confusing talent with genius.

HAROLD LLOYD (1893–1971)

FILMS: 1916–1919: More than 100 one- and two-reelers. 1919: (2-reelers) Bumping into Broadway, Captain Kidd's Kids, From Hand to Mouth, His Royal Slyness. 1920: (2-reelers) Haunted Spooks, An Eastern Westerner, High and Dizzy, Get Out and Get Under; Number, Please. 1921: (3-reelers) Now or Never, Among Those Present, I Do, Never Weaken. Features: 1921—A Sailor-Made Man (Fred Newmeyer). 1922—*Grandma's Boy* (Fred Newmeyer), Dr. Jack (Fred Newmeyer). 1923—*Safety Last* (Fred Newmeyer and Sam Taylor), Why Worry? (Newmeyer and Taylor). 1924 —*Girl Shy* (Newmeyer and Taylor), Hot Water (Newmeyer and Taylor). 1925—*The Freshman* (Newmeyer and Taylor). 1926— For Heaven's Sake (Sam Taylor). 1927—The Kid Brother (Ted Wilde). 1928—*Speedy* (Ted Wilde). 1929—Welcome Danger (Clyde Bruckman). 1930—Feet First (Clyde Bruckman). 1932— Movie Crazy (Clyde Bruckman). 1934—The Cat's Paw (Sam Taylor). 1936—*The Milky Way* (Leo McCarey). 1938—Professor Beware (Elliott Nugent). 1947—*Mad Wednesday* (Preston Sturges).

Harold Lloyd has never achieved the critical eminence of Chaplin and Keaton, although *The Freshman* is one of the authentic comedy classics of the American screen. Lloyd has always seemed less universal than Chaplin, less starkly American than Keaton, less individualistic than both. With Chaplin and Keaton we feel that we shall never see their like again. Lloyd's spiritual facsimile is an even-money bet to turn up at the next convention of the Shriners, the Rotarians, or the Elks.

Lloyd's golden age was almost exclusively in the silents. From *Grandma's Boy* to *Speedy,* Lloyd fulfilled the wildest success fantasies of the so-called Jazz Age. He was less effective in the sound era, and even the very special gifts of Preston Sturges were unable to resurrect Lloyd as a comic favorite in *Mad Wednesday.* Audiences were somewhat baffled and put off by this zany optimist with more energy than charm. Lloyd is hardly the only comedian who failed to cross the sound barrier. Keaton's fall was even more precipitous, and Langdon virtually disappeared.

(Laurel and Hardy are a special case in that their sound personalities represent no particular break with their silent personalities. It is as if the coming of sound were incidental to two careers that were more specialized and limited than those of the more classic clowns. In a sense, Laurel and Hardy brought up the rear in the fullest anal sense, and they never seriously challenged the triumvirate of Chaplin, Keaton, and Lloyd in one era, or the Marx Brothers in another. In the end, they were eclipsed by one of the most minor of all comedy teams, Abbott and Costello.)

Lloyd was something else again. His fall was only partly one of inspiration. His comic type simply became obsolete after the Crash. The aggressive values he had embodied in the giddy twenties seemed downright irresponsible in the hung-over thirties. Lloyd's face did not gain in wisdom or pathos or resignation as it aged. It seemed as smug and complacent in the end as it had in the beginning. The fact that Lloyd never lost his money, but remained as rich as Croesus may have contributed to the absence of pain in his features. Lloyd never even seemed to get old. Money and optimism had cushioned him irrevocably against the metaphysical shock registered in the tortured expressions of Chaplin and Keaton in the dressing-room scene of *Limelight*.

THE MARX BROTHERS (Groucho–1890–1977) (Harpo–1888–1964) (Chico–1886–1961)

FILMS: 1929—*The Cocoanuts* (Robert Florey and Joseph Santley). 1930—*Animal Crackers* (Victor Heerman). 1931—*Monkey Business* (Norman McLeod). 1932—*Horse Feathers* (Norman McLeod). 1933—*Duck Soup* (Leo McCarey). 1935—*A Night at the Opera* (Sam Wood). 1937—A Day at the Races (Sam Wood). 1938—Room Service (William A. Seiter). 1939—At the Circus (Edward Buzzell). 1940—Go West (Edward Buzzell). 1941—The Big Store (Charles Reisner). 1946—A Night in Casablanca (Archie L. Mayo). 1949—Love Happy (David Miller).

The Marx Brothers so completely dominated the slapstick scene in the early sound era that few moviegoers mourned the demise of pantomime. Except for Leo McCarey's relatively integrated

Duck Soup, the Marx Brothers burrowed from within an invariably mediocre mise-en-scène to burst upon the audience with their distinctively anarchic personalities. They were a welcome relief not only from the badness of their own movies but also from the badness of most of the movies around them. Except for Groucho's bad habit of doing double and triple takes after every bon mot to give his audience a chance to laugh, the Marx Brothers have worn reasonably well in the three decades since they burned themselves out somewhere between *A Night at the Opera* and *A Day at the Races.* Their more intellectual admirers have compared them with everyone from the Brothers Karamazov to the Beatles. A case can be made for Groucho as Ivan, Harpo as Aloysha, and Chico as Dmitri. Groucho, the skeptic of the sound track, was often pitted against Harpo's Fool of silence. The highbrows laughed louder at Groucho, but they smiled more sweetly at Harpo. The Fool fell in more easily with the lingering aesthetic guilt over the demise of the silent film. There were really only three Marx Brothers. Zeppo and Gummo never counted, and Alan Jones was never anything more than one of Irving J. Thalberg's stray tenors. However, Groucho was aided in no small measure by the exquisite dignity and self-abasement of Margaret Dumont, one of the greatest character comediennes in the history of the screen. Groucho's confrontations with Miss Dumont seem much more the heart of the Marxian matter today than the rather loose rapport among the three Brothers themselves.

The limiting factor of the Marx Brothers is their failure to achieve the degree of production control held by Chaplin throughout his career, and Keaton and Lloyd in the silent era. The Marx Brothers often had to sit by in compliant neutrality while the most inane plot conventions were being developed. *Monkey Business,* particularly, suffers from a studio-grafted gangster intrigue in mock imitation of the gangster films of the time. It may seem trivial that Chaplin, Keaton, and Lloyd were always trying to get the girl, whereas the Marx Brothers were trying to get the girl for whatever straight man happened to be around at the time, but that is what made Chaplin, Keaton, and Lloyd major and the Marx Brothers minor.

Nonetheless, the best bits of the Marx Brothers were as funny as anything the sound film has produced. For starters, there is Groucho's land auction in *The Cocoanuts,* Harpo's and Chico's bridge game in *Animal Crackers,* Harpo's madness with the passports and the puppets in *Monkey Business,* Harpo's and Groucho's bunny-nightcap confrontation in the magical mirror of *Duck Soup,* and the stateroom scene in *A Night at the Opera.* On the other side of the ledger were a profusion of piano and harp solos, bad puns from Groucho and Chico, and, toward the end, the desecrations of B-picture budgets and shooting schedules. As for the comparison between the Marx Brothers and the Beatles, the Marx Brothers, to borrow Priestley's phrase, tried to be mad in a sane world, whereas the Beatles try to be sane in a mad world.

MAE WEST (1892–1980)

FILMS: 1932—Night After Night. 1933—*She Done Him Wrong, I'm No Angel.* 1934—*Belle of the Nineties.* 1935—*Goin' to Town.* 1936—*Klondike Annie;* Go West, Young Man. 1937—Every Day's a Holiday. 1940—My Little Chickadee. 1943—The Heat's On.

The sad story of Mae West is that she was done in by the bluenoses. Social historians have designated 1934 as the censorridden year that marked the transition from Anita Loos to Louisa May Alcott, from Big Mama to *Little Women,* from such boisterous nymphs as Mae West and Jean Harlow to such bristling nymphets as Shirley Temple and Deanna Durbin. Even before 1934, however, the unexpurgated Mae West was somewhat too salty for the screen. No movie audience shared a stage audience's delight over such a provocative query as "Are you packin' a rod or are you just glad to see me?" The movies were never the ideal medium for such bawdy Broadway clowns as Miss West, Bobby Clark, Jimmy Savo, and a horde of burlesque lechers and Borscht Circuit fag-imitators.

Mae West was at her best under Lowell Sherman's perceptive direction in *She Done Him Wrong* with Cary Grant as her perfect foil. For the rest, her career was a patchwork of bits and lines and scenes. Calling her the Tom Mix of the boudoir, John Grierson praised the emotional resiliency of a line like "Beulah, peel me a grape" as a preferable example for young girls than Greta Garbo's literally dying for love in *Camille*. A life preserver in World War II was named after Mae West, possibly in recognition of the fact that she was one of the few stars of the leg-conscious thirties with more impressive measurements from east to west than from north to south. (Only Lupe Velez comes to mind as a contemporaneous competitor to Mae West in the comic amplitude of her bosom.) The leering image of Mae West complete with an IBM eye inspection of a man's Priapean potentialities is part of the iconography of the thirties.

In a way, Mae West's brand of fun was infinitely more innocent when it was considered infinitely more wicked. The censors were at least gallant enough to treat her conceits as dangerous symptoms of a too healthy heterosexuality. The tendency nowadays is to smile indulgently at the familiar accents of a female impersonator who just happened to be a woman on the side. (Vide Shirley Clarke's *Jason* for the ultimate corruption of the West legend.) The thirties were surprisingly full of fruity character comedians and gravel-voiced bulldyke character comediennes, but it was always played so straight that when Franklin Pangborn or Cecil Cunningham went into their routines, it was possible to laugh without being too sophisticated. Only in retrospect have we come to realize how much depravity lurked under the surface of Hollywood's wholesomeness.

XI.
MISCELLANY

MICHAEL ANDERSON (1920–   )

FILMS: 1952—Waterfront Women. 1955—The Dam Busters, Will Any Gentleman? 1956—1984, Around the World in 80 Days. 1957—Battle Hell (Yangtse Incident). 1958—Chase a Crooked Shadow. 1959—Shake Hands with the Devil, *The Wreck of the Mary Deare.* 1960—All the Fine Young Cannibals. 1961—The Naked Edge. 1964—Flight from Ashiya, Wild and Wonderful. 1965—Operation Crossbow. 1966—*The Quiller Memorandum.*

Michael Anderson's career is so undistinguished until *The Quiller Memorandum* that two conclusions are unavoidable, one that Harold Pinter was the true auteur of *The Quiller Memorandum,* and two that Pinter found in Anderson an ideal metteur en scène for his (Pinter's) very visual conceits. The fact that Michael Anderson was also the director of the much-applauded *Around the World in 80 Days* does not deserve even the dignity of a footnote.

LASLO BENEDEK (1907–1992)

FILMS: 1948—The Kissing Bandit. 1949—Port of New York. 1951—Death of a Salesman. 1952—Storm Over the Tiber. 1954—*The Wild One,* Bengal Brigade. 1957—Affair in Havana. 1962—Malaga. 1966—Namu, the Killer Whale.

The Wild One stands out in the list of Laslo Benedek's credits like a beacon in the darkness. The raffish motorcyclists incarnated in the images of Marlon Brando and Lee Marvin have entered the mythology of the cinema. By contrast, *Death of a Salesman* was atrociously directed away from the expressionistic pseudotragedy of Arthur Miller and Elia Kazan on Broadway to the relatively realistic pseudopathology of Hollywood.

JOHN BRAHM (1893–1982)

FILMS: 1935—Scrooge. 1936—The Last Journey. 1937—Broken Blossoms, Counsel for Crime. 1938—Penitentiary, Girl's School. 1939—Let Us Live, Rio. 1940—Escape to Glory. 1941—Wild Geese Calling. 1942—The Undying Monster. 1943—Tonight We Raid Calais, Wintertime. 1944—*The Lodger, Guest in the House.* 1945—*Hangover Square.* 1946—*The Locket.* 1947—*The Brasher Doubloon,* Singapore. 1951—The ¦Thief of Venice. 1952—The Miracle of Our Lady of Fatima, Face to Face (with Bretaigne Windust). 1953—The Diamond Queen. 1954—The Mad Magician, Die Goldene Pest. 1955—Special Delivery, Bengazi. 1956–1967—Approximately 150 TV films. 1967—Hot Rods to Hell.

John Brahm began his career with conscientious imitations of D. W. Griffith (*Broken Blossoms*) and Fritz Lang (*Let Us Live*). He hit his stride in the forties with a series of mood-drenched melodramas—*The Lodger, Guest in the House, Hangover Square, The Locket, The Brasher Doubloon.* His quiet virtues of visual tastefulness and dramatic balance were unable to sustain his career. He remains a minor example of the studio director cast adrift with the collapse of the studio system.

JACK CONWAY (1887–1952)

FILMS: 1918—Bond of Fear, Because of a Woman, Little Red Decides, Her Decision, You Can't Believe Everything. 1919—Diplomatic Mission, Desert Law. 1920—Riders of the Dawn, Lombardi, Ltd. 1921—Dwelling Place of Light, Money Changers, The Spenders, The U.P. Trail, The Kiss, A Daughter of the Law. 1922—Step On It, A Parisian Scandal, The Millionaire, Across the Dead Line, Another Man's Shoes, Don't Shoot, The Long Chance. 1923—The Prisoner, Sawdust, Quicksands, What Wives Want, Trimmed in Scarlet, Lucretia Lombard. 1924—The Trouble Shooter, The Heart Buster. 1925—The Roughneck, The Hunted Woman, The Only

Thing. 1926—Brown of Harvard, Soul Mates. 1927—The Under-
standing Heart, Twelve Miles Out, Quicksands. 1928—Smart Set,
Bringing Up Father, While the City Sleeps. 1929—Alias Jimmy
Valentine, Our Modern Maidens, Untamed. 1930—They Learned
About Women, Unholy Three, New Moon. 1931—Easiest Way,
Just a Gigolo. 1932—*Arsene Lupin*, But the Flesh Is Weak, *Red
Headed Woman*. 1933—Hell Below, The Nuisance, Solitare Man.
1934—*Viva Villa!*, The Girl from Missouri, The Gay Bride. 1935
—One New York Night, *A Tale of Two Cities*. 1936—*Libeled
Lady*. 1937—Saratoga. 1938—*A Yank at Oxford*, Too Hot to
Handle. 1939—Let Freedom Ring, Lady of the Tropics. 1940—
Boom Town. 1941—Love Crazy, Honky Tonk. 1942—Cross-
roads. 1943—Assignment in Brittany. 1944—Dragon Seed. 1947—
High Barbaree, The Hucksters. 1948—Julia Misbehaves.

Jack Conway was submerged in the Metro studio system, and
few of his films are worth mentioning even in passing, but there
are moments of enchantment in *Arsene Lupin, Red Headed
Woman, Viva Villa!, A Tale of Two Cities, Libeled Lady*, and *A
Yank at Oxford*. Most of the enchantment can be attributed to
such acting luminaries as John Barrymore, Jean Harlow, Ronald
Colman, Wallace Beery, and the very early Vivien Leigh in *A
Yank at Oxford*.

HUBERT CORNFIELD (1929–)

FILMS: 1955—Sudden Danger. 1957—Lure of the Swamp.
1958—Plunder Road. 1959—The Third Voice. 1961—Angel
Baby (with Paul Wendkos). 1962—Pressure Point. 1968—The
Night of the Following Day.

Hubert Cornfield's career seems to have been blighted after a
disagreement with producer Stanley Kramer over *Pressure
Point*. Cornfield seemed to be striving for a Europeanized elegance of form even when his scripts seemed too sordid for serious consideration. It remains to be seen whether Cornfield can
return to the scene with any semblance of unity of style and
content.

WILLIAM DIETERLE (1893–1972)

FILMS: 1929—Behind the Altar. 1931—Der Tanz Geht Weiter, *Last Flight, Her Majesty Love.* 1932—Man Wanted, Jewel Robbery, The Crash, Six Hours to Live, Scarlet Dawn, Lawyer Man. 1933—Grand Slam, Adorable, Devils in Love, Female, From Headquarters. 1934—Fashions of 1934, Fog over Frisco, Madame Du Barry, The Firebird. 1935—Secret Bride, Dr. Socrates, A Midsummer Night's Dream, The Story of Louis Pasteur, Concealment, Men on Her Mind. 1936—The White Angel, Satan Met a Lady. 1937—The Great O'Malley, Another Dawn, Life of Emile Zola. 1938—Blockade. 1939—Juarez, Hunchback of Notre Dame. 1940—The Story of Dr. Ehrlich's Magic Bullet, A Dispatch from Reuters. 1941—*All That Money Can Buy* (Here Is a Man). 1942—Syncopation, *Tennessee Johnson.* 1944—Kismet, *I'll Be Seeing You.* 1945—*Love Letters,* This Love of Ours. 1946—The Searching Wind. 1948—The Accused, Portrait of Jenny. 1949—Rope of Sand. 1950—Paid in Full, *Dark City,* September Affair. 1951—Peking Express, Red Mountain. 1952—*Boots Malone,* The Turning Point. 1953—Salome, Volcano. 1954—Elephant Walk. 1956—Magic Fire. 1957—Omar Khayyam.

William Dieterle seemed less interesting than Michael Curtiz in his (Dieterle's) Warners period and less interesting than Billy Wilder in his (Dieterle's) Paramount period. *All That Money Can Buy,* his most successful work, seems somewhat extraneous to his career. *The Last Flight* evokes tender memories of Helen Chandler and bizarre memories of a bowdlerized version of Hemingway's *The Sun Also Rises. Love Letters* is dominated by the nervous emotionalism of Jennifer Jones, Ayn Rand, Lee Garmes, and Victor Young. But Dieterle was around on the set when many interesting things happened over the years, and it is reasonable to assume that he had something to do with them.

ROY DEL RUTH (1895–1961)

FILMS: 1925—Eve's Lover, Hogan's Alley. 1926—Three Weeks in Paris, The Man Upstairs, The Little Irish Girl, Footloose

Widows, Across the Pacific. 1927—Wolf's Clothing, The First Auto, If I Were Single, Ham and Eggs at the Front. 1928—Five and Ten Cent Annie, Powder My Back, The Terror, Beware of Bachelors. 1929—Conquest, Desert Song, The Hottentot, Gold Diggers of Broadway, Aviator. 1930—Hold Everything, Second Floor Mystery, Three Faces East, Life of the Party. 1931—My Past, Divorce Among Friends, Maltese Falcon, Larceny Lane, Side Show, Blonde Crazy. 1932—*Taxi,* Beauty and the Boss, Winner Take All, *Blessed Event.* 1933—Employees' Entrance, Mind Reader, Little Giant, Bureau of Missing Persons, Captured, *Lady Killer.* 1934—Bulldog Drummond Strikes Back, Upper World, Kid Millions. 1935—Folies Bergere, *Broadway Melody of 1936,* Thanks a Million. 1936—It Had to Happen, Private Number, Born to Dance. 1937—On the Avenue, *Broadway Melody of 1938.* 1938—Happy Landing, My Lucky Star. 1939—Tail Spin, The Star Maker, Here I Am a Stranger. 1940—He Married His Wife. 1941—Topper Returns, The Chocolate Soldier. 1942—Maisie Gets Her Man. 1943—Du Barry Was a Lady. 1944—Broadway Rhythm, Barbary Coast Gent. 1947—It Happened on Fifth Avenue. 1948—The Babe Ruth Story. 1949—Red Light, Always Leave Them Laughing. 1950—The West Point Story. 1951—On Moonlight Bay, Starlift. 1952—About Face, Stop, You're Killing Me. 1953—Three Sailors and a Girl. 1954—Phantom of the Rue Morgue. 1959—The Alligator People.

Roy Del Ruth, like Mervyn LeRoy, switched in the mid-thirties from the hard-boiled world of *Taxi, Blessed Event,* and *Lady Killer* to the gilded musical stage of *Broadway Melody of 1936* and *Broadway Melody of 1938.* On the whole, however, Roy Del Ruth seemed more a trend follower than a trend setter.

GORDON DOUGLAS (1909–1993)

FILMS: 1936—General Spanky. 1939—Zenobia. 1940—Saps at Sea. 1941—Road Show, Broadway Limited, Niagara Falls. 1942—The Devil with Hitler, The Great Gildersleeve. 1943—Gildersleeve's Bad Day, Gildersleeve on Broadway. 1944—A Night of Adventure, Gildersleeve's Ghost, Girl Rush, The Falcon in Hollywood. 1945—First Yank into Hollywood. 1946—San Quentin, Dick Tracy vs. Cueball. 1948—The Black Arrow, If You Knew

Susie, Walk a Crooked Mile. 1949—The Doolins of Oklahoma, Mr. Soft Touch. 1950—The Nevadan, The Fortunes of Captain Blood, Rogues of Sherwood Forest, *Kiss Tomorrow Goodbye,* Between Midnight and Dawn, The Great Missouri Raid. 1951—*Only the Valiant,* I Was a Communist for the FBI, *Come Fill the Cup.* 1952— Mara Maru, The Iron Mistress. 1953—She's Back on Broadway, The Charge at Feather River, So This Is Love. 1954—*Them, Young at Heart.* 1955—The McConnell Story, Sincerely Yours. 1957— Santiago, The Big Land, Bombers B-52. 1958—Fort Dobbs, The Fiend Who Walked the West. 1959—Up Periscope, Yellowstone Kelly. 1961—Gold of the Seven Saints, *The Sins of Rachel Cade,* Claudelle Inglish. 1963—Call Me Bwana. 1964—Robin and the 7 Hoods, Rio Conchos. 1965—*Sylvia, Harlow.* 1966—Stagecoach, Way . . . Way Out. 1967—*Tony Rome.* 1968—The Detective, The Lady in Cement.

Gordon Douglas could be dismissed as an efficient technician without too noticeable a personal style, *Kiss Tomorrow Goodbye, Only the Valiant, Come Fill the Cup, Them, Young at Heart,* and *Tony Rome* to the contrary. However, a director who has lived through Liberace (*Sincerely Yours*) deserves all our compassion, particularly when he didn't shirk his job despite the utmost provocation.

PHILIP DUNNE (1908–1992)

FILMS: 1955—*Prince of Players,* The View From Pompey's Head. 1956—*Hilda Crane,* Three Brave Men. 1958—Ten North Frederick, In Love and War. 1959—Blue Denim. 1961—Wild in the Country. 1962—Lisa. 1966—Blindfold.

Philip Dunne was a prolific and successful screenwriter at Fox with scripts for John Ford (*How Green Was My Valley*), Joseph L. Mankiewicz (*The Ghost and Mrs. Muir*), Elia Kazan (*Pinky*), and Jacques Tourneur (*The Way of a Gaucho*) among many others. Dunne made his directorial debut with *Prince of Players,* the project of an ambitious sensibility. Unfortunately, the public was not electrified by Richard Burton as Edwin Booth. Perhaps it was waiting subconsciously for Burton's Antony to cross the Rubicon of stardom after a tryst on the Tiber. Perhaps the casting of Maggie MacNamara opposite Burton was too much of a handicap. Dunne's civilized taste flickered briefly in the exquisite expressions of Jean Simmons in *Hilda Crane*. The rest is leaden and laborious.

VICTOR FLEMING (1883–1949)

FILMS: 1920—When the Clouds Roll By, The Mollycoddle. 1921—Mamma's Affair. 1922—Woman's Place, Red Hot Romance, Lane That Had No Turning, Anna Ascends. 1923—Dark Secrets, Law of the Lawless, To the Last Man, Call of the Canyon. 1924—Empty Hands, The Code of the Sea. 1925—A Son of His Father, Adventure, The Devil's Cargo, Lord Jim. 1926—Blind Goddess, Mantrap. 1927—Rough Riders, *Way of All Flesh*, Hula. 1928—Abie's Irish Rose, The Awakening. 1929—Wolf Song, *The Virginian*. 1930—Common Clay, Renegades. 1931—Around the World in 80 Minutes. 1932—The Wet Parade, *Red Dust*. 1933—White Sister, *Bombshell*. 1934—*Treasure Island*. 1935—*Reckless*, The Farmer Takes a Wife. 1937—*Captains Courageous*. 1938—Test Pilot. 1939—*The Wizard of Oz, Gone with the Wind*. 1941—Dr. Jekyll and Mr. Hyde. 1942—Tortilla Flat. 1943—*A Guy Named Joe*. 1945—Adventure. 1948—Joan of Arc.

Fleming's work has a Jekyll and Hyde quality of its own. Within the same year, Jekyll could turn out the raucously entertaining *Bombshell* while Hyde was being heavy-handed with *White Sister*. Or is it simply the law of accidents that explains the superiority of *Treasure Island, Captains Courageous,* and *A Guy Named Joe* over *The Virginian, Test Pilot,* and *Tortilla Flat*? Fleming's most popularly remembered films, *Gone with the Wind* and *The Wizard of Oz,* seem extraneous to his career, and such creditable efforts as *Red Dust* and *Reckless* were magnificently remade by Ford (*Mogambo*) and Sirk (*Written on the Wind*), and significantly improved in the process. His last films, *Adventure* and *Joan of Arc* were disastrous failures, yet with somewhat more merit than their reputations would indicate. This mysterious figure probably expressed more of Hollywood's contradictions than did most of his colleagues. Yet, aside from Cukor, he was the only Metro director who could occasionally make the lion roar.

Gone with the Wind is one of the notable exceptions to the notion of directorial authorship. Fleming was actually hired for the job because Clark Gable resented the care George Cukor took with the performances of the ladies in the cast. Some of George Cukor's scenes remain in the film. It can be argued also that David O. Selznick, Ben Hecht, and William Cameron Menzies were particularly influential in the shape the film finally took. That *Gone with the Wind* succeeded as entertainment is due largely to the inspired casting of Vivien Leigh as Scarlett O'Hara. That it failed as personal art is due to the incessant interference with a project that was always too big to be controlled by a single directorial style.

JACK GARFEIN (1930–)

FILMS: 1957—The Young One. 1961—Something Wild.

One of the last and least of Kazan's imitators, Garfein attracted some attention with his first film, and then dispelled any incipient hopes with his second. His style, such as it is, consists of little more than contrived hysteria. Until anger is considered an adequate substitute for talent, Garfein's status will remain dubious.

STUART HEISLER (1894–1979)

FILMS: 1940—*The Biscuit Eater.* 1941—The Monster and the Girl, Among the Living. 1942—The Remarkable Andrew, *The Glass Key.* 1945—Along Came Jones. 1946—Blue Skies. 1947—*Smash-Up, The Story of a Woman.* 1949—*Tulsa,* Tokyo Joe. 1950—Chain Lightning, *Storm Warning.* 1951—Journey Into Light. 1952—*Island of Desire.* 1953—*The Star.* 1954—Beachhead, This Is My Love. 1955—I Died a Thousand Times. 1956—The Lone Ranger, The Burning Hills. 1962—Hitler.

Stuart Heisler's career lacks any overall coherence or control, and some of his projects sound more outrageous than they actually are, but he has had moments of insight and charm scattered like loose beads on a sawdust-covered floor. Conventional film historians would probably single him out for *The Biscuit Eater* and *The Glass Key* in his early Paramount period, but he seemed more interesting directing the mature sexuality of Ginger Rogers in *Storm Warning,* Linda Darnell in *Island of Desire,* Susan Hayward in *Tulsa,* and Bette Davis in *The Star,* projects light years beyond such doomed dada as *The Lone Ranger* and *Hitler.*

STANLEY KRAMER (1913–   )

FILMS: 1955—Not As a Stranger. 1957—The Pride and the Passion. 1958—*The Defiant Ones.* 1959—On the Beach. 1960 —Inherit the Wind. 1961—Judgment at Nuremberg. 1963—It's a Mad, Mad, Mad, Mad World. 1965—Ship of Fools. 1967—Guess Who's Coming to Dinner? 1969—The Secret of Santa Vittoria.

If Stanley Kramer had not existed, he would have had to have been invented as the most extreme example of thesis or message cinema. Unfortunately, he has been such an easy and willing target for so long that his very ineptness has become encrusted with tradition. He will never be a natural, but time has proved that he is not a fake.

JOSHUA LOGAN (1919–1988)

FILMS: 1938—I Met My Love Again (with Arthur Ripley). 1956—*Picnic, Bus Stop.* 1957—Sayonara. 1958—South Pacific. 1960—*Tall Story.* 1961—Fanny. 1964—Ensign Pulver. 1967— Camelot. 1969—Paint Your Wagon.

The promise of *Picnic,* long since betrayed as far as Joshua Logan is concerned, can be attributed to Jo Mielziner's coherent principles of set design. Logan's main function now consists of transporting Broadway's tastelessness to the cinema. The unspeakable quartet of *Sayonara, South Pacific, Fanny,* and *Camelot* invests the director's vulgarity with cosmic dimensions. The last hope of the cinema is that Mr. Logan finds Broadway more congenial and stays there. Unfortunately, the most obscenely lit scrim curtain is no adequate substitute for camera filters and slobbering close-ups, and who can deny a director his addictions?

DAVID MILLER (1909–1992)

FILMS: 1941—*Billy the Kid.* 1942—Sunday Punch, Flying Tigers. 1949—Top o' the Morning, *Love Happy.* 1950—Our Very Own. 1951—Saturday's Hero. 1952—*Sudden Fear.* 1954—Twist of Fate. 1955—Diane. 1956—The Opposite Sex. 1957—*The Story of Esther Costello.* 1959—Happy Anniversary. 1960—*Midnight Lace.* 1961—Back Street. 1962—*Lonely Are the Brave.* 1963—Captain Newman, M.D. 1968—Hammerhead.

How a David Miller cult ever got started is one of the unsolved mysteries of underground criticism. Miller's *Billy the Kid* was actually superior to Vidor's without being particularly distinguished in its own right. *Flying Tigers* proved that no one could plagiarize from Hawks's *Only Angels Have Wings* without equaling the master, *Love Happy* that the Marx Brothers have always needed Leo McCarey and a good script, *The Opposite Sex* that George Cukor was indeed inimitable, and *Back Street* that Douglas Sirk was indeed irreplaceable. Not much is left after the parrot pictures are removed. *Sudden Fear* and *Midnight Lace* are ambitious lady-in-distress thrillers, more aggravating than suspenseful. *The Story of Esther Costello* is notable only for the Rossano Brazzi shock treatment, and *Lonely Are the Brave* is worth mentioning only for the presumption of its producer-star, the estimable Kirk Douglas, who deigned to give discriminating American audiences an honest-to-goodness art film from Hollywood, and then found us all unworthy of the privilege. The basic question remains: Who is David Miller?

JEAN NEGULESCO (1900-1993)

FILMS: 1941—Singapore Woman. 1944—*The Mask of Dimitrios*, The Conspirators. 1946—*Three Strangers*, Nobody Lives Forever. 1947—*Humoresque, Deep Valley.* 1948—*Road House, Johnny Belinda.* 1949—The Forbidden Street. 1950—Under My Skin, Three Came Home, The Mudlark. 1951—*Take Care of My Little Girl.* 1952—Phone Call From a Stranger, Lydia Bailey, Lure of the Wilderness, O. Henry's Full House. 1953—Titanic, How to Marry a Millionaire. 1954—Three Coins in the Fountain, Woman's World. 1955—Daddy Long Legs, The Rains of Ranchipur. 1957—Boy on a Dolphin. 1958—The Gift of Love, A Certain Smile. 1959—Count Your Blessings, The Best of Everything. 1962—Jessica. 1964—The Pleasure Seekers.

Jean Negulesco's career can be divided into two periods labeled B.C. and A.C. or Before Cinemascope and After Cinemascope. *The Mask of Dimitrios, Three Strangers, Humoresque, Deep Valley, Road House, Johnny Belinda* and *Take Care of My Little Girl* are all Before Cinemascope, and all rather competently and even memorably made. Everything After Cinemascope is completely worthless. Negulesco's is the most dramatic case of directorial maladjustment in the fifties.

JOSEPH M. NEWMAN (1909–   )

FILMS: 1942—Northwest Rangers. 1945—Diary of a Sergeant. 1948—Jungle Patrol. 1949—The Great Dan Patch, Abandoned. 1950—*711 Ocean Drive.* 1951—Lucky Nick Cain, The Guy Who Came Back, Love Nest, Smoke Jumpers. 1952—Red Skies of Montana, *The Outcasts of Poker Flat*, Pony Soldier. 1953—Dangerous Crossing. 1954—*The Human Jungle.* 1955—This Island Earth, Kiss of Fire. 1956—Flight to Hong Kong. 1957—Death in Small Doses. 1958—Fort Massacre. 1959—The Gunfight at Dodge City, The Big Circus, Tarzan, The Ape Man. 1961—*King of* *the Roaring Twenties—The Story of Arnold Rothstein,* A Thunder of Drums, The George Raft Story, Twenty Plus Two.

Newman nags the critical conscience as an action director with a soft touch and a soupçon of subtlety. The flickering intelligence of Edmond O'Brien in *711 Ocean Drive,* Dale Robertson in *Outcasts of Poker Flat,* Gary Merrill in *The Human Jungle,* and David Janssen in *King of the Roaring Twenties* lingers in the mind long after their inane intrigues have been forgotten. Most memorable of all are the remarkably subdued performances of Mickey Rooney and Jack Carson in *King of the Roaring Twenties.*

ELLIOTT NUGENT (1899–1980)

FILMS: 1929—Wise Girls. 1932—*The Mouthpiece, Life Begins.* 1933—Whistling in the Dark, *Three-Cornered Moon,* If I Were Free. 1934—Two Alone, Strictly Dynamite, She Loves Me Not. 1935—Love in Bloom, Enter Madame, College Scandal, Splendour. 1936—And So They Were Married, Wives Never Know. 1938—It's All Yours, Professor Beware, Give Me a Sailor. 1939— Never Say Die, *The Cat and the Canary.* 1941—Nothing But the Truth. 1942—The Male Animal. 1943—The Crystal Ball. 1944— *Up in Arms.* 1947—My Favorite Brunette, Welcome Stranger. 1948—My Girl Tisa. 1949—*The Great Gatsby,* Mr. Belvedere Goes to College. 1950—The Skipper Surprised His Wife. 1951— My Brother the Outlaw. 1952—Just For You.

Elliott Nugent has left such a pleasant memory of his stage performances in *The Male Animal* and *The Voice of the Turtle* that it is reasonable to assume that his acting personality can be correlated with some of the subtler touches of directing in *The Mouthpiece, Three-Cornered Moon,* and *The Cat and the Canary.* It is reasonable to assume also that his heart remained in the theatre, and that his position in the cinema is understandably marginal.

ARCH OBOLER (1909–1987)

FILMS: 1945—Bewitched. 1946—The Arnelo Affair. 1950 —*Five*. 1952—Bwana Devil. 1953—The Twonky. 1961—One Plus One.

Arch Oboler came to Hollywood out of the radio tube, but he never showed the visual flair of Orson Welles. His name still reverberates from the "Lights Out" radio series I heard in my childhood. Hence, he is included if only as a reminder of the vanished mystique of radio in the motion picture industry.

RICHARD QUINE (1920–1989)

FILMS: 1951—On the Sunny Side of the Street, Purple Heart Diary. 1952—Sound Off, Rainbow 'Round My Shoulder. 1953— All Ashore, Siren of Bagdad, Cruisin' Down the River. 1954— *Drive a Crooked Road, Pushover,* So This Is Paris. 1955—*My Sister Eileen*. 1956—*Solid Gold Cadillac*. 1957—*Full of Life*, Operation Madball. 1958—Bell, Book and Candle. 1959—It Happened to Jane. 1960—*Strangers When We Meet*, The World of Suzie Wong. 1962—The Notorious Landlady. 1964—Paris When It Sizzles, Sex and the Single Girl. 1965—How to Murder Your Wife, *Synanon*. 1967—Oh Dad, Poor Dad, Mamma's Hung You in the Closet and I'm Feelin' So Sad, *Hotel*. 1969—A Talent for Loving.

Richard Quine's early Columbia films possessed a discreet charm that seemed promising as late as 1957 with *Operation Madball*. The promise has never been fulfilled. At best, Quine has functioned as an inoffensive imitator of his betters. *Pushover* is a poor man's *Double Indemnity. Solid Gold Cadillac* and *Full of Life* are pale copies of Cukor's *It Should Happen to You* and *The Marrying Kind* respectively. Quine's comedy technique for *The Notorious Landlady, How to Murder Your Wife,* and *Sex and the Single Girl* was already ineffectively strenuous before the ultimate disaster of *Oh Dad, Poor Dad, Mamma's Hung You in the*

Closet and I'm Feelin' So Sad. Quine seems more at home with the lower-key seriousness of *Synanon, Hotel,* and *Strangers When We Meet.*

LESLIE STEVENS (1924–   )

FILMS: 1960—Private Property. 1962—Hero's Island.

Leslie Stevens achieved some notice and notoriety with *Private Property,* a film that seems more ambitious than it is. Ted McCord was hired to shoot people through brandy snifters with such affected artiness that McCord should have known better even if Stevens didn't. All that lingers in the mind from *Private Property* is Stevens's flair for feelthy fetishism and the hauntingly stupid blonde beauty of the late Kate Manx, Stevens's wife and garish Galatea. *Hero's Island* is best left to the more esoteric film historians.

EDWARD SUTHERLAND (1895–1974)

FILMS: 1925—Wild, Wild Susan, Coming Through, A Regular Fellow. 1926—It's the Old Army Game, Behind the Front, We're in the Navy Now. 1927—Love's Greatest Mistake, Fireman Save My Child, Figures Don't Lie. 1928—Tillie's Punctured Romance, Baby Cyclone, Number Please. 1929—*Close Harmony, Dance of Life,* Fast Company, The Saturday Night Kid, Pointed Heels. 1930—Burning Up, Paramount on Parade, *Social Lion,* Sap from Syracuse. 1931—Gang Buster, June Moon, Up Pops the Devil, Palmy Days. 1932—Sky Devils, Mr. Robinson Crusoe, Secrets of the French Police. 1933—Murders in the Zoo, International House, Too Much Harmony. 1935—*Mississippi,* Diamond Jim. 1936—*Poppy.* 1937—Champagne Waltz, Every Day's a Holiday. 1939—The Flying Deuces. 1940—The Boys from Syracuse, Beyond Tomorrow, One Night in the Tropics. 1941—The Invisible Woman, Nine Lives Are Not Enough, Steel Against the Sky. 1942—Sing Your Worries Away, Army Surgeon, The Navy Comes Through. 1943—Dixie. 1944—Follow the Boys, Secret Command. 1945—Having Wonderful Crime. 1946—Abie's Irish Rose.

Sutherland's career seemed consistently anachronistic through the thirties and forties, and *Abie's Irish Rose* ended things with a toppling down rather than a tapering off. Nonetheless Sutherland remains interesting as an active transitional figure through the switchover to sound. A taste for the Paramount musical of that era is required for any reconsideration of Sutherland's career.

BURT TOPPER

FILMS: 1958—Hell Squad, War Hero. 1959—Tank Commandos, Diary of a High School Bride. 1964—War Is Hell, The Strangler.

Burt Topper has been discovered by *Cahiers du Cinéma* as one of its little jokes on American film scholarship at the Midi-Minuit level. The joke is wearing thin at a time when American films are consistently reviled in the pages of *Cahiers* all the better to sing the praises of the New Albanian Cinema.

W. S. VAN DYKE (1899–1943)

FILMS: 1918—Men of the Desert, Gift O' Gab. 1919—Lady of the Dugout. 1922—According to Hoyle, Boss of Camp No. 4, Forget Me Not. 1923—Little Girl Next Door, Miracle Workers, Loving Lies, You Are in Danger. 1924—Half-a-Dollar Bill. 1925 —The Beautiful Sinner, Gold Heels, Hearts and Spurs, The Trail Rider, The Ranger of the Big Pines, The Timber Wolf, The Desert's Price. 1926—The Gentle Cyclone, War Paint. 1927—Winners of the Wilderness, California, Heart of the Yukon, Eyes of the Totem, Foreign Devils, Spoilers of the West. 1928—Wyoming, Under Black Eagle, *White Shadows of the South Seas.* 1929—The Pagan. 1931—*Trader Horn,* Never the Twain Shall Meet, Guilty Hands, Cuban Love Song. 1932—*Tarzan, The Ape Man;* Night World. 1933—Penthouse, *Eskimo, Prizefighter and the Lady.* 1934— Laughing Boy, Manhattan Melodrama, *The Thin Man,* Hide-Out.

1935—Forsaking All Others, Naughty Marietta, I Live My Life. 1936—Rose Marie, San Francisco, His Brother's Wife, The Devil Is a Sissy, Love on the Run, *After the Thin Man*. 1937—Personal Property, They Gave Him a Gun, Rosalie. 1938—*Marie Antoinette*, Sweethearts. 1939—Stand Up and Fight, It's a Wonderful World, Andy Hardy Gets Spring Fever, Another Thin Man. 1940— I Take This Woman, I Love You Again, Bitter Sweet. 1941—Rage in Heaven, The Feminine Touch, Shadow of the Thin Man, Dr. Kildare's Victory. 1942—I Married an Angel, Cairo, Journey for Margaret.

Woody Van Dyke made more good movies than his reputation for carelessness and haste would indicate. Perhaps carelessness and haste are precisely the qualities responsible for the breezy charm of *Trader Horn, Tarzan, The Ape Man; Prizefighter and the Lady, The Thin Man, After The Thin Man,* and even the much-maligned *Marie Antoinette*.

DON WEIS (1922–   )

FILMS: 1951—It's a Big Country (with Richard Thorpe, John Sturges, Charles Vidor, Clarence Brown, Don Hartman, William Wellman), Bannerline. 1952—Just This Once, You for Me. 1953— *I Love Melvin*, Remains to Be Seen, A Slight Case of Larceny, *The Affairs of Dobie Gillis*, Half a Hero. 1954—*The Adventures of Hajji Baba*. 1956—Ride the High Iron. 1959—*The Gene Krupa Story*. 1963—*Critic's Choice*. 1964—Looking for Love, Pajama Party. 1965—Billie. 1966—Ghost in the Invisible Bikini.

The Don Weis cultists in Britain and France are not normally frivolous, but just this once it remains to be seen. Beyond the graceful nonsense of *The Affairs of Dobie Gillis* and *The Adventures of Hajji Baba,* it is difficult to discern any stylistic or thematic pattern in a career longer on commission than on conviction. What Weis lacks more than anything else is one eye-popping masterpiece for the objectively inclined American noncultists.

TERENCE YOUNG (1915–   )

FILMS: 1949—One Night with You, *Corridor of Mirrors,* Woman Hater. 1951—They Were Not Divided. 1952—The Valley of the Eagles. 1953—The Frightened Bride. 1954—The Para-trooper (Red Beret). 1955—That Lady. 1956—Safari, Storm Over the Nile. 1957—Zarak, Action of the Tiger. 1958—Tank Force. 1962—Black Tights. 1963—*Dr. No.* 1964—*From Russia With Love.* 1965—The Amorous Adventures of Moll Flanders, *Thunderball.* 1966—The Dirty Game, The Poppy Is Also a Flower. 1967 —*Wait Until Dark.* 1968—Mayerling.

Terence Young did the best of the Bonds, *Wait Until Dark,* and the curiously memorable, baroque, and unoriginal *Corridor of Mirrors.* He seems at home with the sweet lyricism of death, but his overall career is staggeringly undistinguished. Nonetheless, he seems to have come into his own, at least commercially.

AFTERWORD: THE AUTEUR THEORY
REVISITED

One would think that after so many years of furious controversy there would be no need for another article on the auteur theory. Yet all sorts of scholarly books and articles continue to disseminate an astounding amount of misinformation on the origin and evolution of auteurism. What to do? Having been officially credited or blamed for bringing the words *auteur, auteurism,* and *auteurist* into the English language, I seem to be stuck with these tar-baby terms for the rest of my life. My own previous writings on the subject have been compiled in *The Primal Screen,* a little read volume that came out in 1973. "Notes on the Auteur Theory in 1962" first appeared in *Film Culture,* "Notes on the Auteur Theory in 1970" followed in *Film Comment,* and so now in 1977 a pattern of periodicity seems to justify my current endeavor. Also, auteurism seems to have become a scapegoat for just about every cultural affliction associated with the cinema.

For example, Gore Vidal (in the April *American Film*) associates auteurism with the deification of directors over writers in the moviemaking process. Speaking of Renoir's "great heist" of *The Southerner,* Vidal explains: "Renoir was a man who had great trouble speaking English, much less writing it, and the script was written by William Faulkner. According to Zachary Scott, who acted in it, Faulkner really liked the script and would have been pleased to have had the credit. But Renoir so muddled the business that the credit finally read: 'Screenplay by Jean Renoir.'"

Unfortunately, Vidal neglects to mention that *The Southerner* was adapted from a novel entitled *Hold Autumn in Your*

Excerpted from *American Film* 2, no. 9 (July–August 1977). © 1977 The American Film Institute. Reprinted by permission.

Hand by George Sessions Perry, the forgotten man in the anti-Renoir, pro-Faulkner anecdote. Who was George Sessions Perry? I have no idea, and neither, apparently, does Vidal. He is (or was) a veteran of the vast army of virtually anonymous authors who have supplied so many of the stories on the screen. Vidal's anecdote implies that Faulkner thought up the story of *The Southerner* all by himself, and Renoir then stole the script and "muddled" it, whatever that means. The anecdote loses something, if Faulkner is revealed as the middleman in the screenwriting process. Until Vidal is prepared to research how much Faulkner's script owes to Perry's novel, the indictment of Renoir as a plagiarist must be thrown out for lack of evidence. Besides, Renoir's reputation does not rest excessively on *The Southerner* any more than Faulkner's reputation rests on his screenplays, credited or uncredited.

Both Renoir and Faulkner must be evaluated in terms of the total context of their careers. This is one of the basic assumptions of auteurism, one that we have always taken for granted in literature, music, and the fine arts, but one that came very late to cinema because of the lack of archival facilities. Hence, film history existed long before there were qualified historians to appraise it. It might be said that the early auteurists discovered so many lost and forgotten treasures in the cinematheques that a theory of history was thrust upon them. They then suggested thematic and stylistic hypotheses which they sought to establish with the proof of a pattern of achievement. But movies were still alive and kicking, and individual careers were still evolving. Some auteurists had placed their bets on Hawks and Hitchcock, others on Renoir and Rossellini. Violent debates ensued between the partisans of Mizoguchi and Kurosawa, Dreyer and Bergman, Antonioni and Fellini, Walsh and Losey. No auteurist completely agreed with any other.

"The auteur theory itself," I wrote back in 1962, "is a pattern theory in constant flux." Despite all my disclaimers, qualifications, and reservations, however, a composite image of the auteurist emerged in anti-auteurist writings. Auteurists were invariably male (at least according to Pauline Kael). They never bathed because it took time away from their viewing of old movies. They shared a preposterous passion for Jerry Lewis. They preferred trash to art. They encouraged the younger generation not to read books.

Vidal himself seeks to establish a dialectical confrontation between the word and the image: "Movies are stories; only writers can tell stories. So the wrong people are making the movies." It might be argued by the defenders of directors that movies are stories told primarily through pictures, or, at least, movies *should* be stories told primarily through pictures. Vidal has an answer for that, too: "We do need the cameraman, the editor. But above all we need the script."

Vidal's position is not particularly audacious for Hollywood. One can imagine the ghosts of the old Hollywood moguls nodding in agreement with Vidal's summary dismissal of directors. All you need to make a good movie is a good story. Everybody on the Bel Air circuit knows *that*. A few years ago *Esquire* published a screenplay entitled *Two-Lane Blacktop* with a come-on across the cover to the effect that this was going to be the best movie of the year. When the critics and public failed to concur with *Esquire*'s prediction, the magazine sheepishly shifted the blame to director Monte Hellman, accusing him of being an auteur. Actually, *Two-Lane Blacktop* was not a bad movie. Choking on the exhaust fumes of the more vulgar and more violent *Easy Rider,* it never caught on at the box office with its subtly modernist malaise, and a brilliant performance by Warren Oates was wasted. This is one of the problems in resolving arguments between auteurists and anti-auteurists: The two sides can never agree entirely on what is good and what is bad. In opposition to the horror stories of Gore Vidal and Rex Reed, there is even a small cult for the movie version of *Myra Breckenridge.*

If one were to examine the pertinent texts of the fifties, the sixties, or the seventies, one would be hard put to find a single generalization in auteurist criticism sweeping enough to justify the simplistic attacks made against it. For one thing, auteurism did not evolve in a vacuum. In the beginning, particularly, its preoccupation with visual structure and personal style was largely a reaction against the sloganized vocabulary of social significance and socialist realism. The open-minded and open-hearted French attitude toward myth and genre enable a new generation of American critics to rediscover and reclaim the American cinema. Suddenly there was credit to parcel out for Hollywood's long despised output, whereas before the auteurists there was only blame. After years on the front lines, my own attitude to the auteurist controversy may have been summed up in the defiant words sung by the late Edith Piaf: *"Non, non, je ne regrette rien."*

Still, if I had to do it all over again, I would reformulate the auteur theory with a greater emphasis on the tantalizing mystery of style than on the romantic agony of the artists. Why, I wondered back in the mid-fifties, had so many Hollywood movies endured as classics despite the generalized contempt of the highbrows? The auteur theory turned out to be a very workable hypothesis for this task of historical reevaluation. But I was never all that interested in the clinical "personalities" of directors, and I have never considered the interview as one of the indispensable weapons in my critical arsenal.

The interview is an autonomous art form like any other, and it follows that directors who give good interviews do not necessarily make good movies, and directors who give bad interviews do not necessarily make bad movies. I am, if anything, anti-interview in that I believe that a director's formal utterances (his films) tell us more about his artistic personality than do his informal utterances (his conversations).

That is why I was far more strongly influenced by the cinematheque-oriented critics on *Cahiers du Cinéma* before 1960 than the tape-recorder interviewers on *Cahiers du Cinéma* after 1960. It is not a question simply of Truffaut, Godard, Chabrol, Rohmer, Rivette, Valcroze, and others validating their pre-1960 critiques with their post-1960 filmmaking. I doubt that Gore Vidal has any notion of what Truffaut was writing about back in 1954 when Truffaut first articulated *La Politique des Auteurs* as an attack on the tradition of quality in the French cinema. Godard's translated criticism has merely mystified even his most determined American admirers. Having published twelve editions of *Cahiers du Cinéma in English* between 1965 and 1967, I can testify that many of my French-speaking acquaintances in America were frequently unable to decipher the cryptic pronouncements of *Cahiers*.

Indeed, few people seem to be aware that my original article on the auteur theory was largely an examination of André Bazin's critique of *La Politique des Auteurs*. Vidal lumps together all French film critics into one monolithic auteurist block as if *Cahier*ism was a national vice. Yet *Cahiers* never sold more than fifteen thousand copies of any monthly issue, and its opinions were violently opposed by other specialized French film publications, most notably and most persistently by *Positif*, which made a point of preferring Huston to Hitchcock, and Fellini to Rossellini. For every Bazin in French film criticism there were a dozen French Bosley Crowthers and Siegfried Kracauers. One did not have to be an auteurist or a *Cahier*ist to adore Jerry Lewis. He happened to be a very catholic French taste. In fact, the most prominent of the Lewis lovers were on the staff of *Positif*.

Similarly, the auteurists of the fifties and sixties did not introduce the cult of the director. Dwight Macdonald and John Grierson were writing very knowledgeably about Hollywood directors back in the early thirties. The great majority of film histories around the world have been organized in terms of the collected works of individual directors. If, as Vidal implies, all that auteurism represents is an emphasis on directors, this so-called theory should be banished for its banality.

A great deal of confusion has been caused by the assumption that auteurism was inseparably linked with the personal tastes of individual critics. Since I was one of the first two American auteurists (along with the late Eugene Archer), I must bear a large part of the blame for this confusion. Let me state at this point, albeit belatedly, that auteurism and Sarrisism are not identical. Both, I hope, have been evolving over the past quarter of a century on a widening front of scholarly activity. Along the way, certain tendencies have clustered around auteurism to form a basis for discussion. Among these tendencies have been the antimontage writings of André Bazin, the many French meditations on mise-en-scène, Lawrence Alloway's celebrations of pop art, and Peter Wollen's valiant efforts to reconcile auteurism with semiotics. Some of these formulations conflicted with others to such an extent that alleged auteurists were often at each other's throats. I have written extensively on many of these internal conflicts, and I have no desire to rehash them now. What I propose instead is a report on the theoretical fall-out from the polemical explosions of the past. An attempt will be made to add historical perspective to auteurism, and emerge with a usable residue of critical theory for 1977.

Bazin's most striking contribution to film aesthetics was the restoration of interest in the integrity of the visual field. If he did not actually demolish the montage theories of Eisenstein, Pudovkin, Kuleshov, and Vertov, he did succeed in reducing these theories from imperatives to options. Bazin's writings were never systematic enough or comprehensive enough to establish new imperatives, and there is little indication that he ever wished to establish a new orthodoxy to replace the old. But he did change the way many critics looked at motion pictures. No longer was the ambiguity of the individual image disdained for the dialectical conflict between successive images. Examining both the deep focus shots in *Citizen Kane* and the slow pans in *Open City,* Bazin managed to link these two otherwise dissimilar films in a very ingenious concept of optical realism.

When Bazin's writings first began to filter across the Atlantic in the mid-fifties, the American cinema was in the midst of a formal crisis with wide screens. Most American reviewers either ignored the width altogether or dealt with it in isolation from the script. Wide-screen color canvases like *East of Eden* and *Rebel Without a Cause* were reviewed in America as if they were small-screen, black-and-white Philco Television Playhouse productions like *Marty.* I recall Claude Chabrol's attack on my review of *East of Eden* as *"ennuyeux."* He was right to the extent that my critique did not do justice to the film's emotional sweep encompassed in tilted, distended compositions.

American movies are often discriminated against in America because the ear takes precedence over the eye. By contrast, the French were able to provide a detailed visual analysis of American movies precisely because they were undistracted by the dialogue. To an American ear *Rebel Without a Cause* is still gravely flawed by its undigested clinical dialogue. But one would have to be blind to fail to realize that Ray has transcended the tedious social worker rhetoric of the film with a succession of striking initiatory ceremonies all filmed with profound splendor. And it is to our everlasting disgrace that the French understood James Dean on a mythic level long before we did. Similarly, they understood how deeply Alfred Hitchcock's *Vertigo* had influenced Alain Resnais's and Alain Robbe-Grillet's *Last Year at Marienbad*. While the New York critics were honoring Stanley Kramer's *The Defiant Ones,* the *Cahiers* critics were cheering Orson Welles's *Touch of Evil*. Obviously, their eyes were quicker than our ears.

Although in the long run they could not have the last word on the American cinema, they gave many of us the first glimpse of this elusive entity. American film criticism has not been the same since. There was a time when movies were judged almost entirely in terms of an absolute fidelity to social reality. Good intentions alone were too often considered the paving stones to heaven. By establishing the notion of individual creation in even the Hollywood cinema, the French shifted the critical emphasis away from the nature of content to the director's attitude toward content.

This attitude was expressed through a somewhat mystical process called mise-en-scène, defined perhaps most eloquently by French critic-director Alexandre Astruc: "But Mizoguchi knows well that, after all, it is not very important for his film to turn out well; he is more concerned with knowing whether the strongest bonds between himself and his characters are those of tenderness or contempt. He is like the viewer who sees the reflection of pleasure on the features of the one he watches, even though he also knows quite well that it is not this reflection alone which he is seeking but perhaps quite simply the tedious confirmation of something he has always known but cannot refrain from verifying. So I consider mise-en-scène as a means of transforming the world into a spectacle given primarily to oneself—yet what artist does not know instinctively that what is seen is less important than the way of seeing, or of a certain way of needing to see or be seen."

As I wrote some years ago, I would suggest a definition of mise-en-scène that includes all the means available to a director to express his attitude toward his subject. This takes in cutting, camera movement, pacing, the direction of players and their placement in the decor, the angle and distance of the camera, and even the content of the shot. Mise-en-scène as an attitude tends to accept the cinema as it is and enjoy it for what it is—a sensuous conglomeration of all the other arts.

Bazin, Astruc, and Roger Leehardt caused a ferment in film aesthetics by demystifying so-called "pure" cinema. There was no such entity, they insisted. We could now discuss hitherto verboten subjects as adaptations without placing surgical masks over our faces. What were once considered germs from the other arts were now treated as vitamins. Hence, whereas Agee worried that Olivier's film treatment of *Henry V* was not truly cinematic, Bazin applauded Olivier for honoring cinema by honoring theater.

The French critics tended to brush aside the distinctions between cinema as a medium and cinema as an art form. "The cinema is everything," Godard declared. And he meant it. Every scrap of film was grist for his sensibility. The cinema was no longer a holy temple to which only certain sanctified works were admitted. Cinema was to be found on every movie screen in the world, and Hollywood movies were no less cinematic than anything else. There was still room for disagreement in this new critical climate, but the disputes were couched in terms more relative than absolute.

About the time that auteurism was swimming across the English Channel to London's moviemanes, and across the Atlantic to New York's film cultists, pop art exploded all across the cultural landscape, and nothing has seemed the same since. The two movements converged uneasily in the sixties in such multifaceted artifacts as Richard Lester's *A Hard Day's Night* with the Beatles, John Boorman's *Having a Wild Weekend* with the Dave Clark Five, Jean-Luc Godard's *One Plus One* with the

Rolling Stones, the experimental kinetics of Frank Zappa, and the personal appearances on film of Bob Dylan.

Lawrence Alloway, who had coined the term "pop art," proposed "a criticism of movies as a pop art which can have a critical currency beyond that of footnotes and preposterous learning." Alloway thereby came into conflict with the scholarly tendencies of auteurism. The terms in which he defined the cinema—whether as "the index of a Baudelairean art of modern life" with "modernity" defined by Baudelaire as "that which is ephemeral, fugitive, contingent upon the occasion" or as "the art synthesis proposed by Wagner, the total work to which all arts contribute"—were terms that pertained more to sociological criticism than to auteurist criticism. For the hard-core auteurists, the hitherto despised Hollywood movies could be judged as high art. For Alloway, high art had been supplanted by pop art, and new forms of judgment were required. Alloway's stress on the topicality and expendability of movies as consumer products was not without a certain ironic condescension toward the medium. By contrast, most auteurists tended to view movies as sacred relics of a spiritual medium. Their tone was reverent and, hence, vulnerable. Their only excuse (and mine) was that they thought that they were writing only for other believers.

No one to my knowledge has ever commented on the Kierkegaard quotation from *Either/Or* with which I introduced my 1962 auteur article: "I call these sketches shadowgraphs, partly by the designation to remind you at once that they derive from the darker side of life, partly because like other shadowgraphs they are not directly visible. When I take a shadowgraph in my hand, it makes no impression on me, and gives me no clear conception of it. Only when I hold it up opposite the wall, and now look not directly at it, but at that which appears on the wall, am I able to see it. So also with the picture which does not become perceptible until I see through the external. This external is perhaps quite unobtrusive but not until I look through it do I discover that inner picture which I desire to show you, an inner picture too delicately drawn to be outwardly visible, woven as it is of the tenderest moods of the soul."

Kierkegaard's "inner picture" eventually found its way into my essay as "interior meaning," a term that gave me a great deal of trouble at the time, but one that has since come to define what all serious film criticism seeks to discover. Auteurism has less to do with the way movies are made than with the way they are elucidated and evaluated. It is more a critical instrument than a creative inspiration. Peter Wollen has suggested the hypothetical nature of the enterprise, and I will go along with that. The cinema is a deep, dark mystery that we auteurists are attempting to solve. It is a labyrinth with a treacherous resemblance to reality. I suppose that the difference between auteurists and structuralists is the difference between knowing all the questions before finding the answers, and knowing all the answers before formulating the questions.

At this late date I am prepared to concede that auteurism is and always has been more a tendency than a theory, more a mystique than a methodology, more an editorial policy than an aesthetic procedure. Contrary to anti-auteurist legends, auteurist critics around the world are an unruly lot. For the most part, they do not describe themselves as auteurists. They are content to describe the stylistic and thematic epiphanies of their favorite auteurs.

DIRECTORIAL CHRONOLOGY 1915–1967

The directorial chronology between 1915 and 1928 does not purport to be an authoritative critical valuation. This chronology consists simply of (a) authenticated classics and (b) the films of directors whose work in the sound era is of some interest. There are too many gaps in silent film scholarship at this time for a definitive stand. Conversely, the directorial chronology between 1929 and 1967 represents a weighted critical valuation.

1915

D. W. GRIFFITH—*The Birth of a Nation.*

CHARLES CHAPLIN—His New Job, A Night Out, The Champion, In the Park, The Jitney Elopement, By the Sea, The Tramp, Work, A Woman, The Bank, Shanghaied, A Night at the Show.

CECIL B. DE MILLE—*The Cheat,* The Girl of the Golden West, The Warrens of Virginia, The Unafraid, The Captive, Wild Goose Chase, The Arab, Chimmie Fadden, Kindling, Maria Rosa, Carmen, Temptation, Chimmie Fadden Out West.

ALLAN DWAN—A Girl of Yesterday, Jordan Is a Hard Road, The Pretty Sister of Jose, The Dancing Girl, David Harum.

RAOUL WALSH—The Regeneration, Carmen.

1916

D. W. GRIFFITH—*Intolerance.*

CHARLES CHAPLIN—*The Rink, One A.M., The Pawnshop,* Carmen, Police, The Floorwalker, The Fireman, The Vagabond, The Count, Behind the Screen.

ALLAN DWAN—Manhattan Madness, The Half-Breed, The Good Bad Man, An Innocent Magdalene, Betty of Greystone, The Habit of Happiness.

CECIL B. DE MILLE—The Golden Chance, The Trail of the Lonesome Pine, The Heart of Nora Flynn, The Dream Girl.

RAOUL WALSH—Honor System, Blue Blood and Red, The Serpent.

1917

CHARLES CHAPLIN—*Easy Street, The Immigrant, The Cure, The Adventurer.*

ALLAN DWAN—Panthea, The Fighting Odds, His Excellency, the Governor.

CECIL B. DE MILLE—Joan the Woman, A Romance of the Redwoods, The Little American, The Woman God Forgot, The Devil Stone.

RAOUL WALSH—Betrayed, The Conqueror, The Pride of New York, The Innocent Sinner, Silent Lie.

JOHN FORD—Straight Shooting, The Secret Man, A Marked Man, Bucking Broadway.

MAURICE TOURNEUR—The Pride of the Clan.

1918

D. W. GRIFFITH—*Hearts of the World,* The Great Love, The Greatest Thing in Life.

CHARLES CHAPLIN—*Shoulder Arms, A Dog's Life,* The Bond.

ALLAN DWAN—A Modern Musketeer, Mister Fix-It, Bound in Morocco, He Comes Up Smiling.

CECIL B. DE MILLE—The Squaw Man, Old Wives for New, We Can't Have Everything, Till I Come Back to You, The Whispering Chorus.

ERICH VON STROHEIM—Blind Husbands.

KING VIDOR—The Turn in the Road.

FRANK BORZAGE—Flying Colors, Until They Get Me, The Gun Woman, Shoes That Danced, Innocent's Progress, Society for Sale, An Honest Man, The Ghost Flower, The Curse of Iku, Who Is to Blame?

JOHN FORD—Phantom Riders, Wild Women, Thieves' Gold, The Scarlet Drop, Hell Bent, Delirium, A Woman's Fool, Three Mounted Men.

RAOUL WALSH—Woman and the Law, This Is the Life, The Prussian Cur, On the Jump, Every Mother's Son, I'll Say So.

JOHN STAHL—Wives of Men.

1919

D. W. GRIFFITH—*True Heart Susie, Broken Blossoms,* The Girl Who Stayed at Home, A Romance of Happy Valley, Scarlet Days, The Greatest Question, The Fall of Babylon, The Mother and the Law.

CHARLES CHAPLIN—*Sunnyside,* A Day's Pleasure.

KING VIDOR—*The Jack Knife Man,* Better Times, The Other Half, Poor Relations.

ERICH VON STROHEIM—The Devil's Passkey.

ALLAN DWAN—Cheating Cheaters, Soldiers of Fortune, Sahara, The Dark Star, Getting Mary Married.

RAOUL WALSH—Evangeline, Should a Husband Forgive?

CECIL B. DE MILLE—Don't Change Your Husband, For Better for Worse, Male and Female.

JOHN FORD—Roped, A Fight for Love, The Fighting Brothers, Bare Fists, The Gun Packers, Riders of Vengeance, The Last Outlaw, The Outcasts of Poker Flat, Ace of the Saddle, Rider of the Law, A Gun Fightin' Gentleman, Marked Men.

FRANK BORZAGE—Toton, Prudence of Broadway, Whom the Gods Destroy.

JOHN STAHL—Her Code of Honor, Suspicion, Woman Under Oath.

1920

MAURICE TOURNEUR—*The Last of the Mohicans.*

D. W. GRIFFITH—*Way Down East,* The Love Flower, The Idol Dancer.

FRANK BORZAGE—Humoresque.

ALLAN DWAN—Luck of the Irish, A Splendid Hazard, The Forbidden Thing.

KING VIDOR—The Family Honour.

JOHN FORD—The Prince of Avenue A, The Girl in Number 29, Hitchin' Posts, Just Pals.

RAOUL WALSH—From Now On, The Deep Purple, The Strongest.

CECIL B. DE MILLE—Why Change Your Wife, Something to Think About.

JOHN STAHL—Women Men Forget, Woman in His House.

1921

CHARLES CHAPLIN—*The Kid, The Idle Class.*

D. W. GRIFFITH—*Dream Street.*

KING VIDOR—The Sky Pilot, Love Never Dies, Conquering the Women; Woman, Wake Up.

REX INGRAM—The Four Horsemen of the Apocalypse.

FRANK BORZAGE—The Duke of Chimney Butte.

ALLAN DWAN—The Perfect Crime, A Broken Doll, In the Heart of a Fool, The Scoffer.

MAURICE TOURNEUR—The Foolish Matrons.

CECIL B. DE MILLE—The Affairs of Anatol, Forbidden Fruit.

RAOUL WALSH—The Oath, Serenade.

JOHN FORD—The Big Punch, The Freeze-Out, The Wallop, Desperate Trails, Action, Sure Fire, Jackie.

LEO MC CAREY—Society Secret.

JOHN STAHL—The Child Thou Gavest Me, Sowing the Wind.

1922

ROBERT FLAHERTY—*Nanook of the North.*

CHARLES CHAPLIN—*The Pilgrim, Pay Day.*

D. W. GRIFFITH—*Orphans of the Storm*, One Exciting Night.

ERICH VON STROHEIM—*Foolish Wives*, Merry-Go-Round.

FRED NEWMEYER—*Grandma's Boy* (Harold Lloyd).

REX INGRAM—Prisoner of Zenda.

ALLAN DWAN—Robin Hood, The Sin of Martha Queed, Superstition.

KING VIDOR—Peg O' My Heart, Alice Adams, The Real Adventure, Dusk to Dawn.

FRANK BORZAGE—Get-Rich-Quick Wallingford, Back Pay, Silent Shelby, Billy Jim, The Good Provider, Valley of Silent Men, The Pride of Palomar.

JOHN FORD—Little Miss Smiles, Silver Wings, The Village Blacksmith.

RAOUL WALSH—Kindred of the Dust.

CECIL B. DE MILLE—Fool's Paradise, Saturday Night, Manslaughter.

JOHN STAHL—The Song of Life, One Clear Call, Suspicious Wives.

1923

CHARLES CHAPLIN—*A Woman of Paris.*

BUSTER KEATON—*The Three Ages, Our Hospitality.*

D. W. GRIFFITH—*The White Rose.*

JAMES CRUZE—*Hollywood*, Covered Wagon, Ruggles of Red Gap.

ERNST LUBITSCH—Rosita.

KING VIDOR—Wild Oranges, Three Wise Fools, The Woman of Bronze, Happiness.

FRED NEWMEYER and SAM TAYLOR—Safety Last (Harold Lloyd).

REX INGRAM—Scaramouche.

FRANK BORZAGE—Nth Commandment, Children of Dust, Song of Love.

JOHN FORD—Cameo Kirby, Three Jumps Ahead, The Face on the Bar-room Floor.

ALLAN DWAN—Zaza, Glimpses of the Moon, Lawful Larceny, Big Brother.

CECIL B. DE MILLE—Adam's Rib, The Ten Commandments.

RAOUL WALSH—Lost and Found on a South Sea Island.

JOHN STAHL—The Wanters, The Dangerous Age.

1924

ERNST LUBITSCH—*The Marriage Circle, Forbidden Paradise*, Three Women.

BUSTER KEATON—*Sherlock Junior, The Navigator.*

JOHN FORD—The Iron Horse, Hoodman Blind, North of Hudson Bay, Hearts of Oak.

D. W. GRIFFITH—America.

RAOUL WALSH—The Thief of Bagdad.

KING VIDOR—Wine of Youth, His Hour, Wife of the Centaur.

FRED NEWMEYER and SAM TAYLOR—Girl Shy (Harold Lloyd), Hot Water (Lloyd).

VICTOR SEASTROM—He Who Gets Slapped.

ALLAN DWAN—Her Love Story, Manhandled, A Society Scandal, The Wages of Virtue, Argentine Love.

FRANK BORZAGE—Secrets, The Age of Desire.

CECIL B. DE MILLE—Triumph, Feet of Clay.
JOHN STAHL—Husbands and Lovers, Why Men Leave Home.

1925
CHARLES CHAPLIN—*The Gold Rush.*
KING VIDOR—*The Big Parade,* La Boheme, Proud Flesh.
ERNST LUBITSCH—Lady Windermere's Fan, Kiss Me Again.
ERICH VON STROHEIM—Greed, The Merry Widow.
BUSTER KEATON—Go West, Seven Chances.
D. W. GRIFFITH—Sally of the Sawdust, Isn't Life Wonderful, The Royle Girl.
JOSEF VON STERNBERG—The Salvation Hunters.
FRED NEWMEYER and SAM TAYLOR—The Freshman (Harold Lloyd).
HERBERT BRENON—A Kiss for Cinderella, Peter Pan.
JAMES CRUZE—Beggar on Horseback.
HENRY KING—Stella Dallas, Romola.
VICTOR SEASTROM—The Tower of Lies.
SVEND GADE—Siege.
TOD BROWNING—The Unholy Three.
JOHN FORD—Lightnin', Kentucky Pride, The Fighting Heart, Thank You.
FRANK BORZAGE—The Lady, Daddy's Gone a'Hunting, Wages for Wives, The Circle, Lazybones.
RAOUL WALSH—East of Suez, The Spaniard.
ALLAN DWAN—Night Life in New York, Stage Struck, Coast of Folly.
CECIL B. DE MILLE—The Road to Yesterday, The Golden Bed.
JOHN STAHL—Fine Clothes.
ALFRED HITCHCOCK—The Pleasure Garden.

1926
BUSTER KEATON—*The General,* Battling Butler.
ERNST LUBITSCH—*So This is Paris.*
ROBERT FLAHERTY—Moana.
JOSEF VON STERNBERG—The Exquisite Sinner, The Sea Gull.
FRANK CAPRA—The Strong Man.
ALFRED HITCHCOCK—The Lodger, The Mountain Eagle.
RAOUL WALSH—What Price Glory?, The Wanderer, The Lucky Lady, The Lady of the Harem.
KING VIDOR—Bardelys the Magnificent.
MALCOLM ST. CLAIR—The Grand Duchess and the Waiter, A Woman of the World.
HERBERT BRENON—Beau Geste.
CLARENCE BROWN—Flesh and the Devil.
JOHN FORD—Three Bad Men, The Shamrock Handicap, The Blue Eagle.
HOWARD HAWKS—Fig Leaves, The Road to Glory.
FRANK BORZAGE—The First Year, Marriage License, Early to Wed, The Dixie Merchant.
D. W. GRIFFITH—The Sorrows of Satan.
ALLAN DWAN—Tin Gods, Summer Bachelors, Sea Horses, Padlocked.
CECIL B. DE MILLE—The Volga Boatmen.
JOHN STAHL—Memory Lane, The Gay Deceiver.
GREGORY LA CAVA—Woman Handled.

1927
JOSEF VON STERNBERG—*Underworld.*
F. W. MURNAU—*Sunrise.*
KING VIDOR—*The Crowd,* The Patsy.
FRANK BORZAGE—Seventh Heaven.
ERNST LUBITSCH—The Student Prince.
BUSTER KEATON—College.

FRANK CAPRA—Long Pants, For the Love of Mike.
ALFRED HITCHCOCK—The Ring, Easy Virtue, Downhill.
RAOUL WALSH—The Loves of Carmen, The Monkey Talks.
JOHN FORD—Upstream.
HOWARD HAWKS—Paid to Love, The Cradle Snatchers.
CECIL B. DE MILLE—The King of Kings.
VICTOR FLEMING—The Way of All Flesh.
GREGORY LA CAVA—Running Wild.
MAURITZ STILLER—Hotel Imperial.
HARRY D'ARRAST—The Gentleman from Paris.
PAUL LENI—The Cat and the Canary.
LEWIS MILESTONE—Two Arabian Knights.
ALLAN DWAN—The Music Master, Joy Girl; East Side, West Side.
JOHN STAHL—Lovers, In Old Kentucky.
HERBERT BRENON—Sorrell and Son.
ALEXANDER KORDA—The Private Life of Helen of Troy.

1928

CHARLES CHAPLIN—*The Circus.*
JOSEF VON STERNBERG—*The Last Command, Docks of New York,* The Dragnet.
BUSTER KEATON—Steamboat Bill Junior, The Cameraman.
HOWARD HAWKS—A Girl in Every Port, The Air Circus, Fazil.
ERICH VON STROHEIM—The Wedding March, Queen Kelly.
PAUL LENI—The Man Who Laughs.
ERNST LUBITSCH—The Patriot.
KING VIDOR—Show People.
FRANK BORZAGE—Street Angel.
VICTOR SEASTROM—The Wind, The Divine Woman.
F. W. MURNAU—The Four Devils.
VICTOR SCHERTZINGER—Forgotten Faces.
HARRY D'ARRAST—Dry Martini.
ANTHONY ASQUITH—Shooting Stars.
D. W. GRIFFITH—The Battle of the Sexes, Drums of Love.
ALFRED HITCHCOCK—The Farmer's Wife, The Manxman, Champagne.
JOHN FORD—Four Sons, Mother Machree, Hangman's House, Napoleon's Barber, Riley the Cop.
RAOUL WALSH—Sadie Thompson, The Red Dance; Me, Gangster.
TAY GARNETT—The Spieler, Celebrity.
HERBERT BRENON—Laugh, Clown, Laugh.
LEWIS MILESTONE—The Racket.
ALLAN DWAN—French Dressing, Big Noise.
CECIL B. DE MILLE—The Godless Girl.

1929

KING VIDOR—Hallelujah!, Not So Dumb.
ERNST LUBITSCH—The Love Parade, Eternal Love.
JOSEF VON STERNBERG—Thunderbolt, The Case of Lena Smith.
ALFRED HITCHCOCK—Blackmail.
FRANK BORZAGE—The River, Lucky Star, They Had to See Paris.
ROLAND WEST—Alibi.
ROUBEN MAMOULIAN—Applause.
PAUL FEJOS—Lonesome.
JACQUES FEYDER—The Kiss.
JOSEPH SANTLEY and ROBERT FLOREY—The Cocoanuts (The Marx Brothers).
D. W. GRIFFITH—Lady of the Pavements.
HOWARD HAWKS—Trent's Last Case.
JOHN FORD—Strong Boy, The Black Watch, Salute.

RAOUL WALSH—The Cockeyed World, In Old Arizona (with Irving Cummings).
CECIL B. DE MILLE—Dynamite.
ALLAN DWAN—The Iron Mask, Tide of Empire, Frozen Justice, The Far Call, South Sea Rose.
FRANK CAPRA—Flight, The Donovan Affair.
LEO MC CAREY—The Sophomore, Red Hot Rhythm.
PAUL LENI—The Last Warning.
TAY GARNETT—Flying Fools, Oh Yeah!
REX INGRAM—Three Passions.
DAVID BUTLER—Sunny Side Up.
HARRY BEAUMONT—The Broadway Melody.
VICTOR FLEMING—The Virginian.
ALFRED E. GREEN—Disraeli.
EDWARD SUTHERLAND—Close Harmony, Dance of Life, Fast Company, Saturday Night Kid, Pointed Heels.

1930

JOSEF VON STERNBERG—*Morocco, The Blue Angel.*
D. W. GRIFFITH—*Abraham Lincoln.*
HOWARD HAWKS—*The Dawn Patrol.*
JOHN FORD—Men Without Women, Up the River, Born Reckless.
F. W. MURNAU—City Girl (Our Daily Bread).
ALFRED HITCHCOCK—Murder, Juno and the Paycock.
ERNST LUBITSCH—Monte Carlo, Paramount on Parade (with Edmund Goulding, Rowland V. Lee, Victor Schertzinger, Dorothy Arzner, Otto Brower, Victor Heerman, Edwin Knopf, Lothar Mendes, Edward Sutherland, and Frank Tuttle.
GEORGE CUKOR—The Royal Family of Broadway (with Cyril Gardner), Grumpy (with Cyril Gardner).
LEWIS MILESTONE—All Quiet on the Western Front.
TAY GARNETT—Her Man, Officer O'Brien.
GEORGE HILL—The Big House, Min and Bill.
HOWARD HUGHES—Hell's Angels.
HARRY D'ARRAST—Raffles, Laughter.
CLARENCE BROWN—Anna Christie, Romance.
KING VIDOR—Billy the Kid.
FRANK BORZAGE—Song o' My Heart, Liliom.
RAOUL WALSH—The Big Trail.
CECIL B. DE MILLE—Madame Satan.
JOHN CROMWELL—Street of Chance.
JAMES WHALE—Journey's End.
VICTOR HEERMAN—Animal Crackers (The Marx Brothers).
FRANK CAPRA—Ladies of Leisure, Rain or Shine.
LEO MC CAREY—Let's Go Native, Wild Company, Part Time Wife.
JOHN STAHL—A Lady Surrenders.
MERVYN LEROY—Little Johnny Jones, Playing Around, Show Girl in Hollywood, Numbered Men, Broken Dishes, Top Speed, Little Caesar.
WILLIAM WYLER—Hell's Heroes.
HERBERT BRENON—The Case of Sergeant Grischa.
EDWARD SUTHERLAND—Social Lion.
ROBERT MILTON—Outward Bound.

1931

CHARLES CHAPLIN—*City Lights*
F. W. MURNAU—*Tabu* (with Robert Flaherty).
JOSEF VON STERNBERG—*An American Tragedy, Dishonored.*
KING VIDOR—Street Scene, The Champ.

HOWARD HAWKS—The Criminal Code.
D. W. GRIFFITH—The Struggle.
ERNST LUBITSCH—The Smiling Lieutenant.
FRANK BORZAGE—Bad Girl, Doctors' Wives, As Young as You Feel.
JOHN FORD—Arrowsmith, The Seas Beneath, The Brat.
GEORGE CUKOR—Tarnished Lady, Girls About Town.
LEWIS MILESTONE—The Front Page.
CECIL B. DE MILLE—The Squaw Man.
FRANK CAPRA—Dirigible, The Miracle Woman, Platinum Blonde.
ROLAND WEST—The Bat Whispers, Corsair.
ALFRED HITCHCOCK—The Skin Game.
LEO Mᶜ CAREY—Indiscreet.
JOHN STAHL—Seed, Strictly Dishonorable.
ROUBEN MAMOULIAN—City Streets.
ROWLAND BROWN—Quick Millions.
JAMES WHALE—Frankenstein, Waterloo Bridge.
WILLIAM WELLMAN—The Public Enemy, Other Men's Women, Star Witness, Night Nurse, Safe in Hell.
SIDNEY FRANKLIN—The Guardsman, Private Lives.
MERVYN LEROY—Five Star Final.
WILLIAM WYLER—A House Divided.
NORMAN TAUROG—Skippy.
NORMAN MC LEOD—Monkey Business (The Marx Brothers).
WESLEY RUGGLES—Cimarron.
TOD BROWNING—Dracula.
WILLIAM DIETERLE—The Last Flight.

1932
HOWARD HAWKS—*Scarface*, The Crowd Roars, Tiger Shark.
JOSEF VON STERNBERG—*Shanghai Express*, Blonde Venus.
ERNST LUBITSCH—*Trouble in Paradise*, One Hour With You, The Man I Killed, If I Had a Million (with James Cruze, Norman Taurog, Stephen Roberts, Norman Z. McLeod, William Seiter, and Bruce Humberstone).
FRANK BORZAGE—A Farewell to Arms, After Tomorrow, Young America.
GEORGE CUKOR—A Bill of Divorcement, What Price Hollywood, Rockabye.
JOHN FORD—Air Mail, Flesh.
ALFRED HITCHCOCK—East of Shanghai.
CECIL B. DE MILLE—The Sign of the Cross.
TAY GARNETT—One Way Passage.
JOHN STAHL—Back Street.
FRANK CAPRA—American Madness, Forbidden.
LEO MC CAREY—The Kid from Spain.
EDMUND GOULDING—Grand Hotel.
ROUBEN MAMOULIAN—Dr. Jekyll and Mr. Hyde, Love Me Tonight.
MERVYN LEROY—I Am a Fugitive from a Chain Gang, High Pressure, Heart of New York, Two Seconds, Big City Blues, Three on a Match.
ALLAN DWAN—While Paris Sleeps.
ROWLAND BROWN—Hell's Highway.
W. S. VAN DYKE—Tarzan, The Ape Man.
EDWARD F. CLINE—Million Dollar Legs.
JAMES WHALE—The Invisible Man.
TOD BROWNING—Freaks.
RICHARD BOLESLAWSKI—Rasputin and the Empress.
GREGORY LA CAVA—The Half Naked Truth.
VICTOR FLEMING—Red Dust.
JAMES CRUZE—Washington Merry-Go-Round.
LEWIS MILESTONE—Rain.

LOWELL SHERMAN—The Greeks Had a Word for Them.
EDWARD L. CAHN—Law and Order.
ROY DEL RUTH—Blessed Event.
IRVING PICHEL—The Most Dangerous Game.
WILLIAM WELLMAN—The Hatchet Man.
KARL FREUND—The Mummy.
ELLIOTT NUGENT—The Mouthpiece, Life Begins.
CLARENCE BROWN—Emma.
GEORGE FITZMAURICE—As You Desire Me.

1933

ERNST LUBITSCH—*Design for Living.*
GEORGE CUKOR—*Dinner at Eight,* Little Women, Our Betters.
FRANK BORZAGE—*A Man's Castle,* Secrets.
FRANK CAPRA—Lady for a Day, The Bitter Tea of General Yen.
LEO MC CAREY—Duck Soup.
LEWIS MILESTONE—Hallelujah, I'm a Bum!
JOHN FORD—Doctor Bull, Pilgrimage.
SERGEI EISENSTEIN—Thunder Over Mexico.
HOWARD HAWKS—Today We Live.
ROUBEN MAMOULIAN—Queen Christina, The Song of Songs.
JOHN STAHL—Only Yesterday.
MERVYN LEROY—Gold Diggers of 1933, Hard to Handle.
VICTOR FLEMING—Bombshell.
LOWELL SHERMAN—She Done Him Wrong, Morning Glory.
ROWLAND V. LEE—Zoo in Budapest.
MERRIAM C. COOPER and ERNEST SCHOESDACK—King Kong.
ALEXANDER KORDA—The Private Life of Henry VIII.
HARRY D'ARRAST—Topaze.
ELLIOTT NUGENT—Three-Cornered Moon.
JAMES CRUZE—I Cover the Waterfront.
WILLIAM K. HOWARD—The Power and the Glory.
LLOYD BACON—Forty-second Street, The Picture Snatcher, Footlight Parade.
HENRY KING—State Fair.
WILLIAM WYLER—Counsellor at Law.
FRANK LLOYD—Cavalcade, Berkeley Square.
WILLIAM WELLMAN—Heroes for Sale.

1934

HOWARD HAWKS—*Twentieth Century,* Viva Villa! (with Jack Conway).
JOSEF VON STERNBERG—*The Scarlet Empress.*
ROBERT FLAHERTY—*Man of Aran.*
JOHN FORD—The Lost Patrol, Judge Priest, The World Moves On.
FRANK BORZAGE—Little Man, What Now?, No Greater Glory.
ERNST LUBITSCH—The Merry Widow.
FRANK CAPRA—It Happened One Night, Broadway Bill.
KING VIDOR—Our Daily Bread.
CECIL B. DE MILLE—Cleopatra, Four Frightened People.
JOHN STAHL—Imitation of Life.
EDGAR G. ULMER—The Black Cat.
LEO MC CAREY—Belle of the Nineties, Six of a Kind.
G. W PABST—A Modern Hero.
JAMES CRUZE—David Harum.
VICTOR FLEMING—Treasure Island.
VICTOR SCHERTZINGER—One Night of Love.
JOHN CROMWELL—Of Human Bondage.
HENRY HATHAWAY—The Witching Hour.

MARK SANDRICH—The Gay Divorcee.
MERVYN LEROY—Sweet Adeline, Hi Nellie.
W. S. VAN DYKE—The Thin Man.
GREGORY LA CAVA—What Every Woman Knows, The Affairs of Cellini.
PAUL CZINNER—Catherine the Great.
BASIL DEAN—The Constant Nymph.
JAMES WHALE—One More River.
HAROLD YOUNG—The Scarlet Pimpernel.
ALEXANDER HALL—Little Miss Marker.
BEN HECHT and CHARLES MAC ARTHUR—Crime Without Passion.
NORMAN TAUROG—It's a Gift, Mrs. Wiggs of the Cabbage Patch.

1935

JOSEF VON STERNBERG—*The Devil is a Woman*, Crime and Punishment.
JOHN FORD—*Steamboat 'Round the Bend, The Whole Town's Talking*, The Informer.
ALFRED HITCHCOCK—*The 39 Steps, The Man Who Knew Too Much.*
LEO MC CAREY—Ruggles of Red Gap.
GREGORY LA CAVA—She Married Her Boss, Private Worlds.
GEORGE STEVENS—Alice Adams.
HOWARD HAWKS—Barbary Coast.
GEORGE CUKOR—Sylvia Scarlett, David Copperfield.
FRANK BORZAGE—Living on Velvet.
KING VIDOR—So Red the Rose.
JOHN STAHL—The Magnificent Obsession.
CECIL B. DE MILLE—The Crusades.
HENRY HATHAWAY—Peter Ibbetson, Lives of a Bengal Lancer.
BEN HECHT and CHARLES MAC ARTHUR—The Scoundrel, Once in a Blue Moon.
MARK SANDRICH—Top Hat, Follow the Fleet.
VICTOR FLEMING—Reckless.
JAMES WHALE—Bride of Frankenstein.
WESLEY RUGGLES—The Gilded Lily.
FRANK LLOYD—Mutiny on the Bounty.
ROUBEN MAMOULIAN—Becky Sharp.
MICHAEL CURTIZ—Captain Blood, Black Fury.
WILLIAM K. HOWARD—Mary Burns—Fugitive.
BUSBY BERKELEY—Gold Diggers of 1935.
SAM WOOD—A Night at the Opera (The Marx Brothers).
WILLIAM WYLER—The Gay Deception, The Good Fairy.
CLARENCE BROWN—Ah, Wilderness; Anna Karenina.
ROY DEL RUTH—Broadway Melody of 1936.
TOM CONWAY—A Tale of Two Cities.
ALFRED E. GREEN—Dangerous.
CLYDE BRUCKMAN—The Man on the Flying Trapeze.
EDWARD SUTHERLAND—Mississippi, Diamond Jim.

1936

CHARLES CHAPLIN—*Modern Times.*
ALFRED HITCHCOCK—*Secret Agent.*
GREGORY LA CAVA—*My Man Godfrey.*
JOHN FORD—The Prisoner of Shark Island, Mary of Scotland, The Plough and the Stars.
HOWARD HAWKS—Ceiling Zero, The Road to Glory, Come and Get It (with William Wyler).
FRITZ LANG—Fury.
FRANK CAPRA—Mr. Deeds Goes to Town.
KING VIDOR—The Texas Rangers.

CECIL B. DE MILLE—The Plainsman.
FRANK BORZAGE—Desire.
LEO MC CAREY—The Milky Way.
GEORGE STEVENS—Swing Time.
LEWIS MILESTONE—The General Died at Dawn, Anything Goes.
GEORGE CUKOR—Romeo and Juliet.
JOSEF VON STERNBERG—The King Steps Out.
WILLIAM WYLER—Dodsworth, These Three.
RAOUL WALSH—Klondike Annie, Big Brown Eyes.
RENE CLAIR—The Ghost Goes West.
ALEXANDER KORDA—Rembrandt.
ROUBEN MAMOULIAN—The Gay Desperado.
HENRY HATHAWAY—The Trail of the Lonesome Pine; Go West, Young Man.
MICHAEL CURTIZ—Charge of the Light Brigade.
JACK CONWAY—Libeled Lady.
JAMES WHALE—Show Boat.
ALFRED SANTELL—Winterset.
W. S. VAN DYKE—The Great Ziegfeld, San Francisco, After the Thin Man.
DOROTHY ARZNER—Craig's Wife.
LOTHAR MENDES—The Man Who Could Work Miracles.
WILLIAM DIETERLE—The Story of Louis Pasteur.
ARCHIE MAYO—The Petrified Forest.
WILLIAM CAMERON MENZIES—Things to Come.
JAMES CRUZE—Sutter's Gold.
E. A. DUPONT—A Son Comes Home.
TOD BROWNING—The Devil-Doll.
CLARENCE BROWN—Wife Versus Secretary.

1937

ERNST LUBITSCH—*Angel.*
FRITZ LANG—*You Only Live Once.*
FRANK BORZAGE—*History is Made at Night,* Green Light, Mannequin, The Big City.
ALFRED HITCHCOCK—Sabotage.
JOHN FORD—The Hurricane, Wee Willie Winkie.
LEO MC CAREY—The Awful Truth, Make Way for Tomorrow.
GEORGE CUKOR—Camille.
KING VIDOR—Stella Dallas.
FRANK CAPRA—Lost Horizon.
GREGORY LA CAVA—Stage Door.
GEORGE STEVENS—Quality Street, A Damsel in Distress.
JOHN STAHL—Parnell.
TAY GARNETT—Slave Ship, Stand In, Love Is News.
MITCHELL LEISEN—Easy Living; Swing High, Swing Low.
JOHN CROMWELL—The Prisoner of Zenda.
RICHARD THORPE—Night Must Fall.
WILLIAM WELLMAN—A Star Is Born, Nothing Sacred.
VICTOR FLEMING—Captains Courageous.
WESLEY RUGGLES—I Met Him in Paris, True Confession.
MERVYN LEROY—They Won't Forget.
MARK SANDRICH—Shall We Dance?
HENRY HATHAWAY—Souls at Sea.
MICHAEL CURTIZ—Kid Galahad.
ZOLTAN KORDA—Elephant Boy.
JAMES WHALE—The Road Back.
WILLIAM WYLER—Dead End.
WILLIAM DIETERLE—The Life of Emile Zola.

HENRY KOSTER—Three Smart Girls, 100 Men and a Girl.
NORMAN MC LEOD—Topper.
ALEXANDER HALL—Exclusive.
ROUBEN MAMOULIAN—High, Wide, and Handsome.
SIDNEY FRANKLIN—The Good Earth.

1938

GEORGE CUKOR—*Holiday, Zaza.*
HOWARD HAWKS—*Bringing up Baby.*
FRANK BORZAGE—*Three Comrades,* The Shining Hour.
ALFRED HITCHCOCK—The Girl Was Young, The Lady Vanishes.
ERNST LUBITSCH—Bluebeard's Eighth Wife.
JOHN FORD—Submarine Patrol, Four Men and a Prayer.
FRITZ LANG—You and Me.
KING VIDOR—The Citadel.
FRANK CAPRA—You Can't Take It With You.
ANTHONY ASQUITH and LESLIE HOWARD—Pygmalion.
CECIL B. DE MILLE—The Buccaneer.
GEORGE STEVENS—Vivacious Lady.
JOHN STAHL—Letter of Introduction.
HENRY HATHAWAY—Spawn of the North.
MICHAEL CURTIZ—Angels with Dirty Faces, Four Daughters, The Adventures of
    Robin Hood (with William Keighley).
GARSON KANIN—A Man to Remember, Next Time I Marry.
MARK SANDRICH—Carefree.
RICHARD WALLACE—The Young in Heart.
WILLIAM WYLER—Jezebel.
JOHN CROMWELL—Algiers.
WILLIAM DIETERLE—Blockade.
WESLEY RUGGLES—Sing You Sinners.
W. S. VAN DYKE—Marie Antoinette.
HENRY KING—Alexander's Ragtime Band.
JULIEN DUVIVIER—The Great Waltz.
TIM WHELAN—Divorce of Lady X, Action for Slander.
ERICH POMMER—The Beachcomber.
VICTOR SAVILLE—South Riding.
MICHAEL POWELL—The Edge of the World.
ANATOLE LITVAK—The Sisters.
NORMAN TAUROG—Boys Town.
EDMUND GOULDING—The Dawn Patrol, White Banners.
LLOYD BACON—A Slight Case of Murder.

1939

JOHN FORD—*Stagecoach, Young Mr. Lincoln,* Drums Along the Mohawk.
HOWARD HAWKS—*Only Angels Have Wings.*
ERNST LUBITSCH—*Ninotchka.*
LEO MC CAREY—*Love Affair.*
FRANK CAPRA—*Mr. Smith Goes to Washington.*
GEORGE CUKOR—The Women.
ALFRED HITCHCOCK—Jamaica Inn.
JOSEF VON STERNBERG—Sergeant Madden.
RAOUL WALSH—The Roaring Twenties, St. Louis Blues.
KING VIDOR—Northwest Passage.
CECIL B. DE MILLE—Union Pacific.
GEORGE STEVENS—Gunga Din.
VICTOR FLEMING—Gone with the Wind, The Wizard of Oz.
WILLIAM WYLER—Wuthering Heights.

JOHN STAHL—When Tomorrow Comes.
MITCHELL LEISEN—Midnight.
GARSON KANIN—Bachelor Mother, The Great Man Votes.
GREGORY LA CAVA—Fifth Avenue Girl.
EDMUND GOULDING—Dark Victory, The Old Maid, We Are Not Alone.
GEORGE MARSHALL—Destry Rides Again, You Can't Cheat an Honest Man.
WILLIAM K. HOWARD—Back Door to Heaven.
JAY THEODORE REED—What a Life!
ALLAN DWAN—Frontier Marshal.
JOHN CROMWELL—Made for Each Other, In Name Only.
MICHAEL CURTIZ—Dodge City, Daughters Courageous, The Private Lives of Elizabeth and Essex, Four Wives.
ZOLTAN KORDA—Four Feathers.
ROY KELLINO—I Met a Murderer.
BUSBY BERKELEY—Babes in Arms.
VICTOR SCHERTZINGER—The Mikado.
MICHAEL POWELL—The Spy in Black.
WILLIAM DIETERLE—Juarez, Hunchback of Notre Dame.
ANATOLE LITVAK—Confessions of a Nazi Spy.
JOHN FARROW—Five Came Back, Full Confession.
WESLEY RUGGLES—Invitation to Happiness.
GREGORY RATOFF—Intermezzo.
LEWIS SEILER—Dust Be My Destiny.
SAM WOOD—Goodbye, Mr. Chips.

1940

CHARLES CHAPLIN—*The Great Dictator.*
ERNST LUBITSCH—*The Shop Around the Corner.*
HOWARD HAWKS—His Girl Friday.
FRANK BORZAGE—The Mortal Storm, Strange Cargo, Flight Command.
ALFRED HITCHCOCK—Rebecca, Foreign Correspondent.
JOHN FORD—The Grapes of Wrath, The Long Voyage Home.
TAY GARNETT—Seven Sinners, Slightly Honorable.
PRESTON STURGES—The Great McGinty, Christmas in July.
GEORGE CUKOR—The Philadelphia Story, Susan and God.
CECIL B. DE MILLE—Northwest Mounted Police.
WILLIAM WYLER—The Letter.
FRITZ LANG—The Return of Frank James.
RAOUL WALSH—They Drive By Night, The Dark Command.
CAROL REED—Night Train, The Stars Look Down.
GEORGE STEVENS—Vigil in the Night.
LUDWIG BERGER, MICHAEL POWELL, and TIM WHELAN—The Thief of Bagdad.
ROBERT Z. LEONARD—Pride and Prejudice.
MITCHELL LEISEN—Remember the Night; Arise, My Love.
LEWIS MILESTONE—Of Mice and Men, The Night of Nights, Lucky Partners.
GREGORY LA CAVA—-The Primrose Path.
GARSON KANIN—My Favorite Wife, They Knew What They Wanted.
MICHAEL CURTIZ—The Sea Hawk, Virginia City, Santa Fe Trail.
BUSBY BERKELEY—Strike Up the Band.
EDWARD F. CLINE—The Bank Dick, My Little Chickadee, The Villain Still Pursued Her.
JOHN CROMWELL—Victory.
RICHARD THORPE—The Earl of Chicago.
LEE GARMES and BEN HECHT—Angels Over Broadway.
VICTOR SCHERTZINGER—Rhythm on the River, Road to Singapore.
WILLIAM DIETERLE—Doctor Ehrlich's Magic Bullet, A Dispatch From Reuters.
ANATOLE LITVAK—City for Conquest, All This and Heaven Too, Castle on the Hudson.

SAM WOOD—Our Town, Kitty Foyle.
WESLEY RUGGLES—Arizona, Too Many Husbands.
GEORGE MARSHALL—When the Daltons Rode.
TIM WHELAN—Sidewalks of London.
HAL ROACH and D. W. GRIFFITH—One Million B.C.

1941
ORSON WELLES—*Citizen Kane.*
JOSEF VON STERNBERG—*The Shanghai Gesture.*
ALFRED HITCHCOCK—*Suspicion,* Mr. and Mrs. Smith.
JEAN RENOIR—*Swamp Water.*
JOHN FORD—*How Green Was My Valley,* Tobacco Road.
FRITZ LANG—*Man Hunt,* Western Union.
HOWARD HAWKS—Sergeant York, Ball of Fire.
RAOUL WALSH—High Sierra, The Strawberry Blonde, They Died With Their Boots On, Manpower.
PRESTON STURGES—The Lady Eve.
JOHN HUSTON—The Maltese Falcon.
GEORGE STEVENS—Penny Serenade.
GEORGE CUKOR—A Woman's Face, Two-Faced Woman.
KING VIDOR—H. M. Pulham, Esq.
ERNST LUBITSCH—That Uncertain Feeling.
WILLIAM WYLER—The Little Foxes.
FRANK CAPRA—Meet John Doe.
RENE CLAIR—The Flame of New Orleans.
GREGORY LA CAVA—Unfinished Business.
MITCHELL LEISEN—Hold Back the Dawn, I Wanted Wings.
EDMUND GOULDING—The Great Lie.
ALEXANDER HALL—Here Comes Mr. Jordan, Bedtime Story, This Thing Called Love.
WILLIAM DIETERLE—All That Money Can Buy.
ALLAN DWAN—Rise and Shine, Look Who's Laughing.
GABRIEL PASCAL—Major Barbara.
ALEXANDER KORDA—That Hamilton Woman.
ROBERT STEVENSON—Back Street.
GARSON KANIN—Tom, Dick and Harry.
CHARLES VIDOR—Ladies in Retirement.
JOHN CROMWELL—So Ends Our Night.
MICHAEL CURTIZ—The Sea Wolf, Dive Bomber.
HENRY HATHAWAY—The Shepherd of the Hills, Sundown.
GEORGE MARSHALL—Texas.
BRUCE HUMBERSTONE—I Wake Up Screaming.
IRVING RAPPER—Shining Victory.
SAM WOOD—The Devil and Miss Jones.

1942
ORSON WELLES—*The Magnificent Ambersons,* Journey Into Fear (with Norman Foster).
ERNST LUBITSCH—*To Be or Not To Be.*
ALFRED HITCHCOCK—Saboteur.
PRESTON STURGES—Sullivan's Travels, The Palm Beach Story.
RAOUL WALSH—Gentleman Jim, Desperate Journey.
MICHAEL CURTIZ—Casablanca, Yankee Doodle Dandy.
CECIL B. DE MILLE—Reap the Wild Wind.
JACQUES TOURNEUR—The Cat People.
BILLY WILDER—The Major and the Minor.
GEORGE STEVENS—Woman of the Year, Talk of the Town.
JOHN HUSTON—Across the Pacific, In This Our Life.

LEO MC CAREY—Once Upon a Honeymoon.
RENE CLAIR—I Married a Witch.
FRANK BORZAGE—Seven Sweethearts.
DAVID LEAN and NOEL COWARD—In Which We Serve.
ALBERT LEWIN—The Moon and Sixpence.
MERVYN LEROY—Random Harvest, Johnny Eager.
HENRY HATHAWAY—China Girl, Ten Gentlemen From West Point.
ALLAN DWAN—Friendly Enemies, Here We Go Again.
WILLIAM WYLER—Mrs. Miniver.
WILLIAM WELLMAN—Roxie Hart.
SAM WOOD—Kings Row, Pride of the Yankees.
MICHAEL POWELL and EMERIC PRESSBURGER—One of Our Aircraft Is Missing.
STUART HEISLER—The Glass Key.
FRANK TUTTLE—This Gun for Hire.
IRVING RAPPER—Now Voyager, The Gay Sisters.

1943

ALFRED HITCHCOCK—*Shadow of a Doubt.*
FRITZ LANG—*Hangmen Also Die.*
HOWARD HAWKS—*The Air Force.*
ERNST LUBITSCH—Heaven Can Wait.
JEAN RENOIR—This Land Is Mine.
JOHN STAHL—Holy Matrimony, The Immortal Sergeant.
H. C. POTTER—Mr. Lucky.
JACQUES TOURNEUR—I Walked With a Zombie, The Leopard Man.
GEORGE CUKOR—Keeper of the Flame.
FRANK BORZAGE—Stage Door Canteen, His Butler's Sister.
DOUGLAS SIRK—Hitler's Madman.
VINCENTE MINNELLI—Cabin in the Sky, I Dood It.
GEORGE STEVENS—The More the Merrier.
RAOUL WALSH—Northern Pursuit, Background to Danger.
BILLY WILDER—Five Graves to Cairo.
EDMUND GOULDING—Claudia, The Constant Nymph.
RICHARD ROSSEN—Corvette K-225.
VICTOR FLEMING—A Guy Named Joe.
RICHARD WALLACE—The Fallen Sparrow.
ZOLTAN KORDA—Sahara.
CLARENCE BROWN—The Human Comedy.
WILLIAM WELLMAN—The Ox-Bow Incident.
JULIEN DUVIVIER—Flesh and Fantasy.
VINCENT SHERMAN—The Hard Way, Old Acquaintance.
MARK ROBSON—The Seventh Victim, The Ghost Ship.
RAY ENRIGHT—Gung Ho!
LEWIS MILESTONE—The North Star.
IRVING PICHEL—The Moon Is Down.
HERBERT WILCOX—Lassie Come Home.
SAM WOOD—For Whom the Bell Tolls.
MARK SANDRICH—So Proudly We Hail.
NORMAN KRASNA—Princess O'Rourke.
HERMAN SHUMLIN—Watch on the Rhine.

1944

OTTO PREMINGER—*Laura.*
PRESTON STURGES—*The Miracle of Morgan's Creek, Hail the Conquering Hero,*
The Great Moment.
GEORGE CUKOR—*Gaslight,* Winged Victory.
HOWARD HAWKS—*To Have and Have Not.*

ALFRED HITCHCOCK—Lifeboat.
LEO MC CAREY—Going My Way.
FRANK BORZAGE—Till We Meet Again.
ROBERT SIODMAK—Phantom Lady, Christmas Holiday, Cobra Woman.
VINCENTE MINNELLI—Meet Me in St. Louis.
FRANK CAPRA—Arsenic and Old Lace.
BILLY WILDER—Double Indemnity.
EDGAR G. ULMER—Bluebeard.
JOHN STAHL—The Eve of St. Mark, The Keys of the Kingdom.
ARTHUR RIPLEY—Voice in the Wind.
DOUGLAS SIRK—Summer Storm.
RAOUL WALSH—Uncertain Glory.
KING VIDOR—An American Romance.
CECIL B. DE MILLE—The Story of Dr. Wassell.
JOHN CROMWELL—Since You Went Away.
RENE CLAIR—It Happened Tomorrow.
MITCHELL LEISEN—Lady in the Dark.
JEAN NEGULESCO—The Mask of Dimitrios.
ROBERT WISE—Curse of the Cat People.
ANDRE DE TOTH—Dark Waters.
LEWIS ALLEN—The Uninvited, Our Hearts Were Young and Gay.
WILLIAM CASTLE—When Strangers Marry (Betrayed).
JOHN BRAHM—The Lodger, Guest in the House.
CHARLES VIDOR—Cover Girl, Together Again.
CLIFFORD ODETS—None But the Lonely Heart.
EDWARD DMYTRYK—Murder, My Sweet.
FRED ZINNEMANN—The Seventh Cross.
LEWIS MILESTONE—The Purple Heart.
ROY BOULTING—Thunder Rock.
HENRY KING—The Song of Bernadette, Wilson.
ELLIOTT NUGENT—Up in Arms.

1945
JOHN FORD—*They Were Expendable.*
JEAN RENOIR—*The Southerner.*
FRITZ LANG—*Ministry of Fear,* The Woman in the Window, Scarlet Street.
ALFRED HITCHCOCK—Spellbound.
OTTO PREMINGER—Fallen Angel, A Royal Scandal.
ROBERT SIODMAK—The Suspect, Uncle Harry.
JOHN STAHL—Leave Her to Heaven.
RAOUL WALSH—Salty O'Rourke, Objective Burma, The Horn Blows at Midnight.
LEO MC CAREY—The Bells of St. Mary's.
VINCENTE MINNELLI—The Clock, Yolanda and the Thief.
FRANK BORZAGE—The Spanish Main.
BILLY WILDER—The Lost Weekend.
WILLIAM WELLMAN—Story of G.I. Joe.
ELIA KAZAN—A Tree Grows in Brooklyn.
ALLAN DWAN—Brewster's Millions, Getting Gertie's Garter.
COMPTON BENNETT—The Seventh Veil.
RENE CLAIR—And Then There Were None.
EDGAR G. ULMER—Detour, Strange Illusion.
JOSEPH H. LEWIS—My Name Is Julia Ross.
GUSTAV MACHATY—Jealousy.
ROBERT WISE—The Body Snatcher.
MICHAEL CURTIZ—Mildred Pierce.
CLIVE BROOK—On Approval.

DAVID LEAN—Blithe Spirit.

MICHAEL POWELL and EMERIC PRESSBURGER—The Life and Death of Colonel Blimp.

ALBERT LEWIN—The Picture of Dorian Gray.

ALEXANDER KORDA—Vacation From Marriage.

JOHN BRAHM—Hangover Square.

WILLIAM DIETERLE—Love Letters, I'll Be Seeing You.

GEORGE MARSHALL—Murder, He Says; Incendiary Blonde.

MARK ROBSON—Isle of the Dead.

EDWARD DMYTRYK—Cornered.

HENRY HATHAWAY—The House on 92nd Street.

GEORGE SIDNEY—Anchors Aweigh.

WALTER LANG—State Fair.

HERMAN SHUMLIN—Confidential Agent.

JOHN BAXTER—Love on the Dole.

1946

ALFRED HITCHCOCK—*Notorious.*

HOWARD HAWKS—*The Big Sleep.*

JOHN FORD—*My Darling Clementine.*

JEAN RENOIR—*Diary of a Chambermaid.*

FRANK CAPRA—*It's a Wonderful Life.*

ORSON WELLES—The Stranger.

DOUGLAS SIRK—A Scandal in Paris.

ROBERT SIODMAK—The Killers, The Spiral Staircase, The Dark Mirror.

FRANK BORZAGE—I've Always Loved You, The Magnificent Doll.

ERNST LUBITSCH—Cluny Brown.

FRITZ LANG—Cloak and Dagger.

CAVALCANTI, BASIL DEARDEN, and ROBERT HAMER—Dead of Night.

DAVID LEAN—Brief Encounter.

VINCENTE MINNELLI—Ziegfeld Follies.

RAOUL WALSH—The Man I Love.

WILLIAM WYLER—The Best Years of Our Lives.

ARTHUR RIPLEY—The Chase.

JACQUES TOURNEUR—Canyon Passage.

LEWIS MILESTONE—A Walk in the Sun, The Strange Love of Martha Ivers.

ALLAN DWAN—Rendezvous with Annie, Calendar Girl.

CHARLES VIDOR—Gilda.

EDMUND GOULDING—The Razor's Edge.

JOSEPH H. LEWIS—So Dark the Night.

DON SIEGEL—The Verdict.

LAURENCE OLIVIER—Henry V.

SIDNEY GILLIAT—Notorious Gentleman.

MICHAEL POWELL and EMERIC PRESSBURGER—Stairway to Heaven.

JEAN NEGULESCO—Three Strangers, Nobody Lives Forever, Humoresque.

EDGAR G. ULMER—Her Sister's Secret.

TAY GARNETT—The Postman Always Rings Twice.

JOSEPH L. MANKIEWICZ—Dragonwyck, Somewhere in the Night.

JOHN BRAHM—The Locket.

ROY WILLIAM NEILL—Black Angel.

HAROLD CLURMAN—Deadline at Dawn.

JOHN CROMWELL—Anna and the King of Siam.

GABRIEL PASCAL—Caesar and Cleopatra.

ALFRED E. GREEN—The Jolson Story.

MARK ROBSON—Bedlam.

IRVING RAPPER—Deception.

CURTIS BERNHARDT—Devotion, A Stolen Life.

1947

CHARLES CHAPLIN—*Monsieur Verdoux.*
MAX OPHULS—*The Exile.*
CAROL REED—Odd Man Out.
ANTHONY MANN—T-Men.
JOSEPH LOSEY—The Boy With Green Hair.
KING VIDOR—Duel in the Sun.
JEAN RENOIR—Woman on the Beach.
RAOUL WALSH—Pursued, Cheyenne.
JACQUES TOURNEUR—Out of the Past.
ROBERT ROSSEN—Johnny O'Clock, Body and Soul.
DOUGLAS SIRK—Lured.
FRANK BORZAGE—That's My Man.
JOHN FORD—The Fugitive.
ZOLTAN KORDA—The Macomber Affair, A Woman's Vengeance.
HENRY HATHAWAY—Kiss of Death.
CECIL B. DE MILLE—Unconquered.
OTTO PREMINGER—Daisy Kenyon, Forever Amber.
LEO MC CAREY—Good Sam.
JOHN STAHL—The Foxes of Harrow, The Walls of Jericho.
DAVID LEAN—Great Expectations, This Happy Breed.
MICHAEL POWELL and EMERIC PRESSBURGER—Black Narcissus, I Know Where
    I'm Going.
ROBERT WISE—Born to Kill.
CHARLES WALTERS—Good News.
JULES DASSIN—Brute Force.
ANDRE DE TOTH—Ramrod.
BYRON HASKIN—I Walk Alone.
JOSEPH L. MANKIEWICZ—The Ghost and Mrs. Muir.
ROBERT MONTGOMERY—Ride the Pink Horse.
EDMUND GOULDING—Nightmare Alley.
ELIA KAZAN—Gentleman's Agreement, Boomerang!
EDWARD DMYTRYK—Crossfire.
SIDNEY GILLIAT—Green for Danger.
JEAN NEGULESCO—Deep Valley.
IRVING PICHEL—They Won't Believe Me.
DELMER DAVES—Dark Passage, The Red House.
VINCENT SHERMAN—The Unfaithful.

1948

MAX OPHULS—*Letter From an Unknown Woman.*
ORSON WELLES—*The Lady From Shanghai.*
JOHN FORD—*Fort Apache.*
HOWARD HAWKS—*Red River, A Song Is Born.*
FRANK BORZAGE—*Moonrise.*
JOHN HUSTON—Key Largo, The Treasure of the Sierra Madre.
ABRAHAM POLONSKY—Force of Evil.
FRANK CAPRA—State of the Union.
HENRY HATHAWAY—Call Northside 777.
ALFRED HITCHCOCK—Rope, The Paradine Case.
GEORGE CUKOR—A Double Life.
DOUGLAS SIRK—Sleep, My Love.
VINCENTE MINNELLI—The Pirate.
GEORGE STEVENS—I Remember Mama.
FRITZ LANG—The Secret Beyond the Door.
KING VIDOR—On Our Merry Way.
RAOUL WALSH—Silver River, One Sunday Afternoon, Fighter Squadron.

LAURENCE OLIVIER—Hamlet.
MICHAEL POWELL and EMERIC PRESSBURGER—The Red Shoes.
EDGAR G. ULMER—Ruthless.
ALLAN DWAN—The Inside Story, Angel in Exile.
PRESTON STURGES—Unfaithfully Yours.
CHARLES WALTERS—Easter Parade.
ROUBEN MAMOULIAN—Summer Holiday.
BILLY WILDER—A Foreign Affair, The Emperor Waltz.
ANDRE DE TOTH—Pitfall.
ROBERT SIODMAK—Cry of the City.
JEAN NEGULESCO—Johnny Belinda, Road House.
JOHN FARROW—The Big Clock.
MICHAEL GORDON—Another Part of the Forest, An Act of Murder.
EDWARD LUDWIG—Wake of the Red Witch.
JULES DASSIN—The Naked City.
ALFRED WERKER—He Walked by Night.
RICHARD HAYDEN—Miss Tatlock's Millions.
WALTER LANG—Sitting Pretty.
RALPH THOMAS—The Clouded Yellow.
WILLIAM WELLMAN—Yellow Sky, The Iron Curtain.
LEWIS MILESTONE—Arch of Triumph, No Minor Vices.
ROBERT FLAHERTY—Louisiana Story.
CLAUDE BINYON—The Saxon Charm.
FRED ZINNEMANN—The Search.
ANATOLE LITVAK—The Snake Pit; Sorry, Wrong Number.

1949

JOHN FORD—*She Wore a Yellow Ribbon,* Three Godfathers.
MAX OPHULS—*Caught,* The Reckless Moment.
RAOUL WALSH—*White Heat,* Colorado Territory.
HOWARD HAWKS—I Was a Male War Bride.
KING VIDOR—The Fountainhead, Beyond the Forest.
JOSEPH H. LEWIS—Gun Crazy, Undercover Man.
ANTHONY MANN—Border Incident, Side Street, Reign of Terror.
ALFRED HITCHCOCK—Under Capricorn.
GEORGE CUKOR—Adam's Rib; Edward, My Son.
NICHOLAS RAY—They Live By Night.
JOHN HUSTON—We Were Strangers.
DOUGLAS SIRK—Shockproof, Slightly French.
OTTO PREMINGER—Whirlpool, The Fan.
STANLEY DONEN and GENE KELLY—On the Town.
SAMUEL FULLER—I Shot Jesse James.
VINCENTE MINNELLI—Madame Bovary.
CAROL REED—The Fallen Idol.
JOSEPH L. MANKIEWICZ—A Letter to Three Wives, House of Strangers.
ELIA KAZAN—Pinky.
MICHAEL CURTIZ—Flamingo Road, My Dream Is Yours.
BYRON HASKIN—Too Late for Tears.
FRED ZINNEMANN—Act of Violence.
ROBERT ROSSEN—All the King's Men.
JULES DASSIN—Thieves' Highway.
ROBERT WISE—The Set-Up.
EMLYN WILLIAMS—The Woman of Dolwyn.
CECIL B. DE MILLE—Samson and Delilah.
DON SIEGEL—The Big Steal, Night Unto Night.
CHARLES WALTERS—The Barkleys of Broadway.
PRESTON STURGES—The Beautiful Blonde from Bashful Bend.

CLARENCE BROWN—Intruder in the Dust.
MARK ROBSON—Champion, Home of the Brave.
WILLIAM WELLMAN—Battleground.
WILLIAM WYLER—The Heiress.
ELLIOTT NUGENT—The Great Gatsby.
ROBERT SIODMAK—Criss Cross.
JOHN STURGES—The Walking Hills.
ROBERT MONTGOMERY—Once More, My Darling.
RUDY MATE—D.O.A., No Sad Songs for Me.
STUART HEISLER—Tulsa.
ALFRED WERKER—Lost Boundaries.
TED TATZLAFF—The Window.
TERENCE YOUNG—Corridor of Mirrors.

1950

JOHN FORD—*Wagonmaster, Rio Grande,* When Willie Comes Marching Home.
CAROL REED—*The Third Man.*
JOHN HUSTON—*The Asphalt Jungle.*
OTTO PREMINGER—*Where the Sidewalk Ends.*
JOSEPH LOSEY—The Lawless.
ALFRED HITCHCOCK—Stage Fright.
ANTHONY MANN—Winchester 73, Devil's Doorway, The Furies.
NICHOLAS RAY—In a Lonely Place.
JOSEPH L. MANKIEWICZ—All About Eve, No Way Out.
BILLY WILDER—Sunset Boulevard.
ELIA KAZAN—Panic in the Streets.
JULES DASSIN—Night and the City.
FRITZ LANG—American Guerilla in the Philippines, House by the River.
FRANK CAPRA—Riding High.
SAMUEL FULLER—The Baron of Arizona.
ROBERT HAMER—Kind Hearts and Coronets.
JOHN CROMWELL—Caged.
MICHAEL CURTIZ—The Breaking Point.
GEORGE CUKOR—A Life of Her Own, Born Yesterday.
VINCENTE MINNELLI—Father of the Bride.
CHARLES CRICHTON—The Lavender Hill Mob.
CHARLES WALTERS—Summer Stock.
JOSEPH H. LEWIS—Lady Without a Passport.
JACQUES TOURNEUR—The Flame and the Arrow, Stars in my Crown.
JOHN STURGES—Mystery Street.
GORDON DOUGLAS—Kiss Tomorrow Goodbye.
CYRIL ENDFIELD—Sound of Fury.
WILLIAM DIETERLE—Dark City.
RUDY MATE—Union Station.
MARK ROBSON—My Foolish Heart.
HENRY KING—Twelve O'Clock High, The Gunfighter.
FRED ZINNEMANN—The Men.
ANTHONY ASQUITH—The Winslow Boy.
DELMER DAVES—Broken Arrow.
SIDNEY GILLIAT—State Secret (The Great Manhunt).
RICHARD THORPE—Black Hand, Three Little Words.
JOSEPH M. NEWMAN—711 Ocean Drive.
EDWARD DMYTRYK—Give Us This Day.
STUART HEISLER—Storm Warning.

1951

JEAN RENOIR—*The River.*
ALFRED HITCHCOCK—*Strangers on a Train.*

JOSEPH LOSEY—The Prowler, The Big Night, M.
SAMUEL FULLER—The Steel Helmet, Fixed Bayonets.
ANTHONY MANN—The Tall Target.
RAOUL WALSH—Distant Drums, Captain Horatio Hornblower, Along the Great Divide.
BRETAIGNE WINDUST—The Enforcer.
NICHOLAS RAY—On Dangerous Ground, Flying Leathernecks.
KING VIDOR—Lightning Strikes Twice.
GEORGE STEVENS—A Place in the Sun.
VINCENTE MINNELLI—An American in Paris, Father's Little Dividend.
BUDD BOETTICHER—The Bullfighter and the Lady.
ALLAN DWAN—Belle Le Grande.
PRESTON STURGES—Mad Wednesday.
ELIA KAZAN—A Streetcar Named Desire.
BILLY WILDER—Ace in the Hole.
JOHN STURGES—The People Against O'Hara, Kind Lady.
FRANK CAPRA—Here Comes the Groom.
HENRY KOSTER—No Highway in the Sky.
CHRISTIAN NYBY—The Thing.
JACQUES TOURNEUR—Anne of the Indies, Circle of Danger.
ALBERT LEWIN—Pandora and the Flying Dutchman.
JOSEPH L. MANKIEWICZ—People Will Talk.
DAVID LEAN—Oliver Twist.
JOHN BERRY—He Ran All the Way, Tension.
GORDON DOUGLAS—Come Fill the Cup.
HENRY HATHAWAY—Fourteen Hours, The Desert Fox, You're in the Navy Now, Rawhide.
OTTO PREMINGER—The Thirteenth Letter.
STANLEY DONEN—Royal Wedding.
ANTHONY ASQUITH—The Browning Version.
ROY BAKER—Operation Disaster.
WILLIAM WYLER—Detective Story.
FRED ZINNEMANN—Teresa.
ANATOLE LITVAK—Decision Before Dawn.
JOHN HUSTON—The Red Badge of Courage.
ROBERT WISE—The Day the Earth Stood Still.
LASLO BENEDEK—Death of a Salesman.
MARK ROBSON—Bright Victory.

1952

CHARLES CHAPLIN—*Limelight.*
HOWARD HAWKS—*The Big Sky,* Monkey Business, O'Henry's Full House (with Henry Hathaway, Jean Negulesco, Henry King, and Henry Koster).
JOHN FORD—*The Quiet Man.*
GEORGE CUKOR—The Marrying Kind, The Model and the Marriage Broker, Pat and Mike.
FRITZ LANG—Rancho Notorious, Clash by Night.
KING VIDOR—Ruby Gentry.
ANTHONY MANN—Bend of the River.
JOSEPH L. MANKIEWICZ—Five Fingers.
NICHOLAS RAY—The Lusty Men.
CECIL B. DE MILLE—The Greatest Show on Earth.
DOUGLAS SIRK—Has Anybody Seen My Gal?
STANLEY DONEN and GENE KELLY—Singin' in the Rain.
SAMUEL FULLER—Park Row.
LEO MC CAREY—My Son John.
JOSEF VON STERNBERG—Macao.

RAOUL WALSH—The Lawless Breed, The World in His Arms, Glory Alley, Sea Devils, Blackbeard the Pirate.
CAROL REED—Outcast of the Islands.
ELIA KAZAN—*Viva Zapata!*
DAVID LEAN—Breaking Through the Sound Barrier.
JOHN HUSTON—The African Queen.
GEORGE STEVENS—Something to Live For.
CHARLES CRICHTON—The Stranger in Between.
GEORGE SIDNEY—Scaramouche.
ALEXANDER MACKENDRICK—The Man in the White Suit.
ROBERT SIODMAK—The Crimson Pirate.
RICHARD BROOKS—Deadline, U.S.A.
FRED ZINNEMANN—High Noon.
ZOLTAN KORDA—Cry, the Beloved Country.
RICHARD FLEISCHER—The Narrow Margin.
MICHAEL POWELL and EMERIC PRESSBURGER—The Small Back Room.
ANDREW STONE—The Steel Trap.
PAT JACKSON—White Corridors.
WILLIAM WYLER—Carrie.
STUART HEISLER—Island of Desire.
DAVID BUTLER—Where's Charlie.
GOTTFRIED REINHARDT—Invitation.
CHARLES MARQUIS WARREN—Hellgate.

1953

ALFRED HITCHCOCK—*I Confess.*
FRITZ LANG—*The Big Heat,* The Blue Gardenia.
DOUGLAS SIRK—*Take Me to Town,* All I Desire.
CAROL REED—*The Man Between.*
JOHN FORD—Mogambo.
HOWARD HAWKS—Gentlemen Prefer Blondes.
OTTO PREMINGER—Angel Face, The Moon Is Blue.
GEORGE CUKOR—The Actress.
VINCENTE MINNELLI—The Bad and the Beautiful, The Bandwagon, The Story of Three Loves (with Gottfried Reinhardt).
RAOUL WALSH—A Lion Is in the Streets, Gun Fury.
SAMUEL FULLER—Pickup on South Street.
GEORGE STEVENS—Shane.
BILLY WILDER—Stalag 17.
ANTHONY MANN—The Naked Spur, Thunder Bay.
WILLIAM WYLER—Roman Holiday.
STANLEY DONEN—Give a Girl a Break.
ALEXANDER MACKENDRICK—The Story of Mandy.
LASLO BENEDEK—The Wild One.
CHARLES WALTERS—Lilli, Torch Song.
PHIL KARLSON—99 River Street.
DON SIEGEL—Count the Hours.
CURTIS BERNHARDT—Miss Sadie Thompson.
RICHARD BROOKS—Take the High Ground, Battle Circus.
HENRY HATHAWAY—Niagara.
JOHN HUSTON—Moulin Rouge.
FRED ZINNEMANN—From Here to Eternity, The Member of the Wedding.
JOSEPH L. MANKIEWICZ—Julius Caesar.
ELIA KAZAN—Man on a Tightrope.
IDA LUPINO—The Hitch-Hiker.
GEORGE SIDNEY—Kiss Me Kate, Young Bess.
DON WEIS—I Love Melvin, The Affairs of Dobie Gillis, Remains To Be Seen.

RUSSELL ROUSE—Wicked Woman.
GEORGE SEATON—Little Boy Lost.

1954

ALFRED HITCHCOCK—*Rear Window*, Dial M for Murder.
JOHN FORD—*The Sun Shines Bright.*
JEAN RENOIR—*The Golden Coach.*
ROBERTO ROSSELLINI—*The Greatest Love.*
LUIS BUNUEL—*The Adventures of Robinson Crusoe.*
NICHOLAS RAY—Johnny Guitar.
GEORGE CUKOR—A Star Is Born, It Should Happen to You.
RENE CLEMENT—Lovers, Happy Lovers.
JOSEF VON STERNBERG—Anatahan.
DON SIEGEL—Riot in Cell Block 11, Private Hell 36.
ELIA KAZAN—On the Waterfront.
OTTO PREMINGER—River of No Return, Carmen Jones.
DOUGLAS SIRK—Magnificent Obsession, Sign of the Pagan; Taza, Son of Cochise.
FRITZ LANG—Human Desire.
JOSEPH L. MANKIEWICZ—The Barefoot Contessa.
ROBERT ALDRICH—Apache, World for Ransom.
SAMUEL FULLER—Hell and High Water.
HENRY CORNELIUS—Genevieve.
ALLAN DWAN—Silver Lode, Cattle Queen of Montana, Passion.
VINCENTE MINNELLI—Brigadoon.
RAOUL WALSH—Saskatchewan.
DAVID LEAN—Hobson's Choice.
STANLEY DONEN—Seven Brides for Seven Brothers.
BYRON HASKIN—The Naked Jungle.
RICHARD BROOKS—The Last Time I Saw Paris.
DON WEIS—The Adventures of Hajji Baba.
ANTHONY MANN—The Glenn Miller Story.
JOHN HUSTON—Beat the Devil.
BILLY WILDER—Sabrina.
ROBERT WISE—Executive Suite.
RICHARD QUINE—Drive a Crooked Road, Pushover, So This Is Paris.
NUNNALLY JOHNSON—Black Widow.
WILLIAM WELLMAN—The High and the Mighty.
GEORGE SEATON—The Country Girl.

1955

ROBERTO ROSSELLINI—*Strangers.*
ALFRED HITCHCOCK—*To Catch a Thief,* The Trouble With Harry.
DOUGLAS SIRK—*Captain Lightfoot.*
ORSON WELLES—*Othello.*
JOHN FORD—*The Long Gray Line,* Mister Roberts (with Mervyn LeRoy).
NICHOLAS RAY—Rebel Without a Cause, Run for Cover.
ROBERT ALDRICH—Kiss Me Deadly, The Big Knife.
FRITZ LANG—Moonfleet.
PHIL KARLSON—The Phenix City Story, Five Against the House, Hell's Island, Tight Spot.
SAMUEL FULLER—House of Bamboo.
ROBERT PARRISH—The Purple Plain.
KING VIDOR—Man Without a Star.
OTTO PREMINGER—The Man With the Golden Arm, The Court Martial of Billy Mitchell.

HOWARD HAWKS—Land of the Pharaohs.
RAOUL WALSH—Battle Cry, The Tall Men.
VINCENTE MINNELLI—The Cobweb, Kismet.
EDGAR G. ULMER—The Naked Dawn, Murder Is My Beat.
ALLAN DWAN—Tennessee's Partner, Pearl of the South Pacific, Escape to Burma.
CHARLES LAUGHTON—The Night of the Hunter.
STANLEY DONEN and GENE KELLY—It's Always Fair Weather.
ELIA KAZAN—East of Eden.
CHARLES WALTERS—The Tender Trap.
FRANK TASHLIN—Artists and Models, The Lieutenant Wore Skirts.
ANTHONY MANN—The Last Frontier, The Man from Laramie, The Far Country, Strategic Air Command.
DAVID LEAN—Summertime.
JOSEPH H. LEWIS—The Big Combo, The Lawless Street.
CHARLES VIDOR—Love Me Or Leave Me.
RICHARD FLEISCHER—Violent Saturday, The Girl in the Red Velvet Swing, Bandido.
JACQUES TOURNEUR—Wichita.
BUDD BOETTICHER—The Magnificent Matador.
ARTHUR LUBIN—Footsteps in the Fog.
JACK WEBB—Pete Kelly's Blues.
JOHN STURGES—Bad Day at Black Rock.
MELVILLE SHAVELSON—Houseboat.
HENRY KING—Love Is a Many Splendored Thing.
WILLIAM WYLER—The Desperate Hours.
RICHARD BROOKS—The Blackboard Jungle.
GEORGE SIDNEY—The Eddy Duchin Story.
DANIEL MANN—The Rose Tattoo.
DELBERT MANN—Marty.
PHILIP DUNNE—Prince of Players.
HALL BARTLETT—Unchained.

1956

JOHN FORD—*The Searchers.*
ALFRED HITCHCOCK—*The Man Who Knew Too Much, The Wrong Man.*
NICHOLAS RAY—Bigger Than Life, Hot Blood.
BUDD BOETTICHER—Seven Men from Now, The Killer Is Loose.
DOUGLAS SIRK—All That Heaven Allows, There's Always Tomorrow, Battle Hymn.
GEORGE CUKOR—Bhowani Junction.
ROBERT ALDRICH—Attack, Autumn Leaves.
DON SIEGEL—Invasion of the Body Snatchers, Crime in the Streets.
STANLEY KUBRICK—The Killing.
FRITZ LANG—While the City Sleeps, Beyond a Reasonable Doubt.
LAURENCE OLIVIER—Richard III.
KING VIDOR—War and Peace.
ALLAN DWAN—Slightly Scarlet, Hold Back the Night.
RAOUL WALSH—A King and Four Queens, The Revolt of Mamie Stover.
VINCENTE MINNELLI—Lust for Life, Tea and Sympathy.
GEORGE STEVENS—Giant.
CECIL B. DE MILLE—The Ten Commandments.
RICHARD BROOKS—The Last Hunt, The Catered Affair.
ALEXANDER MACKENDRICK—The Ladykillers.
GERD OSWALD—Kiss Before Dying, The Brass Legend.
FRANK TASHLIN—The Girl Can't Help It, Hollywood or Bust.
LEWIS FOSTER—The Bold and the Brave.

ROBERT WISE—Somebody Up There Likes Me.
R. G. SPRINGSTEEN—Come Next Spring.
NORMAN PANAMA and MELVIN FRANK—The Court Jester.
ELIA KAZAN—Baby Doll.
JOHN HUSTON—Moby Dick.
JOSHUA LOGAN—Picnic, Bus Stop.
WILLIAM WYLER—Friendly Persuasion.
CAROL REED—A Kid for Two Farthings, Trapeze.
RUSSELL ROUSE—The Fastest Gun Alive.
ARNOLD LAVEN—The Rack.
HARRY KELLER—The Unguarded Moment.
CORNELL WILDE—Storm Fear.
JOSEPH ANTHONY—The Rainmaker.
PHILIP DUNNE—Hilda Crane.
HARRY HORNER—The Wild Party.
DANIEL MANN—I'll Cry Tomorrow.

1957

JOHN FORD—*The Wings of Eagles, The Rising of the Moon.*
SAMUEL FULLER—*Forty Guns,* Run Of the Arrow, China Gate.
JOSEF VON STERNBERG—*Jet Pilot.*
DOUGLAS SIRK—*Written on the Wind,* Interlude.
JEAN RENOIR—*Paris Does Strange Things.*
GEORGE CUKOR—Les Girls, Wild Is the Wind.
OTTO PREMINGER—Saint Joan.
JOSEPH LOSEY—Time Without Pity.
ALEXANDER MACKENDRICK—Sweet Smell of Success.
ALLAN DWAN—The River's Edge, The Restless Breed.
GERD OSWALD—Crime of Passion, Fury at Showdown, Valerie.
BUDD BOETTICHER—The Tall T, Decision at Sundown.
DON SIEGEL—Baby Face Nelson.
ELIA KAZAN—A Face in the Crowd.
RAOUL WALSH—Band of Angels.
VINCENTE MINNELLI—Designing Woman.
LEO MC CAREY—An Affair to Remember.
BLAKE EDWARDS—Mister Cory.
FRANK TASHLIN—Will Success Spoil Rock Hunter?
JOSEPH H. LEWIS—The Halliday Brand.
PHIL KARLSON—The Brothers Rico.
NICHOLAS RAY—The True Story of Jesse James.
STANLEY DONEN—Funny Face, Kiss Them for Me, The Pajama Game (with
    George Abbott).
ANTHONY MANN—Men at War, The Tin Star.
PAUL WENDKOS—The Burglar.
BILLY WILDER—Love in the Afternoon.
ROBERT WISE—This Could Be the Night, Until They Sail.
DAVID LEAN—The Bridge on the River Kwai.
DICK POWELL—The Enemy Below.
ROBERT MULLIGAN—Fear Strikes Out.
DELMER DAVES—3:10 to Yuma, Cowboy.
JOSE FERRER—The Great Man.
DELBERT MANN—The Bachelor Party.
STANLEY KUBRICK—Paths of Glory.
JOHN HUSTON—Heaven Knows, Mr. Allison.
JOHN FRANKENHEIMER—The Young Stranger.
SIDNEY LUMET—Twelve Angry Men.
FRED ZINNEMANN—A Hatful of Rain.

CHARLES WALTERS—Don't Go Near the Water.
GEORGE SIDNEY—Jeanne Eagels, Pal Joey.
MARTIN RITT—Edge of the City.
JACK GARFEIN—The Strange One.
DAVID MILLER—The Story of Esther Costello.

1958
ALFRED HITCHCOCK—*Vertigo.*
ORSON WELLES—*Touch of Evil.*
DOUGLAS SIRK—*A Time to Love and a Time to Die, Tarnished Angels.*
OTTO PREMINGER—*Bonjour Tristesse.*
NICHOLAS RAY—*Wind Across the Everglades, Bitter Victory,* Party Girl.
JOHN FORD—*The Last Hurrah.*
ANTHONY MANN—Man of the West, God's Little Acre.
RENE CLEMENT—This Angry Age.
FRANK BORZAGE—China Doll.
DON SIEGEL—The Line-Up, A Spanish Affair, The Gun Runners.
ARTHUR PENN—The Left Handed Gun.
BUDD BOETTICHER—Buchanan Rides Alone.
RAOUL WALSH—The Naked and the Dead.
ARTHUR RIPLEY—Thunder Road.
IRVING LERNER—Murder by Contract.
VINCENTE MINNELLI—Gigi, The Reluctant Debutante.
JACQUES TOURNEUR—Curse of the Demon.
LEO MC CAREY—Rally Round the Flag, Boys.
GERD OSWALD—Screaming Mimi.
JOSEPH L. MANKIEWICZ—The Quiet American.
STANLEY DONEN—Indiscreet, Damn Yankees (with George Abbott).
JOSEPH H. LEWIS—Terror in a Texas Town.
BLAKE EDWARDS—This Happy Feeling, The Perfect Furlough.
FRANK TASHLIN—Rock-a-bye Baby, Geisha Boy.
PHIL KARLSON—Gunman's Walk.
SIDNEY LUMET—Stage Struck.
ROBERT WISE—I Want to Live.
IRVIN KERSHNER—Stakeout on Dope Street.
JOHN CROMWELL—The Goddess.
DICK POWELL—The Hunters.
HENRY HATHAWAY—From Hell to Texas.
GEORGE MARSHALL—The Sheepman, Imitation General.
PAUL WENDKOS—The Case Against Brooklyn.
RICHARD BROOKS—Cat on a Hot Tin Roof, The Brothers Karamazov.
CAROL REED—The Key.
RONALD NEAME—The Horse's Mouth.
JOHN HUSTON—The Roots of Heaven.
WILLIAM WYLER—The Big Country.
STANLEY KRAMER—The Defiant Ones.
DELBERT MANN—Separate Tables.
DANIEL MANN—Hot Spell.

1959
ALFRED HITCHCOCK—*North by Northwest.*
JOHN FORD—*The Horse Soldiers, Gideon of Scotland Yard.*
DOUGLAS SIRK—*Imitation of Life.*
HOWARD HAWKS—*Rio Bravo.*
OTTO PREMINGER—*Anatomy of a Murder,* Porgy and Bess.
BLAKE EDWARDS—Operation Petticoat.
VINCENTE MINNELLI—Some Came Running.

SAMUEL FULLER—The Crimson Kimono.
BUDD BOETTICHER—Ride Lonesome, Westbound.
ROBERT ALDRICH—The Angry Hills, Ten Seconds to Hell.
FRANK CAPRA—A Hole in the Head.
BILLY WILDER—Some Like It Hot.
DON SIEGEL—Hound Dog Man, Edge of Eternity.
FRANK TASHLIN—Say One for Me.
SIDNEY LUMET—That Kind of Woman.
CHARLES WALTERS—Ask Any Girl.
GEORGE STEVENS—The Diary of Anne Frank.
JACK CLAYTON—Room at the Top.
JOHN STURGES—Last Train from Gun Hill.
ROBERT WISE—Odds Against Tomorrow.
TONY RICHARDSON—Look Back in Anger.
FRED ZINNEMANN—The Nun's Story.
JOSEPH L. MANKIEWICZ—Suddenly Last Summer.
DELMER DAVES—A Summer Place.
JAMES CLAVELL—Five Gates to Hell.
DELBERT MANN—The Middle of the Night.
JOSEPH ANTHONY—Career.
J. LEE THOMPSON—Tiger Bay.
STANLEY KRAMER—On the Beach.
WILLIAM WYLER—Ben-Hur.

1960
ALFRED HITCHCOCK—*Psycho.*
JOHN FORD—*Sergeant Rutledge.*
JOSEPH LOSEY—Chance Meeting.
GEORGE CUKOR—Heller in Pink Tights, Let's Make Love, Song Without End
    (with Charles Vidor).
OTTO PREMINGER—Exodus.
BUDD BOETTICHER—Comanche Station, The Rise and Fall of Legs Diamond
ELIA KAZAN—Wild River.
BILLY WILDER—The Apartment.
RICHARD BROOKS—Elmer Gantry.
SAMUEL FULLER—Verboten!
VINCENTE MINNELLI—Bells Are Ringing, Home from the Hill.
JOHN STURGES—The Magnificent Seven.
DON SIEGEL—Flaming Star.
ROBERT MONTGOMERY—The Gallant Hours.
ROBERT MULLIGAN—The Rat Race, The Great Impostor.
RAOUL WALSH—Esther and the King.
BLAKE EDWARDS—High Time.
HENRY HATHAWAY—North to Alaska, Seven Thieves.
TAY GARNETT—The Night Fighters.
PHILIP LEACOCK—Take a Giant Step.
STUART ROSENBERG and BURT BALABAN—Murder, Inc.
JOHN HUSTON—The Unforgiven.
PHIL KARLSON—Hell to Eternity, Key Witness.
CHARLES WALTERS—Please Don't Eat the Daisies.
GEORGE SIDNEY—Who Was That Lady?
STANLEY KUBRICK—Spartacus.
HUBERT CORNFIELD—The Third Voice.
JERRY LEWIS—The Bellboy.
RICHARD QUINE—Strangers When We Meet.
RONALD NEAME—Tunes of Glory.
JACK CARDIFF—Sons and Lovers.

JAMES CLAVELL—Walk Like a Dragon.
LESLIE STEVENS—Private Property.
STANLEY DONEN—Once More With Feeling, Surprise Package, The Grass Is Greener.
TONY RICHARDSON—The Entertainer.
JOHN WAYNE—The Alamo.
FRED ZINNEMANN—The Sundowners.
JOSHUA LOGAN—Tall Story.
DANIEL PETRIE—The Bramble Bush.

1961
JOHN FORD—*Two Rode Together.*
BLAKE EDWARDS—*Breakfast at Tiffany's.*
FRANK CAPRA—Pocketful of Miracles.
SAMUEL FULLER—Underworld, U.S.A.
NICHOLAS RAY—The Savage Innocents, The King of Kings.
LUIS BUNUEL—The Young One.
ROBERT MULLIGAN—The Great Impostor.
GERD OSWALD—Brainwashed.
ROBERT ROSSEN—The Hustler.
BYRON HASKIN—Armored Command.
IRVIN KERSHNER—The Hoodlum Priest.
ALEXANDER SINGER—Cold Wind in August.
JEROME ROBBINS and ROBERT WISE—West Side Story.
ANTHONY MANN—El Cid.
ROBERT ALDRICH—The Last Sunset.
RAOUL WALSH—Marines, Let's Go.
MARLON BRANDO—One Eyed Jacks.
JERRY LEWIS—The Ladies' Man.
SETH HOLT—Scream of Fear.
GORDON DOUGLAS—The Sins of Rachel Cade.
ELIA KAZAN—Splendor in the Grass.
KAREL REISZ—Saturday Night and Sunday Morning.
PAUL WENDKOS—Angel Baby.
JACK CLAYTON—The Innocents.
JOSEPH PEVNEY—The Plunderers.
JOSEPH M. NEWMAN—King of the Roaring 20's.
GUY GREEN—The Mark.
JOHN CASSAVETES—Shadows.
CHARLES WALTERS—Two Loves.
PHIL KARLSON—The Young Doctors.
JOHN FRANKENHEIMER—The Young Savages.
JOHN HUSTON—The Misfits.
BILLY WILDER—One, Two, Three.
STANLEY KRAMER—Judgement at Nuremberg.

1962
JOHN FORD—*The Man Who Shot Liberty Valance.*
SAMUEL FULLER—*Merrill's Marauders.*
JOSEPH LOSEY—*The Concrete Jungle.*
VINCENTE MINNELLI—Two Weeks in Another Town, The Four Horsemen of the Apocalypse.
ROBERT ALDRICH—What Ever Happened to Baby Jane?
OTTO PREMINGER—Advise and Consent.
ORSON WELLES—Mister Arkadin.
HOWARD HAWKS—Hatari!
DON SIEGEL—Hell Is for Heroes.

GEORGE CUKOR—The Chapman Report.
FRANK TASHLIN—Bachelor Flat, It's Only Money.
JERRY LEWIS—The Errand Boy.
ARTHUR PENN—The Miracle Worker.
BLAKE EDWARDS—Experiment in Terror.
LEO MC CAREY—Satan Never Sleeps.
STANLEY KUBRICK—Lolita.
SAM PECKINPAH—Ride the High Country, The Deadly Companions.
TONY RICHARDSON—A Taste of Honey, The Loneliness of the Long Distance Runner.
DAVID LEAN—Lawrence of Arabia.
JOHN FRANKENHEIMER—The Manchurian Candidate, All Fall Down, Bird Man of Alcatraz.
SIDNEY LUMET—Long Day's Journey Into Night, A View from the Bridge.
JOHN CASSAVETES—Too Late Blues.
MERVYN LEROY—Gypsy.
PHIL KARLSON—Kid Galahad.
CHARLES WALTERS—Jumbo.
DAVID MILLER—Lonely Are the Brave.
FRANK PERRY—David and Lisa.
DENIS SANDERS—War Hunt.
RICHARD BROOKS—Sweet Bird of Youth.
ELLIOT SILVERSTEIN—Belle Sommers.
JOHN HUSTON—Freud.
WILLIAM WYLER—The Children's Hour.
BRYAN FORBES—Whistle Down the Wind.
GUY GREEN—Light in the Piazza.
DELMER DAVES—Rome Adventure.
PETER USTINOV——Billy Budd.

1963

JOHN FORD—*Donovan's Reef,* How the West Was Won (with Henry Hathaway and George Marshall).
ALFRED HITCHCOCK—The Birds.
SAMUEL FULLER—Shock Corridor.
OTTO PREMINGER—The Cardinal.
VINCENTE MINNELLI—The Courtship of Eddie's Father.
RALPH NELSON—Soldier in the Rain.
NICHOLAS RAY—55 Days at Peking.
ELIA KAZAN—America America.
ORSON WELLES—The Trial.
JERRY LEWIS—The Nutty Professor.
JOHN CASSAVETES—A Child Is Waiting.
PHIL KARLSON—Kid Galahad, Rampage.
STANLEY DONEN—Charade.
JOHN STURGES—The Great Escape.
GEORGE SIDNEY—Bye, Bye, Birdie.
JOAN LITTLEWOOD—Sparrows Can't Sing.
EDWARD LUDWIG—The Gun Hawk.
BLAKE EDWARDS—Days of Wine and Roses.
ROBERT MULLIGAN—To Kill a Mockingbird, Love With a Proper Stranger.
STEVE SEKELY—The Day of the Triffids.
JACQUES TOURNEUR—The Comedy of Terrors.
ROGER CORMAN—The Raven, "X" The Man With the X-Ray Eyes.
LINDSAY ANDERSON—This Sporting Life.
TONY RICHARDSON—Tom Jones.
JOHN SCHLESINGER—Billy Liar.

CLIFF OWEN—The Wrong Arm of the Law.
DON WEIS—Critic's Choice.
FRANKLIN SCHAFFNER—The Stripper.
FRANK TASHLIN—Who's Minding the Store?, The Man From the Diners' Club.
TERENCE YOUNG—Dr. No.
GEORGE ROY HILL—Toys in the Attic.
BILLY WILDER—Irma La Douce.
JOHN HUSTON—The List of Adrian Messenger.
PETER BROOK—Lord of the Flies.
ADOLFAS MEKAS—Hallelujah the Hills.
PAUL WENDKOS—Gidget Goes to Rome.
ROBERT WISE—The Haunting.
BRIAN FORBES—The L-Shaped Room.
ROBERT ALDRICH—4 For Texas.
ROBERT PARRISH—In the French Style.
LESLIE MARTINSON—PT-109.
HALL BARTLETT—The Caretakers.
PETER GLENVILLE—Term of Trial.

1964

JOSEPH LOSEY—*The Servant.*
HOWARD HAWKS—Man's Favorite Sport.
RICHARD LESTER—A Hard Day's Night.
BLAKE EDWARDS—Pink Panther, A Shot in the Dark.
DONALD SIEGEL—The Killers.
SETH HOLT—Station Six—Sahara.
FRANKLIN SCHAFFNER—The Best Man.
CLIVE DONNER—Nothing But the Best, The Guest.
STANLEY KUBRICK—Dr. Strangelove Or: How I Learned to Stop Worrying And
    Love the Bomb.
ALFRED HITCHCOCK—Marnie.
JOHN FORD—Cheyenne Autumn.
ROGER CORMAN—Masque of the Red Death.
GEORGE CUKOR—My Fair Lady.
VINCENTE MINNELLI—Goodbye Charlie.
BILLY WILDER—Kiss Me Stupid.
SAMUEL FULLER—The Naked Kiss.
FRANK TASHLIN—The Disorderly Orderly.
JERRY LEWIS—The Patsy.
RAOUL WALSH—A Distant Trumpet.
PETER TEWKSBURY—Sunday in New York, Emil and the Detectives.
RENÉ CLÉMENT—Joy House.
BURT KENNEDY—Mail Order Bride.
ARTHUR HILLER—The Americanization of Emily.
JACK CLAYTON—The Pumpkin Eater.
BRIAN FORBES—Seance on a Wet Afternoon.
IRVIN KERSHNER—The Luck of Ginger Coffey.
GEORGE SIDNEY—Viva Las Vegas.
CY ENFIELD—Zulu.
DELMER DAVES—Youngblood Hawke.
CHARLES WALTERS—The Unsinkable Molly Brown.
ALEXANDER SINGER—Psyche '59.
ROBERT STEVENSON—Mary Poppins.
JOHN GUILLERMIN—Guns at Batasi.
SIDNEY LUMET—Fail Safe.
RONALD NEAME—The Chalk Garden.
GEORGE MARSHALL—Advance to the Rear.

MARIO BAVA—Black Sabbath.
PETER GLENVILLE—Becket.
MICHAEL CACOYANNIS—Zorba the Greek.
FRED ZINNEMANN—Behold a Pale Horse.
PAUL HENREID—Dead Ringer.
ROBERT LYNN—Dr. Crippen.
JOHN FRANKENHEIMER—Seven Days in May.
R. G. SPRINGSTEEN—He Rides Tall, Taggart.
GEORGE ROY HILL—The World of Henry Orient.
DOUGLAS HEYES—Kitten With a Whip.
MICHAEL ROEMER—Nothing But a Man.

1965

OTTO PREMINGER—*Bunny Lake Is Missing,* In Harm's Way.
WILLIAM WYLER—The Collector.
JOSEPH LOSEY—These Are the Damned, Eva.
BLAKE EDWARDS—The Great Race.
ROBERT MULLIGAN—Baby, the Rain Must Fall.
CLIVE DONNER—What's New Pussycat?
ALEXANDER MACKENDRICK—A Boy Ten Feet Tall, High Wind in Jamaica.
ELLIOT SILVERSTEIN—Cat Ballou.
ROBERT ALDRICH—Hush . . . Hush . . . Sweet Charlotte.
HARVEY HART—Bus Riley's Back in Town.
ROMAN POLANSKI—Repulsion.
JOHN SCHLESINGER—Darling.
BRIAN FORBES—King Rat.
RICHARD QUINE—Synanon.
FRANKLIN SCHAFFNER—The War Lord.
JACK CARDIFF—Young Cassidy.
SAM PECKINPAH—Major Dundee.
RICHARD LESTER—Help!; The Knack . . . and How to Get It.
JOHN BOORMAN—Having a Wild Weekend.
BURT KENNEDY—The Rounders.
NORMAN JEWISON—The Cincinnati Kid.
SETH HOLT—The Nanny.
SIDNEY LUMET—The Hill, The Pawnbroker.
HOWARD HAWKS—Red Line 7000.
SIDNEY FURIE—The Ipcress File, The Leather Boys.
DAVID LEAN—Doctor Zhivago.
HENRY HATHAWAY—The Sons of Katie Elder.
ALEXANDER SINGER—Love Has Many Faces.
ROBERT WISE—The Sound of Music.
J. LEE THOMPSON—Return From the Ashes.
FRED COE—A Thousand Clowns.
GORDON DOUGLAS—Harlow.
VINCENTE MINNELLI—The Sandpiper.
TONY RICHARDSON—The Loved One.
JACK SMIGHT—The Third Day.
MARTIN RITT—The Spy Who Came in from the Cold.
ARTHUR PENN—Mickey One.
STANLEY KRAMER—Ship of Fools.

1966

JOHN FORD—*Seven Women.*
ALFRED HITCHCOCK—*Torn Curtain.*
MICHELANGELO ANTONIONI—*Blow-up.*
JOSEPH LOSEY—*King and Country,* Modesty Blaise.

FRANÇOIS TRUFFAUT—Fahrenheit 451.
BLAKE EDWARDS—What Did You Do in the War, Daddy?
MICHAEL ANDERSON—The Quiller Memorandum.
BURT KENNEDY—The Money Trap.
ROBERT ALDRICH—The Flight of the Phoenix.
GEORGE AXELROD—Lord Love a Duck.
ROBERT MULLIGAN—Inside Daisy Clover.
KAREL REISZ—Morgan!
ANTHONY MANN—The Heroes of Telemark.
BILLY WILDER—The Fortune Cookie.
ARTHUR PENN—The Chase.
JACK SMIGHT—Kaleidoscope, Harper.
PHIL KARLSON—The Silencers.
SIDNEY LUMET—The Group.
JERRY LEWIS—Three On a Couch.
HENRY HATHAWAY—Nevada Smith.
FRANK TASHLIN—The Glass-Bottom Boat, The Alphabet Murders.
BRIAN FORBES—The Wrong Box.
BERNARD GIRARD—Dead Heat On a Merry-Go-Round.
CORNELL WILDE—The Naked Prey.
WILLIAM WYLER—How to Steal a Million.
MIKE NICHOLS—Who's Afraid of Virginia Woolf?
RICHARD BROOKS—The Professionals.
ROMAN POLANSKI—Cul-de-Sac.
FRED ZINNEMANN—A Man For All Seasons.
IRVIN KERSHNER—A Fine Madness.
GEORGE SIDNEY—The Swinger.
STANLEY DONEN—Arabesque.
RICHARD LESTER—A Funny Thing Happened On the Way to the Forum.
JOHN GUILLERMIN—The Blue Max.
CHARLES WALTERS—Walk, Don't Run.
KENNETH ANGER—Scorpio Rising.
ROBERT GIST—The American Dream.

1967
HOWARD HAWKS—*El Dorado.*
JOHN BOORMAN—Point Blank.
BLAKE EDWARDS—Gunn.
ORSON WELLES—Falstaff.
CHARLES CHAPLIN—A Countess From Hong Kong.
JOSEPH LOSEY—Accident.
ROBERT MULLIGAN—Up the Down Staircase.
ARTHUR PENN—Bonnie and Clyde.
FRANCIS FORD COPPOLA—You're a Big Boy Now.
MIKE NICHOLS—The Graduate.
JOHN HUSTON—Reflections in a Golden Eye.
STUART ROSENBERG—Cool Hand Luke.
BUD YORKIN—Divorce American Style.
OTTO PREMINGER—Hurry Sundown.
NORMAN JEWISON—In the Heat of the Night.
ROBERT ALDRICH—The Dirty Dozen.
STANLEY DONEN—Two For the Road, Bedazzled.
DONN PENNEBAKER—Don't Look Back.
ANDY WARHOL—Bike Boy, The Nude Restaurant.
BURT KENNEDY—Welcome to Hard Times, The War Wagon.
ALEXANDER MACKENDRICK—Don't Make Waves.
JAMES CLAVELL—To Sir, With Love.

ELLIOT SILVERSTEIN—The Happening.
IRVIN KERSHNER—The Flim Flam Man.
ROY BOULTING—The Family Way.
PETER BROOK—Marat/Sade.
TERENCE YOUNG—Wait Until Dark.
GORDON DOUGLAS—Tony Rome.
ROMAN POLANSKI—The Fearless Vampire Killers.
BRIAN FORBES—The Whisperers.
BUZZ KULIK—Warning Shot.
FRANK TASHLIN—Caprice.
JOSEPH L. MANKIEWICZ—The Honey Pot.
CLIVE DONNER—Luv.
CORNELL WILDE—Beach Red.
CURTIS HARRINGTON—Games.
PETER TEWKSBURY—Doctor, You've Got to Be Kidding.
JOHN STURGES—Hour of the Gun.
MARTIN RITT—Hombre.
DON CHAFFEY—One Million Years B.C.
PETER GOLDMAN—Echoes of Silence.
TONY RICHARDSON—Sailor From Gibraltar.
T. C. FRANK—Born Losers.
RICHARD LESTER—How I Won the War.
JOSHUA LOGAN—Camelot.
STANLEY KRAMER—Guess Who's Coming to Dinner?

DIRECTORIAL INDEX TO THE AMERICAN CINEMA

By Michael Schwartz and James R. Prickett

The following index contains every English language film made after 1929 and mentioned in this book. In addition, the authors have culled films from fourteen other sources. They are alphabetized computer style: spaces and punctuation are treated as letters. For example, *No, Not Again* would appear before *Noah's Ark* but after *No Time for Sergeants*. Although this index falls short of our original goal (a listing of every American film ever made), it still should go a long way toward ending the tyranny of randomness plaguing those who spend their time watching movies on television.

Abandon Ship; 1957; Richard Sale

Abandoned; 1949; Joseph M. Newman

Abbott and Costello Meet Invisible Man; 1951; Charles Lamont

Abductors, The; 1956; Andrew McLaglen

Abie's Irish Rose; 1946; Edward Sutherland

About Face; 1942; Kurt Neumann

About Mrs. Leslie; 1954; Daniel Mann

Above Suspicion; 1943; Richard Thorpe

Above Us the Waves; 1955; Ralph Thomas

Abraham Lincoln; 1930; D. W. Griffith

Abroad with Two Yanks; 1944; Allan Dwan

Absent-Minded Professor, The; 1960; Robert Stevenson

Accident; 1967; Joseph Losey

Accused, The; 1948; William Dieterle

Ace in the Hole (The Big Carnival); 1951; Billy Wilder

Across the Bridge; 1957; Ken Annakin

Across the Pacific; 1942; John Huston

Across the Wide Missouri; 1951; William Wellman

Act of Love; 1954; Anatole Litvak

Act of Murder, An; 1957; Michael Gordon

Act of Violence; 1949; Fred Zinnemann

Action in the North Atlantic; 1943; Lloyd Bacon

Action of the Tiger; 1957; Terence Young

Actors and Sin; 1952; Ben Hecht

Actress, The; 1953; George Cukor

Ada; 1961; Daniel Mann

Adam and Evalyn; 1950; Harold French

Adam Had Four Sons; 1941; Gregory Ratoff

Adam's Rib; 1949; George Cukor

Address Unknown; 1944; William C. Menzies

Admirable Crichton; 1952; Lewis Gilbert

Adorable; 1933; William Dieterle

Advance to the Rear; 1964; George Marshall

Adventure; 1945; Victor Fleming

Adventure's End; 1937; Arthur Lubin

Adventures in Baltimore; 1949; Richard Wallace

Adventures in Silverado; 1948; Phil Karlson

Adventures of Hajji Baba, The; 1954; Don Weis

Adventures of Huckleberry Finn, The; 1939; Richard Thorpe

Adventures of Huckleberry Finn, The; 1960; Michael Curtiz

Adventures of Marco Polo; 1938; Archie Mayo

Adventures of Mark Twain, The;

1944; Irving Rapper

Adventures of Quentin Durward, The; 1956; Richard Thorpe

Adventures of Robin Hood, The; 1938; Michael Curtiz and William Keighley

Adventures of Sherlock Holmes, The; 1939; Alfred Werker

Adventures of Tom Sawyer; 1938; H. C. Potter and Norman Taurog

Advise and Consent; 1962; Otto Preminger

Affair in Havana; 1957; Laslo Benedek

Affair of the Skin, An; 1963; Ben Maddow

Affair of Trinidad; 1957; Vincent Sherman

Affair to Remember, An; 1957; Leo McCarey

Affairs of Cellini; 1934; Gregory La Cava

Affairs of Dobie Gillis, The; 1953; Don Weis

Affairs of Martha, The; 1942; Jules Dassin

Affairs of Susan, The; 1935; Kurt Neumann

Affairs of Susan, The; 1945; William Seiter

Affectionately Yours; 1941; Lloyd Bacon

African Fury; 1952; Zoltan Korda

African in London, An; 1943; George Pearson

African Queen, The; 1952; John Huston

After Midnight with Boston Blackie; 1943; Lew Landers

After Office Hours; 1935; Robert Z. Leonard

After the Thin Man; 1936; W. S. van Dyke

After Tomorrow; 1932; Frank Borzage

After Tonight; 1933; George Archainbaud

Against All Flags; 1952; George Sherman

Against the Wind; 1948; Charles Crichton

Age of Consent; 1932; Gregory La Cava

Agent 8¾; 1963; Ralph Thomas

Agony and the Ecstasy, The; 1964; Carol Reed

Ah, Wilderness; 1935; Clarence Brown

Aimez-Vous Brahms; 1961; Anatole Litvak

Ain't Misbehaving; 1955; Edward Buzzell

Air Force; 1943; Howard Hawks

Air Mail; 1932; John Ford

Al Capone; 1959; Richard Wilson

Alamo, The; 1960; John Wayne

Albert RN; 1953; Lewis Gilbert

Alexander the Great; 1956; Robert Rossen

Alexander's Ragtime Band; 1938; Henry King

Alfie; 1965; Lewis Gilbert

Alfred the Great; 1968; Clive Donner

Algiers; 1938; John Cromwell

Ali Baba and the Forty Thieves; 1943; Arthur Lubin

Alias Jesse James; 1959; Norman Z. McLeod

Alias Jimmy Valentine; 1929; Jack Conway

Alias Mary; 1935; Kurt Neumann

Alias Mr. Twilight; 1947; John Sturges

Alias Nick Beal; 1949; John Farrow

Alias the Doctor; 1932; Lloyd Bacon

Alibi; 1929; Roland West

Alice Adams; 1935; George Stevens

Alice in Wonderland; 1933; Norman Z. McLeod

All About Eve; 1950; Joseph Mankiewicz

All American, The; 1953; Jesse Hibbs

All Ashore; 1953; Richard Quine

All Fall Down; 1962; John Frankenheimer

All I Desire; 1953; Douglas Sirk

All in Good Time; 1965; John Boulting and Roy Boulting

All My Sons; 1948; Irving Reis

All Night Long; 1961; Basil Dearden

All Over the Town; 1948; Derek Twist

All Quiet on the Western Front; 1930; Lewis Milestone

All That Heaven Allows; 1956; Douglas Sirk

All That Money Can Buy; 1941; William Dieterle

All the Brothers Were Valiant; 1953; Richard Thorpe

All the Fine Young Cannibals; 1958; Michael Anderson

All the King's Horses; 1935; Frank Tuttle

All the King's Men; 1949; Robert Rossen

All the Way Home; 1963; Alex Segal

All the Young Men; 1960; Hall Bartlett

All This and Heaven Too; 1941; Anatole Litvak

All Through the Night; 1942; Vincent Sherman

All Women Have Secrets; 1940; Kurt Neumann

Alligator People, The; 1959; Roy del Ruth

Almost Married; 1932; William C. Menzies

Along Came Jones; 1945; Stuart Heisler

Along the Great Divide; 1951; Raoul Walsh

Along the Mohawk Trail; 1956; Sam Newfield

Alphabet Murders, The; 1966; Frank Tashlin

Always Leave Them Laughing; 1949; Roy del Ruth

Amazing Doctor Clitterhouse, The; 1938; Anatole Litvak

Amazing Transparent Man, The; 1960; Edgar G. Ulmer

Ambassador's Daughter, The; 1956; Norman Krasna

Ambush; 1939; Kurt Neumann

America, America; 1963; Elia Kazan

America's Hidden Weapon (Doc); 1944; William McGann

American Dream, An; 1966; Robert Gist

American Empire; 1942; William McGann

American Guerilla in the Philippines; 1950; Fritz Lang

American in Paris, An; 1951; Vincente Minnelli

American Madness; 1932; Frank Capra

American Romance, An; 1944; King Vidor

American Tragedy, An; 1931; Josef von Sternberg

Americanization of Emily, The; 1964; Arthur Hiller

Among the Living; 1941; Stuart Heisler

Amorous Adventures of Moll Flanders; 1965; Terence Young

Amorous Prawn, The; 1962; Anthony Kimmins

Anastasia; 1956; Anatole Litvak

Anatahan; 1954; Josef von Sternberg

Anatomy of a Murder; 1959; Otto Preminger

Anchors Aweigh; 1945; George Sidney

And Now Tomorrow; 1944; Irving Pichel

And So They Were Married; 1936; Elliott Nugent

And the Angels Sing; 1944; George Marshall

And Then There Were None; 1944; René Clair

Andy Hardy Comes Home; 1958; Howard W. Koch

Andy Hardy Gets Spring Fever; 1939; W. S. van Dyke

Andy Hardy Series; George Seitz

Angel; 1937; Ernst Lubitsch

Angel Baby; 1961; Paul Wendkos

Angel Face; 1953; Otto Preminger

Angel in Exile; 1948; Allan Dwan

Angel on My Shoulder; 1946; Archie Mayo

Angels in the Outfield; 1951; Clarence Brown

Angels over Broadway; 1940; Lee Garmes and Ben Hecht

Angels with Dirty Faces; 1938; Michael Curtiz

Angry Hills, The; 1959; Robert Aldrich

Angry Silence, The; 1959; Guy Green

Animal, The; 1932; Edward H. Griffith

Animal Crackers; 1930; Victor Heerman

Ann Vickers; 1933; John Cromwell

Anna and the King of Siam; 1946; John Cromwell

Anna Christie; 1930; Clarence Brown

Anna Karenina; 1935; Clarence Brown

Anna Karenina; 1948; Julien Duvivier

Anna Lucasta; 1958; Arnold Laven

Annabelle's Affairs; 1931; Alfred Werker

Annapolis Story, An; 1955; Don Siegel

Anne of the Indies; 1951; Jacques Tourneur

Annie Get Your Gun; 1950; George Sidney

Another Dawn; 1937; William Dieterle

Another Part of the Forest; 1948; Michael Gordon

Another Thin Man; 1939; W. S. van

Dyke

Anthony Adverse; 1936; Mervyn Le Roy

Any Number Can Play; 1949; Mervyn Le Roy

Anything Goes; 1936; Lewis Milestone

Apache; 1954; Robert Aldrich

Apache Woman; 1955; Roger Corman

Apartment, The; 1960; Billy Wilder

Appaloosa, The; 1966; Sidney Furie

Applause; 1929; Rouben Mamoulian

Appointment, The; 1968; Sidney Lumet

Appointment in Honduras; 1953; Jacques Tourneur

Appointment with Danger; 1951; Lewis Allen

Appointment with Venus; 1951; Ralph Thomas

Arabesque; 1966; Stanley Donen

Arabian Nights; 1942; Mario Bava and Henry Levin

Arch of Triumph; 1948; Lewis Milestone

Arena; 1953; Richard Fleischer

Arise My Love; 1940; Mitchell Leisen

Arizona; 1941; Wesley Ruggles

Arizona Cyclone; 1942; Joseph H. Lewis

Arizonian, The; 1935; Charles Vidor

Arkansas Traveler, The; 1938; Alfred Santell

Armored Car Robbery; 1950; Richard Fleischer

Armored Command; 1961; Byron Haskin

Army Surgeon; 1942; Edward Sutherland

Arnelo Affair; 1946; Arch Oboler

Around the World; 1943; Allan Dwan

Around the World in 80 Days; 1956; Michael Anderson

Around the World in 80 Minutes; 1931; Douglas Fairbanks and Victor Fleming

Arouse and Beware; 1940; Leslie Fenton

Arrowsmith; 1931; John Ford

Arruza (Doc); 1963; Budd Boetticher

Arsene Lupin; 1932; Jack Conway

Arsenic and Old Lace; 1944; Frank Capra

Art of Love, The; 1965; Norman Jewison

Arthur Takes Over; 1948; Malcolm St. Clair

Artists and Models; 1937; Raoul Walsh

Artists and Models; 1955; Frank Tashlin

Artists and Models Abroad; 1938; Mitchell Leisen

As You Desire Me; 1932; George Fitzmaurice

As You Like It; 1936; Paul Czinner

As Young as You Feel; 1931; Frank Borzage

As Young as You Feel; 1951; Harmon Jones

Ask a Policeman; 1941; Max Varnel

Ask Any Girl; 1959; Charles Walters

Asphalt Jungle, The; 1950; John Huston

Assassin, The; 1953; Ralph Thomas

Assigned to Danger; 1948; Budd Boetticher

Assignment in Brittany; 1943; Jack Conway

Assignment Paris; 1952; Robert Parrish

At Gunpoint; 1958; Alfred Werker

At the Circus; 1938; Edward Buzzell

Atlantis the Lost Continent; 1961; George Pal

Atomic City, The; 1952; Jerry Hopper

Atomic Kid, The; 1954; Leslie H. Martinson

Atomic Man, The; 1956; Kenneth Hughes

Attack; 1956; Robert Aldrich

Attack of the Crab Monsters; 1957; Roger Corman

Auntie Mame; 1958; Morton da Costa

Autumn Leaves; 1956; Robert Aldrich

Avenger, The (Murders); 1934; Louis Brooks

Aviator; 1929; Roy del Ruth

Away All Boats; 1956; Joseph Pevney

Awful Truth, The; 1937; Leo McCarey

B.F.'s Daughter; 1948; Robert Z. Leonard

Babbitt; 1934; William Keighley

Babe Ruth Story, The; 1948; Roy del Ruth

Babes in Arms; 1939; Busby Berkeley

Babes in Bagdad; 1952; Edgar G. Ulmer

Babes on Broadway; 1941; Busby Berkeley

Baby Doll; 1956; Elia Kazan

Baby Face Harrington; 1935; Raoul Walsh

Baby Face Nelson; 1957; Don Siegel

Baby the Rain Must Fall; 1965; Robert Mulligan

Bachelor and the Bobbysoxer; 1947; Irving Reis

Bachelor Apartment; 1931; Lowell Sherman

Bachelor Apartment; 1937; Edward Buzzell

Bachelor Bait; 1934; George Stevens

Bachelor Flat; 1962; Frank Tashlin

Bachelor in Paradise; 1961; Jack Arnold

Bachelor Knight; 1947; Irving Reis

Bachelor Mother; 1939; Garson Kanin

Bachelor Party, The; 1957; Delbert Mann

Bachelor's Affairs; 1932; Alfred Werker

Back Door to Heaven; 1939; William K. Howard

Back Door to Hell; 1964; Monty Hellman

Back from Eternity; 1956; John Farrow

Back Street; 1932; John Stahl

Back Street; 1941; Robert Stevenson

Back Street; 1961; David Miller

Back to Bataan; 1945; Edward Dmytryk

Backfire; 1950; Vincent Sherman

Background to Danger; 1943; Raoul Walsh

Backlash; 1956; John Sturges

Bacon Grabbers (Short); 1929; Lewis R. Foster

Bad and the Beautiful, The; 1953; Vincente Minnelli

Bad Company; 1931; Tay Garnett

Bad Day at Black Rock; 1955; John Sturges

Bad Girl; 1931; Frank Borzage

Bad Lord Byron; 1948; David MacDonald

Bad Seed, The; 1956; Mervyn Le Roy

Bad Sister; 1931; Hobart Henley

Badlanders, The; 1958; Delmer Daves

Bait; 1954; Hugo Haas

Ball of Fire; 1941; Howard Hawks

Bamboo Blonde, The; 1946; Anthony Mann

Band of Angels; 1957; Raoul Walsh

Band Wagon, The; 1953; Vincente Minnelli

Bandido; 1956; Richard Fleischer

Bandit of Sherwood Forest; 1947; George Sherman

Banjo; 1947; Richard Fleischer

Banjo on My Knee; 1936; John Cromwell

Bank Dick, The; 1940; Eddie Cline

Bank Holiday; 1937; Carol Reed

Bannerline; 1951; Don Weis

Barabbas; 1962; Richard Fleischer

Barbarian, The; 1933; Sam Wood

Barbarian and the Geisha, The; 1958; John Huston

Barbary Coast; 1935; Howard Hawks

Barbary Coast Gent; 1944; Roy del Ruth

Barefoot Contessa; 1954; Joseph Mankiewicz

Barkleys of Broadway, The; 1949; Charles Walters

Baron of Arizona, The; 1950; Samuel Fuller

Baroud; 1932; Rex Ingram

Barretts of Wimpole Street, The; 1934; Sidney Franklin

Barretts of Wimpole Street, The; 1957; Sidney Franklin

Bashful Bachelor, The; 1942; Malcolm St. Clair

Bat Whispers; 1931; Roland West

Bataan; 1943; Tay Garnett

Bathing Beauty; 1944; George Sidney

Battle Circus; 1953; Richard Brooks

Battle Cry; 1955; Raoul Walsh

Battle Hell; 1957; Michael Anderson

Battle Hymn; 1956; Douglas Sirk

Battle of Apache Pass, The; 1952; George Sherman

Battle of Britain, The (Doc); 1943; A. Veiller

Battle of Midway, The; 1942; John Ford and Anatole Litvak

Battle of San Pietro, The (Doc); 1944; John Huston

Battle of the Bulge, The; 1965; Ken Annakin

Battle of the Coral Sea; 1959; Paul Wendkos

Battle of the Sexes; 1959; Charles Crichton

Battle of Villa Fiorita; 1964; Delmer Daves

Battleaxe, The; 1960; Godfrey Grayson

Battleground; 1949; William Wellman

Beachhead; 1954; Stuart Heisler

Beach Party; 1963; William Asher

Beach Red; 1967; Cornell Wilde

Beast of the City; 1932; Charles Brabin

Beast with Five Fingers; 1946; Robert Florey

Beat the Devil; 1954; John Huston

Beau Brummel; 1954; Curtis Bernhardt

Beau Geste; 1939; William Wellman

Beautiful Blonde from Bashful Bend, The; 1949; Preston Sturges

Beautiful but Dangerous; 1955; Robert Z. Leonard

Beauty and the Beast; 1962; Edward L. Cahn

Beauty and the Boss; 1932; Roy del Ruth

Beauty for Sale; 1933; Richard Boleslavsky

Beauty Jungle, The; 1964; Val Guest

Beauty Parlor; 1932; Richard Thorpe

Beauty's Daughter; 1935; Allan Dwan

Because of Him; 1946; Richard Wallace

Because They're Young; 1960; Paul Wendkos

Becket; 1964; Peter Glenville

Becky Sharp; 1935; Rouben Mamoulian

Bed of Roses; 1933; Gregory La Cava

Bedazzled; 1968; Stanley Donen

Bedeviled; 1955; Mitchell Leisen

Bedford Incident, The; 1965; James B. Harris

Bedlam; 1946; Mark Robson

Bedside; 1934; Robert Florey

Bedtime Story; 1942; Alexander Hall

Beggar's Opera, The; 1953; Peter Brook

Behind Locked Doors; 1948; Budd Boetticher

Behind the Mask; 1946; Phil Karlson

Behind the Mask; 1960; Brian D. Hurst

Behind the Rising Sun; 1943; Edward Dmytryk

Behold a Pale Horse; 1964; Fred Zinnemann

Behold My Wife; 1935; Mitchell Leisen

Bell for Adano, A; 1945; Henry King

Bell, Book, and Candle; 1958; Richard Quine

Bellboy, The; 1960; Jerry Lewis

Belle le Grande; 1951; Allan Dwan

Belle of New York, The; 1952; Charles Walters

Belle of the Nineties; 1934; Leo McCarey

Belle of the Yukon; 1944; William Seiter

Belle Sommers; 1962; Elliot Silverstein

Bells Are Ringing; 1960; Vincente Minnelli

Bells Go Down, The; 1942; Basil Dearden

Bells of St. Mary's, The; 1945; Leo McCarey

Beloved Brat; 1937; Arthur Lubin

Beloved Enemy; 1936; H. C. Potter

Beloved Infidel; 1959; Henry King

Below Zero (Short); 1930; James Parrott

Ben Hur; 1959; William Wyler

Bend of the River; 1952; Anthony Mann

Bengal Brigade; 1954; Laslo Benedek

Bengal Tiger; 1934; Joe May

Bengazi; 1955; John Brahm

Benjy (Doc); 1951; Fred Zinnemann

Berkeley Square; 1933; Frank Lloyd

Berlin Express; 1948; Jacques Tourneur

Bermuda Affair; 1957; Edward Sutherland

Bespoke Overcoat, The; 1955; Jack Clayton

Best Foot Forward; 1943; Eddie Buzzell

Best Man, The; 1964; Franklin Schaffner

Best Man Wins; 1948; John Sturges

Best of Enemies, The; 1962; Guy Hamilton

Best of Everything, The; 1959; Jean Negulesco

Best Things in Life Are Free, The; 1956; Michael Curtiz

Best Years of Our Lives, The; 1946; William Wyler

Betrayed (When Strangers Marry); 1944; William Castle

Betrayal, The; 1929; Lewis Milestone

Better Tomorrow, A (Doc); 1945; Alexander Hackenschmied

Between Heaven and Hell; 1956; Richard Fleischer

Between Midnight and Dawn; 1950; Gordon Douglas

Between Two Worlds; 1944; Edward A. Blatt

Between Us Girls; 1942; Henry Koster

Beware; 1946; Bud Pollard

Beware My Lovely; 1952; Harry Horner

Beware of Children (No Kidding);

1961; Gerald Thomas
Bewitched; 1945; Arch Oboler
Beyond a Reasonable Doubt; 1956; Fritz Lang
Beyond the Forest; 1949; King Vidor
Beyond the Time Barrier; 1960; Edgar G. Ulmer
Beyond This Place; 1958; Jack Cardiff
Beyond Tomorrow; 1940; Edward Sutherland
Bhowani Junction; 1956; George Cukor
Bible, The; 1966; John Huston
Big Beat, The; 1958; Will Cowan
Big Boodle, The; 1957; Richard Wilson
Big Broadcast, The; 1932; Frank Tuttle
Big Broadcast of 1937; 1936; Mitchell Leisen
Big Broadcast of 1938; 1938; Mitchell Leisen
Big Brown Eyes; 1936; Raoul Walsh
Big Business (Short); 1929; James W. Horne
Big Circus, The; 1959; Joseph M. Newman
Big News; 1929; Gregory La Cava
Big Cage, The; 1933; Kurt Neumann
Big Carnival, The (Ace in the Hole); 1951; Billy Wilder
Big Cat, The; 1949; Phil Karlson
Big Circus, The; 1959; Joseph M. Newman
Big City, The; 1937; Frank Borzage
Big City Blues; 1932; Mervyn Le Roy
Big Clock, The; 1948; John Farrow
Big Combo, The; 1955; Joseph H. Lewis
Big Country, The; 1958; William Wyler
Big Fella; 1938; J. Elder Wills
Big Fisherman, The; 1959; Frank Borzage
Big Gamble, The; 1961; Richard Fleischer
Big Guy, The; 1940; Arthur Lubin
Big Hearted Herbert; 1934; William Keighley
Big Heat, The; 1953; Fritz Lang
Big House, The; 1930; George Hill
Big Jim McLain; 1952; Edward Ludwig
Big Knife, The; 1955; Robert Aldrich
Big Land, The; 1957; Gordon Douglas
Big Leaguer, The; 1953; Robert Aldrich

Big Night, The; 1951; Joseph Losey
Big Noise, The; 1944; Malcolm St. Clair
Big Red; 1962; Norman Tokar
Big Shot, The; 1942; Lewis Seiler
Big Sky, The; 1952; Howard Hawks
Big Sleep, The; 1946; Howard Hawks
Big Steal, The; 1949; Don Siegel
Big Store, The; 1941; Charles Reisner
Big Street, The; 1943; Irving Reis
Big Town Czar; 1939; Arthur Lubin
Big Trail, The; 1930; Raoul Walsh
Big Trees, The; 1952; Felix Feist
Bigamist, The; 1953; Ida Lupino
Bigger than Life; 1956; Nicholas Ray
Bike Boy; 1967; Andy Warhol
Bikini Beach; 1965; William Asher
Bill of Divorcement, A; 1932; George Cukor
Bill of Divorcement, A; 1940; John Farrow
Billy Budd; 1962; Peter Ustinov
Billy Liar; 1963; John Schlesinger
Billy the Kid; 1930; King Vidor
Billy the Kid; 1941; David Miller
Bird of Paradise; 1932; King Vidor
Bird of Paradise; 1951; Delmer Daves
Birdman of Alcatraz; 1962; John Frankenheimer
Birds, The; 1963; Alfred Hitchcock
Birds and the Bees, The; 1956; Norman Taurog
Birth of the Blues; 1941; Victor Schertzinger
Birthday Present, The; 1957; Pat Jackson
Biscuit Eater, The; 1940; Stuart Heisler
Bishop's Wife, The; 1948; Henry Koster
Bitter Creek; 1954; George Waggner
Bitter Harvest; 1963; Peter Graham Scott
Bitter Sweet; 1940; W. S. van Dyke
Bitter Tea of General Yen; 1933; Frank Capra
Bitter Victory; 1958; Nicholas Ray
Black Angel; 1946; Roy William Neill
Black Arrow, The; 1948; Gordon Douglas
Black Castle; 1952; Nathan Juran
Black Cat, The; 1934; Edgar G. Ulmer
Black Cat, The; 1941; Albert S. Rogell
Black Friday; 1940; Arthur Lubin
Black Fury; 1935; Michael Curtiz
Black Gold; 1947; Phil Karlson
Black Gold; 1963; Leslie H. Martinson

Black Hand, The; 1950; Richard Thorpe

Black King, The; 1932; Bud Pollard

Black Knight, The; 1954; Tay Garnett

Black Legion, The; 1936; Archie Mayo

Black like Me; 1964; Carl Lerner

Black Midnight; 1949; Budd Boetticher

Black Narcissus; 1947; Michael Powell and Emeric Pressburger

Black Orchid, The; 1959; Martin Ritt

Black Room; 1935; Roy William Neill

Black Rose, The; 1950; Henry Hathaway

Black Sabbath; 1964; Mario Bava

Black Sheep; 1935; Allan Dwan

Black Sheep of Whitehall, The; 1941; Basil Dearden and Will Hay

Black Shield of Falworth; 1954; Rudolph Mate

Black Sleep, The; 1956; Reginald Le Borg

Black Spurs; 1964; R. G. Springsteen

Black Sunday; 1961; Mario Bava

Black Swan, The; 1942; Henry King

Black Tights; 1962; Terence Young

Black Torment, The; 1964; Robert Hartford-Davis

Black Tuesday; 1955; Hugo Fregonese

Black Watch; 1929; John Ford

Black Waters; 1929; Herbert Wilcox

Black Widow; 1954; Nunnally Johnson

Blackbeard the Pirate; 1952; Raoul Walsh

Blackboard Jungle, The; 1955; Richard Brooks

Blackmail; 1929; Alfred Hitchcock

Blackmail; 1939; H. C. Potter

Blackout; 1950; Robert S. Baker

Blanche Fury; 1947; Marc Allegret

Blaze of Noon; 1947; John Farrow

Blazing Six Shooters; 1940; Joseph H. Lewis

Blessed Event; 1932; Roy del Ruth

Blind Adventure; 1933; Ernest L. Schoesdack

Blind Alibi; 1939; Charles Vidor

Blind Date (Chance Meeting); 1960; Joseph Losey

Blindfold; 1966; Philip Dunne

Blithe Spirit; 1945; David Lean

Blockade; 1938; William Dieterle

Blockheads; 1938; John Blystone

Blonde Bait; 1956; Elmo Williams

Blonde Crazy; 1931; Roy del Ruth

Blonde Inspiration; 1941; Busby Berkeley

Blonde Venus; 1932; Josef von Sternberg

Blondie of the Follies; 1932; Edmund Goulding

Blood Alley; 1955; William Wellman

Blood and Sand; 1941; Rouben Mamoulian

Blood of the Vampire; 1958; Henry Cass

Blood on the Moon; 1948; Robert Wise

Blood on the Sun; 1945; Frank Lloyd

Blossoms in the Dust; 1941; Mervyn Le Roy

Blossoms on Broadway; 1937; Richard Wallace

Blow Up; 1966; Michelangelo Antonioni

Blowing Wild; 1953; Hugo Fregonese

Blue Angel, The; 1930; Josef von Sternberg

Blue Angel, The; 1959; Edward Dmytryk

Blue Denim; 1959; Philip Dunne

Blue Gardenia, The; 1953; Fritz Lang

Blue Lamp, The; 1949; Basil Dearden

Blue Max, The; 1966; John Guillermin

Blue Skies; 1946; Stuart Heisler

Bluebeard; 1944; Edgar G. Ulmer

Bluebeard's Eighth Wife; 1938; Ernst Lubitsch

Blues in the Night; 1941; Anatole Litvak

Bobo, The; 1967; Robert Parrish

Body and Soul; 1931; Alfred Santell

Body and Soul; 1947; Robert Rossen

Body Disappeared, The; 1942; D. Ross Lederman

Body Snatcher, The; 1945; Robert Wise

Bohemian Girl, The; 1936; James W. Horne

Bold and the Brave, The; 1956; Lewis R. Foster

Bombardier; 1942; Richard Wallace

Bombers B-52; 1957; Gordon Douglas

Bombs over Burma; 1942; Joseph H. Lewis

Bombshell; 1933; Victor Fleming

Bondage; 1933; Alfred Santell

Bonjour Tristesse; 1958; Otto Preminger

Bonnie and Clyde; 1967; Arthur Penn

Boom; 1968; Joseph Losey

Boom Town; 1940; Jack Conway

Boomerang; 1947; Elia Kazan
Boots Malone; 1952; William Dieterle
Border Incident; 1949; Anthony Mann
Border Wolves; 1938; Joseph H. Lewis
Borderline; 1930; Kenneth MacPherson
Bordertown; 1935; Archie Mayo
Born Losers; 1967; T. C. Frank
Born Reckless; 1930; John Ford
Born Reckless; 1937; Malcolm St. Clair
Born to Be Bad; 1934; Lowell Sherman
Born to Be Bad; 1950; Nicholas Ray
Born to Dance; 1936; Roy del Ruth
Born to Kill; 1947; Robert Wise
Born to Love; 1931; Paul Stein
Born Yesterday; 1950; George Cukor
Boss, The; 1956; Byron Haskin
Boss of Hangtown Mesa, The; 1942; Joseph H. Lewis
Boston Blackie's Rendezvous; 1945; Arthur Dreifuss
Boston Strangler, The; 1968; Richard Fleischer
Botany Bay; 1953; John Farrow
Bottom of the Bottle, The; 1956; Henry Hathaway
Boudoir Diplomat; 1930; Malcolm St. Clair
Bought; 1931; Archie Mayo
Bounty Hunters, The; 1954; Andre de Toth
Bowery, The; 1933; Raoul Walsh
Bowery Bombshell; 1946; Phil Karlson
Bowery to Broadway; 1945; Charles Lamont
Boy from Oklahoma, The; 1954; Michael Curtiz
Boy on a Dolphin; 1957; Jean Negulesco
Boy Ten Feet Tall, A; 1965; Alexander MacKendrick
Boy with Green Hair, The; 1948; Joseph Losey
Boys, The; 1962; Sidney Furie
Boys from Syracuse, The; 1940; Edward Sutherland
Boys in Brown; 1949; Montgomery Tully
Boys of the City; 1940; Joseph H. Lewis
Boys' Town; 1938; Norman Taurog
Brain Machine, The; 1956; Kenneth Hughes
Brainwashed; 1961; Gerd Oswald

Bramble Bush, The; 1960; Daniel Petrie
Branded; 1951; Rudolph Mate
Brandy for the Parson; 1952; John Eldridge
Brasher Doubloon, The; 1947; John Brahm
Brass Legend, The; 1956; Gerd Oswald
Brat, The; 1931; John Ford
Brats (Short); 1930; James Parrott
Bravados, The; 1958; Henry King
Brave Bulls, The; 1951; Robert Rossen
Brave Don't Cry, The; 1952; Philip Leacock
Brave One, The; 1956; Irving Rapper
Break, The; 1963; Lance Comfort
Break of Hearts; 1935; Philip Moeller
Break to Freedom; 1955; Don McGuire
Breakfast at Tiffany's; 1961; Blake Edwards
Breaking Point, The; 1950; Michael Curtiz
Breaking the Sound Barrier; 1952; David Lean
Breath of Scandal, A; 1960; Michael Curtiz
Brewster's Millions; 1945; Allan Dwan
Bribe, The; 1949; Robert Z. Leonard
Bridal Path, The; 1959; Sidney Gilliat and Frank Launder
Bride by Mistake; 1944; Richard Wallace
Bride Came C.O.D., The; 1940; William Keighley
Bride Goes Wild, The; 1948; Norman Taurog
Bride of Frankenstein, The; 1935; James Whale
Bride of the Gorilla; 1951; Curt Siodmak
Bride of Vengeance; 1949; Mitchell Leisen
Bride Wore Red, The; 1937; Dorothy Arzner
Brides of Dracula, The; 1960; Terence Fisher
Bridge, The (The Spy) (Short); 1932; Charles Vidor
Bridge on the River Kwai; 1957; David Lean
Bridges of Toko-Ri, The; 1955; Mark Robson
Brief Encounter; 1946; David Lean
Brief Moment; 1933; David Burton

Brigadoon; 1954; Vincente Minnelli

Brigand, The; 1952; Phil Karlson

Brigham Young, Frontiersman; 1940; Henry Hathaway

Bright Leaf; 1950; Michael Curtiz

Bright Lights; 1931; Michael Curtiz

Bright Lights; 1935; Busby Berkeley

Bright Victory (Lights Out); 1952; Mark Robson

Brighton Rock; 1946; John Boulting and Roy Boulting

Bring Your Smile Along; 1955; Blake Edwards

Bringing Up Baby; 1938; Howard Hawks

British Agent; 1934; Michael Curtiz

Broad Minded; 1931; Mervyn Le Roy

Broadway; 1929; Paul Fejos

Broadway; 1942; William Seiter

Broadway Bill; 1934; Frank Capra

Broadway Daddy; 1929; Mervyn Le Roy

Broadway Gondolier; 1935; Lloyd Bacon

Broadway Limited; 1941; Gordon Douglas

Broadway Melody, The; 1929; Harry Beaumont

Broadway Melody of 1936; 1935; Roy del Ruth

Broadway Melody of 1938; 1937; Roy del Ruth

Broadway Melody of 1940; 1940; Norman Taurog

Broadway Rhythm; 1944; Roy del Ruth

Broadway Serenade; 1939; Robert Z. Leonard

Broken Arrow; 1950; Delmer Daves

Broken Blossoms; 1937; John Brahm

Broken Dishes; 1930; Mervyn Le Roy

Broken Lance; 1954; Edward Dmytryk

Broken Lullaby (Man I Killed, The); 1932; Ernst Lubitsch

Broken Strings; 1940; Bernard B. Ray

Bronco Buster; 1952; Budd Boetticher

Brother Orchid; 1940; Lloyd Bacon

Brooklyn Orchid; 1942; Kurt Neumann

Brothers, The; 1947; David MacDonald

Brothers in Law; 1956; John Boulting and Roy Boulting

Brothers Karamazov, The; 1958; Richard Brooks

Brothers Rico, The; 1957; Phil Karlson

Browning Version, The; 1951; Anthony Asquith

Brute Force; 1947; Jules Dassin

Buccaneer, The; 1938; Cecil B. de Mille

Buccaneer, The; 1958; Anthony Quinn

Buchanan Rides Alone; 1958; Budd Boetticher

Buck Benny Rides Again; 1940; Mark Sandrich

Buck Privates; 1941; Arthur Lubin

Bucket of Blood, A; 1960; Roger Corman

Buffalo Bill; 1944; William Wellman

Bugles in the Afternoon; 1952; Roy Rowland

Bull Fighters, The; 1945; Malcolm St. Clair

Bulldog Drummond; 1929; F. Richard Jones

Bulldog Drummond Strikes Back; 1934; Roy del Ruth

Bullet for Joey, A; 1955; Lewis Allen

Bullet Is Waiting, A; 1954; John Farrow

Bullets for O'Hara; 1941; William K. Howard

Bullets or Ballots; 1936; William Keighley

Bullfighter and the Lady, The; 1951; Budd Boetticher

Bundle of Joy; 1957; Norman Taurog

Bunny Lake Is Missing; 1965; Otto Preminger

Bureau of Missing Persons; 1933; Roy del Ruth

Burglar, The; 1957; Paul Wendkos

Burn Witch Burn; 1962; Sidney Hayers

Burning Cross, The; 1947; Walter Colmes

Burning Hills, The; 1956; Stuart Heisler

Burning Up; 1930; Edward Sutherland

Bus Riley's Back in Town; 1965; Harvey Hart

Bus Stop (Wrong Kind of Girl); 1956; Joshua Logan

Bushwhackers, The; 1951; Rod Amateau

But the Flesh Is Weak; 1932; Jack Conway

Butterfield 8; 1960; Daniel Mann

Bwana Devil; 1952; Arch Oboler

By Candlelight; 1933; James Whale

By Love Possessed; 1961; John Sturges
Bye Bye Birdie; 1963; George Sidney
Bye Bye Braverman; 1968; Sidney Lumet

Cabin in the Cotton; 1932; Michael Curtiz
Cabin in the Sky; 1943; Vincente Minnelli
Caesar and Cleopatra; 1946; Brian D. Hurst and G. Pascal
Cafe Metropole; 1937; Edward H. Griffith
Caged; 1950; John Cromwell
Cain and Mabel; 1936; Lloyd Bacon
Caine; 1968; Samuel Fuller
Caine Mutiny, The; 1954; Edward Dmytryk
Cairo; 1942; W. S. van Dyke
Calamity Jane; 1953; David Butler
Calcutta; 1947; John Farrow
Calendar Girl; 1947; Allan Dwan
California; 1946; John Farrow
California Straight Ahead; 1937; Arthur Lubin
Call a Messenger; 1939; Arthur Lubin
Call It a Day; 1937; Archie Mayo
Call Me Bwana; 1963; Gordon Douglas
Call Me Madam; 1953; Walter Lang
Call Me Mister; 1951; Lloyd Bacon
Call Northside 777; 1948; Henry Hathaway
Call of the Wild, The; 1935; William Wellman
Callaloo (Doc); 1937; Brian Montagu and Irene Nicholson
Calling Doctor Kildare; 1939; Harold Buquet
Camelot; 1967; Joshua Logan
Camille; 1937; George Cukor
Campbell's Kingdom; 1957; Ralph Thomas
Canary Murder Case, The; 1929; Frank Tuttle and Malcolm St. Clair
Can This Be Dixie; 1936; George Marshall
Can-Can; 1960; Walter Lang
Canadians, The; 1961; Burt Kennedy
Canyon Crossroads; 1955; Alfred Werker
Canyon Passage; 1946; Jacques Tourneur
Cape Fear; 1961; J. Lee Thompson
Caprice; 1967; Frank Tashlin
Captain Blood; 1935; Michael Curtiz
Captain Carey, USA; 1950; Mitchell Leisen
Captain China; 1949; Lewis R. Foster
Captain Clegg; 1962; Peter Graham Scott
Captain Eddie; 1944; Lloyd Bacon
Captain from Castile; 1947; Henry King
Captain Hates the Sea, The; 1934; Lewis Milestone
Captain Horatio Hornblower; 1951; Raoul Walsh
Captain Kidd; 1945; Rowland V. Lee
Captain Lightfoot; 1955; Douglas Sirk
Captain Newman; 1963; David Miller
Captain Scarlett; 1953; Thomas H. Carr
Captain Sinbad; 1963; Byron Haskin
Captain's Paradise, The; 1953; Anthony Kimmins
Captain's Table, The; 1958; Jack Lee
Captains Courageous; 1937; Victor Fleming
Captains of the Clouds; 1942; Michael Curtiz
Captive City, The; 1952; Robert Wise
Captive Heart, The; 1946; Basil Dearden
Capture, The; 1950; John Sturges
Captured; 1933; Roy del Ruth
Carbine Williams; 1952; Richard Thorpe
Card, The; 1952; Ronald Neame
Cardinal, The; 1963; Otto Preminger
Cardinal Richelieu; 1936; Rowland V. Lee
Career; 1939; Leigh Jason
Career; 1960; Joseph Anthony
Carefree; 1938; Mark Sandrich
Caretaker, The; 1963; Clive Donner
Caretakers, The; 1963; Hall Bartlett
Carleton Browne of the F.O.. 1960; John Boulting
Carmen Jones; 1954; Otto Preminger
Carnegie Hall; 1947; Edgar G. Ulmer
Carnival; 1932; Herbert Wilcox
Carolina; 1934; Henry King
Carousel; 1956; Henry King
Carpetbaggers, The; 1964; Edward Dmytryk
Carrie; 1952; William Wyler
Carrington V.C.; 1954; Anthony Asquith
Carry On, Admiral; 1958; Val Guest
Carry On, Nurse; 1960; Peter Rogers
Carry On, Sergeant; 1959; Gerald Thomas
Carson City; 1952; Andre de Toth

Carve Her Name with Pride; 1958; Lewis Gilbert

Casablanca; 1942; Michael Curtiz

Casanova Brown; 1944; Sam Wood

Casanova's Big Night; 1954; Norman Z. McLeod

Casbah; 1948; John Berry

Case Against Brooklyn, The; 1958; Paul Wendkos

Case of Lena Smith, The; 1929; Josef von Sternberg

Case of the Curious Bride; 1935; Michael Curtiz

Case of the Lucky Legs; 1935; Archie Mayo

Cash McCall; 1960; Joseph Pevney

Casino Royale; 1967; John Huston

Cass Timberlane; 1947; George Sidney

Castle on the Hudson; 1940; Anatole Litvak

Cat and the Canary; 1939; Elliott Nugent

Cat and the Fiddle; 1934; William K. Howard

Cat Ballou; 1965; Elliot Silverstein

Cat on a Hot Tin Roof; 1958; Richard Brooks

Cat People; 1942; Jacques Tourneur

Catered Affair, The; 1956; Richard Brooks

Catherine The Great; 1934; Paul Czinner

Cattle Queen of Montana; 1954; Allan Dwan

Caught; 1949; Max Ophuls

Cause for Alarm; 1951; Tay Garnett

Cavalcade; 1933; Frank Lloyd

Cease Fire; 1953; Owen Crump

Ceiling Zero; 1936; Howard Hawks

Centennial Summer; 1946; Otto Preminger

Central Airport; 1933; William Wellman

Centurions, The; 1966; Mark Robson

Ceremony, The; 1963; Laurence Harvey

Certain Smile, A; 1955; Jean Negulesco

Chad Hanna; 1940; Henry King

Chain Lightning; 1950; Stuart Heisler

Chained; 1934; Clarence Brown

Chalk Garden, The; 1964; Ronald Neame

Challenge, The; 1938; Milton Rosmer

Champ, The; 1931; King Vidor

Champagne Waltz; 1937; Edward Sutherland

Champagne Murders, The; 1968; Claude Chabrol

Champion; 1949; Mark Robson

Chance at Heaven; 1933; William Seiter

Chance Meeting (Blind Date); 1960; Joseph Losey

Chances; 1931; Allan Dwan

Chandu the Magician; 1932; William C. Menzies

Chapman Report, The; 1962; George Cukor

Charade; 1963; Stanley Donen

Charge at Feather River, The; 1953; Gordon Douglas

Charge of the Light Brigade; 1936; Michael Curtiz

Charlie Chan at the Olympics; 1937; H. Bruce Humberstone

Charlie Chan at the Opera; 1936; H. Bruce Humberstone

Charlie Chan at the Race Track; 1936; H. Bruce Humberstone

Charlie Chan at Treasure Island; 1939; Norman Foster

Charlie Chan in Panama; 1940; Norman Foster

Charlie Chan in Reno; 1939; Norman Foster

Charlie's Aunt; 1941; Archie Mayo

Chase, The; 1946; Arthur Ripley

Chase, The; 1966; Arthur Penn

Chase a Crooked Shadow; 1958; Michael Anderson

Chasing Trouble; 1940; Howard Bretherton

Cheaper by the Dozen; 1949; Walter Lang

Cheating Cheaters; 1934; Richard Thorpe

Checkers; 1937; H. Bruce Humberstone

Cheers for Miss Bishop; 1941; Tay Garnett

Cheyenne (The Wyoming Kid); 1947; Raoul Walsh

Cheyenne Autumn; 1964; John Ford

Chicago Deadline; 1949; Lewis Allen

Child Is Born, A; 1940; Lloyd Bacon

Child Is Waiting, A; 1962; John Cassavetes

Child of Divorce; 1946; Richard Fleischer

Children at School (Doc); 1937; Basil Wright

Children of Dreams; 1931; Alan Cros-

land
Children on Trial; 1946; Jack Lee
Children's Hour, The; 1962; William Wyler
Chimes at Midnight (Falstaff); 1967; Orson Welles
China; 1943; John Farrow
China Clipper; 1936; Ray Enright
China Doll; 1958; Frank Borzage
China Gate; 1957; Samuel Fuller
China Girl; 1942; Henry Hathaway
China Seas; 1935; Tay Garnett
Chinatown Nights; 1929; William Wellman
China Venture; 1953; Don Siegel
Chocolate Soldier, The; 1941; Roy del Ruth
Christina; 1929; William K. Howard
Christmas Carol, A; 1956; Ralph Levy
Christmas Holiday; 1944; Robert Siodmak
Christmas in July; 1940; Preston Sturges
Christopher Columbus; 1948; David MacDonald
Christopher Strong; 1933; Dorothy Arzner
Chump at Oxford, A; 1940; Alfred Goulding
Cimarron; 1931; Wesley Ruggles
Cimarron; 1960; Anthony Mann
Cimarron Kid, The; 1951; Budd Boetticher
Cincinnati Kid; 1965; Norman Jewison
Cinderella Jones; 1948; Busby Berkeley
Cinderfella; 1960; Frank Tashlin
Circle of Danger; 1951; Jacques Tourneur
Circle of Deception; 1961; Jack Lee
Circus of Horrors; 1959; Sidney Hayers
Circus World; 1964; Henry Hathaway
Citadel, The; 1938; King Vidor
Citizen Kane; 1941; Orson Welles
City Girl (Our Daily Bread); 1930; F. W. Murnau
City Beneath the Sea; 1953; Budd Boetticher
City For Conquest; 1940; Anatole Litvak
City Lights; 1931; Charles Chaplin
City of Fear; 1959; Irving Lerner
City of Shadows; 1955; William Witney
City Park; 1934; Richard Thorpe

City Streets; 1931; Rouben Mamoulian
City Without Men; 1943; Sidney Salkow
Clash by Night; 1952; Fritz Lang
Clash by Night; 1963; Montgomery Tully
Claudia; 1943; Edmund Goulding
Claudelle Inglish; 1961; Gordon Douglas
Clay Pigeon, The; 1949; Richard Fleischer
Cleopatra; 1934; Cecil B. de Mille
Cleopatra; 1963; Joseph Mankiewicz
Climax, The; 1944; George Waggner
Climbing High; 1938; Carol Reed
Clive of India; 1935; Richard Boleslavsky
Cloak and Dagger; 1946; Fritz Lang
Clock, The; 1945; Vincente Minnelli
Close Call for Boston Blackie, A; 1946; Lew Landers
Close Harmony; 1929; John Cromwell and Edward Sutherland
Close Quarters; 1944; Jack Lee
Close to My Heart; 1951; William Keighley
Clown, The; 1953; Robert Z. Leonard
Club Havana; 1946; Edgar G. Ulmer
Cluny Brown; 1946; Ernst Lubitsch
Cobra Woman; 1945; Robert Siodmak and George Waggner
Cobweb; 1955; Vincente Minnelli
Cock-Eyed World, The; 1929; Raoul Walsh
Cockleshell Heroes; 1955; José Ferrer
Cocktail Hour, The; 1933; Victor Schertzinger
Cocoanuts, The; 1929; Joseph Santley and Robert Florey
Code Two; 1953; Fred M. Wilcox
Cohens and Kellys in Trouble; 1933; George Stevens
Cold Wind in August; 1961; Alexander Singer
Colditz Story, The; 1957; Guy Hamilton
Collector, The; 1964; William Wyler
College Coach; 1933; William Wellman
College Confidential; 1960; Albert Zugsmith
College Holiday; 1939; Frank Tuttle
College Scandal; 1935; Elliott Nugent
College Swing; 1938; Raoul Walsh
Colorado Territory; 1949; Raoul Walsh

Comanche; 1956; George Sherman

Come and Get It; 1936; Howard Hawks and William Wyler

Come Back Little Sheba; 1953; Daniel Mann

Come Fill the Cup; 1951; Gordon Douglas

Come Live with Me; 1941; Clarence Brown

Come Next Spring; 1956; R. G. Springsteen

Come On, The; 1956; Russell Birdwell

Come On Leathernecks; 1938; James Cruze

Come On Marines; 1934; Henry Hathaway

Come September; 1961; Robert Mulligan

Comedy of Terrors, The; 1964; Jacques Tourneur

Comet over Broadway; 1938; Busby Berkeley

Comanche Station; 1960; Budd Boetticher

Comancheros, The; 1961; Michael Curtiz

Command Decision; 1949; Sam Wood

Common Clay; 1930; Victor Fleming

Common Lady, The; 1931; Paul Stein

Common Touch; 1941; John Baxter

Company of Cowards; 1964; George Marshall

Company She Keeps, The; 1950; John Cromwell

Compulsion; 1959; Richard Fleischer

Comrade X; 1940; King Vidor

Concealment; 1935; William Dieterle

Concrete Jungle, The; 1962; Joseph Losey

Condemned; 1929; Wesley Ruggles

Coney Island; 1943; Walter Lang

Confessions of a Nazi Spy; 1939; Anatole Litvak

Confessions of Boston Blackie; 1941; Edward Dmytryk

Confidence Girl; 1952; Andrew L. Stone

Confidential Agent; 1945; Herman Shumlin

Confidential Report (Mister Arkadin); 1962; Orson Welles

Confirm or Deny; 1941; Archie Mayo

Connecticut Yankee; 1931; David Butler

Connecticut Yankee in King Arthur's Court, A; 1949; Tay Garnett

Connection, The; 1960; Shirley Clarke

Conqueror, The; 1955; Dick Powell

Conquerors, The; 1932; William Wellman

Conquest; 1929; Roy del Ruth

Conquest (Marie Walewska); 1937; Clarence Brown

Conquest of Space; 1955; Byron Haskin

Conquest of the Air; 1940; Alexander Korda

Conspirators, The; 1944; Jean Negulesco

Constant Nymph, The; 1943; Edmund Goulding

Contact Man, The; 1949; John Farrow

Convention City; 1933; Archie Mayo

Convict Ninety-Nine; 1938; Max Varnel

Cool Hand Luke; 1967; Stuart Rosenberg

Cool Mikado, The; 1963; Michael Winner

Cool Sound from Hell; 1956; Sidney Furie

Cool World, The; 1963; Shirley Clarke

Copacabana; 1947; Alfred E. Green

Copper Canyon; 1950; John Farrow

Corn Is Green, The; 1945; Irving Rapper

Corridor of Mirrors; 1949; Terence Young

Corsair; 1931; Roland West

Corvette K-225; 1943; Richard Rossen

Cottage on Dartmoor; 1929; Norah Baring and Anthony Asquith

Counsel for Crime; 1937; John Brahm

Counsellor at Law; 1933; William Wyler

Count of Monte Cristo; 1933; Rowland V. Lee

Count the Hours; 1953; Don Siegel

Count Your Blessings; 1959; Jean Negulesco

Counterattack; 1945; Zoltan Korda

Counterfeit Traitor, The; 1961; George Seaton

Countess from Hong Kong, A; 1967; Charles Chaplin

Country Doctor; 1936; Henry King

Country Girl, The; 1954; George Seaton

Country Music Holiday; 1958; Alvin Ganzer

Courage of the West; 1937; Joseph H. Lewis

Court Jester, The; 1956; Norman Panama and Melvin Frank

Court-Martial of Billy Mitchell, The; 1955; Otto Preminger

Courtship of Eddie's Father, The; 1963; Vincente Minnelli

Cover Girl; 1944; Charles Vidor

Cowboy; 1958; Delmer Daves

Cowboy and the Lady; 1939; H. C. Potter

Crack in the Mirror; 1960; Richard Fleischer

Crack-Up; 1936; Malcolm St. Clair

Crack Up; 1946; Irving Reis

Cradle Song; 1933; Mitchell Leisen

Craig's Wife; 1936; Dorothy Arzner

Crash, The; 1932; William Dieterle

Crash Dive; 1943; Archie Mayo

Crashout; 1955; Lewis R. Foster

Crazylegs; 1953; Francis D. Lyon

Creature from the Black Lagoon; 1954; Jack Arnold

Creature Walks Among Us; 1957; John Sherwood

Crime and Punishment; 1935; Josef von Sternberg

Crime and Punishment 62; 1958; Denis Sanders

Crime Doctor's Strangest Case; 1943; Eugene J. Forde

Crime in the Museum of Horrors; 1958; Arthur Crabtree

Crime in the Streets; 1956; Don Siegel

Crime of Doctor Crespi; 1935; John Auer

Crime of Doctor Forbes; 1936; George Marshall

Crime of Passion; 1957; Gerd Oswald

Crime School; 1938; Lewis Seiler

Crime Smasher; 1943; James Tinling

Crime Wave; 1954; Andre de Toth

Crime Without Passion; 1934; Ben Hecht and Charles MacArthur

Criminal Code, The; 1931; Howard Hawks

Criminal Court; 1946; Robert Wise

Crimson Kimono, The; 1959; Samuel Fuller

Crimson Pirate, The; 1952; Robert Siodmak

Crisis; 1950; Richard Brooks

Criss Cross; 1949; Robert Siodmak

Critic's Choice; 1963; Don Weis

Crooked Circle; 1932; H. Bruce Humberstone

Crooks in Cloisters; 1964; Jeremy Summers

Crooner; 1932; Lloyd Bacon

Cross Examination; 1932; Richard Thorpe

Cross of Lorraine, The; 1943; Tay Garnett

Crossfire; 1947; Edward Dmytryk

Crossroads; 1942; Jack Conway

Crosswinds; 1951; Lewis R. Foster

Crowd Roars, The; 1932; Howard Hawks

Crowded Day, The (Shop Soiled); 1954; John Guillermin

Crowded Sky, The; 1960; Joseph Pevney

Cruel Sea, The; 1953; Charles Frend

Cruel Tower, The; 1956; Lew Landers

Cruising down the River; 1953; Richard Quine

Crusades, The; 1935; Cecil B. de Mille

Cry Danger; 1951; Robert Parrish

Cry Havoc; 1943; Richard Thorpe

Cry of Battle; 1963; Irving Lerner

Cry of the City; 1948; Robert Siodmak

Cry of the Hunted; 1953; Joseph H. Lewis

Cry Terror; 1958; Andrew L. Stone

Cry the Beloved Country; 1952; Zoltan Korda

Cry Tough; 1959; Paul Stanley

Cry Vengeance; 1954; Mark Stevens

Crystal Ball, The; 1943; Elliott Nugent

Cuban Love Song; 1932; W. S. van Dyke

Cul-de-sac; 1966; Roman Polanski

Curse of Frankenstein; 1957; Terence Fisher

Curse of the Cat People, The; 1944; Gunther Fritsch and Robert Wise

Curse of the Demon; 1958; Jacques Tourneur

Curse of the Werewolf; 1951; Terence Fisher

Custer of the West; 1968; Robert Siodmak

Cynara; 1932; King Vidor

Cyrano de Bergerac; 1950; Michael Gordon

Daddy Longlegs; 1930; Alfred Santell

Daddy Longlegs; 1955; Jean Negulesco

Daisy Kenyon; 1947; Otto Preminger

Dakota; 1945; Joseph Kane

Dam Busters; 1955; Michael Anderson

Damaged Lives; 1933; Edgar G. Ulmer

Dames; 1934; Ray Enright

Damn Citizen; 1957; Robert Gordon

Damn the Defiant; 1962; Lewis Gilbert

Damn Yankees; 1958; Stanley Donen

Damned Don't Cry, The; 1950; Vincent Sherman

Damsel in Distress, A; 1937; George Stevens

Dance, Fools Dance; 1931; Harry Beaumont

Dance of Life; 1929; John Cromwell and Edward Sutherland

Dance with Me, Henry; 1956; Charles T. Barton

Dancing Lady; 1933; Robert Z. Leonard

Dancing Masters, The; 1943; Malcolm St. Clair

Dandy in Aspic; 1968; Anthony Mann

Danger, Love at Work; 1937; Otto Preminger

Danger Signal; 1945; Robert Florey

Dangerous; 1935; Alfred E. Green

Dangerous Age, A; 1956; Sidney Furie

Dangerous Crossing; 1953; Joseph M. Newman

Dangerous Female (The Maltese Falcon); 1931; Roy del Ruth

Dangerous Nan McGrew; 1930; Malcolm St. Clair

Dangerous Number; 1937; Richard Thorpe

Dangerous Paradise; 1930; William Wellman

Dangerously They Live; 1941; Robert Florey

Dangerously Yours; 1933; Frank Tuttle

Dangerously Yours; 1937; Malcolm St. Clair

Dante's Inferno; 1935; Harry Lachman

Darby's Rangers; 1958; William Wellman

Dark Alibi; 1946; Phil Karlson

Dark Angel, The; 1935; Sidney Franklin

Dark at the Top of the Stairs, The; 1960; Delbert Mann

Dark City; 1950; William Dieterle

Dark Command; 1940; Raoul Walsh

Dark Corner, The; 1946; Henry Hathaway

Dark Horse, The; 1932; Alfred E. Green

Dark Intruder; 1965; Harvey Hart

Dark Journey; 1937; Victor Saville

Dark Mirror, The; 1946; Robert Siodmak

Dark Passage; 1947; Delmer Daves

Dark Past, The; 1948; Rudolph Mate

Dark Sands (Jericho); 1937; Thornton Freeland

Dark Victory; 1939; Edmund Goulding

Dark Waters; 1944; Andre de Toth

Darling; 1965; John Schlesinger

Darling, How Could You; 1951; Mitchell Leisen

Darling Lili; 1969; Blake Edwards

Daughter of Dr. Jekyll; 1957; Edgar G. Ulmer

Daughter of Rosie O'Grady, The; 1950; David Butler

Daughter of Shanghai; 1937; Robert Florey

Daughters Courageous; 1939; Michael Curtiz

David and Bathsheba; 1952; Henry King

David and Lisa; 1962; Frank Perry

David Copperfield; 1935; George Cukor

David Harum; 1934; James Cruze

Dawn Patrol, The; 1930; Howard Hawks

Dawn Patrol, The; 1938; Edmund Goulding

Day and the Hour; 1963; René Clément

Day at the Races, A; 1939; Sam Wood

Day of the Arrow; 1965; Sidney Furie

Day of the Outlaw; 1959; Andre de Toth

Day of the Triffids, The; 1963; Steve Sekely

Day Shall Dawn, The; 1959; A. Kardar

Day the Earth Caught Fire; 1962; Val Guest

Day the Earth Stood Still, The; 1951; Robert Wise

Day the World Ended, The; 1956; Roger Corman

Day They Robbed the Bank of England; 1960; John Guillermin

Daybreak; 1932; Jacques Feyder

Daytime Wife; 1939; Gregory Ratoff

Days of Glory; 1944; Jacques Tourneur

Days of Wine and Roses; 1963; Blake Edwards

Dead End; 1937; William Wyler

Dead Heat on a Merry-Go-Round; 1966; Bernard Girard

Dead Image; 1964; Paul Henreid

Dead Men Tell No Tales; 1938; David MacDonald

Dead of Night; 1945; Alberto Cavalcanti and Charles Crichton

Dead Reckoning; 1947; John Cromwell

Dead Ringer; 1964; Paul Henreid

Deadfall; 1968; Bryan Forbes

Deadliest Sin, The; 1956; Kenneth Hughes

Deadline, USA; 1952; Richard Brooks

Deadly at Dawn; 1946; Harold Clurman

Deadly Companions, The; 1962; Sam Peckinpah

Deadly Is the Female; 1949; Joseph H. Lewis

Deadly Mantis, The; 1956; Nathan Juran

Dear Brat; 1951; William Seiter

Dear Brigitte; 1965; Henry Koster

Dear Murderer; 1946; Arthur Crabtree

Death in Small Doses; 1957; Joseph M. Newman

Death of a Champion; 1939; Robert Florey

Death of a Salesman; 1951; Laslo Benedek

Death Takes a Holiday; 1934; Mitchell Leisen

Death Valley Outlaws; 1941; George Sherman

Deathwatch; 1965; Vic Morrow

Deception; 1946; Irving Rapper

Decision at Sundown; 1957; Budd Boetticher

Decision Before Dawn; 1951; Anatole Litvak

Decks Ran Red, The; 1958; Andrew L. Stone

Deep Blue Sea, The; 1955; Anatole Litvak

Deep in My Heart; 1954; Stanley Donen

Deep Valley; 1947; Jean Negulesco

Deep Waters; 1948; Henry King

Defiant Ones, The; 1958; Stanley Kramer

Delicate Delinquent, The; 1957; Don McGuire

Delightfully Dangerous; 1945; Arthur Lubin

Dementia; 1955; John Parker

Dementia; 1962; Francis Ford Coppola

Demetrius and the Gladiators; 1953; Delmer Daves

Demi-Paradise, The; 1943; Anthony Asquith

Denver and the Rio Grande, The; 1952; Byron Haskin

Deported; 1950; Robert Siodmak

Desert Attack (Ice Cold in Alex); 1958; J. Lee Thompson

Desert Fox, The; 1951; Henry Hathaway

Desert Fury; 1947; Lewis Allen

Desert Patrol; 1958; Guy Green

Desert Rats, The; 1953; Robert Wise

Desert Song; 1929; Roy del Ruth

Desert Song, The; 1953; Bruce Humberstone

Desert Song, The; 1943; Robert Florey

Design for Living; 1933; Ernst Lubitsch

Designing Woman; 1957; Vincente Minnelli

Desirable; 1934; Archie Mayo

Desire; 1936; Frank Borzage

Desire in the Dust; 1960; William F. Claxton

Desire Under the Elms; 1958; Delbert Mann

Desiree; 1954; Henry Koster

Desk Set; 1957; Walter Lang

Desperadoes, The; 1943; Charles Vidor

Desperate; 1947; Anthony Mann

Desperate Hours, The; 1955; William Wyler

Desperate Journey; 1942; Raoul Walsh

Desperate Search; 1952; Joseph H. Lewis

Desperate Siege (Rawhide); 1951; Henry Hathaway

Destination Gobi; 1953; Robert Wise

Destination Moon; 1950; Irving Pichel

Destination Tokyo; 1943; Delmer Daves

Destination Unknown; 1933; Tay Garnett

Destroyer, The; 1943; William Seiter

Destry; 1954; George Marshall

Destry Rides Again; 1939; George Marshall

Detective, The (Father Brown); 1954; Robert Hamer

Detective, The; 1968; Gordon Douglas

Detective Story; 1951; William Wyler

Detour; 1946; Edgar G. Ulmer

Devil's Hairpin, The; 1957; Cornell

Wilde

Devil and Daniel Webster; 1941; William Dieterle

Devil and Miss Jones; 1941; Sam Wood

Devil and the Deep; 1932; Marion Gering

Devil at 4 O'clock, The; 1961; Mervyn Le Roy

Devil Dogs of the Air; 1935; Lloyd Bacon

Devil Doll, The; 1936; Tod Browning

Devil Is a Sissy, The; 1936; W. S. van Dyke

Devil Is a Woman, The; 1935; Josef von Sternberg

Devil Makes Three, The; 1952; Andrew Marton

Devil May Care; 1929; Sidney Franklin

Devil Pays Off, The; 1941; John Auer

Devil to Pay, The; 1930; George Fitzmaurice

Devil with Hitler, The; 1942; Gordon Douglas

Devil with Women, A; 1930; Irving Cummings

Devil's Canyon; 1953; Alfred Werker

Devil's Disciple, The; 1959; Guy Hamilton

Devil's Doorway; 1950; Anthony Mann

Devil's in Love; 1933; William Dieterle

Devotion; 1946; Curtis Bernhardt

D.I., The; 1957; Jack Webb

Dial M for Murder; 1954; Alfred Hitchcock

Diamond Head; 1962; Guy Green

Diamond Jim; 1935; Edward Sutherland

Diamond Queen, The; 1953; John Brahm

Diane; 1955; David Miller

Diary of a Chambermaid; 1946; Jean Renoir

Diary of a High School Bride; 1959; Burt Topper

Diary of a Madman; 1963; Reginald Le Borg

Diary of a Sergeant; 1945; Joseph M. Newman

Diary of Anne Frank, The; 1959; George Stevens

Dick Tracy Versus Cueball; 1946; Gordon Douglas

Dimples; 1936; William Seiter

Dinner at Eight; 1933; George Cukor

Diplomaniacs; 1933; William Seiter

Diplomatic Courier; 1952; Henry Hathaway

Dirigible; 1931; Frank Capra

Dirty Dozen, The; 1967; Robert Aldrich

Dirty Game, The; 1966; Christian Jacque and Carlo Lizzani

Disbarred; 1939; Robert Florey

Dishonored; 1931; Josef von Sternberg

Dishonored Lady; 1947; Robert Stevenson

Disobedient; 1954; Charles Frank

Disorderly Orderly, The; 1964; Frank Tashlin

Dispatch from Reuters, A; 1940; William Dieterle

Disputed Passage; 1939; Frank Borzage

Disraeli; 1929; Alfred E. Green

Distant Drums; 1951; Raoul Walsh

Distant Trumpet, A; 1964; Raoul Walsh

Dive Bomber; 1941; Michael Curtiz

Divide and Conquer (Doc); 1943; Frank Capra and Anatole Litvak

Divided Heart, The; 1954; Charles Crichton

Divine; 1935; Max Ophuls

Divine Lady; 1929; Frank Lloyd

Divorce American Style; 1967; Bud Yorkin

Divorce Among Friends; 1931; Roy del Ruth

Dixie; 1943; Edward Sutherland

Dixie Jamboree; 1945; Christy Cabanne

D.O.A.; 1949; Rudolph Mate

Docks of New Orleans; 1948; Derwin Abrahams

Doctor and the Playgirl, The; 1965; William Martin

Doctor at Sea; 1955; Ralph Thomas

Doctor Blood's Coffin; 1960; Sidney Furie

Doctor Broadway; 1942; Anthony Mann

Doctor Bull; 1933; John Ford

Doctor Crippen; 1964; Robert Lynn

Doctor Cyclops; 1940; Ernest L. Schoesdack

Doctor Dolittle; 1967; Richard Fleischer

Doctor Ehrlich's Magic Bullet; 1940; William Dieterle

Doctor in the House; 1955; Ralph Thomas

Doctor Jekyll and Mr. Hyde; 1932; Rouben Mamoulian

Doctor Jekyll and Mr. Hyde; 1941; Victor Fleming

Doctor Kildare's Victory; 1941; W. S. van Dyke

Doctor Monica; 1934; William Keighley

Doctor No; 1962; Terence Young

Doctor Socrates; 1934; William Dieterle

Doctor Strangelove Or: How I Learned to Stop Worrying and Love the Bomb; 1963; Stanley Kubrick

Doctor X; 1932; Michael Curtiz

Doctor You've Got to Be Kidding; 1967; Peter Tewksbury

Doctor Zhivago; 1965; David Lean

Doctor's Diary, A; 1937; Charles Vidor

Doctor's Dilemma; 1958; Anthony Asquith

Doctor's Wives; 1931; Frank Borzage

Doctors Don't Tell; 1941; Jacques Tourneur

Dodge City; 1939; Michael Curtiz

Dodsworth; 1936; William Wyler

Donovan Affair; 1929; Frank Capra

Don Quixote; 1933; John Farrow and G. W. Pabst

Don't Bet on Blondes; 1935; Robert Florey

Don't Bet on Women; 1931; William K. Howard

Don't Bother to Knock; 1952; Roy Baker

Don't Give Up the Ship; 1959; Norman Taurog

Don't Go near the Water; 1957; Charles Walters

Don't Look Back; 1967; Donn Pennebaker

Don't Make Waves; 1967; Alexander Mackendrick

Don't Panic Chaps; 1960; George Pollock

Don't Trust Your Husband; 1948; Lloyd Bacon

Donovan's Brain; 1953; Felix Feist

Donovan's Reef; 1963; John Ford

Doolins of Oklahoma, The; 1949; Gordon Douglas

Doss House; 1932; John Baxter

Double Bunk; 1961; C. M. Pennington-Richards

Double Crossbones; 1950; Charles T. Barton

Double Deal; 1938; Arthur Dreifuss

Double Door; 1933; Charles Vidor

Double Harness; 1933; John Cromwell

Double Indemnity; 1944; Billy Wilder

Double Life, A; 1948; George Cukor

Double Man, The; 1968; Franklin Schaffner

Double Wedding; 1937; Richard Thorpe

Down Among the Sheltering Palms; 1953; Edmund Goulding

Down on the Farm; 1939; Malcolm St. Clair

Down to the Sea in Ships; 1949; Henry Hathaway

Downstairs at Ramsey's; 1969; Mervyn Le Roy

Dracula; 1931; Tod Browning

Dracula; 1958; Terence Fisher

Dracula's Daughter; 1936; Lambert Hillyer

Drag; 1929; Frank Lloyd

Dragnet; 1947; Leslie Goodwins

Dragnet; 1954; Jack Webb

Dragon Murder Case; 1934; H. Bruce Humberstone

Dragon Seed; 1944; Jack Conway

Dragonwyck; 1946; Joseph Mankiewicz

Dream Girl; 1947; Mitchell Leisen

Dream Wife; 1953; Sidney Shelton

Dreamboat; 1952; Claude Binyon

Dressed to Kill; 1954; Roy William Neill

Drive a Crooked Road; 1954; Richard Quine

Drum, The (Drums); 1938; Zoltan Korda

Drum Beat; 1954; Delmer Daves

Drums Along the Mohawk; 1939; John Ford

Drums in the Deep South; 1951; William C. Menzies

Drums of the Jungle (Ouanga); 1935; George Terwilliger

DuBarry Was a Lady; 1943; Roy del Ruth

Dubious Patriots; 1963; Roger Corman

Duck Soup; 1933; Leo McCarey

Duel at Silver Creek, The; 1952; Don Siegel

Duel in the Jungle; 1954; George Marshall

Duel in the Sun; 1947; King Vidor

Duel on the Mississippi; 1955; William Castle

Duffy; 1968; Robert Parrish

Duke Steps Out, The; 1929; James Cruze

During One Night (Night of Passion); 1961; Sidney Furie

Dust Be My Destiny; 1939; Lewis Seiler

Dynamite; 1929; Cecil B. de Mille

Each Dawn I Die; 1939; William Keighley

Eagle and the Hawk, The; 1933; Stuart Walker

Eagle Squadron; 1942; Arthur Lubin

Earl of Chicago, The; 1940; Richard Thorpe

Earth Dies Screaming; 1964; Terence Fisher

Easiest Way; 1931; Jack Conway

East Is East; 1929; Tod Browning

East of Borneo; 1932; George Melford

East of Eden; 1955; Elia Kazan

East of Shanghai; 1932; Alfred Hitchcock

East of Sumatra; 1953; Budd Boetticher

East of the Rising Sun (Malaya); 1949; Richard Thorpe

East of the River; 1940; Alfred S. Green

East Side, West Side; 1949; Mervyn Le Roy

Easter Parade; 1948; Charles Walters

Easy Come, Easy Go; 1947; John Farrow

Easy Living; 1937; Mitchell Leisen

Easy Living; 1949; Jacques Tourneur

Easy to Love; 1934; William Keighley

Easy to Wed; 1946; Edward Buzzell

Easy Way, The (Room for One More); 1952; Norman Taurog

Eddie Cantor Story; 1954; Alfred E. Green

Eddie Duchin Story, The; 1956; George Sidney

Edge of Darkness; 1943; Lewis Milestone

Edge of Eternity; 1960; Don Siegel

Edge of Fury; 1958; Irving Lerner

Edge of Hell; 1956; Hugo Haas

Edge of the City (Man is Ten Feet Tall, A); 1957; Martin Ritt

Edison the Man; 1940; Clarence Brown

Egyptian, The; 1954; Michael Curtiz

Eight Girls in a Boat; 1934; Richard Wallace

Eight Iron Men; 1952; Edward Dmytryk

El Cid; 1961; Anthony Mann

El Dorado; 1967; Howard Hawks

Elephant Boy; 1937; Zoltan Korda and Robert Flaherty

Elephant Walk; 1954; William Dieterle

Elizabeth the Queen (Private Lives of Elizabeth and Essex, The); 1939; Michael Curtiz

Ellery Queen Master Detective; 1940; Kurt Neumann

Elmer Gantry; 1960; Richard Brooks

Elmer the Great; 1933; Mervyn Le Roy

Emil and the Detectives; 1964; Peter Tewksbury

Emma; 1932; Clarence Brown

Emperor Jones, The; 1933; Dudley Murphy

Emperor Waltz, The; 1948; Billy Wilder

Employees Entrance; 1933; Roy del Ruth

Empty Saddles; 1936; Leslie Selander

Enchanted Cottage, The; 1945; John Cromwell

Enchanted Island; 1958; Allan Dwan

End of the Affair, The; 1955; Edward Dmytryk

End of the River, The; 1947; Derek Twist

Enemy General, The; 1960; George Sherman

Enforcer, The; 1951; Bretaigne Windust

Enough to Eat (Doc); 1936; Edgar Anstey

Escape from Devil's Island; 1936; Albert S. Rogell

Escape from San Quentin; 1957; Fred F. Sears

Enter Madame; 1935; Elliott Nugent

Entertainer, The; 1960; Tony Richardson

Erik the Great Illusionist; 1929; Paul Fejos

Errand Boy, The; 1962; Jerry Lewis

Escapade; 1935; Robert Z. Leonard

Escapade; 1955; Philip Leacock

Escape; 1940; Mervyn Le Roy

Escape; 1948; Joseph Mankiewicz

Escape from East Berlin (Tunnel 28); 1962; Robert Siodmak

Escape from Fort Bravo; 1953; John Sturges

Escape from Zahrain; 1961; Ronald Neame

Escape in the Fog; 1945; Budd Boetticher

Escape Me Never; 1935; Paul Czinner

Escape Me Never; 1945; Peter Godfrey

Escape to Burma; 1955; Allan Dwan

Escape to Glory; 1940; John Brahm

Escapement; 1958; Montgomery Tully

Eskimo; 1933; W. S. van Dyke

Espionage; 1936; Kurt Neumann

Espionage Agent; 1939; Lloyd Bacon

Esther and the King; 1960; Raoul Walsh

Eternally Yours; 1939; Tay Garnett

Eureka Stockade; 1948; Harry Watt

Eva; 1963; Joseph Losey

Eve of Saint Mark, The; 1944; John Stahl

Evelyn Prentice; 1934; William K. Howard

Ever in My Heart; 1933; Archie Mayo

Ever Since Eve; 1934; George Marshall

Ever Since Eve; 1937; Lloyd Bacon

Evergreen; 1934; Victor Saville

Every Day Except Christmas (Short); 1957; Lindsay Anderson

Every Day's a Holiday; 1937; Edward Sutherland

Every Girl Should Be Married; 1948; Don Hartman

Every Night at Eight; 1935; Raoul Walsh

Every Sunday; 1936; Felix Feist

Everybody Does It; 1949; Edmund Goulding

Everybody Sing; 1938; Edwin L. Marin

Everything is Thunder; 1936; Milton Rosner

Executive Suite; 1954; Robert Wise

Evils of Chinatown (Souls for Sale); 1963; Albert Zugsmith

Ex-Lady; 1933; Robert Florey

Ex-Mrs. Bradford, The; 1936; Stephen Roberts

Exile, The; 1947; Max Ophuls

Exiles, The; 1961; Kent MacKenzie

Exodus; 1960; Otto Preminger

Experiment in Terror; 1962; Blake Edwards

Experiment Perilous; 1944; Jacques Tourneur

Expert, The; 1932; Archie Mayo

Explosive Generation, The; 1961; Buzz Kulik

Expresso Bongo; 1960; Val Guest

Eye Witness; 1950; Robert Montgomery

Eyes in the Night; 1942; Fred Zinnemann

Eyes of the World; 1930; Henry King

Face Behind the Mask, The; 1940; Robert Florey

Face in the Crowd, A; 1957; Elia Kazan

Face in the Rain, A; 1963; Irvin Kershner

Face of a Fugitive; 1959; Paul Wendkos

Face to Face; 1952; John Brahm and Bretaigne Windust

Facts of Life, The; 1960; Melvin Frank

Fahrenheit 451; 1966; François Truffaut

Fail-Safe; 1963; Sidney Lumet

Fair Warning Mister Moto; 1937; Norman Foster

Fair Wind to Java; 1953; Joseph Kane

Falcon in Hollywood, The; 1944; Gordon Douglas

Fall of the Roman Empire; 1963; Anthony Mann

Fallen Angel; 1945; Otto Preminger

Fallen Idol; 1949; Carol Reed

Fallen Sparrow, The; 1943; Richard Wallace

Falstaff (Chimes at Midnight); 1967; Orson Welles

Fame Is the Spur; 1946; John Boulting and Roy Boulting

Family Doctor; 1957; Derek Twist

Family Way, The; 1967; Roy Boulting

Famous Ferguson Case; 1932; Lloyd Bacon

Fan, The; 1949; Otto Preminger

Fanny; 1961; Joshua Logan

Fanny Hill; 1964; Albert Zugsmith

Far Call, The; 1929; Allan Dwan

Far Country, The; 1955; Anthony Mann

Far From the Madding Crowd; 1967; John Schlesinger

Far Horizons, The; 1955; Rudolph Mate

Farewell to Arms, A; 1932; Frank Borzage

Farewell to Arms, A; 1957; Charles Vidor

Farmer Takes a Wife, The; 1935; Victor Fleming

Farmer's Daughter, The; 1947; H. C. Potter

Fashions of 1934; 1934; William Dieterle

Fast and Furious; 1939; Busby Berkeley

Fast and Loose; 1930; Fred Newmeyer

Fast Company; 1929; Edward Sutherland

Fast Lady, The; 1963; Ken Annakin

Fast Workers; 1933; Tod Browning

Fastest Gun Alive; 1949; Russell Rouse

Fate Is the Hunter; 1964; Ralph Nelson

Father Brown (The Detective); 1954; Robert Hamer

Father Came Too; 1964; Peter Graham Scott

Father Goose; 1964; Ralph Nelson

Father of the Bride; 1950; Vincente Minnelli

Father Takes a Wife; 1941; J. Hively

Father's Little Dividend; 1951; Vincente Minnelli

FBI Story, The; 1959; Mervyn Le Roy

Fear and Desire; 1954; Stanley Kubrick

Fear Strikes Out; 1957; Robert Mulligan

Fearless Fagan; 1952; Stanley Donen

Fearless Vampire Killers, The; 1967; Roman Polanski

Fearmakers, The; 1958; Jacques Tourneur

Feather in Her Hat, A; 1935; Alfred Santell

Feet First; 1930; Clyde Bruckman

Fellow Americans (Doc); 1942; Garson Kanin

Female; 1933; Michael Curtiz and William Dieterle

Female on the Beach; 1955; Joseph Pevney

Feminine Touch, The; 1941; W. S. van Dyke

Feminine Touch, The; 1955; Pat Jackson

Ferry Cross the Mersey; 1964; Jeremy Summers

Ferry to Hong Kong; 1959; Lewis Gilbert

Feudin' Fools; 1952; William Beaudine

Fever in the Blood; 1950; Vincent Sherman

Fiddlers Three; 1944; Harry Watt

Fiend Who Walked the West, The; 1958; Gordon Douglas

Fiend Without a Face; 1958; Arthur Crabtree

Fiesta; 1947; Richard Thorpe

Fifteen Maiden Lane; 1936; Allan Dwan

Fifth Avenue Girl; 1939; Gregory La Cava

Fifty-Five Days at Peking; 1962; Nicholas Ray

Fighter Squadron; 1948; Raoul Walsh

Fighting Back; 1948; Malcolm St. Clair

Fighting Caravans; 1931; Otto Brower and David Burton

Fighting Kentuckian, The; 1949; George Waggner

Fighting Lady, The (Doc); 1943; William Wyler

Fighting Seabees, The; 1944; Edward Ludwig

Fighting 69th, The; 1940; William Keighley

Fighting Sullivans (The Sullivans); 1944; Lloyd Bacon

Fine Madness, A; 1966; Irvin Kershner

Finger of Guilt; 1956; Joseph Losey

Finger Point, The; 1931; John Francis Dillon

Finian's Rainbow; 1968; Francis Ford Coppola

Fire Down Below; 1957; Robert Parrish

Fire over England; 1936; William K. Howard

Fireball, The; 1950; Tay Garnett

Firebird, The; 1934; William Dieterle

Fireman Save My Child; 1932; Lloyd Bacon

Firefly, The; 1937; Robert Z. Leonard

First Legion, The; 1951; Douglas Sirk

First Love; 1939; Henry Koster

First Texan; 1956; Byron Haskin

First Time, The; 1952; Frank Tashlin

First to Fight; 1967; Christian Nyby

First Weapons; 1950; René Wheeler

First Yank into Hollywood; 1945; Gordon Douglas

First Year; 1932; William K. Howard

Five; 1951; Arch Oboler

Five Against the House; 1955; Phil

Karlson

Five Branded Women; 1960; Martin Ritt

Five Came Back; 1939; John Farrow

Five-Finger Exercise; 1962; Daniel Mann

Five Fingers; 1952; Joseph Mankiewicz

Five Gates to Hell; 1959; James Clavell

Five Graves to Cairo; 1943; Billy Wilder

Five Guns West; 1955; Roger Corman

Five Miles to Midnight; 1963; Anatole Litvak

Five Pennies; 1959; Melville Shavelson

Five Star Final; 1931; Mervyn Le Roy

Five Thousand Fingers of Doctor T, The; 1953; Roy Rowland

Fixed Bayonets; 1951; Samuel Fuller

Fixer, The; 1968; John Frankenheimer

Flame and the Arrow, The; 1950; Jacques Tourneur

Flame in the Streets; 1962; Roy Baker

Flame of New Orleans, The; 1941; René Clair

Flame of the Barbary Coast; 1945; Joseph Kane

Flame over India; 1959; J. Lee Thompson

Flame Within, The; 1935; Edmund Goulding

Flaming Star; 1960; Don Siegel

Flamingo Road; 1949; Michael Curtiz

Flesh; 1932; John Ford

Flesh and Fantasy; 1943; Julien Duvivier

Flesh and Flame (Night of the Quarter Moon); 1959; Hugo Haas

Flesh and Fury; 1952; Joseph Pevney

Flesh and the Fiends, The (Mania); 1960; John Gilling

Flight; 1929; Frank Capra

Flight Command; 1940; Frank Borzage

Flight from Ashiya; 1964; Michael Anderson

Flight Nurse; 1953; Allan Dwan

Flight of the Phoenix; 1966; Robert Aldrich

Flight to Hong Kong; 1956; Joseph M. Newman

Flim Flam Man, The; 1967; Irvin Kershner

Flirtation Walk; 1934; Frank Borzage

Florentine Dagger; 1935; Robert Florey

Flowing Gold; 1940; Alfred E. Green

Fly, The; 1958; Kurt Neumann

Fly by Night; 1942; Robert Siodmak

Flying Deuces, The; 1939; Edward Sutherland

Flying Down to Rio; 1933; Thornton Freeland

Flying Fools; 1929; Tay Garnett

Flying Leathernecks; 1951; Nicholas Ray

Flying Serpent, The; 1946; Sherman Scott

Flying Tigers; 1942; David Miller

Fog over Frisco; 1934; William Dieterle

Follies Bergere; 1935; Roy del Ruth

Follow Me Quietly; 1949; Richard Fleischer

Follow That Dream; 1962; Gordon Douglas

Follow the Boys; 1944; Edward Sutherland

Follow the Fleet; 1935; Mark Sandrich

Follow the Leader; 1930; Norman Taurog

Fools for Scandal; 1938; Mervyn Le Roy

Foot and Mouth (Short); 1955; Lindsay Anderson

Footlight Parade; 1933; Lloyd Bacon

Footsteps in the Dark; 1941; Lloyd Bacon

Footsteps in the Fog; 1955; Arthur Lubin

For Heaven's Sake; 1950; George Seaton

For Love or Money; 1963; Michael Gordon

For Me and My Gal; 1942; Busby Berkeley

For the Defense; 1930; John Cromwell

For the Love of Rusty; 1947; John Sturges

For Whom the Bell Tolls; 1943; Sam Wood

Forbidden; 1932; Frank Capra

Forbidden; 1949; George King

Forbidden; 1953; Rudolph Mate

Forbidden Company; 1932; Richard Thorpe

Forbidden Planet; 1956; Fred M. Wilcox

Forbidden Street, The; 1949; Jean Negulesco

Force of Arms; 1951; Michael Curtiz

Force of Evil; 1948; Abraham Polonsky

Foreign Affair, A; 1948; Billy Wilder

Foreign Correspondent; 1940; Alfred Hitchcock

Foreign Intrigue; 1956; Sheldon Reynolds

Forest Rangers, The; 1942; George Marshall

Forever Amber; 1947; Otto Preminger

Forever and a Day; 1943; Frank Lloyd

Forever Darling; 1956; Alexander Hall

Forever Female; 1954; Irving Rapper

Forget Me Not; 1935; Zoltan Korda

Forgotten; 1933; Richard Thorpe

Forgotten Faces; 1929; Victor Schertzinger

Forgotten Faces; 1936; Eqald Dupont

Forgotten Women; 1932; Richard Thorpe

Forsaking All Others; 1934; W. S. van Dyke

For the Love of Mike; 1960; George Sherman

Fort Apache; 1948; John Ford

Fort Algiers; 1953; Leslie Selander

Fort Defiance; 1951; John Rawlins

Fort Dobbs; 1958; Gordon Douglas

Fort Massacre; 1958; Joseph M. Newman

Fort Yuma; 1955; Leslie Selander

Fortune Cookie, The; 1966; Billy Wilder

Fortunes of Captain Blood, The; 1950; Gordon Douglas

Forty Mothers; 1940; Busby Berkeley

Forty Guns; 1957; Samuel Fuller

Forty Pounds of Trouble; 1962; Norman Jewison

Forty-second Street; 1933; Lloyd Bacon

Forty-ninth Parallel (The Invaders); 1942; Michael Powell

Fountain, The; 1934; John Cromwell

Fountainhead, The; 1949; King Vidor

Four-D Man, The; 1959; Irvin S. Yeaworth

Four Daughters; 1938; Michael Curtiz

Four Faces West; 1948; Alfred E. Green

Four Feathers, The; 1929; Merian C. Cooper and Ernest L. Schoesdack

Four Feathers; 1939; Zoltan Korda

Four for Texas; 1963; Robert Aldrich

Four Frightened People; 1934; Cecil B. de Mille

Four Horsemen of the Apocalypse; 1962; Vincente Minnelli

Four Hours to Kill; 1935; Mitchell Leisen

Four Men and a Prayer; 1938; John Ford

Four Mothers; 1940; William Keighley

Four Poster, The; 1952; Irving Reis

Four Wives; 1939; Michael Curtiz

Four's a Crowd; 1938; Michael Curtiz

Fourteen Hours; 1951; Henry Hathaway

Foxes of Harrow, The; 1947; John Stahl

Framed; 1947; Richard Wallace

Franchise Affair, The; 1951; Lawrence Huntington

Francis; 1950; Arthur Lubin

Francis in the Navy; 1954; Arthur Lubin

Francis Joins the Wacs; 1954; Arthur Lubin

Francis of Assisi; 1961; Michael Curtiz

Frankenstein; 1931; James Whale

Fraternally Yours; 1934; William Seiter

Fraulein; 1958; Henry Koster

Freaks; 1932; Tod Browning

Freckles; 1960; Andrew McLaglen

Free and Easy; 1941; George Sidney

Free Soul, A; 1931; Clarence Brown

French Mistress, A; 1959; Roy Boulting

French They Are a Funny Race, The; 1957; Preston Sturges

French Without Tears; 1939; Anthony Asquith

Frenchman's Creek; 1944; Mitchell Leisen

Frenzy; 1969; Alfred Hitchcock

Freud (The Secret Passion); 1962; John Huston

Friday the Thirteenth; 1933; Victor Saville

Frieda; 1947; Basil Dearden

Friendly Enemies; 1942; Allan Dwan

Friendly Persuasion; 1956; William Wyler

Friends and Lovers; 1931; Victor Schertzinger

Fright (Spell of the Hypnotist); 1957; W. Lee Wilder

Frightened Bride, The; 1953; Terence Young

Frisco Jenny; 1933; William Wellman

Frisco Kid; 1935; Lloyd Bacon

Frisco Waterfront; 1935; Arthur Lubin

Frogmen, The; 1951; Lloyd Bacon

From Headquarters; 1933; William Dieterle

From Heaven to Hell; 1933; Eric C. Kenton

From Hell to Texas; 1958; Henry Hathaway

From Here to Eternity; 1953; Fred Zinnemann

From Russia with Love; 1963; Terence Young

From Saturday to Sunday; 1931; Gustav Machaty

From the Earth to the Moon; 1958; Byron Haskin

From the Hip; 1969; Richard Lester

From the Terrace; 1960; Mark Robson

Front Page, The; 1931; Lewis Milestone

Front Page Woman; 1935; Michael Curtiz

Frontier Gal; 1945; Charles Lamont

Frontier Marshall; 1939; Allan Dwan

Frontier Rangers; 1959; Jacques Tourneur

Frozen Justice; 1929; Allan Dwan

Fugitive, The; 1947; John Ford

Fugitive Kind, The; 1959; Sidney Lumet

Full Confession; 1939; John Farrow

Full of Life; 1957; Richard Quine

Fuller Brush Girl, The; 1949; Lloyd Bacon

Fuller Brush Man, The; 1948; Lloyd Bacon

Fun in Acapulco; 1963; Richard Thorpe

Funny Face; 1957; Stanley Donen

Funny Girl; 1968; William Wyler

Funny Thing Happened on the Way to the Forum, A; 1966; Richard Lester

Furies, The; 1950; Anthony Mann

Fury; 1936; Fritz Lang

Fury at Furnace Creek; 1948; H. Bruce Humberstone

Fury at Showdown; 1957; Gerd Oswald

Fuzzy Pink Nightgown, The; 1957; Norman Taurog

G-Men; 1935; William Keighley

Gallant Hours; 1960; Robert Montgomery

Gallant Journey; 1946; William Wellman

Gallant Lady; 1943; William Beaudine

Galloping Major, The; 1951; Henry Cornelius

Gambler and the Lady (Co-Dir); 1952; Patrick Jenkins

Gambling Lady; 1934; Archie Mayo

Gambling Ship; 1933; Louis Gasnier and Max Marcin

Game of Death, A; 1945; Robert Wise

Games; 1967; Curtis Harrington

Gang Buster; 1931; Edward Sutherland

Gang's All Here, The; 1939; Thornton Freeland

Gang's All Here, The; 1943; Busby Berkeley

Gangs of Chicago; 1940; Arthur Lubin

Gangs of New York; 1938; James Cruze

Garden of Allah, The; 1936; Richard Boleslavsky

Garden of Evil; 1954; Henry Hathaway

Garden of the Moon; 1938; Busby Berkeley

Garment Jungle, The; 1957; Vincent Sherman

Gaslight; 1939; Thorold Dickinson

Gaslight; 1944; George Cukor

Gathering of Eagles, A; 1963; Delbert Mann

Gay Bride, The; 1934; Jack Conway

Gay Deception, The; 1935; William Wyler

Gay Desperado, The; 1936; Rouben Mamoulian

Gay Divorcee, The; 1934; Mark Sandrich

Gay Falcon, The; 1941; Irving Reis

Geisha Boy; 1958; Frank Tashlin

Gene Krupa Story, The; 1959; Don Weis

General Died at Dawn, The; 1936; Lewis Milestone

General Spanky; 1936; Gordon Douglas

Genevieve; 1954; Henry Cornelius

Gentle Annie; 1945; Andrew Marton

Gentle Gunman, The; 1952; Basil Dearden

Gentleman From Dixie; 1942; Al Herman

Gentleman Jim; 1942; Raoul Walsh

Gentlemen Marry Brunettes; 1955;

Richard Sale

Gentlemen of the Press; 1934; Millard Webb

Gentlemen Prefer Blondes; 1953; Howard Hawks

Gentlemen's Agreement; 1947; Elia Kazan

George Washington Slept Here; 1942; William Keighley

Geronimo; 1962; Arnold Laven

Getting Gertie's Garter; 1945; Allan Dwan

Ghost and Mrs. Muir, The; 1947; Joseph Mankiewicz

Ghost Breakers, The; 1940; George Marshall

Ghost Goes West, The; 1936; René Clair

Ghost Ship, The; 1943; Mark Robson

GI Honeymoon; 1945; Phil Karlson

Giant; 1956; George Stevens

Giant of Marathon, The; 1960; Jacques Tourneur

Gideon of Scotland Yard; 1959; John Ford

Gidget; 1959; Paul Wendkos

Gidget Goes Hawaiian; 1961; Paul Wendkos

Gidget Goes to Rome; 1963; Paul Wendkos

Gift of Love, The; 1958; Jean Negulesco

Gigi; 1958; Vincente Minnelli

Gigot; 1962; Gene Kelly

Gilda; 1946; Charles Vidor

Gilded Lily, The; 1935; Wesley Ruggles

Gildersleeve on Broadway; 1943; Gordon Douglas

Gildersleeve's Bad Day; 1943; Gordon Douglas

Gildersleeve's Ghost; 1944; Gordon Douglas

Girl Can't Help It, The; 1956; Frank Tashlin

Girl Crazy; 1932; William Seiter

Girl Crazy; 1943; Norman Taurog

Girl He Left Behind, The; 1956; David Butler

Girl from Maxim's; 1933; Alexander Korda

Girl From Missouri, The; 1933; Jack Conway

Girl Getters, The; 1966; Michael Winner

Girl Hunters, The; 1963; Roy Rowland

Girl in Every Port, A; 1952; Chester Erskine

Girl in the News, The; 1940; Carol Reed

Girl in the Red Velvet Swing, The; 1955; Richard Fleischer

Girl in White, The; 1952; John Sturges

Girl Missing; 1933; Robert Florey

Girl Most Likely, The; 1957; Mitchell Leisen

Girl Must Live, A; 1938; Carol Reed

Girl Named Tamiko, A; 1962; John Sturges

Girl of the Golden West; 1938; Robert Z. Leonard

Girl Rush; 1944; Gordon Douglas

Girl Was Young, A; 1938; Alfred Hitchcock

Girl With Green Eyes; 1964; Desmond Davis

Girl's School; 1938; John Brahm

Girls About Town; 1931; George Cukor

Girls in Chains; 1943; Edgar G. Ulmer

Girls on the Beach; 1965; William Witney

Give a Girl a Break; 1953; Stanley Donen

Give Me a Sailor; 1938; Elliott Nugent

Give Me Your Eyes; 1942; Sacha Guitry

Give Me Your Heart; 1936; Archie Mayo

Give My Regards to Broadway; 1947; Lloyd Bacon

Give Us This Day; 1950; Edward Dmytryk

Glad Rag Doll; 1929; Michael Curtiz

Glass-Bottom Boat, The; 1966; Frank Tashlin

Glass Cage, The; 1955; Montgomery Tully

Glass Key, The; 1935; Frank Tuttle

Glass Key, The; 1942; Stuart Heisler

Glass Menagerie; 1950; Irving Rapper

Glass Slipper, The; 1955; Charles Walters

Glass Wall, The; 1953; Maxwell Shane

Glass Web, The; 1954; Jack Arnold

Glenn Miller Story, The; 1954; Anthony Mann

Glory Alley; 1952; Raoul Walsh

Glory Brigade, The; 1953; Robert D. Webb

Glory Guys, The; 1965; Arnold Laven

Go into Your Dance; 1935; Archie Mayo

Go Man Go; 1953; James Wong Howe

Go Naked in the World; 1961; Ranald MacDougall

Go West; 1940; Edward Buzzell

Go West, Young Man; 1936; Henry Hathaway

Go-Getter, The; 1937; Busby Berkeley

God Is My Co-Pilot; 1945; Robert Florey

God's Country and the Woman; 1936; William Keighley

God's Gift to Women; 1931; Michael Curtiz

God's Little Acre; 1958; Anthony Mann

Goddess, The; 1958; John Cromwell

Going Highbrow; 1935; Robert Florey

Going Hollywood; 1933; Raoul Walsh

Going My Way; 1944; Leo McCarey

Going to Town; 1935; Alexander Hall

Gold Diggers of Broadway; 1929; Roy del Ruth

Gold Diggers of 1933; 1933; Mervyn Le Roy

Gold Diggers of 1935; 1935; Busby Berkeley

Gold Diggers of 1937; 1936; Lloyd Bacon

Gold for the Caesars; 1964; Andre de Toth

Gold Is Where You Find It; 1938; Michael Curtiz

Gold of the Seven Saints; 1961; Gordon Douglas

Golden Blade, The; 1953; Nathan Juran

Golden Boy; 1939; Rouben Mamoulian

Golden Coach, The; 1954; Jean Renoir

Golden Earrings; 1947; Mitchell Leisen

Golden Girl; 1951; Lloyd Bacon

Golden Gloves; 1940; Edward Dmytryk

Golden Harvest; 1933; Ralph Murphy

Golden Head, The; 1965; Richard Thorpe

Golden Mask, The; 1954; Charles Brabin

Golden Mistress, The; 1953; Abner Biberman

Golden Salamander, The; 1950; Ronald Neame

Goldfinger; 1964; Guy Hamilton

Goldie Gets Along; 1933; Malcolm St. Clair

Goldstein; 1964; Philip Kaufman

Goldwyn Follies; 1938; George Marshall

Gone Are the Days (Purlie Victorious); 1963; Nicholas Webster

Gone with the Wind; 1939; Victor Fleming

Gonks Go Beat; 1965; Robert Hartford-Davis

Good Companions, The; 1932; Victor Saville

Good Die Young, The; 1955; Lewis Gilbert

Good Earth, The; 1937; Sidney Franklin

Good Fairy, The; 1935; William Wyler

Good Intentions; 1930; William K. Howard

Good Neighbor Sam; 1964; David Swift

Good Morning Boys; 1937; Max Varnel

Good News; 1947; Charles Walters

Good Sam; 1948; Leo McCarey

Goodbye Again; 1933; Michael Curtiz

Goodbye Again; 1961; Anatole Litvak

Goodbye Charlie; 1964; Vincente Minnelli

Goodbye Love; 1933; H. Bruce Humberstone

Goodbye Mr. Chips; 1939; Sam Wood

Goodbye My Fancy; 1951; Vincent Sherman

Goodbye, My Lady; 1956; William Wellman

Goodnight Vienna; 1932; Herbert Wilcox

Goose Steps Out, The; 1942; Basil Dearden and Will Hay

Gorgeous Hussy, The; 1936; Clarence Brown

Gorgon, The; 1964; Terence Fisher

Gorilla, The; 1939; Allan Dwan

Graduate, The; 1967; Mike Nichols

Grand Hotel; 1932; Edmund Goulding

Grand Prix; 1966; John Frankenheimer

Grand Slam; 1933; William Dieterle

Grapes of Wrath, The; 1940; John Ford

Grass Is Greener, The; 1960; Stanley Donen

Great Caruso, The; 1951; Richard Thorpe

Great Dan Patch, The; 1949; Joseph M. Newman

Great Day in the Morning; 1956; Jacques Tourneur

Great Dictator, The; 1940; Charles Chaplin

Great Escape, The; 1963; John Sturges

Great Expectations; 1947; David Lean

Great Flamarion, The; 1945; Anthony Mann

Great Gambini, The; 1937; Charles Vidor

Great Gabbo, The; 1929; James Cruze

Great Garrick, The; 1937; James Whale

Great Gatsby, The; 1949; Elliott Nugent

Great Gildersleeve, The; 1942; Gordon Douglas

Great God Gold; 1935; Arthur Lubin

Great Imposter, The; 1960; Robert Mulligan

Great Jesse James Raid, The; 1953; Reginald Le Borg

Great Lie, The; 1941; Edmund Goulding

Great Locomotive Chase, The; 1956; Francis D. Lyon

Great Lover, The; 1949; Alexander Hall

Great Man, The; 1957; José Ferrer

Great Man Votes, The; 1939; Garson Kanin

Great Man's Lady, The; 1942; William Wellman

Great McGinty, The; 1940; Preston Sturges

Great Missouri Raid, The; 1950; Gordon Douglas

Great Moment, The; 1944; Preston Sturges

Great O'Malley, The; 1937; William Dieterle

Great Race, The; 1964; Blake Edwards

Great Sinner, The; 1949; Robert Siodmak

Great Sioux Uprising, The; 1953; Lloyd Bacon

Great Victor Herbert, The; 1939; Andrew L. Stone

Great Waltz, The; 1938; Julien Duvivier

Great Ziegfeld, The; 1936; Robert Z. Leonard

Greatest Show on Earth, The; 1952; Cecil B. de Mille

Greatest Story Ever Told, The; 1964; George Stevens

Green Berets, The; 1968; John Wayne

Green Eyes; 1934; Richard Thorpe

Green Fields; 1937; Jacob Ben-Ami and Edgar G. Ulmer

Green Glove, The; 1952; Rudolph Mate

Green Goddess, The; 1932; Alfred E. Green

Green Grow the Rushes; 1951; Derek Twist

Green Hell; 1940; James Whale

Green Light; 1937; Frank Borzage

Green Man, The; 1957; Robert Day

Green Mansions; 1958; Mel Ferrer

Green Pastures, The; 1936; Marc Connelly and William Keighley

Greengage Summer, The (Loss of Innocence); 1961; Lewis Gilbert

Greenwich Village Story; 1963; Jack O'Connell

Grip of the Strangler; 1958; Robert Day

Group, The; 1965; Sidney Lumet

Grumpy; 1930; George Cukor and Cyril Gardner

Guardsman, The; 1931; Sidney Franklin

Guess Who's Coming to Dinner; 1967; Stanley Kramer

Guest, The; 1964; Clive Donner

Guest in the House; 1944; John Brahm

Guide for the Married Man; 1967; Gene Kelly

Guilt of Janet Ames, The; 1947; Charles Vidor

Guilty Hands; 1931; W. S. van Dyke

Guinea Pig, The; 1948; John Boulting and Roy Boulting

Gun Battle at Monterey; 1957; Sidney Franklin and Karl K. Hittelman

Gun Crazy; 1949; Joseph H. Lewis

Gun for a Coward; 1957; Abner Biberman

Gun Fury; 1953; Raoul Walsh

Gun Glory; 1957; Roy Rowland

Gun Hawk, The; 1963; Edward Ludwig

Gun Runners, The; 1958; Don Siegel

Gun the Man Down; 1956; Andrew McLaglen

Gun-Slinger, The; 1958; Roger Corman

Gunfight at Dodge City, The; 1959; Joseph M. Newman

Gunfight at the O K Corral; 1957; John Sturges

Gunfighter, The; 1950; Henry King

Gung Ho; 1943; Ray Enright

Gunga Din; 1939; George Stevens

Gunman's Walk; 1958; Phil Karlson

Gunn; 1967; Blake Edwards

Guns at Batasi; 1964; John Guillermin

Guns in the Afternoon (Ride the High Country); 1962; Sam Peckinpah

Guns of Darkness; 1962; Anthony Asquith

Guns of Navarone, The; 1961; J. Lee Thompson

Guns of the Magnificent Seven; 1968; Paul Wendkos

Guns of the Timberland; 1960; Robert D. Webb

Guy Could Change, A; 1946; William K. Howard

Guy Named Joe, A; 1943; Victor Fleming

Guy Who Came Back, The; 1951; Joseph M. Newman

Guy, a Gal and a Pal, A; 1945; Budd Boetticher

Guys and Dolls; 1955; Joseph Mankiewicz

Gypsy; 1962; Mervyn Le Roy

Gypsy and the Gentleman, The; 1958; Joseph Losey

Hail the Conquering Hero; 1944; Preston Sturges

Hairy Ape, The; 1944; Alfred Santell

Half a Hero; 1953; Don Weis

Half a Sinner; 1934; Kurt Neumann

Half a Sixpence; 1968; George Sidney

Half-Naked Truth, The; 1932; Gregory La Cava

Halfway House, The; 1943; Basil Dearden

Hallelujah; 1929; King Vidor

Hallelujah the Hills; 1963; Adolfas Mekas

Hallelujah Trail, The; 1964; John Sturges

Hallelujah, I'm a Bum; 1933; Lewis Milestone

Halliday Brand, The; 1957; Joseph H. Lewis

Halls of Montezuma; 1950; Lewis Milestone

Hamlet; 1948; Sir Laurence Olivier

Hand in Hand; 1960; Philip Leacock

Hands Across the Table; 1935; Mitchell Leisen

Hanging Tree, The; 1959; Delmer Daves

Hangman, The; 1959; Michael Curtiz

Hangmen Also Die; 1943; Fritz Lang

Hangover Square; 1945; John Brahm

Hannibal; 1960; Edgar G. Ulmer

Hans Christian Andersen; 1952; Charles Vidor

Happening, The; 1967; Elliot Silverstein

Happiness Ahead; 1934; Mervyn Le Roy

Happy Anniversary; 1959; David Miller

Happy Is the Bride; 1958; Roy Boulting

Happy Landing; 1937; Roy del Ruth

Happy Road, The; 1957; Gene Kelly

Happy Thieves, The; 1962; George Marshall

Happy Time, The; 1952; Richard Fleischer

Happy Years; 1950; William Wellman

Hard Day's Night, A; 1964; Richard Lester

Hard to Handle; 1933; Mervyn Le Roy

Hard Way, The; 1942; Vincent Sherman

Hard-Boiled Canary, The; 1941; Andrew L. Stone

Hard, Fast and Beautiful; 1951; Ida Lupino

Harder They Fall, The; 1956; Mark Robson

Harlem on the Prairie; 1939; Jed Buell

Harlow; 1965; Gordon Douglas

Harlow; 1965; Alex Segal

Harper; 1966; Jack Smight

Harriet Craig; 1930; Vincent Sherman

Harvey; 1951; Henry Koster

Harvey Girls, The; 1946; George Sidney

Harvey Middleman, Fireman; 1965; Ernest Pintoff

Has Anybody Seen My Gal; 1952; Douglas Sirk

Hasty Heart, The; 1949; Vincent Sherman

Hat Check Girl; 1932; Sidney Lanfield

Hatari; 1962; Howard Hawks

Hatchet Man; 1932; William Wellman

Hatful of Rain, A; 1957; Fred Zinnemann

Haunted England; 1961; Michael Winner

Haunted Palace, The; 1963; Roger Corman

Haunting, The; 1963; Robert Wise

Having a Wild Weekend; 1965; John Boorman

Having Wonderful Crime; 1945;

Edward Sutherland

Having Wonderful Time; 1938; Alfred Santell

He Laughed Last; 1956; Blake Edwards

He Married His Wife; 1940; Roy del Ruth

He Ran All the Way; 1951; John Berry

He Rides Tall; 1964; R. G. Springsteen

He Walked by Night; 1941; Alfred Werker

He Was Her Man; 1934; Lloyd Bacon

He Who Must Die; 1958; Jules Dassin

Hear Me Good; 1957; Don McGuire

Heart of a Child; 1958; Clive Donner

Heart of New York; 1932; Mervyn Le Roy

Heart of the Matter, The; 1954; George More O'Ferrall

Hearts Divided; 1936; Frank Borzage

Hearts in Dixie; 1929; Paul Sloane

Hearts in Exile; 1929; Michaël Curtiz

Heat Lightning; 1934; Mervyn Le Roy

Heat's On, The; 1943; Gregory Ratoff

Heaven Can Wait; 1943; Ernst Lubitsch

Heaven Knows, Mr. Allison; 1957; John Huston

Heavens Above; 1963; John Boulting and Roy Boulting

Heidi; 1937; Allan Dwan

Heiress, The; 1949; William Wyler

Helen Morgan Story, The; 1957; Michael Curtiz

Helen of Troy; 1955; Robert Wise

Hell and High Water; 1954; Samuel Fuller

Hell Bent for Leather; 1960; George Sherman

Hell Below; 1933; Jack Conway

Hell Below Zero; 1954; Mark Robson

Hell Canyon Outlaws; 1957; Paul Landres

Hell Harbor; 1930; Henry King

Hell in the Pacific; 1968; John Boorman

Hell Is a City; 1959; Val Guest

Hell on Frisco Bay; 1955; Frank Tuttle

Hell Squad; 1958; Burt Topper

Hell to Eternity; 1960; Phil Karlson

Hell's Angels; 1930; Howard Hughes

Hell's Five Hours; 1958; Jack L. Copeland

Hell's Headquarters; 1932; Andrew L. Stone

Hell's Heroes; 1930; William Wyler

Hell's Highway; 1932; Rowland Brown

Hell's Island; 1955; Phil Karlson

Hellbent for Glory; 1958; William Wellman

Helldorado; 1935; James Cruze

Heller in Pink Tights; 1960; George Cukor

Hellfire; 1939; R. G. Springsteen

Hellfire Club; 1963; Monty Berman and Robert S. Baker

Hellgate; 1952; Charles Marquis Warren

Hello Dolly; 1968; Gene Kelly

Hello Out There (Never released); 1949; James Whale

Hellzapoppin; 1942; H. C. Potter

Help; 1965; Richard Lester

Helpmates; 1931; James Parrott

Helter Skelter; 1948; Ralph Thomas

Hemingway's Adventures of a Young Man; 1962; Martin Ritt

Henry V; 1945; Sir Laurence Olivier

Her Cardboard Lover; 1942; George Cukor

Her First Mate; 1933; William Wyler

Her Highness and the Bellboy; 1945; Richard Thorpe

Her Majesty Love; 1931; William Dieterle

Her Man; 1930; Tay Garnett

Her Private Life; 1929; Alexander Korda

Her Sister's Secret; 1946; Edgar G. Ulmer

Here Come the Waves; 1944; Mark Sandrich

Here Comes Mister Jordan; 1941; Alexander Hall

Here Comes the Groom; 1951; Frank Capra

Here Comes the Navy; 1934; Lloyd Bacon

Here I Am a Stranger; 1939; Roy del Ruth

Here Is a Man; 1941; William Dieterle

Here We Go Again; 1942; Allan Dwan

Here We Go Round the Mulberry Bush; 1968; Clive Donner

Heritage of the Desert; 1933; Henry Hathaway

Hero's Island; 1963; Leslie Stevens

Heroes for Sale; 1933; William Wellman

Heroes of Telemark; 1966; Anthony Mann

Hi Diddle Diddle; 1943; Andrew L. Stone

Hi Nellie; 1934; Mervyn Le Roy

Hidden Fear; 1957; Andre de Toth

Hide Out; 1934; W. S. van Dyke

High and Dry; 1954; Alexander Mackendrick

High and the Mighty, The; 1954; William Wellman

High Barbaree; 1947; Jack Conway

High Bright Sun, The; 1965; Ralph Thomas

High Command, The; 1936; Thorold Dickinson

High Noon; 1952; Fred Zinnemann

High Pressure; 1932; Mervyn Le Roy

High School Confidential (Young Hellions); 1960; Albert Zugsmith

High Sierra; 1941; Raoul Walsh

High Society; 1955; William Beaudine

High Society; 1956; Charles Walters

High Tension; 1936; Allan Dwan

High Tide at Noon; 1957; Philip Leacock

High Time; 1960; Blake Edwards

High, Wide and Handsome; 1937; Rouben Mamoulian

High Wind in Jamaica; 1965; Alexander Mackendrick

Highway 301; 1950; Andrew L. Stone

Highwayman, The; 1951; Leslie Selander

Hilda Crane; 1956; Philip Dunne

Hill, The; 1965; Sidney Lumet

Hindle Wakes; 1931; Victor Saville

Hindle Wakes; 1950; Arthur Crabtree

His Affair; 1937; William Seiter

His Brother's Wife; 1936; W. S. van Dyke

His Butler's Sister; 1943; Frank Borzage

His Double Life; 1933; Arthur Hopkins and William C. de Mille

His Excellency; 1952; Robert Hamer

His Family Tree; 1935; Charles Vidor

His First Command; 1930; Gregory La Cava

His Girl Friday; 1940; Howard Hawks

His Kind of Woman; 1951; John Farrow

His Majesty O'Keefe; 1953; Byron Haskin

His Woman; 1931; Edward Sloman

History Is Made at Night; 1937; Frank Borzage

History of the Wax Museum; 1933; Michael Curtiz

Hit the Deck; 1955; Roy Rowland

Hitch-Hiker, The; 1953; Ida Lupino

Hitler; 1962; Stuart Heisler

Hitler Gang, The; 1944; John Farrow

Hitler's Children; 1943; Edward Dmytryk and Irving Reis

Hitler's Madman; 1943; Douglas Sirk

Hitting a New High; 1937; Raoul Walsh

H. M. Pulham, Esq.; 1941; King Vidor

HMS Defiant; 1962; Lewis Gilbert

Hobson's Choice; 1954; David Lean

Hold Back the Dawn; 1941; Mitchell Leisen

Hold Back the Night; 1956; Allan Dwan

Hold Everything; 1930; Roy del Ruth

Hold That Blonde; 1945; George Marshall

Hold That Ghost; 1941; Arthur Lubin

Hold Them Navy; 1937; Kurt Neumann

Hole in the Head, A; 1959; Frank Capra

Holiday; 1930; Edward H. Griffith

Holiday; 1938; George Cukor

Holiday in Mexico; 1946; George Sidney

Holiday Inn; 1942; Mark Sandrich

Holly and the Ivy, The; 1953; George More O'Ferrall

Hollywood Boulevard; 1937; Robert Florey

Hollywood Canteen; 1944; Delmer Daves

Hollywood Cavalcade; 1939; Irving Cummings

Hollywood Hotel; 1937; Busby Berkeley

Hollywood or Bust; 1956; Frank Tashlin

Hollywood Revue of 1929; 1929; Charles Reisner

Holy Matrimony; 1943; John Stahl

Holy Terror, A; 1931; Irving Cummings

Hombre; 1967; Martin Ritt

Home at Seven (Murder on Monday); 1952; Ralph Richardson

Home Before Dark; 1958; Mervyn Le Roy

Home from the Hill; 1960; Vincente Minnelli

Home in Indiana; 1944; Henry Hathaway

Home of the Brave; 1949; Mark Rob-

son

Home Sweet Homicide; 1946; Lloyd Bacon

Homecoming; 1948; Mervyn Le Roy

Homely Girl; 1936; Henry Koster

Homicidal; 1961; William Castle

Hondo; 1953; John Farrow

Honey Pot, The; 1967; Joseph Mankiewicz

Honeymoon; 1947; William Keighley

Honeymoon for Three; 1941; Lloyd Bacon

Honeymoon Limited; 1935; Arthur Lubin

Hong Kong Confidential; 1958; Edward L. Cahn

Honky Tonk; 1941; Jack Conway

Honor Among Lovers; 1931; Dorothy Arzner

Hoodlum Priest, The; 1961; Irvin Kershner

Hoodlum Saint, The; 1946; Norman Taurog

Hook, The; 1963; George Seaton

Horizons West; 1952; Budd Boetticher

Horizontal Lieutenant, The; 1962; Richard Thorpe

Horn Blows at Midnight, The; 1945; Raoul Walsh

Horror of Dracula; 1958; Terence Fisher

Horror of It All; 1964; Terence Fisher

Horse Feathers; 1932; Norman Z. McLeod

Horse Soldiers, The; 1959; John Ford

Horse's Mouth, The; 1958; Ronald Neame

Hostage, The; 1956; Harold Huth

Hostages; 1943; Frank Tuttle

Hot Blood; 1956; Nicholas Ray

Hot Enough for June; 1964; Ralph Thomas

Hot for Paris; 1929; Raoul Walsh

Hot Saturday; 1932; William Seiter

Hot Spell; 1958; Daniel Mann

Hot Rods to Hell; 1967; John Brahm

Hot Steel; 1940; Christy Cabanne

Hot Stuff; 1929; Mervyn Le Roy

Hotel Berlin; 1945; Peter Godfrey

Hotel for Women; 1939; Gregory Ratoff

Hotel Imperial; 1939; Robert Florey

Hotel Paradiso; 1966; Peter Glenville

Hotel Sahara; 1951; Ken Annakin

Hottentot, The; 1929; Roy del Ruth

Hound Dog Man; 1959; Don Siegel

Hound of the Baskervilles; 1939; Sidney Lanfield

Hound of the Baskervilles; 1959; Terence Fisher

Hounded (Johnny Allegro); 1949; Ted Tetzlaff

Hounds of Zaroff, The (Most Dangerous Game, The); 1932; Irving Pichel and Ernest L. Schoesdack ·

Hour Before the Dawn, The; 1943; Frank Tuttle

Hour of the Gun; 1967; John Sturges

House by the River; 1950; Fritz Lang

House Divided, A; 1932; William Wyler

House of a Thousand Candles; 1936; Arthur Lubin

House of Bamboo; 1955; Samuel Fuller

House of Connelly, The; 1934; Henry King

House of Fear, The; 1945; Roy William Neill

House of Horror, The; 1929; Benjamin Christensen

House of Rothschild, The; 1934; Alfred Werker

House of Secrets; 1957; Guy Green

House of Strangers; 1949; Joseph Mankiewicz

House of the Seven Hawks, The; 1959; Richard Thorpe

House of Usher, The; 1961; Roger Corman

House of Wax; 1952; Andre de Toth

House of Women; 1962; Walter Doniger

House on 56th Street; 1933; Robert Florey

House on Haunted Hill, The; 1959; William Castle

House on Telegraph Hill, The; 1951; Robert Wise

House on 92nd Street, The; 1945; Henry Hathaway

Houseboat; 1958; Melville Shavelson

How Green Was My Valley; 1941; John Ford

How I Won the War; 1967; Richard Lester

How the West Was Won; 1963; John Ford, Henry Hathaway, and George Marshall

How to Be Very, Very Popular; 1954; Nunnally Johnson

How to Marry a Millionaire; 1953; Jean Negulesco

How to Murder Your Wife; 1964;

Richard Quine

How to Steal a Million; 1966; William Wyler

Howards of Virginia, The; 1940; Frank Lloyd

Huckleberry Finn; 1933; Norman Taurog

Hucksters, The; 1947; Jack Conway

Hud; 1963; Martin Ritt

Hudson's Bay; 1937; Irving Pichel

Hue and Cry; 1946; Charles Crichton

Huk; 1956; John Barnwell

Human Cargo; 1936; Allan Dwan

Human Comedy, The; 1943; Clarence Brown

Human Desire; 1954; Fritz Lang

Human Jungle, The; 1954; Joseph M. Newman

Humoresque; 1947; Jean Negulesco

Hunchback of Notre Dame, The; 1939; William Dieterle

Hungry Hill; 1955; Brian D. Hurst

Hunters, The; 1958; Dick Powell

Hurricane; 1937; John Ford

Hurry Sundown; 1966; Otto Preminger

Hush, Hush, Sweet Charlotte; 1964; Robert Aldrich

Hustler, The; 1961; Robert Rossen

Hypnotised; 1933; Mack Sennett

Hypnotist, The; 1957; Montgomery Tully

I Aim at the Stars; 1960; J. Lee Thompson

I Am a Camera; 1955; Henry Cornelius

I Am a Fugitive from a Chain Gang; 1932; Mervyn Le Roy

I Am a Thief; 1935; Robert Florey

I Believe in You; 1951; Basil Dearden

I Confess; 1952; Alfred Hitchcock

I Could Go on Singing; 1962; Ronald Neame

I Cover the War; 1937; Arthur Lubin

I Cover the Waterfront; 1933; James Cruze

I Died a Thousand Times; 1955; Stuart Heisler

I Don't Care Girl, The; 1953; Lloyd Bacon

I Dood It; 1943; Vincente Minnelli

I Dream of Jeannie; 1952; Allan Dwan

I Dream Too Much; 1935; John Cromwell

I Found Stella Parish; 1935; Mervyn Le Roy

I Hate Your Guts (The Intruder); 1962; Roger Corman

I Have Lived; 1933; Richard Thorpe

I Live for Love; 1935; Busby Berkeley

I Live in Grosvenor Square; 1945; Herbert Wilcox

I Live My Life; 1935; W. S. van Dyke

I Love a Soldier; 1944; Mark Sandrich

I Love Chinatown; 1936; Norman Foster

I Love Melvin; 1953; Don Weis

I Love You Again; 1940; W. S. van Dyke

I Loved You Wednesday; 1933; Henry King

I Married a Doctor; 1936; Archie Mayo

I Married a Monster from Outer Space; 1958; Gene Fowler

I Married a Witch; 1942; René Clair

I Married a Woman; 1958; Hal Kanter

I Married an Angel; 1941; W. S. van Dyke

I Met My Love Again; 1938; Joshua Logan and Arthur Ripley

I Mobster; 1959; Roger Corman

I Remember Mama; 1948; George Stevens

I Saw What You Did; 1965; William Castle

I Sell Anything; 1934; Robert Florey

I Shot Jesse James; 1949; Samuel Fuller

I Stole a Million; 1939; Frank Tuttle

I Take This Woman; 1931; Marion Gering

I Take This Woman; 1940; W. S. van Dyke

I Thank a Fool; 1962; Robert Stevens

I the Jury; 1953; Henry Essex

I Walk Alone; 1947; Byron Haskin

I Wake Up Screaming; 1941; H. Bruce Humberstone

I Walked with a Zombie; 1943; Jacques Tourneur

I Want to Live; 1958; Robert Wise

I Wanted Wings; 1941; Mitchell Leisen

I Was a Communist for the FBI; 1951; Gordon Douglas

I Was a Male War Bride; 1949; Howard Hawks

I Was a Spy; 1933; Victor Saville

I Was Happy Here (Time Lost and Time Remembered); 1966; Desmond Davis

I Was Monty's Double; 1958; John

Guillermin

I Wonder Who's Kissing Her Now; 1947; Lloyd Bacon

I'd Climb the Highest Mountain; 1951; Henry King

I'd Rather Be Rich; 1964; Jack Smight

I'll Be Seeing You; 1944; William Dieterle

I'll Be Yours; 1947; William Seiter

I'll Cry Tomorrow; 1956; Daniel Mann

I'll Never Forget What's 'Is Name; 1968; Michael Winner

I'll Never Forget You; 1951; Roy Baker

I'll See You in My Dreams; 1951; Michael Curtiz

I'll Take Sweden; 1965; Frederick de Cordova

I'm All Right Jack; 1960; John Boulting

I'm No Angel; 1933; Wesley Ruggles

I'm Nobody's Sweetheart Now; 1940; Arthur Lubin

I've Always Loved You; 1946; Frank Borzage

Ice Cold in Alex (Desert Attack); 1958; J. Lee Thompson

Ice Follies; 1939; Reinhold Schunzel

Ice Palace; 1960; Vincent Sherman

Ideal Husband, An; 1948; Alexander Korda

Identity Unknown; 1945; Walter Colmes

Identity Unknown; 1960; Frank Marshall

Idiot's Delight; 1939; Clarence Brown

Idol, The; 1966; Daniel Petrie

Idol of the Crowds; 1937; Arthur Lubin

If; 1968; Lindsay Anderson

If a Man Answers; 1962; Henry Levin

If I Had a Million; 1930; James Cruze and H. Bruce Humberstone

If I Were Free; 1933; Elliott Nugent

If I Were King; 1938; Frank Lloyd

If You Knew Susie; 1948; Gordon Douglas

Illustrated Man, The; 1968; Jack Smight

Imitation of Life; 1934; John Stahl

Imitation of Life; 1959; Douglas Sirk

Immortal Land, The; 1958; Basil Wright

Immortal Sergeant; 1943; John Stahl

Immortal Story, The; 1968; Orson Welles

Impact; 1949; Arthur Lubin

Impatient Maiden; 1932; James Whale

Imperfect Lady; 1947; Lewis Allen

Importance of Being Earnest, The; 1952; Anthony Asquith

Imposter, The (Strange Confession); 1943; Julien Duvivier

In a Lonely Place; 1950; Nicholas Ray

In Caliente; 1935; Lloyd Bacon

In Cold Blood; 1967; Richard Brooks

In Harm's Way; 1964; Otto Preminger

In Love and War; 1958; Philip Dunne

In Name Only; 1939; John Cromwell

In Old Arizona; 1929; Raoul Walsh and Irving Cummings

In Old California; 1942; William McGann

In Old Chicago; 1938; Henry King

In Old Kentucky; 1935; George Marshall

In Our Time; 1944; Vincent Sherman

In Search of the Castaways; 1961; Robert Stevenson

In the Cool of the Day; 1963; Robert Stevens

In the French Style; 1963; Robert Parrish

In the Good Old Summertime; 1949; Robert Z. Leonard

In the Heat of the Night; 1967; Norman Jewison

In the Meantime Darling; 1944; Otto Preminger

In This Our Life; 1942; John Huston

In Which We Serve; 1942; Noel Coward and David Lean

Incendiary Blonde; 1945; George Marshall

Incident at Phantom Hill; 1966; Earl Bellamy

Incredible Shrinking Man; 1957; Jack Arnold

Incredibly Strange Creatures Who Stopped Living and Became Zombies, The; 1962; Ray Dennis Stecker

Indian Fighter, The; 1955; Andre de Toth

Indiscreet; 1931; Leo McCarey

Indiscreet; 1958; Stanley Donen

Inferno; 1952; Roy Baker

Informer, The; 1935; John Ford

Inherit the Wind; 1960; Stanley Kramer

Inn of the Sixth Happiness, The; 1958; Mark Robson

Innocent Eye, The (Short); 1958; John Schlesinger

Innocent Sinners; 1957; Philip Leacock

Innocents, The; 1961; Jack Clayton

Inside Daisy Clover; 1966; Robert Mulligan

Inside Story, The; 1948; Allan Dwan

Inspector, The (Lisa); 1962; Mark Robson

Inspector Calls, An; 1954; Guy Hamilton

Inspector Clouseau; 1968; Bud Yorkin

Inspector General, The (USA); 1949; Henry Koster

Inspiration; 1931; Clarence Brown

Intent to Kill; 1957; Jack Cardiff

Interlude; 1957; Douglas Sirk

Intermezzo, A Love Story; 1939; Gregory Ratoff

International House; 1933; Edward Sutherland

International Spy; 1937; Joseph H. Lewis

Interns, The; 1962; David Swift

Interns Can't Take Money; 1936; Alfred Santell

Intimate Relations (Disobedient); 1954; Charles Frank

Intruder, The; 1953; Guy Hamilton

Intruder, The (I Hate Your Guts); 1962; Roger Corman

Intruder in the Dust; 1949; Clarence Brown

Invaders, The (Forty-Ninth Parallel); 1942; Michael Powell

Invaders from Mars; 1953; William C. Menzies

Invasion of the Body Snatchers; 1956; Don Siegel

Invisible Boy; 1957; Herman Hoffman

Invisible Ghost, The; 1941; Joseph H. Lewis

Invisible Man, The; 1933; James Whale

Invisible Stripes; 1939; Lloyd Bacon

Invisible Woman, The; 1941; Edward Sutherland

Invitation; 1952; Gottfried Reinhardt

Invitation to a Gunfighter; 1964; Richard Wilson

Invitation to the Dance; 1956; Gene Kelly

Ipcress File, The; 1965; Sidney Furie

Irene; 1940; Herbert Wilcox

Irish in Us, The; 1935; Lloyd Bacon

Irma La Douce; 1963; Billy Wilder

Iron Curtain, The; 1948; William Wellman

Iron Duke, The; 1936; Victor Saville

Iron Man; 1931; Tod Browning

Iron Mask, The; 1929; Allan Dwan

Iron Mistress, The; 1952; Gordon Douglas

Iron Petticoat; The; 1956; Ralph Thomas

Iroquois Trail, The; 1950; Phil Karlson

Is Paris Burning?; 1966; René Clement

Isadora; 1968; Karel Reisz

Island of Love; 1963; Morton da Costa

Island in the Sky; 1953; William Wellman

Island in the Sun; 1957; Robert Rossen

Island of Desire; 1952; Stuart Heisler

Island of Doomed Men; 1940; Charles T. Barton

Island of Lost Men; 1939; Kurt Neumann

Island of Lost Souls; 1933; Erle C. Kenton

Isle of Forgotten Sins; 1943; Edgar G. Ulmer

Isle of Fury; 1936; Frank McDonald

Isle of the Dead; 1945; Mark Robson

It All Came True; 1940; Lewis Seiler

It Always Rains on Sunday; 1947; Robert Hamer

It Grows on Trees; 1952; Arthur Lubin

It Had to Be You; 1948; Rudolph Mate

It Had to Happen; 1936; Roy del Ruth

It Happened on Fifth Avenue; 1947; Roy del Ruth

It Happened One Night; 1934; Frank Capra

It Happened One Summer (State Fair); 1945; Walter Lang

It Happened One Sunday; 1945; Karel Lamac

It Happened to Jane; 1959; Richard Quine

It Happened Tomorrow; 1944; René Clair

It Happens Every Spring; 1949; Lloyd Bacon

It Happens Every Thursday; 1953; Joseph Pevney

It Pays to Advertise; 1931; Frank Tuttle

It Should Happen to You; 1954; George Cukor

It Started with Eve; 1941; Henry Koster

It's a Big Country; 1951; Clarence

Brown and Don Hartman
It's a Date; 1940; William Seiter
It's a Great Feeling; 1949; David Butler
It's a Mad, Mad, Mad, Mad World; 1963; Stanley Kramer
It's a Wonderful Life; 1946; Frank Capra
It's a Wonderful World; 1939; W. S. van Dyke
It's All Yours; 1938; Elliott Nugent
It's Always Fair Weather; 1955; Gene Kelly and Stanley Donen
It's in the Bag; 1944; Richard Wallace
It's Love I'm After; 1937; Archie Mayo
It's Only Money; 1962; Frank Tashlin
Ivanhoe; 1952; Richard Thorpe
Ivy; 1947; Sam Wood

Jack London; 1942; Alfred Santell
Jack the Ripper; 1959; Robert S. Baker and Monty Berman
Jackpot, The; 1950; Walter Lang
Jacqueline; 1956; Roy Baker
Jailhouse Rock; 1957; Richard Thorpe
Jalna; 1935; John Cromwell
Jammin' the Blues; 1945; Gjon Mili
Jamaica Inn; 1939; Alfred Hitchcock
Jane Eyre; 1944; Robert Stevenson
Janie; 1944; Michael Curtiz
Japanese War Bride; 1952; King Vidor
Jazz Singer, The; 1952; Michael Curtiz
Jazzboat; 1960; Kenneth Hughes
Jealousy; 1929; Jean De Limur
Jealousy; 1945; Gustav Machaty
Jeanne Eagels; 1957; George Sidney
Jeopardy; 1953; John Sturges
Jericho (Dark Sands); 1937; Thornton Freeland
Jesse James; 1939; Henry King
Jessica; 1962; Jean Negulesco
Jet over the Atlantic; 1959; Byron Haskin
Jet Pilot; 1957; Josef von Sternberg
Jewel Robbery; 1932; William Dieterle
Jezebel; 1938; William Wyler
Jigsaw; 1962; Val Guest
Jim Thorpe—All American; 1951; Michael Curtiz
Jimmy, The Gent; 1934; Michael Curtiz
Jitterbugs; 1943; Malcolm St. Clair
Jive Junction; 1943; Edgar G. Ulmer
Joan of Arc; 1948; Victor Fleming

Joan of Paris; 1942; Robert Stevenson
Joe Dakota; 1957; Richard Basehart
Joe Macbeth; 1955; Kenneth Hughes
John Goldfarb, Please Come Home; 1964; J. Lee Thompson
John Meade's Woman; 1936; Richard Wallace
John Paul Jones; 1959; John Farrow
Johnny Allegro (Hounded); 1949; Ted Tetzlaff
Johnny Angel; 1945; Edwin L. Marin
Johnny Apollo; 1940; Henry Hathaway
Johnny Belinda; 1948; Jean Negulesco
Johnny Concho; 1956; Don McGuire
Johnny Cool; 1964; William Asher
Johnny Come Lately; 1943; William K. Howard
Johnny Eager; 1942; Mervyn Le Roy
Johnny Guitar; 1954; Nicholas Ray
Johnny Norse; 1964; Don Siegel
Johnny O'Clock; 1947; Robert Rossen
Johnny One-Eye; 1950; Robert Florey
Johnny Stool Pigeon; 1949; William Castle
Johnny Tiger; 1966; Paul Wendkos
Joker Is Wild, The; 1958; Charles Vidor
Jokers, The; 1967; Michael Winner
Jolly Bad Fellow, A; 1964; Don Chaffey
Jolson Sings Again; 1950; Henry Levin
Jolson Story, The; 1946; Alfred E. Green
Josephine and Men; 1955; Roy Boulting
Josette; 1938; Allan Dwan
Journal of a Crime; 1934; William Keighley
Journey, The; 1959; Anatole Litvak
Journey for Margaret; 1942; W. S. van Dyke
Journey into Fear (Signed N. Foster); 1942; Orson Welles
Journey into Light; 1951; Stuart Heisler
Journey to the Lost City; 1960; Fritz Lang
Journey's End; 1930; James Whale
Joy House; 1964; René Clement
Joy of Living; 1938; Tay Garnett
Juarez; 1939; William Dieterle
Jubal; 1956; Delmer Daves
Judge Priest; 1934; John Ford
Judgement at Nuremberg; 1961; Stanley Kramer

Judith; 1965; Daniel Mann
Juke Girl; 1942; Curtis Bernhardt
Julia Misbehaves; 1948; Jack Conway
Julie; 1956; Andrew L. Stone
Julius Caesar; 1950; David Bradley
Julius Caesar; 1953; Joseph Mankiewicz
Jumbo; 1962; Charles Walters
June Bride; 1948; Bretaigne Windust
June Moon; 1931; Edward Sutherland
Jungle Book, The; 1942; Zoltan Korda
Jungle Patrol; 1948; Joseph M. Newman
Juno and the Paycock; 1930; Alfred Hitchcock
Jupiter's Darling; 1955; George Sidney
Just a Gigolo; 1931; Jack Conway
Just Across the Street; 1952; Joseph Pevney
Just for You; 1952; Elliott Nugent
Just This Once; 1952; Don Weis
Just William's Luck; 1947; Val Guest

Kaleidoscope; 1966; Jack Smight
Kangaroo; 1952; Lewis Milestone
Kansas City Princess; 1934; William Keighley
Katherine the Last; 1936; Henry Koster
Keep Em Flying; 1941; Arthur Lubin
Keep Your Powder Dry; 1943; Edward Buzzell
Keeper of the Bees; 1947; John Sturges
Keeper of the Flame; 1943; George Cukor
Kelly and Me; 1957; Robert Z. Leonard
Kennel Murder Case; 1933; Michael Curtiz
Kentuckian, The; 1955; Burt Lancaster
Kentucky Kernels; 1934; George Stevens
Kentucky Minstrels; 1935; John Baxter
Kept Husbands; 1931; Lloyd Bacon
Key, The; 1934; Michael Curtiz
Key, The; 1958; Carol Reed
Key Largo; 1948; John Huston
Key to the City; 1950; George Sidney
Key Witness; 1960; Phil Karlson
Keyhole, The; 1933; Michael Curtiz
Keys of the Kingdom, The; 1944; John Stahl
Khartoum; 1966; Basil Dearden
Kid for Two Farthings, A; 1956; Carol Reed
Kid from Brooklyn, The; 1946; Norman Z. McLeod
Kid from Left Field, The; 1953; Harmon Jones
Kid from Spain, The; 1932; Leo McCarey
Kid Galahad; 1937; Michael Curtiz
Kid Galahad; 1962; Phil Karlson
Kid Glove Killer; 1942; Fred Zinnemann
Kid's Million; 1934; Roy del Ruth
Kidnapped; 1938; Alfred Werker
Kidnappers, The; 1953; Philip Leacock
Kill the Umpire; 1950; Lloyd Bacon
Killer Leopard; 1954; Ford Beebe
Killer Is Loose, The; 1956; Budd Boetticher
Killer Shark; 1950; Budd Boetticher
Killer's Kiss; 1955; Stanley Kubrick
Killers, The; 1946; Robert Siodmak
Killers, The; 1964; Donald Siegel
Killing, The; 1956; Stanley Kubrick
Kind Hearts and Coronets; 1948; Robert Hamer
Kind Lady; 1938; George B. Seitz
Kind Lady; 1951; John Sturges
Kind of Loving, A; 1962; John Schlesinger
Kinder; 1955; Laslo Benedek
King and Country; 1964; Joseph Losey
King and Four Queens, The; 1956; Raoul Walsh
King and I, The; 1956; Walter Lang
King and the Chorus Girl, The; 1937; Mervyn Le Roy
King Creole; 1958; Michael Curtiz
King in New York, A; 1957; Charles Chaplin
King Kong; 1933; Merian C. Cooper and Ernest L. Schoesdack
King Murder, The; 1932; Richard Thorpe
King of Gamblers; 1937; Robert Florey
King of Jazz; 1930; J. Anderson
King of Kings; 1961; Nicholas Ray
King of the Jungle; 1933; H. Bruce Humberstone
King of the Khyber Rifles; 1954; Henry King
King of the Roaring Twenties; 1961; Joseph M. Newman
King of the Underworld; 1939; Lewis Seiler

King of the Wild Stallions; 1959; R. G. Springsteen

King of the Zombies; 1941; Jean Yarbrough

King Rat; 1965; Bryan Forbes

King Richard and the Crusaders; 1954; David Butler

King Solomon's Mines; 1937; Robert Stevenson

King Solomon's Mines; 1950; Compton Bennett and Andrew Marton

King Steps Out, The; 1936; Josef von Sternberg

King's Row; 1942; Sam Wood

King's Thief, The; 1955; Robert Z. Leonard

Kings Go Forth; 1958; Delmer Daves

Kings of the Sun; 1963; J. Lee Thompson

Kipps; 1940; Carol Reed

Kismet; 1944; William Dieterle

Kismet; 1955; Vincente Minnelli

Kiss, The; 1929; Jacques Feyder

Kiss and Make Up; 1934; Harlan Thompson

Kiss and Tell; 1944; Richard Wallace

Kiss Before Dying, A; 1956; Gerd Oswald

Kiss Before the Mirror; 1933; James Whale

Kiss For Corliss, A; 1949; Richard Wallace

Kiss in the Dark, A; 1949; Delmer Daves

Kiss Me Deadly; 1955; Robert Aldrich

Kiss Me Kate; 1953; George Sidney

Kiss Me Stupid; 1964; Billy Wilder

Kiss of Death; 1947; Henry Hathaway

Kiss of Fire; 1955; Joseph M. Newman

Kiss the Blood off My Hands; 1948; Norman Foster

Kiss Them for Me; 1957; Stanley Donen

Kiss Tomorrow Goodbye; 1950; Gordon Douglas

Kissin' Cousins; 1963; Gene Nelson

Kissing Bandit, The; 1948; Laslo Benedek

Kitten with a Whip; 1964; Douglas Heyes

Kitty; 1946; Mitchell Leisen

Kitty Foyle; 1940; Sam Wood

Klondike Annie; 1936; Raoul Walsh

Klondike Fury; 1942; William K. Howard

Knack . . . and How to Get It, The;

1965; Richard Lester

Knave of Hearts; 1953; René Clement

Knight Without Armour; 1937; Jacques Feyder

Knights of the Round Table; 1954; Richard Thorpe

Knock on Any Door; 1949; Nicholas Ray

Knock on Wood; 1953; Melvin Frank and Norman Panama

Knute Rockne, All American; 1940; Lloyd Bacon

Kronos; 1957; Kurt-Neumann

L-Shaped Room, The; 1964; Bryan Forbes

Laburnum Grove; 1936; Carol Reed

Lad: A Dog; 1962; Leslie H. Martinson and Avrim Avakian

Lady to Love, A; 1930; Victor Seastrom

Laddie; 1935; George Stevens

Ladies in Love; 1936; Edward H. Griffith

Ladies in Retirement; 1941; Charles Vidor

Ladies Love Danger; 1935; H. Bruce Humberstone

Ladies of Leisure; 1930; Frank Capra

Ladies of the Chorus; 1948; Phil Karlson

Ladies Should Listen; 1934; Frank Tuttle

Ladies They Talk About; 1933; William Keighley

Ladies' Man; 1937; Lothar Mendes

Ladies' Man, The; 1961; Jerry Lewis

Lady and the Monster, The; 1944; George Sherman

Lady Be Good; 1941; Norman Z. McLeod

Lady By Choice; 1934; David Burton

Lady Eve, The; 1941; Preston Sturges

Lady for a Day; 1933; Frank Capra

Lady for a Night; 1941; Leigh Jason

Lady from Cheyenne; 1941; Frank Lloyd

Lady from Shanghai; 1949; Orson Welles

Lady Gambles, The; 1949; Michael Gordon

Lady Godiva; 1956; Arthur Lubin

Lady Hamilton (That Hamilton Woman); 1941; Alexander Korda

Lady in a Jam; 1942; Gregory La Cava

Lady in Question, The; 1940; Charles Vidor

Lady in the Dark; 1944; Mitchell Leisen

Lady in the Lake; 1946; Robert Montgomery

Lady Is a Square, The; 1958; Herbert Wilcox

Lady Is Willing, The; 1942; Mitchell Leisen

Lady Killer; 1934; Roy del Ruth and Leslie Fenton

Lady of Burlesque; 1943; William Wellman

Lady of Scandal; 1930; Sidney Franklin

Lady of the Night; 1933; William Wellman

Lady of the Pavements; 1929; D. W. Griffith

Lady of the Tropics; 1939; Jack Conway

Lady Pays Off, The; 1951; Douglas Sirk

Lady Takes a Chance, A; 1943; William Seiter

Lady Takes a Sailor, The; 1949; Michael Curtiz

Lady Vanishes, The; 1938; Alfred Hitchcock

Lady With a Past; 1932; Edward H. Griffith

Lady Without a Passport; 1950; Joseph H. Lewis

Lady's Morals, A; 1930; Sidney Franklin

Ladybug, Ladybug; 1963; Frank Perry

Ladykillers, The; 1955; Alexander Mackendrick

Lafayette Escadrille (Hell-Bent for Glory); 1958; William Wellman

Land, The; 1942; Robert Flaherty

Land of the Pharaohs; 1955; Howard Hawks

Land We Love, The; 1962; Leslie Stevens

Larceny Inc.; 1942; Lloyd Bacon

Larceny Lane; 1931; Roy del Ruth

Las Vegas Story, The; 1952; Robert Stevenson

Lash, The; 1930; Frank Lloyd

Lassie Come Home; 1943; Fred M. Wilcox

Last Angry Man, The; 1959; Daniel Mann

Last Command, The; 1955; Frank Lloyd

Last Days of Pompeii; 1935; Ernest L. Schoesdack

Last Flight; 1931; William Dieterle

Last Frontier, The; 1956; Anthony Mann

Last Hunt, The; 1956; Richard Brooks

Last Hurrah, The; 1958; John Ford

Last Journey, The; 1936; John Brahm

Last Man to Hang; 1957; Terence Fisher

Last Mile, The; 1959; Howard W. Koch

Last Moment, The; 1967; Paul Fejos

Last of Mrs. Cheney; 1929; Sidney Franklin

Last of Mrs. Cheney, The; 1937; Richard Boleslavsky

Last of the Comanches; 1952; Andre de Toth

Last of the Mohicans, The; 1936; George Seitz

Last of the Pagans; 1935; Richard Thorpe

Last Outpost; 1935; Charles Barton

Last Round-Up; 1934; Henry Hathaway

Last Stand, The; 1938; Joseph H. Lewis

Last Sunset, The; 1961; Robert Aldrich

Last Time I Saw Archie, The; 1961; Jack Webb

Last Time I Saw Paris, The; 1954; Richard Brooks

Last Train from Gun Hill; 1959; John Sturges

Last Voyage, The; 1960; Andrew L. Stone

Last Wagon, The; 1956; Delmer Daves

Last Warning, The; 1929; Paul Leni

Late George Apley, The; 1947; Joseph Mankiewicz

Latin Lovers; 1953; Mervyn Le Roy

Laugh and Get Rich; 1931; Gregory La Cava

Laughing Boy; 1934; W. S. van Dyke

Laughing Sinners; 1931; Harry Beaumont

Laughter; 1930; Harry D'Arrast

Laughter in Hell; 1933; Edward L. Cahn

Laughter in Paradise; 1950; M. Zampi

Laughter in the Dark; 1969; Tony Richardson

Laura; 1944; Otto Preminger

Lavender Hill Mob, The; 1951; Charles Crichton

Law and Disorder; 1958; Charles Crichton and Henry Cornelius

Law and Jack Wade, The; 1958; John Sturges

Law and Order; 1932; Edward L. Cahn

Law of the Tropics; 1941; Ray Enright

Lawless, The; 1950; Joseph Losey

Lawless Street, A; 1955; Joseph H. Lewis

Lawrence of Arabia; 1962; David Lean

Lawyer Man; 1932; William Dieterle

League of Gentlemen; 1961; Basil Dearden

Leather Boys, The; 1963; Sidney Furie

Leave Her to Heaven; 1945; John Stahl

Leech Woman, The; 1960; Edward Dein

Left Hand of God, The; 1955; Edward Dmytryk

Left Right and Centre; 1961; Sidney Gilliat and Frank Launder

Lefthanded Gun, The; 1958; Arthur Penn

Legend of the Lost; 1957; Henry Hathaway

Legend of Tom Dooley; 1959; Ted Post

Legion of Terror; 1937; C. C. Coleman

Lemon Drop Kid, The; 1951; Sidney Lanfield

Lenny Bruce Story, The; 1969; Stuart Rosenberg

Leopard, The; 1963; Luchino Visconti

Leopard Man, The; 1943; Jacques Tourneur

Les Girls; 1957; George Cukor

Les Miserables; 1935; Richard Boleslavsky

Les Miserables; 1952; Lewis Milestone

Let Freedom Ring; 1939; Jack Conway

Let Us Live; 1939; John Brahm

Let 'em Have It; 1935; Sam Wood

Let No Man Write My Epitaph; 1959; Philip Leacock

Let the People Sing; 1942; John Baxter

Let There Be Light (Doc, Suppressed); 1945; John Huston

Let's Do It Again; 1953; Alexander Hall

Let's Fall in Love; 1934; David Burton

Let's Go Native; 1930; Leo McCarey

Let's Live a Little; 1948; Richard Wallace

Let's Make it Legal; 1951; Richard Sale

Let's Make Love; 1960; George Cukor

Let's Rock; 1958; Harry Foster

Let's Sing Again; 1936; Kurt Neumann

Let's Talk It Over; 1934; Kurt Neumann

Letter, The; 1940; William Wyler

Letter for Evie, A; 1945; Jules Dassin

Letter from an Unknown Woman; 1948; Max Ophuls

Letter of Introduction; 1938; John Stahl

Letter to Three Wives, A; 1949; Joseph Mankiewicz

Letty Lynton; 1932; Clarence Brown

Libel; 1960; Anthony Asquith

Libeled Lady; 1936; Jack Conway

Lieutenant Wore Skirts, The; 1956; Frank Tashlin

Life Begins; 1932; Elliott Nugent

Life Begins at Forty; 1935; George Marshall

Life for Ruth; 1962; Basil Dearden

Life of Emile Zola, The; 1937; William Dieterle

Life of Her Own, A; 1950; George Cukor

Life of Jimmy Dolan; 1933; Archie Mayo

Life of the Party; 1930; Roy del Ruth

Life of Vergie Winters; 1934; Alfred Santell

Life with Father; 1947; Michael Curtiz

Lifeboat; 1944; Alfred Hitchcock

Light in the Piazza, The; 1961; Guy Green

Light That Failed, The; 1939; William Wellman

Light Touch, The; 1951; Richard Brooks

Lightnin'; 1930; Henry King

Lightning Strikes Twice; 1951; King Vidor

Lights Out (Bright Victory); 1952; Mark Robson

Lili; 1953; Charles Walters

Lilies of the Field; 1963; Ralph Nelson

Liliom; 1930; Frank Borzage

Liliom; 1933; Fritz Lang

Lilith; 1963; Robert Rossen

Lilly Turner; 1933; William Wellman

Limehouse Blues; 1936; Alexander Hall

Limelight; 1936; Herbert Wilcox

Limelight; 1952; Charles Chaplin
Line-Up, The; 1958; Don Siegel
Lion, The; 1962; Jack Cardiff
Lion Has Wings, The; 1940; Brian D. Hurst
Lion Is in the Streets, A; 1953; Raoul Walsh
Liquidator, The; 1965; Jack Cardiff
Lisa; 1962; Philip Dunne
Lisbon; 1956; Ray Milland
Lisbon Story, The; 1946; Paul L. Stein
List of Adrian Messenger, The; 1963; John Huston
Listen, Darling; 1938; Edwin L. Marin
Little Ballerina; 1947; Lewis Gilbert
Little Big Shot; 1935; Michael Curtiz
Little Boy Lost; 1953; George Seaton
Little Caesar; 1930; Mervyn Le Roy
Little Colonel, The; 1935; David Butler
Little Foxes, The; 1941; William Wyler
Little Fugitive, The; 1953; Engel Morris
Little Giant; 1933; Roy del Ruth
Little Hut, The; 1957; Mark Robson
Little Johnny Jones; 1930; Mervyn Le Roy
Little Kidnappers, The; 1954; Philip Leacock
Little Lord Fauntleroy; 1936; John Cromwell
Little Man What Now; 1934; Frank Borzage
Little Minister, The; 1934; Richard Wallace
Little Mother; 1935; Henry Koster
Little Mr. Jim; 1946; Fred Zinnemann
Little Nellie Kelly; 1940; Norman Taurog
Little Old New York; 1940; Henry King
Little Savage; 1959; Byron Haskin
Little Shepherd of Kingdom Come; 1961; Andrew McLaglen
Little Shop of Horrors, The; 1961; Roger Corman
Little Women; 1933; George Cukor
Little Women; 1949; Mervyn Le Roy
Littlest Rebel, The; 1936; David Butler
Live Wires; 1946; Phil Karlson
Lively Set, The; 1964; Jack Arnold
Lives of a Bengal Lancer; 1935; Henry Hathaway
Living Idol, The; 1957; Albert Lewin
Living in a Big Way; 1947; Gregory La Cava
Living It Up; 1954; Norman Taurog
Living on Velvet; 1935; Frank Borzage
Lloyds of London; 1936; Henry King
Local Boy Makes Good; 1931; Mervyn Le Roy
Locket, The; 1946; John Brahm
Lodger, The; 1941; John Brahm
Lolita; 1962; Stanley Kubrick
Lone Ranger, The; 1956; Stuart Heisler
Lone Star; 1951; Vincent Sherman
Lone Wolf Returns; 1935; Roy William Neill
Lone Wolf Spy Hunt, The; 1939; Peter Godfrey
Long John Silver; 1955; Byron Haskin
Loneliness of the Long-Distance Runner; 1962; Tony Richardson
Lonely Are the Brave; 1962; David Miller
Lonely Man, The; 1957; Harry Levin
Lonelyhearts; 1958; Vincent J. Donehue
Long Day's Journey into Night; 1962; Sidney Lumet
Long Gray Line, The; 1955; John Ford
Long Haul, The; 1957; Kenneth Hughes
Long Hot Summer, The; 1957; Martin Ritt
Long Long Trailer, The; 1954; Vincente Minnelli
Long Memory, The; 1953; Robert Hamer
Long Night, The; 1947; Anatole Litvak
Long Ships, The; 1963; Jack Cardiff
Long Voyage Home, The; 1940; John Ford
Longest Day, The; 1962; Ken Annakin and Bernhard Wicki
Look Back in Anger; 1958; Tony Richardson
Look Who's Laughing; 1941; Allan Dwan
Looking for Trouble; 1934; William Wellman
Looking Forward; 1933; Clarence Brown
Lord Jim; 1964; Richard Brooks
Lord of the Flies, The; 1962; Peter Brook
Lord Love a Duck; 1966; George Axelrod

Lorna Doone; 1951; Phil Karlson

Loss of Innocence; 1961; Lewis Gilbert

Lost Angel; 1944; Roy Rowland

Lost Boundaries; 1949; Alfred Werker

Lost Command; 1966; Mark Robson

Lost Horizon; 1937; Frank Capra

Lost Lady, The; 1932; William Wellman

Lost Moment, The; 1947; Martin Gabel

Lost Patrol, The; 1934; John Ford

Lost Squadron, The; 1932; George Archainbaud

Lost Weekend, The; 1945; Billy Wilder

Lost World, The; 1960; Irwin Allen

Lottery Bride, The; 1930; Paul Stein

Louisiana; 1947; Phil Karlson

Louisiana Story; 1948; Robert Flaherty

Lovable Cheat, The; 1949; Richard Oswald

Love Affair; 1932; Thornton Freeland

Love Affair; 1939; Leo McCarey

Love and the Devil; 1929; Alexander Korda

Love Before Breakfast; 1936; Walter Lang

Love Crazy; 1941; Jack Conway

Love Happy; 1949; David Miller

Love Has Many Faces; 1964; Alexander Singer

Love in Bloom; 1935; Elliott Nugent

Love in Las Vegas (Viva Las Vegas); 1964; George Sidney

Love in the Afternoon; 1957; Billy Wilder

Love Is a Ball; 1963; David Swift

Love Is a Many Splendored Thing; 1955; Henry King

Love Is a Racket; 1932; William Wellman

Love Is Better Than Ever; 1952; Stanley Donen

Love Is Dangerous; 1933; Richard Thorpe

Love Is Like That; 1933; Richard Thorpe

Love Is News; 1937; Tay Garnett

Love Letters; 1945; William Dieterle

Love Live and Laugh; 1929; William K. Howard

Love Me Forever; 1935; Victor Schertzinger

Love Me or Leave Me; 1934; Charles Vidor

Love Me or Leave Me; 1955; Charles Vidor

Love Me Tender; 1956; Robert D. Webb

Love Me Tonight; 1932; Rouben Mamoulian

Love Nest; 1951; Joseph M. Newman

Love on the Dole; 1940; John Baxter

Love on the Run; 1936; W. S. van Dyke

Love Parade, The; 1929; Ernst Lubitsch

Love Racket, The; 1930; William Seiter

Love Slaves of the Amazon; 1957; Curt Siodmak

Love Trap; 1929; William Wyler

Love Under Fire; 1937; George Marshall

Love with a Proper Stranger; 1963; Robert Mulligan

Loved One, The; 1964; Tony Richardson

Lovely to Look At; 1952; Mervyn Le Roy

Lover Come Back; 1961; Delbert Mann

Lovers, Happy Lovers; 1954; René Clement

Lovers and Lollipops; 1955; Engel Morris and Ruth Orkin

Loves of a Dictator, The; 1935; Victor Saville

Loves of Carmen, The; 1948; Charles Vidor

Lure of the Wilderness; 1952; Jean Negulesco

Luck of Ginger Coffey, The; 1963; Irvin Kershner

Lucky Cisco Kid; 1940; H. Bruce Humberstone

Lucky Ghost; 1941; Jed Buell

Lucky Jim; 1957; John Boulting and Roy Boulting

Lucky Jordan; 1942; Frank Tuttle

Lucky Me; 1954; Jack Donahue

Lucky Nick Cain; 1951; Joseph M. Newman

Lucky Partners; 1940; Lewis Milestone

Lucky Star; 1929; Frank Borzage

Lucretia Borgia; 1935; Abel Gance

Lucy Gallant; 1955; Robert Parrish

Lullaby of Broadway; 1951; David Butler

Lure of the Swamp; 1957; Hubert Cornfield

Lured (Personal Column); 1947; Douglas Sirk

Lust for Life; 1956; Vincente Minnelli

Lusty Men, The; 1952; Nicholas Ray

Luv; 1967; Clive Donner

Lydia; 1941; Julien Duvivier

Lydia Bailey; 1952; Jean Negulesco

M; 1951; Joseph Losey

Macabre; 1958; William Castle

Macao; 1952; Josef von Sternberg

Macbeth; 1950; Orson Welles

Macbeth; 1961; George Schaefer

Machine Gun Kelly; 1958; Roger Corman

Macomber Affair, The; 1947; Zoltan Korda

Mad About Men; 1954; Ralph Thomas

Mad About Music; 1938; Norman Taurog

Mad Doctor of Market Street, The; 1942; Joseph H. Lewis

Mad Dog Coll; 1961; Burt Balaban

Mad King; 1933; John Farrow

Mad Magician, The; 1954; John Brahm

Mad Martindales, The; 1942; Alfred Werker

Mad Miss Manton; 1938; Leigh Jason

Mad Room, The; 1968; Bernard Girard

Mad Wednesday; 1947; Preston Sturges

Mad Woman of Chaillot, The; 1968; Bryan Forbes

Madame Bovary; 1949; Vincente Minnelli

Madame Butterfly; 1932; Marion Gering

Madame Curie; 1943; Mervyn Le Roy

Madame DuBarry; 1934; William Dieterle

Madame Satan; 1930; Cecil B. de Mille

Madame Spy; 1942; Roy William Neill

Madame X; 1929; Lionel Barrymore

Madame X; 1937; Sam Wood

Madame X; 1965; David Lowell Rich

Made for Each Other; 1939; John Cromwell

Madeleine; 1950; David Lean

Mademoiselle Fifi; 1944; Robert Wise

Madigan; 1968; Don Siegel

Madison Avenue; 1962; H. Bruce Humberstone

Madonna of Avenue A; 1929; Michael Curtiz

Madonna of the Seven Moons; 1944; Arthur Crabtree

Maggie, The; 1953; Alexander Mackendrick

Magic Face, The; 1951; Frank Tuttle

Magic Fire; 1956; William Dieterle

Magic Town; 1947; William Wellman

Magnetic Monster, The; 1953; Curt Siodmak

Magnificent Ambersons, The; 1942; Orson Welles

Magnificent Doll, The; 1946; Frank Borzage

Magnificent Dope, The; 1942; Walter Lang

Magnificent Fraud; 1939; Robert Florey

Magnificent Matador, The; 1955; Budd Boetticher

Magnificent Obsession; 1935; John Stahl

Magnificent Obsession; 1954; Douglas Sirk

Magnificent Seven, The; 1960; John Sturges

Magnificent Showman, The; 1963; Henry Hathaway

Magnificent Yankee, The; 1950; John Sturges

Maid of Salem; 1936; Frank Lloyd

Mail Order Bride; 1964; Burt Kennedy

Main Attraction, The; 1962; Daniel Petrie

Main Street to Broadway; 1953; Tay Garnett

Maisie Gets Her Man; 1942; Roy del Ruth

Major and the Minor, The; 1942; Billy Wilder

Major Dundee; 1965; Sam Peckinpah

Majority of One, A; 1961; Mervyn Le Roy

Make a Wish; 1937; Kurt Neumann

Make Haste to Live; 1954; William Seiter

Make Mine a Double; 1962; Darcy Conyers

Make Mine Laughs; 1949; Richard Fleischer

Make Way for Tomorrow; 1937; Leo McCarey

Malaga; 1961; Laslo Benedek

Malaya (East of the Rising Sun); 1949; Richard Thorpe

Male Animal, The; 1942; Elliott Nugent and Wolfgang Reinhardt

Malta Story, The; 1954; Brian D. Hurst

Maltese Falcon, The (Dangerous Female); 1931; Roy del Ruth

Maltese Falcon, The; 1941; John Huston

Mambo; 1955; Robert Rossen

Mammy; 1930; Michael Curtiz

Man About Town; 1939; Mark Sandrich

Man Alone, A; 1955; Ray Milland

Man at the Carlton Tower, The; 1962; Robert Tronson

Man Between, The; 1953; Carol Reed

Man Called Back; 1932; Robert Florey

Man Called Peter, A; 1955; Henry Koster

Man Could Get Killed, A; 1965; Cliff Owen

Man Crazy; 1953; Irving Lerner

Man-Eater of Kumaon; 1948; Byron Haskin

Man for All Seasons, A; 1966; Fred Zinnemann

Man from Del Rio; 1956; Harry Horner

Man from Frisco; 1944; Robert Florey

Man from Laramie, The; 1955; Anthony Mann

Man from Morocco, The; 1945; Max Greene

Man from Planet X, The; 1951; Edgar G. Ulmer

Man from the Alamo, The; 1953; Budd Boetticher

Man from the Diner's Club, The; 1963; Frank Tashlin

Man from Tumbleweeds, The; 1940; Joseph H. Lewis

Man from Wyoming, A; 1930; Rowland V. Lee

Man Hunt; 1941; Fritz Lang

Man I Killed, The (Broken Lullaby); 1932; Ernst Lubitsch

Man I Love, The; 1929; William Wellman

Man I Love, The; 1946; Raoul Walsh

Man in a Cocked Hat; 1960; Roy Boulting and Jeffrey Dell

Man in the Iron Mask; 1940; James Whale

Man in the Middle; 1964; Guy Hamilton

Man in the Moon; 1961; Basil Dearden

Man in the Net, The; 1959; Michael Curtiz

Man in the Saddle; 1951; Andre de Toth

Man in the Trunk, The; 1942; Malcolm St. Clair

Man in the Vault; 1956; Andrew McLaglen

Man in the White Suit, The; 1952; Alexander Mackendrick

Man Is Ten Feet Tall, A (Edge of the City); 1957; Martin Ritt

Man of a Thousand Faces; 1957; Joseph Pevney

Man of Aran; 1934; Robert Flaherty

Man of Sentiment; 1933; Richard Thorpe

Man of the Forest; 1933; Henry Hathaway

Man of the West; 1958; Anthony Mann

Man of the World; 1931; Richard Wallace

Man on a String; 1960; Andre de Toth

Man on a Tightrope; 1953; Elia Kazan

Man on America's Conscience, The (Tennessee Johnson); 1942; William Dieterle

Man on Fire; 1957; Ranald MacDougall

Man Proof; 1937; Richard Thorpe

Man to Man; 1931; Allan Dwan

Man to Remember, A; 1938; Garson Kanin

Man Upstairs, The; 1958; Don Chaffey

Man Wanted; 1932; William Dieterle

Man Who Broke the Bank at Monte Carlo; 1935; Stephen Roberts

Man Who Came Back, The; 1931; Raoul Walsh

Man Who Came to Dinner, The; 1941; William Keighley

Man Who Dared, The; 1946; John Sturges

Man Who Knew Too Much, The; 1935; Alfred Hitchcock

Man Who Knew Too Much, The; 1956; Alfred Hitchcock

Man Who Shot Liberty Valance, The; 1962; John Ford *

Man Who Talked Too Much, The; 1940; Vincent Sherman

Man Who Watched Trains Go By, The; 1952; Harold French

Man Who Wouldn't Talk, The; 1960; Herbert Wilcox

Man with a Gun; 1955; Richard Wil-

son

Man with a Million; 1954; Ronald Neame

Man with the Golden Arm, The; 1955; Otto Preminger

Man with the X-Ray Eyes, The; 1963; Roger Corman

Man with Two Faces; 1934; Archie Mayo

Man without a Star; 1955; King Vidor

Man's Castle, A; 1933; Frank Borzage

Man's Favorite Sport; 1964; Howard Hawks

Manchurian Candidate, The; 1962; John Frankenheimer

Mandalay; 1934; Michael Curtiz

Mandy; 1952; Alexander Mackendrick

Manhandled; 1944; Lewis R. Foster

Manhattan Parade; 1932; Lloyd Bacon

Manhattan Melodrama; 1934; W. S. van Dyke

Mania (The Flesh and the Fiends); 1960; John Gilling

Manila Calling; 1942; Herbert Leeds

Mannequin; 1937; Frank Borzage

Manpower; 1941; Raoul Walsh

Manslaughter; 1930; George Abbott

Manuela; 1956; Guy Hamilton

Mara Maru; 1952; Gordon Douglas

Maracaibo; 1958; Cornell Wilde

Marat/Sade; 1967; Peter Brook

March of Time (1936–38, Doc); 1936; Edgar Anstey

Marco Polo; 1962; Hugo Fregonese

Mardi Gras; 1958; Edmund Goulding

Margie; 1946; Henry King

Margin for Error; 1943; Otto Preminger

Marie Antoinette; 1937; W. S. van Dyke

Marie Gallante; 1934; Henry King

Marie Walewska (Conquest); 1937; Clarence Brown

Marines, Let's Go; 1961; Raoul Walsh

Marjorie Morningstar; 1957; Irving Rapper

Mark, The; 1961; Guy Green

Mark of the Vampire; 1935; Tod Browning

Mark of Zorro, The; 1940; Rouben Mamoulian

Marked Woman; 1937; Lloyd Bacon

Marnie; 1964; Alfred Hitchcock

Marriage of Convenience; 1960; Clive Donner

Married and in Love; 1940; John Farrow

Marry Me Again; 1953; Frank Tashlin

Marrying Kind, The; 1952; George Cukor

Martin Luther; 1953; Irving Pichel

Marty; 1955; Delbert Mann

Mary Burns—Fugitive; 1935; William K. Howard

Mary Jane's Pa; 1935; William Keighley

Mary of Scotland; 1936; John Ford

Mary, Mary; 1963; Mervyn Le Roy

Mary Poppins; 1964; Robert Stevenson

Mary Stevens, M.D.; 1933; Lloyd Bacon

Maryland; 1940; Henry King

Mask of Dijon, The; 1946; Lew Landers

Mask of Dimitrios, The; 1944; Jean Negulesco

Mask of Fu Manchu, The; 1932; Charles Vidor

Mask of the Avenger; 1951; Phil Karlson

Masque of the Red Death; 1964; Roger Corman

Masquerade; 1965; Basil Dearden

Masquerade in Mexico; 1945; Mitchell Leisen

Masquerader; 1933; Richard Wallace

Massacre; 1934; Alan Crosland

Master of Ballantrae, The; 1953; William Keighley

Master of the World; 1961; William Witney

Master Race, The; 1944; Herbert Biberman

Mata-Hari; 1932; George Fitzmaurice

Matchmaker, The; 1958; Joseph Anthony

Mating Season, The; 1951; Mitchell Leisen

Matrimonial Bed, The; 1930; Michael Curtiz

Matter of Morals, A; 1961; John Cromwell

Maybe It's Love; 1930; William Wellman

Mayerling; 1968; Terence Young

Mayor of 44th Street, The; 1942; Alfred E. Green

Mayor of Hell; 1933; Archie Mayo

Maytime; 1938; Robert Z. Leonard

McConnell Story, The; 1955; Gordon Douglas

McLintock; 1963; Andrew McLaglen

Me and My Gal; 1932; Raoul Walsh

Me and the Colonel; 1958; Peter Glenville

Meet Boston Blackie; 1941; Robert Florey

Meet Danny Wilson; 1951; Joseph Pevney

Meet John Doe; 1941; Frank Capra

Meet Me at Dawn; 1947; Thornton Freeland

Meet Me at the Fair; 1952; Douglas Sirk

Meet Me in St. Louis; 1944; Vincente Minnelli

Meet Nero Wolfe; 1936; Herbert Biberman

Meet the Missus; 1940; Malcolm St. Clair

Meet the Stewarts; 1942; Alfred E. Green

Meet the Wildcat; 1940; Arthur Lubin

Melancholy Dame; 1929; Octavius Roy Cohen

Melba; 1953; Lewis Milestone

Member of the Wedding, The; 1952; Fred Zinnemann

Memory for Two; 1946; Del Lord

Memphis Belle, The (Doc); 1943; William Wyler

Men, The; 1950; Fred Zinnemann

Men Are Not Gods; 1937; Walter Reisch

Men Are Such Fools; 1938; Busby Berkeley

Men in Exile; 1937; John Farrow

Men in War; 1957; Anthony Mann

Men in White; 1934; Richard Boleslavsky

Men O'War (Short); 1929; Lewis R. Foster

Men of Destiny; 1942; Ray Enright

Men on Her Mind; 1935; William Dieterle

Men with Wings; 1938; William Wellman

Men Without Law; 1937; Lewis Seiler

Men Without Women; 1930; John Ford

Merely Mary Ann; 1931; Henry King

Merrill's Marauders; 1962; Samuel Fuller

Merrily We Go to Hell; 1932; Dorothy Arzner

Merrily We Live; 1938; Norman Z. McLeod

Merry Andrew; 1957; Michael Kidd

Merry Widow, The; 1934; Ernst Lubitsch

Message to Garcia; 1935; George Marshall

Mexicans; 1945; Alfred Santell

Miami Exposé; 1956; Fred F. Sears

Mickey One; 1965; Arthur Penn

Mickey the Kid; 1939; Arthur Lubin

Middle of the Night; 1959; Delbert Mann

Midnight; 1934; Chester Erskine

Midnight; 1939; Mitchell Leisen

Midnight Alibi; 1934; Alan Crosland

Midnight Intruder; 1937; Arthur Lubin

Midnight Lace; 1960; David Miller

Midnight Lady; 1932; Richard Thorpe

Midnight Mary; 1933; William Wellman

Midshipman Easy; 1936; Carol Reed

Midsummer Night's Dream, A; 1935; William Dieterle and Max Reinhardt

Mighty Barnum, The; 1936; Walter Lang

Mighty Joe Young; 1949; Merian C. Cooper and Ernest L. Schoesdack

Mikado, The; 1939; Victor Schertzinger

Mildred Pierce; 1945; Michael Curtiz

Milky Way, The; 1936; Leo McCarey

Million Dollar Legs; 1932; Eddie Cline

Million Dollar Mermaid; 1952; Mervyn Le Roy

Millionairess, The; 1960; Anthony Asquith

Min and Bill; 1930; George Roy Hill

Mind Benders, The; 1963; Basil Dearden

Mind Reader; 1933; Roy del Ruth

Mine Own Executioner; 1947; Anthony Kimmins

Ministry of Fear; 1945; Fritz Lang

Miniver Story, The; 1950; H. C. Potter

Minstrel Man; 1944; Joseph H. Lewis

Miracle, The; 1959; Irving Rapper

Miracle at Morgan's Creek, The; 1944; Preston Sturges

Miracle in Soho; 1957; Julian Amyes

Miracle in the Rain; 1955; Rudolph Mate

Miracle of Our Lady of Fatima, The; 1952; John Brahm

Miracle of the Bells, The; 1948; Irving Pichel

Miracle on 34th Street; 1947; George

Seaton

Miracle Woman; 1931; Frank Capra

Miracle Worker, The; 1962; Arthur Penn

Miracles for Sale; 1939; Tod Browning

Mirage; 1965; Edward Dmytryk

Miranda; 1948; Ken Annakin

Misfits, The; 1961; John Huston

Miss London LMT; 1943; Val Guest

Miss Sadie Thompson; 1954; Curtis Bernhardt

Miss Susie Slagle's; 1946; John Berry

Miss Tatlock's Millions; 1948; Richard Haydn

Missing Juror, The; 1945; Budd Boetticher

Mission to Moscow; 1943; Michael Curtiz

Mississippi; 1935; Edward Sutherland

Mississippi Gambler, The; 1953; Rudolph Mate

Mister 880; 1950; Edmund Goulding

Mister and Mrs. Smith; 1941; Alfred Hitchcock

Mister Arkadin (Confidential Report); 1962; Orson Welles

Mister Belvedere Goes to College; 1949; Elliott Nugent

Mister Blandings Builds His Dream House; 1948; H. C. Potter

Mister Buddwing; 1965; Delbert Mann

Mister Cory; 1957; Blake Edwards

Mister Deeds Goes to Town; 1936; Frank Capra

Mister Drake's Duck; 1950; Val Guest

Mister Hobbs Takes a Vacation; 1962; Henry Koster

Mister Lucky; 1943; H. C. Potter

Mister Moses; 1965; Ronald Neame

Mister Moto Takes a Vacation; 1939; Norman Foster

Mister Moto's Last Warning; 1939; Norman Foster

Mister Music; 1950; Richard Haydn

Mister Peabody and the Mermaid; 1948; Irving Pichel

Mister Perrin and Mr. Traill; 1948; Lawrence Huntington

Mister Roberts; 1955; Mervyn Le Roy and John Ford

Mister Robinson Crusoe; 1932; Edward Sutherland

Mister Sardonicus; 1961; William Castle

Mister Skitch; 1933; James Cruze

Mister Smith Goes to Washington; 1939; Frank Capra

Mister Washington Goes to Town; 1940; Jed Buell

Mister Soft Touch; 1949; Gordon Douglas

Mob, The; 1951; Robert Parrish

Moby Dick; 1956; John Huston

Model and the Marriage Broker, The; 1952; George Cukor

Model Wife; 1941; Leigh Jason

Modern Hero, A; 1934; G. W. Pabst

Modern Times; 1936; Charles Chaplin

Modesty Blaise; 1966; Joseph Losey

Mogambo; 1953; John Ford

Mole People, The; 1956; Virgil Vogel

Moment of Indiscretion; 1958; Max Varnel

Moment to Moment; 1966; Mervyn Le Roy

Momma Don't Allow (Short); 1955; Karel Reisz and Tony Richardson

Money and the Woman; 1940; William K. Howard

Money Trap; 1966; Burt Kennedy

Mongols, The; 1961; Andre de Toth

Monkey Business; 1931; Norman Z. McLeod

Monkey Business; 1952; Howard Hawks

Monkey on My Back; 1957; Andre de Toth

Monkey's Uncle, The; 1965; Robert Stevenson

Monsieur Verdoux; 1947; Robert Florey and Charles Chaplin

Monsoon; 1952; Clarence Brown

Monster and the Girl; 1941; Stuart Heisler

Montana Belle; 1952; Allan Dwan

Montana Moon; 1930; Malcolm St. Clair

Monte Carlo; 1930; Ernst Lubitsch

Monte Carlo Story, The; 1957; Samuel Taylor

Moon and Sixpence, The; 1942; Albert Lewin

Moon Is Blue, The; 1953; Otto Preminger

Moon Is Down, The; 1943; Irving Pichel

Moon over Harlem; 1939; Edgar G. Ulmer

Moon over Her Shoulder; 1941; Alfred Werker

Moon Spinners, The; 1964; J. Neilson

Moonfleet; 1955; Fritz Lang

Moonlight in Havana; 1942; Anthony Mann

Moonrise; 1948; Frank Borzage

Moontide; 1942; Archie Mayo

More the Merrier, The; 1943; George Stevens

Morgan; 1966; Karel Reisz

Morgan the Pirate; 1960; Andre de Toth

Morning After, The; 1934; Allan Dwan

Morning Departure; 1950; Roy Baker

Morning Glory; 1933; Lowell Sherman

Morocco; 1930; Josef von Sternberg

Mortal Storm, The; 1940; Frank Borzage

Most Dangerous Game, The (Hounds of Zaroff); 1932; Irving Pichel and Ernest L. Schoesdack

Most Dangerous Man Alive; 1961; Allan Dwan

Mother Didn't Tell Me; 1950; Claude Binyon

Mother Is a Freshman; 1949; Lloyd Bacon

Mother Wore Tights; 1947; Walter Lang

Moulin Rouge; 1934; Sidney Lanfield

Moulin Rouge; 1953; John Huston

Mountain, The; 1956; Edward Dmytryk

Mountain Justice; 1937; Michael Curtiz

Mountain Music; 1937; Robert Florey

Mourning Becomes Electra; 1947; Dudley Nichols

Mouse on the Moon, The; 1963; Richard Lester

Mouse That Roared, The; 1959; Jack Arnold

Mouthpiece, The; 1932; Elliott Nugent

Move Over Darling; 1963; Michael Gordon

Movie Crazy; 1932; Clyde Bruckman

Mrs. Mike; 1949; Louis King

Mrs. Miniver; 1942; William Wyler

Mrs. Parkington; 1944; Tay Garnett

Mrs. Skeffington; 1944; Vincent Sherman

Mrs. Wiggs of the Cabbage Patch; 1934; Norman Taurog

Mudlark, The; 1950; Jean Negulesco

Mummy, The; 1932; Karl Freund

Mummy, The; 1959; Terence Fisher

Mummy's Ghost, The; 1944; Reginald Le Borg

Murder; 1930; Alfred Hitchcock

Murder at Dawn; 1932; Richard Thorpe

Murder at the Gallop; 1963; George Pollock

Murder at the Vanities; 1934; Mitchell Leisen

Murder by Contract; 1958; Irving Lerner

Murder He Says; 1945; George Marshall

Murder in Reverse; 1945; Montgomery Tully

Murder in Soho; 1939; Norman Lee

Murder, Inc.; 1960; Burt Balaban and Stuart Rosenberg

Murder Is My Beat; 1955; Edgar G. Ulmer

Murder Most Foul; 1964; George Pollock

Murder My Sweet; 1944; Edward Dmytryk

Murder on Diamond Row; 1937; William K. Howard

Murder on Lenox Avenue; 1941; Arthur Dreifuss

Murder on Monday (Home at Seven); 1952; Ralph Richardson

Murder She Said; 1963; George Pollock

Murders (The Avenger); 1934; Louis Brooks

Murders in the Rue Morgue; 1932; Robert Florey

Murders in the Zoo; 1933; Edward Sutherland

Muscle Beach (Short); 1948; Irving Lerner

Muscle Beach Party; 1964; William Asher

Music Box; 1932; James Parrott

Music for Millions; 1944; Henry Koster

Music Goes Round, The; 1936; Victor Schertzinger

Music in the Air; 1934; Joe May

Music Man, The; 1962; Morton da Costa

Muss Em Up; 1936; Charles Vidor

Mutiny on the Bounty; 1935; Frank Lloyd

Mutiny on the Bounty; 1962; Lewis Milestone

My Best Gal; 1944; Anthony Mann

My Blue Heaven; 1950; Henry Koster

My Brother Talks to Horses; 1947; Fred Zinnemann

My Brother the Outlaw; 1951; Elliott

Nugent
My Cousin Rachel; 1953; Henry Koster
My Darling Clementine; 1946; John Ford
My Dream Is Yours; 1949; Michael Curtiz
My Fair Lady; 1964; George Cukor
My Favorite Blonde; 1942; Sidney Lanfield
My Favorite Brunette; 1947; Elliott Nugent
My Favorite Spy; 1942; Tay Garnett
My Favorite Spy; 1951; Norman Z. McLeod
My Favorite Wife; 1940; Garson Kanin
My Foolish Heart; 1949; Mark Robson
My Forbidden Past; 1951; Robert Stevenson
My Geisha; 1962; Jack Cardiff
My Girl Tisa; 1948; Elliott Nugent
My Heart Belongs to Daddy; 1942; Robert Siodmak
My Kingdom for a Cook; 1943; Richard Wallace
My Learned Friend; 1943; Basil Dearden and Will Hay
My Life with Caroline; 1941; Lewis Milestone
My Little Chickadee; 1940; Eddie Cline
My Lucky Star; 1938; Roy del Ruth
My Man and I; 1952; William Wellman
My Man Godfrey; 1936; Gregory La Cava
My Man Godfrey; 1957; Henry Koster
My Name Is Julia Ross; 1945; Joseph H. Lewis
My Pal Gus; 1952; Robert Parrish
My Pal the King; 1932; Kurt Neumann
My Past; 1931; Roy del Ruth
My Sister Eileen; 1955; Richard Quine
My Six Convicts; 1952; Hugo Fregonese
My Son; 1949; George Cukor
My Son John; 1952; Leo McCarey
My Son, My Son; 1940; Charles Vidor
My Son, The Hero; 1943; Edgar G. Ulmer
Mysterious Crossing; 1936; Arthur Lubin
Mysterious Island, The; 1960; Cyril Endfield
Mystery in Mexico; 1948; Robert Wise

Mystery in Swing; 1938; Arthur Dreifuss
Mystery Street; 1950; John Sturges
Mystery Submarine; 1950; Douglas Sirk

Nabonga; 1944; Sam Newfield
Naked and the Dead, The; 1958; Raoul Walsh
Naked City, The; 1948; Jules Dassin
Naked Dawn, The; 1955; Edgar G. Ulmer
Naked Edge, The; 1961; Michael Anderson
Naked Jungle, The; 1954; Byron Haskin
Naked Kiss, The; 1964; Samuel Fuller
Naked Maja, The; 1959; Henry Koster
Naked Prey, The; 1966; Cornell Wilde
Naked Runner; 1967; Sidney Furie
Naked Spur, The; 1953; Anthony Mann
Naked Street, The; 1955; Maxwell Shane
Namu, The Killer Whale; 1966; Laslo Benedek
Nana; 1934; Dorothy Arzner
Nancy Steele Is Missing; 1937; George Marshall
Nanny, The; 1965; Seth Holt
Narrow Margin, The; 1952; Richard Fleischer
Nation Aflame, A; 1938; Victor Halperin
National Velvet; 1945; Clarence Brown
Naughty Baby; 1929; Mervyn Le Roy
Naughty Marietta; 1935; W. S. van Dyke
Naughty Nineties, The; 1945; Jean Yarbrough
Navajo; 1952; Norman Foster
Navy Blues; 1929; Clarence Brown
Navy Blues; 1941; Lloyd Bacon
Navy Comes Through, The; 1942; Edward Sutherland
Navy Wife; 1956; Edward L. Bernds
Nazi Agent; 1942; Jules Dassin
Nazis Strike, The (Doc); 1943; Frank Capra and Anatole Litvak
Negro Soldier, The (Doc); 1944; Frank Capra
Negro Sailor, The (Doc); 1945; Henry Levin
Nell Gwyn; 1935; Herbert Wilcox
Nevada Smith; 1966; Henry Hathaway
Nevadan, The; 1950; Gordon Douglas

Never Fear; 1950; Ida Lupino

Never Give a Sucker an Even Break; 1941; Eddie Cline

Never Let Go; 1963; John Guillermin

Never Let Me Go; 1953; Delmer Daves

Never Love a Stranger; 1958; Robert Stevens

Never on Sunday; 1960; Jules Dassin

Never Say Die; 1939; Elliott Nugent

Never Say Goodbye; 1956; Jerry Hopper

Never So Few; 1959; John Sturges

Never the Twain Shall Meet; 1931; W. S. van Dyke

Never Wave at a WAC; 1953; Norman Z. McLeod

New Adventures of Don Juan, The; 1948; Vincent Sherman

New Divorce; 1936; Robert Florey

New Faces; 1954; Harry Horner

New Interns, The; 1964; John Rich

New Lot, The (Doc); 1942; Carol Reed

New Mexico; 1951; Irving Reis

New Moon; 1930; Jack Conway

New Moon; 1940; Robert Z. Leonard

New Orleans; 1947; Arthur Lubin

New York Confidential; 1955; Russell Rouse

New York Nights; 1929; Lewis Milestone

New York Town; 1941; Charles Vidor

Next of Kin; 1941; Thorold Dickinson

Next Time I Marry; 1938; Garson Kanin

Next to No Time; 1958; Henry Cornelius

Next Voice You Hear, The; 1950; William Wellman

Niagara; 1953; Henry Hathaway

Niagara Falls; 1941; Gordon Douglas

Nicholas Nickleby; 1947; Alberto Cavalcanti

Nick Carter—Master Detective; 1939; Jacques Tourneur

Night After Night; 1932; Archie Mayo

Night and Day; 1946; Michael Curtiz

Night and the City; 1950; Jules Dassin

Night Angel; 1931; Edmund Goulding

Night at Earl Carroll's, A; 1940; Kurt Neumann

Night at the Opera, A; 1935; Sam Wood

Night Before the Divorce, The; 1942; Robert Siodmak

Night Boat to Dublin; 1941; Lawrence Huntington

Night Fighter, The; 1960; Tay Garnett

Night Flight; 1933; Clarence Brown

Night Has a Thousand Eyes, The; 1948; John Farrow

Night Holds Terror, The; 1955; Andrew L. Stone

Night in Casablanca; 1946; Archie Mayo

Night into Morning; 1951; Fletcher Markle

Night Must Fall; 1937; Richard Thorpe

Night Must Fall; 1963; Karel Reisz

Night Nurse; 1931; William Wellman

Night of Adventure, A; 1944; Gordon Douglas

Night of Mystery, A; 1937; E. A. DuPont

Night of Nights, The; 1940; Lewis Milestone

Night of Passion (During One Night); 1961; Sidney Furie

Night of the Eagle; 1962; Sidney Hayers

Night of the Following Day; 1968; Hubert Cornfield

Night of the Generals; 1967; Anatole Litvak

Night of the Hunter, The; 1955; Charles Laughton

Night of the Iguana; 1964; John Huston

Night of the Quarter Moon (Flesh and Flame); 1959; Hugo Haas

Night Parade; 1929; Malcolm St. Clair

Night People; 1954; Nunnally Johnson

Night Song; 1947; John Cromwell

Night Tide; 1961; Curtis Harrington

Night to Remember, A; 1942; Richard Wallace

Night to Remember, A; 1958; Roy Baker

Night Train; 1939; Carol Reed

Night Train for Inverness; 1959; Ernest Morris

Night unto Night; 1949; Don Siegel

Night Walker, The; 1964; William Castle

Night Without Sleep; 1952; Roy Baker

Night World; 1932; W. S. van Dyke

Nightfall; 1956; Jacques Tourneur

Nightmare; 1942; Tim Whelan

Nightmare; 1956; Maxwell Shane

Nightmare Alley; 1947; Edmund Goulding

Nine Hours to Rama; 1963; Mark Robson

Nine Men; 1944; Harry Watt

Nine Lives Are Not Enough; 1941; Edward Sutherland

Nineteen-Eighty-Four; 1956; Michael Anderson

Ninety-Nine River Street; 1953; Phil Karlson

Ninotchka; 1939; Ernst Lubitsch

Nitwits; 1935; George Stevens

No Down Payment; 1957; Martin Ritt

No Greater Glory; 1934; Frank Borzage

No Highway in the Sky; 1951; Henry Koster

No Kidding (Beware of Children); 1961; Gerald Thomas

No Love for Johnnie; 1961; Ralph Thomas

No Man of Her Own; 1932; Wesley Ruggles

No Man of Her Own; 1950; Mitchell Leisen

No Minor Vices; 1948; Lewis Milestone

No More Ladies; 1935; Edward H. Griffith

No More Orchids; 1932; Walter Lang

No One Man; 1932; Lloyd Corrigan

No Parking; 1938; Carol Reed

No Room for the Groom; 1952; Douglas Sirk

No Sad Songs for Me; 1950; Rudolph Mate

No Time for Comedy; 1940; William Keighley

No Time for Flowers; 1952; Don Siegel

No Time for Love; 1943; Mitchell Leisen

No Time for Sergeants; 1958; Mervyn Le Roy

No Trees in the Street; 1958; J. Lee Thompson

No Way Out; 1950; Joseph Mankiewicz

No Way to Treat a Lady; 1968; Jack Smight

Noah's Ark; 1929; Michael Curtiz

Nob Hill; 1945; Henry Hathaway

Nobody Lives Forever; 1946; Jean Negulesco

Nobody's Darling; 1943; Anthony Mann

None but the Brave; 1964; Frank Sinatra

None but the Lonely Heart; 1944; Clifford Odets

None Shall Escape; 1944; Andre de Toth

North by Northwest; 1959; Alfred Hitchcock

North Star, The; 1943; Lewis Milestone

North to Alaska; 1960; Henry Hathaway

North West Frontier; 1959; J. Lee Thompson

North West Mounted Police; 1940; Cecil B. de Mille

Northern Pursuit; 1943; Raoul Walsh

Northwest Outpost; 1947; Allan Dwan

Northwest Passage; 1939; King Vidor

Northwest Rangers; 1942; Joseph M. Newman

Not as a Stranger; 1955; Stanley Kramer

Not of This Earth; 1957; Roger Corman

Not So Dumb; 1930; King Vidor

Not Wanted; 1949; Ida Lupino

Nothing but a Man; 1964; Michael Roemer

Nothing but the Best; 1964; Clive Donner

Nothing but the Truth; 1931; Victor Schertzinger

Nothing but the Truth; 1941; Elliott Nugent

Nothing Sacred; 1937; William Wellman

Nothing to Lose; 1953; Lewis Gilbert

Notorious; 1946; Alfred Hitchcock

Notorious but Nice; 1933; Richard Thorpe

Notorious Gentleman; 1947; Sidney Gilliat

Notorious Landlady, The; 1962; Richard Quine

Now and Forever; 1934; Henry Hathaway

Now Voyager; 1942; Irving Rapper

Nowhere to Go; 1959; Seth Holt

Nude Restaurant, The; 1967; Andy Warhol

Nuisance, The; 1933; Jack Conway

Number Seventeen; 1932; Alfred Hitchcock

Numbered Men; 1930; Mervyn Le Roy

Nun's Story, The; 1959; Fred Zinnemann

Nurse Edith Cavell; 1939; Herbert Wilcox

Nutty Professor, The; 1963; Jerry Lewis

O Dreamland (Short); 1953; Lindsay Anderson

O. Henry's Full House; 1952; Howard Hawks and Henry King

O'er Hill and Dale; 1931; Basil Wright

O'Shaughnessy's Boy; 1935; Richard Boleslavsky

Objective Burma; 1945; Raoul Walsh

Obliging Young Lady; 1942; Richard Wallace

Obsession; 1934; Maurice Tourneur

Ocean's Eleven; 1960; Lewis Milestone

October Man, The; 1947; Roy Baker

Odd Man Out; 1947; Carol Reed

Odds Against Tomorrow; 1959; Robert Wise

Odette; 1950; Herbert Wilcox

Of Human Bondage; 1934; John Cromwell

Of Human Bondage; 1946; Edmund Goulding

Of Human Bondage; 1963; Kenneth Hughes

Of Human Hearts; 1938; Clarence Brown

Of Mice and Men; 1940; Lewis Milestone

Offbeat; 1960; Cliff Owen

Officer O'Brien; 1930; Tay Garnett

Oh, For a Man; 1930; Hamilton MacFadden

Oh Men, Oh Women; 1957; Nunnally Johnson

Oh, Mister Porter; 1939; Max Varnel

Oh Yeah; 1929; Tay Garnett

Oil for the Lamps of China; 1935; Mervyn Le Roy

OK Roberta; 1934; William Seiter

Okay America; 1932; Tay Garnett

Oklahoma; 1955; Fred Zinnemann

Oklahoma Kid; 1939; Lloyd Bacon

Old Acquaintance; 1943; Vincent Sherman

Old Bones of the River; 1939; Max Varnel

Old Dark House, The; 1932; James Whale

Old Dark House, The; 1963; William Castle

Old Maid, The; 1939; Edmund Goulding

Old Man and the Sea, The; 1958; John Sturges

Old Yeller; 1957; Robert Stevenson

Oliver; 1968; Carol Reed

Oliver Twist; 1951; David Lean

Olsen's Big Moment; 1934; Malcolm St. Clair

Omar Khayyam; 1957; William Dieterle

On Approval; 1944; Clive Brook

On Borrowed Time; 1939; Harold S. Bucquet

On Dangerous Ground; 1951; Nicholas Ray

On Moonlight Bay; 1951; Roy del Ruth

On Our Merry Way; 1947; King Vidor

On the Avenue; 1936; Roy del Ruth

On the Beach; 1959; Stanley Kramer

On the Night of the Fire; 1939; Brian D. Hurst

On the Riviera; 1951; Walter Lang

On the Run; 1963; Robert Tronson

On the Sunny Side; 1942; Harold Schuster

On the Sunny Side of the Street; 1951; Richard Quine

On the Threshhold of Space; 1956; Robert D. Webb

On the Town; 1949; Stanley Donen and Gene Kelly

On the Waterfront; 1954; Elia Kazan

On Velvet; 1938; Widgey Newman

On with the Show; 1929; Alan Crosland

On Your Toes; 1939; Ray Enright

Once a Gentleman; 1930; James Cruze

Once a Thief; 1965; Ralph Nelson

Once in a Blue Moon; 1935; Ben Hecht

Once in a Lifetime; 1932; Russell Mack

Once More with Feeling; 1960; Stanley Donen

Once More, My Darling; 1949; Robert Montgomery

Once upon a Honeymoon; 1942; Leo McCarey

Once upon a Time; 1944; Alexander Hall

One Crowded Night; 1940; Irving Reis

One Desire; 1955; Jerry Hopper

One Foot in Heaven; 1941; Irving Rapper

One Foot in Hell; 1960; James B. Clark

One Hour with You; 1932; George Cukor and Ernst Lubitsch

One Hundred Men and a Girl; 1937;

Henry Koster

One Mile from Heaven; 1937; Allan Dwan

One Million, BC (Sig. Hal Roach); 1940; D. W. Griffith

One Million Years BC; 1967; Don Chaffey

One Minute to Zero; 1952; Tay Garnett

One More River; 1934; James Whale

One More Spring; 1935; Henry King

One Mysterious Night; 1944; Budd Boetticher

One New York Night; 1935; Jack Conway

One Night in the Tropics; 1940; Edward Sutherland

One Night of Love; 1934; Victor Schertzinger

One Night with You; 1949; Terence Young

One Plus One; 1961; Arch Oboler

One Romantic Night; 1930; Paul Stein

One Sunday Afternoon; 1933; Stephen Roberts

One Sunday Afternoon; 1948; Raoul Walsh

One That Got Away, The; 1957; Roy Baker

One Third of a Nation; 1939; Dudley Murphy

One Touch of Venus; 1948; William Seiter

One Way Passage; 1932; Tay Garnett

One Way Ticket; 1935; Herbert Biberman

One Woman's Story; 1949; David Lean

One-Eyed Jacks; 1961; Marlon Brando

One-Way Street; 1951; Hugo Fregonese

One, Two, Three; 1961; Billy Wilder

Onionhead; 1958; Norman Taurog

Only Angels Have Wings; 1939; Howard Hawks

Only the Brave; 1930; Frank Tuttle

Only the Valiant; 1951; Gordon Douglas

Only Yesterday; 1933; John Stahl

Operation CIA; 1965; Christian Nyby

Operation Crossbow; 1965; Michael Anderson

Operation Disaster; 1951; Roy Baker

Operation Madball; 1957; Richard Quine

Operation Pacific; 1951; George Waggner

Operation Petticoat; 1959; Blake Edwards

Operation Stogie; 1960; Ernest Morris

Operator 13; 1934; Richard Boleslavsky

Opposite Sex, The; 1956; David Miller

Orchestra; 1942; Archie Mayo

Orchids to You; 1935; William Seiter

Orders to Kill; 1957; Anthony Asquith

Oscar Wilde; 1960; Gregory Ratoff

OSS; 1946; Irving Pichel

Othello; 1955; Orson Welles

Other Love, The; 1947; Andre de Toth

Other Men's Women; 1931; William Wellman

Ouanga (Drums of the Jungle); 1935; George Terwilliger

Our Betters; 1933; George Cukor

Our Blushing Brides; 1930; Harry Beaumont

Our Daily Bread (City Girl); 1930; F. W. Murnau

Our Daily Bread; 1934; King Vidor

Our Leading Citizen; 1939; Alfred Santell

Our Man Flint; 1965; Daniel Mann

Our Man in Havana; 1960; Carol Reed

Our Modern Maidens; 1929; Jack Conway

Our Mother's House; 1967; Jack Clayton

Our Town; 1940; Sam Wood

Our Very Own; 1950; David Miller

Our Vines Have Tender Grapes; 1945; Roy Rowland

Out of the Fog; 1941; Anatole Litvak

Out of the Past; 1947; Jacques Tourneur

Out of this World; 1945; Hal Walkon

Outcast; 1936; Robert Florey

Outcast, The; 1952; William Witney

Outcast Lady; 1934; Robert Z. Leonard

Outcast of the Islands; 1952; Carol Reed

Outcasts of Poker Flat, The; 1952; Joseph M. Newman

Outlaw, The; 1943; Howard Hughes

Outrage; 1950; Ida Lupino

Outrage, The; 1964; Martin Ritt

Outward Bound; 1930; Robert Milton

Over My Dead Body; 1942; Malcolm St. Clair

Over the Hill; 1931; Henry King

Over the Moon; 1940; Robert E. Sherwood

Over Twenty-One; 1945; Charles Vidor

Overland Stage Riders; 1938; George Sherman

Overlanders, The; 1946; Harry Watt

Ox Bow Incident (Strange Incident); 1943; William Wellman

Pacific Rendezvous; 1942; George Sidney

Pack Up Your Troubles; 1932; George Marshall

Pack Up Your Troubles; 1939; H. Bruce Humberstone

Pagan, The; 1929; W. S. van Dyke

Pagan Love Song; 1950; Robert Alton

Page Miss Glory; 1935; Mervyn Le Roy

Paid; 1930; Sam Wood

Paid in Full; 1950; William Dieterle

Painted Lady, The; 1931; Howard Higgin

Painted Veil, The; 1934; Richard Boleslavsky and W. S. van Dyke

Pajama Game, The; 1957; George Abbott and Stanley Donen

Pal Joey; 1957; George Sidney

Paleface, The; 1948; Norman Z. McLeod

Palm Beach Story, The; 1942; Preston Sturges

Palm Springs Weekend; 1963; Norman Taurog

Palmy Days; 1931; Edward Sutherland

Panama Hattie; 1943; Norman Z. McLeod

Pandora and the Flying Dutchman; 1951; Albert Lewin

Panic Button; 1964; George Sherman

Panic in the Parlor; 1957; Gordon Parry

Panic in the Streets; 1950; Elia Kazan

Panic in the Year Zero; 1962; Ray Milland

Panthers Moon; 1950; George Sherman

Parachute Jumper; 1933; Alfred S. Green

Paradine Case, The; 1947; Alfred Hitchcock

Paradise in Harlem; 1939; Joseph Seiden

Paramount on Parade; 1930; Dorothy Arzner and Otto Brower

Paratrooper, The (Red Beret); 1954; Terence Young

Pardners; 1956; Norman Taurog

Pardon Us; 1931; James Parrott

Paris Bound; 1929; Edward H. Griffith

Paris Blues; 1961; Martin Ritt

Paris Does Strange Things; 1957; Jean Renoir

Paris Holiday; 1958; Gerd Oswald

Paris Honeymoon; 1939; Frank Tuttle

Paris in Spring; 1935; Lewis Milestone

Paris Underground; 1946; Gregory Ratoff

Paris When It Sizzles; 1963; Richard Quine

Park Row; 1952; Samuel Fuller

Parnell; 1937; John Stahl

Parole Fixer; 1940; Robert Florey

Parrish; 1961; Delmer Daves

Part Time Wife; 1930; Leo McCarey

Party, The; 1968; Blake Edwards

Party Girl; 1958; Nicholas Ray

Party's Over, The; 1963; Guy Hamilton

Passage to Marseilles; 1944; Michael Curtiz

Passion; 1954; Allan Dwan

Passport to Hell, A; 1932; Frank Lloyd

Passport to Pimlico; 1948; Henry Cornelius

Password Is Courage, The; 1962; Andrew L. Stone

Pat and Mike; 1952; George Cukor

Patch of Blue, A; 1965; Guy Green

Paths of Glory; 1957; Stanley Kubrick

Patsy, The; 1964; Jerry Lewis

Patterns; 1956; Fielder Cook

Pawnbroker, The; 1965; Sidney Lumet

Pay or Die; 1960; Richard Wilson

Payment on Demand; 1951; Curtis Bernhardt

Pay-Off, The; 1935; Robert Florey

Payroll; 1961; Sidney Hayers

Peace of Britain (Doc); 1936; Paul Rotha

Pearl of the South Pacific; 1955; Allan Dwan

Peeper, The (Peeping Tom); 1960; Michael Powell

Peer Gynt; 1941; David Bradley

Peking Express; 1951; William Dieterle

Penitentiary; 1938; John Brahm

Pennies from Heaven; 1937; Norman Z. McLeod

Penny Paradise; 1938; Carol Reed

Penny Princess; 1951; Val Guest

Penny Serenade; 1941; George Stevens

Penrod and Sam; 1937; William McGann

Penthouse; 1933; W. S. van Dyke

People Against O'Hara, The; 1951; John Sturges

People Will Talk; 1935; Alfred Santell

People Will Talk; 1951; Joseph Mankiewicz

Pepe; 1960; George Sidney

Perfect Day (Short); 1929; James Parrott

Perfect Furlough, The; 1958; Blake Edwards

Perfect Marriage, The; 1946; Lewis Allen

Perfect Specimen, The; 1937; Michael Curtiz

Perfect Strangers; 1950; Bretaigne Windust

Perfect Understanding; 1933; Cyril Gardner

Perilous Journey, A; 1953; R. G. Springsteen

Perils of Pauline; 1947; George Marshall

Personal Column (Lured); 1947; Douglas Sirk

Personal Property; 1937; W. S. van Dyke

Pete Kelly's Blues; 1955; Jack Webb

Peter; 1935; Henry Koster

Peter Ibbetson; 1935; Henry Hathaway

Petrified Forest, The; 1936; Archie Mayo

Petulia; 1968; Richard Lester

Petty Girl; 1950; Henry Levin

Peyton Place; 1957; Mark Robson

Phaedra; 1962; Jules Dassin

Phantom Killers, The; 1943; William Beaudine

Phantom Lady; 1944; Robert Siodmak

Phantom of the Opera, The; 1943; Arthur Lubin

Phantom of the Opera, The; 1954; Roy del Ruth

Phantom of the Opera, The; 1962; Terence Fisher

Phantom of the Rue Morgue; 1954; Roy del Ruth

Phantom Riders; 1940; Jacques Tourneur

Phenix City Story, The; 1955; Phil Karlson

Phffft; 1954; Mark Robson

Philadelphia Story, The; 1940; George Cukor

Phone Call from a Stranger; 1952; Jean Negulesco

Piccadilly; 1929; E. A. Dupont

Piccadilly Incident; 1946; Herbert Wilcox

Pickup; 1951; Hugo Haas

Pickup on South Street; 1953; Samuel Fuller

Picnic; 1956; Joshua Logan

Picture of Dorian Gray, The; 1945; Albert Lewin

Picture Snatcher; 1933; Lloyd Bacon

Pied Piper, The; 1942; Irving Pichel

Pied Piper of Hamelin, The; 1959; Bretaigne Windust

Pieges; 1939; Robert Siodmak

Pigeon That Took Rome, The; 1962; Melville Shavelson

Pigskin Parade; 1936; David Butler

Pilgrimage; 1933; John Ford

Pillow Talk; 1958; Michael Gordon

Pilot No. 5; 1943; George Sidney

Pimpernel Smith; 1942; Leslie Howard

Pin-Up Girl; 1944; H. Bruce Humberstone

Pink Panther, The; 1964; Blake Edwards

Pink String and Sealing Wax; 1945; Robert Hamer

Pinky; 1949; Elia Kazan

Pirate, The; 1948; Vincente Minnelli

Pirates of Capri, The; 1949; Edgar G. Ulmer

Pirates of Tortuga, The; 1961; Robert D. Webb

Pit and the Pendulum, The; 1961; Roger Corman

Pitfall, The; 1948; Andre de Toth

Pittsburgh Kid, The; 1942; Jack Townley

Place in the Sun, A; 1951; George Stevens

Place to Live, A (Doc); 1941; Irving Lerner

Plainsman, The; 1936; Cecil B. de Mille

Planter's Wife, The; 1952; Ken Annakin

Platinum Blonde; 1931; Frank Capra

Platinum High School (Trouble at 16); 1960; Albert Zugsmith

Play Dirty; 1968; Andre de Toth

Play It Cool; 1962; Michael Winner

Planet of the Apes; 1968; Franklin Schaffner

Playboy of the Western World, The; 1962; Brian D. Hurst

Playing Around; 1930; Mervyn Le Roy

Please Believe Me; 1950; Norman Taurog

Please Don't Eat the Daisies; 1960; Charles Walters

Pleasure Cruise; 1933; Frank Tuttle

Pleasure Garden, The; 1954; James Broughton

Pleasure of His Company, The; 1961; George Seaton

Pleasure Seekers, The; 1964; Jean Negulesco

Plough and the Stars, The; 1936; John Ford

Plunder of the Sun; 1953; John Farrow

Plunder Road; 1957; Hubert Cornfield

Plymouth Adventure; 1952; Clarence Brown

Pocketful of Miracles; 1961; Frank Capra

Poe's Tales of Terror; 1962; Roger Corman

Point Blank; 1967; John Boorman

Pointed Heels; 1929; Edward Sutherland

Police Dog; 1955; Derek Twist

Polly of the Circus; 1932; Alfred Santell

Pollyanna; 1960; David Swift

Pony Express; 1953; Jerry Hopper

Pony Soldier; 1952; Joseph M. Newman

Pool of London; 1950; Basil Dearden

Poppy; 1936; Edward Sutherland

Poppy Is Also a Flower, The; 1966; Terence Young

Porgy and Bess; 1959; Otto Preminger

Pork Chop Hill; 1959; Lewis Milestone

Port Afrique; 1956; Rudolph Mate

Port of New York; 1949; Laslo Benedek

Port of Seven Seas; 1938; James Whale

Portrait in Black; 1960; Michael Gordon

Portrait of a Mobster; 1961; Joseph Pevney

Portrait of Jason; 1967; Shirley Clarke

Portrait of Jennie; 1947; William Dieterle

Possessed; 1931; Clarence Brown

Possessed; 1947; Curtis Bernhardt

Postman Always Rings Twice, The; 1946; Tay Garnett

Pot Carriers, The; 1962; Peter Graham Scott

Power, The; 1968; Byron Haskin and George Pal

Powder River; 1953; Louis King

Power and the Glory; 1933; William K. Howard

Practically Yours; 1944; Mitchell Leisen

Prelude to War (Doc); 1942; Frank Capra

Premature Burial, The; 1961; Roger Corman

Presenting Lily Mars; 1943; Norman Taurog

President Vanishes, The; 1934; William Wellman

President's Analyst, The; 1967; Theodore J. Flicker

Pressure Point; 1962; Hubert Cornfield

Prestige; 1932; Tay Garnett

Pretty Baby; 1950; Bretaigne Windust

Preview Murder Mystery; 1936; Robert Florey

Price of Fear, The; 1956; Abner Biberman

Pride and Prejudice; 1940; Robert Z. Leonard

Pride and the Passion, The; 1957; Stanley Kramer

Pride of the Bowery; 1941; Joseph H. Lewis

Pride of the Marines; 1945; Delmer Daves

Pride of the Yankees; 1942; Sam Wood

Prime Minister, The; 1941; Thorold Dickinson

Primrose Path; 1940; Gregory La Cava

Prince and the Pauper, The; 1937; William Keighley

Prince and the Showgirl, The; 1957; Sir Laurence Olivier

Prince of Foxes; 1949; Henry King

Prince of Players; 1955; Philip Dunne

Prince Valiant; 1954; Henry Hathaway

Prince Who Was a Thief; 1951; Rudolph Mate

Princess and the Pirate, The; 1944; David Butler

Princess and the Plumber, The; 1930; Alexander Korda

Princess Comes Across; 1937; William K. Howard

Princess O'Rourke; 1943; Norman Krasna

Prison Nurse; 1938; James Cruze

Prisoner, The; 1955; Peter Glenville

Prisoner of Japan; 1942; Arthur Ripley

Prisoner of Shark Island, The; 1936; John Ford

Prisoner of War; 1954; Andrew Marton

Prisoner of Zenda, The; 1937; John Cromwell

Prisoner of Zenda, The; 1952; Richard Thorpe

Private Affairs of Bel Ami, The; 1947; Albert Lewin

Private Angelo; 1949; Peter Ustinov

Private Detective 62; 1933; Michael Curtiz

Private Hell 36; 1954; Don Siegel

Private Life of Adam and Eve, The; 1961; Albert Zugsmith

Private Life of Don Juan; 1934; Alexander Korda

Private Life of Henry VIII; 1933; Alexander Korda

Private Lives; 1931; Sidney Franklin

Private Lives of Elizabeth and Essex, The (Elizabeth the Queen); 1939; Michael Curtiz

Private Navy of Sgt. O'Farrell; 1968; Frank Tashlin

Private Number; 1936; Roy del Ruth

Private Property; 1960; Leslie Stevens

Private War of Major Benson, The; 1955; Jerry Hopper

Private Worlds; 1935; Gregory La Cava

Private's Affair, A; 1959; Raoul Walsh

Private's Progress; 1955; John Boulting and Roy Boulting

Privilege; 1967; Peter Watkins

Prize, The; 1963; Mark Robson

Prize of Arms; 1962; Cliff Owen

Prizefighter and the Lady; 1933; W. S. van Dyke

Probation; 1932; Richard Thorpe

Prodigal, The; 1955; Richard Thorpe

Professional Soldier; 1935; Tay Garnett

Professional Sweetheart; 1933; William Seiter

Professionals, The; 1966; Richard Brooks

Professor Beware; 1938; Elliott Nugent

Promoter, The (The Card); 1952; Ronald Neame

Proud and the Profane, The; 1956; George Seaton

Proud Ones, The; 1956; Robert D. Webb

Proud Rebel, The; 1958; Michael Curtiz

Proud Valley, The; 1940; Pen Tennyson

Prowler, The; 1951; Joseph Losey

Psyche '59; 1964; Alexander Singer

Psycho; 1960; Alfred Hitchcock

PT-109; 1963; Leslie Martinson

Public Enemy, The; 1931; William Wellman

Public Hero Number One; 1935; J. Walter Ruben

Pumpkin Eater, The; 1963; Jack Clayton

Punch and Judy Man, The; 1962; Jeremy Summers

Purchase Price; 1932; William Wellman

Purlie Victorious (Gone Are the Days); 1963; Nicholas Webster

Purple Heart, The; 1944; Lewis Milestone

Purple Heart Diary; 1951; Richard Quine

Purple Mask, The; 1955; H. Bruce Humberstone

Purple Plain, The; 1955; Robert Parrish

Purple Stream, The; 1961; Clive Donner

Pursued; 1947; Raoul Walsh

Pushover; 1954; Richard Quine

Pygmalion; 1938; Anthony Asquith and Leslie Howard

Quality Street; 1937; George Stevens

Quarterback, The; 1940; H. Bruce Humberstone

Quatermass II; 1956; Val Guest

Queen Bee; 1955; Ranald D. MacDougall

Queen Christina; 1933; Rouben Mamoulian

Queen of Blood; 1966; Curtis Harrington

Queen of Spades, The; 1948; Thorold Dickinson

Question Seven; 1961; Stuart Rosenberg

Quick Before It Melts; 1964; Delbert Mann

Quiet American, The; 1958; Joseph Mankiewicz

Quiet Man, The; 1952; John Ford
Quick Millions; 1931; Rowland Brown
Quick Millions; 1939; Malcolm St. Clair
Quiet One, The; 1948; Sidney Meyers
Quiller Memorandum, The; 1966; Michael Anderson
Quitter, The; 1934; Richard Thorpe
Quo Vadis; 1951; Mervyn Le Roy

Rabbit Trap, The; 1958; Philip Leacock
Rabbit, Run; 1969; Jack Smight
Racers, The; 1955; Henry Hathaway
Rack, The; 1956; Arnold Laven
Racket, The; 1951; John Cromwell
Racket Busters; 1938; Lloyd Bacon
Racetrack; 1933; James Cruze
Raffles; 1930; Harry D'Arrast and George Fitzmaurice
Raffles; 1939; Sam Wood
Rafter Romance; 1934; William Seiter
Rage in Heaven; 1941; W. S. van Dyke
Rage of Paris, The; 1938; Henry Koster
Raging Sea, The; 1969; Cornell Wilde
Raid, The; 1954; Hugo Fregonese
Railroaded; 1947; Anthony Mann
Rain; 1932; Lewis Milestone
Rain People, The; 1969; Francis Ford Coppola
Rain or Shine; 1930; Frank Capra
Rainbow Jacket, The; 1954; Basil Dearden
Rainbow on the River; 1936; Kurt Neumann
Rainbow over Broadway; 1933; Richard Thorpe
Rainbow Round My Shoulder; 1952; Richard Quine
Rainmaker, The; 1956; Joseph Anthony
Rains Came, The; 1939; Clarence Brown
Rains of Ranchipur, The; 1955; Jean Negulesco
Raintree County; 1957; Edward Dmytryk
Raisin in the Sun, A; 1961; Daniel Petrie
Rally Round the Flag Boys; 1958; Leo McCarey
Ramona; 1936; Henry King
Rampage; 1963; Phil Karlson
Rancho Notorious; 1952; Fritz Lang
Random Harvest; 1942; Mervyn Le Roy

Rango; 1931; Ernest L. Schoesdack
Ransom; 1956; Alex Segal
Rapture; 1965; John Guillermin
Rare Breed, The; 1965; Andrew McLaglen
Rasputin and the Empress; 1932; Richard Boleslavsky
Rat Race, The; 1960; Robert Mulligan
Raven, The; 1935; Louis Friedlander
Raven, The; 1963; Roger Corman
Raw Deal; 1948; Anthony Mann
Raw Wind in Eden; 1958; Richard Wilson
Rawhide (Desperate Siege); 1951; Henry Hathaway
Rawhide Years, The; 1956; Rudolph Mate
Razor's Edge, The; 1946; Edmund Goulding
Reach for Glory; 1963; Philip Leacock
Reach for the Sky; 1956; Lewis Gilbert
Reaching for the Moon; 1930; Edmund Goulding
Reaching for the Sun; 1940; William Wellman
Ready for the People; 1964; Buzz Kulik
Real Glory, The; 1939; Henry Hathaway
Reap the Wild Wind; 1942; Cecil B. de Mille
Rear Window; 1954; Alfred Hitchcock
Rebecca; 1940; Alfred Hitchcock
Rebecca of Sunnybrook Farm; 1932; Alfred Santell
Rebecca of Sunnybrook Farm; 1938; Allan Dwan
Rebel in the Ring; 1964; Jay O. Lawrence
Rebel Without a Cause; 1955; Nicholas Ray
Reckless; 1935; Victor Fleming
Reckless Moment; 1949; Max Ophuls
Recoil; 1963; Paul Wendkos
Red Badge of Courage, The; 1951; John Huston
Red Ball Express; 1952; Budd Boetticher
Red Beret (The Paratrooper); 1954; Terence Young
Red Danube, The; 1949; George Sidney
Red Dust; 1932; Victor Fleming
Red Garters; 1954; George Marshall
Red Headed Woman; 1932; Jack Conway

Red Hot Rhythm; 1929; Leo McCarey
Red House, The; 1947; Delmer Daves
Red Light; 1949; Roy del Ruth
Red Line Seven Thousand; 1965; Howard Hawks
Red Menace, The; 1949; R. G. Springsteen
Red Mountain; 1951; William Dieterle
Red Planet Mars; 1952; Harry Horner
Red Pony, The; 1949; Lewis Milestone
Red River; 1948; Howard Hawks
Red Shoes, The; 1948; Michael Powell and Emeric Pressberger
Red Skies of Montana; 1952; Joseph M. Newman
Red Sundown; 1956; Jack Arnold
Red, Hot and Blue; 1949; John Farrow
Redhead and the Cowboy, The; 1951; Leslie Fenton
Reflections in a Golden Eye; 1967; John Huston
Registered Nurse; 1934; Robert Florey
Reign of Terror; 1949; Anthony Mann
Reluctant Debutante, The; 1958; Vincente Minnelli
Remains to Be Seen; 1953; Don Weis
Remarkable Andrew, The; 1942; Stuart Heisler
Remarkable Mr. Pennypacker, The; 1959; Henry Levin
Remember Last Night; 1934; James Whale
Remember the Day; 1941; Henry King
Remember the Night; 1940; Mitchell Leisen
Remote Control; 1930; Malcolm St. Clair
Rendezvous; 1935; William K. Howard
Rendezvous with Annie; 1946; Allan Dwan
Renegades; 1930; Victor Fleming
Reno; 1939; John Farrow
Repeat Performance; 1948; Alfred Werker
Report from the Aleutians (Doc); 1942; John Huston
Repulsion; 1965; Roman Polanski
Requiem for a Heavyweight; 1962; Ralph Nelson
Rescue, The; 1929; Herbert Brown
Reserved for Ladies; 1932; Alexander Korda
Restless Breed, The; 1957; Allan Dwan
Retreat, Hell; 1952; Joseph H. Lewis
Return from the Ashes; 1965; J. Lee Thompson
Return of Doctor X, The; 1939; Vincent Sherman
Return of Frank James, The; 1940; Fritz Lang
Return of October, The; 1948; Joseph H. Lewis
Return of the Seven; 1966; Burt Kennedy
Return of the Texan; 1952; Delmer Daves
Return of the Vampire; 1943; Lew Landers and Kurt Neumann
Return of Wild Bill, The; 1940; Joseph H. Lewis
Return to Paradise; 1953; Mark Robson
Reunion in France; 1942; Jules Dassin
Reunion in Vienna; 1933; Sidney Franklin
Revenge of Frankenstein, The; 1958; Terence Fisher
Revenge of the Creature; 1955; Jack Arnold
Revolt, The; 1935; Lloyd Bacon
Revolt of Mamie Stover, The; 1956; Raoul Walsh
Revolt in the Desert; 1937; Zoltan Korda
Rhapsody; 1954; Charles Vidor
Rhapsody in Blue; 1945; Irving Rapper
Rhubarb; 1950; Arthur Lubin
Rhythm on the River; 1940; Victor Schertzinger
Rich Man's Folly; 1931; John Cromwell
Rich People; 1930; Edward H. Griffith
Richard III; 1955; Sir Laurence Olivier
Ride Back, The; 1957; Allen Miner
Ride Em Cowboy; 1942; Arthur Lubin
Ride Lonesome; 1959; Budd Boetticher
Ride the High Country; 1962; Sam Peckinpah
Ride the High Iron; 1956; Don Weis
Ride the Pink Horse; 1947; Robert Montgomery
Ride the Wild Surf; 1964; Don Taylor
Ride Vaquero; 1953; John Farrow
Riders of the Purple Sage; 1941; James Tinling
Riding High; 1950; Frank Capra
Riding Shotgun; 1954; Andre de Toth
Riffraff; 1946; Ted Tetzlaff
Right Cross; 1950; John Sturges

Right to Live; 1935; William Keighley

Right to Romance; 1933; Alfred Santell

Ring of Spies; 1964; Robert Tronson

Ring of Steel (Doc); 1942; Garson Kanin

Ringer, The; 1952; Guy Hamilton

Rings on Her Fingers; 1942; Rouben Mamoulian

Rio; 1939; John Brahm

Rio Bravo; 1959; Howard Hawks

Rio Conchos; 1964; Gordon Douglas

Rio Grande; 1950; John Ford

Rio Rita; 1942; S. Sylvan Simon

Riot, The; 1969; Buzz Kulik

Riot in Cell Block 11; 1954; Don Siegel

Riptide; 1934; Edmund Goulding

Rise and Fall of Legs Diamond, The; 1960; Budd Boetticher

Rise and Shine; 1941; Allan Dwan

Rising of the Moon, The; 1957; John Ford

Risk, The; 1961; John Boulting and Roy Boulting

Risky Business; 1939; Arthur Lubin

River, The; 1929; Frank Borzage

River, The (Doc); 1938; Pare Lorentz

The River; 1951; Jean Renoir

River Beat; 1953; Guy Green

River of No Return; 1954; Otto Preminger

River's Edge, The; 1957; Allan Dwan

River's End; 1931; Michael Curtiz

Road Back, The; 1937; James Whale

Road House; 1948; Jean Negulesco

Road Show; 1941; Gordon Douglas

Road to Bali, The; 1953; Hal Walter

Road to Glory, The; 1936; Howard Hawks

Road to Hollywood, The; 1933; Bud Pollard

Road to Hong Kong, The; 1962; Norman Panama

Road to Rio; 1948; Norman Z. McLeod

Road to Singapore, The; 1940; Victor Schertzinger

Road to Utopia; 1946; Hal Walker

Road to Zanzibar; 1941; Victor Schertzinger

Roaring Twenties, The; 1939; Raoul Walsh

Robbery Under Arms; 1957; Jack Lee

Robe, The; 1953; Henry Koster

Roberta; 1935; William D. Seiter

Robin and the Seven Hoods; 1964; Gordon Douglas

Robin Hood of El Dorado; 1935; William Wellman

Robinson Crusoe; 1953; Luis Buñuel

Robinson Crusoe on Mars; 1964; Byron Haskin

Rock-A-Bye Baby; 1958; Frank Tashlin

Rockabye; 1932; George Cukor

Rocketship XM; 1950; Kurt Neumann

Rocky; 1948; Phil Karlson

Rocky Mountain; 1950; William Keighley

Rogue Song, The; 1930; Lionel Barrymore

Roger Touhy, Gangster; 1944; Robert Florey

Rogues of Sherwood Forest; 1950; Gordon Douglas

Roman Holiday; 1953; William Wyler

Roman Scandals; 1933; Frank Tuttle

Roman Spring of Mrs. Stone; 1961; J. Quintero

Romance; 1930; Clarence Brown

Romance and Riches; 1937; Alfred Zeisler

Romance of Rosy Ridge; 1947; Roy Rowland

Romance on the High Seas; 1948; Michael Curtiz

Romanoff and Juliet; 1961; Peter Ustinov

Rome Adventure; 1962; Delmer Daves

Rome Express; 1932; Walter Forde

Romeo and Juliet; 1936; George Cukor

Rookery Nook; 1930; Herbert Wilcox

Room at the Top; 1958; Jack Clayton

Room for One More (The Easy Way); 1952; Norman Taurog

Room Service; 1938; William Seiter

Rooney; 1958; George Pollock

Roots of Heaven, The; 1958; John Huston

Rope; 1948; Alfred Hitchcock

Rope of Sand; 1949; William Dieterle

Rosalie; 1937; W. S. van Dyke

Rose Marie; 1936; W. S. van Dyke

Rose of Washington Square; 1939; Gregory Ratoff

Rose Tattoo, The; 1954; Daniel Mann

Roseanna McCoy; 1949; Irving Reis

Rose Marie; 1936; W. S. van Dyke

Rosemarie; 1954; Mervyn Le Roy

Rosemary's Baby; 1968; Roman Polanski

Rotten to the Core; 1965; John Boulting and Roy Boulting

Roughly Speaking; 1945; Michael Curtiz

Rounders, The; 1965; Burt Kennedy

Roxie Hart; 1942; William Wellman

Royal Family of Broadway, The; 1930; George Cukor and Cyril Gardner

Royal Scandal, A; 1945; Otto Preminger

Royal Wedding; 1951; Stanley Donen

Ruby Gentry; 1952; King Vidor

Ruggles of Red Gap; 1935; Leo McCarey

Rulers of the Sea; 1939; Frank Lloyd

Rumba; 1934; Marion Gering

Run for Cover; 1955; Nicholas Ray

Run for the Sun; 1956; Roy Boulting

Run of the Arrow; 1957; Samuel Fuller

Run Silent Run Deep; 1958; Robert Wise

Runaway Bus, The; 1954; Val Guest

Running Man, The; 1963; Carol Reed

Russians Are Coming, The Russians Are Coming, The; 1966; Norman Jewison

Ruthless; 1948; Edgar G. Ulmer

Saadia; 1954; Albert Lewin

Sabotage; 1937; Alfred Hitchcock

Saboteur; 1942; Alfred Hitchcock

Sabrina; 1954; Billy Wilder

Sabu and the Magic Ring; 1958; George Blair

Sad Horse, The; 1959; James B. Clark

Saddle the Wind; 1958; Robert Parrish

Sadie McKee; 1934; Clarence Brown

Safari; 1940; Edward H. Griffith

Safari; 1956; Terence Young

Safe in Hell; 1931; William Wellman

Safecracker, The; 1958; Ray Milland

Safety in Numbers; 1938; Malcolm St. Clair

Sahara; 1943; Zoltan Korda

Sailor Be Good; 1933; James Cruze

Sailor from Gibraltar; 1967; Tony Richardson

Sailor Takes a Wife, The; 1946; Richard Whorf

Sailor's Lady; 1940; Allan Dwan

Sailor's Luck; 1933; Raoul Walsh

Saint Benny the Dip; 1951; Edgar G. Ulmer

Saint Joan; 1957; Otto Preminger

Saint Martin's Lane (Sidewalks of London); 1938; Tim Whelan

Saint Strikes Back, The; 1939; John Farrow

Saint's Vacation, The; 1941; Leslie Fenton

Salerno Beachhead (Walk in the Sun); 1946; Lewis Milestone

Sally and Saint Anne; 1952; Rudolph Mate

Salome; 1953; William Dieterle

Salty O'Rourke; 1945; Raoul Walsh

Salute; 1929; John Ford

Salute to France (Alleg. Doc); 1944; Garson Kanin and Jean Renoir

Salvation Nell; 1931; James Cruze

Sammy Going South; 1962; Alexander Mackendrick

Sammy the Way Out Seal; 1963; Norman Tokar

Samson and Delilah; 1949; Cecil B. de Mille

San Antonio; 1945; David Butler

San Diego I Love You; 1945; Reginald Le Borg

San Francisco; 1936; W. S. van Dyke

San Francisco (Doc); 1945; W. S. van Dyke

San Quentin; 1937; Lloyd Bacon

San Quentin; 1946; Gordon Douglas

Sanctuary; 1961; Tony Richardson

Sand Castle, The; 1960; Jerome Hill

Sand Pebbles, The; 1966; Robert Wise

Sanders of the River; 1935; Zoltan Korda

Sandpiper, The; 1965; Vincente Minnelli

Sands of Iwo Jima; 1949; Allan Dwan

Santa Fe; 1951; Irving Pichel

Santa Fe Trail; 1940; Michael Curtiz

Santiago; 1957; Gordon Douglas

Sap from Syracuse; 1930; Edward Sutherland

Sapphire; 1959; Basil Dearden

Saps at Sea; 1940; Gordon Douglas

Sarah and Son; 1930; Dorothy Arzner

Saratoga; 1937; Jack Conway

Saratoga Trunk; 1945; Sam Wood

Saskatchewan; 1954; Raoul Walsh

Satan Bug, The; 1964; John Sturges

Satan Meets a Lady; 1936; William Dieterle

Satan Never Sleeps; 1962; Leo McCarey

Saturday Night and Sunday Morning; 1960; Karel Reisz

Saturday Night Kid, The; 1929; Edward Sutherland

Saturday Night Out; 1963; Robert Hartford-Davis

Saturday's Children; 1929; Gregory La Cava

Saturday's Children; 1940; Vincent Sherman

Saturday's Hero; 1951; David Miller

Savage Innocents, The; 1961; Nicholas Ray

Savage Sam; 1963; Norman Tokar

Saxon Charm, The; 1948; Claude Binyon

Say It in French; 1938; Andrew L. Stone

Say One for Me; 1959; Frank Tashlin

Sayonara; 1957; Joshua Logan

Scandal in Paris, A; 1946; Douglas Sirk

Scandal Sheet; 1931; John Cromwell

Scandal Sheet; 1952; Phil Karlson

Scapegoat, The; 1958; Robert Hamer

Scaramouche; 1952; George Sidney

Scared Stiff; 1953; George Marshall

Scarface; 1932; Howard Hawks

Scarlet Clue, The; 1945; Phil Rosen

Scarlet Coat, The; 1955; John Sturges

Scarlet Dawn; 1932; William Dieterle

Scarlet Empress; 1934; Josef von Sternberg

Scarlet Hour, The; 1956; Michael Curtiz

Scarlet Pimpernel, The; 1933; Harold Young

Scarlet Street; 1945; Fritz Lang

Scavengers, The; 1959; John Cromwell

Scene of the Crime; 1949; Roy Rowland

Scent of Mystery; 1960; Jack Cardiff

School for Scoundrels; 1960; Robert Hamer

School for Secrets; 1946; Peter Ustinov

Scorpio Rising; 1966; Kenneth Anger

Scotland Yard; 1941; Norman Foster

Scotland Yard; 1930; William K. Howard

Scotland Yard Triumphs (One Epis); 1964; Clive Donner

Scoundrel, The; 1935; Charles MacArthur and Ben Hecht

Scream of Fear; 1961; Seth Holt

Screaming Mimi; 1958; Gerd Oswald

Scrooge; 1935; John Brahm

Sea Chase, The; 1955; John Farrow

Sea Devils; 1953; Raoul Walsh

Sea Hawk, The; 1940; Michael Curtiz

Sea of Grass, The; 1947; Elia Kazan

Sea Shall Not Have Them, The; 1953; Lewis Gilbert

Sea Wolf, The; 1941; Michael Curtiz

Sealed Verdict; 1947; Lewis Allen

Seance on a Wet Afternoon; 1964; Brian Forbes

Search, The; 1948; Fred Zinnemann

Searchers, The; 1956; John Ford

Searching Wind, The; 1946; William Dieterle

Seas Beneath, The; 1931; John Ford

Season of Passion; 1961; Leslie Norman

Second Chance; 1953; Rudolph Mate

Second Floor Mystery; 1930; Roy del Ruth

Second Greatest Sex, The; 1955; George Marshall

Second Time Around, The; 1961; Vincent Sherman

Seconds; 1966; John Frankenheimer

Secret Agent; 1936; Alfred Hitchcock

Secret Beyond the Door; 1948; Fritz Lang

Secret Bride; 1935; William Dieterle

Secret Ceremony; 1968; Joseph Losey

Secret Command; 1944; Edward Sutherland

Secret Door, The; 1962; Gilbert L. Kay

Secret Garden, The; 1949; Fred M. Wilcox

Secret Invasion, The; 1964; Roger Corman

Secret Life of an American Wife, The; 1968; George Axelrod

Secret Life of Walter Mitty; 1947; Norman Z. McLeod

Secret of My Success, The; 1965; Andrew L. Stone

Secret of the Chateau; 1935; Richard Thorpe

Secret of the Incas; 1954; Jerry Hopper

Secret Passion, The (Freud); 1962; John Huston

Secret People, The; 1950; Thorold Dickinson

Secret Place, The; 1956; Clive Donner

Secret Service; 1932; J. Walter Ruben

Secret Six, The; 1931; George Hill

Secret War of Harry Frigg; 1968; Jack Smight

Secret Ways, The; 1961; Phil Karlson

Secrets; 1933; Frank Borzage

Secrets of a Co-Ed; 1942; Joseph H.

Lewis
Secrets of the French Police; 1932; Edward Sutherland
Secrets of Wu Sin; 1933; Richard Thorpe
Seed; 1931; John Stahl
Sellout, The; 1951; Gerald Mayer
Seminole; 1953; Budd Boetticher
Senator Was Indiscreet, The; 1948; George F. Kaufman
Send Me No Flowers; 1964; Norman Jewison
Sensation; 1935; Brian D. Hurst
Sensation Hunters; 1933; Charles Vidor
Sensations of 1945; 1944; Andrew L. Stone
Separate Tables; 1958; Delbert Mann
Sepia Cinderella; 1947; Arthur Leonard
September Affair; 1950; William Dieterle
September Storm; 1960; Byron Haskin
Serenade; 1956; Anthony Mann
Sergeant Deadhead; 1965; Norman Taurog
Sergeant Madden; 1939; Josef von Sternberg
Sergeant Rutledge; 1960; John Ford
Sergeant Ryker; 1968; Buzz Kulik
Sergeant York; 1941; Howard Hawks
Sergeants Three; 1961; John Sturges
Servant, The; 1964; Joseph Losey
Servant's Entrance; 1934; Frank Lloyd
Service De Luxe; 1938; Rowland V. Lee
Service for Ladies; 1931; Alexander Korda
Set-Up, The; 1949; Robert Wise
Seven Brides for Seven Brothers; 1954; Stanley Donen
Seven Cities of Gold; 1955; Robert D. Webb
Seven Days in May; 1964; John Frankenheimer
Seven Days' Leave; 1930; Richard Wallace
Seven Days to Noon; 1948; John Boulting and Roy Boulting
Seven Men from Now; 1956; Budd Boetticher
Seven Eleven Ocean Drive; 1950; Joseph M. Newman
Seven Footprints to Satan; 1929; Benjamin Christensen
Seven Seas to Calais; 1962; Rudolph

Mate
Seven Sinners; 1940; Tay Garnett
Seven Sweethearts; 1942; Frank Borzage
Seven Thieves; 1960; Henry Hathaway
Seven Women; 1966; John Ford
Seven Women from Hell; 1961; Robert D. Webb
Seven Wonders of the World; 1956; Tay Garnett
Seven Year Itch, The; 1955; Billy Wilder
Seventh Cavalry, The; 1956; Joseph H. Lewis
Seventh Cross, The; 1944; Fred Zinnemann
Seventh Dawn, The; 1964; Lewis Gilbert
Seventh Heaven; 1937; Henry King
Seventh Veil, The; 1946; Compton Bennett
Seventh Victim, The; 1943; Mark Robson
Seventh Voyage of Sinbad; 1958; Nathan Juran
Sex and the Single Girl; 1964; Richard Quine
Sex Kittens Go to College; 1960; Albert Zugsmith
Shadow of a Doubt; 1943; Alfred Hitchcock
Shadow of the Thin Man; 1941; W. S. van Dyke
Shadow on the Mountain; 1931; Arthur Elton
Shadow on the Wall, The; 1948; Pat Jackson
Shadowed; 1946; John Sturges
Shadows; 1961; John Cassavetes
Shake Hands with the Devil; 1959; Michael Anderson
Shakedown, The; 1929; William Wyler
Shall We Dance; 1937; Mark Sandrich
Shamrock Hill; 1949; Arthur Dreifuss
Shane; 1953; George Stevens
Shanghai Cobra, The; 1945; Phil Karlson
Shanghai Express; 1932; Josef von Sternberg
Shanghai Gesture, The, 1941; Josef von Sternberg
She; 1935; Irving Pichel
She Couldn't Take It; 1935; Tay Garnett
She Done Him Wrong; 1933; Lowell Sherman

She Goes to War; 1929; Henry King

She Got What She Wanted; 1930; James Cruze

She Had to Eat; 1937; Malcolm St. Clair

She Knew All the Answers; 1940; Richard Wallace

She Loves Me Not; 1934; Elliott Nugent

She Married Her Boss; 1935; Gregory La Cava

She Wore a Yellow Ribbon; 1949; John Ford

She-Gods of Shark Reef; 1957; Roger Corman

She's Back on Broadway; 1953; Gordon Douglas

Sheepman, The; 1958; George Marshall

Sheik Steps Out, The; 1937; Irving Pichel

Shenandoah; 1965; Andrew McLaglen

Shepherd of the Hills, The; 1941; Henry Hathaway

Sheriff of Fractured Jaw, The; 1958; Raoul Walsh

Sherlock Holmes; 1932; William K. Howard

Sherlock Holmes and the Voice of Terror; 1942; John Rawlins

Shining Hour, The; 1938; Frank Borzage

Ship of Fools; 1965; Stanley Kramer

Ship's Cafe; 1935; Robert Florey

Shipmates Forever; 1935; Frank Borzage

Shock Corridor; 1963; Samuel Fuller

Shock Treatment; 1963; Denis Sanders

Shockproof; 1949; Douglas Sirk

Shoot First; 1953; Robert Parrish

Shoot to Kill; 1960; Michael Winner

Shop Around the Corner, The; 1940; Ernst Lubitsch

Shop Soiled (The Crowded Day); 1954; John Guillermin

Shopworn Angel; 1929; Richard Wallace

Shopworn Angel; 1938; H. C. Potter

Short Cut to Hell; 1956; James Cagney

Shot in the Dark, A; 1964; Blake Edwards

Shotgun; 1955; Leslie Selander

Show Boat; 1936; James Whale

Show Girl in Hollywood; 1930; Mervyn Le Roy

Show Goes On, The; 1935; Kurt Neumann

Show of Shows, The; 1929; John Adolfi

Show Them No Mercy; 1935; George Marshall

Showboat; 1929; Harry Pollard

Showboat; 1936; James Whale

Showboat; 1951; George Sidney

Shrike, The; 1955; José Ferrer

Side Show; 1931; Roy del Ruth

Side Street; 1929; Malcolm St. Clair

Side Street; 1949; Anthony Mann

Sidewalks of London (St. Martin's Lane); 1938; Tim Whelan

Siege at Red River; 1954; Rudolph Mate

Siege of Pinchgut, The; 1958; Harry Watt

Sign of the Cross, The; 1932; Cecil B. de Mille

Sign of the Pagan; 1954; Douglas Sirk

Sign of the Ram; 1948; John Sturges

Silencers, The; 1966; Phil Karlson

Silk Hat Kid; 1935; H. Bruce Humberstone

Silk Stockings; 1957; Rouben Mamoulian

Silver Bullet, The; 1942; Joseph H. Lewis

Silver City; 1951; Byron Haskin

Silver Cord; 1933; John Cromwell

Silver Lode; 1954; Allan Dwan

Silver Queen; 1942; Lloyd Bacon

Silver River; 1948; Raoul Walsh

Sin Takes a Holiday; 1930; Paul Stein

Sin Town; 1942; Ray Enright

Sinbad the Sailor; 1947; Richard Wallace

Since You Went Away; 1944; John Cromwell

Sincerely Yours; 1955; Gordon Douglas

Sinful Davey; 1969; John Huston

Sing Baby Sing; 1936; Sidney Lanfield

Sing Your Way Home; 1945; Anthony Mann

Sing Your Worries Away; 1942; Edward Sutherland

Singapore; 1947; John Brahm

Singapore Woman; 1941; Jean Negulesco

Singer Not the Song, The; 1960; Roy Baker

Singin' in the Rain; 1952; Stanley Donen and Gene Kelly

Singing Blacksmith, The; 1938; Edgar G. Ulmer

Singing Kid, The; 1936; William

Keighley

Singing Marine, The; 1937; Ray Enright

Singing Outlaw; 1937; Joseph H. Lewis

Single Standard, The; 1929; J. Robertson

Sinister Man, The; 1961; Clive Donner

Sink the Bismarck; 1960; Lewis Gilbert

Sinners in Paradise; 1938; James Whale

Sinners in the Sun; 1932; Alexander Hall

Sins of Rachel Cade, The; 1961; Gordon Douglas

Siren of Bagdad; 1953; Richard Quine

Siren of the Tropics; 1937; Dave Goldberg and Jack Goldberg

Sirocco; 1951; Curtis Bernhardt

Sisters, The; 1938; Anatole Litvak

Sitting Pretty; 1933; Harry Joe Brown

Sitting Pretty; 1948; Walter Lang

Six Bridges to Cross; 1955; Joseph Pevney

Six Hours to Live; 1932; William Dieterle

Six of a Kind; 1934; Leo McCarey

Skidoo; 1968; Otto Preminger

Skin Game, The; 1931; Alfred Hitchcock

Skipper Surprised His Wife, The; 1950; Elliott Nugent

Skippy; 1932; Norman Taurog

Skirts Ahoy; 1952; Sidney Lanfield

Sky Devils; 1932; Edward Sutherland

Sky's the Limit, The; 1943; Edward H. Griffith

Skylark; 1941; Mark Sandrich

Slattery's Hurricane; 1949; Andre de Toth

Slave Ship; 1937; Tay Garnett

Sleep My Love; 1948; Douglas Sirk

Sleeping Tiger, The; 1954; Joseph Losey

Slight Case of Larceny, A; 1953; Don Weis

Slight Case of Murder, A; 1938; Lloyd Bacon

Slightly French; 1949; Douglas Sirk

Slightly Honorable; 1940; Tay Garnett

Slightly Married; 1932; Richard Thorpe

Slightly Scarlet; 1956; Allan Dwan

Slime People, The; 1963; Robert Hutton

Small Town Girl; 1936; William Wellman

Small World of Sammy Lee; 1962; Kenneth Hughes

Smallest Show on Earth, The; 1957; Basil Dearden

Smart Woman; 1931; Gregory La Cava

Smart Woman; 1948; Edward A. Blatt

Smarty; 1934; Robert Florey

Smash-Up; 1947; Stuart Heisler

Smashing Time; 1967; Desmond Davis

Smilin' Through; 1932; Sidney Franklin

Smilin' Through; 1941; Frank Borzage

Smiling Lieutenant, The; 1931; Ernst Lubitsch

Smoke Jumpers; 1951; Joseph M. Newman

Smoky; 1946; Louis King

Smooth as Silk; 1946; Charles T. Barton

Snake Pit, The; 1949; Anatole Litvak

Snake Woman, The; 1960; Sidney Furie

Sniper, The; 1952; Edward Dmytryk

Snowball; 1960; Pat Jackson

Snows of Kilimanjaro, The; 1952 Henry King

So Big; 1932; William Wellman

So Big; 1953; Robert Wise

So Dark the Night; 1946; Joseph H. Lewis

So Ends Our Night; 1941; John Cromwell

So Evil, My Love; 1947; Lewis Allen

So Proudly We Hail; 1943; Mark Sandrich

So Red the Rose; 1935; King Vidor

So This Is Love; 1953; Gordon Douglas

So This Is New York; 1948; Richard Fleischer

So This Is Paris; 1954; Richard Quine

Soak the Rich; 1936; Ben Hecht

Social Lion; 1930; Edward Sutherland

Sodom and Gomorrah; 1963; Robert Aldrich and Sergio Leone

Soldier in the Rain; 1963; Ralph Nelson

Soldier of Fortune; 1955; Edward Dmytryk

Soldier's Plaything; 1931; Michael Curtiz

Soldiers Three; 1951; Tay Garnett

Solid Gold Cadillac; 1956; Richard

Quine

Solitaire Man; 1933; Jack Conway

Solomon and Sheba; 1959; King Vidor

Some Came Running; 1959; Vincente Minnelli

Some Like It Cool; 1961; Michael Winner

Some Like It Hot; 1959; Billy Wilder

Some People; 1962; Clive Donner

Somebody Up There Likes Me; 1956; Robert Wise

Someone to Remember; 1943; Robert Siodmak

Something for the Birds; 1952; Robert Wise

Something of Value; 1957; Richard Brooks

Something to Live For; 1952; George Stevens

Something to Shout About; 1943; Gregory Ratoff

Something to Sing About; 1937; Victor Schertzinger

Something Wild; 1961; Jack Garfein

Somewhere in the Night; 1946; Joseph Mankiewicz

Son of a Sailor; 1933; Lloyd Bacon

Son of Ali Baba; 1953; Kurt Neumann

Son of Dracula; 1943; Robert Siodmak

Son of Flubber; 1963; Robert Stevenson

Son of Frankenstein; 1939; Rowland V. Lee

Son of Fury; 1942; John Cromwell

Son of Kong; 1933; Ernest L. Schoesdack

Son of Paleface; 1952; Frank Tashlin

Son of the Gods; 1930; Frank Lloyd

Son-Daughter, The; 1932; Clarence Brown

Song and Dance Man, The; 1936; Allan Dwan

Song Is Born, A; 1948; Howard Hawks

Song O' My Heart; 1930; Frank Borzage

Song of Bernadette, The; 1944; Henry King

Song of Ceylon; 1934; Basil Wright

Song of Freedom; 1937; J. Elder Wills

Song of Love; 1947; Clarence Brown

Song of Songs; 1933; Rouben Mamoulian

Song of Surrender; 1949; Mitchell Leisen

Song of the Thin Man; 1947; Edward Buzzell

Song to Remember; 1945; Charles Vidor

Song Without End; 1960; George Cukor and Charles Vidor

Sons and Lovers; 1960; Jack Cardiff

Sons of Katie Elder; 1965; Henry Hathaway

Sophomore, The; 1929; Leo McCarey

Sorority Girl; 1957; Roger Corman

Sorority House; 1939; John Farrow

Sorry Wrong Number; 1948; Anatole Litvak

SOS Iceberg; 1933; Tay Garnett

Soul Kiss; 1930; Sidney Franklin

Souls at Sea; 1937; Henry Hathaway

Souls for Sale (Evils of Chinatown); 1963; Albert Zugsmith

Sound and the Fury, The; 1957; Martin Ritt

Sound of Fury, The; 1950; Cyril Endfield

Sound of Music, The; 1965; Robert Wise

Sound Off; 1952; Richard Quine

South Pacific; 1958; Joshua Logan

South Riding; 1938; Victor Saville

South Sea Rose; 1929; Allan Dwan

Southerner, The; 1945; Jean Renoir

Spanish Affair; 1958; Don Siegel

Spanish Earth, The; 1937; Joris Ivens

Spanish Gardener, The; 1956; Philip Leacock

Spanish Main, The; 1945; Frank Borzage

Spare the Rod; 1961; Leslie Norman

Sparrows Can't Sing; 1963; Joan Littlewood

Spartacus; 1960; Stanley Kubrick

Spawn of the North; 1938; Henry Hathaway

Special Agent; 1935; William Keighley

Special Delivery; 1955; John Brahm

Spectre of the Rose; 1946; Ben Hecht

Spell of the Hypnotist (Fright); 1957; W. Lee Wilder

Spellbound; 1945; Alfred Hitchcock

Spencer's Mountain; 1963; Delmer Daves

Spendthrift; 1936; Raoul Walsh

Spider and the Fly, The; 1951; Robert Hamer

Spider Woman, The; 1944; Roy William Neill

Spiral Road, The; 1962; Robert Mulligan

Spiral Staircase, The; 1946; Robert Siodmak

Spirit of St. Louis, The; 1957; Billy Wilder

Spirit of the People; 1940; Max Gordon

Spirit of West Point, The; 1947; Ralph Murphy

Spitfire; 1934; John Cromwell

Spitfire; 1943; Leslie Howard

Splendor in the Grass; 1961; Elia Kazan

Splendour; 1935; Elliott Nugent

Split Second; 1952; Dick Powell

Spoilers, The; 1930; Edwin Carewe and David Burton

Spoilers, The; 1942; Frank Lloyd

Spoilers, The; 1956; Jesse Hibbs

Spree; 1967; Mitchell Leisen

Spring in Park Lane; 1948; Herbert Wilcox

Spring Offensive (Doc); 1940; Humphrey Jennings

Spring Parade; 1940; Henry Koster

Spring Reunion; 1957; Robert Pirosh

Spring Song; 1947; Montgomery Tully

Springfield Rifle; 1952; Andre de Toth

Spy, The (The Bridge) (Short); 1932; Charles Vidor

Spy of Napoleon; 1936; Maurice Elvey

Spy 13; 1934; Richard Boleslavsky

Spy Ring, The; 1938; Joseph H. Lewis

Spy Who Came in From the Cold, The; 1965; Martin Ritt

Squadron 992; 1940; Harry Watt

Squall, The; 1929; Alexander Korda

Squaw Man, The; 1931; Cecil B. de Mille

St. Louis Blues; 1939; Raoul Walsh

St. Valentine's Day Massacre; 1967; Roger Corman

Stage Door; 1937; Gregory La Cava

Stage Fright; 1950; Alfred Hitchcock

Stage Struck; 1936; Busby Berkeley

Stage Struck; 1958; Sidney Lumet

Stagecoach; 1939; John Ford

Stagecoach; 1966; Gordon Douglas

Stagedoor Canteen; 1943; Frank Borzage

Stakeout on Dope Street; 1958; Irvin Kershner

Stalag 17; 1953; Billy Wilder

Stalking Moon, The; 1968; Robert Mulligan

Stand in; 1937; Tay Garnett

Stand Up and Fight; 1939; W. S. van Dyke

Standing Room Only; 1944; Sidney Lanfield

Stanley and Livingstone; 1939; Henry King

Star, The; 1953; Stuart Heisler

Star; 1968; Robert Wise

Star Dust; 1940; Walter Lang

Star in the Dust; 1956; Charles Haas

Star Is Born, A; 1937; William Wellman

Star Is Born, A; 1954; George Cukor

Star Maker, The; 1939; Roy del Ruth

Star of Midnight; 1935; Stephen Roberts

Star of Texas; 1953; Thomas H. Carr

Star Spangled Rhythm; 1943; George Marshall

Star Witness; 1931; William Wellman

Starlift; 1951; Roy del Ruth

Stars and Stripes Forever; 1952; Henry Koster

Stars in My Crown; 1950; Jacques Tourneur

Stars Look Down, The; 1939; Carol Reed

Stars over Broadway; 1935; William Keighley

State Department—File 649; 1949; Peter Stewart

State Fair; 1933; Henry King

State Fair (It Happened One Summer); 1945; Walter Lang

State Fair; 1962; José Ferrer

State of the Union; 1948; Frank Capra

Station Six-Sahara; 1964; Seth Holt

Stay Away, Joe; 1968; Peter Tewksbury

Steamboat 'Round the Bend; 1935; John Ford

Steel Against the Sky; 1941; Edward Sutherland

Steel Cage, The; 1954; Walter Doniger

Steel Claw, The; 1961; George Montgomery

Steel Helmet, The; 1950; Samuel Fuller

Steel Highway; 1930; William Wellman

Steel Trap, The; 1952; Andrew L. Stone

Stella Dallas; 1937; King Vidor

Stingaree; 1934; William Wellman

Stolen Heaven; 1938; Andrew L. Stone

Stolen Holiday; 1936; Michael Curtiz

Stolen Hours, The; 1963; Daniel Petrie

Stolen Sweets; 1934; Richard Thorpe

Stop Me Before I Kill; 1961; Val Guest

Stop Train 349; 1964; Rolf Haedrich

Stop You're Killing Me; 1953; Roy del Ruth

Storm, The; 1930; William Wyler

Storm Fear; 1956; Cornell Wilde

Storm in a Teacup; 1937; Victor Saville

Storm over the Nile; 1956; Zoltan Korda and Terence Young

Storm over the Tiber; 1952; Laslo Benedek

Stormy Weather; 1943; Andrew L. Stone

Story of Dr. Wassell, The; 1944; Cecil B. de Mille

Story of Esther Costello, The; 1957; David Miller

Story of GI Joe; 1945; William Wellman

Story of Louis Pasteur, The; 1936; William Dieterle

Story of Mankind, The; 1957; Irwin Allen

Story of Mandy, The; 1953; Alexander Mackendrick

Story of Three Loves, The; 1953; Vincente Minnelli and Gottfried Reinhardt

Story of Vernon and Irene Castle, The; 1939; H. C. Potter

Story of Will Rogers, The; 1952; Michael Curtiz

Story on Page One, The; 1960; Clifford Odets

Stranded; 1935; Frank Borzage

Strange Cargo; 1940; Frank Borzage

Strange Confession (The Imposter); 1943; Julien Duvivier

Strange Fascination; 1952; Hugo Haas

Strange Illusion; 1945; Edgar G. Ulmer

Strange Incident (Ox Bow Incident); 1943; William Wellman

Strange Interlude; 1932; Robert Z. Leonard

Strange Interpretation; 1946; Anthony Mann

Strange Lady in Town; 1955; Mervyn Le Roy

Strange Love of Martha Ivers; 1946; Lewis Milestone

Strange Love of Molly Louvain; 1932; Michael Curtiz

Strange One, The; 1957; Jack Garfein

Strange People; 1933; Richard Thorpe

Strange Wives; 1935; Richard Thorpe

Strange Woman, The; 1945; Edgar G. Ulmer

Stranger, The; 1946; Orson Welles

Stranger at My Door; 1956; William Witney

Stranger in Between, The; 1952; Charles Crichton

Stranger in Town, A; 1956; George Pollock

Stranger on Horseback; 1955; Jacques Tourneur

Stranger on the Prowl; 1953; Joseph Losey

Stranger on the Run; 1967; Don Siegel

Stranger Wore a Gun, The; 1953; Andre de Toth

Stranger's Return, The; 1933; King Vidor

Strangers All; 1935; Charles Vidor

Strangers in the City; 1962; Rick Carrier

Strangers in the Night; 1944; Anthony Mann

Strangers of the Evening; 1932; H. Bruce Humberstone

Strangers on a Train; 1951; Alfred Hitchcock

Strangers When We Meet; 1960; Richard Quine

Strangler, The; 1964; Burt Topper

Stranglehold; 1962; Lawrence Huntington

Stranglers of Bombay; 1959; Terence Fisher

Strategic Air Command; 1955; Anthony Mann

Stratton Story, The; 1949; Sam Wood

Strauss' Great Waltz; 1935; Alfred Hitchcock

Strawberry Blonde, The; 1941; Raoul Walsh

Street of Chance; 1930; John Cromwell

Street of Chance; 1942; Jack Hively

Street Scene; 1931; King Vidor

Street with No Name, The; 1948; William Keighley

Streetcar Named Desire, A; 1951; Elia Kazan

Strictly Dishonorable; 1931; John Stahl

Strictly Dynamite; 1934; Elliott Nugent

Strike Me Pink; 1936; Norman Taurog

Strike Up the Band; 1940; Busby

Berkeley

Stripper, The (Woman of Summer); 1963; Franklin Schaffner

Strong Boy; 1929; John Ford

Struggle, The; 1931; D. W. Griffith

Student Prince, The; 1954; Richard Thorpe

Studs Lonigan; 1960; Irving Lerner

Submarine Command; 1951; John Farrow

Submarine D-1; 1937; Lloyd Bacon

Submarine Patrol; 1938; John Ford

Subterraneans, The; 1960; Ranald MacDougall

Sudden Danger; 1955; Hubert Cornfield

Sudden Fear; 1952; David Miller

Suddenly It's Spring; 1946; Mitchell Leisen

Suddenly Last Summer; 1959; Joseph Mankiewicz

Suez; 1938; Allan Dwan

Suitable Case for Treatment; 1965; Karel Reisz

Sullivan's Travels; 1942; Preston Sturges

Sullivans, The (Fighting Sullivans); 1944; Lloyd Bacon

Summer and Smoke; 1960; Peter Glenville

Summer Holiday; 1948; Rouben Mamoulian

Summer Place, A; 1960; Delmer Daves

Summer Stock; 1950; Charles Walters

Summer Storm; 1944; Douglas Sirk

Summertime; 1955; David Lean

Sun Also Rises, The; 1957; Henry King

Sun Comes Up, The; 1948; Richard Thorpe

Sun Shines Bright, The; 1954; John Ford

Sunday Dinner for a Soldier; 1944; Lloyd Bacon

Sunday in New York; 1964; Peter Tewksbury

Sunday Punch; 1942; David Miller

Sunday Sinners; 1941; Arthur Dreifuss

Sundown; 1941; Henry Hathaway

Sundowners, The; 1960; Fred Zinnemann

Sunny Side Up; 1929; David Butler

Sunrise at Campobello; 1960; Vincent J. Donehue

Sunset Boulevard; 1950; Billy Wilder

Sunset Pass; 1933; Henry Hathaway

Sunshine Susie; 1931; Victor Saville

Surprise Package; 1960; Stanley Donen

Surrender; 1931; William K. Howard

Surrender; 1950; Allan Dwan

Susan and God; 1940; George Cukor

Susan Lennox, Her Fall and Rise; 1931; Robert Z. Leonard

Susan Slade; 1961; Delmer Daves

Suspense; 1947; Frank Tuttle

Suspicion; 1941; Alfred Hitchcock

Sutter's Gold; 1936; James Cruze

Suzy; 1936; George Fitzmaurice

Swamp Water; 1941; Jean Renoir

Swan, The; 1956; Charles Vidor

Swanee River; 1940; Sidney Lanfield

Sweepings; 1933; John Cromwell

Sweet Adeline; 1934; Mervyn Le Roy

Sweet and Lowdown; 1944; Archie Mayo

Sweet Bird of Youth; 1962; Richard Brooks

Sweet Ride, The; 1968; Harvey Hart

Sweet Smell of Success; 1957; Alexander Mackendrick

Sweethearts; 1938; W. S. van Dyke

Swimmer, The; 1968; Frank Perry

Swing High, Swing Low; 1937; Mitchell Leisen

Swing Parade of 1946; 1946; Phil Karlson

Swing Time; 1936; George Stevens

Swing Your Lady; 1938; Ray Enright

Swinger, The; 1966; George Sidney

Swiss Family Robinson, The; 1960; Ken Annakin

Swiss Miss; 1938; John Blystone

Sword of Lancelot; 1963; Cornell Wilde

Swordsman, The; 1947; Joseph H. Lewis

Sylvia; 1965; Gordon Douglas

Sylvia Scarlett; 1935; George Cukor

Symphony of Six Million; 1932; Gregory La Cava

Synanon; 1965; Richard Quine

Syncopation; 1942; William Dieterle

System, The; 1964; Michael Winner

T-Men; 1947; Anthony Mann

Tabu; 1931; F. W. Murnau and Robert Flaherty

Tail Spin; 1939; Roy del Ruth

Taggart; 1964; R. G. Springsteen

Take a Giant Step; 1960; Philip Leacock

Take a Letter, Darling; 1942; Mitchell

Leisen

Take Care of My Little Girl; 1951; Jean Negulesco

Take Me Out to the Ball Game; 1949; Busby Berkeley

Take Me to Town; 1953; Douglas Sirk

Take One False Step; 1949; Chester Erskine

Take the High Ground; 1953; Richard Brooks

Tale of Five Cities, A; 1951; Montgomery Tully

Tale of Two Cities, A; 1935; Jack Conway

Tale of Two Cities, A; 1957; Ralph Thomas

Tales of Hoffman; 1952; Michael Powell

Tales of Manhattan; 1942; Julien Duvivier

Talk of the Devil; 1937; Carol Reed

Talk of the Town; 1942; George Stevens

Tall Lie, The; 1952; Paul Henreid

Tall Men, The; 1955; Raoul Walsh

Tall Story; 1960; Joshua Logan

Tall T, The; 1957; Budd Boetticher

Tall Target, The; 1951; Anthony Mann

Tamahine; 1963; Philip Leacock

Taming of the Shrew, The; 1929; Samuel Taylor

Tanganyika; 1954; Andre de Toth

Tank Commandos; 1959; Burt Topper

Tank Force; 1958; Terence Young

Tarantula; 1956; Jack Arnold

Taras Bulba; 1962; J. Lee Thompson

Tarawa Beachhead; 1958; Paul Wendkos

Target for Tonight; 1941; Harry Watt

Tarnished Angels, The; 1958; Douglas Sirk

Tarnished Heroes; 1961; Ernest Morris

Tarnished Lady; 1931; George Cukor

Tartars, The; 1960; Richard Thorpe

Tarzan and the Amazons; 1945; Kurt Neumann

Tarzan and the Leopard Woman; 1946; Kurt Neumann

Tarzan Escapes; 1936; Richard Thorpe

Tarzan Finds a Son; 1939; Richard Thorpe

Tarzan the Ape Man; 1932; W. S. van Dyke

Tarzan the Ape Man; 1959; Joseph M.

Newman

Tarzan's New York Adventure; 1942; Richard Thorpe

Tarzan's Peril; 1951; Byron Haskin

Task Force; 1949; Delmer Daves

Taste of Fear; 1962; Seth Holt

Taste of Honey; 1962; Tony Richardson

Taxi; 1932; Roy del Ruth

Taza, Son of Cochise; 1954; Douglas Sirk

Tea and Sympathy; 1956; Vincente Minnelli

Teacher Was a Sexpot; 1960; Albert Zugsmith

Teacher's Pet; 1952; Fred Seaton

Teahouse of the August Moon, The; 1956; Daniel Mann

Teen Age Rebel; 1956; Edmund Goulding

Teenage Doll; 1957; Roger Corman

Tell England; 1931; Anthony Asquith and Geoffrey Barkas

Tell Me Lies; 1968; Peter Brook

Tell No Tales; 1939; Leslie Fenton

Ten Commandments, The; 1956; Cecil B. de Mille

Tender Comrade; 1943; Edward Dmytryk

Ten Gentlemen from the West Point; 1942; Henry Hathaway

Ten Dollar Raise; 1935; George Marshall

Ten Little Indians; 1965; George Pollock

Ten North Frederick; 1958; Philip Dunne

Ten Seconds to Hell; 1959; Robert Aldrich

Ten Wanted Men; 1955; H. Bruce Humberstone

Tender Is the Night; 1962; Henry King

Tender Trap, The; 1955; Charles Walters

Tenderfoot, The; 1932; Ray Enright

Tennessee Champ; 1954; Fred M. Wilcox

Tennessee Johnson (Man on America's Conscience, The); 1942; William Dieterle

Tennessee's Partner; 1955; Allan Dwan

Teresa; 1951; Fred Zinnemann

Term of Trial; 1963; Peter Glenville

Terminus (Short); 1960; John Schlesinger

Terrible Beauty, A (Night Fighters,

The); 1960; Tay Garnett

Terror in a Texas Town; 1958; Joseph H. Lewis

Terror of the Tongs; 1961; Anthony Bushell

Terror on a Train (Time Bomb); 1953; Ted Tetzlaff

Tess of the Storm Country; 1932; Alfred Santell

Terror Street; 1953; Montgomery Tully

Test Riot; 1938; Victor Fleming

Texan, The; 1930; John Cromwell

Texas Carnival; 1951; Charles Walters

Texas Rangers, The; 1936; King Vidor

Texas Rangers; 1951; Phil Karlson

Texas Stagecoach; 1940; Joseph H. Lewis

Thank You Mister Moto; 1937; Norman Foster

Thank Your Lucky Stars; 1943; David Butler

Thanks a Million; 1935; Roy del Ruth

That Brennan Girl; 1946; Alfred Santell

That Certain Woman; 1937; Edmund Goulding

That Darn Cat; 1965; Robert Stevenson

That Funny Feeling; 1965; Richard Thorpe

That Gang of Mine; 1940; Joseph H. Lewis

That Hamilton Woman (Lady Hamilton); 1941; Alexander Korda

That I May Live; 1937; Allan Dwan

That Kind of Girl; 1962; Robert Hartford-Davis

That Kind of Woman; 1959; Sidney Lumet

That Lady; 1955; Terence Young

That Lady in Ermine; 1948; Ernst Lubitsch and Otto Preminger

That Touch of Mink; 1962; Delbert Mann

That Uncertain Feeling; 1941; Ernst Lubitsch

That's My Boy; 1952; Hal Walker

That's My Man; 1946; Frank Borzage

Their Big Moment; 1934; James Cruze

Thelma Jordan; 1949; Robert Siodmak

Them; 1954; Gordon Douglas

There Goes Kelly; 1945; Phil Karlson

There Goes My Heart; 1938; Norman Z. McLeod

There's Always Tomorrow; 1956; Douglas Sirk

There's No Business like Show Business; 1954; Walter Lang

These Are the Damned; 1965; Joseph Losey

These High Grey Walls; 1939; Charles Vidor

These Thousand Hills; 1959; Richard Fleischer

These Three; 1936; William Wyler

They All Come Out; 1939; Jacques Tourneur

They All Kissed the Bride; 1942; Alexander Hall

They Came from Outer Space; 1950; Jack Arnold

They Came to Cordura; 1959; Robert Rossen

They Dare Not Love; 1941; James Whale

They Died with Their Boots On; 1941; Raoul Walsh

They Drive by Night; 1940; Raoul Walsh

They Flew Alone; 1942; Herbert Wilcox

They Gave Him a Gun; 1937; W. S. van Dyke

They Had to See Paris; 1929; Frank Borzage

They Knew What They Wanted; 1940; Garson Kanin

They Learned About Women; 1930; Jack Conway

They Live by Night; 1949; Nicholas Ray

They Live in Fear; 1944; Josef Berne

They Made Me a Criminal; 1939; Busby Berkeley

They Met in Bombay; 1941; Clarence Brown

They Rode West; 1954; Phil Karlson

They Were Expendable; 1945; John Ford

They Were Not Divided; 1951; Terence Young

They Were Sisters; 1945; Arthur Crabtree

They Who Dare; 1955; Lewis Milestone

They Won't Believe Me; 1947; Irving Pichel

They Won't Forget; 1937; Mervyn Le Roy

Thief of Bagdad, The; 1940; Zoltan Korda

Thief of Baghdad; 1961; Arthur Lubin

Thief of Venice, The; 1951; John Brahm

Thieves Highway; 1949; Jules Dassin

Thin Man, The; 1934; W. S. van Dyke

Thin Man Goes Home, The; 1944; Richard Thorpe

Thin Red Line, The; 1964; Andrew Marton

Thing, The; 1951; Christian Nyby

Things to Come; 1936; William Cameron Menzies

Think Fast Mister Moto; 1937; Norman Foster

Third Day, The; 1965; Jack Smight

Third Man, The; 1950; Carol Reed

Third Voice, The; 1960; Hubert Cornfield

Thirteen Hours by Air; 1936; Mitchell Leisen

Thirteen Rue Madeleine; 1946; Henry Hathaway

Thirteen West Street; 1962; Philip Leacock

Thirteenth Chair; 1929; Tod Browning

Thirteenth Hour, The; 1947; William Clemens

Thirteenth Letter, The; 1950; Otto Preminger

Thirty; 1959; Jack Webb

Thirty-Day Princess; 1934; Marion Gering

Thirty-nine Steps, The; 1935; Alfred Hitchcock

Thirty-nine Steps, The; 1959; Ralph Thomas

Thirty-six Hours; 1964; George Seaton

This Above All; 1942; Anatole Litvak

This Angry Age; 1958; René Clement

This Could Be the Night; 1957; Robert Wise

This Day and Age; 1933; Cecil B. de Mille

This Earth Is Mine; 1959; Henry King

This England; 1941; David MacDonald

This Gun for Hire; 1936; Robert Florey

This Gun for Hire; 1942; Frank Tuttle

This Happy Breed; 1947; David Lean

This Happy Feeling; 1958; Blake Edwards

This Is Korea (Doc); 1951; John Ford

This Is My Love; 1954; Stuart Heisler

This Is My Street; 1964; Sidney Hayers

This Is the Army; 1943; Michael Curtiz

This Is the Night; 1932; Frank Tuttle

This Island Earth; 1955; Joseph M. Newman

This Land Is Mine; 1943; Jean Renoir

This Love of Ours; 1945; William Dieterle

This Man in Paris; 1939; David MacDonald

This Man Is Dangerous; 1952; Felix Feist

This Man Is Mine; 1934; John Cromwell

This Man Is News; 1938; David MacDonald

This Man Reuter (Dispatch From Reuters, A); 1940; William Dieterle

This Man's Navy; 1945; William Wellman

This Reckless Age; 1932; Frank Tuttle

This Side of Heaven; 1934; William K. Howard

This Sporting Life; 1963; Lindsay Anderson

This Thing Called Love; 1929; Paul Stein

This Was Japan; 1945; Basil Wright

This Way Please; 1937; Robert Florey

Thomas Crown Affair, The; 1968; Norman Jewison

Thoroughbreds Don't Cry; 1937; Alfred E. Green

Those Calloways; 1965; Norman Tokar

Those Magnificent Men in Their Flying Machines; 1965; Ken Annakin

Those We Love; 1932; Robert Florey

Thousand Clowns, A; 1965; Fred Coe

Thousand Eyes of Dr. Mabuse, The; 1961; Fritz Lang

Thousands Cheer; 1943; George Sidney

Three Brave Men; 1956; Philip Dunne

Three Came Home; 1950; Jean Negulesco

Three Cheers for the Irish; 1940; Lloyd Bacon

Three Coins in the Fountain; 1954; Jean Negulesco

Three Comrades; 1938; Frank Borzage

Three Cornered Moon; 1933; Elliott Nugent

Three Daring Daughters; 1948; Fred M. Wilcox

Three Faces East; 1930; Roy del Ruth

Three Faces of Eve, The; 1957; Nunnally Johnson

Three for the Show; 1955; H. C. Potter

Three Ghosts; 1935; H. Bruce Humberstone

Three Godfathers; 1948; John Ford

Three Guys Named Mike; 1951; Charles Walters

Three Hats for Lisa; 1965; Sidney Hayers

Three Hundred Spartans, The; 1962; Rudolph Mate

Three Husbands; 1950; Irving Reis

Three Installations (Short); 1951; Lindsay Anderson

Three Little Words; 1950; Richard Thorpe

Three Maxims, The; 1936; Herbert Wilcox

Three Men in a Boat; 1957; Ken Annakin

Three Men on a Horse; 1936; Mervyn Le Roy and Archie Mayo

Three Musketeers, The; 1939; Allan Dwan

Three Musketeers, The; 1948; George Sidney

Three on a Couch; 1966; Jerry Lewis

Three on a Match; 1932; Mervyn Le Roy

Three Passions; 1929; Rex Ingram

Three Ring Circus; 1954; Joseph Pevney

Three Sailors and a Girl; 1953; Roy del Ruth

Three Secrets; 1950; Robert Wise

Three Smart Girls; 1937; Henry Koster

Three Smart Girls Grow Up; 1939; Henry Koster

Three Strangers; 1946; Jean Negulesco

Three Stripes in the Sun; 1955; Richard Murphy

Three Violent People; 1956; Rudolph Mate

Three Worlds of Gulliver; 1960; Jack Sher

Three-ten to Yuma; 1957; Delmer Daves

Thrill of It All, The; 1963; Norman Jewison

Thrill of Youth; 1932; Richard Thorpe

Thru Different Eyes; 1942; Thomas Loring

Thunder Bay; 1953; Anthony Mann

Thunder Below; 1932; Richard Wallace

Thunder Birds; 1942; William Wellman

Thunder of Drums; 1961; Joseph M. Newman

Thunder on the Hill; 1951; Douglas Sirk

Thunder over the Plains; 1953; Andre de Toth

Thunder Road; 1958; Arthur Ripley

Thunder Rock; 1944; John Boulting and Roy Boulting

Thunderball; 1965; Terence Young

Thunderbolt; 1929; Josef von Sternberg

Thunderhoof; 1948; Phil Karlson

Thundering Herd; 1934; Henry Hathaway

Thursday's Children (Short); 1953; Lindsay Anderson and G. Brenton

Ticket to Tomahawk, A; 1950; Richard Sale

Tickle Me; 1965; Norman Taurog

Ticklish Affair, A; 1963; George Sidney

Tide of Empire; 1929; Allan Dwan

Tiger Bay; 1933; J. Elder Wills

Tiger Bay; 1959; J. Lee Thompson

Tiger Shark; 1932; Howard Hawks

Tiger Walks, A; 1964; Norman Tokar

Tight Little Island; 1950; Alexander Mackendrick

Tight Spot; 1955; Phil Karlson

Till the Clouds Roll By; 1946; Richard Whorf

Till the End of Time; 1946; Edward Dmytryk

Till We Meet Again; 1940; Edmund Goulding

Till We Meet Again; 1944; Frank Borzage

Timberjack; 1955; Joseph Kane

Timbuktu; 1959; Jacques Tourneur

Time Bomb (Terror on a Train); 1953; Ted Tetzlaff

Time Gentlemen Please; 1952; Lewis Gilbert

Time Limit; 1957; Karl Malden

Time Lost and Time Remembered (I Was Happy Here); 1966; Desmond Davis

Time Machine, The; 1960; George Pal

Time of Your Life, The; 1948; H. C. Potter

Time Out for Romance; 1937; Malcolm St. Clair

Time Out of Mind; 1947; Robert Siodmak

Time Out of War (Short); 1954; Denis Sanders

Time to Love and a Time to Die, A; 1958; Douglas Sirk

Time Without Pity; 1957; Joseph Losey

Timetable; 1955; Mark Stevens

Tin Pan Alley; 1940; Walter Lang

Tin Star, The; 1957; Anthony Mann

Tingler, The; 1959; William Castle

Titanic; 1953; Jean Negulesco

Titfield Thunderbolt, The; 1953; Charles Crichton

Tip on a Dead Jockey; 1957; Richard Thorpe

To Be a Man; 1962; Irving Lerner

To Be or Not to Be; 1942; Ernst Lubitsch

To Catch a Thief; 1955; Alfred Hitchcock

To Each His Own; 1946; Mitchell Leisen

To Have and Have Not; 1944; Howard Hawks

To Hell and Back; 1955; Jesse Hibbs

To Kill a Mockingbird; 1963; Robert Mulligan

To Mary with Love; 1936; John Cromwell

To Paris with Love; 1955; Robert Hamer

To Please a Lady; 1950; Clarence Brown

To Sir, With Love; 1967; James Clavell

To the Last Man; 1933; Henry Hathaway

To the Victor; 1948; Delmer Daves

Toast of New York; 1937; Rowland V. Lee

Tobacco Road; 1941; John Ford

Today We Live; 1933; Howard Hawks

Together Again; 1944; Charles Vidor

Tokyo File 212; 1951; Dorrell McGowan and Stuart McGowan

Tokyo Joe; 1949; Stuart Heisler

Tom Brown of Culver; 1932; William Wyler

Tom Brown's School Days; 1940; Robert Stevenson

Tom Jones; 1963; Tony Richardson

Tom Sawyer; 1930; John Cromwell

Tom Thumb; 1958; George Pal

Tom, Dick and Harry; 1941; Garson Kanin

Tomorrow and Forever; 1945; Irving Pichel

Tomorrow and Tomorrow; 1932; Richard Wallace

Tomorrow Is Another Day; 1951; Felix Feist

Tomorrow the World; 1944; Leslie Fenton

Tomorrow We Live; 1942; Edgar G. Ulmer

Tonight or Never; 1931; Mervyn Le Roy

Tonight We Raid Calais; 1943; John Brahm

Tonight We Sing; 1953; Mitchell Leisen

Tony Rome; 1967; Gordon Douglas

Too Hot to Handle; 1938; Jack Conway

Too Late Blues; 1962; John Cassavetes

Too Late for Tears; 1949; Byron Haskin

Too Much Harmony; 1933; Edward Sutherland

Too Much Too Soon; 1958; Art Napoleon

Too Young to Love; 1961; Muriel Box

Too Young to Marry; 1931; Mervyn Le Roy

Top Hat; 1935; Mark Sandrich

Top o' the Morning; 1949; David Miller

Top Secret Affair; 1957; H. C. Potter

Top Speed; 1930; Mervyn Le Roy

Topaz; 1969; Alfred Hitchcock

Topaze; 1933; Harry d'Arrast

Topper; 1937; Norman Z. McLeod

Topper Returns; 1941; Roy del Ruth

Topper Takes a Trip; 1938; Norman Z. McLeod

Torch Song; 1953; Charles Walters

Torment; 1949; John Guillermin

Tormented; 1960; Bert I. Gordon

Torn Curtain; 1966; Alfred Hitchcock

Tornado; 1943; William Berke

Torpedo Alley; 1953; Lew Landers

Torrid Zone; 1940; William Keighley

Tortilla Flat; 1942; Victor Fleming

Touch of Evil; 1958; Orson Welles

Touch of Larceny, A; 1959; Guy Hamilton

Toughest Man in Arizona, The; 1953; R. G. Springsteen

Tovarich; 1937; Anatole Litvak

Toward the Unknown; 1956; Mervyn Le Roy

Tower of London; 1940; Rowland V. Lee

Tower of London; 1962; Roger Corman

Town, The (Doc); 1944; Josef von Sternberg

Town like Alice, A; 1954; J. Lee Thompson

Town on Trial; 1956; John Guillermin

Town Tamer; 1965; Leslie Selander

Town Without Pity; 1961; Gottfried Reinhardt

Toy Tiger; 1956; Jerry Hopper

Toys in the Attic; 1963; George Roy Hill

Track of the Cat; 1954; William Wellman

Track the Man Down; 1956; R. G. Springsteen

Trade Winds; 1938; Tay Garnett

Trader Horn; 1931; W. S. van Dyke

Trail of the Lonesome Pine, The; 1936; Henry Hathaway

Trail of the Vigilantes; 1940; Allan Dwan

Train, The; 1964; John Frankenheimer

Traitors, The; 1963; Robert Tronson

Transatlantic; 1931; William K. Howard

Trapeze; 1956; Carol Reed

Trapped; 1949; Richard Fleischer

Traveller's Joy; 1949; Ralph Thomas

Treasure Island; 1934; Victor Fleming

Treasure Island; 1950; Byron Haskin

Treasure of Lost Canyon, The; 1952; Ted Tetzlaff

Treasure of Pancho Villa; 1955; George Sherman

Treasure of the Golden Condor; 1953; Delmer Daves

Treasure of Ruby Hills; 1955; Frank McDonald

Treasure of the Sierra Madre, The; 1948; John Huston

Tree Grows in Brooklyn, A; 1945; Elia Kazan

Trent's Last Case; 1929; Howard Hawks

Trial; 1955; Mark Robson

Trial, The; 1963; Orson Welles

Trial and Error; 1962; Jerome Hill

Trial of Vivienne Ware; 1932; William K. Howard

Trials of Oscar Wilde, The; 1960; Kenneth Hughes

Tribute to a Bad Man; 1956; Robert Wise

Trip, The; 1967; Roger Corman

Trip to Paris, A; 1938; Malcolm St. Clair

Trouble Along the Way; 1953; Michael Curtiz

Trouble at 16 (Platinum High School); 1960; Albert Zugsmith

Trouble in Paradise; 1932; Ernst Lubitsch

Trouble with Harry, The; 1955; Alfred Hitchcock

Troublemaker, The; 1964; Theodore J. Flicker

True Confession; 1937; Wesley Ruggles

True Glory, The; 1945; Garson Kanin and Carol Reed

True Story of Jesse James, The; 1957; Nicholas Ray

Trunk Conveyor (Short); 1954; Lindsay Anderson

Truth About Spring, The; 1965; Richard Thorpe

Tudor Rose; 1936; Robert Stevenson

Tugboat Annie; 1933; Mervyn Le Roy

Tulsa; 1949; Stuart Heisler

Tunes of Glory; 1960; Ronald Neame

Tunnel 28 (Escape from East Berlin); 1962; Robert Siodmak

Tunnel of Love; 1958; Gene Kelly

Turn of the Furrow (Doc); 1944; Peter Baylis

Turn the Key Softly; 1953; Jack Lee

Turning Point, The; 1952; William Dieterle

Tuttles of Tahiti, The; 1942; Charles Vidor

Twelve Angry Men; 1957; Sidney Lumet

Twelve O'clock High; 1950; Henry King

Twentieth Century; 1934; Howard Hawks

Twenty Million Miles to Earth; 1957; Nathan Juran

Twenty Mule Team; 1940; Richard Thorpe

Twenty One Days Together; 1940; Basil Dean

Twenty Plus Two; 1961; Joseph M. Newman

Twenty Thousand Leagues Under the Sea; 1954; Richard Fleischer

Twenty Thousand Years in Sing Sing; 1933; Michael Curtiz

Twenty-three Paces to Baker Street; 1956; Henry Hathaway

Twist of Fate; 1954; David Miller

Two Against the World; 1932; Archie Mayo

Two Alone; 1934; Elliott Nugent

Two and Two Make Six; 1960; Freddie Francis

Two Before Zero; 1962; William Faralla

Two Black Sheep; 1935; Arthur Lubin

Two Down, One to Go (Doc); 1945; Frank Capra

Two Faces of Dr. Jekyll; 1960; Terence Fisher

Two Fisted; 1935; James Cruze

Two Flags West; 1950; Robert Wise

Two for the Road; 1967; Stanley Donen

Two for the Seesaw; 1962; Robert Wise

Two for Tonight; 1935; Frank Tuttle

Two Guns and a Badge; 1954; Lewis D. Collins

Two in a Taxi; 1941; Robert Florey

Two Left Feet; 1964; Roy Baker

Two Loves; 1961; Charles Walters

Two Men; 1934; John Farrow

Two Mrs. Carrolls, The; 1947; Peter Godfrey

Two O'Clock Courage; 1945; Anthony Mann

Two on the Tiles; 1950; John Guillermin

Two Rode Together; 1961; John Ford

Two Seconds; 1932; Mervyn Le Roy

Two Sinners; 1935; Arthur Lubin

Two Smart People; 1946; Jules Dassin

Two Thousand and One—A Space Odyssey; 1968; Stanley Kubrick

Two Weeks in Another Town; 1962; Vincente Minnelli

Two Weeks to Live; 1943; Malcolm St. Clair

Two Years Before the Mast; 1946; John Farrow

Two-Faced Woman; 1941; George Cukor

Two-Fisted Rangers; 1940; Joseph H. Lewis

Two-Headed Spy, The; 1959; Andre de Toth

Two-Way Stretch; 1961; Robert Day

Twonky, The; 1953; Arch Oboler

Tycoon; 1947; Richard Wallace

Ugly American, The; 1963; George Englund

Uncertain Glory; 1944; Raoul Walsh

Unchained; 1955; Hall Bartlett

Uncle, The; 1966; Desmond Davis

Uncle Harry; 1945; Robert Siodmak

Unconquered; 1947; Cecil B. de Mille

Undead, The; 1958; Roger Corman

Under a Texas Moon; 1930; Michael Curtiz

Under Capricorn; 1949; Alfred Hitchcock

Under Eighteen; 1932; Archie Mayo

Under Fire; 1957; James B. Clark

Under My Skin; 1950; Jean Negulesco

Under Pressure; 1935; Raoul Walsh

Under Pup, The; 1939; Richard Wallace

Under the Red Robe; 1937; Victor Seastrom

Under the Tonto Rim; 1933; Henry Hathaway

Under the Yum Yum Tree; 1963; David Swift

Under Two Flags; 1936; Frank Lloyd

Under Your Spell; 1936; Otto Preminger

Undercover Man, The; 1949; Joseph H. Lewis

Undercurrent; 1946; Vincente Minnelli

Underground; 1930; Anthony Asquith

Undertow; 1949; William Castle

Underwater; 1955; John Sturges

Underworld U.S.A.; 1961; Samuel Fuller

Undying Monster, The; 1942; John Brahm

Unearthly Stranger; 1963; John Krish

Unfaithful; 1931; John Cromwell

Unfaithful, The; 1947; Vincent Sherman

Unfaithfully Yours; 1948; Preston Sturges

Unfinished Business; 1941; Gregory La Cava

Unforgiven, The; 1960; John Huston

Unguarded Moment, The; 1956; Harry Keller

Unholy Garden, The; 1931; George Fitzmaurice

Unholy Partners; 1941; Mervyn Le Roy

Unholy Three, The; 1930; Jack Conway

Unholy Wife; 1957; John Farrow

Uninvited, The; 1944; Lewis Allen

Union Pacific; 1939; Cecil B. de Mille

Union Station; 1949; Rudolph Mate

Unknown Guest; 1943; Kurt Neumann

Unmarried; 1939; Kurt Neumann

Unsinkable Molly Brown, The; 1964; Charles Walters

Unsuspected, The; 1947; Michael Curtiz

Untamed; 1929; Jack Conway

Untamed; 1955; Henry King

Untamed Frontier; 1952; Hugo Fregonese

Until I Die; 1940; Ben Hecht

Until They Sail; 1957; Robert Wise

Up from the Beach; 1965; Robert Parrish

Up in Arms; 1944; Elliott Nugent

Up in Mabel's Room; 1944; Allan Dwan

Up Periscope; 1959; Gordon Douglas

Up Pops the Devil; 1931; Edward Sutherland

Up the Creek; 1958; Val Guest

Up the Down Staircase; 1967; Robert Mulligan

Up the River; 1930; John Ford

Upper World; 1934; Roy del Ruth

Uptown New York; 1932; Victor Schertzinger

Upturned Glass, The; 1947; Lawrence Huntington

USA (The Inspector General); 1949; Henry Koster

Vacation from Marriage; 1945; Alexander Korda

Vagabond King, The; 1930; Ludwig Berger

Vagabond King, The; 1956; Michael Curtiz

Valerie; 1957; Gerd Oswald

Valiant, The; 1929; William K. Howard

Valiant, The; 1962; Roy Baker

Valley of Decision, The; 1945; Tay Garnett

Valley of the Eagles, The; 1952; Terence Young

Valley of the Giants; 1938; William Keighley

Vanessa—Her Love Story; 1935; William K. Howard

Vanishing Virginian, The; 1941; Frank Borzage

Variety Girl; 1947; George Marshall

Varsity Show; 1937; William Keighley

Venetian Bird; 1953; Ralph Thomas

Vengeance Valley; 1951; Richard Thorpe

Vera Cruz; 1954; Robert Aldrich

Verboten; 1960; Samuel Fuller

Verdict, The; 1946; Don Siegel

Vertigo; 1958; Alfred Hitchcock

Very Honorable Man, A; 1934; Lloyd Bacon

Very Important Person; 1961; Ken Annakin

Very Special Favor, A; 1965; Michael Gordon

Vice Squad; 1931; John Cromwell

Vice Squad; 1953; Arnold Laven

Vice Versa; 1948; Peter Ustinov

Vicious Years, The; 1950; Robert Florey

Victim; 1961; Basil Dearden

Victoria the Great; 1937; Herbert Wilcox

Victors, The; 1962; Carl Foreman

Victory; 1940; John Cromwell

View from Pompey's Head, The; 1955; Philip Dunne

View from the Bridge; 1962; Sidney Lumet

Vigil in the Night; 1940; George Stevens

Vikings, The; 1958; Richard Fleischer

Villa Rides; 1968; Buzz Kulik

Village Tale; 1935; John Cromwell

Violent Men, The; 1955; Rudolph Mate

Violent Moment; 1958; Sidney Hayers

Violent Playground; 1957; Basil Dearden

Violent Saturday; 1955; Richard Fleischer

VIP'S, The; 1963; Anthony Asquith

Virgin Island; 1958; Pat Jackson

Virgin Queen, The; 1956; Henry Koster

Virginia; 1941; Edward H. Griffith

Virginia City; 1940; Michael Curtiz

Virginian, The; 1929; Victor Fleming

Virtue; 1932; Eddie Buzzell

Virtuous Sin; 1930; George Cukor and Louis Gasnier

Visit, The; 1964; Bernard Wicki

Visit to a Small Planet; 1960; Norman Taurog

Viva Cisco Kid; 1940; Norman Foster

Viva Las Vegas (Love in Las Vegas); 1964; George Sidney

Viva Villa; 1934; Howard Hawks and Jack Conway

Viva Zapata; 1952; Elia Kazan

Vivacious Lady; 1938; George Stevens

Voice in the Wind; 1944; Arthur Ripley

Voice of Bugle Ann; 1936; Richard Thorpe

Voice of the Turtle; 1948; Irving Rapper

Voice of the World; 1932; Arthur Elton

Volcano; 1953; William Dieterle

Voltaire; 1933; John G. Adolphi

Voodoo Island; 1957; Reginald Le Borg

Von Ryan's Express; 1965; Mark Robson

Wackiest Ship in the Army, The; 1960; Richard Murphy

Wagonmaster; 1950; John Ford

Wagons Roll at Night, The; 1941; Ray Enright

Waikiki Wedding; 1937; Frank Tuttle

Wait Till the Sun Shines Nellie; 1952; Henry King

Wait Until Dark; 1967; Terence Young

Wake Island; 1942; John Farrow

Wake Me When It's Over; 1960; Mervyn Le Roy

Wake of the Red Witch; 1948; Edward Ludwig

Wake Up and Dream; 1934; Kurt Neumann

Wake Up and Dream; 1945; Lloyd Bacon

Wake Up and Live; 1937; Sidney Lanfield

Wakefield Express (Short); 1952; Lindsay Anderson

Walk a Crooked Mile; 1948; Gordon Douglas

Walk, Don't Run; 1966; Charles Walters

Walk East on Beacon; 1952; Alfred Werker

Walk in the Sun (Salerno Beachhead); 1946; Lewis Milestone

Walk like a Dragon; 1960; James Clavell

Walk on the Wild Side; 1962; Edward Dmytryk

Walk Softly Stranger; 1950; Robert Stevenson

Walking Dead, The; 1936; Michael Curtiz

Walking down Broadway; 1932; Erich von Stroheim

Walking Hills, The; 1949; John Sturges

Walking My Baby Back Home; 1953; Lloyd Bacon

Walking on Air; 1946; Aveling Ginever

Walls of Jericho, The; 1947; John Stahl

Waltz of the Toreadors; 1962; John Guillermin

Wanda, Elyse, and Patti; 1944; John Farrow

Wanted for Murder; 1945; Lawrence Huntington

War and Peace; 1956; King Vidor

War Arrow; 1954; George Sherman

War Comes to America (Doc); 1945; Anatole Litvak

War Game, The; 1967; Peter Watkins

War Hero; 1958; Burt Topper

War Hunt; 1962; Denis Sanders

War Is Hell; 1964; Burt Topper

War Lord, The; 1965; Franklin Schaffner

War Lover, The; 1962; Philip Leacock

War of the Satellites; 1959; Roger Corman

War of the Worlds, The; 1953; Byron Haskin

War Wagon, The; 1967; Burt Kennedy

Ware Case, The; 1938; Robert Stevenson

Warlock; 1959; Edward Dmytryk

Warning Shot, The; 1967; Buzz Kulik

Warpath; 1951; Byron Haskin

Washington Merry-Go-Round; 1933; James Cruze

Wasp Woman; 1959; Roger Corman

Watch on the Rhine; 1943; Vincent Sherman and Herman Shumlin

Watch Your Stern; 1960; Gerald Thomas

Waterfront Women; 1952; Michael Anderson

Waterloo Bridge; 1940; Mervyn Le Roy

Wave, The (Doc); 1935; Fred Zinnemann and Muriel Gomez

Wave, A Wac and a Marine, A; 1944; Phil Karlson

Way Ahead, The (Doc); 1942; Carol Reed

Way Down East; 1935; Henry King

Way Down South; 1939; Bernard Vorhaus

Way of a Gaucho; 1952; Jacques Tourneur

Way Out West; 1937; James W. Horne

Way to the Gold, The; 1957; Robert D. Webb

Way to the Stars, The; 1945; Anthony

Asquith
Way Way Out; 1966; Gordon Douglas
Wayward Bus, The; 1957; Victor Vicas
We Are Not Alone; 1939; Edmund Goulding
We Are the Lambeth Boys; 1958; Karel Reisz
We Dive at Dawn; 1943; Anthony Asquith
We Live Again; 1934; Rouben Mamoulian
We Sail at Midnight (Doc); 1943; John Ford
We Were Strangers; 1949; John Huston
We'll Bury You; 1962; Jack Leewood and Jack W. Thomas
We're No Angels; 1955; Michael Curtiz
We're Not Dressing; 1934; Norman Taurog
We're Not Married; 1952; Edmund Goulding
Weary River; 1929; Frank Lloyd
Wedding Night, The; 1934; King Vidor
Wedding Present; 1936; Richard Wallace
Wedding Rehearsal; 1932; Alexander Korda
Weddings and Babies; 1958; Morris Engel
Wee Willie Winkie; 1937; John Ford
Week-End at the Waldorf; 1945; Robert Z. Leonard
Weekend with Father; 1951; Douglas Sirk
Welcome Danger; 1929; Clyde Bruckman
Welcome Stranger; 1947; Elliott Nugent
Welcome to Hard Times; 1967; Burt Kennedy
Wells Fargo; 1937; Frank Lloyd
West Eleven; 1963; Michael Winner
West of Shanghai; 1937; John Farrow
West of Zanzibar; 1953; Harry Watt
West Point Story, The; 1950; Roy del Ruth
West Point Widow; 1941; Robert Siodmak
West Side Story; 1961; Jerome Robbins and Robert Wise
Westbound; 1959; Budd Boetticher
Western Approaches; 1944; Pat Jackson

Western Union; 1941; Fritz Lang
Westerner, The; 1940; William Wyler
Westward the Women; 1951; William Wellman
Wet Parade, The; 1932; Victor Fleming
Wharf Angel; 1934; William C. Menzies
What a Life; 1939; Jay Theodore Reed
What a Way to Go; 1964; J. Lee Thompson
What a Widow; 1930; Allan Dwan
What Did You Do in the War, Daddy; 1966; Blake Edwards
What Ever Happened to Baby Jane; 1962; Robert Aldrich
What Every Woman Knows; 1934; Gregory La Cava
What Next, Corporal Hargrove; 1945; Richard Thorpe
What Price Glory; 1952; John Ford
What Price Hollywood; 1932; George Cukor
What's New Pussycat; 1965; Clive Donner
When in Rome; 1951; Clarence Brown
When Ladies Meet; 1933; Harry Beaumont
When Ladies Meet; 1941; Robert Z. Leonard
When Strangers Marry (Betrayed); 1944; William Castle
When the Daltons Rode; 1953; George Marshall
When the Lights Go On Again; 1944; William K. Howard
When Thief Meets Thief; 1937; Raoul Walsh
When Tomorrow Comes; 1939; John Stahl
When We Are Married; 1943; John Baxter
When Willie Comes Marching Home; 1950; John Ford
When Worlds Collide; 1951; Rudolph Mate
When You're in Love; 1937; Robert Riskin
Where Danger Lives; 1950; John Farrow
Where Love Has Gone; 1964; Edward Dmytryk
Where No Vultures Fly; 1951; Harry Watt
Where the Sidewalk Ends; 1950; Otto Preminger
Where the Spies Are; 1965; Val Guest

Where's Charlie; 1952; David Butler

Where's Jack; 1968; James Clavell

While Paris Sleeps; 1932; Allan Dwan

While the City Sleeps; 1956; Fritz Lang

Whirlpool; 1949; Otto Preminger

Whisky Galore; 1948; Alexander Mackendrick

Whisperers, The; 1967; Bryan Forbes

Whistle at Eaton Falls, The; 1951; Robert Siodmak

Whistle Down the Wind; 1962; Bryan Forbes

Whistling in the Dark; 1933; Elliott Nugent

White Angel; 1936; William Dieterle

White Banners; 1938; Edmund Goulding

White Bondage; 1937; Nicholas Grinde

White Christmas; 1954; Michael Curtiz

White Cliffs of Dover; 1944; Clarence Brown

White Corridors; 1950; Pat Jackson

White Feather; 1955; Robert D. Webb

White Heat; 1949; Raoul Walsh

White Heat; 1955; Gordon Douglas

White Hunter; 1937; Irving Cummings

White Savage; 1943; Arthur Lubin

White Sister; 1933; Victor Fleming

White Tie and Tails; 1946; Charles T. Barton

White Tower, The; 1950; Ted Tetzlaff

White Witch Doctor; 1953; Henry Hathaway

White Woman; 1933; S. Walker

White Zombie; 1932; Victor Halperin

Who Killed Aunt Maggie; 1940; Arthur Lubin

Who Killed Teddy Bear; 1965; Joseph Cates

Who Was That Lady; 1960; George Sidney

Who's Afraid of Virginia Woolf; 1967; Mike Nichols

Who's Been Sleeping in My Bed; 1963; Daniel Mann

Who's Minding the Store; 1963; Frank Tashlin

Whole Town's Talking, The; 1935; John Ford

Whoopee; 1930; Thornton Freeland

Why Must I Die; 1960; Roy del Ruth

Wichita; 1955; Jacques Tourneur

Wicked; 1931; Allan Dwan

Wicked as They Come; 1955; Kenneth Hughes

Wicked Woman; 1953; Russell Rouse

Wide Boy; 1952; Kenneth Hughes

Widow, The; 1955; Lewis Milestone

Wife of Monte Cristo, The; 1946; Edgar G. Ulmer

Wife Takes a Flyer, The; 1942; Richard Wallace

Wife Versus Secretary; 1936; Clarence Brown

Wife Wanted; 1946; Phil Karlson

Wild and the Willing, The; 1962; Ralph Thomas

Wild and Wonderful; 1963; Michael Anderson

Wild Angels, The; 1966; Roger Corman

Wild Bill Hickock Rides; 1941; Ray Enright

Wild Blue Yonder, The; 1951; Allan Dwan

Wild Boys of the Road; 1933; William Wellman

Wild Bunch, The; 1968; Sam Peckinpah

Wild Company; 1930; Leo McCarey

Wild Geese Calling; 1941; John Brahm

Wild Girl; 1932; Raoul Walsh

Wild Gold; 1934; George Marshall

Wild Harvest; 1947; Tay Garnett

Wild Horse Mesa; 1933; Henry Hathaway

Wild Horse Rodeo; 1937; George Sherman

Wild in the Country; 1961; Philip Dunne

Wild Is the Wind; 1957; George Cukor

Wild One, The; 1953; Laslo Benedek

Wild Orchids; 1929; Sidney Franklin

Wild Party, The; 1956; Harry Horner

Wild River; 1960; Elia Kazan

Will Any Gentlemen; 1955; Michael Anderson

Will Success Spoil Rock Hunter; 1957; Frank Tashlin

Willie Boy; 1968; Abraham Polonsky

Wilson; 1944; Henry King

Winchester 73; 1950; Anthony Mann

Wind Across the Everglades; 1958; Nicholas Ray

Wind Cannot Read, The; 1958; Ralph Thomas

Window, The; 1949; Ted Tetzlaff

Wing and a Prayer; 1944; Henry Hathaway

Winged Victory; 1944; George Cukor

Wings for the Eagle; 1942; Lloyd Bacon

Wings in the Dark; 1935; James Flood

Wings of Eagles, The; 1957; John Ford

Wings of the Hawk; 1953; Budd Boetticher

Wings of the Navy; 1939; Lloyd Bacon

Winner Take All; 1932; Roy del Ruth

Winning Team, The; 1952; Lewis Seiler

Winslow Boy, The; 1948; Anthony Asquith

Winter Meeting; 1947; Bretaigne Windust

Winterset; 1936; Alfred Santell

Wintertime; 1943; John Brahm

Wise Girls; 1929; Elliott Nugent

Wishing Well Inn; 1958; Maurice Elvey

Witching Hour, The; 1934; Henry Hathaway

With a Song in My Heart; 1951; Walter Lang

Within the Law; 1939; Gustav Machaty

Without Love; 1945; Harold S. Bucquet

Without Reservations; 1946; Mervyn Le Roy

Witness for the Prosecution; 1958; Billy Wilder

Wives and Lovers; 1963; John Rich

Wives Never Know; 1936; Elliott Nugent

Wives of Reno; 1934; H. Bruce Humberstone

Wives Under Suspicion; 1938; James Whale

Wizard of Oz, The; 1939; Victor Fleming

Wolf Hunters, The; 1950; Budd Boetticher

Wolf Man; 1948; George Waggner

Wolf Song; 1929; Victor Fleming

Woman Accused; 1933; Paul Sloane

Woman Chases Man; 1937; John Blystone

Woman from Monte Carlo; 1932; Michael Curtiz

Woman Hater; 1949; Terence Young

Woman in a Dressing-Gown; 1957; J. Lee Thompson

Woman in Green, The; 1945; Roy William Neill

Woman in Question, The; 1950; Anthony Asquith

Woman in Red; 1935; Robert Florey

Woman in Room 13; 1932; Henry King

Woman in the Hall, The; 1947; Jack Lee

Woman in the Wind; 1939; John Farrow

Woman in the Window, The; 1945; Fritz Lang

Woman Obsessed; 1959; Henry Hathaway

Woman of Dolwyn, The; 1949; Emlyn Williams

Woman of Straw; 1964; Basil Dearden

Woman of Summer (The Stripper); 1963; Franklin Schaffner

Woman of the Town; 1943; George Archainbaud

Woman of the Year; 1942; George Stevens

Woman on the Beach, The; 1947; Jean Renoir

Woman Rebels, A; 1936; Mark Sandrich

Woman They Almost Lynched; 1953; Allan Dwan

Woman to Woman; 1929; Victor Saville

Woman Trap; 1929; William Wellman

Woman Wise; 1937; Allan Dwan

Woman's Face, A; 1941; George Cukor

Woman's Secret, A; 1949; Nicholas Ray

Woman's Temptation, A; 1959; Godfrey Grayson

Woman's Vengeance, A; 1947; Zoltan Korda

Woman's World; 1954; Jean Negulesco

Women, The; 1939; George Cukor

Women Everywhere; 1930; Alexander Korda

Women of All Nations; 1931; Raoul Walsh

Women Without Names; 1940; Robert Florey

Women Won't Tell; 1933; Richard Thorpe

Wonder Bar; 1934; Lloyd Bacon

Wonder Man; 1945; H. Bruce Humberstone

Wonder of Women; 1929; Clarence Brown

Wonderful Country, The; 1959; Robert Parrish

Wonderful Life; 1964; Sidney Furie

Wooden Horse; 1950; Jack Lee

Words and Music; 1948; Norman Taurog

World and the Flesh; 1932; John Cromwell

World Changes, The; 1933; Mervyn Le Roy

World for Ransom; 1954; Robert Aldrich

World in His Arms, The; 1952; Raoul Walsh

World Moves On, The; 1934; John Ford

World of Henry Orient, The; 1964; George Roy Hill

World of Suzie Wong, The; 1960; Richard Quine

World Premiere; 1941; Ted Tetzlaff

Wreck of the Mary Deare, The; 1959; Michael Anderson

Written on the Wind; 1957; Douglas Sirk

Wrong Again (Short); 1929; Leo McCarey

Wrong Arm of the Law, The; 1963; Cliff Owen

Wrong Box, The; 1966; Bryan Forbes

Wrong Kind of Girl (Bus Stop); 1956; Joshua Logan

Wrong Man, The; 1956; Alfred Hitchcock

Wrong Road, The; 1937; James Cruze

Wuthering Heights; 1939; William Wyler

Wyoming; 1940; Richard Thorpe

Wyoming Renegades; 1955; Fred F. Sears

Yangtse Incident; 1956; Herbert Wilcox

Yank at Eton, A; 1942; Norman Taurog

Yank at Oxford, A; 1938; Jack Conway

Yank in the RAF, A; 1941; Henry King

Yank in Vietnam, A; 1964; Marshall Thompson

Yankee Doodle Dandy; 1942; Michael Curtiz

Yearling, The; 1946; Clarence Brown

Yellow Balloon, The; 1953; J. Lee Thompson

Yellow Canary, The; 1963; Buzz Kulik

Yellow Rolls-Royce; 1964; Anthony Asquith

Yellow Sky; 1948; William Wellman

Yellow Teddybears, The; 1963; Robert Hartford-Davis

Yellow Ticket; 1931; Raoul Walsh

Yellowstone; 1936; Arthur Lubin

Yellowstone Kelly; 1959; Gordon Douglas

Yes, My Darling Daughter; 1939; William Keighley

Yield to the Night; 1956; J. Lee Thompson

Yolanda and the Thief; 1945; Vincente Minnelli

You and Me; 1938; Fritz Lang

You Came Along; 1945; John Farrow

You Can't Cheat an Honest Man; 1939; George Marshall

You Can't Get Away with Murder; 1939; Lewis Seiler

You Can't Run Away from It; 1956; Dick Powell

You Can't Take It with You; 1938; Frank Capra

You for Me; 1952; Don Weis

You Gotta Stay Happy; 1947; H. C. Potter

You Know What Sailors Are; 1954; Ken Annakin

You Must Be Joking; 1966; Michael Winner

You Only Live Once; 1937; Fritz Lang

You Said a Mouthful; 1932; Lloyd Bacon

You Were Meant for Me; 1947; Lloyd Bacon

You're a Big Boy Now; 1967; Francis Ford Coppola

You're in the Army Now; 1937; Raoul Walsh

You're in the Navy Now; 1951; Henry Hathaway

Young America; 1932; Frank Borzage

Young and the Brave, The; 1963; Francis D. Lyon

Young as You Feel; 1940; Malcolm St. Clair

Young at Heart; 1954; Gordon Douglas

Young Captives, The; 1959; Irvin Kershner

Young Cassidy; 1965; Jack Cardiff

Young Dillinger; 1965; Terry O. Morse

Young Doctor Kildare; 1938; Harold Bucquet

Young Doctors, The; 1961; Phil Karl-

son
Young Eagles; 1930; William Wellman
Young Hellions (High School Confidential); 1960; Albert Zugsmith
Young Ideas; 1943; Jules Dassin
Young in Heart, The; 1938; Richard Wallace
Young Land, The; 1959; Ted Tetzlaff
Young Lions, The; 1958; Edward Dmytryk
Young Lovers, The; 1949; Ida Lupino
Young Lovers, The; 1954; Anthony Asquith
Young Man with Ideas; 1952; Mitchell Leisen
Young Mister Pitt, The; 1940; Carol Reed
Young Mr. Lincoln; 1939; John Ford
Young Nowheres; 1929; Frank Lloyd
Young One, The; 1960; Luis Buñuel
Young Ones, The; 1961; Sidney Furie
Young People; 1940; Allan Dwan
Young Philadelphians, The; 1959; Vincent Sherman
Young Racers, The; 1963; Roger Corman
Young Savages, The; 1961; John Frankenheimer

Young Stranger, The; 1957; John Frankenheimer
Young Tom Edison; 1940; Norman Taurog
Youngblood Hawke; 1964; Delmer Daves
Younger Generation; 1929; Frank Capra
Your Cheatin' Heart; 1964; Gene Nelson
Your Past Is Showing; 1958; M. Zampi
Youth on Trial; 1945; Budd Boetticher

Zarak; 1957; Terence Young
Zaza; 1938; George Cukor
Zenobia; 1939; Gordon Douglas
Zero Hour; 1957; Hall Bartlett
Ziegfeld Follies; 1946; Vincente Minnelli
Ziegfeld Girl; 1941; Robert Z. Leonard
Zoo in Budapest; 1933; Rowland V. Lee
Zombies, The; 1933; Victor Halperin
Zorba the Greek; 1964; Michael Cacoyannis
Zulu; 1964; Cy Enfield

ANDREW SARRIS is film critic for the *New York Observer* and professor of cinema at Columbia University. He is a member of the National Society of Film Critics and the New York Film Critics Circle. Mr. Sarris was film critic for the *Village Voice* from 1960 to 1989, editor-in-chief of *Cahiers du Cinema in English* from 1965 to 1967, and an associate editor of *Film Culture* from 1955 to 1965. He is the author of *The Films of Josef von Sternberg, Interviews with Film Directors, The Film, Confessions of a Cultist, The Primal Screen, The John Ford Movie Mystery,* and *Politics and Cinema.*